The Hibernensis • BOOK 2

Studies in Medieval and Early Modern Canon Law

Kenneth Pennington, General Editor

Studies in Medieval and Early Modern Canon Law

VOLUME 17 • BOOK 2

The Hibernensis

Translation, Commentary, and Indexes

Roy Flechner, Editor

The Catholic University of America Press
Washington, D.C.

The Catholic University of America Press thanks the author for preparing this camera-ready publication for printing.

The paper used in this publication meets the minimum requirements of American National Standards for Information Science—Permanence of Paper for Printed Library Materials, ANSI, Z39.48-1984.

∞

ISBN: 978-0-8132-3221-8

Hibernensis: Translation

Observing the numerousness of copies of synodal texts, and foreseeing that the obscurity of a great many of them will be less useful to the uninitiated, and also anticipating that the inharmonious diversity of the rest would be destructive rather than constructive, I have provided a brief, clear, and harmonious exposition in a single volume out of the great forest of authors, adding many things, reducing many things, excerpting many things word-for-word, asserting more things following the sense with the order of the words disregarded;[1] seeking this alone in all things: that the things that might appear as recommendations should not be imputed to my judgement. I have prefixed names of individuals to individual testimonies, lest whatever someone may call uncertain should shine less brightly. But let this not deceive the reader, that when he turns to the general titles, which we prefixed by necessity, he ought to observe the numbers diligently; by which numbers, when they are observed, he will find the matter that he wishes without delay. The prologue ends.[2]

Concerning the synod

Concerning the word 'synod'

In the books of etymologies: 'Synod' is translated 'company' or 'assembly'. The word 'council' is drawn from Roman custom, for when cases were being dealt with, everyone gathered together and debated with a common interest. Whence 'council' also takes its name from 'common interest', as if it were 'council', that is, as if it were 'I revolve' (*conuerso*). For they are [like] eyelids (*cilia*).[3]

Whence also a judicial assembly (*considium*) is a council (*concilium*)—that is, a council decree of itself[4]—the letter 'd' changing to 'l'. An assembly is a gathering or congregation, from 'coming together' (*coeundo*), that is, from 'convening together' (*conueniendo*).

However, Cicero says: 'synod' is a Latin noun; saying, 'a synod is a congregation of the elders'.

Concerning the principal synods

In the books of etymologies: However, of all the councils, we find that there are four venerable synods which principally encompass the whole faith, just as there are the four Gospels or as many rivers of paradise. The first, the Nicaean synod of 318 bishops, took place during the reign of Constantine Augustus. In it was condemned the blasphemy of the Arian heresy, which the same Arius espoused concerning the inequality of the Holy Trinity. The second synod, of 150 fathers, was convened under Theodosius the Elder at Constantinople. In condemning Macedonius who denied that the Holy Spirit was the Lord, it demonstrated that the Holy Spirit is consubstantial with the father and son. The third, the Ephesian synod of 200 bishops, was held under Theodosius Augustus the Younger. This synod, by just anathema, condemned Nestorius, who espoused that there were two persons in Christ. The fourth, the Chalcedonian synod of 630 *sacerdotes*, was held under the *princeps*[5] Marcian. In which a sentence of the fathers condemned Eutyches, the Constantinopolitan abbot, who propagated the single nature of the word of God and the flesh, and his defender, Dioscorus, at one time bishop of the Alexandrians, and, once more, the same Nestorius together with the other heretics; the same synod proclaimed that Christ the Lord was born of a virgin such that in him there was a substance of both the divine and human.

From Dionysius's preface to Stephen[6] concerning different synods

At Nicaea 20 rulings. At Ancyra 24 rulings. At Caesarea 14 rulings. At Antioch 26 rulings. At Laodicea in Phrygia 58 rulings. At Constantinople 13 rulings. At Chalcedon 27 rulings. At Gangra 20 rulings. Rulings of the Sardican[7] synod 20. At Carthage in Africa 138 rulings. It ends amen.

Concerning the days for convening synods

The synod of Antioch said: For the sake of ecclesiastical expediency and for addressing the things that meet with doubt and controversy, it was most opportunely decided that in each and every province councils of bishops ought to be repeated twice a year: the first after the third week of the Paschal feast, so that a synod may be convened in the fourth week of Pentecost, after the metropolitan bishop has given notice to the provincials. Let the second synod take place in October, that is on the fifteenth of the month of October. In these councils there shall be present presbyters, deacons, and all others who feel themselves aggrieved. And let the judgement of the synod explore matters. Let none celebrate councils at their own sees, save those in whom metropolitan prerogatives are seen to have been invested.

1 Concerning the bishop

1.1 Concerning the word 'bishop'

The word 'bishop' is drawn from Greek, changing 'os' into 'us', rendering that which in Latin is called 'overseer' or 'superintendent', because he oversees the conduct and the way of life of the people under him and superintends the care of his subjects.

Isidore said: Looking (*scopus*) is indeed the intention, therefore, in Latin we can say that a bishop superintends.

And it is not the presider who enjoys respect, but he who helps by administering care to others, namely to his subjects.

Paul: He who desires the office of a bishop, desires good work.

Isidore: However, the episcopal office, as a certain wise man said, denotes burden rather than honour. Note that bishops are designated *sacerdotes*,[8] and likewise presbyters are deemed to be *sacerdotes*.[9]

Likewise: Let it be known that bishops and presbyters assumed their appellations from the new law. However, *sacerdotes* are so named both in the old and in the new law. Let the bishop know that he is designated *pontifex* and *antistes* and chief *sacerdos*.

That a man who was polluted by a second or illicit marriage ought not be ordained bishop

A Roman synod says: If someone after baptism should be joined by a second marriage, or should have a concubine, he may not be a bishop, or presbyter, or deacon, or, in short, be numbered among those who serve in the sacred ministry.

Isidore said in the books concerning the offices: For if someone who has already been placed in the episcopal office or the office of presbyter had committed a mortal sin, he ought not offer loaves to the Lord. All the more so let him not be ordained if he has been found to be a sinner prior to his ordination.

1.2 Concerning those who assume the title of bishop undeservedly

Not all bishops are considered true bishops.

Augustine: The more a bishop desires honour, the more he is weighed down by danger.

Jerome: The bishop, while he is so named, must take care not to forget the work of his episcopal office.

Many bishops desire the honorific title but avoid the work of their office.

1.3 Concerning the origin of the *sacerdos* in both laws

Isidore: Aaron was the first to receive the sacerdotal title in the law[10] and the first to wear a pontifical robe. He offered sacrifices, with the Lord commanding and saying to Moses: Receive Aaron and his sons. You will bring the father with his sons to the entrance of the tabernacle etc.

In which place Aaron ought to be perceived as the chief *sacerdos*, which is to say that he prefigured the bishop, and his sons heralded the figure of presbyters.

Moses, however, represents the figure of Christ.

And in the New Testament the pontifical order begins after Christ with Peter the apostle and Jacob the bishop of bishops.

1.4 Concerning the laying on of hands on the bishop

Isidore: That bishops are ordained by a laying on of hands is an ancient institution. For the patriarch Isaac, placing his hand upon Jacob's head, blessed him. Similarly Jacob blessed his sons. But also Moses, placing his hand upon Joshua's head, gave him the spirit of courage and leadership over the people of Israel. Thus also our Lord Jesus Christ blessed his apostles by the laying on of a hand; and by the command of the Holy Spirit, a hand was placed by the apostles upon Paul and Barnabas towards the episcopate, and thus they were sent to evangelise etc.

The synod of Carthage said: When a bishop is ordained, let two bishops impose their hands, and let them hold a book of the Gospels over his head, that is, above his neck, and after one of them utters a blessing, let all the other bishops who are present extend their hands over his head, following on the hand of the bishop.

1.5 That a single bishop should not ordain another

Isidore: Furthermore, a bishop should not be ordained by a single bishop, but by all the fellow-provincial bishops, lest something contrary to faith be attempted through the tyrannical authority of one bishop. On account of this, he is invested by all who are convened, and by no fewer than three who are present, while the others give their consent in writing.

The synod of Carthage said: Then, let the bishop be ordained with the consent of the clerics and laymen and the bishops of the whole province and especially the metropolitan—either by letter, or by a representative, or in person.

1.6 Concerning the staff and ring of the bishop

When he is consecrated he is given a staff, so that by its sign he may rule and correct the community subject to him, and sustain the weaknesses of the weak. A ring is also given him to signify pontifical honour or a seal of secrets, lest the sacraments of God be revealed to the unworthy.

Gregory: What is signified by the staff if not pastoral care? For the staff sustains, defends, and governs.

Let the *chorepiscopi*, that is, the deputies of bishops or bishops of a single community, be ordained by a single bishop. They are ordained only by the bishop of the nearest *ciuitas*.

1.7 Concerning the one who is to be ordained

Paul: If someone desires the office of a bishop, he desires good work. The church seeks as a *sacerdos* a man of a single wife, or a virgin.

That no one ought to be ordained hastily, lest another's sin should harm you

Likewise, the same authority: Lay not hands lightly upon any man, lest you be a partaker of other men's sins. Keep yourself chaste.

The same: Not a neophyte, lest, puffed up with pride, he should think himself ordained not so much to the service of humility, but for the exercise of secular power.

Isidore: For how will a secular man fulfil a sacerdotal ministry whose duty he did not grasp and its instruction he did not accept? Or how will he teach, when he himself has not learned? For nowadays we often see that many ordain not those whom the church chooses, but either those whom they love themselves, or those who allure them by service and obedience, or those on whose behalf a wicked man entreats, and—to mention the worst cases—those who secured their ordination by means of gifts. Others make their sons or relatives successors and strive to hand down the dignity of superintending to their descendants; though even Moses, the friend of God, could not do this, but chose Joshua from another tribe, that we may know that the leadership of the people must not be determined by blood, but by a life of merit.

A synod says: Before a bishop is ordained, let it be examined whether he is prudent by nature, whether he is ready to listen, whether his manners are temperate, whether he is sober, whether he leads a chaste life, whether he is kind to the lowly, whether he is merciful, whether he is learned, whether he is versed in the law of the Lord, whether he is careful with the sense of scripture, and above all, whether he proclaims the proofs of faith in simple terms.

1.8 Concerning the bishop's conduct

Isidore: His speech ought to be pure and candid, full of severity and honesty, full of sweetness and grace, concerned with the mystery of law, with the teaching of the faith, with the virtue of self-restraint, with the discipline of justice; above all, his special duty is to read the scripture, inspect the canons thoroughly, imitate the examples of saints in fasts and vigils, commit himself to prayers, be in peace with the brethren, care for the poor, feed the hungry, clothe the naked, receive pilgrims, redeem captives, look after widows and orphans. Whose dwelling place ought to be a refuge for all. For the layman admits one or two in order to fulfil the obligation of hospitality. If, however, the bishop should not admit everybody, he is savage.

A synod says: Let no bishop invade the *parochia*[11] of another, or ordain a cleric belonging to another's church, or receive payment in return for ordination, or receive the gifts of the wicked, which the most high condemns, or travel without a presbyter, etc. He is at peace with everybody, he does not condemn anyone without reason, he does not excommunicate anyone save for the savage, such that he knows to correct his subjects and does not exercise the power of severity through immoderate authority. The bishop ought not be obstinate but modest. It is necessary for the bishop to have knowledge of scripture. For should he not be erudite, he will serve only himself; but if he should be, he can teach others and persecute adversaries.

Likewise: He who reproves the sins of others must himself be a stranger to sin.

For how dare he reprove his subjects, when they can accuse him of the same things? Wherefore he who has failed to do righteous things, would cease to teach righteous things.

Likewise: He who admonishes others to live virtuously, ought first to correct himself.

Likewise, Dionysius Exiguus: And if a bishop or presbyter should offer above the altar any sacrifice besides that which is ordained by the Lord, namely honey or milk, or fortified wines instead of wine, and certain cooked dishes, or birds or other animals or vegetables, he does so contrary to custom. Let him be deposed at the proper time. Let nothing be permitted to be offered at the altar when the holy offering is celebrated, except new ears of grain and oil for lamps and *thymiama*, that is, incense.

Let all other *adom* firstfruits[12] be given to the bishop and presbyters.

1.9 Concerning the amount of time the bishop ought to be absent from the church

The synod of Sardica says: Let it not be permitted to any bishop to be absent from the church for more than three weeks.

Likewise, a Hibernian synod said: It is the duty of the bishop not to be absent from his church for even one Sunday.[13] If, however, he has been absent for more than two, he should be sent into exile. If, however, he has neglected to celebrate a solemnity in his church, let him be demoted.

1.10 Concerning different duties of the bishop

Let a bishop's guest-chamber not be far from the church.

Let a bishop not concern himself with the interests of his household, but he should be free only to read, and pray, and preach the word of God.

Let a bishop sit in a higher seat than the assembly of the presbyters. But inside the dwelling, let him concede that he is a colleague of the presbyters.

Let a bishop have simple furniture, and a table, and modest nourishment, and claim the power of his dignity in faith and in the merits of a good life.

Let a bishop not read the books of pagans; however, he may read books by heretics, depending on the occasion and need.

Let a bishop not undertake the administration of wills.

Let a bishop not look after widows, and orphans, and pilgrims himself, but through an archpresbyter and an archdeacon.

Let a bishop not litigate about worldly things even if he is challenged.

Let a bishop be permitted to be absent from a synod on account of a sufficiently urgent cause; if he should send a representative in his place, he shall accept anything that the synod has decided provided that the truth of the faith be safeguarded.

Let a bishop or cleric not move from a lowly to a higher place through ambition.

Let a bishop not ordain clerics without an assembly of his presbyters, in order that he might ask the *ciues* to be witnesses.

Let a bishop not presume to judge a case without the presence of his clerics, otherwise the bishop's verdict will be void, unless it should be confirmed in the presence of his clerics.

Let a bishop, whenever sitting, not suffer his presbyters to stand.

Let a bishop use church property as if it were a deposit, not as his own property.

Let a bishop not forbid anyone from entering the church to hear the word of God, be it a heretic, a Jew, a pagan, until the dismissal of the catechumens.

1.11 Concerning the ages at which one is raised to the episcopal office

The episcopal age is reckoned with respect to three criteria.

The first, concerning virginity and ecclesiastical institutions

The synod of Carthage: But a lad who was given to ecclesiastical services since infancy, should remain a lector or exorcist up until his twentieth year. A porter and subdeacon four years, a deacon five, a presbyter in his thirtieth year, a bishop in his fortieth, a *sacerdos* in his thirtieth (or his sixtieth year) for in that year Christ began to preach.[14]

The second, concerning a young man of one wife

The same synod: But one who lived virtuously from the beginning of adolescence to his thirtieth year, content with a single wife who was a virgin at the time of marriage: five years a subdeacon and five years a deacon, in his fortieth let him be a presbyter, in his fiftieth a bishop.

The third, concerning an aged layman

The same synod: But if he should be a layman of advanced age, and if it be necessary that he should be made a bishop, let him be a lector for two years, five a subdeacon, five a deacon; after twelve years let him be chosen to replace a presbyter or bishop.

Likewise: There is another, different, time in which one may not become a bishop, or presbyter, or deacon, to wit: If one should enter upon another marriage after baptism or have a concubine, he may not be a bishop, or presbyter, or deacon, or, in short, be numbered among those who serve in the sacred ministry.

If one should marry a widow and a divorced woman, or a harlot, or a female slave, or one of those who are sold for public spectacles, he may not be a bishop, or presbyter, or deacon, or be numbered among those who serve in the sacred ministry.

1.12 That the one who is to be ordained must not be summoned from another place, except by necessity

An Alexandrian synod: Only then may one be chosen from another church: if no worthy candidate has been found from among the clerics of that *ciuitas*[15] for which someone ought to be ordained.

1.13 Concerning the need to undo unlawful ordinations

The same synod: If ordinations have been performed unlawfully, let them be annulled. Similarly, let those who ordained be completely deprived of the power of ordination, lest respect for religion should be dimmed.

1.14 That bishops have authority to bind and loose

Gregory the Roman: Bishops receive the authority to bind and loose. A great honour has befallen them who are allotted a position of ruling, but the honour carries a heavy burden. It is surely unfitting that he who does not know how to keep control over his own life, should become the judge of another's.

Peter says of Clement the Roman, his successor: I have deemed him, before others, honouring God, loving men, careful in speech, devoted to studies, sober, kind, just, forbearing, wise. On account of which I hand over to him the power to bind and loose. For he will bind what ought to be bound, and loose what ought to be loosed.

1.15 That a bishop is the image of Christ

Augustine said: Christ bears the image of God, just as a bishop bears the image of Christ.

1.16 That no one ought to judge bishops

In the Ecclesiastical History: King Constantine said to the bishops: You cannot be judged by men. Await, therefore, the judgement of God alone amongst yourselves, etc.

Gildas said: Indeed, *sacerdotes*[16] and bishops have a terrible judge, to whom it belongs, and not to us, to judge them in both worlds.

Likewise: It is better not to judge fellow bishops and fellow abbots and fellow subjects.

1.17 That a bishop chooses his successor while he is still alive and of sound mind

In the Ecclesiastical History: A certain Alexander, quite famous by distinction of confession,[17] was elected bishop of the church of Jerusalem, while Narcissus, who formerly held the pontifical office there, was still alive.

Likewise, a little further on: When he was already old and unable to perform the service of the pontificate, divine inspiration, by means of manifest revelations, summoned the same Alexander, who was already bishop of another place, to the aid of old Narcissus.

Likewise: Anatolius left many writings in that matter, through which salutary learning is known to those who wish to learn it. He was the first upon whom Theotechnus, holding the priesthood of Caesarea, laid hands to make him a bishop. Whence for some time he presided over the church of Caesarea with the same Theotechnus.

The synod of Sardica said: If we should submit our souls and necks to the bishop, it is all the more fitting that he ought to govern the church and ordain a successor.[18]

Origen: Why does it seem right to you to change our governor's decision? For if God entrusted him with greater things, why do we not entrust him with the smallest of things?

1.18 That the election of the worthy candidates ought to take place after the death, or at the deathbed, of the retiring bishop

A synod said: Let no bishop appoint a successor while he is alive, but let the worthy ones elect a worthy candidate after his death.

Likewise, a synod ruled that a bishop ordain his successor on his deathbed with the consent of the synod and according to the will of the same region, lest it be void.

1.19 That a bishop was elected from another race

Following fifteen bishops of the circumcision, who presided over the city of Jerusalem after Jacob, Mark was the first of the gentiles to be elected bishop of the same see. Thereafter innumerable other gentiles followed.

Likewise, Mark, the disciple of Peter, Jewish by race, presided over Alexandria, the city of the Egyptians. Likewise, Alexander, a Cappadocian by race, arriving as a guest for the sake of worshipping and seeing the holy places, was unanimously elected bishop of the church of Jerusalem. Likewise, Anatolius the Alexandrian presided over the Caesarean church and then presided over the Laodicean church.

1.20 That a *sacerdos* should not minister in the presence of an infirm bishop

If a bishop has suffered infirmity or dimness of his senses or has lost the ability to speak, let him not allow presbyters to perform in his presence the things that are performed only by bishops, but let him summon a bishop, to whom he should entrust that which needs to be performed.

That eunuchs may accept the episcopal office

Dionysius Exiguus: A eunuch, whose virile organs were amputated through a plot carried out by men or through persecution or if he was born with this condition, is worthy to be made bishop. If, however, he has cut them off himself, i.e. if someone amputated them for him at his request, he is not to become a bishop, but he is also not a cleric. He who is a killer of his own self is also inimical to the work of God.

1.21 That a bishop does not give away any church property without consultation with his clerics

A bishop's benefaction, or sale, or a deposit of ecclesiastical property shall be void without written approval from his clerics.[19]

1.22 Concerning the need to excommunicate a bishop who seized the property of another

A synod: A bishop who seized the *parochia*[20] of another bishop, must be excommunicated from the peace,[21] mass, and table, unless he does penance in proper order.

Let a bishop not leave for another *parochia* and abandon his, unless he does so by a decision of many bishops and especially their earnest request.

He who has slain a bishop or presbyter must be sent to the king for judgement.

Likewise, Dionysius Exiguus and Laurence, highly accomplished Greek authors, say concerning the same matter: A bishop, although urged by many, is not permitted to seize the *parochia* of another and forsake his own, which he has relinquished, unless perchance he is compelled by a reasonable cause, like being able to confer quickly more profit on those living there, and really to provide something else for religion's sake. This he cannot do by himself, but by a decision of many bishops and especially their request.

2 Concerning the presbyter and *sacerdos*[22]

2.1 Concerning the word 'presbyter'

'Presbyter' is a Greek word, rendering that which in Latin is called 'senior'. Isidore: Presbyters are so called for their merit and wisdom, not for their age, as it is said in Proverbs: The glory of old men is their grey head. What is this grey head? Without doubt it is wisdom, of which it has been written: The grey head of men is prudence.

Concerning the origin of *sacerdos*, that is, concerning the *sacerdotes* of the law of nature[23]

Sacerdotes are so called because they provide sacred leadership to the people.

2.2 Concerning the origin of presbyters

Isidore: The order of presbyters takes its beginning from the sons of Aaron, who were called *sacerdotes* in the Old Testament. They are the ones who are now called presbyters. And they who are designated chiefs of *sacerdotes* are now[24] called bishops, even though Melchisedech was the first to offer a sacrifice before Aaron, and after him Abraham, and Isaac, and Jacob. But they did so of their own volition, not by sacerdotal authority.

2.3 That presbyters are ordained

The synod of Carthage: When a presbyter is ordained, while the bishop is blessing him and holding a hand over his head, let all presbyters who are present place their hands by the bishop's hand, over his head.

2.4 Concerning the similarity and difference between the ministry of a bishop and a presbyter[25]

Isidore said concerning presbyters: To them, as to bishops, was given the dispensation of God's ministries. For they preside over the church of Christ. And they are consorts of bishops in confecting[26] the divine body and blood and likewise in apostolic teaching and the duty of preaching. Only the ordination and consecration of clerics must be reserved for the chief *sacerdos* on account of his authority, lest—if the discipline of the church is claimed by many—it should disturb the harmony and generate scandals; whence he [the presbyter] is second in grade [to the bishop] but nearly conjoined.

Concerning the presbyter's manner of life

A presbyter is blameless, a man of a single wife, without blemish, not quarrelsome, not greedy, not irascible, not proud, not villainous,[27] he does not appear in the presence of the poor without the bishop's consent.[28]

2.5 Concerning the reasons why the *sacerdotes* of the law of nature,[29] the first of whom was Melchisedech, were offering[30]

Jerome: Melchisedech offered in three ways. First, he offered for himself, so that he might not be made proud by worldly goods, nor despair by evils, and that he might do away with his own evils. Second, for his family, that it might live in worldly comfort. Third, in prefiguration of the body of Christ.

Gregory: One reads that Job made an offering to the Lord for his sons, in which he joined together three things. First, that he should not be made proud by the wealth of his sons. Second, also for his sons, that they may not sin in their good fortune, as he said: Lest perhaps my sons should sin in the Lord. Third, in prefiguration of Christ, through which he was deemed worthy not to sin in his afflictions, as Job did not sin with his lips, nor in all these things.

2.6 Concerning the things for which the *sacerdotes* of the law of the letter, the first of whom was Aaron, were offering[31]

In the first place, Aaron was offering for himself and for his sons. Second, for the sins of the people. Third, in prefiguration of Christ, just as the other *sacerdotes* were offering.

2.7 Concerning the four kinds of offerings in the law of the letter that prefigure Christ

Isidore: Four principal kinds of offerings are described at the beginning of Leviticus. First, an immaculate calf of the herd. Second, a lamb of the flock. Third, a turtledove and dove. Fourth, moistened fine unleavened flour, anointed with oil, baked in the oven. All the remaining were offered by the representatives of the people, according to the nature of the cases. Thus the first, a calf of the herd, represented Christ, descendant of the line of the patriarchs, who tamed the land of our flesh by the plough of his cross. Second, a sacrifice from the sheep, namely Christ, styled a lamb on account of his innocence. Third, a sacrifice of a turtledove and dove, namely the flesh of Christ joined to the Holy Spirit. Fourth, fine flour, which prefigures the figure of the church—which, as if it were the fine wheat of the threshing floor, was gathered from the many seeds of the believers—and by the mill of the law and the Gospels was separated letter from spirit, anointed with the oil of the Holy Spirit.

2.8 Concerning the things for which Christ, the first *sacerdos* of the New Testament, offered

Augustine said: Christ offered in many ways. First, for his own weak flesh. Second, for the apostles on account of future temptations. Third, as an example to the church thereafter. Fourth, for the souls released from hell at the hour of his death.

Whence Paul said: If the blood of calves and goats, and the ashes of a heifer being sprinkled, has redeemed the sins of men, how much more the blood of Christ has redeemed us.

2.9 Concerning the ways in which the church offers nowadays

A Hibernian synod: Nowadays the church offers to the Lord in many ways. First, for itself. Second, for the commemoration of Jesus Christ, who says: Do this in commemoration of me. Third, for the souls of the dead.

2.10 Concerning the varied offerings in the four laws

Melchisedech offered wine and bread, Job holocausts, Aaron lambs and calves and doves and turtledoves, Christ offered his body and blood.

That a sordid life does not affect the ministry of the one who ministers

In the life of the saints one reads:[32] There was a solitary man, and a presbyter used to come to him and consecrate his offering for him for communion. A certain person appearing before the old man made accusations against the presbyter, who regularly came to discharge his ministry. The old man was tempted to believe that he[33] should not minister to him,[34] and he[35] left. Then the old man experienced a vision, and he saw the likeness of a golden well and exceptionally clean water. He also saw a leper drawing it up and pouring it into a vessel. He was eager to drink, but he did not want to on account of the leper who was drawing water. And behold, there came a voice to him, saying: Why do you not drink from this water? What is wrong with the one who fills? For he only fills and pours it back into a vessel. Then the old man changed his mind, summoned the presbyter, and made him sanctify his offering, as before.

2.11 Concerning the entitlements[36] of a *sacerdos* from the people

The law says: The firstfruits of the whole people of Israel will belong to the priests, both the tithes and the majority of the firstborn.

Likewise: They shall eat the victim both for sin and for trespass, and every vowed thing in Israel and all the libations of all things that are offered shall belong to the priests, as well as firstfruits of your foodstuffs.

Likewise: I have taken the consecrated breast and the right shoulder from the children of Israel in perpetual right, and they shall belong to the priests.

Likewise: They who serve the altar partake from the altar.

Likewise: Aaron did not make his own vestments, but Moses and others. This signifies that all the necessities of the priest are to be provided by the *princeps*.[37]

It should be noted that Aaron did not make the tabernacle himself, but the people and the craftsmen on the advice of Moses. This signifies that it is not for *sacerdotes* to build churches.

Likewise: Aaron did not hand out the sacrifices, except for a few. But the people did. He only used to place his hand over its head. This signifies that *sacerdotes* do not prepare food.

Likewise: Aaron never carried the tabernacle and its utensils, but only wrapped [them]. This signifies that ministers are identified with *sacerdotes*.

2.12 Concerning punishments for those who resist the *sacerdos*

The Law says: He who will be proud and refuse to obey the commandment of the *sacerdos*, who ministers at that time, let that man die and you shall take away the evil from Israel.

Likewise: If someone has contradicted the *sacerdos*, let him die.

Likewise: Let no one dare to resist the *sacerdotes*, for they are ministers of God.

2.13 Concerning unworthy buyers of the priesthood and sellers of the gift of God

Gregory Nazianzen:[38] We declare that whoever is eager to buy this gift by making a gift, while he cares not for the office but for the title, is not a *sacerdos*. Just as the one who, being reluctant, refuses, and when being sought, flees, must be removed from the holy altars.[39] Thus also he who ventures too far or obtrudes himself inappropriately, must, without doubt, be rejected. For he who ascends to the altar in this manner, what does he do, except by increasing decrease and by climbing externally, descend internally into the depths?

Luke in the Acts of the Apostles: Peter says to Simon Magus: Let your money be with you unto perdition; for you reckoned that the gift of God might be purchased with money.

In the temple doves were being sold. What do the doves signify, except the gift of the Holy Spirit? But they who were selling them signify those who receive worldly gifts in return for the laying on of hands.

2.14 That it is necessary to give to the *sacerdotes* a part of the property of every deceased person

A Hibernian synod decreed: Since Aaron exacted a part of every offering, whether from the *princeps* or from the servant, thus also a *sedatium*[40] must be given from the property of every deceased person.

2.15 Concerning the common *sedatio*

The synod of Carthage[41] said: If the *sedatium* should be moderate, it ought not be rejected. If great, it should be accepted up to the value of a cow. The king and the bishop, whose *monachus* he is, and the brethren are exempt from this *sedatium*.[42]

A Hibernian synod resolved that in respect to this *sedatium*, a sheep or its value as determined by prescribed measures are levied.

2.16 Concerning the *communio*

A Hibernian synod: The word *communio* is this: it consists of *uiaticum*,[43] that is, protection for the way (*uia*). For it protects the soul until it will stand before the tribunal of Christ, to whom it carries its deeds, as if it has borne them. The archangel cannot lead it to [eternal] life until God has judged it, nor can the Devil carry it off to punishment, unless the Lord has damned it.

2.17 Concerning reproving wicked *sacerdotes*

Ezekiel said: Woe to the priests who consume the sins of my people; which is to say that they either eat their sacrificial victims and do not pray for those [who offered the victims] or consume the sacrifices and do not reproach the wicked.

Likewise, Gregory: Wicked *sacerdotes* are the cause of the people's ruin.

No one is more harmful to the church than he who, while behaving perversely, assumes the title and order of sanctity. For no one presumes to contradict this delinquent. And, as a warning, the blame greatly increases, because a sinner is honoured in accordance with the reverence owed to the rank.

2.18 Concerning punishing the most wicked among *sacerdotes*

The Law says: Aaron bore the iniquity of the sons of Israel.

And if he has done this again through negligence or if he has not done this in good faith, but either through envy, or through greedy desire for the possessions of another, like the sons of Aaron offering strange fire, or out of regard for foodstuffs and through negligence of the ministry, like the sons of Eli the priest, or out of disputes with the leadership, like Core, he shall be put to death.

2.19 That *sacerdotes* have no inheritance except the Lord

The law says: You will not give them an inheritance in Israel, for I am their inheritance.

But let it be known that the six cities of refuge of Israel with their precincts, belonged to the *sacerdotes*.

Concerning the *sacerdos*'s rite in regard to the *princeps*[44] and people

In the first place, the *sacerdos* should offer for himself, lest his sins should infect the people, for [it has been said], 'wicked *sacerdotes*, etc.' Then, for the people, as he said: He shall bear their iniquity etc.

2.20 That the surplus property of *sacerdotes* should be given to churches

A synod decreed that any surplus which a *sacerdos* may have, he should give to the church; and what he took of the church's property, the church shall take of his surplus property.

2.21 Concerning *sacerdotes*, that they may not seek payment for their ministering

Jerome: Let a *sacerdos* not seek payment for ministering; let him give freely, for he has received freely.

2.22 Concerning *sacerdotes*, that they may not accept gifts from the wicked

A synod ruled that a *sacerdos* may not accept the gifts of someone whose conscience he does not know. As the host does not help the one, so the gifts of the wicked harm the other.

A Fervensian synod:[45] Gifts of the wicked, which have been rejected by God, should be rejected by saints.

Likewise, a synod: The gifts of those who oppress the poor, should be refused by *sacerdotes*.

2.23 That essential provisions and clothing do not harm, unless you receive superfluous gifts [of them]

A Roman synod, concerning the offerings of these things:[46] Be content only with clothing and food, and reject all other gifts of the wicked, which the most high condemns, since the lamp takes nothing but that by which it is fed.

2.24 That a *sacerdos* should accept the gifts of the wicked, so that they may be spent for the poor and for [redeeming] captives

Martin: Next, Lycontius, having experienced divine kindness, came quickly to him. He also offered a hundred pounds of silver, which the blessed man neither rejected nor accepted, but before that sum touched the confines of the monastery, he designated it for the redemption of captives. And when it was suggested to him that some of it should be reserved for the monastery's expenses, saying that there was little food for all and many lacked clothing, he said: Let the church feed and clothe us.

2.25 Concerning an occasion on which *sacerdotes* must be absent from the church, and on penance for those who are absent for longer

A Hibernian synod decreed that a *sacerdos* may be absent from his church only for a single day. If he be absent for two, let him do seven days of penance on bread and water. If, however, a dead man has been brought into the church in his absence, he ought to be made to do penance because he is guilty of this crime.

Likewise: If he was absent on a single Sunday, let him do twenty days of penance on bread and water. If, however, he was absent on two or three, he should be deprived of the honour of his rank.

2.26 That a *sacerdos* ought not regard offered gifts as his own, but as the church's

A synod says: *Sacerdotes*, to whom something is given by others either as a conjoint gift to them and the church, or separately, shall not consider it as their own, but as a grant to the church, since it is judged that he, who gives, offers it for the redemption of his soul rather than for the well-being of the *sacerdos*. For it is fair that just as a *sacerdos* holds what has been given to the church, so should the church receive what is left to the *sacerdos*.

Indeed, perhaps something is granted in trust either in the name of the *sacerdos* or of the church, to profit someone else afterwards; that is, the church will not be able to reckon it or retain it amongst its belongings.

2.27 That clergy of the high orders ought not have secular responsibilities

Let a bishop or presbyter or deacon never assume secular responsibilities, and let them be demoted if otherwise.

The synod of Chalcedon decreed, the holy council ruled, that no bishop, or monk, or presbyter, or cleric should hold possessions for himself or implicate himself in secular affairs, except for the sake of caring for foundlings, or orphans, or widows, and especially for people who are in need of help, for fear of the Lord. For if anyone transgresses he will be subject to the rebukes of the church.

3 Concerning the Deacon

3.1 Concerning the word 'deacon'

Diaconos is a Greek word, pronounced 'deacon' in Latin, which means 'minister', because he ministers to the altar.

3.2 Concerning the origin of deacons in both laws

The order of deacons drew its origin from the tribe of Levi. For the Lord instructed Moses, that through the ordination of Aaron the priest and his sons, the tribe of Levi should be ordained again in the service of the divine cult, and they should be consecrated to the Lord for all their firstborn, and serve God for Israel. They should also carry the ark and the tabernacle and all its vessels, and it has been commanded that they serve in the tabernacle from the age of twenty-five and above.

In the new law, however, we read the following in the Acts of the Apostles about their origin: Then the twelve apostles calling together the multitude of the disciples, said: Seek from among you seven men of good reputation, full of the Holy Spirit and wisdom, whom we may appoint over this matter. But we will give ourselves continually to prayer and to the ministry of the word.

3.3 Concerning the deacon's ordination

A synod: When a deacon is ordained, let only the bishop who blesses him place a hand over his head, since he is consecrated not to the *sacerdotium* but to the ministry.

3.4 Concerning the deacons' earnestness

The apostle said: Deacons in like manner ought to be grave and chaste, not double-tongued, not given to much wine, not greedy for shameful gain, holding the service of faith in pure conscience. And let these also first be proved, and so let them minister, having no crime.

Isidore said: They are, without a doubt, chaste, i.e. abstaining from lust. Not double-tongued, so that they do not disturb those who have peace.

Not given to much wine, for where there is drunkenness, lust is granted free rein, and also rage. Not greedy for shameful gain, lest they pursue worldly gains through their heavenly ministry.

3.5 Concerning the difference between the service[47] of the *sacerdos* and of the deacon

Isidore: They (*sc.* deacons) instruct all with a clear voice, in the manner of a herald, whether in praying or in genuflecting; they also call upon the Lord that we may have ears for hearing; they also read the Gospel. Without them a *sacerdos* has a title, but no office. For just as consecration belongs to the function of a *sacerdos*, so does dispensing the sacrament belong to the function of a *minister*.[48] The former he commanded to pray, the latter to sing psalms; the former sanctifies the offerings, the latter dispenses what has been sanctified. The *sacerdotes* themselves are not permitted to take the chalice from the Lord's table through presumption, unless it has been presented to them by the deacon.

And it ought to be known that, in the Law, Levites were reckoned to be guardians of vessels from their fiftieth year. Thus also in the New Testament the sacristans of the churches are in advanced age and are to be regarded as venerable old men.

3.6 Concerning the robes of the deacon

Isidore: Those who stand at the altar dressed in white, so that they may have eternal life, let them also abase themselves, white and immaculate, before hosts, namely clean in body, of unblemished modesty.

A synod: A deacon wears white only during the eucharist.

3.7 Concerning the deacon's subjection

A synod: The deacon shall know himself to be the minister of the presbyter, so that bishops may honour the presbyters.[49]

3.8 Concerning the distribution of the eucharist by the deacon

A synod: If necessity compels, let a deacon hand out the eucharist to the people, with a presbyter taking responsibility.

3.9 Concerning the deacon's speech in the presence of presbyters

A synod: Let a deacon speak when questioned before presbyters.

3.10 Concerning the deacon not occupying the presbyter's chair

The synod of Nicaea: Deacons may not take precedence over presbyters, nor sit in the sight of presbyters.

4 Concerning the subdeacon

4.1 Concerning the word 'subdeacon'

Among the Greeks it is pronounced 'apodiaconos'; in Latin, however, as 'subdiaconus', namely, an under-minister, because the subdeacons obey the offices of the Levites.

4.2 Concerning the ministry of subdeacons

Isidore: They receive the offerings from the people in the temple of God, they offer the vessels of the body and blood of Jesus Christ to the deacon at the altar. About whom it pleased the fathers that those, who are ordained to the holy ministeries be free from any carnal uncleanness, in accordance with that which the prophet says to them: Be clean, you who carry the vessels of the Lord.

4.3 Concerning the ordination of the subdeacon

A synod: When the subdeacon is ordained, since he is not confirmed by the laying on of hands, let him receive an empty paten from the bishop's hand and an empty chalice. And from the archdeacon let him receive a pitcher with water for washing hands, namely a cup with water and a towel.

4.4 Concerning the origin of subdeacons in both laws

Subdeacons are found in Ezra, where they are called Nazarenes,[50] namely the ones humbly serving God. Of their order was Nathanael, who, in the Gospel, admonished by divine revelation, was deemed worthy to confess the saviour, the Lord having declared: Behold an Israelite man in whom there is no guile.

5 Concerning lectors

5.1 Concerning the origin of lectors

Lectors are they who proclaim the word of God, to whom it is said: Cry, cease not, lift up your voice like a trumpet. Those who recited the divine books drew their origins from the prophets and the law.

5.2 Concerning the lector's ordination

A Roman synod: When the lector is ordained, the bishop introduces him to the community, making known his faith, way of life, and talent. Thereafter, the community watching, let him also give him a book, from which he will read, saying to him: Take, and be the revealer of God's word; if you fulfil the office faithfully and beneficially, you shall have a share with those who ministered the word of God.

5.3 Concerning the one who should be elected lector

Isidore: However, the one who is advanced to this sort of rank will be imbued with doctrine and books, and so adorned with the knowledge of meanings and words, that he shall know how to distinguish sentences, where a compound is joined, at which point speech should be paused, where the final sentence should end, namely distinguishing types of pronunciation, and so forth.

5.4 Concerning the voice of lectors

The same said: Moreover, the voice of lectors ought to be plain and clear, suited to every type of pronunciation, full of manly vigour, avoiding a common and rustic tone, not meek, but not boastful, not ragged, not delicate, and not feminine.

6 Concerning the exorcist

6.1 Concerning the origin of exorcists

The first to assume this grade was Ezra, who ordered that there be *disposssitores* in Solomon's temple, whom Ezra refers to as administrators of the temple, and whom the church now calls God's exorcists. Just as a prudent and good administrator knows his lord's property and oversees all the measures of [his] wealth, so the exorcist brings the secrets of the whole kingdom of God under his care, in the same manner that he commits the sacraments to memory.

6.2 Concerning the exorcist's ordination and ministry

A Roman synod: When the exorcist is ordained, he receives from the bishop's hand a little book, in which the exorcisms have been written, the bishop having said to him: Take, and commit them to memory, and have the power of laying on of hands upon the possessed, whether he be baptised or a catechumen.

7 Concerning the doorkeeper

7.1 Concerning their origin in the law

Doorkeepers are they who were called porters of the temple in the Old Testament, who were in charge of Jerusalem's gates, and who took turns guarding all the interiors and exteriors of the temple.

7.2 Concerning their ministry in the new law

In short, they come between the sacred and profane. They admit only the faithful into the church. For they are authorised to admit the good and reject the unworthy. And through them we enter the church.

7.3 Concerning the doorkeeper's ordination

A Roman synod: When a doorkeeper is ordained, after he has been instructed by the archdeacon on the manner in which he ought to behave in the house of God, let the bishop, at the archdeacon's recommendation, give him the keys of the church from the altar, saying: Behave as though you will render an account unto God for the things which these keys open.

8 Concerning the recapitulation of the seven grades

8.1 Concerning the grades that Christ participated in

He was a doorkeeper when he opened the gates of hell. He was an exorcist when he expelled the seven demons from Mary Magdalene. He was a lector when he opened the book of Isaiah. He was a subdeacon when he turned water into wine at Cana in Galilee. He was a deacon when he washed the feet of the disciples. He was a *sacerdos* when he received bread and broke it and blessed it. He was a bishop when he raised his hands to the heavens and blessed his apostles.

8.2 Concerning the difference between the grades

It is the duty of the bishop to judge and interpret and consecrate and confirm and ordain and baptise and offer. The *sacerdos*, however, ought to offer and bless and govern well and teach and baptise. The levite, namely the minister, ought to minister at the altar and baptise and give communion. It is the duty of the subdeacon to serve the water at the altar to the deacon and to clean the altar. The exorcist ought to expel demons and tell those who take communion to ask to be cleansed by the water of ministry. The lector ought to read out to him, who preaches, and to recite the lections and bless the new loaves and firstfruits. The doorkeeper ought to sound the bell, open the church and the *sacrarium* and the book being used for preaching or reading.

9 Concerning the acolyte and psalmist and cleric

9.1 Concerning the acolyte's ordination

A Roman synod: When the acolyte is ordained, he is also taught by the bishop how he ought to perform his duty, but let him receive a candlestick with wax from the archdeacon, so that he may know that he is charged with lighting the church's lamps. Let him also receive an empty small jug for supplying wine for the eucharist of the body of Christ.

9.2 Concerning the psalmist's origin, his voice and his duties

Isidore: David and Asaph stood out as precedents for the psalmists. After the death of Asaph, his sons were installed in that order by David, and they were psalmists by hereditary succession, just like the sacerdotal order. The church drew on that ancient custom as an example of supporting the psalmists, by whose songs the minds of the hearers are aroused to the love of God. Their voice, however, will not be rough, nor hoarse or dissonant, but melodious, agreeable, clear, and sharp, having a sound and melody suitable for holy religion, and it should not be redolent of the musical or theatrical art, but cause greater compunction to the hearers.

Concerning the psalmist's ordination

He is ordained without the bishop's command, but by the decision of the presbyter alone, saying to him: See that what you sing with your mouth, you believe with your heart, and what you believe with your heart, you show forth with deeds.

Psalmist is Greek, in Latin it is *cantator*; a psalm being a *canticum*. But a psalm is divine while a *canticum* is human.

Concerning the cleric

Concerning the word 'cleric'[51]

Clerics, who serve the church of Christ, their epithet is translated in the first place from the meaning of the term in Latin. For what is called *kleros* in Greek, is designated *sors* of God in Latin.[52] Therefore, they are called clerics either because they are of the Lord's lot (*sors*), or because the same Lord is their lot, namely the share of the clerics. For the same is the share of the Lord; or he ought to show that he is the kind of person to have the Lord as his share, so that he may possess the Lord and may himself be possessed by the Lord.

Isidore: Consequently, therefore, they are commonly called clerics either because they are allotted a place in the Lord's inheritance, or because the same Lord is their lot, the Lord having said: I am their inheritance.

That all who have ecclesiastical grades are designated clerics

Therefore, all who have been ordained to the grades of the ministry of the church are known generically as clerics.

That clerics ought to be judged before the abbot, not before secular [judges]

The synod of Laodicea: If a cleric has a grievance against another cleric, let him not bypass his own bishop and rush to secular judgements, but first let the case be aired before his own bishop; or, at least, with the advice of the same bishop they shall submit to the judgement of those who are acceptable to both parties. If, however, someone should do anything other than this, he shall be subjected to canonical punishments.

Concerning the clerics' case against the bishop

The same synod: But if a cleric has a case against another cleric, let it be judged before their own bishop. If, however, against his own bishop, let it be judged before the synod of the province.

That clerics ought not attend parties

The synod of Antioch: Christians going to weddings ought not applaud or dance, but respectfully dine or lunch; as is proper for Christians.

Likewise, the same synod: That *sacerdotes* and clerics ought not attend any public spectacles, feasts, or weddings; but it is appropriate that before the dancers enter, they ought to get up and leave.

Concerning clerics or bishops having a case against the metropolitan bishop

The synod of Laodicea: If a bishop or cleric has a grievance against the metropolitan bishop of his province, let him appeal to the primate of the province or the see of the royal city of Constantinople, and let them be judged there.

Concerning the tempering of the clerics' voice

Basil determined the measure of the voice by the standard of audibility. If the voice should be lower and more subdued than the occasion requires, it should rightly be regarded as a murmur or mutter, rather than speech. If, however, it should be louder than the occasion requires—when he to whom we speak could hear even if we spoke more quietly—this will also not be a voice, but a shout, which is inconstant.

That clerics are not to be tied to their *loca*, unlike their superiors

The synod of Nicaea: Clerics must not be restricted to their own churches in times of danger, or persecution, or if their search for a better rule compels them to leave. Senior grades, however, ought not abandon their own churches, but ought to be committed to its every need.

10 Concerning various matters pertaining to clerics

A cleric should represent his profession in both dress and appearance. Let him not seek embellishment for his feet or shoes.

A cleric should not live with unrelated women.

A cleric should not stroll through streets and alleyways, unless he is on compelling and very important business related to his office.

A cleric should prepare his own food and clothing through workmanship or agriculture, as long as it does not harm his office.

A cleric who wanders out among worldly people or in a public place, not in order to buy something, should be demoted from his office.

A cleric envying the successes of the brethren, while he is in this vice, should be demoted.

A cleric being scurrilous and making foul jokes should be demoted.

A cleric clinging to his office amidst temptations should be raised to higher grades.

A cleric singing between courses at a meal, not edifying faith but only profaning ears, should be excommunicated.

A cleric who breaks a fixed fast without being compelled by necessity is to be regarded as less worthy.

A cleric should avoid both the feasts and the solemnities of heretics and schismatics.

A cleric, although versed in God's word, should obtain food by means of his own productive work.

A cleric who thinks that a bishop ruled unfairly against him should go before a synod.

A cleric is not allowed to demand the death of someone. And we ought not censure the powers granted by God for punishing the wicked, even after baptism, lest we should be seen to diverge from the Lord's discipline or go against the Lord's authority. However, all things done with those powers will be kept in the account to be rendered [to God]. However, so long as the authority of the laws is exercised against the wicked, the one ordering their death will be immune.[53]

Clerics possessed by the devil should be demoted.

A cleric is not allowed to associate with unrelated women, but he may live only with his mother, maternal aunt, daughter, sister, or granddaughter; this offence is perceived to be different from all others that nature established.

A cleric who, not being ill, is absent from the night office, should be deprived of his stipend.

A cleric who makes a slanderous remark, especially against *sacerdotes*, should be compelled to ask forgiveness. Should he refuse, let him be demoted and not be recalled to office until he makes satisfaction.

A cleric who, amidst temptations, turns away from his office or fulfills it negligently, should be removed from office.

A cleric who swears must be excommunicated.

A cleric should neither groom his hair nor shave his beard.

A cleric should not desert his own church.

A cleric should not accept interest payments and not pursue shameful gain. If one should be found planning something like this, let him be ejected from the clergy.

Clerics who disagree over a certain matter and it has been proven that one of them provoked an enemy [of the other] to slay or injure him, it is more fitting that he be called a killer than a cleric and regarded as a stranger by all the righteous.

A cleric ought not accept interest payments, since he will not attain a heavenly abode, because he gave his money to interest payments.

That all clerics ought not engage in secular businesses

The synod of Chalcedon: It has come to the attention of the holy synod that certain men who appear to have been included among the clergy, have rented the estates of others for the sake of shameful gain, and have taken on secular business with the greatest concern for their own profit, caring little for the ministry of God, but running around to the houses of worldly men, assuming responsibilities for patrimonies out of greed for property. The holy and great council decreed that henceforth, no bishop or cleric or monk should rent estates or implicate himself in secular affairs unless perchance laws require unavoidable care of foundlings or the bishop of a *ciuitas* orders him to take care of ecclesiastical property or the interests of orphans and widows and people who lack provision, and of persons, who have the greatest need of the help of the church, and the occasion demands it for fear of God. However, should anyone try to transgress the statutes, he shall be subject to ecclesiastical rebukes of this kind.

Concerning the Christian

Concerning the word 'christ'

In the Ecclesiastical History: Therefore, then, when many among the Hebrews in past times were solemnly anointed to the same purpose with the consecrated oil of the anointed (*christus*) they were, on account of this, ordained either as kings, or prophets, or priests. Nevertheless, none of them could give his own name to the nations or disciples or followers and call his own disciples 'anointed', except he alone who is the true anointed, and he was anointed not by man-made oil, but by the paternal spirit. He made the peoples of his followers and the universal nation throughout the whole world known by the perennial word 'Christians', from the word of his name and of the true anointed.

Concerning the proper conduct of the Christian

Augustine: Who deems himself Christian, save he who follows Christ's doctrine and imitates his example? But you think he is a Christian whose bread never sates hunger, whose drink never quenches thirst, whose table no one knows, by whose help no pauper is supported, whose goodness no one is familiar with, whose pity no one knows. Let not someone like this be called a son of God. A Christian is he who shows mercy to all, who feels the grief of another as if it were his own, who is moved to tears by the tears of others, whose home is shared by all, whose door is closed to no one, whose table no pauper is a stranger to, whose goodness all know, who serves God by day and night, who is made poor to the world that he may become rich to God, who desires heavenly rather than earthly things, who spurns human things, that he may know heavenly things.

Concerning those who think they are righteous, but are not

Gildas: While they eat bread by the measure, they boast about it beyond measure; while they use water, at the same time they drink the cup of hatred; while they take dry dishes, they are full of disdains; while they expend themselves on vigils, they rebuke others who are overcome by sleep. They prefer fasting to charity, vigils to justice, their own contrivances to concord, the enclosure of their cell to humility, [and], finally, man to God. They fast, which, unless it is pursued through other virtues, profits nothing. But they who perform charity, proclaim with the *cithara* of the Holy Spirit.[54]

Isaiah: All our justices are like the rag of a menstruous woman, etc.

In the Gospel, the Pharisee boasts, saying: I give thanks to my God that I am not like this publican, etc. Concerning them, Paul says: Not knowing the justice of God and seeking to establish their own, they are not humbled to the justice of God.

Concerning the need to restrain the clothes of Christians

Jerome: Their clothing is neither too clean, nor too dirty, and not outlandish, lest a crowd of passers-by encounter you and you should be pointed at.

Gregory: Surely, no one seeks special clothes for any other reason than vainglory: that he may appear more distinguished than others. That he seeks expensive clothes only out of vainglory is borne out by the very fact that no one wants to wear expensive clothes where he cannot be seen by others.

That a true Christian ought to adopt seven [characteristics] of Christ, along with his epithet

Jerome: A Christian ought to adopt, along with his epithet, seven [characteristics] from Christ. To be poor, as the Lord, who said: The son of man does not have, etc. Humble, as the Lord [said]: Learn of me, because I am meek, etc. Not quarrelsome, as his Lord, of whom it is said: He did not quarrel, nor did he raise his voice, etc. Not angry, as the Lord who was mild. Not greedy, as the Lord, who said: If you want to be perfect, etc. A good host, as the Lord, who said: He who shall receive one of them, etc. Not reviling, as the Lord: When he was reviled, he did not revile.

Concerning those, to whom the name 'Christian' pertains

Augustine: 'Christian' is a name of justice, goodness, integrity, patience, prudence, humility, innocence, piety.

11 Concerning sinners in orders

11.1 That it is uncertain whether, after a lapse, a bishop may be restored to the grade he held

Jerome said: Whoever did not guard the dignity of the divine grade, let him be content with saving his own soul. However, whether or not they should return to the same grade, I know not. God knows.

Patrick the bishop says: He who sins in orders, ought to be excommunicated, since the dignity of this title is great. Nevertheless, he can redeem his soul after penance; whether or not it is difficult to return to the former grade, I know not. God knows.

Origen: Judas Iscariot fell from his grade and did not attain it again.

Likewise, a synod: Whoever fell while in orders, shall rise without being in orders.

11.2 Concerning the ministry that a sinner in orders exercises after penance

Augustine: He who lapsed from his grade, let him be content after his penance to administer baptism, to give communion to the infirm, and to minister at the altar.

11.3 Concerning the decree of the synods about the fallen grades

A Hibernian synod decreed that they shall go into exile and minister there under the abbot's supervision.[55]

The *Hibernenses*[56] adjudge more charitably, owing to the paucity of *sacerdotes*, that after penance they should be consecrated by a laying on of hands, and minister in silence under the sign of penance until death, never acting according to their own will.

11.4 A discourse concerning restoration of the grade

Isidore, likewise: John wrote to the angel of the church of Ephesus: Be mindful whence you have fallen, and do your former works, and do penance; or else I will come to you, and will move your candlestick from its place. Hiereneus and Primasius[57] say this about those who fall from their grade.

In the angel, he indicates the head of the church, namely the *sacerdos*, according to Malachias, who says: The lips of the *sacerdos* will keep knowledge, and they will seek the law from his mouth, because he is the angel of the Lord. The candlestick of the angel, however, is understood to be the sacerdotal teaching or the dignity of the power that he holds. Consequently, the candlestick is the gift of dignity of the *sacerdos*. According to John, it (*sc.* the candlestick) will be completely removed when, after the offence has occurred, penance is neglected and wrongs, though admitted, are not lamented. For he did not say: Because you have fallen I will remove your candlestick; but: Unless you do penance, I will remove your candlestick.

Likewise: It should be noted that the sons of Aaron, when they sinned, and likewise the sons of Eli, were not demoted.

11.5 Concerning the reason why some are restored, but others cannot be

Isidore in a letter concerning sacerdotal penance: In one place one reads that in a lapse of the corporeal variety, the grade of dignity must be restored after penance, and elsewhere, that the right to the former rank must never be recovered after an offence of this sort. And this contradiction is thus discerned: the canon instructs that those who have performed penance and a fitting confession of sins return to their former grade. But, on the other hand, those who are not reformed from the vice of corruption, but strive to vindicate, by some rash and superstitious claim, this carnal offence which they commit, may not, under any circumstance, receive either the grade of dignity or the grace of communion.

11.6 Concerning the penance of a *sacerdos* who falls beneath his grade

Isidore: However, that [rule], which by judgement of the canons allows that a penitent *sacerdos* be restored to his former status after seven years, they did not enact on their own authority, but rather by the ruling of divine judgement. For one reads that when Mary, the prophetess sister of Aaron and Moses, committed the offence of defamation against her brother, she was struck by the mark of leprosy right there and then; but when Moses asked that she be healed, He ordered that she leave the camp for seven days, and return once she is healed. Thus Mary, the sister of Aaron, is interpreted as the flesh of the *sacerdos*. She, while given to pride [and] is tainted by the filthy stains of corruptions, is detained outside the camp for seven days; which is to say, let [the *sacerdos*] be banished from the company of the holy church for seven years; these years having elapsed, after the correction of vices he receives the right of his place and his former dignity.

Concerning law

Concerning the essence of the definition of law and on the word 'law'

Isidore, in the books of etymologies, concerning law:[58] Law is the ordinance of the people, which the elders enacted with the commoners. For what a king or emperor established is called a constitution or edict. A fair constitution is twofold, pertaining both to the law and to customs. Between law (*lex*) and custom (*mos*) there is this difference, that law (*lex*) is written, while custom (*mos*) is usage (*consuetudo*) ratified by its antiquity, or unwritten law (*lex non scripta*). For law (*lex*) in the strict sense is so named from 'reading' (*a legendo*), because it is written. Custom (*mos*) is longstanding usage (*longa consuetudo*), taken likewise from *mores*. *Consuetudo* moreover is a certain *ius* established by *mores*, which is accepted in lieu of law when law is found wanting. Nor does it matter whether it exists in writing or in reason, seeing that reason commends a law. Indeed if law depends upon reason, the law will consist of everything that already agrees with reason, provided that it accords with religion, befits orderly conduct, and that it befits or profits welfare through reason. *Consuetudo* is so called because it is in common use (*communi est usu*).

Concerning the three things of which law consists

Isidore: Every law either permits something, such that a valiant man may seek his reward, or forbids such that it is not permitted to marry a sacred virgin, or punishes such that he who commits murder should be punished by death.[59]

Concerning the reason why law was made

Laws were made in order to restrain human audacity for fear of them, that innocence may be safe in the midst of reprobates, and that by threatening punishment, the propensity of the same reprobates to injure will be curbed. Human life is controlled either by the reward of law or its punishment.[60]

Concerning the binary state of law

Likewise, Isidore in the fifth book concerning the law: All laws are either divine or human. The divine is in accord with nature, the human is in accord with *mores*. And therefore the latter disagree [among themselves], because different laws suit different peoples. *Fas* is divine law. *Ius* is human law. To cross through a stranger's property is just (*fas*) but not legal (*ius*).

Concerning *ius*

In many ways *ius* is a general term in the law, and law (*lex*) is a species of *ius*. It is called *ius* because it is just (*iustum*). Every *ius* is in accord with laws and *mores*. Law is a written constitution. *Mos* is usage ratified by antiquity or unwritten law. Law is either natural,[61] or civil, or of nations.[62]

Natural *ius* is common to all nations because it exists everywhere by natural instinct (not kept by any regulation) such as in the union of man and woman, the succession and education of children, a common possession for all, a single freedom for all, and the acquisition of what is taken from the sky, the earth, and the sea. Also the return of something which was deposited, and of money which was entrusted, [and] the repulsion of violence by force. Now this, or whatever is similar to it, is never unjust, but is held to be natural and fair.[63]

Civil *ius* is that which each individual people or city established specially for itself, for human and divine cause.

Ius of nations is occupying places, building, fortification, wars, captivities, enslavement beyond borders, treaties of peace, truces, the pledge not to molest embassies, the prohibition of marriage between different races. And it is called *ius* of nations because nearly all nations employ this *ius*.[64]

Likewise, in the same book: *Iura* are things that are possessed by us lawfully and do not belong to someone else. Property (*res*) is so named from holding by right, and 'lawful ownership' (*ius*) from holding lawfully. For this is justly possessed which is possessed by right, and this is rightly possessed which is justly held, and this is justly held which is well held. But what is possessed unfairly is the property of another. However, he possesses unfairly who abuses his own property or takes the things of another. He possesses justly, who is not surrendered to greed. But whoever is held by greed is the possessed, not the possessor.[65]

Concerning the things which law ought to comprise

In the books of etymologies: Law shall be just, feasible, in agrement with nature, in agreement with the custom of the country, appropriate to place and time, necessary, useful, and also clear, lest in its obscurity it should contain something deceitful, and it should be written not for private convenience, but for the common benefit of the citizens.[66]

Concerning transgressing laws

Clement: Laws that are not easily transgressed have been instituted by men in each and every district or kingdom, either by being committed to writing or by continuing in use.

Concerning observing and rejecting the old law

Eucherius: Question: What of the Old Testament ought we to relinquish, and what ought we to observe? Response: We ought to observe the commands that pertain to the correction of life and *mores*; but relinquish the ceremonies and rites of sacrifices, which once conveyed the figures and shadows of things to come.[67]

Jerome: In regard to precepts that pertain to life, we ought not evoke allegory, nor should we seek a knot in a bulrush.[68]

Concerning the authors of laws

In the books of etymologies: Moses of the Hebrew people was the first to lay down the holy laws by sacred letters. King Phoroneus was the first to write laws and judgements for the Greeks. Mercury Trimegistus first gave laws to the Egyptians. Solon was the first to establish rules (*iura*) for the Lacedaemonians,[69] by the authority of Apollo. Numa Pompilius, who succeeded Romulus in the kingship, first established laws for the Romans.[70]

Concerning the five laws

The apostle said: The law of nature, the law of the letter, the law of the prophets, the law of successive authors up to Christ, the new law.[71]

12 Concerning fasting

Concerning the word 'fast'

In the books of etymologies: Fasting is parsimony of sustenance, abstinence from foods, whose name is drawn from a certain portion of the intestines, always thin and empty, which is commonly called *ieiunium.* Whence the noun *ieiunium* is derived, because by fasting the intestines may be emptied and cleaned out.[72]

Concerning the three kinds of gluttony

Cassian: There are three kinds of gluttony: the first which compels the monk to eat before the designated hour, the second is to fill the stomach with any dish whatsoever, the third is to crave delicacies. From the first kind there arises contempt towards the monastery, and dread of and intolerance towards the same dwelling place, and thereafter a rapid flight follows. From the second arises the fire of excess and lust. From the third, avarice, [there stems] the noose; by which vice we are not content with the existing flavours of dishes, but we look with untrammelled licence that some flavouring be sprinkled on them. Concerning the nature of this vice, a certain old philosopher said: My father left me indebted to many creditors. I gladly paid the others in full, and I was released by them; for one [of them] there is daily satisfaction, and I cannot be released from him.[73]

That fasting also benefits laymen

Isidore: In the calculation of Lent this sum of legal tithes is paid. A whole year, when decimated, equals thirty-six. Sundays, on which fasts are remitted, are subtracted from the forty-day period (i.e. Lent), and also these days—nearly a tenth of the whole year—on which we go to church and offer the offerings of our labours to God in a sacrifice of rejoicing. Indeed, those who are perfected are not held by the laws of this forty-day period, as our Cassian said, nor are they content with the small requirements of this canon. For, indeed, it is for those who are enthralled by secular pleasures and business all through the year, that the *principes* of churches ruled that at least in these days—as if bound by a certain legal necessity—they are compelled to call upon God.

Concerning fasting, that it should not be according to one's own preference

Basil: The measure of fasting ought not be determined by individual preference, but according to the command and regulation of those who serve God together, and just as the unanimity in all things is related of those, who are said in the Acts of the Apostles to have had one heart and one soul.

12.1 Concerning the compelling need to eat in the morning

Luke in the Acts of the Apostles: And when it began to be light, Paul besought them all to take food.

Likewise: When he had said these things, taking bread, he gave thanks to God in the sight of them all, and when he had broken bread, he began to eat.

12.2 Concerning keeping a fast, because it benefits much

The people of Nineveh fasted for three days, by which it deserved to receive mercy and indulgence. The people of God fasted before eating the Pasch, by which it deserved to cross the sea with dry feet, and to see its enemies drowned by the sea. Moses fasted in the desert, by which he deserved to hear God's mystery. Joshua son of Nun ordered the people to fast before crossing the Jordan, by which he deserved to overthrow Jericho and exterminate the Canaanites. David fasted after his sin, by which he deserved to undo his wrongdoing, as he said: I humbled my soul in fasting. Isaiah imposed fast and prayer on the people of Israel, by which he deserved that 185 thousand Assyrians be destroyed. Christ fasted forty days and nights, by which he overcame his adversary, and angels ministered to him. Peter fasted, by which he deserved to see the angel releasing him from prison. John the evangelist fasted, by which he deserved to hear the divine mystery dictated to him by an angel. Paul fasted, by which he deserved to be cured of his blindness and receive baptism.

Jerome said: Adam was in paradise so long as he did not eat. But as soon as he ate he was expelled; and since she was a virgin in paradise, he knew his wife only afterwards.[74]

Jerome: Some bread and water was given by an angel sitting under a leafy tree to the fasting Elijah when Jezabel wanted to kill him; not wine, nor meat, knowing that the prophet would not otherwise be able to overcome temptations, unless he was toughened through fasts.

Fasting is parsimony of sustenance, and abstinence from foods. It has three kinds: I, as I have said; II, watching (*statio*), namely observance of days, as the fourth day of the week and the sixth day of the week, and the forty days (i.e. Lent); III, abstinence from foods affecting the humours.

Daniel, conscious of things to come, was styled 'man of wants' because he did not eat the food of lust, nor drink the drink of desire.

John, the precursor of the Lord, was nourished by locusts and wild honey in the wilderness, not by the flesh of animals; teaching a doctrine of severity both by word and deed.

Jerome: And when, in the Gospel, a certain man possessed by a demon, whom the apostles were unable to set free, was brought to the Lord; asking, they heard: This kind is cast out by nothing, save by fasting and prayer. See how great is the power of fasts, that fasts would be able to achieve what the apostles could not.

And elsewhere one reads: Filthy spirits appear in greater numbers where they see more food and drink.

That temptation does not inflame those who fast

Gregory: Temptation does not inflame a body broken by fasting. Whence also the flame of the Babylonian fire did not consume the three fasting youths, even though it touched them.

12.3 Concerning the praise of fasting

Isidore said: Fasting is a holy thing, a heavenly deed, the entrance to the kingdom, the image of the future; for he who behaves in a holy manner is joined to God, is alienated to the world, becomes spiritual. For by means of it vices are crushed, the flesh is humbled, the devil's temptations are defeated.

Jerome: Fasting castigates the body, fasting curbs vices, incites the virtues of the soul.

Augustine: Fasting reveals mysteries, removes vices, illuminates the soul.

12.4 That fasting is futile without other virtues

Isaiah: Behold, you fast for debates and strife.

Jerome: When you abstain from your own things, do not seek what is not yours. For he who deprives himself of lawful things and seeks what is unlawful, gains nothing, but doubles his punishments.

Concerning fasting being futile to those who abound in wickedness

Likewise, elsewhere, the same: It is of no use to suppress the exterior character and damn the interior.

Isidore: Fasts with good deeds are pleasing to God. However, they who abstain from foods and behave badly are like demons, who take no food, but are always wicked.

Likewise, the son of Sirach: He who washes himself after touching the dead and then touches him again, what does his washing avail? So a man who fasts for his sins, and does the same again, what does his humbling himself profit him? Who will hear his prayer?

12.5 Concerning the futility of fasting without charity

Gildas said: Abstinence from bodily food is useless without charity. Those who do not fast unduly or abstain over much from God's creation, while being careful in the sight of the Lord to preserve within them a clean heart—on which, as they know, their life ultimately depends—are better than those who do not eat flesh or take pleasure in the food of this world, or travel in carriages or on horseback, they regard themselves as superiors to the rest of men: to these death has entered through the windows of their pride.[75]

12.6 Concerning fasting with almsgiving

The son of Sirach: When you fast, feed the poor; then the cry of your hunger shall be heard in heaven.

Jerome: Fasting with almsgiving is twice as good.

12.7 Concerning the futility of fasting without almsgiving

Jerome: Many clerics fast through proud arrogance, giving nothing of their own to the needy, but saving it all for their meal time. It is better to share what is yours with others, than to fast with a great many people.

Jerome said: In this place it is shown that, through fasting, that troublesome race could be cast out.[76]

That a fast ought not be halved

Isaiah, likewise: Woe to you who strike the chest and fast undutifully.

And elsewhere: There ought not be a halved fast.

12.8 That fasting ought to be tempered

Isidore: Excessive enfeeblement of the body crushes the strength of the soul and weakens the competence of the mind. The body must not be subjected to immoderate fasting. For whatever is moderate is healthy, but whatever is excessive and exceeds the right measure is dangerous; like water, for instance: if rain clouds provide too much water, not only would it be of no use, but also bring danger.

That abstinence is better than any fast

Jerome: I do not say that we should undertake weekly, nor double and multiple fasts, but at least a few days without the excess of food.

The same: You shall have daily fasts and refection, avoiding saturation. For it is of no use for you to bear on an empty stomach for two or three days, if at the same time your mind is overwhelmed by vices. If fasts are compensated for by saturation, the mind immediately grows numb, and the irrigated soil of the body germinates thorns and thistle.

A synod: He who is filled to the brim by evils from within and tormented from without, forsakes the grimacing frugality of the flesh and does not seek the consolation of the soul.

12.9 Concerning the praise of abstinence

Jerome: Let your fasts be pure, continuous and moderate; namely, to be hungry every day and eat every day.

Paul: Do not still drink water, but use a little wine for your infirmities.

Concerning healing a delinquent, and on the sanctification of the healed

Jerome: Sanctify the fast, proclaim the cure. Abstinence heals the wounds of a delinquent and fasting sanctifies those who are healed.

12.10 Concerning the good and expedient fast

Isaiah says: Is not this rather the fast that I have chosen? Loose the oppressive bonds, undo every wicked knot, break your bread for the hungry, etc.

12.11 Concerning the variety of fasting

Paul: One man judges one day to be different from another, another believes that all days are the same: namely, he prescribes[77] either two days a week, or abstinence unto death, as it is said: Sanctify the fast, proclaim the cure.

12.12 That demons assault through immoderate foods

Clement: Through immoderate food and drink demons solicit to sin those who exhibit an inclination to sin, who, while they seem to wish to fulfil the needs of nature, not holding to moderation, leave room for the same demons to enter them.

Concerning the demons that we overcome through fasting

Jerome said: By fasting, the demons fear us, and especially the demon of fornication and gluttony, for flesh and blood—i.e. fornication and gluttony which we overcome through fasting—will not possess the Lord's kingdom.

12.13 That a single measure of fasting should not be applied to all

Basil: The quantity and quality of food shall be tempered. Nor is it possible for all the brethren to maintain a single order or measure and rule. They who are healthy can all abstain to the same degree. However, it ought to be modified for those who are different.

12.14 Concerning exemption from fasting for the sake of kindness

A synod says: For the sake of kindness and love, it is better to offer the newly arrived brethren *uirtus*, and loosen the strictness of abstinence and the hardship of daily impositions; for fasting is pleasing to the Lord when it has been consumed with the fruits of charity.

In the Ecclesiastical History one reads: A certain Alcibiades was among those who were imprisoned for Christ's sake. He led a harsh and austere life, not wanting to take food, consuming only bread and salt with water. When he wanted to practise this severe life also in prison, it was revealed to Attalus that Alcibiades was doing wrong in not using the things which God has created and in leaving these things to others as a kind of scandal. Having learned this Alcibiades began to take all with thanksgiving; for the things that the spirit revealed to the one, so that he might instruct, the same spirit prevailed upon the other, so that he might follow.

That abstinence from foods may be loosed

A synod says: Concerning abstinence from foods without break the *Romani* decided that the advent of Christ the bridegroom shall find none of our laws of fasting. What difference is there between a Christian and a Novatian, except that a Novatian abstains continually, but a Christian fasts from time to time, so that place, time, and person may be observed in all things.[78]

12.15 Concerning fasting from which no place, nor time, nor person can exempt

Jeremiah: The word of the Lord, which was declared to Jeremiah by the Lord in the days of Joakim the son of Josias king of Judah, saying: Go to the house of the Rechabites, and speak to them, and bring them into the house of the Lord, into one of the treasure chambers, and you shall give them wine to drink. And I took Jezonias the son of Jeremiah the son of Habsanias and his brethren and all his sons and the whole house of the Rechabites. And I brought them into the house of the Lord, and I set before the sons of the house of the Rechabites pots full of wine and cups, and I said to them: Drink the wine. And they answered: We will not drink wine, because Jonadab the son of Rechab, our father, commanded us, saying: You shall drink no wine, neither you, nor your children, for ever, neither shall you build houses, nor sow seed, nor plant vineyards, nor have any houses, but you shall dwell in tents all your days, that you may live many days upon the face of the earth, in which you sojourn. We therefore obey the voice of Jonadab the son of Rechab, our father, in all things that he commanded us. And Jeremiah said to the house of the Rechabites: Thus says the Lord our God: Because you have obeyed the commandment of Jonadab your father and have kept all his precepts and have done all that he commanded you, therefore, thus says the Lord of host the God of Israel: A man of the race of Jonadab the son of Rechab shall never fail to stand before me.

Peter the apostle says in regard to the same matter: Nor is it just, on account of friendship with someone, that the precepts of truth be abrogated or relaxed.

Likewise: It is sin to reject every good command.

Likewise: Let us teach our external senses to serve our internal senses. Peter says this in regard to fasting and labour.

Concerning fasting for the living

Isaac fasted for the barren Rebecca, and God opened her womb.

Likewise: The people of Israel fasted, by which it deserved to be freed from Sennacherib, etc.

Concerning fasting for the dead

In the Life of the Monks: A certain bishop took the servant of another bishop, and he died in his absence, and he fasted three days, and the Lord revived him.

Likewise: A certain widow fasted for her dead son and God revived him.

That fasting is forbidden on Sunday

A Roman synod: They who persistently fast on Sunday, it is to be believed that they are not catholics.

Likewise, the synod of Gangra: If someone fasts on the Lord's day on account of what he believes to be continence, or [on account of] stubbornness, let him be anathema.

That it is necessary to fast on the fourth and sixth day of the week

In the life of the saints: He taught that the truly lawful fasts ought not be broken, namely on the fourth and sixth day of the week, except in times of pressing necessity. For on the fourth day Judas contemplated betraying the Lord and on the sixth day Christ was crucified. Thus he who dissolves the established fasts when there is no pressing necessity either betrays the saviour as a fellow-traitor or crucifies him with the crucifiers.

That it is necessary to fast on feastdays

Augustine: We fast, dearest brothers, on the feastdays of gentiles, and we lament the stupidity of these wretched men with true and perfect love.

13 Concerning almsgiving

13.1 Concerning the word 'alms'

Origen said: *Elemosyna* in Hebrew, in Latin it means 'the work of my God'; thus *El* is God, i.e. my [God], *mosyna* is 'work'.[79] This word designates work that is not so much human as it is divine. Hence God is called merciful, i.e. pitiful and heart. Since you show mercy, he shall show mercy by means of the heart. Likewise, Christ said: When you give alms, do not invite your father and mother, and so forth until he says: But invite the poor.

13.2 Concerning the praise of almsgiving

Augustine said: Almsgiving is holy, it increases the things of the present, purges sins, multiplies the years, ennobles the mind, extends boundaries, cleans all things, and so forth until he said: It frees from punishment, joins us to the angels, separates us from demons, builds an unshatterable wall around the soul, banishes demons, welcomes angels.

Jerome: Alms penetrate the firmament, precede the giver, knock on the kingdom's door, convene the angels, summon God's help; they are a wonderful, soundless trumpet. The Lord says through Isaiah:[80] I prefer mercy to sacrifice.

Likewise: As water quenches a fire, so alms extinguish sin.

Likewise, in Tobias: For alms deliver from every sin and from death.

That the poor who are not religious should not be ministered to

In the Gospel: Amen I say to you, as long as you did it to one of these my least brethren, you did it to me.

Jerome in his commentary on Matthew: We understood clearly that in every pauper Christ being hungry is fed, being thirsty is quenched, being a guest is given shelter, being naked is clothed, being detained in prison he is comforted by collocutors; but it seems to me that that which follows—'as long as you did it to one etc.'—is not said of the poor in general, but only of those who are poor in spirit, to whom, extending his hand, he said: My brethren and my mother, these are the ones who do the will of my Father.

13.3 That alms avail the sinner

Daniel said to king Nabuchodonosor: Wherefore, O king, let my counsel be acceptable to you, and redeem your sins with alms, and your iniquities with works of mercy for the poor. Perhaps God will forgive your transgressions.

Jerome: The king showed mercy to the poor as he was advised and, therefore, the verdict against him was lifted after twelve months. They who make bold promises of pardon to sinners act rashly. But if it is promised to Nabuchodonosor, the perpetrator of iniquities, how much more so to those who do lesser evils. Now, it is on account of this that Nabuchodonosor is spared punishment: lest it should appear that compassion towards the poor does not profit. But because of pride he lost the kingship that had been preserved through almsgiving.

13.4 That almsgiving alone, in the absence of other virtues, does not free

Gregory says: What good is it to render one's possessions to God, but render one's self to the devil?

Likewise: I seek not the things that are yours, but you.

13.5 That praise is not to be sought in a sincere almsgiving

The Lord says in the Gospel: Let not your left hand know what your right hand does.

Likewise: When you do an almsdeed, sound not a trumpet before you.

Likewise: When you do an almsdeed, let only God see. When you fast, however, let your face be glad.

Concerning the manner in which almsgiving should be performed

Christ said: When you give alms, do not call your father or mother or neighbour or brother or sister or the rich, but the poor, and so forth, as above.

13.6 That alms are to be given from your own possessions, not from others'

Solomon says: The ransom of a man's soul are his riches.

The law says: The things of another must not be sacrificed to God.

Wisdom: Give alms from your own possessions, not from others'.

The Lord said: Go, sell all that you have, and give to the poor.

Augustine: Alms must be given from one's own possessions, that he may delight in God's fellowship by means of his own possessions, and enjoy the best of things.

Isidore: You should not show yourself merciful from spoils exacted from another; instead minister to the poor from your own just labours.

Likewise: Give alms out of your own wealth.

13.7 Concerning alms from theft or spoils

A synod: Alms from theft, spoils, interest payments, loot, or fraud, give as little benefit as if they did not exist; but it is nevertheless better to give them away than to use them as one's own, lest one's own possessions should also become illicit.

Patrick, likewise: It is plainer than daylight that alms offered by faithless pagans ought not be accepted into the church.

13.8 Concerning the difference between fasting and almsgiving

Jerome: It is good to fast, brothers, but it is better to give alms. If one can do both, the two are good. But if not, then almsgiving by itself suffices without fasting. Fasting without almsgiving is entirely without benefit; fasting with almsgiving is twice as good; but fasting without almsgiving is no good at all. Fasting without almsgiving is like an oil lamp which is lit without oil: it can produce smoke, but not light. So fasting without almsgiving crucifies the flesh, but does not brighten the soul by the light of charity.

14 Concerning prayer

14.1 That prayer should be continuous

Paul: Pray without ceasing. The law, however, shows what it means to pray without ceasing, the Lord having said: And these words which I command you today shall be in your heart, and you shall tell them to your children, and you shall meditate upon them sitting in your house and walking on your journey and sleeping and rising, and you shall bind them as a sign on your hand, and they shall remain between your eyes, and you shall write them on the threshold of your house.

14.2 That assiduous prayer is very effective

Paul: The continual prayer of a just man does much in the eyes of God.

Moses prayed and averted God's wrath from the people that was entreating an idol. Moses prayed in the battle against Amalek, and when his hands slacked, Israel was put to flight, and when his hands were raised, Amalek was put to flight. Elijah prayed and sealed the heavens for three years and six months. David prayed for himself and was freed. Isaiah prayed for the king and people and was heard clearly by God. Jonah prayed in the belly of the whale and was set free. Daniel prayed from the lions' den and was deemed worthy to be heard. Elisha prayed to Elijah that he might receive double his spirit. Ezechias prayed in his infirmity and God added fifteen years to his life. And there are many other examples besides. The most blessed Hannah prayed that she might be worthy to bear children, and she was found worthy.

Concerning prayer for other living persons and for the infirm

The apostle: If someone falls ill, let him gather the presbyters, and they pray for him.

Concerning the distinction between prayer, request, and supplication

Paul to Timothy: I desire therefore, first of all, that supplications, prayers, requests, and thanksgivings be made.

Eucherius: Supplications are made for past and present sins, prayers for asking for those things we hope for, requests when we intervene on behalf of others, thanksgivings when we obtain the things that we ask for, or certainly when we repay God's immense kindness with thanksgivings and praises.

14.3 That prayer is better than reading

Isidore in the book concerning the nature of things: We are cleansed by praying, we are instructed by reading; it is good to do both, if this is permitted. If it is not permitted, it is better to pray than to read. He who wants to be with God always, must pray frequently, and also read frequently. For when we pray, we speak to God. However, when we read, God speaks to us.

Concerning the benefit of reading and meditating upon it

Jerome: All that progress comes from reading and meditating. What we do not know, we learn from reading. What we put out of our minds, we retain through meditation.

14.4 That prayer is futile without good deeds

Christ in the Gospel: Not every one that says to me, Lord, Lord, shall enter into the kingdom of heaven, but he who does the will of my father who is in heaven, etc.

14.5 Concerning the futility of prayer which seeks praise

In the Gospel: And when you pray, do not be as the hypocrites, who pray in corners of squares, that they may be seen by men. Amen I say to you, they have received their due.

Concerning prayer being heard late by God

Gregory: Is it of any wonder that we, who hear the Lord's commands either late or never, are late to be heard by the Lord when we pray?

14.6 Concerning the place of prayer

Augustine: Holiest Christians, why are you so sluggish in coming to the house of God?

Likewise: You are lazy, Christians, in cultivating your soil.

Likewise: You say: I pray in my home, I keep vigils in my bedroom. Well then, God made the tabernacle of the testimony for no reason.[81]

David says: I will come into your house, I will worship; as far as: Your. Hannah, Samuel's mother, did not pray in her bed, but hastened to the house of prayer, and so undid the fetter of infertility.

That a voiced cry is futile without a cry from the heart

In a psalm: I have cried to the Lord with my voice, etc.

Augustine in the *decades*: He did not say to shout with a corporeal voice, which is sent forth with a cry of tormented air, but by the voice of the heart, which is inaudible to men. It sounds to God like a cry; by which voice Susanna was heard, and concerning which voice the Lord himself taught that it proceeds from sleeping chambers, namely from the depth of the heart, with no sound.

15 Concerning caring for the dead

15.1 Concerning the four ways in which the living help the dead

Origen said: The souls of the dead are released in four ways: either by the offerings of presbyters or bishops to God, or by the prayer of saints, or by the almsgiving of relatives, or by fasting of relatives.

15.2 Concerning those for whom one ought to offer

A synod said: The church offers for the souls of the dead in four ways: for those who were very good there are thanksgivings, in which an offering has no [sin] to erase; for the very wicked, the living are consoled; for the ones who were not very good, [we offer] that their forgiveness may be complete; for the ones who were not very wicked, [we offer] that their damnation may be more tolerable.

Concerning the three kinds of offerings according to Augustine[82]

Augustine said: There are three kinds of offerings: for the very good there are thanksgivings, that is, they give thanks to God because they lived well; for the ones who were not very wicked, who benefit from sacrifices if they have already done something of merit during their lives, there are propitiations; for the very wicked, if there are no merits that can help the dead, nevertheless there should be consolations of the living, namely the poor.

A Roman synod: The very good do not need assistance after death, since they freed themselves while they were alive. For the very wicked assistance is not necessary, since concerning them it has been ruled that it is not fruitful, with the exception of almsgiving that should be received from the living and distributed among the poor. For those who were not very wicked and for those who were not very good, offering and prayer and almsgiving and fasting must be performed, provided that they professed their faith in life.

15.3 Concerning sacrificing for the dead

Gregory, in the Life of the Fathers,[83] relates that two women, excommunicated by Benedict for despising their cleric, and buried in a church, were wandering outside [it] when the church steward was saying: If there be anyone who does not communicate, let the excommunicated depart. And no one could see them except their nurse, who told Benedict, who told her to offer for their sake. And they ceased to wander outside their tomb.

Likewise: A certain boy went to his parents without Benedict's permission, died, and was buried, and was then cast out of his tomb. The parents told Benedict of this, and he said: Place this Lord's body on his breast. Henceforth he remained in the tomb.

Likewise: For thirty days Gregory offered thirty hosts for his doctor, who was freed from the punishment and showed himself [to Gregory].

Likewise, Gregory: A woman freed her husband from the seven seals by seven sacrifices.

15.4 Concerning praying for the dead

Gregory in the Life of the Fathers:[84] A certain man who died in sin, revealed himself to a bishop in the baths, and said to him: I have been assigned to a place of punishment, for I have sided with Laurence against Symmachus.[85] But I beseech you to pray for me, and in this you will know if you have been heard: You will not find me here. And he prayed for him and never encountered him again.

Likewise, in the Life of the Monks: A certain bishop had a disobedient minister who died. Thence he revealed himself to the bishop and asked him to pray to the Lord for him. And he, praying, was heard by God, and released the minister from his punishment.

15.5 Concerning fasting for the dead

In the book of Kings: Philistines placed the corpses of Saul's sons on a cross; for this reason the inhabitants of Jabesh Gilead from beyond the Jordan came to Mount Gelboe,[86] carried the bodies and fasted alongside them, and the Lord sent rain upon them as a sign of mercy.

Likewise: Saul's concubine spread a tunic over the bodies of Saul's grandsons, who were slain by the Gabaonites and did so by the Lord's command. She placed another over a rock, she fasted for them, and the Lord sent rain upon her as a sign that the descendant of a bad stock was worthy of mercy.

15.6 Concerning giving alms for the dead

Jerome said: Almsgiving must not be refused, for it either atones for sins, or lightens punishments, or provides forgiveness in the future.

Likewise: Judas Maccabee offered silver for his men who fell in battle, who previously worshipped idols in secret. He would not have done this, had he not known that it would help them in the resurrection.

A certain dying boy was seen by his mother more than once in mourning clothes, thirsty and hungry. Which thing his mother told a certain wise man, who said: Offer the clothing and food for him. And she offered. Henceforth he appeared in white clothes with fine ornaments.

15.7 Concerning the value of the redeemed soul

The law says: The man who shall have promised his soul to the Lord, shall give the price according to value. If it be a man from twenty years old unto sixty years old, he shall give fifty shekels[87] of silver. If a woman, thirty. But from the fifth year until the twentieth, if it be a man, he shall give twenty shekels, if it be a woman, ten. From one month until the fifth year, for a male five shekels, if it be a female, three. If he be poor, he shall give as much as the priest judged fair.

15.8 Concerning forgiveness which is not to be sought after death, if it has not been sought in life

Solomon says: Whatsoever your hand is able to do, do it immediately, for neither work nor reason nor wisdom nor knowledge shall be in hell, whither you are hastening.

Gregory: It is as if he had said: Do in life that which can redeem you. For when you do not do it, it does not profit for it to be done for you.

Faustus said: I do not deceive you when I say that that which does not benefit after death, I do not recommend. I advise, therefore, that you emend your life and obtain merit either by prayer or by almsgiving. For how can a dead man benefit from a living voice which he does not hear, or from alms which he did not give?

John says in his first epistle: He who knows his brother to sin, but not mortally, let him ask on his behalf, and God shall give life to him; but not to them, who sin unto death. There is a sin unto death, for that I say not that any man ask. If it is a capital offence for which commensurate penance is not done, it is as though great sins go without penance.

Origen: Do what is enough when it benefits you, and then, even if you should be snatched quickly [from this life], you will be redeemed either by offerings to God or alms of the relatives or the prayer of saints.

Jerome attests: He who does not deserve to receive the host in his life, how will it be able to help him after death?

Give not that which is holy to dogs.

Jerome: This is to offer sacrifice for a sinner who lived out his life like a dog.

Concerning the dead who benefit from the compassion of the living

Augustine: I urge that thing be done before death, which I know will be of benefit after death. For if a body has done good in life, then it would be expedient to offer for its sake after death.

Concerning the dead who do not benefit from the compassion of the living

Likewise: There are those whom none of these things help, whose faults are so bad, that they do not deserve to be helped by such things.

Jerome: Whoever has not received a *uiaticum*[88] of life while alive, it cannot help him after death.[89]

Gregory: O man, do not seek remission for your sins after death, unless you have already sought it in life. The prophet says: Redeem, brother, your sins with alms. He did not say: Someone else will redeem.

Likewise, the psalmist: He shall not redeem, man shall redeem, etc.

15.9 Concerning caring for those who have been borne away by sudden death

The synod of Carthage said: Penitents, who carefully adhere to the laws of penance, if perchance they died on the road or in the sea, where they could not be succoured, let their memory be commemorated by alms and prayers and offerings.

16 Concerning testimony

Concerning the word 'testimony'

A testimony is so called because it is a reminder to witnesses to testify for establishing credence. A testament, however, is so called because it is afterwards a monument for the testator.[90] Those are called witnesses who are regularly added to a testament as signatories to whatever testament they sign.

Concerning the five types of testimony

In the books of etymologies one reads under the tenth heading concerning arguments, where he said: A testimony consists of an external thing. It is divided in five ways. First, by the character. Second, by the distinct authority of nature. Third, by the time of the authorities. Fourth, by the sayings and deeds of the ancestors. Fifth, by tortures. A testimony is everything that is taken from an external thing for establishing credence. It is not just anybody whose testimony carries weight for establishing credence, but he who ought to be praisworthy for the probity of his ways. The authority of nature is the type consisting most especially of virtue. There are many testimonies that confer authority, namely intelligence, wealth, age, fortune, skill, custom, necessity, and the combination of chance occurrences. Credence is sought from the sayings and deeds of the ancestors when the sayings and deeds of ancient times are remembered. Credence is established by tortures. Afterwards no one is believed to want to lie.

Concerning the three things by which a witness is evaluated

A witness is evaluated with regard to condition, nature, and conduct. Condition: whether one is free, not a slave. For often, a slave, out of fear of the master, suppresses testimony of the truth. Nature: whether one is man, not woman. For a woman always says changeable and fickle things.[91] Conduct: whether one is upright and untainted in deed. For if good conduct will be missing, he will lack trustworthiness. For justice cannot keep company with the wicked. There are, however, two kinds of witnesses: either those telling what they have seen, or those revealing what they have heard. For witnesses do wrong in two ways: either when they relate falsehoods, or cover up truthful words by silence.[92]

16.1 That hasty testimony should not be accepted

In Proverbs, Solomon: A hasty witness frameth a lying tongue.

The synod of Carthage: No one may admit the testimony of one who litigates frequently and is quick to accuse, except after thorough examination.

16.2 Concerning the three individuals to whom a false witness is harmful

Isidore: A false witness is harmful to three individuals: first, to God, whom he scorns through perjury. Then to the judge, whom he deceives by lying. Finally to the innocent, whom he oppresses by bearing false witness.

Likewise: Liars cause those speaking the truth not to be believed.

16.3 Concerning those who must not be admitted as witnesses

The synod of Sardica said: Now, witnesses must not be admitted to testify, who are not admitted as accusors, nor those whom the accusor has brought with him from his own household.

The testimony of a young boy is inadmissible.

The same synod: One is not admitted as witness before his fourteenth year.[93]

Jerome: A false witness is not only he who changes, but he who does not understand the right sense of the things that have been said.

A Hibernian synod: The testimony of a sinner is not admitted since he testifies evil testimony concerning himself every day. If he has not fulfilled the things that he avowed in baptism, how will he be considered a truthful witness by others?[94] How will a testimony of a worldly person contending in this world in respect of worldly matters be credible, as he has not made himself dead to the world?

The testimony of a woman is not admitted, just as the apostles did not accept the women's testimony concerning the resurrection of Christ.[95]

16.4 That the character of witnesses must be scrutinised

A synod said: Both he who accuses and he who is being accused must be asked about their manner of life.

For a holy man certainly ranks higher than two or more false witnesses; his word is superior to their oath.

Augustine, likewise: Though there be two or three false witnesses, they are like one, or they do not even fill the role of one. And a single honest witness is as though there are two or three, on account of the triune Lord present in him, for he is God's temple, the apostle having said: You, however, are God's temple.

16.5 That testifying should not always be avoided

Origen: Arrogance should not be guarded against so much, that truth is forsaken.

Isidore: Liars cause those speaking the truth not to be believed.

Concerning the sin of suppressing testimony

In Leviticus: If a soul sin, and hear the voice of one swearing, and is a witness either because he himself has seen or is privy to it: if he does not utter it, he shall bear his iniquity.

That giving false testimony and believing him who gives it are one and the same

In the books concerning the nature of things: He will be condemned by the Lord, who either gives or believes a false testimony against an innocent. For not only is he culpable, who bears false witness against another, but also he who hastily lends an ear to accusations. He who suppresses the truth for fear of authority provokes the wrath of the same truth[96] from heaven.

Concerning the rejection of a lie

The law: You shall not receive the voice of a lie, neither shall you join your hand to bear false witness for a wicked person.

Concerning condemning a lie

Micha says: A lie, O brother, is no trivial offence; earthly kings also punish it. For the falsehoods of offenders condemn them either to exile or to execution by the sword. If this is the custom of the present world, where there is no real truth, how much more so is lying a great offence in the eyes of the God of truth.

16.6 Concerning catholics testifying thoughtlessly

A Hibernian synod: But if the rest of the catholics, following those who are worldly, have dared to overswear[97] concerning a matter about which they are ignorant and which is contested by many, whether it be true or not, let them do penance by fasting after the manner of those who swear a false oath. For they have rashly surrendered their souls into the hands of reprobates.

16.7 Concerning forbidding the testimony of a single witness[98]

We ought not punish anyone [on the testimony] of a single witness.

Likewise, in the law: One witness shall not stand against any man, but in the mouth of two or three witnesses every word shall stand.

In Deuteronomy: Let no man be put to death, when only one bears witness against him.

16.8 Concerning perfect testimony by many witnesses

Deuteronomy says: He who is to be slain shall perish by the mouth of two or three witnesses.

Likewise: It is resolved that wherever there be contention, many shall bear witness, lest there should be either an unjust punishment or a deprivation of the next of kin.

Likewise, the law: No one shall be condemned by the testimony of a single witness.

In the Gospel, John: He who has sent me, and also the works that I do, bear witness of me.

Likewise: Christ did not ascend to the mountain alone, but with Peter, and Jacob, and John, and Moses, and Elijah.

16.9 Concerning the need to fear the testimony even of several witnesses

Two witnesses, judges of Israel, bore false witness against Susanna.

In a psalm: Unjust witnesses have risen up against me.

In the Gospel: Last of all there came two false witnesses.

Likewise, in the law: You shall not yield to the opinion of the majority, such that you stray from the truth.

Likewise, in the law: Ten spies contradicted two spies.

A synod: The testimony of several witnesses must also be feared, whether they be friends or reckless people or stand to lose money.

Whence it is said: Gifts blind the eyes of the wise. Hence also witnesses corrupted by the reward of resurrection[99] have borne false witness.

16.10 Concerning the testimony of the living binding on the dead

In Jesus Nave:[100] The children of Judah came to Joshua in Galgal, and Caleb the son of Jephone spoke to him: You know what the Lord spoke to Moses concerning me and you. And Moses swore: The land which your foot will tread upon shall be your possession and your children's forever, because you have followed the Lord our God. Give, therefore, this mountain, which the Lord promised. Joshua blessed him and gave him possession of Hebron.

Gregory says in the homilies: If a living person has bound[101] over the dead, let the living approach and bind the word of the dead, and the heir shall grant what the living binds.

In the Life of the Fathers:[102] A dying man asked another man for his grave. The latter said: It cannot hold us both. The first man said: Maybe it could. Thereafter, when the same man died, he was buried in it. And others, who heard what he promised to him, came and said to him: Give your brother the grave which holds you both. The same interred man moved himself, and his companion was buried with him.

In the Life of the Monks: A certain dying monk bequeathed his cell to his minister. Thereafter he went before the bishop and confirmed [the agreement],[103] and received it.

In the truth of the Hebrews, Origen: When Moses divided the land of the Amorrhites, the grandchildren of Laban the Syrian came to Moses, saying: Do not cross the border that Jacob and Laban made. Moses said: Confirm what you say. Thereafter they confirmed their border.[104]

A holy synod said: What the living have attested over the dead should be given by the heirs, lest it should be as a sin to the dead.

16.11 That it is not easy to bind[105] a testimony on the dead

In the Life of the Monks of Egypt, bishop Obius said: Let everyone who has testified over the dead produce witnesses, and bind on the dead in the presence of all, and decimate what the dead had promised, as if he himself has been decimated.

In the annals, Origen said: When Jacob opened the wells of his father Isaac, which the Philistines sealed, the inhabitants of the land said: Why has he done this? And answering, he says: Because they were my father's. They said: Let us go to witnesses, and in their presence confirm the price or the word, how much and how many.

The synod of Anchyra: Every purchase or exchange shall be confirmed by witnesses and in writing, for after a party's death it is not easily confirmed.

16.12 Concerning the testimony of the dead binding on the living

In the books of etymologies, concerning a testament: A testament is so called because, unless the testator died, one could not confirm or know what was written in it, because it is closed and sealed; whence it is called 'testament' because it is not valid until after the erection of the testator's tomb.[106]

Paul said: A testament is of force after men are dead. That is, the testament of the redemption of the people's iniquities was confirmed by the sprinkling of animal blood, that is, of a goat, or a calf, or a red cow. All the more so the testament of the redemption of the sins of the new people was confirmed by Christ's sprinkled blood for all dead men. It is like this that the testament is confirmed: if the death of the testator should intercede, namely of Christ, who in his death attested that our life is assured.

In sacred scripture, however, 'testament' is not only the term for that which is not valid unless the testators are dead, but they called every pact and covenant 'testament'. For Laban and Jacob made a testament that was also valid among the living.[107]

16.13 Concerning two living persons contradicting [each other's testimony]

Deuteronomy: If a lying witness stand against a man, accusing him of a transgression, both of them shall stand before the Lord in the sight of the priests and the judges that shall be in those days. And when they have found that the false witness has told a lie against his brother, they shall render to him as he planned to do to his brother, and you shall take away the evil out of the midst of your people, that others hearing may fear, and may not dare to do such things. You shall not pity him, but shall require life for life, eye for eye, tooth for tooth, hand for hand, foot for foot.

Likewise, in Numbers: When two people disagree among themselves, let them stand at my altar.

Likewise, in Deuteronomy: He shall receive according to the evil that he meant to inflict on his brother.

The synod of Sardica: It is resolved that a lying accusor should be punished or condemned to exile, until he repents.

A synod: Let those who falsely accused their brethren not take communion, until the end of their lives.

The synod of Arles: Whoever has given testimony about another, shall swear by the holy Gospels and must remain in the judgement of God, who said: Revenge is mine, and I shall repay.

16.14 Concerning a holy man being accused, how should he defend himself

A Roman synod: In regard to a dispute between two people with no witnesses, they decided that he who is being vindicated shall testify by the four Gospels before he takes communion and then be subject to the ordeal by fire.[108]

16.15 That the oath of the majority should prevail

The synod of *Consul*[109] said: Concerning those who quarrel over anything whatsoever, if one brings one or more witnesses, and the other none, the oath of the majority should prevail.

17 Concerning offerings

17.1 That those things that are given in an offering fall to the Lord's possession

The law says: Everything that is consecrated to the Lord, whether it be man, or beast, or field, shall not be sold, neither may it be redeemed. Whatsoever is once consecrated to God shall be holy of holies to the Lord. And any consecration that is offered by man shall not be redeemed.

17.2 Concerning houses and estates offered to God, being redeemed by their former lord with a fifth of their value

The law: When a man shall vow his house and sanctify it to the Lord, the priest shall consider it, whether it be good or bad, and it shall be sold according to the price that he has appointed. But if he that vowed should wish to redeem it, he shall give the fifth part of the value over and above, and shall have the house.

17.3 Concerning those who reclaim the things sanctified to God

Ananias and Sapphira, reclaiming[110] part of what they have given to the Lord, are punished by death.

Isidore: Therefore, Ananias and Sapphira died first in the sight of the church, that it might be observed what a great sin it is to reclaim from the church what has been offered, and that the rest might be deterred by this example.

The law: If any one eats of or takes back from the sanctified things through ignorance, let him add the fifth part with that which he ate, and he shall give it to the priest into the sanctuary.

Likewise: If any one has taken back through force, let him return it in full, and give the fifth part with it.

A synod: He who carries off consecrated catholic hosts shall be excommunicated.

Concerning those who deny offerings

The synod of Arles: Clerics and also laymen who have taken it upon themselves to retain offerings of kinsmen that have either been granted or bequeathed by testaments, or were unwilling to offer that which they have given, the holy synod decreed that, like slayers of the poor, let them be excluded from churches until they return it.

Likewise, the synod of Agde: If a cleric has defrauded the church, let him be sent into exile.[111]

Gregory: Do not defraud your sheepfold. And if someone has defrauded, he is anathema and must be cast out.

Augustine: If the gifts of God to man are without repentance, how much more should the gifts of man to God be without repentance.

Jerome: He who removes what he has given to God is a robber of both his own property and another's, for the earth is the Lord's and the fullness thereof.

Augustine: If one has removed what he has given to God, he must be removed from his grade and damned by the church, and ought not be received.

The synod of Nicaea: He who removes what has been given to God, is a robber and a despoiler of the whole church, and he removes the offerings of the whole world.

A synod: Whatever had been given to the church of God in what manner soever, we do not allow it to be alienated from the church.

17.4 Concerning the four offerings of the church of God

In the law, concerning the four foods of *sacerdotes*: The first, Aaron and his sons ate in the tabernacle.

In Leviticus: The breast also that is offered, and the right shoulder that is separated, you shall eat in a most clean place, and they are set aside from the peace offerings for your children, etc.

The second, the sons of Aaron ate at the gate of the tabernacle.

The third, both sexes ate in the court.

The fourth, the whole family ate with the servants and slaves. These four signify the four offerings of the church of God.

As Origen says: A place with tombs[112] of saints given to the church ought to be inhabited only by saints, and it is not fitting that it be without a *sacerdos*. However, an estate with no tombs given to the church, even if it is near a *ciuitas*,[113] only men, that is the church's community,[114] shall reside in it. But an estate not adjacent to the church, both sexes shall reside in it. [As for] the fourth: movable property, [namely] cows, and sheep, etc. It may also be given to laymen, namely to Christians or *monachi*.[115]

As David: And he gave them the lands of the gentiles; as far as: They possessed.

The law: He gave you the inheritance of the gentiles, flowing with milk and honey, and you did not obey my commandments; I will, therefore, take you from the land.

In the Gospel: Others have laboured before you, and you have entered into their labours; and so forth, as far as: Keep my commandments.

Gregory: With what audacity do we accept God's offerings, when we do not observe his commandments, and so on and so forth?

A holy synod said: We decree that the things that have been offered for souls be not taken outside the church.

Jerome: They who strive for what is worldly should be deprived of offerings. For Christ cast out those selling and buying in the temple, and he subdued them with whips, saying: My house, etc.

Concerning tithes[116]

The law: You shall not delay to offer your tithes and firstfruits to the Lord.

Augustine: Tithes are demanded out of debt. What if God were to say: Indeed, man is mine, mine is the earth which you cultivate, mine are the seeds that you strew, mine are the animals that you wear out, mine is the heat of the sun; and since all are mine, you, who apply your hands, deserved only a tenth. But keep nine tenths, give me a tenth. If you will not give me a tenth, I shall carry off a sheep. If you will give me a tenth, I shall increase the nine tenths. Thus far Augustine.

Tithes and firstfruits of livestock and crops and every pecuniary thing are rightly commanded to be given to the Lord, who inflicted ten plagues on Egypt in order to free them, and destroyed all the firstborn of the Egyptians in the final plague. And it is not superfluous to give the first to him, who grants us the second and third and so forth; nor is it extraordinary to give a tenth part to him, who bestows the other nine parts on us.

That it is fitting for the poor to receive tithes every third year

In Deuteronomy: The third year you shall separate another tithe of all things that grow to you at that time, and shall lay it up within your gates. And the Levites who have no other part nor possession, and the stranger, and the orphan, and the widow, who are within your gates, shall eat and be filled. Firstfruits of harvests, firstborn of animals: tenths ought to be offered from both.

The weight of firstfruits must be known, that is *gomor*,[117] which according to some is nine loaves, or twelve.[118]

Likewise, the authors said: Tithes of livestock need only have been offered once, and, therefore, that which remained of the livestock was the holy of holies, as it is said: Whatsoever is once consecrated shall be holy of holies; that is, there is no need to offer a tenth of them again.

17.5 Concerning the church dealing more charitably with those who reclaim offerings

A synod: Everyone who dares to bear off offerings sanctified to God shall declare to the Lord what he has borne off. And let the church choose whether it shall receive the value of that which he has borne away, or a satisfaction through penance.

17.6 Concerning those who remove the offerings of the dead

The synod of Vaison: They who withhold the offerings of the deceased faithful, or return them later, are to be cast out of the church like infidels. Such people must be thought of as slayers of the poor or the dead[119] and lacking faith in God's judgement. There is a unanimous verdict of the fathers in this matter, which said: Taking away anything from a friend is theft; however, defrauding the church of God is sacrilege.

Concerning stripping the church

Gregory: If one has stripped the church, let him be anathema.

A synod: Thieves and bandits and robbers must be cast out of the church.

Likewise: If no human penance is exacted for removing God's gifts, small wonder that removing men's gifts goes without penance.[120]

17.7 That churches must not be despoiled even if their *principes*[121] are wicked

Jerome: Even if *principes* are wicked, they destroy themselves; but God's church is without blame.

The *Romani* say: Let no one dare strip a church, of whatever sort its *principes*.

17.8 Concerning offerings being removed if necessity compels

The canonical rule says: Possessions that each and everyone has given to the church of his own free will, or bequeathed by any kind of deeds and contracts, or by any kind of declaration, we do not allow them to be alienated from the church.

Let no one remove the offerings of the church, unless compelled by necessity to be generous towards one's betters, or, of course, towards pilgrims, out of regard for religion; so that they (i.e. superiors, pilgrims, etc.) might enjoy these things for as long as they shall live, and then let them be returned to the possession of the former church.[122]

17.9 Concerning an offering or vow of a *monachus*[123] being of no value without the abbot's consent

The synod of Agde: If someone has given and accepted offerings other than the bishop and the one who has been appointed by him for showing mercy to the poor, let the one who gives and the one who has accepted be anathema.

Origen: Every *monachus* without an abbot—and, sometimes, if the abbot is absent—has no right over anything. But if the abbot has permitted, he may hand over a few things.

A Roman synod: Whoever vows a vow without the abbot's permission, let it be overturned by the abbot.

17.10 Concerning the inutility of an offering made by a person under tribute[124]

In the Life of the Monks: A certain peasant gave a golden dish as an offering to his *sacerdos*, who asked him whether he lived under the rule of an abbot or under royal tribute, and he ascertained that he was subject to a king, and he said: I shall not accept what belongs to another, lest I lose my own.

17.11 Concerning the need to reclaim offerings that boys made to an evil end; if they are for a catholic purpose, they ought not be reclaimed

In the Life of the Monks we read that one of the two sons of an artisan, whose father was delayed while being away on business, sold a golden dish and his father's hut and his horse; and the other son gave his keys[125] to the church as an offering. Afterwards the father returned and reclaimed [the gifts]; then the abbot proclaimed: Revoke what has been given to the world, leave what has been given to the church.

Augustine: Children who have vowed to God in any way whatsoever, the vow shall be upheld, lest those who are cleansed by baptism be held responsible for the offence of violating their duty.

In Genesis: The two sons of Isaac, Jacob and Esau, made an exchange in their father's absence; and he did not go back on his decision [to make Jacob heir], for Esau sold his birthright for his own satisfaction.

The prodigal son, in the Gospel: The father did not reclaim what he sold.

17.12 Concerning whether to reclaim or not to reclaim the offerings of boys

In Numbers: If a father kept silent about his son's or daughter's vow, he shall be bound by the vow.[126] If he did not keep silent about the son's or daughter's vow, whatever they gave or promised shall be void.

Likewise: If a woman vows anything, and binds it by an oath, being in her father's house, and is but yet a girl in age, if her father knew the vow that she has promised, and the oath wherewith she has bound her soul, and kept silent, she shall be bound by the vow. Whatsoever she promised and swore, she shall fulfill in deed. And a little further on, he said: When the wife in the house of her husband bound herself by vow and oath, if her husband heard and did not remain silent, but gainsaid it, she shall not be bound by the promise. If she vows and binds herself by oath to afflict her soul by fasting or abstinence from other things, it shall depend on the wish of her husband, whether she shall do it or not do it. But if the husband hearing it remained silent and defers a statement until another day, whatever she had vowed and promised, she shall fulfil.

In the book of histories we read that a certain boy bound himself by oath without his father's knowledge, and this was revealed to the abbot, who asked the permission of the father, who was not pleased with the oath, and it was undone.

Jerome: One who bound a child or person of unsound mind by a disadvantageous contractual bond, shall himself be bound.[127]

Likewise, a senate[128] says: We have decreed that no one shall bind the infirm or the young, for both these grades are not numbered among the *perfecti*.[129]

17.13 Concerning receiving offerings from sinners in times of need

In Daniel: King Nebuchadnezzar advanced Daniel to a high station, and gave him many and great gifts, and he made him governor over all the provinces of Babylon.

In Exodus: So Jethro the kinsman of Moses offered holocausts and sacrifices to God, and Moses and Aaron and all the elders of Israel came to eat bread with him before the Lord.

17.14 Concerning an offering by a free man which is not to be reclaimed

In the law: Aaron placed a hand over the head of the sacrifice in the entrance to the tabernacle. This signifies that anything given to the church voluntarily, and with a blessing said and sung, cannot be reclaimed by anyone.

Likewise: A sacrifice for a sin and an offence belonged to the *sacerdotes* in perpetual right, and likewise that which is given to the church.

Likewise: Silver and gold, which were given at the dedication of the temple, belonged to God in perpetual right; and no one reclaimed what was left over.

In the law: Everything that is consecrated to the Lord, whether it be man, or beast, or field, shall not be sold, neither may it be redeemed.

17.15 Concerning offerings removed in past times that are to be restored to their former owners

In the Ecclesiastical History: We have also enacted the following by this law, that if any houses or estates or any farms belongings to the Christians and our fathers, have been appropriated by decrees to the treasury, or if they were claimed by another, or if they were destroyed or given to another as a gift, we command that all these be restored to their former ownership, and that all things be returned to their owners.

In the chronicles: Diocletian and Maximian reigned for twenty years. Diocletian, having burned sacred books, persecuted Christians worldwide. Galerius succeeded him for two years. Constantine succeeded Galerius in the kingship for thirty years, and having turned Christian, gave Christians licence to congregate freely and build basilicas in Christ's honour.

In the same: Thrasamund, king of the Vandals, reigned 17 years. He closed down catholic churches and sent 120 bishops into exile in Sardinia. He was succeeded in the kingship by Childeric, who was bound by oath by Trasemund not to show favour to the catholics in his kingdom. Before he assumed the kingship, he ordered that the bishops be returned from exile, and commanded that their churches be restored to them.

17.16 That it is not fitting that offerings granted to the church be used freely

Jerome in his commentary on Matthew: All who are sustained by the temple's alms and by the things that are offered to the use of the church, but use them to other ends by means of which they satisfy their wishes, are like the scribes who paid for a lie and the blood of the saviour.[130]

Jerome: All who misuse the things that are offered to the church to other ends by means of which they satisfy their wishes, are like the scribes who paid for a lie and the blood of the saviour.[131]

18 Concerning the law of burial[132]

18.1 Concerning burying husbands and wives in the same grave

Eucherius says: Hebron is the city of the four men, for in it were buried the three patriarchs in a double cave with their three wives, namely Abraham with Sarah, Isaac with Rebecca, Jacob with Lia, moreover Adam, and also Eve.

Tobias says to his son: When God shall receive my soul, you shall bury my body, and you shall have honour with your mother all the days of her life. And when her time has run out, bury her next to me in one grave.

Jerome: A single grave joins them, who were joined by one marriage, for the flesh is one; and let no man separate what God joined. For man is the woman's head, the head of man is Christ, the head of Christ is God.

Augustine: Let each and every woman follow her husband in both life and death.

In the Acts of the Apostles: And, rising up, they buried the man, and coming in, found his wife dead, and carried her to her husband.

18.2 That one should be buried in the ancestral cemetery[133]

A Roman synod decreed: Let a man or woman be buried in their ancestral cemetery. For it is said: Cursed be the man who is not buried in the grave of his fathers. Jacob, before he died, entreats his son Joseph to return his body to the paternal grave. Likewise, Joseph afterwards entreats the sons of Israel to carry his bones back to the promised land, saying: Carry my bones with you out of this place. Note that Jacob died in Egypt and is thus carried back to the land of Canaan, to signify that anyone dying among his friends, must be buried beside the remains of his fathers. Joseph, however, who died in Egypt, is buried there, but commands that his bones be carried away. For the former, being clean and holy, is not buried among commoners in the land in which he died, but carried back to the grave of his fathers. The latter, as though being contaminated by the Egyptians' way of life, and being involved with strange women, died in Egypt and his bones, like clean things, were carried back, that he may serve as an example of shifting relics in times of trials and migrations.

The Ecclesiastical History says: Philip and his four daughters were buried in one grave in Hierapolis.

That it is considered a disaster for someone not to be buried in an ancestral cemetery

In the book of Kings: The word of the Lord came to the prophet who brought him back, and it cried out to the man of God who came from Judah, saying: Thus says the Lord: Because you have disobeyed the mouth of the Lord, and have not kept the commandments which the Lord your God commanded you, and you have returned and eaten bread, and drunk water in the place wherein he commanded you that you should not eat bread, nor drink water, your dead body shall not be buried in the cemetery of your fathers.

18.3 That a man ought to be buried in the church whose *monachus* he is

A synod decreed: If one has been joined to a church, he shall be buried in it.

A Hibernian synod: Since a *monachus* has not had any freedom in life beyond the abbot's command, how much more so in death.

18.4 That a wife is free after the death of her husband; as in life, so in death

Jerome: A man or woman ought to honour their spouse. However, she shall be buried in the ancestral cemetery or by the church to which she has been joined.

Paul: A woman is bound by her man's law as long as he lives; but after her husband's death she is free from the man's law. For if she is allowed to marry, then all the more she shall have freedom regarding her burial.[134]

18.5 That a lot must be cast between the church and the ancestral cemetery

Origen said: If any secular person has wished, let the lot be between the church and the ancestral cemetery, but he ought to bestow the majority of his gifts on his church, and only a few on the ancestral cemetery, in honour of the ancestors.

Jerome: If a man or woman has a church, s/he is buried in it; otherwise s/he is buried in the ancestral cemetery and ought to honour the sepulchre of her/his spouse.

18.6 Concerning the burial of someone who has attached himself to two abbots[135]

A Hibernian synod: If anyone commended his soul and body and all that he possesses to God and his *princeps*, namely a holy abbot, and if thereafter he departed to another abbot and commended his soul and all that he possesses to him, to whom shall all these belong? Without doubt all his property belongs to the first abbot if he (i.e. the first abbot) did not tacitly approve[136] his vow[137] while he was still alive. Clearly the recent abbot shall have his body, clothing, horse, and cow, or if he has been of high status, two horses with a chariot and the accoutrements of his bed and the vessel from which he drank.[138] For how ought the former abbot offer for the soul of a *monachus* who left him?

That each man ought to purchase a grave

Observe that Abraham paid for the right of burial.

The same synod: Every interred body owes[139] [the value of] a cow and a horse and clothing and the accoutrements of its bed, and none of these are given in return for other debts, for they are due to his body as what is proper to it.[140]

Concerning the need not to retain the dead

In books: Cursed be every man who is not buried etc.

Likewise, Obius: Each and every person is buried in his own grave.

Likewise: You shall not retain anybody's *monachus*, neither in life nor in death. For a basilica,[141] that is a royal residence, ought not hold the untrustworthy and unworthy. For if it has retained him, it should be considered a den of thieves or house of avarice. Iosias fell in Charchamis and was buried there; thereafter he was taken to Jerusalem.[142]

Concerning the transmigration of martyrs

In the catalogue: Luke, however, was buried in Constantinople, to which city, in the thirtieth year of Constantine, his bones were translated together with the relics of Andrew the apostle, as an example to us, etc.

18.7 Concerning retaining the dead

The same synod: Whoever departed from his church and was buried in another church, if his kinsman comes, wishing to move the dead body, he shall pay the burial price of the former burial, namely [the value of] a cow and his communal clothing, and he shall ask the *princeps* of the place to dig up his grave.[143] If, however, the same community has performed the rites for the mercy of the soul on the seventh day, the friend shall pay the price and the *sedatium*.[144] If the *sacerdos* has demanded it, let it be so, on condition that he was a *monachus*. But if he was a *peregrinus*, he leaves behind only his clothing.[145]

In the Life of the Monks: A certain cleric dying in another church was buried there. However, when his kinsmen demanded his body, it was not released, but obstinately detained. Whence they went to bishop Obius, who said: It must not be detained nor released for free.

Jerome: Where any man has fallen, let him remain buried there.

It is not the sepulchre that confers the spiritual quality of life, but how one lived that confers one's merit.

18.8 That it is of no use to bury the wicked in holy places

Gregory in the Life of the Fathers:[146] If heavy sins do not weigh them down, it is expedient for the dead to be buried in a church, because their relatives, arriving at the holy places, pour prayers to God for the interred. But if heavy sins do weigh them down, the graves[147] are placed in the church not for absolution, but to await worse damnation.

Likewise, Gregory: A certain nun was buried in a church by the altar. She appeared to the keeper of the church with half of her body consumed by fire, as though she were carved in the middle, and the other half, namely the lower, remained untouched. For the same woman was a virgin, but she nevertheless did not avoid foolish talk and effrontery.

Likewise, Gregory: A patrician, Valerian by name, purchased a place of burial in a church. Thereafter he died, and was buried in it then, that very night, Faustus the martyr appeared to the keeper of the church, saying: Tell the bishop to cast out the stinking flesh that he placed here; if he will not do so, he shall die on the thirtieth day. The keeper, however, was afraid to tell the bishop, and was admonished a second time, but refused; and on the thirtieth day he suddenly died.[148]

Likewise, Gregory: A *defensor*[149] of a church, Valentine by name, a man given to worldly pursuits, was buried in the church of the martyr Syrus. In the middle of the night, with a thundering noise, tied up, he was dragged by his feet out of the church by foul spirits. The keepers of the church observed this. And he was lain in another place.

Likewise, Gregory: Someone was buried by his wife in the church of the holy Ianuarius, and one night he cried, saying: I am burning, I am burning! The keeper of the church informed his wife, who sent others to inspect him. They found his clothing, but they did not find his body.

Likewise, Gregory: They whose sins are not remitted cannot be aided by holy places after their death.

Likewise: You see that holy places do not set free but, rather, condemn folly.

18.9 Concerning the example of joint burial of husbands and wives, if they are of equal merit

Gregory said concerning the grave of Benedict's sister, who was buried in the grave that he made for himself, that they whose mind was always one in the Lord, should also not be apart in burial.

19 Concerning the order of invoking authoritative sources[150]

Innocent says concerning sources in which there is authority to loose and bind: The twenty-two books of the Old Testament, and the four Gospels together with all the writings of the apostles. Should an answer not present itself, turn to the divine texts that are called *hagiographa* in Greek.[151] If you do not find the answer in them, reach for the catholic histories of the catholic church, written by catholic doctors.[152] If they do not have it, examine the canons of the apostolic see. If they do not have it, consult examples of saints, which have been acutely examined. But if, after consulting all of these, the essence of the matter is not clearly revealed, convene the elders of the province and ask them.[153] For that which is sought by many giving an opinion on one issue is more easily found. For the true surety, the Lord, said: Should two of you come together upon the earth in my name, concerning any thing whatsoever they shall ask, it shall be done for them.

20 Concerning the province[154]

20.1 Concerning the word 'province'

Ambrose: A province is derived from 'distant vicinity' (*porro uicina*),[155] that is with respect to three things: one law, one language, one rule.[156]

20.2 Concerning the structure of a province[157]

Augustine said in the books about the city:[158] It is undoubtedly a province, which has ten *ciuitates*[159] and one king and three lesser ones under him and one bishop and other lesser ones, ten judges, to whose judgement all the cases of the *ciuitates* are referred. And should difficult cases arise, they are to be referred to the judgement of all ten judges.

Jerome: Where one custom and one lordship prevail, there is a province.

Concerning the division of the world

In the books of etymologies:[160] The elders divided the earth into the three parts of the world, Europe, Asia, Africa, the parts into provinces, the provinces into regions, the regions into places, the places into territories, the territories into estates, the estates into hundreds, the hundreds into *iugera*, the jugers into climes, then the climes into *actus*, into *perticae*, into paces, grades, cubits, feet, palms, ounces, and digits.

20.3 Why a province should not be debased, that it may judge its own cases

A Roman synod: Let no province be debased, but let it have its own judges and bishops.

Likewise: Presbyters and clerics who take their cases overseas should not be admitted to communion.

Likewise: Whoever shall have a case, let him be judged by his own judges and should not go over to others on account of wandering and in brazen contempt of his homeland; but let him be judged before the metropolitan bishop of his province.

The canons of the Romans say: A case of any province is not to be referred to another. If, however, major cases[161] have arisen, they are to be referred to the chief city.[162]

20.4 Concerning scorning a province that has no worthy persons for judges

A Hibernian synod: The seat of the patriarchs and the throne of law and the sacerdotal order, was despised and degraded, when it did not have kings and judges and worthy persons, save those who have been summoned to it from other provinces.

That important and uncertain cases are investigated by other *ciuitates*[163]

Roman canons: However, should major cases arise,[164] let them be referred to the chief city.

Likewise: Messengers were sent from Jerusalem to Rome on account of various cases.

Likewise: The Roman church sent messengers to Alexandria on account of various cases concerning the reckoning of Easter.

20.5 Concerning going to other provinces for judgement

A Roman synod says: Should questions arise in any province whatsoever, and should no resolution be reached between the disputing clerics, let them be referred to the greater see. And if they are not easily discussed there, let them be judged where a synod has been convened.

Patrick said: Should any questions arise in this island, let them be referred to the apostolic see.[165]

Note that Moses took advice from a man of another province.[166]

20.6 Concerning provinces and persons that must be avoided in judgement

A Roman institution says: Be careful not to refer cases to other provinces or churches that espouse another doctrine or religion, whether they be

Jews, who serve shadow rather than truth, or Britons, who are opposed to all and have cut themselves off from Roman doctrine and the unity of the church,[167] or heretics, even if they be learned and well versed in ecclesiastical matters.

21 Concerning Judgement

Concerning the word 'judgement'

In the eighteenth book of the etymologies: Judgement (*iudicium*) is so called as if it were 'a saying of the law' (*iuris dictio*), and justice (*iustitia*) as if it were 'the state of law' (*iuris status*). 'Judgement', however, was first called *inquisitio*, whence we also call the agents of judgements *praepositi* or *quaesitores*.

'Business' (*negotium*), however, signifies many things: sometimes a deed of some sort, of which the antonym is 'leisure', sometimes 'bringing charges', that is, a legal dispute.[168] And it is called 'business' (*negotium*) as if it were 'no leisure' (*nec otium*), i.e. 'without leisure' (*sine otio*). It is called *negotium* in legal cases, *negotiatio* in commerce, where something is given, that more may be gained.

'Dispute' (*iurgium*) is so called as if it were 'chatter of law' (*iuris garrium*), for they who plead a case, debate according to the law. 'Litigation' (*lis*) first received its designation from a dispute about borders (*limes*). Of which Virgil says: A boundary was drawn, that it may settle a dispute over an estate.[169]

Causa comprises either an argument or proof. An argument delivered by witnesses or documents never constitutes proof, but investigation alone reveals (*inuenit*) the truth, whence it is also called 'argument', that is 'a revealed argument' (*argumentum inuentum*).[170] Evidence (*probatio*), however, comprises witnesses and the confirmation of written records.

21.1 Concerning the ones worthy of judging

Isidore in the books of etymologies: In every judgement three people are sought: a judge, a prosecutor, a defendant, and three witnesses. A judge (*iudex*) is so called as if he were telling the law (*ius dicens*) to the people, or disputing by means of the law. However, to dispute by means of the law is to judge justly. For he is not a judge, if there is no justice in him.

A prosecutor (*accusator*) is so called as if it were 'towards the accusor' (*ad accusator*), for he summons to a lawsuit (*ad causam*) the person whom he accuses.

A defendant (*reus*) is named after the thing (*res*) of which he is accused, even if he is not guilty of an offence. He is nevertheless called a defendant as long as he is being accused of something.

Witnesses (*testes*) used to be called *superstites* in ancient times, because they were brought forward 'over the status' (*super statum*) of the lawsuit. Now with part of the noun removed, namely the first, they are called witnesses (*testes*).

Gregory Nazianzen[171] said: In all ecclesiastical cases three people must be chosen as judges: a bishop, a *scriba*,[172] a man contemptuous of all secular transactions.[173] Let the bishop summon the elders and the *scriba*. Let the *scriba* consult scripture. Hence Faustinus said: I have examined and questioned and reached a verdict. Let the *contemptibilis*[174] summon all the legal experts,[175] especially his own conscience.

Gregory Nazianzen:[176] In secular legal disputes let a king and an elder and a legal expert[177] sit in judgement. Let the king summon the *scriba*, and the *scriba* pronounce judgement in the king's presence. Let the elder summon all those and pronounce judgement. Let the legal expert summon the elders and fellow-provincials, lest he should judge rashly.[178]

21.2 Concerning many kinds of judges for many kinds of cases

The *Romani* say: There are fifteen judges. The first is the bishop, the second the *sacerdos*, the third the judge, the fourth the king, the fifth the *scriba*. As the Lord says in the law: And you shall come to the *sacerdotes* of the Levitical race, and to the judges, who shall be at that time, and you shall beseech those who shall judge truthfully to you, and you shall do whatsoever they shall say, both those who preside in the place, which the Lord shall choose, and those who have taught you according to the law. The sixth judge is the elder, as the son of Sirach says: O how good and how pleasant is the truthful judgement from the lips of a grey head. The seventh is a gentile in his gentility, like the verdict concerning the gods Minerva and Neptune in the dispute over territory, conducted before Cecrops, as the chronicles relate.[179] The eighth is a person of another race, as Moses received advice from Jethro, a relative of his of another race. The ninth is a holy rustic, as Alexander, the bishop of Jerusalem, says to Demetrius: What you added in your letter is unheard of, nor should it ever happen at any time that laymen should dispute in the presence of bishops. The tenth is the *contemptibilis*, as Paul says: Appoint as judges those who are contemptuous of the church.[180] The eleventh is the wise man, as Paul: I speak to your shame. If there is no wise man among you, who would be able to judge between his brethren? But brother goes to law with brother, and that before unbelievers. The twelfth is the artisan skilled in his craft. In the history, John the apostle says to two young brothers: Go to the goldsmiths and jewellers, until they shall assess whether it be real gold and real gems. The thirteenth is the word, as in the Gospel: The word that I have spoken will itself judge you. The fourteenth is fire. Paul: Of what sort is the work of each man, fire shall show. The fifteenth is that, of which it is said: God is a just judge etc.

Concerning having many judges in one nation

Moses said to the Lord: I am not able alone to bear all this people, because it is burdensome for me. But if it seem unto you otherwise, I beseech you to kill me, and let me find grace in your eyes, that I be not afflicted with such great evils. And the Lord said to Moses: Gather unto me seventy men of the elders etc. whom you know to be ancients and masters of the people, bring them to the entrance to the tabernacle of the covenant, and make them stand there, that I may come down and speak with you, and I shall take from your spirit and give to them, that they may bear with you the burden of the people, and you may not be burdened alone.

21.3 Concerning lesser judges seeking advice from senior judges on an uncertain judgement

Deuteronomy: When you perceive an ambiguous judgement, and you see that the words of the judges vary, arise, and go forth, and go up to the place, which the Lord your God has chosen, and you shall come to the judge who shall be at that time, and he shall judge truthfully for you.

Likewise: Ask your father and he will declare, etc.

Solomon: Every old man shall be modest.

21.4 Concerning the place in which judges ought to judge

Moses judged at the entrance of the tabernacle, that he might convene a multitude of the people and the elders at the entrance of the tabernacle. Solomon judged at the entrance of the tabernacle.

In Deuteronomy: You shall appoint judges and magistrates in all your gates, which the Lord your God shall give you in all your tribes, that they may judge the people in judgement.

The boy Jesus was found disputing in the temple among the elders and, as we have written above: Arise and go up to the place, which the Lord has chosen.

Whence the prophet, lamenting, said: There is no one to judge in the gate.

Likewise: Solomon judged at the entrance of the temple.

21.5 Concerning the three things that a judge needs[181]

Jerome: A judge needs three things: a seat of judges, sobriety of senses, consent[182] of the majority.

Origen: Every judge needs three things, to wit: dignity of place, the testimony of good people, sobriety of conduct.

Augustine: Each and every person who lives not according to his own judgement, but by the example of the elders, cannot be deceived by any means.

21.6 Concerning the three ways in which judges ought to judge

Augustine: Judges must judge in three ways: According to nature, namely by investigating facts and by corroborating facts, and by the correspondence with precedents, and according to the words of scripture.

Likewise: Every truth is recognised in three ways: When it does not contravene nature, and when it is consistent with the words of scripture, and when it does not depart from the opinions of the wise.

Whence Solomon: As the faces of them who look therein shine in water, so the hearts of men are laid open to the wise. Thence he judged between the women who fought over the child.

Patrick: Seek the examples of the elders, where you shall find no deceit.

Gregory: Adapt your judgement to the words of scripture.

That the sense of scripture should not be distorted[183]

Jerome: It is as though it were a noble and not a depraved way of reasoning, to distort the meaning, and to drag scripture against its will towards one's own interpretation.[184]

It must be diligently observed, that when God's law is read, it should not be understood according to one's own interpretation. For there are many things in the divine scriptures that can be made to agree with an understanding that each and every person contrives independently. This should not be.

21.7 Concerning the declaration of the judges, that they seek peace

Zechariah said: Love truth and peace, says the omnipotent Lord.

Solomon said: Love justice, you who judge the earth.

The Lord says: I give you my peace, I leave you my peace.

Paul: Have salt in you, and have peace among you.

Gregory: Clearly what is meant by salt is the wisdom of the word. 'And have peace', that through all that you say, you should, with careful attention, keep the unity of the faith. Therefore, he who strives to speak wisely, should be very careful not to disrupt the unity of the hearers with his words.

Likewise, Gregory: Let the ones sowing discord hear: Blessed are the peacemakers, for they shall be called children of God. And likewise, on the other hand, let them gather. But if they who make peace are called children of God, then without doubt they who disturb peace are Satan's children.

Peter in Clement: Where truth is dispensed peacefully, justice is found in deeds.

21.8 Concerning the things that peace comprises

Jerome: Peace consists of many things: love of neighbour, knowledge of God, contempt of the world, visitations of angels, serenity in things of the present, contemplation of future things.

Concerning certain judgements of the law

Going into your neighbour's vineyard, you may eat as many grapes as you please. But you must not carry any out with you. If you go into your friend's cornfield, you may break the ears, and rub them in your hand, but not reap them with a sickle.

Likewise, in the law: If any man harm a field or a vineyard of another, and set his beast to feed upon that which belongs to others, he shall restore the best of whatsoever he has in his own field or in his vineyard, according to the estimation of the damage.

Likewise, in the law: If a man uncover a cistern and dig it out, and does not cover it, and an ox or an ass fall into it, the owner of the pit shall pay the price of the beasts. What has died, however, shall be his.

Likewise: If a fire breaking out catch the ears of grain, and burn the threshing ground or the crops or the vines or the field or catch stacks of grain or stalks of grain standing in the fields, he that kindled the fire shall make good the loss.

21.9 That there should be a unanimous sentence

Paul: I beseech you, brethren, by the name of our Lord Jesus Christ, that you all speak the same thing, that there be no schisms among you. But instead, be perfect in the same mind and in the same judgement.

A synod says: If anyone dare break the unity which no man can undo nor remove, let him be anathema.

Concerning conflicting judgements given by the same judge

In the books of Kings: And when Mephibosheth, the son of Jonathan, the son of Saul, came to David, he fell on his face and worshipped, and David said: Mephibosheth? And he answered: Behold your servant. And David said to him: Fear not, for I will show you mercy for Jonathan your father's sake, and I will restore to you all the lands of Saul your father, and you shall eat bread at my table always. He, worshipping, said: Who am I but your servant? Then the king called Siba the servant of Saul, and said to him: All that belonged to Saul, and all his house, I have given to your master's son. You, therefore, and your sons shall work the land for him, and bring in food for your master's son, that he may be maintained. And Siba had fifteen sons and twenty servants.

And later, in another part of these books one reads: And when David was a little past the top of the hill, Siba the servant of Mephibosheth came to meet him with two asses, laden with two hundred loaves of bread and a hundred bunches of raisins, a hundred cakes of figs, and vessels of wine. And the king said to Ziba: What mean these things? And Ziba answered: My lord the king, so that the king's household may sit and prepare loaves and figs for your servants to eat and the wine to drink if any man be faint in the desert. And the king said: Where is your master's son? And Ziba answered the king: He remained in Jerusalem, saying that today will the house of Israel restore me the kingdom of my father. And the king said to Ziba: I give you all that belonged to Mephibosheth. And Ziba said: I worship you for I found grace before you.

Likewise, later we read there: But Mephibosheth the son of Saul came down to meet the king, and he had neither washed his feet, nor trimmed his beard, nor washed his garments from the day that the king went out, until the day of his return in peace. And when he met the king at Jerusalem, the king said to him: Why have you not come with me, Mephibosheth? And he answering, said: My lord, O king, my servant Ziba despised me, for I your servant told him to saddle me an ass, that I might ascend with the king, for I am lame. Moreover he also accused me, your servant, before you, my lord the king. But you my lord the king are as an angel of the Lord, do what pleases you. For all of my father's house were no better than worthy of death. And you have set me your servant among the guests of your table. What just complaint, therefore, have I, or what right to cry any more to the king? Then the king said: Why say any more? What I have said is determined: You and Ziba divide the possessions. And Mephibosheth answered the king: By all means, let him receive all, now that my lord the king has arrived home safely.

That is, as if he were to say: I do not need these things, my lord having returned to his house in peace.

21.10 Concerning persons not to be admitted to judgement

In the law: Judge in a just manner, whether he be one of your country or a stranger, so that there may be no difference of persons.[185] So you shall hear the little as well as the great, because it is the judgement of God.

In Deuteronomy: You shall neither do that which is unjust, nor judge unjustly, nor consider the person of the poor, nor honour the countenance of the mighty. Judge your neighbour justly.

Likewise: You shall not follow the multitude to do evil, neither shall you yield in judgement to the opinion of the majority, such that you stray from the truth. Neither shall you pity a poor man in a dispute.

Isidore: Nor ought the bishop favour the mighty, such that contrary to justice he grieves a poor man, nor deny justice to the mighty for the sake of the poor.

Jerome: You shall not lean to any side. For when you have lost your way, it does not matter whether you lean right or left.

21.11 Concerning the need to avoid perverting judgement by acting rashly

In the Gospel: Judge not, that you may not be judged. For with what judgement you judge, you shall be judged.

Jerome in his commentary on Matthew: The Lord determines that we should not pass judgement quickly where there is doubt, but reserve the final decision to God's judgement, so that when the time of judgement will arrive, he will not cast out anyone by suspicion of an offence from the company of saints, but the obvious criminal.

Likewise, in the book of soliloquies: In doubtful cases, reserve the uncertain verdict that you are unable to reach to the judgements of God; submit to divine judgement that which God reserved for his judgement. Let us not judge in uncertain cases before the coming of the Lord, who exposes, in the light, what is hidden.

Basil said: When the Lord says at one time, 'judge not, that you may not be judged', he did not by any means restrict our capacity to judge, but he teaches us to know about the deferral[186] of judgement, that we may know what to judge. If, therefore, something is placed in our power or our judgement and it is uncertain, we ought not make judgement about it.

Augustine: It is better to suffer for the truth than to be rewarded for idolatry.[187]

That judgements should take into account time and places[188]

In the book of soliloquies: Be mindful also of what is appropriate for every occasion; what, where, when, of what kind. When you have to debate cases, observe the rule that pertains to things and time.

Eucherius said: It is not that justice is diverse, but that there are changeable circumstances that cannot go in like manner. And it is necessary that diverse things accord with diverse circumstances or places.[189]

Iunilius:[190] What are the things that we ought to pay attention to in understanding divine scripture? That the things that are said should be in agreement with the one speaking; that they be not inconsistent with the reasons for which they were said; that they be in agreement with respect to times, places, sequence, intention.[191]

That a judge should fear no one

Jerome: A judge must be chosen who does not fear anybody in adjudication, nor strive after gain.

21.12 Concerning ecclesiastical judges, of what sort they ought to be

Patrick said: Ecclesiastical judges ought not have fear of men, but rather fear of God, for fear of God is the inception of wisdom. Judges of the church of God ought not have worldly wisdom, for worldly wisdom is stupidity in the eyes of God; instead they should have God's wisdom. Ecclesiastical judges ought not receive gifts, for gifts blind the eyes of the wise and change the words of the just. Ecclesiastical judges ought not observe the difference of persons in judgement, for there is no respect of persons with God.[192] Ecclesiastical judges ought not hold to secular shrewdness, but divine examples, for a servant of God ought not be shrewd or crafty. Ecclesiastical judges ought not pass such swift judgement before they know what is right, for it is written: Judge, do not be hasty. Ecclesiastical judges ought not be changeable in judgement, for David says: What I have said is determined. And, elsewhere: What I have written I have written. Ecclesiastical judges ought not tell a lie, for lying is a grave offence, but ecclesiastical judges ought to pass a just judgement, for what judgement they shall have judged, they shall themselves be judged.

21.13 Concerning the four principal ways of perverting judgement

Isidore says: Human judgement is perverted in four ways: by fear, cupidity, hatred, love. By fear, when we are scared to speak the truth for fear of someone's might. By cupidity, when we are corrupted by profiting from someone's gift. For often the rich man quickly bribes the judge, but the poor man, while having nothing to offer, is not only denied a hearing, but also oppressed in defiance of the truth. By hate, while we strive against this or that adversary. By love, when we seek to show favour to a friend or to relatives. For these four reasons equity is often violated and innocence is often injured. Some add a fifth kind: idolatry.[193]

Augustine: It is better to suffer for the truth, than to be rewarded for idolatry.[194]

Concerning the ones perverting judgement by means of gifts

In the books of Kings: It came to pass that when Samuel was old, that he appointed his sons to be judges over Israel. Now the name of his firstborn son was Joel, and the name of the second was Abia, judges in Bersabee. And his sons walked not in his ways, and they took bribes and perverted judgement

21.14 Concerning other ways in which judges are influenced

There are five ways beyond that, in which judges are influenced: The first, by wicked servants; the second, pride; the third, anger; the fourth, private grief; the fifth, hidden envy.

Isidore: For the most part, judges are good, but they have wicked servants. Their appearance is, as someone said, like that of a Scylla, who is herself unquestionably human, but surrounded by canine heads. Not otherwise does it happen to certain powerful men that the inhumanity of their wicked servants throws their humanity into confusion.

The second way: Isidore: Verbose and proud judges that want to appear wise do not investigate cases but disrupt the order of judgement; being unsatisfied with their own office, they take over others'.

Isidore: Some, when they begin to judge, become annoyed, and turn the very sentence of judgement into insanity. An irate judge is not able to fully weigh a judgement, for he cannot see through the fog of rage. He who considers the matter after driving away anger reaches an understanding without disturbing the equity.

Gregory: The bishop ought to examine the cases of his subjects in accordance only with the scrutiny of his inner judge, that nothing human should contaminate what he dispenses by virtue of being God's deputy; lest private grief should make a concern for correction more harsh; lest latent jealousy taint the serenity of judgement or reckless anger perturb [it].

21.15 Concerning the anger of pleaders, that it disrupts the system of judgement

Peter in Clement: For many, in the heat of debates, when they realise that their error is being refuted, immediately begin to grow agitated as a defensive measure, and pick a quarrel, lest it become plain to all that they have been defeated. And, therefore, I often implore that an investigation be held with patience and calm, so that if something is seen to be stated inaccurately, it may be revisited and set out more clearly. For it happens every now and again that one thing is said and another is heard, either because it is conveyed less clearly, or heeded less attentively.

Isidore: Those who pursue forensic matters ought to forsake worldly concerns on account of the love for one's neighbour; or else, if love for one's neighbour persists, let them pursue worldly business. But since it is very rare that charity prevails among contenders, their contention must be laid aside so that love of neighbour may survive. For the ancients called forensic eloquence snarling eloquence, because the pleaders in struggles over cases provoke each other to the point of insult.

Concerning contenders, that they make all things doubtful through controversy

In the book of Clement it is said: What argument is beyond contradiction? And what argument is there that cannot be refuted by a counter argument? And it is for this reason that men cannot reach any result with respect to understanding and knowledge through this kind of disputation, and they sooner die before they find the answer. And, therefore, all things are doubtful.[195]

Concerning a judge's ignorance, that it harms many

Nothing is worse, than if someone believes he knows something he does not, and asserts that what is false is true. It is as though an inebriated man thinks himself sober but nevertheless behaves as an inebriated man would. He nevertheless thinks himself sober, and wants to be acknowledged as such by all. So are they who do not know the truth, but nevertheless reach some kind of verdict, and they do bad as if it were good, and rush towards ruin as if it were salvation. On account of this it is first and foremost necessary to arrive at the knowledge of truth, so that, as if with a light kindled from it for ourselves, we may drive away the shadows of error.

Peter says: What might not be clear to one man, can be investigated by many. For often common report can also have the appearence of prophecy.

It also often happens that he who has defended the truth does not always obtain it, for the hearers can either be drawn to another conclusion, or show no interest in a superior opinion.

21.16 That a verbal offence is no less severe than a physical offence

Augustine: Let none among the learned and the wise think that lying by the words of the tongue is less dangerous than shedding blood by the hands.

21.17 Concerning the testing of judges

Solomon said: Give an occasion to a wise man so that he become more wise.

Likewise, the same: Every wise man gives thanks to the one who refutes him.

Likewise: Rebuke a wise man, and he will love you.

Likewise: Iron sharpens iron, a wise man is improved by a wise man.

Paul: Test all things, hold fast that which is good.

Theophilus the bishop says to the elders: Test what you say.

Concerning the disposition of judges

The son of Sirach: Seek not to be made a judge, unless you have strength enough to extirpate iniquities, lest you tremble before the face of the powerful.

Concerning those who judge contrary to truth

Augustine: No reasonable man ought to be opposed to the truth, no Christian to faith, no religious man to scripture, no catholic to the church.

21.18 Concerning the remonstration following the loss of a truthful judgement

Ezekiel: The judge who used to judge truthfully in the gate has perished.

Likewise: You have turned your judgement into wormwood.

Likewise: Woe to you that call evil good, and good evil.

21.19 Concerning the difficulty of correcting a teacher or judge, if they erred

The Lord in the Gospel: You are the salt of the earth. But if the salt lose its savour, wherewith shall it be salted?

Jerome: But if a teacher err, by what teacher shall he be corrected?

21.20 That the verdict of good judges is to be left unchanged

The law: Do not contradict a judge.

In Deuteronomy: If, however, someone will be proud, refusing to obey the commandment of the priest who ministers at that time to the Lord his God and his judge's decree, that man shall be removed,[196] and you shall take away the evil from Israel.

Likewise: Respect the person of the elder.

Likewise: Touch not my anointed ones.

The synod of Laodicea: However, no thoughtless person is permitted to appeal against the decisions of judges who were elected by common consent. Let no bishop give him communion, until he obeys the judges.

Jerome: Let no one dare contradict the words of judges.

Likewise: Let no one change what judges establish, lest he be damned.

Likewise: Should anyone dare to subvert the words of the just, let him be condemned to punishment.

Likewise, the Lord: You shall not disparage.

Concerning culpable judges

Patrick said: Judges who do not judge justly according to the judgement of the holy church are not judges but charlatans.

In the Gospel: They brought him before Caiphas, the high priest.

Jerome: Moses was ordered by God to demand that pontiffs succeed their fathers, and a lineage of descent be formed for *sacerdotes*. According to Josephus, Caiphas purchased the pontificate from Herod for one year. No wonder, therefore, that a wicked *pontifex* should judge wickedly. It is a sin to use words for deception and not for what they were created. They are wicked judges in respect to the truth of a sentence, so long as they assert the inequality of a person. For they often hurt the just by recklessly defending the wicked.[197]

In Proverbs, Solomon: Every just man is able to judge, but a liar is slow to judge truthfully.

David judged quickly, without delay, in the matter concerning the women.

Christ judged quickly [and] justly in the matter concerning the tribute.

21.21 Concerning the judgement of good judges being decided by the sword of the Holy Spirit

Ambrose: But we must not go there,[198] whither the malice of perfidious men leads us, when judges are unable to judge by any other means save by the Holy Spirit. Accordingly, the noble judgement of Solomon must be followed, by which he judged between the women who quarrelled over the child.

Concerning praising a good judge and condemning a wicked one

In Deuteronomy: If there be a controversy between men, and they call upon the judges, they shall give the prize of justice to him whom they perceive to be just, and they shall condemn the wicked of wickedness.

21.22 Concerning choosing a good judge

The law: And you shall come to the priests of the Levitical race and to the judge that shall be at that time. And you shall ask of them who shall judge truthfully, and you shall do whatsoever they shall tell you.

21.23 That age or race should not be sought in judgement, but [only] the truth

Jerome: Age must not be taken into account in judgement, but rather sobriety and truth must be proclaimed.

Moses took advice from Jethro, of another nation.

The son of Sirach: O how good and how pleasant is the truthful judgement from the lips of a grey head.

Solomon: The understanding of a man is his grey head.

Isidore: What is this grey head? It is undoubtedly prudence.

Paul: When I was a child, I spoke with children.

Jesus interpreted in the temple despite being only twelve years of age.

Daniel judged the old despite being only a youth.

Joseph formed judgements as an adolescent in Egypt.

21.24 Concerning refusing to accept gifts in return for revealing the truth

Daniel said to Evilmerodach:[199] Let your rewards be with you unto perdition, and the gifts of your house give to another. But I shall read this writing to you, O king, and show you the interpretation thereof.

Jerome: Let us imitate Daniel, who, despising the king's rewards, reveals the truth without payment; by which deed Daniel fulfilled the Gospel, which says: Freely have you received, freely give.

21.25 Concerning the need to avoid gifts that pervert true judgement

The Lord in the law: You shall not accept gifts which blind the eyes of the wise and change the words of the just.

21.26 Concerning the judgement of clerics, that it be not amongst the wicked or the faithless

Paul: Put away the evil one from among yourselves. Dare any of you, having a grievance, go to be judged before the unjust and not before the saints? Or know you not that the saints shall judge this world? Therefore, they who judge even the smallest matters are unworthy of this. Or know you not that we shall judge angels? Are they not greater than you? If, therefore, you have judgements of things pertaining to this world, set them to be judged before those who are the most despised in the church.

Gregory: That[200] the ones who are adorned by spiritual gifts should not discharge earthly obligations. And more explicitly, he would say:[201] They who are incapable of penetrating the innermost things, should at least apply themselves to pressing matters outside [the church].

Patrick said: Any secular *sapiens*, if he is truly wise, should not partake in ecclesiastical adjudication.

A synod says: A cleric who takes his case, be it just or unjust, to be judged before a judge of another faith, should be excommunicated.

Peter says to Clement: If some folk dispute among themselves outside the tribe, they should not be judged by secular judges, but let every matter whatsoever be scrutinised by the presbyters of the church, and people should obey their decisions in every way.

21.27 That a cleric ought to pursue his case without litigation

The synod of Orléans:[202] If a bishop should have supposed that anything was to be reclaimed, whether from the church or from his own property, and there should be no denouncement or contention or accusation, it is not proper to remove him from communion on account of his dispute.

Likewise, a synod: Let no one presume, under any circumstance, to bring an accusation before a secular judge, without the bishop's permission; but if he has been accused, he may respond. Let him not bring, or dare to bring, a criminal suit to secular judgement.

21.28 Concerning laymen not judging before bishops, or a *scriba*, or *contemptibilis*[203]

Gregory Nazianzen:[204] If a bishop or a *scriba* should be present, let them pass judgement; because it is not proper for laymen to dispute in the presence of bishops or *scribae* or holy men. Hence Alexander, bishop of Jerusalem, said to Demetrius, king of the Greeks: Let it never be heard, nor should it happen, that laymen should dispute in the presence of bishops.

Whence Paul: Put away evil from among yourselves.

21.29 That it is necessary that clerics should not be judged by laymen, but laymen be judged by clerics

In the Ecclesiastical History: King Constantine said to the 318 bishops who came to him: God made you *sacerdotes* and gave you power to judge even us, and, therefore, we are judged justly by you. You, however, cannot be judged by men; await, therefore, the judgement of God alone. And your judgements, whatever they may be, shall await his scrutiny. For you have been given to us as gods, and it is not appropriate that man should judge gods, but that he alone should judge, of whom it is said: God stood in the congregation of gods, etc.

That a judge ought to judge quickly

Solomon decided about the questions of the women without delay. Nathan judged David quickly. Peter judged Ananias and Sapphira without delay. Christ judged quickly on the matter of caesar's tribute.

Gregory: Judges ought to observe three things: to inquire without discrimination, to judge without delay, not to withhold the truth.

Origen: A judge must crush an injustice,[205] condemn deceit, decide the truth without delay, not seek praise for it, not receive gifts which blind the eyes of the wise.

That a judge ought not judge quickly

Solomon: Judge, do not be hasty. A wise man will hold his peace until the time is right.

Patrick said: It is not appropriate for judges of the church to be swift in judgement.

Job: Every case which I knew not, I examined most diligently.

Jerome: When cases were being brought, they all gave their full attention, that nothing truthful may remain hidden.

That a judge ought not be changeable in his judgement

Pilate in the Gospel: What I have written I have written.

David: What I have said is fixed.

Jerome said: Truth must not be changed.

Likewise: Let a judge decide and not change. For if he should change, let him be demoted.

That an unjust[206] judgement should be overturned

Paul: Every knot of injustice will be undone.

Jerome said: It is better to change than to confirm what does not seem to be true.

21.30 That a *princeps* should abide judgement[207] with his servant

In Isaiah: Judge between me and my vineyard.

Likewise: Let us stand judgement together.

Likewise: He who is wise judges between me and this people.

Augustine: A bishop embroiled in a legal case with the infirm should be judged by greater bishops.

Job: I did not despise to abide judgement with my servant, etc.

21.31 That a *monachus* ought not litigate against[208] his *princeps*

In the law: Do not contend with your elders. Whoever despises his *princeps*, let God despise him.

Augustine: He whom God sent to govern the church should not be despised.

Jerome: Let the church's authority curb every pride.

Likewise: Whoever, through insubordinate pride, has dared to rise up against his head, should be condemned.

Likewise: It is not proper for the limbs to rise against the head.

Likewise: There is need to heal this recent vice among *monachi*, by which each and every one wants to litigate against his *princeps*.

22 Concerning truth

Concerning refusing to accept gifts in return for revealing the truth

Daniel said to Balthasar: Let your rewards be with you, and the gifts of your house give to another. But I shall read this writing to you, O king, and show you the interpretation thereof.

Jerome says: Let us imitate Daniel, who, despising the king's rewards, reveals the truth for no price; by which deed Daniel fulfilled the Gospel, which says: Freely have you received, freely give.

The Lord in the law: Do not accept gifts which blind even the eyes of the wise, and change the verdicts of the just.

22.1 That truth must be judged by whichever mouth utters it

Gildas: Truth shines to the wise man from the mouth of whoever utters it.

That truth is more precious than anything

Peter: For, most certainly, neither friendship, nor kinship, nor the loftiness of the reign, ought to be more precious to man than truth; indeed, truth is not lacking in reason, and in truth there is no lie.

Concerning those who judge contrary to truth

Augustine said: No reasonable man ought to be opposed to truth, no Christian to faith, no religious man to scripture, no catholic to the church.

That it is not appropriate to withhold the truth

Isaiah said: Woe to me, because I am a man polluted by my lips.

Concerning the distinction between lie and truth

Clement said: There is, therefore, this distinction: What is frequently said by God to be true, either through the prophets, or through various visions, is always true. However, what is taught by demons is not always true. It is, therefore, clear that things in which there is an occasional lie, are not spoken by the true God. For in truth there is never a lie.

22.2 That the truth is not loved

In Isaiah: Speak unto us what we wish and pleasing words, or else you will die.

King Zedechiah said to Isaiah: You shall not preach God's words to the people, lest they shall kill you.

Paul: Telling the truth, I have become your enemy.

Jerome: Three things induce hatred: If you have spoken the truth, if you have been good, if you become full of riches.

Likewise, the philosopher: Indulgence begets friends, truth begets hatred.[209]

A sermon: The truth is bitter, and so are they who proclaim it.

Augustine: Truth can be oppressed, but it cannot be defeated.

22.3 Concerning unsettling the truth

The son of Sirach: Truth is unsettled, it is not broken. Truth is thrown into disarray not on account of itself, but on account of those who proclaim it.

That truth must not be suppressed on account of humility

In the Gospel of John: If I shall say that I know him not, I shall be like you, a liar.

Augustine in his commentary on John: Arrogance, therefore, should not be avoided such that truth is forsaken.[210]

22.4 Concerning the three ways of identifying truth

Augustine: There are three ways to identify what is true: when it does not contravene nature, and when it is consistent with the words of scripture, and when it does not differ from the opinions of the wise.

That the truth does not always prevail

Clement: However, it often happens that he who has defended the truth, does not always obtain it, for the hearers can either be drawn to another conclusion, or show no interest in a superior opinion.

22.5 Concerning wise men who see into people's hearts

Solomon: As the faces of them that look therein, shine in the water, so the hearts of men are laid open to the wise.

Concerning old men

Concerning respecting the old man

The law says: Respect the person of the elder.

Likewise: Rise up before the hoary head.

Concerning the modesty of old men

Solomon: Every old man shall be modest.

That the iniquity of old men should be guarded against

Daniel: Iniquity has been found among the elders of Israel.

Likewise: Iniquity came forth from the elders.

23 Concerning lordship and subjection

23.1 Concerning lords being kind to their *serui*[211]

Paul: The head cannot say to the feet: I have no need of you; but much more those that seem to be the more feeble members of the body are necessary.

Paul: Masters, cease threatening your subjects.

23.2 Concerning the subjection of *serui* to their lords

Paul: *Serui,* be obedient to them that are your lords according to the flesh, with fear and trembling, just as to Christ. Not serving to the eye, but as to the Lord. Knowing that, whatsoever good thing any man shall do, the same shall he receive from the Lord, whether he be bond, or free.

Likewise: *Serui,* be obedient to your masters, not only to the good, but also to the difficult.

23.3 Concerning the church's lordship over its subjects

It is the duty of a man of such meekness to be blameless, not puffed up with pride, not violent, not given to wine, not a beater.

23.4 Concerning the subjects' subjection to higher powers

Paul: *Serui,* be subject to every human authority for God's sake: whether it be to the king as the one of superior grade, or to governors as sent by him for the punishment of evildoers, but for the praise of the good.

Paul to the Romans: Be subject to all higher powers, for there is no power but from God. And those that are, are ordained of God. Therefore, he who resists power resists God. You want, however, not to be afraid of power: do good and you shall have praise from the same power. For he is God's minister to you unto good. But if you do that which is evil, fear; for he does not bear a sword in vain.

Concerning those who cast off the yoke of servitude under the pretext of Christianity

A Neocaesarean synod:[212] Should anyone, under the pretext of divine veneration, teach a slave[213] to despise his own lord, so that he would depart from his service and cease to serve him with goodwill and every respect, let him be anathema.

24 Concerning kingship

Concerning the word 'kingship'

Isidore in the books of etymologies: 'Kingship' is derived from 'kings'. For just as kings (*reges*) are so called from 'reigning' (*regendo*), so 'kingship' from 'kings'. For one who does not correct does not reign. By doing right the name of king is sustained, by doing wrong it is lost. Hence also among the elders there was such a proverb: You will be a king if you do right, if not you will not be.

24.1 Concerning the king's ordination[214]

In the book of Kings: Samuel took a little vial of oil and poured it upon Saul's head, and kissed him, and said: Behold, the Lord anointed you to be prince over his inheritance.

Concerning reproving kings

The book of Solomon's Wisdom: Hear therefore, O kings, and understand; learn, O judges of the ends of the earth; give ear, you who rule the multitude and who please yourselves in masses of nations. For power is given you by God and strength by the most high, who will examine your works and inspect your thoughts. For when you were ministers of his kingdom, you did not judge rightly, nor kept the law of justice, nor went by his will. Horribly and speedily will he appear to you, for a most severe judgement shall be for them who bear rule. For to him who is little, mercy is granted.[215]

Solomon: The mighty shall be mightily tormented.

That a young brother precedes his elder brothers to the kingship[216]

In the books of Kings: Isai therefore brought his seven sons before Samuel. Samuel said to Isai: Are all your sons here? He answered: There remains yet a young one, who tends to the sheep. And Samuel said: Rise, send and fetch him. He sent therefore and brought him. Now, he was ruddy and beautiful to behold, and of a comely face. And the Lord said: Arise, and anoint him, for this is he. Then Samuel took the horn of oil, and anointed him in the midst of his brethren.

Concerning the different phases of the reign

In the proverbs of the Greeks one reads: According to the experts, the following are the five phases of the reign: the first is the phase of labour, when it is strived for through wars and through crushing enemies. The second phase is when, in increments, it grows like the moon waxes into fullness. The third is the phase of fullness, when it does not sustain injury from anyone anywhere. The fourth phase, as I have said, is when it fades. The fifth is the phase of struggling and contradiction. For it cannot show favour to anybody, and nothing can help it. These are the five phases of the kingship of certain kings.[217]

That a foreign king is called upon to reign over another city

In the chronicles: Severus ruled eighteen years. Severus was from the province of Tripoli, the city of Leptis. He was the only Roman emperor up to the present day from Africa.

Concerning the two virtues of a king

In the book of etymologies: There are two principal royal virtues: justice, but mercy is praised more highly in kings. For justice by itself is severe. Whence it is said: Mercy and truth preserve the king.

24.2 Concerning the king's ordination by lot[218]

Samuel said to the sons of Israel: Now stand before the Lord by your tribes and by your families. And Samuel brought to him all the sons of Israel, and the lot fell on the tribe of Benjamin and the kindreds thereof, and the lot fell on the kindred of Metri, and it came to Saul the son of Cis.

24.3 That the deeds of bad kings are destructive[219]

Patrick: The ninth grade of abuse is the iniquitous king: although he wants to be the ruler of others, he does not preserve the dignity of his title in himself. For the title 'king' implies that he should assume[220] the office of leadership of all his subjects. But how will he be able to correct others, who does not correct his own manners to prevent them from becoming wicked? The iniquity of the iniquitous king shatters the peace of peoples, raises stumbling blocks before the kingship, strips the earth of its fruits, slackens the subjection of the people, makes ready for the deaths of friends, provokes on all sides the incursions of enemies into the province, unleashes beasts to mangle domestic animals, stirs up storms, inhibits the fertility of the land and the produce of the sea, sets lightening on fire, burns up the blossoms of the trees, casts down fruit before it is ripe. Not only does it sully the face of the present reign, but also casts a shadow over sons and grandsons, so that they may not inherit the kingdom. On account of the sacrilege of kings Saul, Jeroboam, Ahab, and others, God extinguished their seed, so that it might not reign.

24.4 That the deeds of good kings are efficacious[221]

Patrick: This is, therefore, the justice of a just king: he does not judge anyone unjustly, he is a defender of strangers and widows and orphans, he prevents thefts, punishes adultery, he does not sustain the unchaste and the buffoons, he does not exalt the iniquitous, he casts out the impious from the land, he does not allow killers and perjurers to live, he defends churches, he feeds the poor with alms, he appoints the just over the affairs of the kingdom, he has elders and wise men and sober men as councillors, he does not heed the superstitions of magicians, oracles and augurs, he bravely and justly defends the homeland against its enemies, he has faith in God through all things, he does not puff up his mind out of prosperity, he bears all hardship with patience, he has catholic faith in God, he does not allow his sons to behave impiously, he persists in prayer at fixed times, he does not eat before the designated hour. The king's justice is the people's peace, the fatherland's protection, the commoners' freedom, the nation's defence, the welfare of the weak, the joy of men, the temperance of weather, the serenity of the sea, the fertility of the land, the consolation of the poor, the sons' inheritance, hope of future blessing, abundance of crops, fecundity of trees.

Elsewhere one reads: The kingdom's prosperity is in the king's mercy, the exaltation of his name in his generosity, and his longevity in his truthful judgement.

Solomon: Mercy and truth preserve the king, and his throne is strengthened by clemency.

24.5 That it is not proper for a young man to reign

Solomon: Woe to you, O city, whose king is a child.

Isaiah: I will give children to be their princes.

24.6 Concerning a king not having many wives

In the books of Kings: A king shall not have many wives, who may disquiet his soul.

A synod: The more dignity a king receives, the more fear he ought to have. For many women deprave his soul; if his mind is distracted by a multitude of women, he is more likely to lapse into a great sin.

24.7 That a brief and just reign is better than a long and wicked one

Gregory Nazianzen:[222] A brief and lawful reign is much better than a long tyranny; and it is better to have a small share with justice, than many possessions with injustice.

24.8 Concerning the one not protecting a king

David to Abner, Saul's keeper: As the Lord liveth, you are the sons of death, for you have not protected your master, the Lord's anointed.

Concerning the one slaying a king

David to Abisai: Kill him not. For who shall raise his hand against the Lord's anointed, and shall be guiltless?

24.9 Concerning paying tribute[223] to the king

Christ said: Render unto caesar the things that are caesar's, and to God the things that are God's.

Jerome: But what are these, that are caesar's? These are service, tribute, honour, fear. What are these that are God's? Tithes, firstfruits, an offering, fear. Christ rendered tribute for himself and Peter, saying: Render unto them for my sake and yours.

Paul: Render to all men their dues: tribute, to whom tribute is due; tax, to whom tax; honour, to whom honour; fear, to whom fear.

Likewise: Joseph has rendered tax to the king, to God fear.

Joseph went up to Judea, that he may render tribute for himself and Mary.

Augustine said: In the days of tribute Judas of Galilee rose in revolt. He inferred from the law[224] that they who offer tithes to the temple, ought not render tributes. This heresy grew so strong that it disturbed the populace. Whence this question was addressed to the Lord: whether or not tribute may be given to caesar.

Luke said: There went out a decree from caesar Augustus, that everyone throughout the world should declare the value of their property.

Likewise: Christ rendered tribute for himself and Peter, saying: Render unto them for my sake and yours.

Joseph obtained all of Egypt for Pharaoh by establishing a levy of the fifth part.[225]

24.10 That a king's tribute must not be levied from the church

Christ said: And so the children of the kingdom are free in every kingdom.

Augustine said: If these children are free from tribute in each and every earthly kingdom, all the more so the children of His kingdom, to whom all earthly kingdoms are subject.

Jerome in his commentary on Matthew: Our Lord was the son of God both according to the flesh and the spirit, and he descended from the line of David, or by the word of the Almighty. Therefore he did not owe tributes as the son of the king, but had to fulfil all justice as one who assumed the humility of the flesh. He bore the cross for us, and rendered tributes, but we do not render tributes for his honour and we, as though the king's children, are also immune from taxes.

Ambrose: Christ asks about the image of the world: the image of God is one thing, the image of the world another. Christ does not have the image of caesar, for he is the image of God, who said: This is not my kingdom. Nor does Peter possess anything of this world, who said: We leave everything for your sake. It is not found in Jacob and John, who are sons of thunder, but caesar's image is found in the sea of this world. On account of which Christ did not give from his own, but rendered to the world what belonged to the world.

Ambrose: A catholic church is free from all tribute. However, should a burden be imposed upon it by reason of a wicked *princeps*,[226] it ought to be restored to its former liberty. For a wife owes no tribute as long as she is joined to a man, namely the church. She says, 'his left is under my head', namely the work of the present world, 'and his right embraces me', namely future life.

Jerome: The pressure from rulers can be sustained by the church, so long as it is not being weighed down by worldly burdens.

Likewise, Ambrose: And you, if you do not want to owe anything to the earthly king, relinquish all that you have and follow Christ.

24.11 That things belonging to the poor should not be rendered as tribute

Jerome: But more simply the Lord gave us this as an example, that he considered it as an impious deed to render as tribute that which belongs to the poor, namely the money that Judas kept in bags.

24.12 Concerning the severity of the king's rule

Samuel told the words of the Lord to the people of Israel, who were asking the Lord for a king: This will be the right of the king who shall reign over you: he will take your sons, and put them in his chariots, and will make them his horsemen, and his running footmen to run before his chariots. And the king will appoint of them to be his tribunes, and centurions, and the ploughmen of his fields, and the reapers of his corn, and the smiths of his weapons and chariots. The king will also take your daughters as makers of his ointments, and his cooks, and bakers. And he will take your fields, and your vineyards, and your best olive groves, and give them to his servants and slaves. Moreover he will take the tenth of your corn, and of the revenues of your vineyards, to give to his eunuchs and servants.

Your servants also and handmaids, and the best of your young men, and your donkeys he will take away, and put them to his work. Your flocks also he will tithe. And you shall be his servants.

On account of which Saul, who did all those things, fell in battle with his son

Likewise: Solomon's son, forsaking the elders' advice, accepting the advice of the young, oppressed his people, on account of which his kingdom was divided from his hand.

24.13 Concerning punishing those who disobey the king's law

In Ezra: Artaxerxes, the king of the Persians, says to Ezra, the swift scribe of the law of Moses: You, Ezra, according to the wisdom of your God, which is in your hand, appoint judges and magistrates, that may judge all the people that is beyond the river, that is, for them who know the law of your God; but also teach the ignorant freely. And whosoever will not observe the law of your God and the law of the king diligently, judgement shall be executed upon him, either unto death, or unto banishment, or to the confiscation of goods, or at least to prison.

Likewise: And proclamation was made in Judah and Jerusalem to all the children of the captivity, that they should assemble together into Jerusalem. And that whosoever would not come within three days, according to the counsel of the elders, all his substance will be taken away.

Concerning punishing the recklessness of those who contradict the decrees of the whole people

In the books of Judges: There was a certain Levite, who dwelt on the side of Mount Ephraim, who took a wife of Bethlehem Judah, up to the point where it is said: The sun went down upon them when they were by Gabaa, which is in the tribe of Benjamin, and they turned into it, to lodge there, etc.

And the children of Israel said: They had bound themselves when they were in Maspha, that whosoever were absent should be slain. And the children of Israel being moved with repentance for their brother Benjamin said: One tribe is taken away from Israel; whence shall they take wives? For we have all in general sworn not to give our daughters to them. Therefore they said: Who is there of all the tribes of Israel, that came not up to the Lord in Maspha? And behold the inhabitants of Jabesh Gilead were found not to have been in that army, when they were in Shiloh, no one of them was found there. So the sons of Israel sent ten thousand of the valiant men, to whom they said: Go and put the inhabitants of Jabesh Gilead to the sword, with their wives and their children. Every male, and all women that have known men, you must kill. And there were found of Jabesh Gilead four hundred virgins that had not known the bed of a man, and they brought them to God's camp Shiloh. And they sent messengers to the children of Benjamin, who were at the rock of Remmon, etc.

24.14 That a king must rule leniently

Ezra says: There was a great cry of the people, and of their wives against their Jewish brethren, on account of the burden of the rule on both men and women, sons and daughters, fields and fruits, livestock and all possessions. For they possess all things, and we have nothing in our power. And I was exceedingly angry when I heard their cry according to these words. And my heart contemplated, and I rebuked the nobles and magistrates, and said to them: Let none of you exact interest payments of your brethren.[227] And I said to them again: The thing you do is not good. Why do you not walk in the fear of our Lord, that you be not reproached by your enemies? Restore, therefore, to them this day their fields, their vineyards, their oliveyards, and their houses. And they said: We shall do this, as you say, and we shall restore to them all that is theirs.

In the chronicles: Antoninus Pius imposed lighter taxes and released debts throughout the Roman kingdom, whence he was styled father of the nation, and consequently he received this as a surname.

Likewise, in the same: Titus governed so kindly, that he never punished anybody, and even released those who were convicted of conspiring against him. Among other things, he is credited with the famous saying, that each day in which he did nothing good was lost.

Likewise, in the chronicles: Curtius, namely the consul of Salassus, was burned alive with four cohorts in the island of Arada, because he had exacted tributes[228] too heavily.

Concerning the lightness of tribute

In the chronicles one reads: Marcus Antonius, Lucius Aurelius Commodus, gave much to many, and they remitted the payment that was owed to the treasury by the provinces. They burned the tablets of the debtors in the middle of the forum of the Roman city and, that no single good thing should be lacking, they tempered each and every severe law with new regulations.

24.15 Concerning moderate rule

Jerome: There are seven things that befit each king: to fear God, to judge truthfully, to be humble towards good men, to be proud towards the wicked, to feed the poor, to help the church of God, to be the same among kinsmen and strangers. They must be careful, for it is said: By me kings reign and obtain their rule.

Likewise, Jerome: Every ordination is from God, all malicious deeds from the devil. And so Maximianus, king of the Romans, fell in battle for oppressing the church of God.

24.16 That lords ought not seize by force, nor defraud

Moses: I did not harm anyone, nor did I touch the donkey of another.

Job: I did not defraud anyone, I did not touch the ox and sheep of another, nor have I taken away anything by force, I loved my elders as my fathers, I nourished the young, fed the poor.

Orosius: To be a good shepherd is to shear the sheep, not flay them.

Jerome: To be a good shepherd is to rule one's subjects, not to oppress them, to distribute everything equally.

Origen: The same Tiberius, moreover, governed the republic with such great and dignified moderation for the greater part of his reign, that he wrote to certain governors who urged him to increase the provinces' tributes, that to be a good shepherd is to shear, not to flay.

24.17 That the word of a king, either dead or alive, slays his enemy

David says to Solomon: You know what Joab the son of Sarvia did to the two *principes* of Israel, to Abner the son of Ner, and to Amasa the son of Jether, whom he slew, and shed the blood of war in time of peace. You also, do not lead his grey head to hell in peace. Whence Solomon sent

Banaias the son of Joiada, and he slew Joab as he held on to the horns of the altar.

As one reads in the same place: Joab fled therefore into the tabernacle of the Lord and grabbed hold of the horns of the altar. And Solomon sent Banaias the son of Joiada saying: Go, kill him, and you shall cleanse from me and from the house of my father the blood shed by Joab. And a little later he said: So Banaias went up, and setting upon him slew him, and he was buried in his house in the desert.

Herod sent agents and killed the children in Bethlehem. Herod sent, and beheaded John.

Whence Jerome says: The king's word is a sword for beheading, a rope for hanging, it casts into prison, condemns to exile.

Augustine: Fear the king's word; it punishes the enemy, honours the friend.

Gregory: If the king's tongue condemns and slays, how much more so the word of God, who is the avenger both here and in the future.

24.18 That the word of a king protects the enemy or the conquered, but then for the sake of mercy

Moses pleaded on behalf of the people, saying: If you do not remit this people that sin, strike me off from the book that you have written for me.

The widow pleaded before David on behalf of her son who killed his brother, saying: All his kin seeks my son, to deliver him for his brother, and because of that I shall be deprived of both my sons. To whom David said: As the Lord liveth, not one of your son's hairs shall fall to the earth.

Likewise: Zedechiah's word released Isaiah[229] from punishment and from prison.

Whence Jerome: The king's word is the consolation of the infirm, the liberation of the defeated, the opening of prisons, the remuneration of the good people. Whence someone said: Would that the king's word had released me and ordered to set me free, like it released Joseph from prison, and freed Daniel from the lions' den, and Mardochai from his troubles.

24.19 That a king or sinner should not be flattered

Concerning losing God's grace while pursuing the ruler's grace

Ambrose: They who seek the grace of the emperor, have lost the grace of God.

Concerning the folly of pleasing wicked men

Gregory: It is truly foolish if we seek to please them, whom we know not to be pleasing to God.

25 Concerning lots

25.1 Concerning casting a lot in doubtful and uncertain matters

The son of Sirach says: A lot is cast in doubtful matters, that God may decide in the sight of man. Whence it is said that a lot falls because it comes from above and is controlled by God.

Augustine: A lot is not a bad thing, but a thing that intimates divine will to us, when there is human doubt.

And the same says: By the hands of the saints, lots reveal the things that are in God's hidden judgement.

And the same says: The things that are granted by lot, are usually granted by divine intervention.

25.2 That there is no human choice in lots, but only the will of God

In Paralipomenon: There is no choice in lots, but rather the will of God.

Hence Solomon: Lots are cast into the lap, but are governed by the Lord.

Origen: It is up to us to choose two out of many, but it is up to God to decide between the two.

Whence the apostles pray: You, Lord, who know the hearts of men, show us which of these two you have chosen to take the place of this ministry and apostleship, from which Judas was deprived.

25.3 That lots should not always be believed, but God

Augustine: Lots should not always be cast, for they sometimes deceive.

Whence someone said: Lots rule, namely demons.

Jerome said in his commentary on Jonah, where it is said, 'the lot fell on Jonah', saying thus: We ought not be quick in taking this as an example for trusting lots, nor associate it with the testimony from the Acts of the Apostles, where Matthew was elected to the apostolate by lot, because the privileges of the few cannot become a law for all. For instance, the ass spoke in condemnation of Balaam, and Pharaoh and Nebuchadnezzar saw the future in the judgement of their dreams, and nevertheless they did not recognise the Lord revealing [the future]. Caiphas also prophesied, while being unaware that it would be expedient for one to die for all. Thus also here a fugitive is apprehended by lot, not on account of the powers of the lot-casters, and especially not of the pagans, but on account of his will, who governs uncertain lots.

25.4 Concerning the four cases in which one reads that a lot was cast

In the scriptures, there are four types of lot. First, over the king, over the tribes, as Samuel gathered all the tribes of Israel, and the lot fell on Benjamin; and so forth, as far as: Saul the son of Cis. Concerning this lot, one reads in the canon [of scripture]: The lot suppresses disagreements, and determines between the mighty. Second, a lot is cast over the priesthood, like the twenty-four elders in the ministry of the temple, of whom the eighth in line was Abia. And in the New Testament they appointed two, namely Barsabas and Matthias, and so on until it says: And the lot fell on Matthias, and he was numbered with the eleven apostles. Concerning this lot Jerome said: They appointed two apostles equal in merit, but it was up to God to prefer one over the other. Third, a lot is cast over a case of uncertain sin, as one reads regarding Achan who stole the golden rule. And concerning the prophet Jonah, where one reads: Come, let us cast lots, that we may know on account of whose evil this storm is upon us.

Concerning this lot Jerome said: We should not trust lots on the basis of this example.

Augustine said: Lots should not always be cast, for they sometimes deceive.

Fourth, over territories and fields, as it is said to Joshua: You shall divide the land by lot to this people. Concerning this lot it is said: The lines are fallen unto me in magnificent places. Whence an 'inheritance' is sometimes 'a share', as Peter says to Simon Magus: You have no share in this life.[230]

In a psalm David said: The Lord will not leave the rod of sinners over the lot of the just.

Likewise, in another context it is said: And upon my vesture they cast a lot, and my lots are in your hands.

25.5 That a lot ought to be cast in doubtful matters

A Hibernian synod: A lot ought to be cast between two doubtful things, or between two equal things, or between two equally catholic things.

26 Concerning offences and their punishments

26.1 Concerning the ways in which a clandestine offence is exposed

Jerome: Any clandestine offence is discovered in three ways: by lot, by the Holy Spirit, by natural prudence.

For in the law Joshua son of Nun discovered Achan's sin by lot, as [one reads] that a lot fell on the tribe of Judah; and so forth, as far as: And he found Achan the son of Charmi.

Jonah's offence was also discovered by lot, as [one reads] that the lot fell on Jonah.

With the help of the Holy Spirit, Daniel discovered the sin of the wicked judges of Israel, and freed Susanna.

Peter also discovered the sin of Ananias and Sapphira, saying: You deceived the Holy Spirit.

With prudence, as Jerome says, Solomon judged between the two women, and he discovered the sin of one and the truth of another.

With prudence David also discovered the sin of Saul, who wished to kill him; whence he said: You have made uncertain and hidden things manifest to me.

26.2 Concerning a manifest offence

The law says: Every guilty man shall be brought to the city gate and punished in the presence of witnesses.

Likewise: He who has struck a man shall be put to death

26.3 Concerning the number of witnesses that attest an offence

The law says: No one ought to be punished on account of a single witness, but every word in the mouth of two or three witnesses shall stand.

26.4 Concerning the three persons who are to be summoned for a punishment

Jerome: Three persons must be summoned to the punishment of the guilty: the king, that he may correct the offence; the bishop, that he may temper the king's rage; the people, that they may be terrified by this example.

26.5 Concerning punishments for offences

In the old law there were five punishments: The first was stoning, as each and every one struck[231] Achan for three reasons: First, that the sign of his sin should endure; second, lest his friends should exact vengeance together; third, lest the king should suffer retribution for punishing him. The second punishment was burning by fire, as Judas said of Thamar: Bring her out that she may be burned. The third was punishment by slaying with a sword, as Phinees cut down the harlot together with her man, that they might die a quick death. The fourth is the cross, but in the Old Testament this was a servile punishment. The fifth was amputation of limbs, as the fingers and toes of Adonibezec were severed by the people of Israel.

26.6 Concerning punishments for offences in the New Testament

In the New Testament, however, as Jerome says, there are three punishments. The first is the cross, consecrated by the example of Christ. Hence

Andrew addressed it, saying: Hail the cross, hail the cross, that bore the grace and beauty of the Lord's limbs. The second is amputation of limbs. Here Jerome said: The Roman church adopted the practice of amputating limbs from the Philistines. For it is fitting that he who robbed the church from within or without be separated from his limbs, so that he might always retain the sign of his shame and wrongdoing. This practice, however, was taken up by the people of Israel, who, as we have said above, amputated Adonibezec's limbs. The third is casting into prison, so that he who was inspired by the devil to commit an offence might perish enveloped in darkness. The fourth is penance with exile, so that he who was a stranger to God's commandments might live in a state of alienation from his friends and province.

Concerning the eight varieties of punishments

In the books of etymologies: Tullius wrote that there are seven varieties of punishments in the laws, namely: a fine, imprisonment, beatings, compensation in kind, shaming, exile, servitude, and death. The first, a fine (*damnum*), is derived from diminution (*diminutio*). The second, prison (*uincula*), is derived from binding (*uinciendo*),[232] that is, confining. The third, beatings (*uerbera*), are so called because when they are applied, they vibrate (*uerberant*) the air. The fourth, compensation in kind, is similar to revenge, as one ought to suffer just as he has done. The fifth, shaming, because whoever is caught committing an offence, ceases to have an honest name. Now, shame (*ignominium*) is so called as if it were 'without name' (*sine nomine*). The sixth, exile (*exilium*), is so called as if it were 'beyond the earth' (*extra solum*). The seventh, to serve, is derived from serving. For among the ancients, those who were spared death in battle, and were taken to servitude, are called servile. The eighth is death. Indeed, deaths have different causes, of which there are the cross (*crux*), or the pillory (*patibulum*), on which hanged people are crucified (*cruciantur*) or suffer (*patiuntur*), whence they take their name.

Concerning punishing an unlawful union

The law: If any man commit adultery with the wife of another, and defile his neighbour's wife, let them be put to death, both the adulterer and the adulteress. If a man lie with his stepmother, and discover the shame of his father, let them both be put to death; their blood be upon them. If any man lie with his daughter-in-law, let both die, because they have committed an offence; their blood be upon them. If any man after marrying the daughter, marry her mother, he has committed an offence; he shall be burned alive with her, neither shall so great an offence remain in your midst. If any man lie with his daughter-in-law,[233] let both die, because they have committed an offence; their blood be upon them. He who shall copulate with any beast or cattle, dying let him die, the beast shall also be killed. If any man take his sister, the daughter of his father, or the daughter of his mother, and see her nakedness, and she behold her brother's shame, they have committed a nefarious deed; they shall be slain in the midst of their people. If any man lie with a woman during her period, and uncover the fountain of the blood, both shall be killed in the midst of their people. But if they did this unknowingly, they shall live, and wash their garments.[234] If any man lie with the wife of his father or uncle, and uncover the shame of his near kin, both shall bear their sin, they shall die without their children. He who marries his brother's wife, does an unlawful deed: he uncovered his brother's nakedness. They shall die without children.

26.7 Concerning punishing a relative, if it is deserved

In the book of Kings: A stubborn son, scorning his father's warnings, they shall take him and bring him to the elders, and the inhabitants of the city shall overwhelm him, and you shall take away the evil.

The law says: Each man shall kill his brother, and friend, and neighbour.

Likewise: Do not pity your brother, nor conceal him, let your hand be first upon him.

Moses: If any man be on the Lord's side, let him join with me, and let every man kill his own brother.

Concerning those who ought to be pardoned through mercy

In a psalm: The Lord is gracious and merciful, patient and plenteous in mercy.

The law: Do not be mindful of the injustice to your citizens.

Likewise: The earth is full of the Lord's mercy.

Likewise: If his children forsake my law, etc.; as far as: My mercy I will not take away from them.

Christ: Love your enemies.

Likewise: Forgive and you shall be forgiven.

Likewise: If you have not remitted their sins, your father will not remit your sins to you.

Likewise: I desire mercy rather than sacrifice.

Likewise: Peter asks: And if my brother offend against me, how many times shall I forgive him? Up to seven times? The truth responded: I say not to you, up to seven times, but up to seventy times seven.

Likewise: the Lord, prescient, pleaded: Father, forgive them, etc.

Likewise, Stephen, saying: Lord, lay not this sin to their charge, etc.

Concerning the severity of punishment

In a psalm: God, the Lord of revenges, etc.; as far as: You who judges the earth.

Likewise: You shall have no mercy on all workers of iniquity.

The law, likewise: Whoever will shed innocent blood, his own blood will be shed.

Likewise: You shall not take payment from him who is guilty of blood, but he shall die forthwith.

Likewise: Be angry, and sin not.

Likewise: The just man shall rejoice when he shall see revenge, he shall wash his hands in the blood of the sinner.

Likewise, Jeremiah: Cursed be he who withholds his sword from blood in the day of vengeance.

The law, likewise: He who has killed with the sword, ought to be killed by the sword.

26.8 Concerning punishment not being prohibited in the New Testament, and on those worthy of inflicting punishment

Jerome: Whoever strikes the wicked insofar as they are wicked, and has implements for killing, that he may strike the most villainous, is the Lord's minister.

Likewise: A king surrounds enemies, and binds, and punishes, because the church punishes no one.[235]

Jerome: Punishing killers and wicked men is not considered shedding of blood, but serving the laws. And as *sacerdotes* spare sinners, they bring about the ruin of churches.[236]

Augustine: What is this vanity, to spare one and lead all others into danger? For the populace is polluted by a single sinner.

Jerome: He who does not kill a thief, himself destroys the helpless. They put to death the souls that do not die, and they revive the souls that do not live.

Gregory: Whoever condemns the just, puts the one who is not dying to death, and whoever strives to release an offender from punishment, seeks to revive the one who will not live.

26.9 Concerning punishment in the New Testament

Augustine: Nor here is there a prohibition against that punishment, for it also leads towards correction. For it is an aspect of mercy. Nor does it impede that intention by which one is prepared to bear even more from him, whom he wants to be corrected. But no one is fit to administer punishment, except he who—through great love—has overcome hatred, by which men who wish to avenge themselves are accustomed to punish.[237] For the following is not to be feared: that the parents should seem to hate their young son; let him be beaten by them when sinning, that he might not increase in sin.[238] And certainly, through perfect imitation of the love of God the Father himself, an example is laid down to us, when he says in what follows: Love your enemies, etc. And nevertheless, concerning the same thing it is said through the prophet: For he whom the Lord loves he chastises, and he scourges every son whom he receives.

For great and holy men who were already fully aware that this death, which releases the soul from the body is not to be feared, nevertheless[239] punished many sins by death after the manner of those who fear it. By which means fear was more effectively struck in the observers, while this death did not harm the ones who were being punished by death.[240] They to whom God gave such judicial discretion did not decide rashly. By which discretion Elijah punished many by death, both by his own hand and by fire demanded from heaven. And also other great and divine men, being guided by the same Holy Spirit, did not act rashly in human affairs. Therefore, after that, he taught them what it means to love your neighbour as yourself. And after the Holy Spirit, which he sent, was poured out, such punishments did not desist, although they were much less frequent than in the Old Testament. For also Ananias and his wife fell lifeless by the words of Peter the apostle. And if the heretics deny this book, and also refuse to believe the Old Testament, let them observe Paul the apostle, saying of a certain heretic—whom he handed over to Satan for the destruction of the flesh—that his soul shall be saved. And if they refuse to understand death in this case—for perhaps it is uncertain—let them acknowledge that a punishment was inflicted by the apostle through Satan; which he did not do so much out of hatred, but out of love, is made clear by that addition: That his soul should be saved. Or let them turn their attention to the very same books, whose authority they themselves value greatly, for it is written there that Thomas the apostle wished a terrible death unto someone who slapped him; he nevertheless recommended that his soul be spared in the afterlife. A dog brought the palm, torn from the body of the dead man, who was killed by a lion, to the tables at which the apostle was feasting.

Augustine said in the Enchiridion: Thomas, however, said: It is better that forgiveness be given to you in the afterlife, where there is no end to scourges. Here, in this world, a transitory punishment is given to you, that you yourself may perish. Whoever corrects by striking a person over whom he is given power, or coerces by other disciplinary means and nevertheless forgives from his heart the sins of the one by whom he has been harmed or wronged, or prays that he should be forgiven, gives alms not only by forgiving and praying, but also by reproving and administering corrective punishment.

26.10 Concerning severe punishments for grave sins

The origin of every sin is pride, by means of which the devil was made; he was created by God a good angel by nature, and thereafter he is damned in perpetuity.[241] Adam, the first man, with all his kind, is damned to death for transgressing a divine commandment. Cain, the first murderer, incurred seven punishments, either because he carried out one punishment for each of seven generations begotten of him, or because he sinned in seven ways through his soul. The soul is, however, tripartite: irascible, desirous, rational; and the body is, however, quadripartite: fire, air, water, earth, other.[242]

Jerome said: These are his seven sins, the first of which is that he divides badly, namely between himself and his brother. The second is that he envied his brother. The third, that he was angry. The fourth, that he slew. The fifth, that he lied. The sixth, that he had bad faith. The seventh, that he despaired.

Seventy times sevenfold punishments were exacted from Lamech, the first adulterer and murderer. The deluge wiped out the iniquity of the world.

Confusion of languages damned the vainglory of the builders of the tower; and as a result of a unnatural sin, fire consumed Sodom and Gomorrha. Egypt, while cruelly holding God's people captive, was afflicted by ten plagues, and finally drowned in the Red Sea. Core also, having sacrificed an unworthy sacrifice to God, is consumed with his kin by strange fire. The earth opened and swallowed Dathan, and enclosed the congregation of Abiron. Because David arrogantly counted the people, seventy thousand men of his army were killed. The two sons of Aaron, offering strange fire, died by their sacrifices; and seven hundred thousand of the Hebrews died in the wilderness for transgressing a commandment. When the three youths were cast into the furnace by Nebuchadnezzar, a fire consumed the Chaldeans. In vengeance for the cross, eleven times a hundred thousand Hebrews perished in Jerusalem by sword and hunger, and one hundred thousand were publicly sold.

26.11 Concerning severe punishments for minor sins

In the law: Gathering firewood on the Sabbath in the presence of the people, a boy was slain.

Likewise, in the law: He who curses his father or mother, shall be condemned to death.

In the books of Kings: God was angry at Uziah on account of his rashness, and raising the ark, after an ox has knocked it over, he dies.[243]

Likewise: Forty-two boys say to Elisha, 'up you go, you bald head', and two bears devoured twelve of them.[244]

Moses did not enter the promised land owing to a minor departure from the faith expressed in a single word.

Zachary, father of John the Baptist, contradicting the angel on one point, was made dumb for nine months.

Christ says: Whosoever shall say to his brother, 'Raca' (i.e. a term of contempt) and 'You Fool', shall be surrendered to the council and to hell fire.

Ananias and Sapphira, lying about their money, died in Peter's presence.

Likewise: The innkeeper died for striking Thomas; for he who transgresses one commandment, becomes the breaker of all.

Gez, Elisha's helper, is struck down by leprosy for lying.

Likewise: Dathan and Abiron and Core were exterminated in a single day. Dathan and Abiron, descendants of Ruben, contested the leadership with Moses; the earth absorbed them together with 150 men. But Core, a descendant of Levi, contested the priesthood with Aaron; fire consumes him together with 500 men.

26.12 Concerning light punishments for grave sins

Daniel says to Nebuchadnezzar: Redeem your sins by your almsgiving.

Solomon: Just as water extinguishes fire, so almsgiving extinguishes sin.

Ezekiel, nay rather the Lord speaking through him: If I have said to a wicked man, 'dying you shall die', if he should convert from his wicked ways, he shall live and not die.

Likewise: In what day soever the sinner shall be converted from his wicked ways, all his iniquities shall be cast into oblivion.

Christ: Many sins are forgiven her, because she has loved much.

Likewise: You have been made whole, sin no more!

In the epistles he says: Purge your iniquities first, and you shall be saved.

Paul, who persecuted the church of God, was converted to the Lord after three days of blindness in Damascus.

Likewise, the apostle: He who stole, let him now steal no more, but labour with his hands, that he may have something to repay those in want.

Jacob said: Confess your sins one to another and be saved.

Tobias: Alms cleanse sins and deliver from death.

Jerome: The Lord is patient and full of mercy, such that he grants eternal life to brief and strict penance.[245]

In the annals: It is said that a certain gentile, while being in danger on a ship, exclaimed: I profess and worship the God of the Hebrews. And it is said that he was deemed to merit life.

26.13 Concerning delayed punishments for sinners

The Lord avenged himself upon Adam after 930 years. Cain, who committed fratricide, was not killed immediately, but he lived for seven generations.

Lamech, the kin-slayer of a kin-slayer, is exterminated after a long time.[246]

Similarly, the sinning Saul does not die quickly, of whom the Lord said: I am sorry I ordained Saul king.

Solomon having sinned, vengeance is exacted from his son.

The sins of the sons of Jacob were avenged upon the third and fourth generation.

The Lord says to Moses concerning the Canaanites: Their iniquities have not yet ceased.

In the prophets: God does not wish death upon a sinner, but that he may convert and live.

Jerome: The Lord threatens to kill sinners, but he waits for many years, just as he waited on the Jews for 42 years after the passion of our Lord Jesus Christ.

Pelagius said: Many even protest to their own injury, 'Why does God not punish at once?', not understanding that if it were so, hardly anyone would have remained, nor ever would any of the unrighteous have become righteous.

26.14 Concerning punishing sinners quickly

In the law: Mary is quickly struck by leprosy.

The two sons of Aaron die quickly.

The two sons of Eli quickly succumb to death.

In the book of Kings: Uziah dies quickly for touching the ark.

In the New Testament: Judas Iscariot is consumed in penalty.

Ananias and Sapphira die quickly.

Olympius the Arian bishop dies quickly of combustion in the sight of all, for blaspheming the Holy Trinity in the baths.

Arius himself, opposing the faith of Christ, dies quickly, his guts having poured out.

26.15 Concerning taking note of the diversity of God's judgements in both testaments

Augustine said: Note the diversity of God's judgement in both: in one, there is the severity of truth and the speediness of God's mercy, lest he should add sins onto sins. In the other, a measure of patience and expectation of penance are presumed, either because this life is like smoke, or a dream, or a shadow, in comparison with the afterlife.

Likewise, Augustine: One must not inquire why the Lord judges sometimes slowly, sometimes quickly, sometimes harshly, sometimes lightly, for Solomon says: You must not know much, and seek not the things that are more sublime than you.

Paul said: Unsearchable are his ways, and his judgements inscrutable.

Gregory: Who knows God's hidden judgements? What we are unable to fathom in the divine way of thinking, we ought to fear rather than investigate.

26.16 Concerning the four reasons[247] why God does not punish quickly

Augustine: There are four reasons[248] why God does not punish quickly: the first, that his patience may be shown. On account of which David says: The Lord is patient and plenteous in mercy. The second, that man be without excuse. On account of which it is said: You are without excuse, O man. The third, because the merits of martyrs plead on their behalf, as Stephen pleaded. The fourth, so that sins be added to sins, that they be punished with the devil at the end of the world. Whence it is said in the law: I shall add new sins upon old sins. For these are the vessels of wrath. And in the Apocalypse, John: They who are filthy, let them be filthy still.

26.17 Concerning the three reasons[249] why God punishes quickly

Augustine said: There are also three reasons[250] why God punishes quickly: the first, that he may display his power and strike fear in others. The second: lest sins should be added, they are consumed quickly in punishment. On account of which Paul said: I delivered that sort of man, etc.; and as Thomas quickly took vengeance upon the innkeeper, that the Lord might show him mercy in the future. The third, because the souls of the saints cry under God's altar: Avenge our blood; and: How long does he not avenge our blood?

26.18 That punishments for a sin are changed according to the sinner's choice

In the book of Kings David is told: A choice of three things is given you; choose one: either three years of famine shall come to you, or you shall flee three months before your adversaries, or for three days there shall be a pestilence in your land. David says: It is better that I should fall into the hands of the Lord, than of men. And there died of the people from Dan to Bersabee seventy thousand men, because David counted the people.

That killing is a greater sin than mistreating[251] the bodies of the slain

In the Gospel of John: Fear not them who kill the body, and afterwards can do nothing.

Concerning this Augustine interpreted thus: How is it that they cannot do anything? What if, when they have killed, they should throw the body to be mangled by beasts and torn by birds? It seems that savageness can still do something. But to whom does it do it? For he has passed on. The body is there, but there is no consciousness. The dwelling place lies there, the dweller departed. For this reason they can do nothing. They can do nothing to the unfeeling.

In Genesis too, no blame was imputed to the ten sons of Jacob for rushing against [the slain] Shechem and Hemor, after their two brothers (*sc.* the two sons of Jacob: Simeon and Levi) killed them. But Simeon and Levi were held responsible for the greatest offence, for being the first to taint their father's good faith.

That he who wishes evil is culpable, just as he who does evil

In the books of Kings: Then Bathsheba came to king Solomon, to speak to him for Adonias. And the king arose to meet her, and bowed to her, and sat down upon his throne, and [his mother] said to him: I desire one small petition of you, do not turn me away. And the king said to her: My mother, ask, for I must not turn you away. And she said: Let Abisag the Sunamitess be given to Adonias your brother as wife. And king Solomon answered his mother and said: Why do you ask Abisag the Sunamitess for Adonias my brother? Ask for him also the kingdom; for he is my elder brother. Then king Solomon swore by the Lord, saying: Let the Lord do these things to me and add these things, because Adonias has spoken this word against his own life. And king Solomon sent by the hand of Banaias, who slew him, and he died.

26.19 Concerning the guilt of offenders coming upon those who forgive them

The law says: If you forgive a man worthy of death, your soul shall be for his soul.

Likewise: Whoever releases the one condemned to death, declares himself to be liable in his place. He is guilty of whatsoever offence he dismissed.

In the book of Kings: As Achia, the man of God, says to Ahab, the king of Israel, concerning Benadad: Because you let go out of your hand a man worthy of death, your soul shall be for his soul, and your people for his people.

Likewise: Jeremiah cried: You shall not defend the Lord's fugitives.

Likewise: Egypt was destroyed for receiving the Lord's fugitives.

Likewise: The tribe of Benjamin is wholly annihilated and exterminated for defending the offenders of a single city.

Likewise: Josias, endeavouring to defend Charcamis, is slain with his army by king Pharaoh Nechao, who replied to messengers that were sent to him: I come not against you, but I fight against another house, against which the Lord has commanded me to go.

26.20 Concerning those helping apostates in good faith

Rahab the prostitute, defending Joshua's messengers, the enemies of Jericho, is saved with all the members of her household.

Likewise: Israel, the people of God, is blamed for not defending Samson, but handing him over to the Philistines, their enemies.

Likewise: Joshua defended the Gabaonites, the enemies of God, when they were disguised, and he is praised for receiving those who came.

Likewise: Christ defended the woman who was an enemy of the Pharisees, but we do not know whether she merited punishment or not.

Likewise: Abraham strove before the Lord to defend the Sodomites, the enemies of God.

Likewise, in Martin: For there was solicitude on Martin's part to free not only Christians but also heretics.

Concerning punishment brought upon the kinsman of the sinner

In Genesis: I will require the blood of man at the hand of a man, and of his kinsman, and his brother.

That consent is a slightly lesser [offence] than perpetration

Paul said: Not only they who do shall perish, but they also who consent to those who do.

Basil asks if he who consents to another's sin is also guilty of sin. The revealed judgement replied through the words of the Lord, which He uttered to Pilate, saying: He who has delivered me to you, has the greater sin. And this demonstrates that Pilate too, since he consented to them who delivered the Lord, had sinned, albeit not as much as they. This [principle], however, is also shown in Adam's assenting to Eve.

26.21 That there is a similar punishment for defendants and defenders of the accused

Jerome said: The defender of the wicked will be destroyed, and let the defended as well as the defender be condemned to a similar punishment.

Likewise: Do not defend unjustly, lest you be justly bound, and subject to another's punishment.[252]

Whence Paul pleaded for the exceedingly honest servant whom he has received.

26.22 Concerning the need to denounce those who do not receive God's wanderers[253]

In Isaiah the Lord says to Moab and Ammon: You did not defend my people, but betrayed it and did not meet the thirsty with bread and water.

Likewise: The people of God are blamed for not defending Samson, but handing him over to the Philistines, etc.

26.23 Concerning a church defending both the worthy and unworthy

Origen said: A dove is a simple bird, which feeds and protects the chicks of others; so too ought the church to be.

For we know that the city of refuge does not only defend the just, but also the unjust, that his case may be heard.

Not only did Abraham defend Lot the just from the kings' hand, but also the Sodomites, the enemies of God.

Moses defended a people inimical to God, and prayed for it.

Christ defended the woman, the enemy of the scribes and Pharisees.

Likewise: He defended the daughters of Jethro the Midianite.

Ruben, striving to defend Joseph the inimical brother, is blessed.

Jacob defended the daughters of Laban the Syrian.

Jerome: The church defends those whom it receives into its bosom, in the manner of a hen that receives both its own chicks and the chicks of others.

26.24 Concerning the need to punish the naiveté of one who receives fugitives

In the prophets: The upright and naive people who received Jonah, a fugitive from God, were punished, and their ship encountered danger.

On account of which Jerome says: Whence we know that the things that men believe to be expedient, are turned against them to destroy them. If the ignorant are punished, how much more so the knowing.

Whence he added: They who are conscious of offences, are guilty.

26.25 Concerning punishment of the one intervening in fights

The law says: If two men have a quarrel together, and one begin to fight against the other, and if the other's wife, wishing to deliver her husband out of the hand of the stronger, shall put forth her hand, and take him by his privates, you shall cut off her hand, nor shall you be moved with any pity in her regard.

26.26 That slaying the wicked on festive days is not forbidden, if they have committed an offence on a festive day

In the chronicles one reads concerning the Jews: They ought to be slain on the days on which they crucified the saviour.

That the man on whose account others have been slain, is himself guilty of their deaths, even though he did not wish it

In the books of Kings: David says to Abiathar, the son of Achimelech: I knew that day when Doeg the Edomite was there, that without doubt he would tell Saul. I am to blame [for the death] of all the souls of your father's house.

27 Concerning cities of refuge

Concerning the word 'city'

In the books of etymologies: A city (*ciuitas*) is a multitude of people joined by a bond of association. It is so called from 'civilians' (*ciuiles*), namely from the same residents of the town (*urbs*). For the walls themselves are the town. The citizens (*ciues*) are not called stones, but inhabitants. A town (*urbs*) is so called from a circular enclosure (*orbis*), because ancient cities (*ciuitates*) were arranged in circles, or from a circular part of the plough, by means of which the walls were marked out.

27.1 Concerning the names and number of the cities of refuge

The law says: And they appointed Cedes in Galilee of Mount Naphtali, and Shechem in Mount Ephraim, and Kiriath-Arba, the same is Hebron in the mountain of Judah. And beyond the Jordan facing Jericho to the east, they appointed Bosor, which is upon the deserted plain of the tribe of Ruben, and Ramoth in Gilead of the tribe of Gad, and Gaulon in Bashan of the tribe of Manasseh.

27.2 Concerning those whom the city of refuge defends

In the law: He who slays a man involuntarily, and he was not lying in ambush, but God delivered him into his hands, I will appoint you a place to which he must flee.

In Deuteronomy: This shall be the law of the killer who flees, whose life is to be saved. He who has killed his neighbour ignorantly, and who is proved to have had no hatred against him yesterday and the day before, but to have gone with him to the forest to chop wood, and if in cutting down the tree the axe slipped out of his hand, and the iron slipping from the handle struck his friend, and killed him, he shall flee to one of the cities aforesaid, and live; nor a kinsman of him whose blood was shed, driven by his grief shall take his life.

27.3 That offenders who are under the cities' protection ought to make satisfaction to those whom they offended

The synod of Agde said: It is resolved that killers be not driven away quickly from the church's doors. Let them be free of all punishment, at least so that they may make satisfaction to those against whom they have injured.[254]

27.4 That killers ought to do penance in a church

Jerome: The church should not forgive secular offenders, but let them be received in its bosom, and constrained to make satisfaction.

To whom it has been said: Whatsoever you shall bind upon the earth, etc.

27.5 That a killer who killed involuntarily should be slain if he is apprehended by an avenger outside the city of refuge

The law says: If the killer be found without the limits of the cities that are appointed for the fugitives, and be struck by him who is the avenger of blood, he who killed him shall be without blame.

27.6 Concerning penance for involuntary manslaughter

Dionysius: Let those who have killed involuntarily, be received into the church's communion through seven years of penance; let those who persist in this state be admitted.

The Roman ruling maintains. First decision: He who has become a fugitive for having shed blood, let him be handed over [to the church] for penance; let him be healed especially by achieving reconciliation with the kinsmen of the victim.[255] Second decision: Let him be condemned to seven years of exile, or let him stay in the bosom of a sheltering church for the rest of his life.

27.7 Concerning those whom the city of refuge does not defend

In Exodus: If a man kill his neighbour intentionally and by lying in ambush, you shall tear him away from my altar, that he may die.

In Deuteronomy: If any man hating his neighbour lie in ambush for him, and rise and strike him and he die, and he flee to one of the cities aforesaid, the ancients of his city shall send and take him out of the place of refuge and deliver him into the hand of the kinsman of him whose blood was shed, and he shall die, nor shall you pity him.

27.8 That offenders must not be killed within the precincts of the city of refuge

In Paralipomenon: Joiada the priest said to the captains and the chiefs of the army of Israel: Take her forth, that is Gotholia,[256] outside the precinct of the temple, and let her be killed with the sword.

A synod: He ordered this that she might not be killed inside the temple.

27.9 That no person of faith be easily rejected from the bosom of the church[257]

The synod of Agde said: Every faithful person who took refuge within the bosom of the church—that is, the mother—should not easily be sent away, but let him be healed in that church by making satisfaction, to the sum that true judges have adjudicated.

Likewise: It is resolved that if someone has entered the city of refuge after committing an unlawful deed, he shall not be removed until the elders of the city have decided his case with the consent of the clerics.

27.10 Concerning the different kinds of penance for killers who kill intentionally

Dionysius: Those who have killed of their own volition should submit themselves to unceasing penance, but towards the end of their lives let them obtain perfection, that is, the grace of Christ's communion.

A Hibernian synod says: Let all killers, if they have been wholeheartedly converted, perform seven years of strict penance under the rule of a monastery.[258]

Patrick: A Christian who has murdered or fornicated, or consulted an augur in the manner of pagans, shall perform a year's penance for each offence; and, having completed it, he shall afterwards be freed by a *sacerdos* in the presence of witnesses.

27.11 That it is not appropriate for a church to drive away those who flee to it; or, if she does drive them away, not to death or maiming

A Roman synod says of killers and adulterers and thieves: If they have fled to the church, we have decided the following: that which the ecclesiastical canons have decreed and the Roman law stipulated, must be observed, namely that they should not, under any circumstances, be taken away from the premises of the church or the residence of the bishop, nor should they be handed over to anyone else, unless oaths are taken on the four Gospels. They should be spared death or physical harm and all forms of punishment, so that he may come to an agreement by compensating him to whom he is liable for an offence. But if someone has been convicted of breaking his oaths, he is guilt of perjury; let him be segregated not only from the communion of the church and all its clerics, but also from the company of catholics. But if the one against whom he is guilty refuses to allow the contention to be put aside, and the same guilty person has left the church out of fear, he shall not be sought by the clerics of the church.

27.12 That the church does not defend offenders at all costs

Augustine said: The church should not defend those guilty of blood, lest she become a party to the shedding of blood. For if the Lord held them in prison, you must not free them, whom the Lord did not free.

Gregory Nazianzen said: Two things must by guarded against in the church: not to loosen what must not be loosened, and not to bind what must not be bound.

Likewise: If you defend the guilty, take care not to harm others. Beware of mercy by which you become unmerciful to others.

27.13 That they who sin in a holy place, must also be killed there

Phinees killed a man and a harlot in a place of saints.

Isaiah said: He behaved badly in a place of saints.

Jerome: Whoever has defiled what is holy, holy things will not protect him.

The Jews were killed in Jerusalem on Easter.

Christ subdued and drove out the evildoers in the temple with whips.

Paul: If any man violate the temple of God, God shall destroy him.

Jerome: If the *locus* itself were helpful, Satan would not have fallen from heaven.

Gregory: Adam, the first man, was expelled from paradise after his sin, and he is punished by death. He who cast away divine eminence is deprived of the eminence of the place.

Concerning the manner in which the church ought to defend an offender

The synod of Agde: It is resolved that killers be not driven away quickly from the church's gates, and let them be free of all punishment, so that they may make satisfaction to those whom they have injured.[259]

27.14 That, in the New Testament, nearly everyone in the church was to die a spiritual death

Augustine: Offenders must be restrained insofar as they are offenders, not released insofar as they are kinsmen.

Gregory: Put up your sword into its place. This sentence of the Lord must be noted, so that the church should not allow corporeal punishment, and it rightly, without discrimination, carries the sword of the word of God, which penetrates deeper than any double-edged sword.

A Roman synod: The church was not created for defending offenders, but for persuading judges to inflict a spiritual death on those who have fled into the bosom of the church.

28 Concerning theft

Concerning the word 'theft'

In the books of etymologies: Theft (*furtum*) is the clandestine carrying away,[260] i.e. as if it were a secret, of another's property. It is so called from *furuus*, i.e. dark, for it is concealed. Theft, however, was a capital offence among the ancients, subject to fourfold punishment, i.e. four for one.

28.1 Concerning forbidding theft

Exodus says: You shall not steal. For theft, as another person says, comprises five wrongs. The first, hatred of one's neighbour, contravenes the following: Love your neighbour, etc., and love your enemies, etc. The second, greed for another's property, contravenes the following: You shall not covet the property of your neighbour. The third, gluttony, as one reads: They, whose stomach is a god. The fourth, perjury. For he who steals will rashly commit perjury, Solomon having said: And lest, being compelled by poverty, I should steal, and forswear the name of the Lord my God. The fifth, leaving your brother's mind in suspense in relation to diverse matters, which is forbidden, for: Do not leave your brother's mind in suspense for a bad cause.

28.2 That it is all the same to God whether anyone steal small or great things

Jerome in his commentary on the epistle to Titus: Let a thief be judged not only in great matters, but also in small matters. For the issue is not what the thief took, but the thieving mindset. Just as in cases of adultery or fornication, fornication or adultery are no different if she is pretty or deformed, rich or poor, a harlot or adulteress; but of whatever sort she may be, fornication and adultery remain the same. Thus also in theft: however much the slave has carried off, he incurs the charge of theft.

That a thief is not deserving of death, but of retribution

Orosius says: Here emerged a little of that ancient Roman appetite for excessive praise, even for kin-slaying. For Fabius Censorius slew his son Fabius Buteo, who was accused of theft. Indeed, the offence that the father deemed worthy of punishing by kin-slaying, not even the laws punished in the case of anyone, except by a large fine, or the remotest exile.

In the books of etymologies: A *crimen* is so called from lacking (*carendo*), the likes of which are theft, falsification, and other things that do not kill, but defame.

28.3 Concerning punishing theft severely

Exodus: If any man steal an ox or a sheep and sell it, he shall restore five oxen for one ox, and four sheep for one sheep.

And this is observed in the New Testament, as in Luke, when Zacheus said to the saviour: If I have wronged anyone, I restore fourfold. And the Lord praised him.

If he does not have the means to make restitution for the theft, he shall himself be sold. If that which he stole be found with him, alive, either ox, or ass or sheep, he shall restore double. If someone has stolen inanimate movable property[261] he shall restore double.

If a man entrusts money or any vessel to his friend, and they be stolen away from him who received them, if [the thief] be found, he shall restore double.

Likewise, in the same: He who has stolen a man and sold him, being convicted of wrongdoing, shall be put to death.

28.4 Concerning perceiving the diversity of compensation due for stealing animals

Origen: In the case of an ox five are restored, because an ox has five uses: to be sacrificed, to transport, to serve in God's temple, to protect the cows, to plough. Others, however, say that ox is a generic noun, and applies to both sexes.

Jerome: A cow also has four uses: to be sacrificed, to console the elderly, to feed the young, to plough in Palestine. Likewise, a sheep has four uses: to satisfy with flesh, to be sacrificed, to feed with milk, to clothe with wool. And therefore this is the number that thieves restore, so that they restore double to the Lord, to whom these animals are accustomed to be offered, and double to their neighbour, to whom these belong.

28.5 Concerning diverse punishments for theft, and the causes for diversity

Thieves occasionally restore double, occasionally fourfold, occasionally fivefold, occasionally sevenfold, occasionally they themselves are sold, occasionally they are put to death, occasionally they are stoned, and all their kin, and livestock, and wealth, and residences are burned.

Sometimes double is restored, as we have said concerning unclean animals and inanimate movables,[262] or if the animal which he stole be found alive with the one who stole it.

Sometimes fourfold, as we have said concerning the sheep.

Sometimes fivefold, as we have said concerning the ox.

Sometimes sevenfold, as one reads in Proverbs: And if he be caught, he shall restore sevenfold. For Solomon, observing the growing iniquity of the people, added three above and beyond the law, that he might cut back the people's vices; or, more accurate still, as Origen said: They are one and the same, that which Solomon says and the law, namely that if a thief has been caught, he shall restore fourfold in accordance with the law and his honour-price.[263] Whence Solomon said: And all the substance of his house.

Sometimes a thief is sold: If a thief has been caught, and he does not have the means to make restitution, he shall be a slave, but his kinsman will have the right of redeeming him.

Sometimes a thief is put to death: For if a thief is killed at night, the killer is innocent.

A Hibernian synod: For a thief caught with the stolen goods during the day, is bound with fetters. Should he be found to be wealthy, let him restore sevenfold. Should he be poor and have little property, he shall hand over all his household goods. However, should he be so poor that he has nothing to give in restitution for the theft, let him then be sold into servitude. Sometimes a thief is sold. If a thief has been caught, and he does not have the means to make restitution, he shall be a slave, but his kinsman will have the right of redeeming him.

The law: If a thief be found breaking open a house or undermining it, and be wounded so as to die, he who slew him shall not be guilty of blood. But if he did this when the sun is risen, he has committed murder, and he himself shall die.

Sometimes a thief is stoned, and all his kin with all his property are set on fire, as it is written in the law: Then Joshua and all Israel with him took Achan, the son of Charmi, and the silver and the scarlet garment, and the golden rule, his sons also and his daughters, his oxen and sheep, the tent also, and all the goods, and they brought him to the valley of Achor, where Joshua said: Because you have troubled us, may God trouble you this day. And all Israel stoned him, and all the things that were his were consumed with fire. Note that this punishment is worse than all other punishments of thieves, because he was responsible for a disaster not only to himself, but to the whole people.

28.6 Concerning theft committed in a church

A Hibernian synod decreed: A first theft in a church is nevertheless restored in turn and atoned for through penance prescribed by the judgement of the *sacerdos;* and the church does this as an indulgence.[264] And if a second theft is committed, a double or fourfold restoration is made. But should the possessions of a secular person be stolen,[265] and the church be catholic and free from tribute, let the owner be entitled to restitution,[266] and his *usura*[267] shall belong to the church. But if the church has been under royal tribute, let the owner receive the same restitution, and the *usura* shall be both the king's and the church's.

Concerning penance to someone stealing in a church

Patrick said: He who has stolen possessions from a holy church or from within an ecclesiastical settlement where martyrs and bodies of saints lie sleeping, let a lot be cast over the following three options; either he lose a hand or a foot; or he be imprisoned, fasting for as long as the elders have decided, and restore, in full, what he removed; or let him be cast into exile, and restore double, and swear that he will not return until he has completed his penance, and after the penance he shall be a *monachus*.

28.7 Concerning penance to someone stealing, if it be not from a church

Patrick: He who has committed theft, let him perform half a year's penance, let him live twenty days on bread and water, and restore the things that he stole, provided that they can be restored, and in this manner he may be readmitted into the church.

Vinnian says: If a cleric has committed theft, let him restore fourfold, and perform one-year's penance.

28.8 Concerning curing theft leniently

The apostle says: He who used to steal, let him now steal no more, but work hard, that he may have something to share with those in want.

Solomon: The fault is not so great when a man has stolen, for he steals to fill his hungry soul. It is as though he proclaims: If any man has been compelled by hunger, there is a lesser guilt if he steals. But it must be noted that he does not say: There is no guilt; rather: The guilt is not great. As David did in the temple, when he was hungry, and the ones who were with him ate the priestly loaves. And as Christ allowed his disciples to pluck the ears of grain.

The synod of Nicaea: A cleric entering into business with stolen goods and interest payments for shameful gain should be demoted from the clergy and alienated from the ecclesiastical rule.

Gregory: Charity does not seek the things of others. Who seeks that which is not his own, except he who seeks financial profit and interest payments?

Concerning perceiving the diversity of compensation due for theft in the Old and New Testaments

Origen said: It must be noted why the Bible presents this diversity in compensation. For sometimes he will restore double, as in the case of unclean animals and movables,[268] for it is said in Luke: If a thief be caught, he shall restore double. Sometimes sevenfold, as in Solomon. These are held to be diverse, for Solomon, observing the growing iniquity of the people, added three above and beyond the law, that he might cut back the people's vices. By so doing he joined law and nature into one,[269] to wit: four for the law, three for nature; or, more accurate still, according to Origen: They are one and the same, that which Solomon said and the law, namely that if a thief has been caught, he shall restore fourfold in accordance with the law and his honour-price,[270] i.e. three, on account of which Solomon added: All the substance of his house.

29 Concerning deposits[271]

29.1 Concerning theft of a deposited thing, according to Mosaic law

Exodus says: If a man deposits money or a vessel with his friend for him to watch over, and they be stolen away from him who received them; if the thief be found he shall restore double. If the thief be not known, the owner of the residence shall be brought to Gods,[272] and shall swear that he did not lay his hand upon his neighbour's goods with the intention of perpetrating fraud, either upon the ox, or the ass, nor did anything that may cause damage; the case of both parties shall come before Gods,[273] and if they so decide, he shall restore double.

That is, if the person to whom something is entrusted is not of such high status to be beyond suspicion but he is compelled to swear to you that that which has been deposited was lost as a result of the keeper's negligence, or whether he intentionally allowed thieves to enter the place where it has been deposited, or whether his own chattels were spared while the other's vanished, and so forth. [Only] then is he forced to restore double, in the manner of a thief who stole a chattel,[274] or because a living animal was found with him; he shall therefore restore double. For if the person should be of such dignity as to be beyond suspicion, or if that which has been deposited was lost as a result of negligence or carelessness, or stolen together with his own chattels, that man must be compelled to make good only the loss.[275]

Origen says: He who swears, let him not make restitution, for he is innocent.

Jerome: He who is found guilty of an offence after he has sworn, shall be punished by beating.

This depositing is said to have taken place not only in the tabernacle, but also between husband and wife. For there is a great difference between a deposit given by one spouse to another, and that which a person deposits in a church. It is perhaps for this reason that, in the law, compensation is given with oaths, that neither the owner of the residence, who is making restitution, be obliged to restore fourfold like a thief, nor the owner of the thing that has been lost, shall depart in sadness, on account of the deposit, without compensation. And, likewise, no one minding property would grow careless in minding his neighbour's property. Therefore, also nowadays one ought to judge in this manner, should a dispute arise between laymen because of a lost deposit.

Origen, likewise:[276] 'And if they so decide, he shall restore double': our Lord deposited our soul with us. And 'should it be lost' due to negligence or theft,[277] i.e. from one's *mores*, God demanded that double should be restored.

Likewise: This old man rebuts us: If he restores double, why does he swear beforehand?

Origen, likewise, in the annals of the Hebrews:[278] 'To Gods' means 'to the *sacerdotes*'. 'He shall be brought', i.e. to (?) the martyrs, and he shall depart, innocent.[279]

Jerome, likewise: He who refuses after [giving] an oath, shall be punished by beating, and the one who swore must be handed over to the judgement of God, who said: Revenge is mine, I shall repay, etc.

Concerning the need to return a loan or not to return it

The law: If a man ask for any of these things as a loan, and it be hurt or die, the owner not being present, he shall be obliged to make restitution. But should the owner be present, he shall not make restitution, especially if it were borrowed for the pay of his work.

29.2 That a lost deposit is to be returned in the New Testament

Jerome: Whoever has lost a deposit of his neighbour through negligence shall restore the value of that which has been lost; and if it be through theft, he shall restore double.

Origen: If you have received a deposit, take care lest it perish. For if it should perish, you shall make restitution for your negligence.

The synod of Sardica: If any man deposited property, it is decided that he should receive that which he has deposited.

Augustine: Do not neglect what your neighbour deposited with you, lest, being condemned before a judge, you are sentenced to restore that which you have neglected.

Concerning denying a thing deposited, or any other thing

In Leviticus: Whosoever shall sin, and despising the Lord, shall deny to his neighbour the thing committed to his trust, or shall by force extort anything, or commit deceit, or find a thing lost, and denying it, shall also swear, and shall do any other of the many things wherein men are wont to sin: being convicted of the offence, he shall restore all that he would have gotten by fraud, in full, and also restore the fifth part to the owner, to whom he brought loss. And for his sin he shall offer a ram without blemish.

Jerome said: Simple-minded folk reckon this saying thus: if five numbers are subtracted and one is added, it seems that about six are due in restitution. But they who have been versed in the discipline of numbers derive another, far different figure from that biblical expression. For in Greek it is also called *coioht*,[280] which is a word for a number that can be said to mean 'above five'. Another five should be added beyond the initial five, and then another one on top of that, for the word to be understood on its own terms:[281] whoever steals restores fivefold, and another five besides, and another one is added on top of that.

Concerning making restitution of a thing deposited by saints

Peter in Clement, to the presbyters: Above all, avoid avarice which, by the opportunity of present wealth, keeps men from the eternal goods. Make sure that weights, measures, and scales are optimally calibrated for each and every place. Faithfully return things that have been deposited with you.

29.3 Concerning the living attesting over the dead in the matter of a deposited thing

In the Ecclesiastical History: Spyridon, bishop of Cyprus, a man of the order of the prophets, had a daughter named Irene, who died a virgin after she had ministered to him. After her death a man arrived, saying that he deposited something with her. The father had no knowledge of this. He was unable to find what he was looking for anywhere in the house. The man persisted and claimed that he too would die soon, unless he got back the deposited thing. Moved by his tears, the old man went to his daughter's grave, and called her by her name, and then she said from the grave: What is it that you want, father? He replied: Where did you put his deposit? And she, pointing to the place, said: You shall find it buried there. When he returned to the house, he found it where she, from the grave, said it would be, and returned it to the claimant.

Likewise, in the Life of the Fathers of Egypt:[282] A certain monk who received a deposit of a brother for safekeeping, died, and the angel that accompanied him refused to allow him to enter the resting-place of souls until he showed that which has been deposited with him. Whence he returned in the flesh and showed the thing sought to one of the brethren. If such things are demanded from the dead, how much more so are the deposits of the living demanded from the living.

29.4 Concerning a deposit of livestock

Jacob replied to Laban: The rams of your flock I did not eat, nor did I show you that which the beast had taken; I made good all the damage, whatsoever was lost by theft, you exacted it of me.

Likewise, Exodus: If a man deliver ass, ox, and sheep, and any animal, to his neighbour's custody, and it die or be hurt or be taken by beasts, and no man saw it, there shall be an oath in public that he did not put forth his hand to his neighbour's goods. And the owner shall accept the oath, and he (i.e. the borrower) shall not be compelled to make restitution; but if it were stolen, he shall make the loss good to the owner; if it were eaten by a beast, let him bring to him that which was slain, and he shall not make restitution.

Concerning neglecting to return a deposit

A Hibernian synod, likewise: If it has been taken away by force, he shall not make restitution; if through negligence, he shall make restitution, even if he was not aware of the damage. If the animals have not come back even though he leaves them under watch, he shall restore half. If, however, another man was keeping watch on another man's day, he whose day it is shall make restitution.

Concerning a thing lost

In Augustine's homilies: If any man has lost something, and said, 'the Lord gave, and the Lord has taken away', through this passage, pleasing to God, he shall either receive a crown if he is just, or forgiveness if he is a sinner.

Likewise, another says: Do not perish along with the damage.

29.5 That things entrusted to the church should not be returned[283]

Origen: If a deposited thing is accepted [on the understanding] that it might be restored, it must not be accepted; just as the one that is blameless should not assume the sin of another.[284]

Likewise, Origen: A place of refuge ought not harm, nor be harmed by another.

The synod of Arles: It is decided that the church should burden no one, for the church receives, nourishes, satiates, and it is never liable for anyone's sin.

The synod of Amiens: If a cleric receives a deposit, and it has vanished as a result of theft, there shall be an oath, and he shall not make restitution. For if it (i.e. the church) has made restitution, he (i.e the depositor) should not accept it; and if it (i.e. the church) has not recovered [his chattels], then it is not a city of refuge. If, however, it is not a city of refuge, it cannot protect.[285]

A Hibernian synod: Let everything that has been deposited for safekeeping be returned, except things deposited with the mother church of all the baptised. Just as every mother does not compensate her son for a lost deposit, thus also every church ought not restore the deposits of her children, even if they were lost.[286]

Likewise, the same synod: If someone (*sc.* the owner of a house) has been found in possession of the keys to his house,[287] and a thief broke into it,[288] and stole another's deposit, he who received (*sc.* the owner of the house) shall not make restitution, but all his household shall make an oath, especially if it has been stolen together with his own chattels.[289]

Concerning uncertain deposits

The synod of Vaison: The following has been decreed according to the statutes of the most faithful princes: that the church, to which it (*sc.* the deposit) is lost, should seek the deposit over a period of forty days. If, however, by the end of this period the identities of the depositors should not be known, let it be sought once more, mercifully, for ten days. If anyone shall bring false accusations against the ones seeking, [for] not having sought it, let him be regarded as a killer.[290]

30 Concerning fathers and sons

Concerning the word 'father' and the designation 'children'

In the books of etymologies: A father (*pater*) is so called because he engenders a son when *patratio* has been performed. For *patratio* is the consummation of sexual intercourse. A child (*filius*) is so called because he is of the father. Children are designated in four ways: by nature, by imitation, by adoption, and by instruction. By nature, as when the Jews are called the children of Abraham. By imitation, as those of the gentiles who imitated the faithfulness of Abraham, as when the Gospel says: the Lord is able to raise up children to Abraham from these stones. There is also adoption, which everybody is familiar with in human society, or as we, as the sons of God not by nature, but by adoption, say: Our father who art in heaven. By instruction, however, as when the apostle called 'his sons', those to whom he preached the Gospel, as he says: My children, whom I have brought forth.[291]

Isidore: Children (*filii*), however, are called *liberi* (lit. 'free') in the laws, so that by this word they might be distinguished from slaves, because just as the slave is under the power of his master, so a child is under the power of his father. Whence also there is emancipation for a son, that he might be free of his father, just as there is manumission for the slave, that he might be freed from his master.

30.1 That a soul must be put to death for its own sin

The law said: The soul that sinned, let it die.

The law says: Let children not be put to death for their fathers, nor fathers for sons, but every one shall die for his own sin.

In the book of Kings: Amasias, the king of Israel, struck down his servants to death, who had slain his father. But the children of the killers he did not put to death.

30.2 Concerning the sin of the father being visited only upon his sons

In the books of Kings: The first son whom Bathsheba bore to David, was quickly snatched by death on account of David's sin.

Likewise: Solomon's sin was avenged against his son, Rehoboam.

30.3 That the iniquity of the fathers is transmitted for several generations

In Exodus the Lord says: I am the Lord, mighty and jealous, visiting the iniquity of the fathers upon the third and fourth generation of them that hate me.

Whence the sin of Ruben was avenged upon Dathan and Abiron, and the sin of Levi upon Core, and the sin of Simeon upon his tribe, not having an inheritance in Israel, except with Judah.

On account of that it is said: Your father was an Amorrhite, your mother a Hittite, and the sin of Saul is handed down to his successors.

30.4 Concerning the iniquity of the children affecting their parents

In the books of Kings it is said to Eli the priest: Why have you cast in the dust my sacrifice and my gifts, which I commanded to be offered in the temple? Why have you honoured your sons more than me, such that you ate the firstfruits of the people of Israel?

Likewise, the Lord: I shall take vengeance on the house of Eli for the iniquities of his sons because, despising God, they spoke evil, and he did not correct them.

30.5 That it harms a father to raise his children badly

In the book of Kings: For I have foretold unto him, that I will condemn his house unto eternity, because he knew that his sons did evil, and did not correct them.

Jerome said: To rule badly is to do evil. And whoever does not know how to rule his own house cannot rule others. And with what impudence dare he correct others when he does not govern his own?

That one ought to correct his sons not only by word, but also by force

In the books of Kings: Now Eli was very old, and he heard all that his sons did to Israel, and how they lay with the women who waited at the entrance to the tabernacle, and he said to them: Why did you do these kinds of things, which I hear, very wicked things, from all the people? Do not do my sons, for it is not just a rumour that I hear, that you cause the people of the Lord to transgress.

30.6 That fathers are not affected by the iniquity of their sons

In the annals of the Hebrews: Noah corrected Ham as much as he could, but the latter spurned his father's advice. Therefore, it is said that Noah said with a clear voice: Let Ham be cursed. Abraham distanced himself and his son Isaac from the sons of the concubines, and sent them away to remote regions, because he had foreknowledge that they would behave wickedly and he did not give them an inheritance, but gifts.

Whence Origen said: Were the patriarch to know that they would be well behaved, he would never have sent them away. Isaac loved Esau, but nevertheless sent him away for wounding his soul with strange women.[292] David sent Absalom away for spurning his advice and following the young men's counsel. David chastised Solomon thus: With the holy one you will be holy, etc.

30.7 Concerning the truth of the fathers passing to their sons

The law says: I made up my mind to destroy you, but for the sake of Abraham and Isaac and Jacob I shall not do it.

John the metropolitan: After committing adultery and murder David did penance, as a result of which he obtained justice, which benefitted future generations after his death. And to Solomon too, who was worthy of a thousand deaths, the Lord granted the entire kingdom for David's sake, saying: I shall tear the kingdom from your hands and deliver it to your servant. But, nevertheless, I shall not do this in your time because of your father David, but I shall claim it from the hands of your son.

The son of Sirach: A father builds a house and makes his son rich; the mother, however, [makes] a daughter.

Daniel: Free us on account of Abraham and Isaac and Jacob.

Likewise, the three youths say: We have sinned unto you, O Lord, and you delivered us unto the hands of our enemies; but free us on account of the merits of our fathers.

Likewise, Jacob against Laban: Unless the fear of Isaac had stood by me, perhaps you would have sent me away naked.

30.8 That the truth of the father does not help a wicked son

The prophet says: That soul that sins, let it die. But the man who performs justice shall live in his justice.

Likewise: If he has begotten a virulent and bloodthirsty son, who does not walk in the path of his just father, let him die in his sin and not live his life.

Likewise: He who has carried out all these iniquities, let him die, and his blood be upon him.

Likewise: Noah's justice did not edify Ham and his descendants.

Likewise: Isaac's justice did not edify Esau.

Likewise: Aaron's justice did not edify his two wicked sons.

Likewise: David's justice did not edify Absalom.

Likewise: Solomon's justice did not edify Rehoboam.

Likewise: Ezechias's justice did not edify Manasseh.

On account of this Augustine, speaking as the character of a reckless son: If my father's justice does not free me from my iniquities, I shall do penance, and my justice shall free me and my descendants.

Whence it is said to David concerning his justice and his descendants: If they have profaned my justices and my commandments, etc.

30.9 That the justice of the father confers honour on a good heir

Jerome said: The justice of the father confers honour on a good heir and edifies his house for him.

Whence David: I have not seen the just forsaken, nor his seed seeking bread.

30.10 That the descendants are cursed for lapsing from their good parents

The prophet says: Cursed are these descendants, who lapsed from their good parents.

Whence John said: Do not say 'Abraham is our father', etc.

In the annals of the Latins, it is said by the character of the son: My father lived justly, I unjustly. The saying is true: A dry branch is born of a green tree.

30.11 That the justice of the sons does not edify unjust fathers

The prophet says: The son who witnessed the sins of the father, and was afraid, and did not do as he did shall not perish in the iniquity of the father, but live in his own justice. The father, however, if he has been taken away with violence, shall die in his own iniquity, and his son shall not bear the iniquity of the father. The justice of the just shall be upon him.

Likewise: Every man shall die in his own sins, which he has sinned.[293]

Jerome said in the letter concerning Thecla:[294] The following two are contrasted: the good son of the unjust father and the green branch of the dry tree; just as the green branch does not edify the dry tree, so a good son does not edify an unjust father.

Likewise, Origen remarks: The cinnamon tree is ever green, and produces sweet fruit, but its root, under the earth, is bitter and dry. And should one of its green parts come into contact with the root, the juniper dries, and it becomes harmful to livestock. That of which the fruit is salutary, the mother of which is harmful and destructive.[295]

30.12 Concerning fathers behaving patiently towards their sons, that is: concerning a father correcting them according to the Lord's doctrine

Isaiah said: I implored you, as a father implores his son.

Likewise, Solomon: He who spares the rod hates his son.

Likewise, Paul: Fathers, provoke not your children to anger, but teach them with the discipline and correction of the Lord.

30.13 Concerning the sons' dutifulness towards their parents

The law says: Honour your father and your mother, etc., that you may be longlived upon the earth, and that things may be well for you on earth.

The son of Sirach: Honour your father, and forget not the groanings of your mother. Remember that you would not have existed were it not for them, and repay them as they have done for you.

Gregory: The blessing of the father confirms the sons' houses.

Solomon: Sons are the crown of their fathers.

Likewise: A wise son cheers his father.

Paul: Children, obey your parents, for this is just.

Likewise: Dutifulness is profitable to all things; it holds the good of the present life, and the promise of that which is to come.

Concerning honouring parents

The law: Honour your father, etc.

Let each fear his father and mother.

Jerome: They should not be honoured for creating life. Nevertheless, they must be loved and honoured for their role in procreation.

30.14 Concerning sons who are undutiful towards their parents

The Lord says in Exodus: He who strikes his father or mother, shall be put to death.

Likewise: He who curses his father or mother, shall be put to death.

Likewise: Cursed be he who does not honour his father and mother, and all the people shall say Amen.

In Deuteronomy: If a man have a proud and unruly son, who will not hear the commandments of his father or mother, and being corrected, refuses to obey, they shall take him and bring him to the elders of his city, and to the gate of judgement, and shall say to them: This our son is rebellious and stubborn, he will not listen to our admonitions, he gives himself to revelling, and to debauchery and banquetings. The peoples of the city shall stone him, and he shall die, that you may take away the evil out of the midst of you, and all those hearing it may be afraid.

Augustine: Honour your father and your mother, that honour may be shown to you by God and men. How dare you invoke God the father, when you disrespect your parents?

30.15 That parents must not be neglected, even on account of divine worship

A synod: Those who cease to support their parents under the pretext of divine worship, and do not pay their due respect, let them be anathema.

Likewise: We decree that whoever abandoned his father or mother in a time of need must be excommunicated.

Origen: Honour your father and your mother, that honour may be shown to you by God and men. How dare you invoke the father of piety, when you disrespect your parents?

30.16 Concerning dishonouring wicked parents[296]

The Lord in the Gospel: Do not call any one your father or mother upon the earth. For one is your father, who is in heaven.

Likewise, in the Gospel, a certain man says: Let me bury my father. The Lord replied: Leave the dead to bury their dead.

Jerome: How many monks, when they keep company with their parents, lose their souls!

Likewise: The sons of Zebedei left their father on the boat and followed Christ.

Jerome: Let us render unto our parents the things that belong to our parents; yet, if they are alive, to God.

Basil: For we should love our parents as our own flesh; if they have prevented us from entering upon the service of Christ, we are not obliged to furnish them with a grave.

30.17 That the parents are not the creators of life, but God

Clement: Why should we love our parents? Because they appear to create life? They are by no means the creators of our life, but its governors. For they do not give life, but carry out the duty of bringing us into this life. The creator of our life is God alone, who created us from nothing.

30.18 Concerning the right of the firstborn as against his brothers[297]

The law says: A father shall give his firstborn a double share of everything he has. For he is the first of his children.

'Double', as some say, is this: of the field, and livestock, and all the wealth, and blessing, both of the firstborn and firstfruits.

Alternatively: In his last days the father divides his inheritance and wealth equally between his sons and himself, as if he were one of the sons. He puts aside a share of the inheritance, which he entrusts to his firstborn, and it shall be his in perpetual right. But after the death of the firstborn, it shall be divided between his heir and his brothers and their successors.

30.19 Concerning those who despise their children under the pretext of religion

A holy synod says: If any man has abandoned his children, and ceased to nourish them, and has stopped caring for them under the pretext of divine worship, let him be anathema without protest.

Likewise: Whosoever begot sons for the sake of posterity, ought to nourish them, lest he become a killer or despiser of his own flesh. For the scripture says: Do not despise your own flesh.

Jerome: Whoever has taken part in carnal copulation, must take part in the rearing.

Concerning the inutility of children

Jerome, in the struggle against Jovinian: And of what use is it to rear a child at home, who might either die before you, or behave perversely, or when you reach old age, you will seem to him to die too slowly? However, friends and relatives, whom you choose with consideration, are better and more secure heirs than those whom—whether you like it or not—you are compelled to have. Though it is a more certain legacy, while you are still alive, to use your property well than, having acquired it with your own labour, to leave it to uncertain uses.

30.20 That God is to be put before children

The Lord in the Gospel: Whoever does not leave his house, or father, or mother, or sons, or daughters, is not worthy of me.

Jerome: If you want to be the Lord's disciple, leave your sons or daughters.

Augustine: If you want to follow Christ, you ought to be free. Whoever does not renounce the ones he loves, i.e. a son or daughter, cannot be the Lord's disciple.

A synod: We decree that every penitent shall leave all his possessions to his sons and, being free, await Christ, who will provide all that is necessary.

31 Concerning parents, their heirs, and children

31.1 That dutifulness towards the parents protects their heirs in the kin land[298] in perpetuity

Jeremiah: Thus says the Lord of hosts the God of Israel: Because you have obeyed the commandment of Jonadab your father, and have kept all his precepts, therefore there shall not be wanting an heir of your race forever.

Concerning the entitlement[299] of the firstborn

The law said: A father shall give his firstborn a double share of everything he has. For he is the first of his children.

'Double', namely of all the father's wealth, except the division of the land, which is divided equally among the heirs.

Or as others reckon: 'Double', that is, in the field, in livestock, and in all wealth, and in the blessing, both of the firstborn and firstfruits.

Alternatively: In his last days the father divides his inheritance and wealth equally between his sons and himself, as if he were one of the sons. He puts aside a share of the inheritance and all the wealth, which he entrusts to his firstborn, and it shall be his in perpetual right.

But others say that after the death of the firstborn, it shall be divided between his heir and his brothers or their successors.

Concerning a division between the son of the favourite and hated wives

In Deuteronomy: If a man have two wives, one beloved, and the other hated, and he has had children by them, and the son of the hated be the firstborn, and the man means to divide his substance among his sons, he may not make the son of the beloved the firstborn and prefer him, but he shall acknowledge the son of the hated wife as the firstborn, and shall give him a double share and the firstborn from among the livestock. For this reason Hebron was given to Caleb, the son of the hated wife.

31.2 That the father's blessing confirms the heirs

Solomon: The father's blessing increases one's years.

Gregory: The fathers' blessing confirms the houses of their sons.

31.3 That the inheritance of a son who dies before his father should be given to Christ, to whom the son migrated

Augustine says in the book concerning heirs: It often happens, however, that one of his sons dies, and his father does not send his share after him, and his share is not offered to Christ, to whom the son has passed away. How will you dare to go to your son, whose share you did not send to him in heaven?

31.4 Concerning a father not dividing the inheritance between his sons according to love

The law says: A father may not leave the inheritance to the son of his beloved wife instead[300] of the son of his hated wife. But should the son of the hated be the firstborn, he shall have a double share, namely of the inheritance, and livestock, and blessings.

31.5 That a father may give a share to one of the sons ahead of his brothers

The law says: Jacob gave a share in Shechem to his son Joseph. As he said: I give you a share beyond your brothers, which I took out of the hand of the Amorrhite.

31.6 That a father can appoint his grandsons in lieu of his sons

The law says: Jacob ordained his grandsons Ephraim, the younger, and Manasseh, saying: The older shall serve the younger.

After these things, Joseph was told that his father was sick. And, taking his two sons, Manasseh and Ephraim, he set out, and the old man was told: Behold your son Joseph comes to you. And being strengthened he sat up in his bed, and to the ones who came to him, he said: God Almighty appeared to me at Luza, which is in the land of Canaan. And he blessed me, and said: Behold, I will cause you to increase and multiply, and I will make of you a multitude of people, and I will give this land to you and to your seed after you for an everlasting possession. So your two sons who were born in the land of Egypt before I came hither to you, Ephraim and Manasseh, shall be mine, just as Ruben and Simeon.

That a father can prefer the younger brother over the older

Jacob preferred Ephraim, the younger, over Manasseh, saying: The older shall serve the younger.

David preferred Solomon, the younger, over Adonias.

Moses was preferred to Aaron, even though he was the younger.

In Exodus: And Moses was eighty years old and Aaron eighty-three when he spoke to Pharaoh.

31.7 That other sons are deprived of an inheritance for the beloved son's sake

Simeon and Levi, transgressing their father's oath, were deprived of their share in the promised land.

31.8 Concerning dividing the inheritance among the brothers by lot

The law: Joshua cast lots before the Lord in Shiloh, and divided the promised land into nine parts for the children of Israel.

31.9 That the inheritance of a man with no sons, is reserved for his daughter, and then to other heirs[301]

The law says: When a man dies without a son, his inheritance shall pass to his daughter. If he have no daughter, his brothers shall succeed him. And if he have no brothers, you shall give the inheritance to his father's brothers. But if he have no paternal uncle, the inheritance shall be given to them who are the next of kin.

31.10 That the inheritance is reserved for legitimate sons

In Genesis: Abraham left all that he possessed to his son Isaac.

Likewise: Isaac kept the inheritance for Jacob.

Likewise: Jacob kept a share for his son Joseph.

Likewise: Caleb left Hebron to his sons.

Likewise: Joshua, dying, gave Mount Ephraim to his sons as an inheritance.

Likewise: David left an inheritance to Solomon.

Likewise: Tobias, dying, left all his property to his sons.

A synod says: A father ought not defraud his son, but grant him gifts and leave him an inheritance.

Likewise, Jerome said: Just as every father keeps his inheritance for his sons, thus also God keeps one for the saints.

Likewise, Christ put forward a parable in the Gospel, saying: A certain rich man divided his inheritance among his sons.

Likewise: Do not despise your own flesh.

That the inheritance of a son who dies before his father must be given to God, and not reserved for the other sons

Augustine said in the books concerning heirs: Do not heap yourselves up with vacuous fleeting treasures. Do not increase your wealth under the pretext of piety; saying: I shall reserve great things for my sons. Why would you not rather reserve it for him who created you from nothing and for him who feeds you and your sons? Nor is it better to bequeath to your son than to your creator. Men who behave obediently out of greed are liars. It often happens, however, that one of the sons dies, and his father does not send his share after him, and his share is not offered to Christ, to whom the son has passed away. How will you dare to go to your son, whose share you did not send to him in heaven, even though the Lord said, 'store up treasures for yourselves in heaven'? For what is kept here may perish; but a treasure forever remains there, where Christ is its guardian. For how dare you ask Christ for an inheritance, when you trick Christ out of your inheritance?

Jerome said: Hand over all your property to God, who created you, and nourishes you, and feeds your children.

Likewise: The following practice[302] is observed by our fathers according to the flesh: that anyone who dies leaves his property to his sons or brothers. God, however, who granted everything, who nourishes the sons and the father, should not be in want.

31.11 Concerning lavishing gifts on the sons of concubines[303]

In Genesis: Abraham gave all that he possessed to Isaac; to the children of the concubines, however, he granted gifts; and he separated them from his son Isaac.

31.12 That the inheritance should be reserved entirely for the sons, but also for God

Augustine said in the books concerning heirs: Do not increase your wealth under the pretext of piety, saying: I shall keep these things for my sons. Why would you not rather keep it for him who created you from nothing, who feeds you and maintains your sons? Is it not better to store up for your creator, than your sons?

Likewise, Augustine: How dare you ask Christ for an inheritance when you defraud Christ of your inheritance?

Jerome: When anyone dies, let him entrust all his property to God, who said to you: Store up treasures for yourselves in heaven.

31.13 Concerning dividing the inheritance into three parts

Origen said in the books concerning heirs: Let a dying father leave a third part to his sons, and a third to caesar, and a third to the church. If he shall not have a church, let him leave it to the poor. If he shall not have a caesar, let him divide it between his sons and the church. If he shall not have a caesar nor a church, let him divide it between his sons and the poor.

A synod: Let every inheritance that is subject to the tribute of a king and bound to a church be divided into three parts. The first part is given to the heirs without the casting of lots, just as in the law when a man has died: he shall leave a share to his sons and brothers, and it may not be transferred to another tribe. The second to the kings, for it is said: Render unto them for my sake and yours. The third to God, to whom it is said: Arise, O God, pass judgement on the earth, etc.

Likewise: Joseph restores all of Egypt to Pharaoh's authority, but nevertheless leaves a portion to his heirs.

Likewise: Paul gave only one portion to God, and another to the king, and another he saved for himself and for his heirs after him.

Concerning dividing a territory between the king and the church

In the Gospel: Render unto caesar the things that are caesar's, and to God the things that are God's. Note that he did not say: Render unto your sons, or brothers, or kinsmen. If he shall not have a caesar, let the entire tribute be given to God. For it is said: If you want to be perfect, go, etc., because the land is the Lord's.

Thence Peter said: We leave everything to you, etc. For, to them, greater things are increased a hundredfold on earth and in the afterlife. For he ought to cast away the other portion of worldly things, lest he be burdened by tribute. For Paul said: What has justice in common with iniquity, or light with darkness? But if you shall have wished it, it is not possible. The Lord said to Peter: Render unto them for my sake and yours. Note that Peter did not divide the whole of what he came by, but gave it to caesar, and gave himself to God.

A synod: Every territory in which a church or altar shall be established is divided into two parts: between the church and king. For Shiloh, where the ark was, belonged only to God and the king, and Jerusalem, where the temple was, was a dwelling place only for God and the king.

That an inheritance of a kinsman must not be held back by force or other means

Isaiah: Woe to you who join house to house, estate to estate, and couple field to field.

Another: Woe to him, who increases what is not his.

A synod: No one can tell the difference between one who seizes the property of others and a conniving thief.

31.14 That a church ought to give its share to the kinsmen of the deceased

A synod determined: When a person dies, he entrusts all that he has to God, and let him render a portion to caesar, and let God, through human agency, give to his (i.e. the deceased's) sons or kinsmen.

31.15 Concerning inheritances that have been neglected for a long time returning to their own heirs

The true angel became a demon by his own doing. He wickedly occupied a world that was not his own. After the passion of the son of man, the demon was ejected from his inheritance. The true heir was restored, as it is said: Jesus comes to his own; and this: All power was given to me in heaven and in earth.

Likewise: Adam was cast out of paradise. He was separated from his inheritance for 5228 years. After the Lord's passion he returned to his inheritance.[304]

Likewise: The race of Ham expelled the race of Sem from Syria, and Abraham, whose great-great-great-great grandfather was Sem, came to the inheritance of his line.

As one reads in the Conferences: For insofar as an old tradition teaches us, the children of Sem were once allotted the lands of the Canaanites, into which the children of Israel were led, and which later the descendants of Ham came to possess violently and forcibly through a wicked act of invasion. In which instance God's most righteous judgement is confirmed, for he drove away the latter from the places that were not their own, which they had maliciously occupied, and restored to the former the ancient property of their fathers, which was allocated to their family in the division of the world.

Likewise: After the temple was burned down and Jerusalem destroyed, the people of Israel spent seventy years in captivity, and gentiles came to own it. But after the expulsion of the gentiles, Israel returned to its own inheritance.

Likewise, in the books of Kings: Elisha spoke to the woman, whose son he had restored to life: Leave your land and wander upon the earth, for the Lord shall summon a famine over the earth, and it shall last seven years. She obeyed and wandered, and after a number of years she returned, and spoke to the king for her house and for her lands. And the king sent word through his crier, saying: Restore her the revenues of all her lands, from the day that she left.

31.16 Concerning things fixed for a long time and not changed

The Amorrhites took over by force a part of the land of Moab, namely from Aroer up to Mount Gilead, and after God reversed the Amorrhites' fortune Moab and Ammon sought the land from the children of Israel. And they were unable to obtain it, but Moses divided it into three parts for the children of Israel.

In the annals it is said: The portion that was given to the tribe of Dan came from the land of Damascus and was not returned.

Likewise: The suburbs of Ekron and Ashdod were from the land of the Philistines, and fell to the tribe of Judah by lot.

Concerning the wife, that she is the heir of the husband and the sons

In the book of Ruth: Then Boaz, taking ten men of the elders of the city, said to them: Sit here. They sat down, and he spoke to his kinsman: Naomi, who is returned from the country of Moab, sells a parcel of land that belonged to our brother Elimelech. I wish you to hear this, and to announce this to you before all hearers, elders of my people. If you will take possession of it by the right of kindred, buy it and possess it. But if it displease you, tell me so, that I may buy. For there is no near kinsman besides you, who are first, and me, who am second. But he answered: I will buy the field. And Boaz said to him: When you buy the field at the woman's hand, also Ruth the Moabitess, who was the wife of the deceased, you must take her, to raise up the name of your kinsman in his inheritance. He answered: I yield up my right of next of kin, for I must not cut off the posterity of my own family. You may make use of my privilege, which I profess I do willingly forego.

31.17 That a father will give his daughter an inheritance along with her brothers

In the law: Caleb gave an inheritance to his daughter Axa, at her request.

In the book of Joshua: And Caleb said: He who shall smite Kiriath-Sepher, and take it, I will give him Axa my daughter as wife. And Othoniel the son of Cenez, the younger brother of Caleb, took it. And he gave him Axa his daughter as wife. And as they were going together, she was moved by her husband to ask a field of her father, and she sighed as she sat on her donkey. And Caleb said to her: What is wrong? And she answered: Give me a blessing; you have given me a southern and dry land, join to it a land that is watered. And Caleb gave her the upper and the lower watery ground.

At the end of the book of Job: And there were not found in all the earth women so beautiful as the daughters of Job. And their father gave them inheritance among their brothers.

Origen in the annals of the Hebrews: Jacob gave a share to his daughter Dina, who remained a widow after her husband.

31.18 That, according to [the law of] nature,[305] a daughter does not receive a share in the division of the inheritance along with her brothers

It is not said to Eve, 'Cursed is the earth in your work', but to Adam.

Nor is it said to Eve: You shall have dominion over all these things. But it is said: He brought them to Adam, etc.

Likewise: Noah divided the whole world among his sons, not his daughters.

Likewise: The promised land is divided among men.

Jerome: Just as the land is cursed on account of man's sin, so he divides it as an inheritance.

Augustine: In the same manner that a man works and protects his inheritance, so he possesses the earth as his inheritance. It is the woman's role to give birth, to nourish, to be subject to her husband's power, to work in the house.

31.19 That women divide the inheritance

Origen says: Rahab, the prostitute in Jericho, received her father's inheritance, such that she was mistress to her brothers.

Jerome: God wiped both sexes clean of Adam's sin, and if they receive an equal share in the heavenly inheritance together, why shall they not hold an equal share in the earthly?

The law says: The daughters of Salphaad, of the tribe of Manasseh, came to Moses in the plains of Moab, saying: Our father died having no sons, nor was he in the sedition of Core and Dathan, but he died in his own sin. Why should we be deprived of his inheritance?

Likewise, in the book of Numbers: Moses answered the children of Israel, and said by the command of the Lord: Rightly hath the tribe of the children of Joseph spoken. And this is the law promulgated by the Lord upon the daughters of Salphaad: Let them marry whomever they will, so long as they be men of their own tribe, lest the possession of the children be mingled from tribe to tribe. For all men shall marry wives of their own tribe and kindred: And all women shall take husbands of the same tribe, so that the inheritance shall remain in the families, lest the tribes be mingled one with another, but they should remain just as they were separated by the Lord. And the daughters of Salphaad did as was commanded. And Maala, and Thersa, and Hegla, and Melcha, and Noa were married to the sons of their uncle by their father, of the family of Manasseh, who was the son of Joseph. And the possession that had been allotted to them remained in the tribe and family of their father.

Moses referred this question to the judgement of the Lord, who said: The daughters of Salphaad demand a just thing. Give them an inheritance among their brothers.

But the Lord commanded that they marry men from their own tribe, lest the inheritance be transferred from one tribe to another. Whence it is to be understood what the Lord said to this end: Let no man be joined to a woman, unless she be from his own tribe, that the inheritance might not be transferred from one tribe to another.[306]

31.20 Concerning the things that ecclesiastical authors have to add concerning female heirs

A Hibernian synod: Ecclesiastical authors have many things to add here: that female heirs guarantee by means of 'paying sureties' and 'enforcing sureties',[307] that the inheritance shall not be alienated.

For the Lord says: Their inheritance shall be transferred to their father's brothers, and therefrom to the next in kin. Let it be known whether they shall give a share to the Lord: if their kinsmen do not object, what they shall give to the Lord will be the Lord's. Otherwise the donation shall be invalidated.

However, it will be deemed proper to offer to the Lord livestock and clothing and vessels, if, indeed, they are rightfully theirs. It shall be permissible to give to the girls serving them sheep and wool and—if by chance they have had carers who are close kin—a share of the inheritance as payment for their servitude and care.

Let it be known what they shall grant by means of a testament, to wit: cows, clothing, and vessels. Let it be known what they shall give to the servants (*ministri*), to wit: a share of the sheep and wool. If, however, the servants (*ministri*) have been kinsfolk, they shall give them a portion of the inheritance. And if they have had a paternal church,[308] they shall leave it a portion of the inheritance. And if they will have sons by men of their own kindred, they shall transmit the inheritance [to them].[309]

31.21 That those ministering to the sick obtain an inheritance

Gregory Nazianzen: Whoever nurses the sick, let him obtain their inheritance.

For Christ says: I was sick and you visited me; possess, therefore, my inheritance!

Jerome: There is no difference between nursing the sick and waiting on Christ; for he must be nourished, because Christ was sick.

31.22 Concerning the testament of the sick

A Hibernian synod: The testament of the sick is that he must give his carer (*minister*) a share of the movables, and another share to the heirs, and another share to the church as payment for burial. The inheritance, however, is divided between the kingdom and the church and the heirs. If, however, he shall not have a kingdom, the third part shall belong to his caregivers (*ministri*). If, however, he shall not have a church, his kinsfolk and caregivers (*ministri*) should divide it [among themselves].

31.23 Concerning a dispute between two joint heirs of two deceased fathers

A synod: In a dispute between joint heirs of two fathers, he shall be chosen who is older and prudent and dignified in his conduct and has a good conscience. And let it be trusted what he says; or let things be judged by lot,[310] which settles all doubtful cases, or decided by able judges.

Likewise: The heirs of the dead should be determined in the following manner: if one shall have witnesses, let him summon them. If not, seniority should be taken into account, and nobility, and rank, and the quality of the claim.[311] If, however, they shall waver, let them submit to the judgement[312] either of lots, or proof, which supersedes all things, or truthful judges who do not lean towards either party.

Likewise, the synod of Ancyra ruled: If two people dispute in the absence of the dead, their dispute can be settled in four ways: either by lot, which reveals what is unseen, or let them divide what they fight over, or let one yield by a payment, or let them give it to the *sacerdotes*.

That correcting good sons who are fit to inherit, is expedient to the father

The son of Sirach says: He who loves his son frequently corrects him, that he may rejoice in his latter end. And he who instructs his son shall be gladdened in him, and he does not grope after the doors of his neighbours, and he shall glory in him in the midst of his servants. He who teaches his son will send his enemy into jealousy. His father is dead, and yet it is as if he were not dead; for he has left one behind him who is like himself. While he lived he looked and rejoiced in him, and in his own death he was not sorrowful, neither was he confounded before his enemies. For he shall leave behind a defender of the house, who will also requite kindness to his friends.

Concerning adopted sons

Augustine says: It is a simple matter that they whom it concerns may notice[313] that Joseph was able to have two fathers: one who begot him, and another who adopted him. For the ancient custom of adoption prevailed also among the people of God, so that sons, whom they did not themselves beget, they made their own, just as Jacob adopted Joseph's sons as his own sons.

In the Chronicles one reads: Nerva died from an illness in the gardens of Sallust in his seventy-second year, when he had already adopted Trajan as his son.

In the books of etymologies: An adoptive son is one who is handed over by the power of his legitimate father, or grandfather, or great-grandfather, to the power of another through a transferral. And he bears the name of both, like Fabius Aemilius, or Scipio Paulinus.

Origen: Therefore Jugurtha, the adopted son and heir of Micipsa, king of the Numidians, became chief among his natural sons. He despised the sons, his joint heirs; indeed, he killed Hiempsal, and exiled the defeated Adherbal from Africa.

In the books of etymologies: Children are designated in four ways: by nature, by imitation, by adoption and by instruction.[314]

Augustine says in the books of the Enchiridion: It cannot be said that everything that is begotten by another, i.e. as worms are begotten by flesh, can be described as the offspring of the one by which it was begotten. Likewise, it does not follow that all who are said to be the children of a certain person can be said to have been begotten by him; for instance, like they who are adopted. Also, they who are called the children of hell were not born from hell, but are prepared for it.

In the books of etymologies: A pro-heir (*proheres*) acts as an heir, as if it were 'for an heir' (*pro heres*). For he is either instated or substituted.

32 Concerning debts, pledges,[315] and interest payments

32.1 Concerning repaying debts

Job says: I have paid the debt of each and every one.

In the book of Kings: Repay your debtor.

Paul to the Romans: Render to all men their dues.

The synod of Arles: Insofar as you want a debt to be repaid to you, you yourself ought to repay.

A Roman synod: Any man who, in the manner of pagans, should cheat over what is owed to his brother is to be excommunicated until he has repaid it.

Likewise: How dare you ask God to remit your debt, when you have not repaid the debt of your neighbour?

32.2 Concerning repaying debts quickly

Moses: Do not withhold a brother's debt.

Solomon: Do not withhold a debt of your neighbour.

Concerning the one withholding a debt

Jerome: Any man who withholds a debt shows himself to be covetous of another's wealth, and behaves like a robber, and commits the offence of theft.

That a debt ought to be repaid even after the death of the person by whom it is owed[316]

In the Life of the Fathers:[317] A certain married man was sent to hell for dying without repaying a debt to his brother. Whence he appeared to his wife and asked her to settle the debt and make an offering for him.

In the books of Kings: Elijah[318] told the woman who outlived her husband to repay a debt for the sake of her sons, saying: Go, sell the oil, and repay your creditor.

32.3 Concerning remitting debts to the enfeebled and the needy

Clement: There is, therefore, as we have said, necessary inequality in the arrangement of the world. So long as men cannot know everything, nor master every craft, all are in need of the experience and help of others. And on account of this it is necessary that one should work and another pay this worker's wage; that one should serve and another give orders; that one should be ruled and another rule. But divine mercy converts this inequality, which is part and parcel of human life, into an opportunity for justice and mercy and humanity: that while these relationships prevail among men, each man should have cause to behave justly towards him, to whom the wage of labour has been paid, and to be merciful to him, who perhaps due to being enfeebled or beleaguered by need, is unable to repay his debt.

Augustine: He who remits a debt to the needy performs a Christian deed.

Origen: He who demands a debt from the needy becomes an extorter of another's property.

Faustus: If you should lend things that are your own, be careful not to exact the things of another; for if the person to whom you lent does not have the means to repay, you extort the things of another. For it was on account of need that the Lord remitted his servant.

Augustine in the books concerning the purity of the heart: He who, of his own volition, or owing to poverty, shall refuse to repay a debt, let it be remitted to him. For he refuses on account of two reasons: either because he does not have the funds, or because he is greedy and covetous of another's property.

Ezekiel: He does not oppress a needy man, and he returned the pledge of the debtor.

32.4 Concerning the four things that should accompany debts[319]

A Roman debate says: Four things accompany a debt: 'paying sureties' and 'enforcing sureties',[320] worthy witnesses, writing. If all these have wavered or if one has been missing, there shall be a binding with an oath, and the debts shall be paid.

Concerning a loan

The son of Sirach: Many have looked upon a thing lent as a thing found, and have given trouble to them who helped them. Till he receives, he kisses the hands of the lender, and in promises he humbles his voice. And when payment is due, he will ask for time, and will return tedious and murmuring words, and will complain of the time. And if he be able to pay, he shall stupidly refuse, and return an insult.

Likewise, the same says: Today a man lends, and tomorrow he asks it again, and such a man as this is hateful.

32.5 Concerning wages being paid quickly to labourers

The law says: You shall not refuse the wage of your brother or a stranger who dwells in your land, but you shall pay him the wages of his labour the same day, before sunset, because he is poor, and with it maintains his life; lest he cry against you to the Lord, and it be reckoned against you as a sin.

Likewise: Do not detain the wages of your labourer with you until morning.

In the prophets: The wages of your labourers cry to me from the earth.

Likewise: You have not returned the pledge of your neighbour, nor have you paid the wages of labourers.

Job: I have never defrauded any labourer.

Tobias: May the wages of labourers not linger with you.

In the Gospel: The Lord rendered payment to the harvesters of his vineyard.

Likewise, in the same: A denarius to each.

The Lord in the Gospel: After one hour's work, he gave them a denarius.

32.6 Concerning wages not being paid quickly to labourers

A synod: The work of labourers is to be considered, and then the wages ought to be paid.

Likewise: Every labourer ends his work quickly, that he may be paid quickly.

Likewise: Every labourer only performs eye-service, [and] therefore a foreman must be appointed to him.

Likewise: A labourer abandons the sheep, since he is only a hireling, and he does not assemble the dispersed, nor does he mend what is broken.

32.7 Concerning giving goods without recompense

In Paralipomenon: Amasias, the king of Israel, took from Israel a hundred valiant men, and gave them a hundred talents of silver. A man of God came to him, and said: O king, the army of Israel shall not go out with you, for God is not with Israel and all the children of Ephraim. And the man of God said: And if you think that battles consist in the strength of the army, the Lord will make you to be overcome by your enemies. And the man of God said: Send them away from you. And king Amasias said to the man of God: What will then become of the hundred talents which I have given to the soldiers of Israel? And the man of God answered: Leave them, because the Lord is rich enough to be able to give you much more than this.

32.8 Concerning accepting a pledge

The law says: If your brother owes you something, having not the means to repay you, accept a pledge from him and keep it, that you may receive what he owes.

32.9 Concerning the amount to be pledged and the procedure involved in it

A Hibernian synod decreed that the fifth part of a debt is rendered as a pledge, as it is said in the law: Render the fifth part. And if he has not paid what he pledged by the designated time, he will never pay it, and he shall return the entire debt, unless you remit his debt.[321]

32.10 That a pledge should be accepted with compassion

Ezekiel says of the just man: He does not oppress a needy man, and returns the security to the debtor.

The law says: When you shall ask back of your neighbour anything that he owes to you, you shall not go into his house to take away a pledge, but you shall stand outside and he shall bring out to you what he has. If he be poor, the pledge shall not lodge with you that night, but you shall restore it to him before sunrise, that he, sleeping, may bless you, and you may have justice before God.

Likewise, in the law: You shall not take the millstone or clothing of your neighbour as a pledge, because by means of these his life is sustained.

32.11 Concerning paying back interest[322]

Jerome in the books concerning the monastic rule: All that you have received must be returned together with the interest. For a long delay incurs interest.

The Lord in the Gospel claimed his money with interest.

Gregory says in the homilies: He who has accepted the money of another man, it must be returned to him, and received with interest. And the longer it stays with him, the more the interest ought to increase. For in the same manner that one gives a loan in order to gain interest, so he who has given alms shall be rewarded with good things.

32.12 That interest must not be sought

The law says: You shall not lend to your brother money with interest payments.

Likewise, the law: If you have given something to your kinsman or to a stranger, you shall not claim it with interest.

David, praising the holy man, says: He whose money; as far as: Do not receive.

Ezekiel: He shall give his bread to the hungry, and cover the naked, and shall not give his money to interest payments, nor take any surplus.

Jerome: There is no difference between demanding interest payments and defrauding or robbing.

Origen: Adapt yourself to your brother and accept what you have given. Do not ask anything beyond.

A holy synod: If anyone has been caught receiving interest payments, or engaging in business for shameful gain, he should be deposed from the clergy.

33 Concerning sureties, and 'paying sureties', and 'enforcing sureties'[323]

33.1 That a 'paying surety', or surety who vouches on behalf of a stranger, is liable to pay[324]

Be not among them who join their hands,[325] and offer themselves sureties for the debts of others. For if you have not the means to restore, what cause is there, that he should take the covering from your bed?

Solomon: If you have engaged fast your hand to a stranger, you should not care to be freed.

Likewise: He who is surety for a stranger shall be afflicted with evil.

Likewise: Take away the garment of him who went surety for an outsider and engaged fast his hand for strangers; take a pledge from him.

33.2 That a cleric ought not be a surety

A synod: A cleric who commits himself to acts of surety should be demoted.

Patrick: If a cleric has been a surety for a pagan in whatsoever amount, and it so happens—as well it might—that the pagan by some ruse defaults [upon the cleric], the cleric must pay the debt from his own means. For should he contend with him in arms, let him be reckoned to be outside the church.[326]

33.3 Concerning those who are not fit to undertake suretyship

A Hibernian synod: It is not fitting for a surety to be either a slave, or a stranger, or an imbecile, or a *monachus*, unless ordered by his abbot, or a son, unless ordered by his father, or a woman, unless she is an abbess (*domina*), both virgin and holy.[327]

33.4 Concerning the time in which a 'paying surety' ought to pay

A Hibernian synod says that a 'paying surety' pays the debt of those on behalf of whom he fixed his hand, in such a manner that, [after the first time he gives notice], he shall wait fifteen days for the debtor to settle the debt, after the second time twenty days, after the third time thirty days, and after the fourth time forty days. Thereafter let him repay the debt without giving it another thought.

Likewise: Others, on the other hand, say that if [he is acting] on behalf of a living debtor, he shall wait ten days the first time, and five the second; but if on behalf of a dead one, thirty days.[328]

33.5 Concerning the manner in which the debtor pays the surety

In the decision of the same synod: Let a debtor repay what the surety paid and insofar as he was inconvenienced [in paying].[329] Should, however, the surety be charitable, he shall not demand an interest, but only the amount that he paid and insofar as he was inconvenienced. But should he be uncharitable, interest is accrued for a single year; let the entire debt be repaid as well as the fifth part of the debt for every month of that year.[330]

33.6 That one ought not buy or sell anything without 'paying sureties' and 'enforcing sureties'[331]

Jeremiah says: The word of the Lord came to me, saying: Behold, Hanameel your cousin, the son of Sellum shall come to you, saying: Buy my field, which is in Anathoth. For it is apt for you, on account of your kinship, that you should buy it. And take the sealed deed of purchase, and the assurances (*stipulationes*), and the ratifications (*ratas*)[332] with the seals that are on the outside.

A holy synod decreed that every sale should be confirmed in four ways, to wit: by 'paying sureties', and 'enforcing sureties', and witnesses, and a written attestation,[333] in which they (i.e. transactions) are recorded.

Augustine: If you have sold or purchased, provide 'paying sureties', and 'enforcing sureties', and written attestations. For any purchase without these shall be void.

Jerome: No one ought to remove the inheritance of a kinsman without solid payment, and assurances and ratifications[334] remaining afterwards in the record, because this is what Jeremiah did.

33.7 Concerning the law[335] of 'enforcing sureties' and witnesses

A Hibernian synod: If there shall be a single 'enforcing surety', they shall cast lots, and [both creditor] and debtor shall swear one over the other. But if one party shall have two or three witnesses, the oath shall be from the majority, and the debtor shall repay. However, should the 'enforcing sureties' disagree among themselves, they shall cast lots, unless there be witnesses. And should one party be found to be lying, he shall either pay the debt or he shall do penance equivalent to the value of the debt.[336]

33.8 Concerning a resistant debtor

The same synod: Every debtor who resists witnesses and 'enforcing sureties' shall be cast out until he has performed a penance prescribed by judges.

Patrick says: For should he have contended with arms, let him be cast out of the church.

34 Concerning oath-taking

34.1 Concerning swearing an oath

The servant swore to Abraham. Now Abraham was old and advanced in age, and the Lord had blessed him. And he said to the elder servant of his house, who was ruler over all he had: Put your hand under my thigh, that I may make you swear by the Lord God of heaven and earth, that you take not a wife for my son of the daughters of the Canaanites, among whom I dwell, etc. And a little later it is said: The servant therefore put his hand under the thigh of Abraham his lord, and swore to him upon this word.

Jacob swore to Laban before the heap of the testimony. Laban answered him: The daughters are mine and the children, and your flocks, and all things that you see are mine. Come therefore, let us enter into a league, that it may be for a testimony between me and you. And Jacob took a stone, and set it up for a title, etc. And a little later he said: And Jacob swore by the name of his father Isaac.

Isaac swore to Abimelech and Phicol. In Genesis: To which place when Abimelech, and Ochozath his friend, and Phicol chief captain of his soldiers came from Gerara, Isaac said to them: Why have you come to me, a man whom you hate and have cast out from among you? And they answered: We saw that the Lord is with you, and therefore we have said: Let there be an oath between us, and let us make a covenant, etc. And a little further on: He made them a feast, and after they had food and drink, arising in the morning, they swore one to another.

Moses swore to Jethro, the priest of Midian.

Joshua swore that he would not rest until he destroyed Achis too.

Likewise: Joshua swore to the Gabaonites.

Likewise: I have given you the land, as I have sworn to your fathers.

David says: The Lord hath sworn, and he shall not repent.

In the books of Kings: Saul to David: Swear to me by the Lord, that you will not destroy my seed after me.

Paul: I speak the truth in Christ, I lie not, my conscience bearing me witness in the Holy Spirit.

Likewise: An oath is the end of a dispute.

Jerome: I testify to Jesus and his holy angels.

The prophet: The Lord lives, and my soul lives.

Ezechias: The Lord lives, who created this soul.

In the law: Render your vows to the Lord.

34.2 Concerning taking precautions about an oath

Isidore in the books concerning the nature of things: One must, therefore, be careful of swearing, and it must not be done, except in times of need.

Swearing does not conflict with the teachings of the Lord, but when we swear, we chance upon the offence of perjury. As one who does not speak cannot lie, so he who is not inclined to swear, shall not be able to commit perjury.

Likewise: He who fears perjury never swears.

Origen: Everyone who is bold in swearing, is close to lying.

Likewise, the same: A man swearing boldly, whatever good he may have done will perish, and the punishment shall remain upon him in the future.

Solomon: A man who swears much shall be filled with iniquity, and he shall not be justified, and a scourge shall not depart from his house. And if he shall have sworn in vain, his sin shall be upon his house. And if he dissemble it, he offends double. And if he swear in vain, he shall not be justified, for his house shall be filled with his punishment.

Augustine: Woe to them who want to swear in order to gain transitory possessions, whereby they lose the eternal.

34.3 That one must not swear by what is created, but only by the creator

The Lord in the Gospel: You shall not swear at all, neither by heaven, for it is the throne of God, nor by the earth, for it is his footstool.

Jerome: The sense of this passage teaches that one should not swear by any created thing, but by the creator, as it is customary for the prophets to say: The Lord, by whom I stand today, lives. For everything by which one swears, one also loves.

34.4 That a Christian ought not swear, but only say

In the Gospel: But I tell you not to swear under any circumstances. Let your speech be: yes, yes, no, no. More than this is from the evil one.

Jerome: The word of the just is received in lieu of an oath.

A Roman synod: Three things must be removed from the church: an oath, contention, interest payments and every kind of secular business.

In the Ecclesiastical History: When a man by the name of Basilides was asked, for some reason, to take an oath in the presence of his colleagues, who challenged his vows and oaths, he said that he was not permitted to swear under any circumstances because he was a Christian.

34.5 Concerning dissolving an oath

Jerome: Three kinds of oaths must be dissolved. If you have taken an oath to murder or commit another evil, do not fulfil it, as Paul said: Undo every unjust bond.

The first: When someone swears to do evil, like murder or any evil of this type.

Isidore in the books of the nature of things: An oath by which an evil is rashly promised must not be kept; for instance, if someone who has been joined to an adulteress, should promise to stay with her forever. It is more tolerable not to fulfil an oath, than to perpetuate a state of disgraceful immorality.

Whence it is said: Undo every unjust bond.

Likewise: Perverse oaths are reversed.

The second: When someone swears unscrupulously, not reckoning it a sin.

Origen: Others swear in vain, with no expediency to themselves or to others; it seems better to dissolve than fulfil such oaths.

A synod: It must be considered praiseworthy to dissolve a reckless agreement; it is not dishonesty, but only correction of rashness.[337]

In the book of Kings Saul vowed that Jonathan would be killed, and he was not killed, nor was he blamed for this vow, for he vowed according to his own will, not God's.

For Saul says to Jonathan: May God do so and so to me, and add these things, for dying you shall die, Jonathan. And the people said to Saul: Shall Jonathan really die, who has wrought this great salvation in Israel? This is not right; as the Lord liveth, not a single hair of his head shall fall to the ground; that is, because Jonathan and his armour-bearer slew twenty thousand Philistines in one day.

The third is: If a woman, a girl in age, being in her father's house, bind herself by an oath, if her father knew the vows and immediately gainsaid them, both her vows and her oaths shall be void, and she shall not be culpable.[338]

A Hibernian synod: The oath of a son or a daughter without their father's knowledge, the oath of a *monachus* without the abbot's knowledge, the oath of a slave without his master's knowledge, shall be void.

Jerome: He who wickedly binds an oath on a person of unsound mind, or a child, or the infirm, shall be held guilty for the oath, if it was taken in the absence of their guardians.

34.6 Concerning not dissolving an oath

The law: If any of the men make a vow, or bind himself by an oath, let him not make his word void, but fulfil all that he promised.

Likewise, the law: If a woman bind herself by an oath, and so forth; until he said: If her father held his peace for a day, she shall be bound by the vow.

Likewise: That which has once left your lips, you shall observe as though you have promised it to the Lord your God.

Jerome: Do everything that you vowed, lest you be found guilty of perjury.

For he said in the Gospel: Perjurers shall not possess the kingdom of heaven.

Origen: Most swearing is to be discouraged, but after an oath has been taken, it must be fulfilled rather than annulled. Jephte swore a reckless oath, and did not dissolve it.

34.7 That many are deceived through oaths

Isidore in the books concerning the nature of things: Many swear falsely in order to deceive, as they use the confidence that an oath inspires to lend credence to their words, and so, through deception, while they perjure and lie, they deceive the gullible man. Sometimes those led astray are deceived by false tears; and the teary-eyed are trusted, who should not have been believed.

34.8 Concerning a false oath

Isidore in the same books: By whatsoever verbal ingenuity one swears, nevertheless God, who is a witness to our conscience, perceives [the oath] in exactly the same manner as he, to whom the oath is given, understands it. For he is twice as guilty, who both takes God's name in vain, and ensnares his fellow man.

34.9 Concerning the vice of compelling an audience to swear

Isidore in the same books: We say most things without swearing, but due to the incredulity of those who do not believe what we say, we are compelled to swear. And through such necessity, we form a habit of swearing. Many who are not moved to put trust in a statement are slow to believe. But they who compel those speaking to them to swear commit a great offence.

34.10 That the evil of someone committing perjury and someone concealing perjury is alike

In Leviticus: The one that sins and hears the voice of one swearing, and is a witness either because he himself has seen, or he is privy to it, unless he utters it, he shall bear his iniquity.

34.11 Concerning performing penance for perjury and the alms to be given for it

In Leviticus: The person who swears falsely that he would do something either evil or good, and forgot, and afterwards remembers, let him do penance for his sin, and offer a lamb, or a she-goat, or two turtledoves, or two young pigeons.

34.12 What is the difference between an oath and God's repentance?[339]

Isidore in the books concerning the nature of things: Swearing is that providence of God by which he commanded not to break agreements.

Likewise: God's repentance, however, is the changing of matters; but to fail to regret is to fail to revoke decisions; as in that [passage]: The Lord has sworn and he will not repent; i.e. whoever swore, will not be made to recant.

34.13 Concerning the accused concluding his case by making an oath or standing by the altar[340]

The synod of Sardica said: It is decided that one who is accused—that is, if he has been afraid of the rash power of the multitude—should choose for himself a nearby place to which he can easily summon witnesses, where the case might be concluded either by oath, or beside the altar.

The synod of Arles: If one has given testimony over another, he shall swear by the Holy Gospels that he shall submit to the judgement of God, who said: Revenge is mine, and I shall repay.

34.14 Why an oath rests with the majority

The synod of *Consul*:[341] They who dispute what case soever, if one should have a witness or many, and the other be without witness, the oath shall rest with the majority.

Concerning him who swears, how should he be quitted

A Roman synod says of two parties that dispute with no witnesses: The one who is being vindicated testifies by the four Gospels before the *sacerdos* dispenses the host, and let him be subject to ordeal by fire.[342]

35 Concerning the jubilee[343]

35.1 Concerning the seven-year jubilee, and the fifty-year jubilee, and the seven-day jubilee; it is the following

On the seventh year he makes a year of remission, and it is observed not only on the seventh, but on the seventh of sevenths, not only in days, but also in years. They designate a fiftieth year, which they call a jubilee, in which there is remission of land and freeing of slaves, and restitution of property that had been obtained for a price.

35.2 Concerning the Sabbath of years, namely on the minor jubilee of the noble Hebrews

In Deuteronomy: In the seventh year you shall make a remission, which shall be celebrated in this order: he to whom anything is owing from his friend and brother and neighbour cannot suddenly demand it back, because it is the year of remission of God. Of the foreigner or stranger you shall exact it; of your countryman and neighbour you shall not have power to demand it again.

35.3 That freeborn captives must be released on the same Sabbath

The Lord says by Jeremiah: I made a covenant with your fathers[344] in the day that I brought them out of the land of Egypt, out of the house of bondage, saying: At the end of seven years, let every man release his brother being a Hebrew, who has been sold to him. He shall serve you six years,[345] and you shall let him go free from you in the seventh year.

35.4 Concerning the price of an estate[346] that has been sold, and on the reversal of the jubilee

The law says: And if a man sold a field of his possession, the price of this field shall be rated according to the measure of the seed. If, however, the ground be sowed with thirty bushels of barley, it shall be sold for fifty shekels of silver. And in the fiftieth year, namely at the end of the jubilee, it shall be restored to its former owner, without him having to pay anything.

Concerning deducting past time

If he vow his field immediately from the beginning year of the jubilee, as much as it may be worth, at so much it shall be rated. But if some time after, the priest shall reckon the money according to the number of years that remain until the jubilee, it shall be deducted from the price. And if he who vowed will want to redeem his field, he shall add the fifth part of the valuation, and shall possess it. And if he will not want to redeem it, but it be sold to any man other than he who vowed it, he may not redeem it any more.

35.5 Concerning the three things that we need when buying an estate[347]

Jeremiah: Take the sealed deed of your purchase, and the assurances (*stipulationes*), and the ratifications (*ratas*), and the seals that are on the outside.[348]

35.6 Concerning three types of things that have been sold, which return on the jubilee

The law says: For all that is sold—of the fields, and possessions, and slaves—shall be sold under the condition of redemption of the jubilee, namely of the fiftieth year.

35.7 Concerning the time at which neglected property is forfeit in respect to its former ownership[349]

Augustine says in the books concerning the synclitic virgin:[350] Do not strive after things which, having grown old, reason has cast into oblivion, or those which have grown old in the memory of the fathers.

Origen: Whoever has alienated his property for the length of the reigns of three successive kings or bishops[351] shall not easily reclaim it.

A Hibernian synod: Anything whatsoever that has been alienated for fifty years, namely up to the jubilee, passes[352] over to the ownership of a single party without protest or excommunication, it shall never return.[353]

Concerning those who were cast out not returning

The angel cast out of heaven shall never reclaim his former liberty. Adam, who was cast out of paradise, will never return to it physically. The race of Ham, having been cast out of Syria, does not return to it again, and so on and so forth.

Concerning fixed things without change

The law: Do not shift the bounds which your fathers have set.

In Proverbs: Pass not beyond the ancient bounds which your fathers have set.

Likewise: Touch not the bounds of your children.

In Deuteronomy: Cursed be he who changes his neighbour's landmarks, which his fathers fixed to mark their property, and a daughter's vow with the father holding his peace, and a wife's vow, with her husband approving.

A synod: Three things are unchangeable: the word of a king, the word of a bishop, the word of a *scriba*. On account of which it is said: What I have written, I have written.

In the Gospel: Heaven and earth shall pass, but my words shall not pass.

Concerning changes without blame

In the law: the sacrifice of livestock. In the New Testament: the sacrifice of virtues.

Eusebius of Caesarea: It seems to be appropriate to change a verdict, when a better and more righteous argument supersedes it, not by human persuasion, nor by deceitful eloquence, but by an argument from divine scripture.

Cassian: It is better for us to change a verdict than suffer the loss of a thing wholesome and perfect.

Concerning returning things that have long been neglected to their proper owners

In the books of histories: We decree, he said, if any houses, or estates, or any farms have been seized from Christians, either by the treasury, or through their being granted as gifts, we order that all these be restored to their previous ownership.

A synod: The truth never grows old.

Likewise: A lie must be erased.

In the chronicles: Diocletian reigned for twenty years; he burned sacred books, and ordered the confiscation of Christian property. Galerius succeeded him. Galerius reigned two years. Constantine, reigning thirty years, restored to the Christians everything that belonged to them.

35.8 That the laws of the jubilee are also observed in the era of the New Testament

A synod said concerning things that have been sold as normal: Since the truth never grows old, the laws of the jubilee, that is, of every fiftieth year, are to be observed, so that claims that have become uncertain through lapse of time may not be affirmed; and therefore every business transaction should be confirmed in writing.[354]

35.9 Concerning a house that is not returned even on the jubilee

The law says: He who sells a house within the walls of a city shall have the liberty to redeem it, until one year be expired. If he has not redeemed it, and the whole year be fully out, the buyer shall possess it and his posterity forever, and it cannot be redeemed, not even in the jubilee.

That things granted to someone temporarily pass into his ownership[355]

In the books of Kings: And David said to Achis: If I have found favour in your sight, let a place be given me in one of the cities of this country, that I may dwell there; for why should your servant dwell in the royal city with you? Then Achis gave him Siceleg that day, for which reason Siceleg is of the kingdom of Judah unto this day. And the time that David dwelt in the country of the Philistines was four months.

Concerning others who resist the jubilee against you, and concerning things that the jubilee does not conclude

In the debate of the elders: If someone, being proud on account of his faculty of judgement, has said: You turn the world backwards, it has long been abolished, you denounce praiseworthy practices, you lose a generation, answer him: The truth has arisen from the earth, and erased every lie.

Whence Paul: The old things have passed away; behold all things are made new.

35.10 Concerning things that the jubilee does not frustrate

A Hibernian synod: You shall reply to those who put forward the jubilee against you: The jubilee year applies to things that were sold or changed hands, between their own joint heirs[356] and catholic men; it does not apply to property deposited in ancient times, nor does it apply to things that have been seized by force, nor does it apply to things that are without price, nor does it apply to things that are sold of the inheritances of others, nor does it apply to things that are exchanged between the king and the church—for so long as the king does not misappropriate the church's property, the churches [shall not misappropriate] the rights of the king—it does not apply to things that occur between the brethren, for brother does not defraud brother.

35.11 Concerning the three reasons for which the jubilee, namely the remission of God, was established

It has been established for three reasons: first, on account of lack of food and money. Second, on account of slaves, who were customarily sold without being redeemed. Third, lest there be whispering among the people that does not know the appointed time at which it should buy or sell anything.

36 Concerning the *principatus*[357]

Concerning the word *princeps*

In the books of etymologies: *Princeps* designates both dignity, and temporal sequence, just as in this Virgilian example it stands for 'first' (*primus*): First Turnus hurled a burning torch. *Princeps* is derived from the notion of 'taking' (*capiendi*) because he 'takes' first (*primus capiat*); it is analogous to a citizen of a municipality (*municeps*) in that he 'takes' official duties (*munia capit*).

36.1 Concerning ordaining a *princeps* by lot

Luke in the Acts of the Apostles: And they appointed two, namely Barsabas and Matthias. And praying, they said: You, Lord, who know the hearts of all men, show us which of these two you have chosen to take the place of this ministry and apostleship, from which Judas has fallen, and may he have his place. And they gave them lots in their bosom, and the lot fell upon Matthias, and he was numbered with the eleven apostles.

36.2 Concerning the four kinds of ordination

Jerome: There are four kinds of ordination in the law: the first by God alone, as Moses was ordained, and also Fabius, in Rome, on whom a pigeon landed as he was coming from the field.

The second, by God and man, as Joshua the son of Nun was ordained by God and Moses.

The third, by man alone, but with God's permission, as Gothoniel was ordained after Jesus Nave,[358] because the people, forsaken by its leader, said: Who will go before us? The Lord said: Judas shall walk before you. After that they ordained themselves *principes*, some were good, others bad.

The fourth is an ordination by a reprobate, as in the case of Abimelech, who slew his seventy brothers, the sons of his father Gideon.

Likewise, in the books concerning the offices: The varieties of the apostles correspond to these four types. One type was by God alone, like Moses; another type was by man and God, like Joshua; the third by man alone, just as in these days persons are chosen as successors among the *sacerdotes* by the support of the people and by those in power; the fourth by themselves, like the pseudo-prophets and pseudo-apostles.

36.3 Concerning good *principes*

Gregory the Roman: They who are able to subdue the tides of excesses within themselves, ought to be responsible for pastoral care.

Gregory: If, therefore, he expertly lies, he should not dare assume the leadership. If vice reigns within him [then] he, who is depraved through his own criminal ways, may not seek to intervene for the faults of others. For when an objectionable man is sent to intercede, the mind of the irate is provoked towards worse things.

Gregory: It is a custom of correct behaviour that one who has not yet learned to obey should not dare to rule, lest he demand the same obedience of his subjects, which he does not know to give his superiors.

Gregory: It is a matter of concern, that a load of worries plagues the mind of each and every bishop. And whenever the mind is divided between many matters, little attention is paid to individual matters.

Gregory: The abuse that is visited upon someone tests what kind of person he is beneath the surface. For as proud men revel in honours, so most humble men revel in being despised.

Gregory: Many things seem good, but are not, because they are not done in good faith. For when the intention is bad, all work that proceeds from it is depraved, even though it might seem right. And on that account there are some who seek to do good, that they might overshadow the merit of another's work, and they do not relish the good that they do, but only the praise for the good by which they debase others.

Gregory: Evil men are to be tolerated with amiability when they congregate where others are found who may be helped towards goodness. But where there is no fruit of goodness present whatsoever, the harvest of evil labour is sometimes superfluous, especially if things that are capable of bearing better fruit to God, are available from a neighbouring place. For saints, when they realise that their labour bears no fruit, migrate with their fruit to another place, to labour.

Gregory: If an immoderate rebuke assaults the mind of a reproved person beyond what is necessary, it frequently slips towards hatred.

Gregory: The nobility of descent is prone to beget an ignobility of mind in some, so that they who remember that they were superior to others, are less censuring of themselves in this world.[359]

A Hibernian synod: Every *princeps* ought to be earth for nourishing, a leader for reforming, an anchor for stabilising, a hammer for striking, tongs for holding, a sun for illuminating, dew for making moist, a slate for writing, a book for reading, a mirror for reflecting, dread for terrifying. His image should be seen in all good things, so that he might be all things to all things.

36.4 Concerning reproving bad *principes*

Gregory Nazianzen: It alarms me to see dogs pursue the pastoral office, especially when they have not prepared themselves in any way for pastoral training, but they have learned only to tear apart and destroy the labours of others, for it is always easier to destroy than preserve.

Isaiah: Woe to you, princes of Israel.

Jeremiah: Woe to the pastors, who destroy and tear the sheep of my pasture, says the Lord.

Ezekiel: Woe to the shepherds of Israel who fed themselves, and did not watch over their flock, nor feed it. They drank the milk from the flocks, and covered themselves with the wool, and killed that which was fat. But my flock they did not feed, says the Lord. The weak they did not strengthen, that which was broken they did not bound up, and that which was driven away they did not bring back again, and that which was lost they did not seek, but they ruled over them with rigour, because there was no good shepherd.

Jerome: It is not a simple thing to stand in the place of Peter and Paul, to hold the seat of those reigning with Christ. Whence it is said: It is not those who occupy the positions of the holy who are the sons of the holy, but those who do the work of the holy.

Jerome: The sin of a great man is looked upon as a grave fault. For the more honourable a person is, the more serious the sin.

A certain Origen: Having taken up the church of God, they are raised up by sacred business, and they look down on everybody with arrogant pride. I call these dogs rather than *principes*.

36.5 That *principes* are not to be blamed for a small offence

Gregory: Subjects must be warned not to pass rash judgement on the conduct of their superiors, if they should happen to see them act inappropriately.

For this reason David did not strike down Saul, who went to relieve himself, but cut the hem of his robe.

Gildas: Mary was punished by leprosy for siding with Aaron in blaming Moses on account of his Ethiopian wife. We, who disparage good *principes* for trivial faults, must be afraid of this example.

36.6 Concerning the people's subjection to the *princeps*

The law: Let the people of the earth obey God and their *princeps*, and let them not contradict him.

Ezekiel: Let each and every one of you fear your *princeps* and honour him.

Patrick: You are ministers, and each and every one of you should fear his *princeps*, to whom he tends and ministers.

The synod of Arles: Whoever has contravened a precept of the *princeps*, should be cast out of the church.

36.7 That the *principatus* is not sought, except by someone who was formerly a subject

A synod: It is the duty of him who wants to be a *princeps*, to be a *monachus* first, and of him who wants to inherit, to be pious first, and of him who wants to teach, to be a pupil first.

36.8 Concerning the penance for disobeying a *princeps*

In the books of Kings: He who has not obeyed the *princeps* shall be put to death.

In the books of Joshua one reads: And Ruben and Gad replied to Joshua: All that you have commanded us we will do, and wherever you shall send us, we will go. As we obeyed Moses, so will we obey you, only the Lord be with you as he was with Moses; he who has contradicted you and has not obeyed all the words that you have commanded, let him die.

Now, however, let him do penance, as much as judges of the church have adjudicated.[360]

36.9 Concerning the rights[361] of the *princeps* as against the people

Ezekiel says: All the people of the land shall be bound to these firstfruits for the prince in Israel.

Patrick: You are Christ's ministers, and each and every one of you should be familiar with his *princeps*, to whom he tends and ministers.

That a *princeps* ought to appoint an heir in his lifetime

In the law: Abraham made Isaac heir in his lifetime.

Isaiah said to king Ezechias: Take order for your house before you die.

Origen in the annals: Noah divided the world between his sons before he died.

A synod: The bishop who presides over the church summons the elders and makes known his choice, namely a man whose virtues are of equal merit to his, lest a dispute should arise after his death.

Likewise: Let the presiding bishop choose one or two with the consent of the clerics, lest the *parochia* and the *monachi* be without a leader.[362]

Likewise: Christ, before his passion, ordained Peter, saying: You are Peter, etc.

Likewise: Peter, before his passion, said in the presence of the brethren: Hear me, O brethren, the day of my death is near. I ordain Clement, I hand over to him the throne of teaching doctrine, for he was my companion in all things.

Concerning the conduct of the elected heir who is to be ordained[363]

Peter said of Clement: I have learned by experience that he, more than others, honours God, is devoted to studies, sober, kind, just, tolerant, familiar with mankind, diligent, careful in learning.

That a *princeps* ought to be ordained after the death of the former

David is ordained after Saul's death. Solomon is ordained after David's death. Rehoboam is ordained after Solomon's death with the consent of the people. Matthias was ordained after the death of Judas Iscariot.

Paul to the Hebrews: A testament is of force upon dead men, otherwise it is as yet of no strength, while the testator lives.

A synod: Let no bishop appoint a successor while he is alive, lest contentions should arise, but let the worthy ones elect a worthy candidate after his death

Likewise, a synod ruled that a bishop ordain his successor on his deathbed with the consent of a synod and according to the will of his region, lest it be null and void.

Likewise: Whoever opposed the decree of the *princeps* and the congregation[364] is not a Christian but a heretic.

Jerome: Then is a successor ordained: when the incumbent is not removed, nor is one being ordained over him.[365]

36.10 Concerning the kindness and humility of a *princeps* towards the people

Job: I have despised no man, and I have been humble to all men.

Moses: I have not been burdensome unto this people, nor have I taken away another man's donkey by force.

Likewise, in the law: Moses was an exceptionally meek man before the Lord.

Gregory in the homilies: A *princeps* does not condemn anyone undeservedly.

The same: A *princeps* ought to be meek. For a grade of kindness has been conferred on him, not pride.

Paul: It is fitting that a man of this sort be mild, not haughty, nor proud.

36.11 That a *princeps* ought to minister not less than he is ministered to

Christ says: Whosoever will want to be the greater among you, let him be your minister.

Jerome: A *princeps* ought to be both a servant and a minister, because he received a grade of ministry, as Christ said: The son of man is not come to be ministered unto, but to minister.

36.12 That a *princeps* ought not have a house of his own in his *ciuitas*[366]

Augustine in the homilies: A *princeps* ought to behave as a guest, and let him not have a house of his own, like Christ, who said: The son of man has no place to lay his head.

36.13 That he ought not keep his own wealth for himself

Jerome: Thus it is right that the *princeps* of the church should know that he has nothing of his own, but he ought to collect all things through the hand of a minister, to clothe the naked, to receive the needy, to honour the elders, to minister to all, according to the example set by Christ when he said: I did not come to be ministered unto, but to minister. Observe that Christ believed that Judas's purse was meant to feed the poor, knowing that he had no possessions of his own.

36.14 That a *princeps* ought to have a minister

Moses had as his minister the son of Nun, without whose advice he did nothing.

Likewise: Abraham had a minister, to whom he entrusted all that he had.

David also had many ministers.

Pharaoh, the king of Egypt, ordained Joseph, who became prefect of all of Egypt.

And Potiphar also ordained him prefect of his household.

And the Lord Jesus had ministers to whom he entrusted purses of oil and sweet spice. After the Lord's passion, the apostles ordained seven deacons who ministered to them.

A synod: It is the duty of a *princeps* to dispense all matters by the hands of his ministers for the benefit of the *parochia* and his subjects and the poor.

36.15 That a *princeps* ought not give away anything, except small things, without conferring with his subjects

A synod says: He ought not do anything without consulting his subjects, except a few things with respect to releasing captives, and consoling the poor and the widows, and he should do such things if the clerics are absent.[367]

36.16 Concerning the servants' obedience to the *princeps*

In Genesis: The servant obeyed Abraham and did not alter his words.

The Lord, therefore, helped him. Joshua obeyed Moses and did nothing without his advice, whence he deserved to lead the people.

Likewise, Moses says: The Lord shall send a prophet, etc.

The apostles were deserving of the apostolate thanks to their devotion to their ministry, such that Christ distributed the loaves in their hands to the crowds. Stephen, by his devotion to the ministry that was enjoined to him, deserved to receive the Holy Spirit.

In the Gospel: because you have been faithful over a few things, I shall set you over many things.

36.17 Concerning excommunicating the one who opposes the *princeps*

Origen: Whoever opposes his lord through arrogant pride, or tears apart the community of the brethren, let him be anathema and he must be cast out.

36.18 Concerning the one opposing the *princeps* who ordains his heir

A synod: Whoever shall have opposed the decree of the *princeps* and the synod concerning the ordination of an heir, is not a Christian but a heretic.

Origen: Why does it seem right to you to change our governor's decision? For if God entrusted him with greater things, why do we not entrust him with the smallest of things?

36.19 That the *princeps* alone ordains his successor

The Lord alone ordained Samuel, he alone ordained Moses in the desert, he alone ordained Jeremiah, he alone ordained Isaiah, he alone ordained Peter and Andrew, he alone ordains Paul.

36.20 Concerning the consent of the people with the *princeps* in the ordination of a successor[368]

Moses ordained Aaron in the presence of many of the sons of Israel.

Saul was ordained by Samuel with the people's consent.

David was ordained by Samuel with the people's consent.

Jacob was ordained with the consent of the Christian people.

Matthias was ordained with the consent of the Christian people.

A synod says: We prescribe that no *princeps* should be ordained, unless the assembled clergy and the *parochia* are in unison.

Jerome: The ordination shall be void, unless he should be ordained in the presence of all.

Origen: Three things are needed in an ordination: the consent of the worthy, many witnesses, the choice of the *princeps*. For thus Peter ordained Clement.

That the *princeps* alone ordains his successor

The Lord ordained Samuel, and Moses, and all the prophets, and the apostles.

A synod of the Romans: If we entrust our soul and necks to the bishops, how much more so he should govern the church and ordain a successor.

Origen: Why does it seem right to you to change our governor's decision? For if God entrusted him with great things, why do we not entrust him with the smallest of things?

36.21 That every *princeps* must take care not to govern his church badly

Jerome said: A *princeps* must be mindful of three things: he should not manage the church's property badly lest he should strip the tabernacle of God; and he should not only see himself responsible for feeding and clothing his subjects, but also for their spiritual well-being; and he should nominate a worthy successor, while no one is able to change his decision.

36.22 That the blood of the subjects is required at the rulers' hands, but if they have rebuked them it is not required, even if they did not obey

Isaiah says: Their priests were of no benefit to them. Dumb dogs are not able to bark. You milk your sheep and eat them. I shall avenge their blood from your hands, says the almighty Lord.

The Lord said: Unless you proclaim to the wicked man his wickedness, I will require his blood at your hand.

Gregory: The blood of a dying man is required at the hand of the one watching over him, for the sin of a dependant is imputed to the guilt of the superior, if he remained silent.

Whence also the following is added: If you have admonished him, and he has not reformed his impiety and his impious way, he dies in his iniquity. You, however, have saved your soul.

Jerome: We shall render account not only for our sins, but for the sins of the ones whose gifts we misuse, and whose well-being we were never concerned with, and for this reason wicked *principes* are to be charged, and they must be examined, whether they are good or evil.

As Paul said: Not all bishops are considered true bishops. You think of Peter, but reflect also on Judas. You observe Stephen, but observe also Nicolas.

That many contract[369] their depravity from the depravities of others

Gregory says: There are also many who contract[370] their depravity from the depravities of others. For they observe others as they do such things, and believe that they are entitled to do the same.

36.23 Why evil *principes* come to occupy the places of saints

John Cassian says: The tombs[371] of saints are inhabited by sinners because the souls of the saints have no need for the things that they left behind; for they follow the lamb of God wherever he goes, in the manner of angels. Of whom it is said: On whom the angels desire to look. And this is all the more true when the souls of the saints, or certain merits of the same saints, are seen by God to have even a tiny defect, on account of which an evil man is left at their tombs, so that their faults are condemned through the guilt of a living man. Or because it is a small matter with the Lord to damn a sinner to be outraged by his own sin, but the tombs of the saints are violated under his name. He conceded, therefore, that the sinner be made wealthy by these riches, that he may resemble Judas Iscariot, to whom the Lord gave his gold and silver, but not to the other apostles, who, thinking nothing of the world, were longing for eternal life. But he, placing his faith in riches, was denied life.

36.24 Concerning others who aspire to the *principatus* undeservedly, that is, either fools or men who have only recently been converted from the world

Gregory: How dare he assume the pastoral office, who did not first learn medicine of souls?

Gregory Nazianzen: It alarms me to see dogs pursue the pastoral office.

A synod: We decree that he should learn what he teaches, that he should be moulded by what he holds, and that he should glow like a lamp placed upon a lampstand, so that the onward rushing wind shall not extinguish the kindled flame of learning, but increase it.

36.25 Concerning laymen striving after the *principatus*

The prophet says: They whose hands are full of blood may not approach my altar.

In the books of Kings: David, a bloody man, shall not build a house for me.

Gregory Nazianzen: Some, puffed up by their desire for honour, are tonsured after the death of their bishops, and suddenly go from being laymen to being *principes*, and shamelessly usurp the leadership of the religious vocation, though they have not yet learned to be simple soldiers. It is to be wondered what they—who are not afraid to take the place of a teacher before they reached the end of their pupillage—shall teach their subjects.

Likewise: Nor have I received them who, by living honourably, do not wash away the offence they have admitted.

36.26 That those who do not govern their house well, are undeserving of the *principatus* of the church

Gregory Nazianzen: He who does not possess the sense to govern himself, and did not wipe away his own faults, nor corrected the transgression of his sons, is to be called a shameless dog rather than a *princeps*. For it is said to Eli the priest: You have honoured your sons more than me.

Likewise: He knew that his sons acted wickedly, and did not correct them.

Likewise: Anyone who does not know how to govern his house well, how can he govern the church of God?

Concerning not refusing the *principatus*

In the law: Aaron had been prepared, he did not decline his ordination.

In Isaiah, the Lord says: Whom shall I send? And who shall go from us? Isaiah replied: Lo, here I am, send me.

Gregory Nazianzen: I have been silent, I will not be silent forever. You have me as your shepherd, hold tight, O most holy flock, you have my subjection. Render me your blessing.

Jerome, seeing Bethlehem, said: This is my rest for ever and ever, etc.

That the *principatus* is not to be obtained quickly

In the law: Moses frequently declined, and he did not assume the leadership, except through signs.

Likewise: Gideon the son of Joash apologised for the ignobility of his descent, and he did not assume the leadership, except through signs.

Jeremiah feared his young age, saying: I am a child.

Solomon: The inheritance to which one hurries at the beginning, at the end shall be without a blessing.

Concerning wicked men who buy the *principatus*

In the Acts of the Apostles Peter said to Simon Magus: Let your money be with you unto perdition; for you thought that the gift of God may be purchased with money.

Gregory: Whoever wishes to buy this gift with money, while caring for the title rather than the office, we have decreed not to be a *sacerdos*.

36.27 That it is neither descent nor the [status of his] church, that give standing to a *princeps*, but his conduct

Gregory Nazianzen: We who govern ought to earn our reputation not from our churches, nor from the dignity of our descent, but from the nobility of our ways; nor from the fame of the *urbes*, but from the purity of faith.

36.28 Concerning the penance of one who blasphemes against a good *princeps*

Patrick said: Whoever murmurs blasphemous words against a good *princeps* because of hatred or jealousy, should do penance on bread and water for seven days, following the example of Mary, who murmured against Moses.

36.29 Concerning a *princeps* to be wary of

Gregory the Roman: One must take diligent care not to find a wolf when seeking a shepherd. For there are many superiors who are more eager in their desire for money than for souls.

36.30 That fools ought not be permitted to govern

The synod of the whole world and Patrick decreed: A fool should not be permitted to govern under any circumstances, but he should carry out his duties under the rule of a catholic abbot.

36.31 Concerning evil men in the last days

Jeremiah says: In the last days shall come the worst times. Men shall be lovers of themselves, covetous, arrogant, proud, blasphemers, disobedient to parents, ungrateful, impure, without affection, without peace, slanderers, unrestrained, cruel, hating of what is good, traitors rather than lovers of God, having an appearance of piety, but denying the power thereof.

36.32 Concerning persisting in one's vocation

Gildas: Let every man, wherein he was called, therein abide [with God], so that the leader may not be removed except by the will of his subjects, nor the subject obtain the place of his superior without the recommendation of an elder.

36.33 That *principes* anointed by God, even wicked ones, must not be demoted

The Lord did not demote Solomon, worthy of a thousand deaths.

Augustine: David called Saul 'the Lord's anointed' after God departed from him, for he was not unaware that there is divine transmission of the royal line.

Jerome: I am sorry I ordained Saul king. And, nevertheless, he did not demote him.

That one ought to submit to wicked *principes*

Peter: Submit to your lords, not only to the gentle ones, but also to the froward, namely the quarrelsome.

Likewise: The sons of Eli were wicked, but nevertheless the priesthood and the gifts of the people were not removed from them.

Annam and Caiphas, although they crucified Christ, were not deprived of secular riches by the Lord.

Christ also, although he knew that Judas would be a traitor, did not take away the purse that he lent him.

Likewise: A bishop who has been ordained must not be stripped of his ordination if he sinned. Insofar as he has been ordained, he must be excommunicated as a sinner.

36.34 Concerning expelling wicked *principes*

The proud angel was cast out of heaven. Adam, after the sin, was expelled from paradise to earth.

Concerning deserting wicked *principes*

Jeroboam,[372] the iniquitous king, was deserted by ten tribes. All heretics, even if they are *principes* of great *urbes*, their heresy having been revealed, are expelled from their sees with the consent of a synod.

36.35 That *principes* ought not despise their *monachi*

Paul: The head cannot say to the feet: I have no need of you; rather, those that seem to be the more feeble members of the body are all the more necessary.

Concerning a church murmuring against a wicked *princeps*

Gregory in the homilies: Let us hear what a voice told the blessed Job: Let my land cry against me, and with it the furrows thereof mourn, if I have eaten its fruits without money.

Gregory: For 'the land cries' against its owner when a church justly murmurs against its shepherd. 'Its furrows also mourn', if the hearts of the hearers—which were furrowed by the voice of preaching from the fathers and the vigour of a verbal charge—notice something that they deplore about the life of the shepherd. 'Whose fruit the good owner does not eat without money', because the just shepherd pays in advance a talent of his word, lest he take from the church a tribute in the form of provisions, and incur damnation.

36.36 That a church ought not be dispersed through disobedience; rather it must be gathered together, like sheep in a sheepfold

A Hibernian synod: Should any disobedience arise through discord between a *princeps* and his *monachi,* the shepherd should not scatter his flock, nor the sheep flee the shepherd, but they should conclude a peace between themselves.

David: I will go in to the altar of my God.

Gregory Nazianzen argues thus, saying: No one has the power to drive me away from this altar. You should never defraud your sheepfold, the feet should not rise against the head, nor the head reckon that the feet are apart from it.

That the *principes* ought not own church property

In the Acts of the Apostles: And the multitude of believers had but one heart and one soul, nor did anyone say that any of the goods are his possession, but they held all things in common, etc.

Jerome: *Principes* who break away from the unity of the church and reserve property for themselves, by whose example all perish, should be called rapacious wolves rather than *principes*, and it is said of their church: You have made it a den of thieves.

Likewise: The priests in Jerusalem acquired gold and silver, reserving it as their own property to the ruin of the people.

Augustine: It is not my place to describe the conduct of a *princeps*, lest one of you should be offended. They invade the property of others, take away the *parochiae* of others, receive alms from the wicked, they reserve property for themselves without their clerics' knowledge, and they do not govern their flock.

That a *princeps* ought not own personal property

In the decisions of the synod of Ancyra: So long as the bishop who presides over a church is alive, the faithful [should know] from the church what property belongs to the church, and the faithful should know from the bishop what property is the bishop's. For if it happens that the bishop depart from this world, the property of the church shall not perish, and the things belonging to the bishop shall not pass over to the church. For it is considered just in the sight of God that a bishop may leave his property to whomever he pleases, and the things that are the church's remain with the church.

The synod of Chalcedon: Clerics are not permitted to plunder the possessions of their *princeps* after his death. If, however, they have dared do so, they should be deposed from their grade.

Origen: Every *princeps* ought to have property by which to feed the poor and the widows and the servants (*ministros*); or, should he have sons, the property of the church should also be reserved for them.[373]

That a *princeps* ought not seize the *parochia* of another

Paul: I have so preached the Gospel of Christ where Christ was not named, lest I should build upon another man's foundation.[374]

A synod: A bishop who seizes the *parochia* of another bishop, must be excommunicated.

36.37 Concerning avoiding wicked *principes*

Ezekiel says: You ought to avoid the suspicious ones for the sake of your conscience, but not to excommunicate them as true culprits from the table, from mass, and from the community, because we cannot say to them that they live wickedly.[375]

Gildas: Unless they perform correct penance, we should ban those whom we know without doubt to be fornicators from the peace,[376] and mass, and the table of whichever order they belong to, according to this rule: If any man who is named a brother, while being a fornicator, etc.

Concerning various cases

It is better for a man to be married and have faith than be continent and not have faith.

Long after the sin, chastity is an imitation of virginity.

A man of faith who is tainted by pollution,[377] is better than proud chastity.

Silence must always be observed, especially by every guest at the table.

Dignity[378] consists of three things: property, justice, worthwhile commitment.

Change from bad to good and from good to bad can occur so long as one is alive. But when we shall have departed from the light of this world, a good person will never be able to be bad, nor can he who is bad become good.

It is better to pray with a silent heart, without the sound of your voice, than to use only words, without reflecting with the mind.

Surplus riches are the property of the poor. True honour shall not be denied to any worthy man; the words of the wise—sparks from a fire,[379] i.e. a furnace—shall not be proclaimed to any unworthy man.

The son of Sirach says: From the parents: home and the son's country. But from God: a good wife. The present life is not life, but slow death.

Augustine: It is twice the sin to do evil near [the relics of] martyrs; a double punishment of angelic prohibition follows.

Augustine said: Where men become evil, there also malignant spirits reside. Let anyone who does not want to slay his kinsman not nourish the beast. For if he has caused harm, let him pay a soul for a soul and damage for damage.

Augustine: It is a sin to use words for deception, and not for what they were created.

In the proverbs, Gregory: Our inner person was created in God's image in six ways: without movement, invisible, quick, incorporeal, delicate, eternal. It is not unjust to slay the ones who persecute this image[380] unjustly.

36.38 That a *princeps* ought not regard what is given him as his own property, but the church's

A synod: Bishops who are given something, either jointly with their church or separately, shall not reckon it as their own, but among the assets of the church.

37 Concerning teachers[381]

37.1 Concerning the entitlements of a good teacher

Luke: Remain in the same house, eating and drinking such things as they have.

Gregory: It is fitting that we receive worldly support from those to whom we offer the rewards of the heavenly country.

Whence Paul, considering it to be a very small matter, says: If we have sown unto you spiritual things, is it a great matter if we reap your carnal things?

In which thing it must be considered that two different payments are owed for each of our works: one along the journey, and the other in the heavenly country; one that supports us in our work, and the other that repays us in the resurrection.

In the Gospel: The workman is worthy of his food and clothing.

Paul: They who serve the altar, partake with the altar.

Likewise: The Lord ordained that they who preach the Gospel should live out of the Gospel.

Gregory interpreted thus, saying: Presbyters are held in double honour, especially those who labour in word and in teaching. It is just as shameful to demand these things as it is for you not to offer them. And what is more incongruous than support not to be given to those who fight, and fruit of the vine to those who plant, and sheep's milk to the shepherds?

The law says: You shall not muzzle the ox that treads out on the threshing floor.

37.2 Concerning the honour due to a good teacher

Jerome: If the heralds of falsehood are held by kings to be worthy of honour, how much more so the heralds of truth.

Origen: If the tablets, skins, and the ministers of the tabernacle are being honoured, namely the builders, the artisans, and the setters of gems, how much more so the pillars, namely the *principes*, *sacerdotes*, and teachers of the church.

37.3 That teachers should have the reward of their teaching with God

Paul: He who ministers seed to the sower, will also give bread to eat.

37.4 That teachers ought to fulfil what they teach

Gregory said: It is fitting that one first clean himself and thus clean others, be made wise and thus make others wise, be made a lamp and thus cast light on others, first approach the Lord and thus cause others to approach the Lord.

Isaiah: Woe to me, because I am a man polluted by my lips.

Likewise: Mute dogs do not bark beside the truth.

The prophet: Woe to me, who preaches to you, if I should not fulfil.

In the Gospel: Woe to you, scribes and Pharisees, who lay heavy burdens on men's shoulders and refuse to touch them even with a finger.

Paul: I chastise my body and bring it into subjection, lest perhaps, while preaching to others, I myself should be rejeted.

Origen: A teacher who teaches and does not fulfil is like a rod (*uirga*) beating the air: a sound is produced, without giving virtue (*uirtus*).

Gregory: It is necessary that the hand that takes care to remove dirt, should aspire to be clean, lest it dirty even more whatever things it touches, if in pursuing dirty things it takes on the mire.
{Gregory, concerning the rooster.}

That teachers ought to take advice from their underlings

In the Gospel: And Jesus to his assembled disciples: I have compassion on the multitudes, because they continue with me now three days, etc.

Jerome: And he calls his disciples, and tells them what he is about to do, either that he may give the example[382] of a teacher by taking counsel with the young ones and the disciples, or that they might comprehend the magnitude of the sign through a story.

37.5 That the teachings of a wicked teacher must be followed, but not his deeds

In the Gospel: The scribes and the Pharisees sat upon the chair of Moses. Whatsoever they shall say to you, do; but do not do according to their deeds.

The philosopher said: If a prudent man had found a golden nugget in the mud, would he not take it and keep it as a great prize?

Jerome: As water[383] flowing through moist and filthy ashes washes and is not itself washed, so good teaching through a wicked teacher washes the souls of the believers from the filth of sinners.

Likewise: Just as clean water found in a filthy pit both washes and cleans, thus also good teaching through a wicked teacher.

Likewise: Just as the skin of a pomegranate is bitter, but that which is hidden inside is sweet and saturating, so is good teaching through a wicked teacher.

Isidore: He who teaches well and lives wickedly is like a cymbal: it makes a sound for others, but itself remains without the capacity for feeling.

Likewise: He who teaches well and lives wickedly, benefits the living because he teaches well, but murders himself because he lives wickedly; just as a *sacerdos* who behaves respectfully, as a *sacerdos* should, his ministry is helpful to himself and others. But when he lives contemptibly, being indeed helpful to others by speaking, he kills his own self by living in a depraved manner. And, as a consequence, that which is dead in him belongs to him; but that which is alive in him, namely his holy ministry, is estranged from him. He who teaches well and lives wickedly is like a candle: as it offers to show good light to others, it consumes and extinguishes itself by its own adverse forces.

37.6 That a wicked teacher is to be condemned

In the Gospel: But if the salt lose its savour, wherewith shall it be salted? It is good for nothing any more but to be cast out, and to be trodden on.

Jerome: But if a teacher err, with which teacher shall he be corrected?

Likewise: A slave who knows his master's wish and does not do it, shall be beaten by flogging.

A synod: He must be honoured insofar as he is a man, dishonoured insofar as he is disobedient.

37.7 That learned justice is better than holy rusticity

Jerome: Holy rusticity is expedient to itself alone, and as much as it edifies by meritorious living, by that much it harms the church of Christ, if it does not stand up to those who oppose it.[384]

Augustine: Learned wisdom is better, and no less edifying than holy rusticity.

Daniel says that the righteous—namely the learned and the understanding—shine like the stars, but the untaught are like the firmament. You see how different they are, although according to the Hebrew truth we read otherwise, etc.

37.8 That holy rusticity has no discretion

Augustine: It is necessary to be careful of rusticity, lest it subtract or add [to the words of scripture]. For in those two, while the mind of the rustic is satisfied, there is danger. And while he believes that what he does is right, the mind is puffed up, and falls into pride, and he despises the words of scripture.

37.9 Concerning rusticity striving against wisdom

Solomon: And the words of the mouth of a wise man are grace, but the lips of a fool shall throw him down headlong.

Jerome interpreted, saying: Foolishness, if it is content with its rusticity, has less evil. But now it wages war, and strives to suppress the grace of wise eloquence by the flood of its words, and whatever wisdom an untaught man has encountered, having been stirred by jealousy, he does not accept it.

37.10 That holy rusticity ought to be ruled, not rule

Jerome says: Holy rusticity is put to good use when it is reformed under the direction of a monastery and an abbot, and taught by the words of scripture.

37.11 That holy rusticity is better than wisdom that achieves little

A synod of Narbonne: It is is certain that, among the elect, rusticity is better than [a state of] sinful knowledge. The peoples ought rather to receive perfect teaching from a cleric who is upright and not corrupt.

The synod of Arles: Untaught rusticity, being holy nevertheless, collects by example and deed. But learned knowledge, being sinful nevertheless, scatters by example, not fulfilling what it teaches by the mouth.

37.12 Concerning a comparison between holy rusticity and sinful knowledge

Gregory the Roman: Let us compare, if you will, the untaught ignorance of another, and our learned knowledge. We, devoid of virtues, speak, and as though, standing between fruit-bearing trees, smell the fruit but do not eat it; that man does not cease to pick the fruits of virtues, though he does not know how to smell.

37.13 Concerning the usage of the words of scripture

Jerome said: The words of scripture are a stimulus with which to motivate, milk with which to nourish, oil with which to heat, a rod with which to correct, salt with which to flavour, a lamp with which to illuminate, water with which to wash, wine with which to inebriate.

The same says: Reading the scriptures edifies the untaught, corrects the learned, sustains the poor, humbles the king, purifies the soul, gladdens the mind, exalts the lowborn, crushes the proud, it is an iron wall.

Concerning the stature of a teacher who does not teach

Isaiah: Woe to me, because I have been silent, because I am a man polluted by my lips.

Likewise: Mute dogs do not bark beside the truth.

Woe to me, who preaches to you, if I should not fulfil.

37.14 Concerning resenting wise men who fulfil little

The prophet: Woe to you, for you have wisdom for doing evil.

Likewise: Wisdom departs from the wise. Note that heresy has been spread throughout the world by the wise.

Likewise: There was none who would cry out and move a wing.

37.15 That it is more difficult to reform an erring wise man, than a rustic

Jerome: If a rustic has erred, inasmuch as he is rustic, the more easily he is reformed. But if a wise man has erred, the wiser he is, the less he submits to correction. On account of which it is said: If a teacher has erred, wherewith shall the teacher be corrected? For he distorts the words of scripture and bends them to his own understanding.[385]

Origen: If a teacher has erred, and has become entrenched in his understanding, no one can correct him, except through royal or episcopal authority.

37.16 Concerning correcting teachers, because heresy emanates from them

A synod: Note that heresy has been spread throughout the world by the wise.

37.17 Concerning not saddening a good teacher

Peter says: Whoever saddens the teacher of truth sins against Christ and angers the father of all, and shall be without life.

That it is no lesser reward to fill [people] with the nourishment of the word than with worldly bread

Gregory in the homilies: There are two kinds of alms. The one, that a morsel be offered to the hungry; the other, that teaching be administered to a hungry soul. Perhaps he who has a tongue does not have bread to offer the hungry, but he can confer a greater thing.[386] For it is better to refresh with the nourishment of the word the mind that will live than to sate with bread the stomach of the mortal flesh.

That no one should change the words of scripture, nor their sense

In the Gospel: And last of all there came two false witnesses, and said: This man said: I am able to destroy the temple of God, and after three days to rebuild it.

Jerome: In what way are they false witnesses if they say what we read that the Lord said? But a false witness is not only one who changes, but one who does not understand the words in the same sense in which they were said. The Lord, however, was speaking about the temple of his body, and on account of these words they falsely accused him. And after the things heard were slightly changed,[387] they made a false accusation appear true. And the saviour said: Destroy this temple. Those men distort and say: I am able to destroy the temple of God. 'You', he said, 'destroy', not 'I'. For it is forbidden that we bring death upon ourselves. Thereafter they distort to 'after three days to rebuild it', thus it would appear that he spoke specifically of the Jewish temple. The Lord, in order to show that a living soul is the temple, said: 'and after three days I shall resuscitate it'. For it is one thing to rebuild, and another to resuscitate.

That it is not permitted to distort the sense of scripture

Jerome: I say nothing of those similar to me, who, if perchance they have come to the holy scriptures after reading secular literature, delight the ear of the people with eloquent speech, believing whatever they say to be God's law; they do not deem it worthy to know what the prophets and apostles believed, but they only adapt texts to suit their own interpretation, as though it were a noble and not a depraved way of saying, to distort the meanings, and to drag scripture against its will towards one's own interpretation.

Clement: It must be diligently observed, that when God's law is read, it should not be understood according to one's own interpretation. For there are many things in the divine scriptures that can be made to agree with a sense that each and every person contrives independently. This should not be.

Iunilius said:[388] What are the things that we ought to observe in understanding divine scripture? That they should be in harmony with the things that the Lord says; that they be not inconsistent with the reasons for which they were said; that they be in agreement with respect to times, places, sequence, intention.

That a wise man helps a wise man, but a fool agrees with him

In the proverbs of the Greeks: A wise man helps another wise man, and a fool imparts foolish wisdom. When a fool agrees with a wise man, they are called two wise men. When a wise man clings to a fool, two fools come into being.

37.18 That a teacher must consider what, who,[389] to whom, when, and how he speaks

Gregory: And a teacher ought to consider what he says, to whom he speaks, when he speaks, how he speaks. For if one of these shall be missing, the discourse will not be appropriate. And we ought to consider what we say, also according to Paul's call: Let our speech be seasoned with the salt of grace. And we must also consider when we ought to speak, because often, even if reproof is put off, after a while it is well received. And the prophet proclaims that the tongues of flatterers are not to be deferred to a later time; he said: Let them who blush for shame be presently confounded, who say to me: Well done, well done! And we must also consider to whom we speak, because often one person accepts a word of reproof, that another person does not accept. And we must also consider in what way we speak, because often the words of reproof that restore one man to spiritual health, injure another. Whence Paul said, admonishing Titus, saying: Rebuke with all authority. And exhorting Timothy, he says: Entreat, rebuke in all patience and teaching. For we offend in two ways: either when we say unjust things or hold back just things.

37.19 Concerning the duty of reproving teachers who do not defend the church

The prophet: You have not gone up from the opposite side, nor have you set up a wall for the house of Israel, to stand in battle in the day of the Lord.

Gregory interpreted this, saying: Clearly 'to go up from the opposite side', is to go against the powers of this world with a free voice, for the sake of defending the flock; and 'to stand in battle in the day of the Lord', is to resist depraved fighters by means of the love of justice.

38 Concerning *monachi*[390]

38.1 Concerning the word '*monachi*'

A Hibernian synod: *Monachus* is a Greek word, in Latin it is *unalis*, either because, being alone, he leads a solitary life in the desert, or because he lives in the world without worldly hindrance, or because he lives this life alone, even though he dwells among many.

38.2 Concerning the origin and foundation of *monachi*

Isidore: The forerunners of this vocation were Elijah, and his disciple Elisha, and other prophets who, after leaving the townships, dwelled by the waters of the Jordan. But in the Gospel, John the Baptist stood out as the founder of this vocation, who lived alone in the desert, eating nothing but locusts and wild honey. Then most noble forerunners of this way of life appeared anew: Paul and Anthony, Hilary, Macarius, and other fathers, by whose example the sacred institution of *monachi* prospered throughout the world.

Concerning the three impurities of a *monachus*

In the life of the saints, the shepherd abbot: One who is quarrelsome is not a *monachus*. One who repays evil for evil is not a *monachus*. One who is prone to anger is not a *monachus*.

38.3 Concerning the different kinds of *monachi*

Isidore said: There are six kinds of *monachi*, of which three are superior, but all others inferior and must be avoided at all costs. The first kind is that of the cenobites (*cenobites*), namely of those living together in emulation of the saints who, in the time of the apostles in Jerusalem, after selling all their property and giving it away to the needy, lived in holy communion of life, without owning any property, but held all things in common, having one heart and one soul in God. And it is their mode of life (*institutio*) that monasteries draw their origins from. The second kind is that of the hermits, who, retreating far from men to pursue and inhabit uninhabited and desolate places are seen to imitate Elijah and John, who entered desert retreats. Having incredible contempt for the world, they truly delight in solitude, being nourished by dry herbs, being content with bread and water alone, which is brought to them regularly; and thus, so separated and far from the sight of all men, engage only in divine conversation, to which they commit themselves to with pure minds. And for the sake of his love, they relinquish contact not only with the world, but also with people. The third kind is that of the anchorites, who, readied by the coenobitical way of life, shut themselves in remote cells, far from the sight of men; they do not allow anyone access to them, but persist steadfastly, living solely in meditative contemplation (*theorica*). They are chosen, through obedience, to that contemplative life, only after being confirmed by the judgement of their *coenobia* in all the disciplines of the monastery for thirty years.[391] The fourth kind is of the ones who flatter themselves by appearing as anchorites, who, as Cassian said, are seen in their early days to seek the perfect way of life of the *coenobium* with brief enthusiasm, but immediately grow lukewarm, and think little of renouncing their former habits and lifestyle, nor are they content to bear the yoke of humility, and resent submitting themselves to the authority of their superiors. They seek separate cells and long to sit alone, so that, being troubled by no one, they would be considered meek and humble. The fifth kind is that of the wanderers (*circumcilliones*), who wander under the visage of *monachi*, carrying around hypocrisy, going around provinces, being sent nowhere, being planted nowhere, staying nowhere, sitting nowhere. Some make up things that they never saw, valuing their own opinions as those of God. Others trade in limbs of martyrs. Others make their phylacteries broad, and enlarge their fringes, winning glory from men. Others let their hair grow long, lest their sanctity be valued less when they are tonsured than when long-haired; so that, clearly, whoever might see them, recalls the ancients we read about, Samuel and Elijah and the rest. Others insist they have honours, which they did not receive. Others say falsely that they heard that their parents and relatives are coming to that region,[392] and they are going to visit them. They all beg, they all demand either something of value for their profitable[393] poverty, or a price for their fake sanctity. The sixth kind is also the worse and must be avoided, which sprang from Ananias and Sapphira in the dawn of the church, and was cut down by the severity of the apostle Peter. And they are called sarabites (*sarabitae*), or hermits (*eremitae*) in the Egyptian language because they separate themselves from coenobitic discipline, and pursue their wishes freely.

In the catalogue: There are said to be four kinds of *monachi*. The first is the hermits, who have nothing in common with the world, but live by the labour of their own hands, and do not accept the gifts of others. They embrace the contemplative (*theorica*) and active (*actualis*) life. But some of them keep themselves free for prayer, and [thereby] rely on others for sustenance. The second are the cenobites, who live communally in emulation of the family of the apostles, and do not wear a thick garment.[394] They never have any free time, but they either read, or pray, or serve their neighbour. The third kind is that of the vagabonds, who wish to have the title '*monachi*', but refuse to abide by their customs. They consort with loose women, tell stories about monasteries, live under no rule, busy themselves with secular affairs; danger rather than reward awaits them; and they should beware what someone says: Woe to me, a sinner, for I bear the name of a false *monachus*. The fourth kind is that of the sarabites, who provide for their own needs, make their home in a fortress or monastery, they always arrive laden, they have a garden arranged with herbs, they spend Lent or [Holy] Week in the communion of a monastery, and pass the rest of the time serving themselves. These are serious in speech, nothing is pleasing to them except what they themselves arrange. They are not joined to any grade; [they are] not *monachi*, nor clerics, nor *plebiles*, nor laymen.

Jerome says in his letter to Benedict:[395] There are four kinds of *monachi*. The first is that of the cenobites, soldiering under a rule and an abbot. This is the most worthy kind. The second is that of the anchorites, who live by their own labour and do not receive support from the *plebs*. The third kind is of the ones who live in pairs, or groups of three, or four, or five, without a shepherd, nor do they follow the example of the elders, but say that they are looked after by the Lord. This kind is guilty of no small offence. The fourth kind, of the *gyrouagi*, who lodge throughout the provinces, is better not to mention.[396] Let us return to the most worthy kind, which soldiers under a rule and an abbot.

38.4 That a *monachus* ought not be without an abbot

Gregory: Just as fish are unable to live on land without water, so a *monachus* ought not live without an abbot.

Augustine: Who steers the ship when the helmsman departs? Who protects the sheep from the ambushes of wolves, if the shepherd is not on the watch? Who can resist brigands and thieves if he does not have a watchman?

A synod: *Monachi* ought not be without leadership, not even for one hour, lest the wind of discord and dissent scatter the church.

Concerning the unity of the *monachi* and offering all of one's property

In the Acts of the Apostles: And the multitude of believers had but one heart and one soul, and no separation between them, neither did anyone say that any of his [former] possessions were his own, but all things were common unto them, and great grace was in them all. For neither was there any one needy among them. For as many were owners of lands or houses [they] sold them, and brought [the price] before the feet of the apostles. And distribution was made to everyone according to his need.

But a certain man named Ananias, with Sapphira his wife, sold a piece of land, and lied about the earnings from the land, his wife being privy to this, and bringing a certain part of it before the feet of the apostles. But Peter said to him: Ananias, why has Satan tempted your heart to lie to the Holy Ghost, so that you lie about the earnings from the land? Whilst it remained, did it not remain to you? And after it was sold, was it not in your power? Why have you conceived this evil deed in your heart? You have not lied to men, but to God. And Ananias hearing these words fell down and died.

In the Gospel: Christ to the wealthy man: If you want to be perfect, go sell what you have, and give it to the poor, and come follow me, and you shall have treasures in heaven.

38.5 That a *monachus* ought not have property

Gildas says:[397] Any secular possessions that a *monachus* has accumulated, ought to be reckoned as excesses and riches; and what he is compelled to have, by necessity and not by choice, shall not be held against him, lest he perish by poverty.

Concerning a fugitive *monachus*

The synod of Arles: Let no abbot receive a *monachus* migrating to another church without his abbot's permission, or against the abbot's will, or without written approval; but wherever he shall be, let him be called back to his abbot's authority.

38.6 That a *monachus* must not be detained by his abbot

Gildas says:[398] A lenient abbot should not detain a *monachus* of his who strives after a stricter way of life.

38.7 Concerning receiving and not receiving fugitive *monachi*

A synod: We decree that *monachi* who flee from wicked *principes* ought to be received by another church, that their case may be examined.

Gildas:[399] They who come to you from a worse place seeking perfection, whose abbot has so far fallen away from the work of God that he deserves to be barred from the table of holy men and loaded with the offence of fornication, not just on suspicion but on a clear and manifest wrong; receive such *monachi* who flee to you from hell fire, with no scruple, without any consultation with their abbot.

The synod of Arles decreed that we should not turn away fugitives fleeing the vices of their *principes* and the injustice of the place. We know that Peter had received those fleeing from Jerusalem. Paul received Onesimus, Philemon's servant. Thus the Lord received the two sons of Zebedee, after they left their father.

Gregory: Whoever flees the evils of this world and its vices, and the injustice of a church, should always be received rather than rejected.

That a *monachus* of another should not be received

But we ought not receive them, whose abbot we do not bar from the table of holy men for reason of notoriety, against his will. And this is all the more true for those who come to us from holy abbots who are not under any kind of suspicion, except for possessing livestock, and vehicles, or on account of the custom of their country, or for their infirmity. These are things that do less harm to their owners if they are possessed in humility and patience, than is done to those who drag ploughs and plunge spades in the ground in presumption and pride.[400]

The synod of Nicaea: Those who flee from their church, we decree that they ought not be received in another church, but compelled to return to their own churches. They who run off without a letter from their abbot should not be received in any monastery.

Likewise: When in a shipwreck, let anyone who can swim swim.

38.8 That a *monachus* ought to hand over to his abbot any acquisitions

A synod says: A *monachus* who, in open defiance, begins to wander around remote places, such that he presumed to have property of his own, all that he acquired, should be turned over to the abbot, according to the monastery's rule, and he should be recalled to oversight, just as an escapee.

38.9 That a *monachus* of a slightly more lenient rule must not be received

Gildas:[401] An abbot of a stricter rule should not receive the *monachus* of another, slightly more lenient abbot; and the one who is more lenient, should not detain a *monachus* of his who strives after a stricter way of life.

38.10 That both must be excommunicated: a fugitive *monachus* and the one who receives him

The synod of Nicaea: If someone receives the *monachus* of another, both must be excommunicated.[402]

Patrick: Whoever has been excommunicated by some cleric and received by another, they should be corrected by the same penance.

38.11 Concerning excommunicating a vagrant *monachus*

Patrick said: A vagrant *monachus* wandering through the lay community without consulting his abbot should be excommunicated.

38.12 That a *monachus* ought to desert a very wicked abbot

Jerome: A wolf must be avoided, a good shepherd must be flocked to, a den of thieves must be deserted, a sheepfold must be sought.

Augustine: Sheep flee from the voice of an unknown shepherd, and seek remote places; so do the sheepfolds of a wicked *princeps*.

38.13 That a *monachus* ought not enlist in two churches

The synod of Chalcedon says that a cleric ought not enlist simultaneously in churches of two *ciuitates*, [namely] the one in which he was initially ordained, and that to which he fled, as if it were to a shepherd, out of greed for inane glory; and those who do so ought to be recalled to their church in which they have originally been ordained, and minister there only.

38.14 Concerning the penance of a *monachus* who has begotten children

An Alexandrian synod: *Monachi* who beget children should be shut in prison, bemoaning this great offence with continual lamentation, so that, even at the point of death, the grace of communion be allowed solely on account of mercy.

38.15 That *monachi* ought not withdraw from the congregation

The synod of Agde: *Monachi* are not permitted to withdraw from the congregation to solitary cells, unless perchance—having been tested after worthy labours—they should receive permission from their abbots, but only for having separate cells, while remaining within the confines of the same monastery.

38.16 That a *monachus* ought not build a cell without his abbot's permission

The synod of Orléans: No *monachus* driven by ambition and vanity, should dare build a cell without his abbot's permission.

39 Concerning excommunication

39.1 Concerning the regulation of excommunication

In the Gospel: If your brother shall offend against you, go, and rebuke him between you and him alone. If he will listen to you, you have won over your brother. But if he will not listen to you, take with you one or two more, that every word may stand in the mouth of two or three witnesses. And if he will not listen to them, tell the church. And if he will not listen to the church, let him be to you as the pagan and publican.

Concerning the manner of excommunication, in what way he who is excommunicated, should be excommunicated

Paul said: You may not communicate at the table or in prayer. For what company does light hold with darkness and Belial with the just?

A Roman synod decreed that there are three modes of excommunication, to wit: from communion, and table, and mass.[403]

A Hibernian synod says there are six modes: from celebrating together, from sharing a table, from cohabitation, from blessing, from absolution, from socialising, from gifts.[404]

39.2 That the wicked must be excommunicated

Augustine: He who befriends God's enemy declines God's friendship, and he who is subject in his mind to God's truth shall resist the enemies of truth.

That the table of the wicked must be excommunicated[405]

Christ, before his passion, did not eat in Jerusalem, but went to Bethany. Abraham avoided the feasts of the Chaldeans. Tobias abstained from the foods of the gentiles. Moses did not eat from Pharaoh's table. Judas Maccabee cast out the tables of the gentiles. God delivered the manna to his people, so that it would not be polluted by the foods of the gentiles. David avoided sitting at Saul's table. Daniel cursed the foods of the Chaldean king, as one reads in that place. Daniel decided in his heart that he should not be polluted by the king's meal or by drinking his wine.[406]

Origen in the annals: Ezekiel excommunicated the messengers of Babylon.

The Lord expelled those wearing a dirty garment from the house of the wedding.

Paul: Not at the table, nor in prayer, etc.

In the proverbs of the Greeks: Just as no one is able to take or lick honey from the tongue of a serpent, or the sharp blade of a sword, or fiery iron, so the elect saints are not able to accept gifts or rewards from evil men and sinners.

And Origen said: If paradise cast out the excommunicated Adam, how much more so the church.

That the clean ought to excommunicate the unclean

The Lord expelled the man wearing a dirty garment from the house of the wedding.

Jerome said: If your own sins do not harm, why do you share in the sins of others?

39.3 Concerning not saying '*aue*' and not receiving sinners

John says in the second epistle: If any man come to you, and bring not this doctrine, receive him not into the house, nor say '*aue*' to him. For he who greets him, shares with his wicked works.

The son of Sirach: If you do good, know to whom you do it. Be merciful and do not receive a sinner.

39.4 That no one ought to be excommunicated quickly[407]

Gildas said: Noah did not wish to keep his son Ham, *scriba* of the magic art, away from the ark or from sharing his table. Abraham did not shudder from Aner and Escol when he was warring with the five kings. Lot did not curse the feasts of the Sodomites. Isaac did not forbid Abimelech and Ochozath and Phicol, leader of the army, to share his table: but they swore oaths to each other after eating and drinking. Jacob was not afraid of contact with his sons, whom he knew to be idolaters. Joseph did not refuse to share the table and cup of Pharaoh. Aaron did not spurn the table of the priest of the idols of Midian. Moses, too, lodged and feasted in peace together with Jethro. Christ did not avoid the feasts of pagans, so as to save all sinners and prostitutes.[408] Thus far Gildas.

But let it be known that the patriarchs did these things out of compelling necessity.

Paul feasted with gentiles.

Our Lord Christ did not openly excommunicate Judas.

39.5 That kinsmen must be excommunicated

Jerome in his epistles concerning food and clothing: Aaron says: How many *monachi*, while they show mercy to a father, mother, brother, sister, or any other relative, lose their souls! We are not permitted to be polluted on account of our father and mother. How much more so our brothers and sisters and cousins!

Gregory: When we join ourselves to friends incautiously, we are bound by the sins of others.

39.6 That the one who receives the excommunicated must be excommunicated

The synod of Ancyra said: Whoever communicates with the excommunicated should himself be excommunicated.

39.7 That alms of an excommunicated man must not be accepted

Patrick: If a cleric has been excommunicated, neither should his alms be received in church.

39.8 That an excommunicated man ought not offer, nor baptise, but only pray

Patrick: If a man has been excommunicated, let him pray alone from that moment on, nor is he permitted to offer or baptise, until he reforms himself.

39.9 That everyone has to clean himself first, and thus excommunicate others

Jerome in the books concerning the status of *monachi*: Some *monachi*, being puffed up in pride of their status and religion, avoid the feasts of others, when in fact they need to clean themselves from within, after the example of the Lord, saying: Physician, heal yourself first.

Augustine: Some excommunicate others for the sake of sobriety, not understanding that the sins of others are extraneous, but theirs are their own.

In the Gospel: And why do you see the mote that is in your brother's eye, and see not the beam that is in your own eye?

39.10 That the ones who go to the grocery market must not be excommunicated[409]

Paul: Whatsoever is sold in the grocery market, eat, asking no question for conscience's sake, for the earth is the Lord's, and the fullness thereof.

Likewise: If any of the non-believers invite you to dinner and you want to go, eat anything that is set before you.

39.11 That food and drink do not blemish a man as much as a depraved thought and deed

A synod: Food and drink do not stain a man as much as a depraved thought and deed blemish him; you can live without the first, but never without yourself.

39.12 Concerning excommunicating heretics

A Roman synod: A cleric should avoid the feasts and company of heretics.

Likewise: One must not pray with heretics.

In the Ecclesiastical History: And there are those who heard that John, the Lord's disciple, when he went to the baths in Ephesus to wash, and saw Cerinthus there, it is said he immediately leaped out, and left without washing, saying: Let us flee from this place, lest even the baths themselves, in which Cerinthus, the enemy of truth, washes, shall sink.

Likewise, in the same: Once, when Polycarp met Marcion, who asked him 'do you recognise us?', he replied: 'I know, I know Satan's firstborn'.

39.13 That good men cannot exist without the bad, and the bad without the good

Grain is pressed under the chaffs on the threshing floor, and they are not separated by any other means, except by the wind. So too the human race, living in the world in a mixed state, until Christ shall separate the grain from the chaffs, namely the just from the sinners, with his winnowing shovel, as it is said: Suffer both to grow, etc.

Likewise: Flowers grow among thorns.

Likewise: The rose that emits a pleasant scent grows with the thorn that pricks.

Adam begot the first two sons; one was chosen and the other a reprobate. Abraham also begot two sons; one was chosen and the other wanton. The three sons of Noah were in the ark, two were chosen and one a reprobate. Isaac begot two sons, one good and the other a reprobate. Jacob begot twelve sons, one of whom was sold because of his innocence, namely Joseph, the remaining eleven were the sellers and killers. Christ chose twelve apostles, and one of them was the betrayer of the saviour, namely the one who picked him out.

Likewise: Seven deacons were ordained by the apostles, but whereas six persisted in the faith, one became the founder of the Nicolaitan heresy.

Isidore: The tabernacle is constructed of different materials, some precious, others cheap. By means of which it is shown that in the church some are holy, others are sinners.

39.14 That it is better to withdraw from the wicked, lest one perish together with them

Noah is commanded to enter the ark quickly, lest he die with the wicked.

Likewise: The angels dragged Lot away from the Sodomites, lest he perish with them.

Likewise: The people of Israel is told to depart far from the tents of Dathan and Abiron.

Likewise: It is said to the people of Israel in Babylon: Go out from the midst of Babylon.

God said to Moses and Aaron: Go out and part from this people, for I shall destroy it.

Likewise: Joshua's spies said to Rahab: Whoever we shall find in your house, we shall not kill; whoever shall have gone outside, his blood shall be upon him.

David asks: Do not deliver me together with the sinners.

Likewise, a synod: Every cleric who wishes to observe public games, should be demoted.

Likewise: Any cleric who has died in battle, or in a riot, or in the public games of the pagans, let it not be pleaded for him either by oblation or prayer, but let him fall into the hands of a judge; he shall, nevertheless, not be deprived of burial.

That the church must not have faith in the powers of the world

Augustine: Whoever is nourished in the bosom of the mother church and shelters under the shade of God's wings, should distance himself far from the influences of the wicked and the protection of demons.

Concerning the understanding of divine books

Augustine said: And in divine books[410] we should love that which is certain that he, whom we ought to read, said. If this is concealed from view, let us love that which accords with the context of scripture. But if this is not forthcoming, then that which is consistent with the catholic faith should be loved. For if the place, the time, and the person, that are observed shall be in agreement with all things. . .[411]

{L} Gregory the bishop says.

That it does not harm the good to be found in the company of the wicked

Noah's ark and the tabernacle and the temple accommodated both the good and the wicked.

The two sons of Aaron were found in the company of the wicked.

Jerome: The church of the present is nourished by both the clean and the unclean.

Paul: In a large house there are many vessels.

Only the future church will be clean; consequently it is said to her: Come, you, who are the blessed of my father.

39.15 That it does not harm the good to die with the wicked

Christ was cut down among the wicked, and nearly all the martyrs died among the wicked.

Likewise: Judas Maccabee offered for the men who died in battle among the wicked.

40 Concerning the bequests of the dead[412]

40.1 Concerning not changing bequests of a *princeps*

Jacob, dying, gave a share of the estate to his son Joseph, and his brothers did not change it.

Origen said in the annals of the Hebrews: Moses bequeathed an inheritance to Jethro, the priest of Midian, in the land of Canaan, and it was fixed.

Jesus, dying, bequeathed his tunic to John.

In the chronicles: A dying king bequeathed his kingdom to the Romans.[413]

Jerome said in the book concerning the state of the *monachi* of Egypt: A certain *princeps*, dying, bequeathed a small field near the *ciuitas* by means of a testament, and since the *monachi* of the *ciuitas* attempted to change it, the case was reported and reached the bishop. And because he did not know what kind of verdict to pass, the following night an angel appeared to him in the form of someone bequeathing a little field, and said: Let the testament of the *princeps* be upheld; whoever should change the testament, let him be anathema.

40.2 Concerning a *princeps* or bishop bequeathing his own property

A synod: Every *princeps* can bequeath his property [to be given away] after his death.

The synod of Ancyra says that a bishop may bequeath the clothes that he wears, both the robe[414] and the woven fabric.

40.3 That a *princeps* may bequeath church property

Jerome said in the questions: Jacob, bishop of Jerusalem, left his episcopal see intact and undivided to his heirs and successors. Peter left a wholesome Antioch to the brethren, according to the books of histories.

Jerome: The Lord's tunic was seamless, to signify that the church is not impaired in any way at the death of a *princeps*.

A synod: Every Christian *princeps* should leave the church the way he found it. Upon his death, let him bequeath nothing without the consent of the clerics, lest he be burdened with curses after his death.

40.4 That a *princeps* may bequeath some of the church's property

A Hibernian synod: Upon his death, a *princeps* can also bequeath some of the church's property, that is, up to the value of an *ancilla*,[415] either from the movables, or the land.

The synod of Agde said: Surely, if the *princeps* has freed any of the slaves of the church, it is proper that it be upheld by his successors. But we command this, that it should not exceed twenty silver solidi and a measure of the land and a little house and a garden; the church shall repossess anything given above and beyond this measure.

A Hibernian synod said: The testament of a bishop or a *princeps* is ten scruples for the *sacerdos* who hands him the host, a mantle for the poor man, provisions of food for the widow, communal clothing for the servant (*minister*), and even these should be confirmed by the clerics.

40.5 That a bishop may bequeath all his property to whomever he wishes, but nothing of the church's property

The synod of Antioch: So long as the bishop who presides over a church is alive, the faithful should know from the church what property belongs to them (i.e. to the church), and the faithful should know from the bishop what property belongs to the bishop. For if it happens that the bishop depart from this world we may know, thanks to reliable records, what things belong to the church, so that they will not fall into ruin and perish, and so that the property that is shown to be the bishop's should not, under some pretext, pass over to the church. For it is considered just and acceptable in the sight of God and men, that a bishop may leave his property to whomever he wishes in God, and the things that are the church's, should remain with the same church—Origen: Every *princeps* ought to have property by which to feed the poor and those who serve him, or his sons, should he have any—lest the church suffer any loss and the bishop be punished with confiscation under the pretext of the church, and they who belong to him be sued, and he shall be burdened with curses after his death.

A Roman synod: Presbyters and deacons should not try to do anything before [the death of] the bishop. For the people of the Lord was entrusted to him, and he shall render an account for their souls. And let the bishop's own property be known, and let that of the Lord also be known; so that the bishop, as he is dying, may have power to do whatever he wishes with the property, to leave it to whomever he wishes, thereby the property that is shown to be the bishop's should not be lost under the pretence of its being the property of the church. For perhaps he has a wife, or sons, or relatives, or slaves. And this is considered just among God and men, that the church should suffer no loss because it does not know the bishop's property, nor the bishop or his relatives be punished with confiscation on account of some pretext of the church, and they who belong to him be sued, and both sides be disgraced with *iniuriae*.[416]

40.6 That a *monachus* cannot bequeath anything without the abbot's permission

The *Romani* say: A dying *monachus* cannot bequeath anything, but he shall leave everything to the abbot. For since he should have no property of his own in his life, how much more so in death.

Likewise: He who has done nothing in his life without the abbot's permission, why should he be exposed as a thief in death? He who gives and he who receives is a thief and robber.

40.7 Concerning a *monachus* bequeathing a few things, but only with his abbot's permission

Origen: Every *monachus* with no abbot, or if the abbot should be absent, has no power over anything. But if the abbot has allowed it, he may bequeath a few things.

In the Life of the Monks: A certain dying *monachus* bequeathed his hut to another brother, who refused to accept it in the abbot's absence until an angel came having the appearance of the abbot, and said: Take it.

40.8 That a person under tribute bequeaths nothing[417]

In the Life of the Monks: A rustic bequeathed a bronze dish to a *sacerdos* as a gift. The latter asked if he lived under the rule of an abbot or king, and learned that he was subject to a king, and said: I shall not accept what belongs to another, lest I lose my own.

A Hibernian synod: Just as a *monachus* shall not dare bequeath anything without the abbot's permission, so he who is under tribute shall not have the power to grant anything upon his death, unless he was commanded by his lord.

40.9 Concerning one living under tribute bequeathing what belongs to him

A Hibernian synod: If anyone has been under royal tribute or an abbot, and bequeathed anything, he is not able to revoke it if his lord knew about it and held his peace for two days; but if [he did not hold his peace], let it be void.

Concerning a bequest of children to be revoked, and not revoked

A synod: If a young boy in the age of childhood, or a young girl, have wanted to bind themselves by oath against their father's will, they shall give nothing, nor bequeath anything. But if they have come of age, and should have something of their own that does not belong to the paternal property (*substantia*), they may bequeath it to God.

40.10 Concerning the bequest of a woman living in marriage

A Hibernian synod: If her husband has held his peace for two days, he shall not take back whatever she gave. But if he has not held his peace, her testament shall be void, except the entitlement of her body, [and anything up to the value of] the mantle and the cow together with her body. And should she have a church that she has served, she shall give the church a third of her property with her husband's consent, as long as she shall be with her husband, but her husband shall divide. The rest however, shall belong to her husband and her children.

A synod: If her husband has held his peace for a number of days, he shall not take back what the wife gave. But if he has not held his peace, her testament shall be void, except that which is given under the law of burial.[418] If a woman has joined herself to a certain church by a monastic vow, she shall give the church a third of her property with her husband's consent. And she shall give a few gifts to her father's and mother's families, distributed by her husband. All the rest shall belong to her children and husband.

Concerning a bequest of a *monachus* who departs to another abbot

A synod: If a *monachus* of a certain abbot departed to another abbot, what shall he commend to both? It is as follows: he shall give all that he possesses to his former abbot, but let him leave his body, and his ordinary outfit, and the vessel from which he drinks, and a cow or its value, and the horse on which he sits, to the most recent abbot.[419] The former shall have the rest. For how can the former abbot offer a *uiaticum*,[420] when he has left him?

Concerning someone who removes what he has bequeathed to God

A synod: We do not allow anything whatsoever that has been given to the church of God by whatever means, to be alienated from the church.

Jerome: Anyone who removes what he has given to God is a robber of both his own property and another's, for the earth is the Lord's, etc.

Augustine: Anyone who has removed what he has given to God, must be cast out of his grade, and damned by the church, and ought not be received.

41 Concerning the church and the world

Concerning the word 'church'

Isidore in the books of etymologies: 'Church' (*ecclesia*) is a Greek word, which is rendered 'calling together' (*conuocatio*) in Latin, because it calls everyone together to itself. 'Catholic' [means] 'universal'. For unlike the assembly places of heretics, it is not in various parts of the territories, but diffused throughout the world.

41.1 Concerning the true church having only three kinds of people[421]

Jerome: The church preserves and nurtures only three [ways of life]: the contemplative life, the active life, and the penitential life. The church does not accept, nor preserve, any other [way of life].

41.2 Concerning the three things of which a church ought not make use[422]

Origen: The church ought [to observe] three things: not to receive the gifts of the wicked, which the most high condemns, not to seize the property of another, and not to accept the price of innocent blood, as [it is said]: You shall not take the payment of innocent blood.

That *defensores*[423] must be sought to protect the church

The synod of Nicaea said: On account of the affliction suffered by the poor at the hands of persecutors, by whose molestations the church is constantly worn down, it has been agreed[424] by all emperors that *defensores* be appointed[425] against the powers of the wealthy, with the oversight of the bishops.

41.3 That a church must not be plundered by the laity[426]

Gregory: If someone has stripped the church, let him be anathema.

The synod of Agde: If someone defrauded the church of God, let him be punished by exile.[427]

A synod: Thieves and bandits and robbers must be cast out of the church.

Concerning the difference between defrauding one's friend and the church

Likewise, the synod of Vaison: If you have defrauded a friend, it is theft. Defrauding the church, however, is sacrilege.

41.4 Concerning a church suffering itself to be plundered[428]

Luke: And him who takes away your cloak from you, forbid not to take your coat also. Give to everyone who asks anything of you. He who takes away your goods, ask them not back from him.

Paul to the Corinthians: Why not rather let yourselves suffer wrong? But you do wrong and defraud, and that even to your brothers.

Pelagius: It is as if he were to say: When, according to the teachings of the Gospel and the Lord's example, you ought to have endured with patience the wrong that has been done to you; on the contrary, you not only do not endure, but also inflict harm on those who do nothing against you.

Nechias:[429] If a debtor is to be required or forced to pay, defer it; if a judge must be inconvenienced, let it go.

Jerome: If a dove has seen another bird snatch the food of its chicks, it does not move a feather, nor claw, nor beak, nor does it croak. So too the church of God, which is the true dove, shall not go after the things that have been seized from it.

Origen: A sheep renounces its fleece for the person shearing it, nor does it open its mouth. So too the church ought to renounce its fleece for the one who robs it and makes away with it. For the more deprived it is of worldly things, the more it is increased in spiritual things. And the more it asks or demands of worldly things, the more it is deprived of spiritual things.

On account of this it is said: He who strives for worldly things shall not possess heavenly things.

Augustine: If any man has lost anything, and said, 'the Lord gave, and the Lord has taken away', thanks to this utterance, pleasing to God, he shall either receive a crown if he is just, or the forgiveness of sins, if he is a sinner.

In the Gospel of Matthew: And if a man will contend with you in judgement, and take away your tunic, let go your cloak also unto him; that is, that no one shall use the cold and their righteousness as an excuse to strip.

41.5 Concerning a dispute being forbidden with the unjust and the just alike

Solomon says: Contend not with the ungodly.

Isaiah: Behold, you fast for debates and strife.

Paul: For, when there is among you envying and dispute, are you not carnal and walk you not according to man?

Concerning dispute itself

Philip: A dispute is when something is defended not by reason, but by temperamental obstinacy, and where truth is not sought so much as attention is worn down.

41.6 Concerning the church, that it may not seize the whole

Aaron the *sacerdos* was given only a portion by the people; only the suburbs were given to the tribe of Levi.

Jerome: Give a portion to them, who are seven, and also to them, who are eight. That is, a portion to the church, which is the eighth, and let a portion be left to worldly people, who are seven.

A synod: No one ought defraud sons or brothers or kinsmen.

Likewise: Let the church receive nothing except the portion of God; when the heir of the world shall come, he shall take back the things that are the world's.

Concerning the church having to preserve the things that have been offered for their own heirs

The *Romani* say: Let the church preserve the things that are given to it, until the son of the donor shall come, or his brother, or a kinsman, and all things shall be restored to their former ownership.

That he who joins himself to a church is not deprived of the inheritance of his fathers

In Deuteronomy: If a Levite go out of any one of your cities throughout all the land in which he dwells, and wants to come, desiring the place which the Lord shall choose, he shall minister in the name of his Lord, like all his brethren the Levites, who shall stand at that time before the Lord. He shall receive the same portion of food that the rest do, besides that which is due to him in his own city, out of paternal succession.

That the inheritance of a just brother must not be taken away on account of an undutiful brother

In the parables of the Greeks: The inheritance of a just brother is not to be taken away by the affairs of an unjust brother. In all truth, the just cannot be grieved on account of the unjust, if they have been separated from each other by evils.[430]

That plotting is not permitted in a church

The synod of Chalcedon: The offence of conspiring and plotting is entirely prohibited also by secular laws; it is all the more fitting to warn that it not be committed in the church of God. Therefore, should clerics or *monachi* be found to be plotters or conspirers or laying traps for bishops or clerics, let them be cast out from their particular grade entirely.

41.7 Concerning two churches disputing over a single estate

A synod: Let inquiries be made about the estate in the written record of both churches. Should nothing be found in the written record, let inquiries be made among the elders and neighbours concerning the length of time that it was with the other [church], and if it remained [with that church] for a confirmed jubilee without conflict,[431] let it remain [with it] in perpetuity. But if no elders have been found, let them divide it in two among themselves, and the one that is nearer to it shall pay [the other] a sum that judges have adjudicated.[432]

41.8 Concerning the proprietary right of the church not lapsing, even after a long time

A synod: If a bishop, for the sake of charity, has given farmsteads to the clerics or *monachi* to cultivate or hold for a limited period of time, even if long periods of time are shown to pass, they shall revert back to the church.

In the Ecclesiastical History: We have enacted the following: that if any houses, or fields, or any landed estates have been seized from Christians, either into the royal treasury, or given away as gifts, we command that all these be restored to their former Christian owners, and that all belongings be restored to their proprietors.

In the chronicles: Diocletian reigned for twenty years; having burned sacred books, he commanded that the property of Christians be seized. Galerius succeeded him for two years. Constantine succeeded Galerius for thirty years. He gave Christians licence to congregate freely, and restored their property to them after many years.

41.9 That it is forbidden to covet the property of others

Isaiah said: Woe to you who join house to house, estate to estate, and lay field to field, even to the boundary of a place. Do you alone dwell in the midst of the earth?

The prophet: Woe to him who heaps up that which is not his own.

In the Gospel: You grind the faces of the poor.

Jerome: Do not strive after the property of others, lest you lose your own.

Gregory: The true shepherd is he who looks after his own property, and does not seek what belongs to others.

The law says: You shall not covet your neighbour's property.

41.10 That the church may accept everything that is given to it

One reads in the law that spoils taken from enemies in battles were divided, and he commanded that a share be given to God from both; that is, God commanded that a share of the fighters' [spoils] be given to God, and Aaron and his sons, and that [a share of the spoils of] the remainder of the multitude be given to the Levites.

Daniel accepted the gifts of the wicked king.

David gave a share of the spoils of the Philistines to God's tabernacle.

God commanded Eleazar the priest to examine Core's pans, which were consumed by fire, and shape them into the plates of the altar.

Abraham offered Melchisedech part of the spoils from the war with the five kings.

A synod: The church ought not seek to acquire, nor reject what has been given.

41.11 Concerning a church being blasphemed by secular persons

Isaiah said: Be ashamed, O Sidon, for the sea spoke. Sidon is a thing sold, namely the church; the sea is the world.

Jerome in his commentary: But we live on an island so long as we are pounded by the temptations of this world. And on our every side, on an island or in a boat, we are beaten by the currents of the sea. But the hunters of this island are from Sidon, which is translated 'huntress', and where hunters lived. Of whom it is said in David: My soul has been delivered as a sparrow out of the snare of the hunters.

Paul: Giving no offence to any man, that our ministry be censured by others, who are outside.

Is the name of Christ not blasphemed by you?

Likewise: Providing good things, not only in the sight of God, but also in the sight of men.

Jerome: When the church sins, it is condemned by wicked men.

Augustine: When we behave well, we get praise from God; when we behave wickedly, we are blamed without respect by the wicked.

41.12 Concerning the correction of secular persons by the church

Paul: Them that sin reprove in the sight of all.

Christ: Woe to you scribes and Pharisees.

Paul: O senseless Galatians, who bewitched you?

David: You fools, be wise at last.

In the Apocalypse: Such as I love, I rebuke and correct. Be zealous therefore, and do penance.

John the Baptist: You brood of vipers, who has instructed you to flee from the wrath to come?

Jerome: You who do no good are bent on evil.

That it is not an offence to reprove someone in truth

Paul says to the Galatians: When Peter came to Antioch, I withstood him to his face, because he had been blamed. For before someone came from Jacob, he ate with the Gentiles. But when he came, he withdrew himself, fearing them who were of the circumcision. And to his hypocrisy the rest of the Jews consented, so that Barnabas was led with them into that hypocrisy.

Concerning reproving moderately

The apostle said to Timothy: Do not rebuke an elderly man, but entreat him as a father; young men as brothers; old women as mothers; young women as sisters, in all chastity. Honour widows, who are widows indeed. But if any widow have children, or grandchildren, let her learn first to govern her own house, and to repay her relatives. For this is acceptable before the Lord.

Concerning secular persons, how frequently they ought to receive the eucharist

The synod of Agde: And secular persons who do not receive communion at Christmas and Easter and Pentecost should be deemed not to be catholics.

That the slaves of clerics must not be harassed

The synod of Arles: If someone should believe that the slaves of clerics are slaves of his own who fled to the church and must be seized, let him be punished by damnation throughout all churches.

41.13 Concerning the ones fostered by the church

The synod of Narbonne: We allow a son to leave his monastery only out of faithful duty, since according to the teachings of the Gospel one ought to assist parents in times of need. But after their death, we should regard him as an outsider, unless he returns to his monastery. Christ did not release his disciple to go to bury his father.

The synod of Nicaea says: If someone was reared in a monastery and educated up to the highest grade of learning and then left, unless he returns he must be condemned on the charge of being a deserter and sinner.

Jerome: Whoever has been reared and educated under a rule should not be received by another church.

Augustine: Dear boy, you must remain where you have acquired the highest grade of learning, lest, being a wanderer, you be called a deserter.

41.14 Concerning the three things that are demanded of a church

Jerome: Three things are demanded of a church: a *monachus* who lived and dwelled in it for many years, and a fosterling educated as far as the highest grade of learning, and a penitent completing his penance.

41.15 Concerning a church not retaining anybody by force

Jacob says to Ermogenis in the Passions of the Apostles: It is not our way to convert someone who is unwilling.

In the conflict of Sylvester one reads: This is the difference between human and divine service: that human service is required, and divine service is voluntary. For God is worshipped by means of the mind, and venerated with sincere human love. On account of this we are deemed to be true Christians, not compelled by need, but by free judgement, not coming to the Lord through human fear, seeking rather that they be joined to the Christians by rational thinking.

Paul persuades, he does not command; he asks, he does not frighten.

Christ left the seat of the law and followed Mary and Joseph.

In the Life of the Monks: A certain bishop said of a certain fosterling who deserted his monastery: Do not curse him insofar as he is a fosterling, nor bless him insofar as he is a deserter.

A synod: If someone left of his own volition, let it be recorded in the presence of witnesses, and be left to God [to judge].

41.16 That payment for ecclesiastical ministry must not be sought, and penance must not be let slip[433]

Jerome: Teaching and baptism ought to be dispensed without payment and delay. Not so penance, which must always be overseen and controlled, lest it lapse.

41.17 That it is not permitted to eat or sleep in a church

The synod of Laodicea: It is not permitted to eat carnal food nor prepare couches for sleeping in the house of God; on account of which Christ forced out the sellers and buyers, saying: My house shall be called a house of prayer.

That it is not permitted to seek worldly gain from religion

In the Gospel: My house shall be called the house of prayer. But you have made it a den of thieves.

Jerome in his commentary: For he who strives to make worldly gain of religion is a thief, and turns God's temple into a den of thieves; and his worship is not so much the worship of God but a pretext for doing business.

Concerning quarrelsome persons being cast out of the church

The synod of Arles: They who flare up in public quarrels must be removed from the fellowship of the church, until they return to peace.

41.18 Concerning the division of a *parochia* between bishops

The synod of Sardica said: Where there have been two shares, let the bishops divide their shares equally between them, that is, let some places (*loca*) belong to one, others to the other. And let him divide, who spent a longer time in the episcopal office, and the junior shall choose. And should there be a single place (*locus*), let it belong to him to whom it is closer. And if it is equally close to both sees, let it belong to him whom the community has chosen. And if the old catholics shall claim it as their own, and the others, who have recently been converted, as theirs, let the will of the majority be preferred to the minority. But if the parts of the community are divided equally, let it be entrusted to the bishop of greater seniority. But if many places are found in which there should be two parts that cannot be divided equally, or if they should be of an odd number, or should a place be left over, what should apply in this case is that which has been said above concerning a single place.[434]

41.19 That division is better than discord

A synod: It is better to divide than always disagree. For division brings forth peace, but disagreement destroys.

In the era of the judges the priesthood was divided. Four soldiers divided Christ's clothes. There were three altars in a single temple, and likewise in the tabernacle.

41.20 Concerning not dividing the church or *parochia* of a single monastery

In the law: There was one priesthood and one priest. And when the priesthood was divided, it was reputed to the people's blame, and God threatens vengeance against the people. Note that when the tabernacle was disassembled, the sacrifices and holocausts ceased; but when it was assembled, then there were sacrifices to the Lord in it.

Likewise: Christ's tunic was not divided. This signifies that the church of God is not divided, for there is one faith and one baptism. The clothes, however, signify the parts of the world, the soldiers, the four Gospels.[435]

Satan is the first to shatter the unity.[436] Whence many divisions emerged in the world. Note that before the law [was proclaimed], Noah and Abraham were commanded to erect an altar, albeit in different places. In this manner, after the law was pronounced, nature is joined to nature.

41.21 Concerning the severity of retribution due to those who abandon young children in the church of God

A Hibernian synod: Let those who abandon young children in a church of God without the abbot's knowledge do penance for three and a half years if there are bishops buried or present in it. But if they committed homicide in it, let them do penance for seven years. This rule is due to the fact that a bishop has seven grades and the church is septiform. If, however, it has no bishops, but instead it is a small church, let them do penance for a year and a half.

Concerning the senior bishop dividing and the junior choosing

A Roman synod: Let the senior bishop divide and the junior choose, for Abraham divided, Lot only chose.[437]

41.22 Concerning young children being abandoned in a church[438]

The same said:[439] A child who has been brought [to the church] is its slave, unless he is redeemed through payment. Should he behave impudently, if he shall correct himself as best he can, his offensive behaviour shall not stain the church. A child who has been brought to the church, if he has left it within a period of one hundred days, the church shall have no power over him,[440] but he will belong to those raising him. If the church received money from his parents in whatever amount, after the fashion of fosterers, he will be the child of his parents. If the young child has died through negligence, let them do penance for seven years, for they have killed Christ. Hence others judge that they who abandoned young children do penance for seven years, so that they may endure as much trouble as they have inflicted on the church.

41.23 Concerning rebuking those seeking money

A Roman synod: Whoever wanders around the brethren, bearing the appearance of being needy, asking for various things, should not be received by the brethren, unless he has a recommendation from some catholic kinsmen.

A synod says: They who collect ecclesiastical belongings for the support of life in the name of mercy, let authority be taken away from them if they are found not to have redeemed any captives. And let what they have accumulated for the redemption of captives be distributed; and let them be as strangers to Christians until they perform three years of penance.

Patrick: If someone has sought to redeem captives in the community independently, without the abbot's permission, he deserves to be excommunicated.

41.24 That a collection of money must not be rebuked, if it be done out of compelling necessity

Patrick: If someone has received the bishop's permission, and the price of a captive has been collected, let him not ask any more than that which necessity demands. If anything is left over, let him place it over the altar, and let it be given to the needy and the captives. Let him not give it to another. And if he has, he has committed a sin.

Likewise: If someone collects money in the name of mercy, he should not dare despoil the church of God, but rather kings and commoners, for whom it is better to give than to hoard.

Concerning the need not to shatter the unity and harmony of the church

A synod: Whoever dares shatter the unity that no man can dissolve or censure, let him be anathema.

Paul: I beseech you, brothers, by the name of our Lord Jesus Christ, that you all speak the same thing, and that there be no schisms among you; but that you be perfect in the same mind and in the same opinion.

41.25 Concerning the church releasing a prisoner

A Hibernian synod: If the church has released a captive from imprisonment, let it claim from him the fetters of punitive penance.[441] But if he has not completed his penance and committed an offence, no curse should come upon the church of God. For the church has the power to bind and loose, and she is free, and each and every one is a debtor to her.

41.26 Concerning a church under tribute[442] not releasing a captive

The same synod: Should the church be under royal tribute, or constrained by certain earthly bonds, it is not worthy of releasing a captive, for should it release him, it shall pay that which is due for his offences.

41.27 That a Catholic church is free not to pay the debts of the wicked

The same synod: A church shall not make satisfaction for the suffering caused by the offences of others. Just as the offences of demons shall not be claimed from God and his angels, so the offences of the devil's limbs shall not be claimed from the limbs of Christ, namely the saints; neither those of the of *monachi* who flee from the church, nor those of wicked strangers, nor those of them, who are cast upon the church, namely wicked collectors,[443] nor those of secular kinsmen. But let secular persons make satisfaction to the church for the offences of other secular persons, which they committed in a church. Similarly, the offence of a wicked brother shall not taint a religious brother who makes satisfaction for the former's offence, neither in a spiritual way, nor in an earthly way.

41.28 Concerning the stages of an offence of a sinning brother[444]

The same synod: First, the offence of every wicked man shall be claimed from his movable property and livestock. Second, if he does not have movable property or livestock, it shall be claimed from his lands.[445] If he does not have lands, it shall be claimed from his king. If he does not have a king, it shall be claimed from the person who furnished the offender with weapons and clothing. But if not, it shall finally be claimed from him who fed him and gave him a bed. But if none of these are found, and if he commits an offence in a church, let it be sought from the chief king of the province in which the church is.

41.29 That the blame of sinners does not come upon the church, even if it feeds them

The same synod: If the church gives food to someone who committed an offence, the offence of the wicked person shall not be claimed from the church on account of the food given to the wicked person by it, because it is the true dove. For a dove does not only tend to its own chicks, but to all birds that open their mouths. Thus the church serves everyone equally, the Lord having said: Be you therefore perfect, as also your heavenly father is perfect, who makes his sun to rise upon both good and bad, upon both just and unjust.

41.30 That secular people do not fix liability by oath upon the deceased [*princeps*] of a church[446]

The same synod: A church defends itself even after the death of its *princeps*, and no oath fixes liability on it, namely, on the deceased [*princeps*], for their words are alive, on account of this scriptural example: And our fathers have told us; they have not been hidden from their children. And it fixes liability upon the secular dead, and therefore no liability is fixed by oath upon it, because it is free, and not a prison.

Concerning the tribe

Concerning the word 'tribe'

In the books of etymologies: Tribes are another name for divisions and various assemblies of peoples. And they are called tribes because in the beginning the Romans were divided into three categories by Romulus: senators, and soldiers, and plebeians. Although the tribes are now multiplied, they retain their original name.

Concerning the population of the tribe of Judah

The law: The Lord spoke to Moses in the desert of Sinai in the tabernacle of the covenant, the first day of the second month, the second year of their going out of Egypt, saying: Take the sum of all the congregation of the children of Israel, etc., by their families, and houses, and the names of every one, as many as are of the male sex from twenty years old, etc.

Of the sons of Judah, by their generations and families and houses of their kindreds, and by the names of every one from twenty years old and upward, all that were able to go forth to war were reckoned up to 74,600.

But afterwards, when Joshua [counted] his tribe in the plains of Moab, this is the number of those from twenty years old and upwards: 70,500.

Concerning consanguinity in a single tribe

In the book of etymologies: Consanguinity, therefore, is reckoned as far as the sixth degree of kinship, for just as the generation of the world and the presence of man is brought to an end in six ages, the propinquity of relation has been bounded by as many grades.

Concerning the difference between agnates and cognates in the tribe

In the books of etymologies: Agnates (*agnati*) are so called because they take the place (*accidant*) of children (*nati*), when there are no sons. Therefore they are acknowledged to rank first in the family, for they descend from persons of the male line, for example a brother born of the same father, or a brother's son, or grandson, or a paternal uncle.

Cognates are so called because they are joined by the propinquity of relationship (*cognatio*). And they are ranked after agnates because they descend from persons of the female line, and they are not agnates, but instead are related by natural law.

Concerning the difference between a people (*populus*) and a community (*plebs*) in the tribe

Isidore: 'People' is a human multitude (*humana multitudo*), joined together by legal agreement and common concord. A people is different from communities (*plebes*) in that all citizens are a 'people', including the elders of the city; a community (*plebs*) comprises the remaining commoners (*uulgus*) without the elders of the city. Therefore 'people' designates the whole city, but the commoners are 'community' . And 'community' (*plebs*) is so called from 'plurality' (*pluralitas*). For the number of the junior ones is greater than that of the senior ones. 'Commoners' (*uulgus*) are a multitude settled all about, as if it were, each one where he wishes (*uult*).

Concerning the genealogy of the tribe of Judah according to Matthew

The book of the generation of Jesus Christ, the son of David, the son of Abraham. Abraham begot Isaac, Isaac begot Jacob, Jacob begot Judas, Judas begot Phares, Esron, Aram, Aminadab, Naasson, Solomon, Boaz, Obed, Jesse, David—XIIII[447]—Solomon, Rehoboam, Abia, Asa, Josaphat, Joram—here he (i.e. the evangelist) omitted three—Uziah, Joatham, Achaz, Ezechias, Manasseh, Amon, Josias begot Jechonias, Jechonias, Salathiel, Zorobabel, Abiud, Eliacim, Azor, Sadoc, Achim, Eliud, Eleazar, Mathan, Jacob, Joseph the husband of Mary, of whom was born Christ, who is called Jesus. XIV.[448]

Behold in this genealogy the tribe of Judas spans nearly three eras of the world, with the exception of Abraham and Isaac and Jacob, that is three from Abraham to David, and four from David to Jechonias, and the five from Jechonias to Christ. Observe the number [of figures of] the tribe of Judah in this genealogy consists of thirty-seven men from Judas to Joseph, with the exception of the three that the evangelist omitted, namely Ochozias, and Joash, and Amasias.

Concerning the genealogy of the tribe of Judah according to Luke

And Jesus was beginning about the age of thirty years; being, as it was supposed, the son of Joseph, who was of Eli, who was of Melchi, who was of Levi, who was of Melchi, who was of Janne, who was of Joseph, who was of Mathathias, who was of Amos, who was of Nahum, who was of Hesli, who was of Nagge, who was of Mathathias, who was of Semei, who was of Joseph, who was of Judah, who was of Joanna, who was of Reza, who was of Salathiel, who was of Neri, who was of Melchi, who was of Addi, who was of Cosan, who was of Helmadan, who was of Her, who was of Jesus, who was of Eliezer, who was of Jorim, who was of Mathat, who was of Levi, who was of Simeon, who was of Judas, who was of Joseph, who was of Jona, who was of Eliakim, who was of Melea, who was of Menna, who was of Mathatha, who was of Nathan, who was of David, who was of Jesse, who was of Obed, who was of Boaz, who was of Solomon, who was of Naasson, who was of Aminadab, who was of Aram, who was of Esron, who was of Phares, who was of Judas, who was of Jacob, who was of Isaac, who was of Abraham, who was of Thare, who was of Nachor, who was of Sarug, who was of Ragau or Reu, who was of Heber Sale, who was of Cainan, who was of Arphaxad, who was of Sem, who was of Noah, who was of Lamech, who was of Methusaleh, who was of Enoch, who was of Jared, who was of Malaleel, who was of Cainan, who was of Henos, who was of Seth, who was of Adam.[449]

Behold this genealogy of the tribe of Judah from Joseph until Judah himself, comprises 53 men.[450] But notice that there are two different genealogies for the same tribe. Because according to Matthew's genealogy, reckoned through Solomon, he counts 26 men between Solomon and Joseph. But the same genealogy according to Luke, places 40 other men between Nathan son of David and Joseph. Although it is the same tribe, there are two different genealogies.

Concerning the names of the sons of David

In the books of Kings: These are the names of the seven sons of David who were born to him when he ruled in Hebron: Amon, Achinoam, Caleb, Absalom, Adonias, Saphathia, Jethraam. When he subsequently ruled in Jerusalem eleven sons were born to him, whose names are these: Samua, and Sobab, and Nathan, and Solomon, and Jebahar, and Elisua, and Nepheg, and Japhia, and Elisama, and Elioda, and Eliphaleth.

Concerning the difference between the genealogies of the Gospels

In the Ecclesiastical History: In the pedigree that Matthew delineates, which begins with David and continues through Solomon, he makes the third from the end to be Mathan, who is said to have begotten Jacob, the father of Joseph. Luke, tracing the progression of generations from David through Nathan, says the third in the same place is none other than Melchi. Therefore it is incumbent upon us to show how, according to Matthew, Joseph is said to have been fathered by Jacob, who is descended from Solomon, but according to Luke, from Eli, who is descended from Nathan. This is the solution: Mathan and Melchi, at different times, begot sons by the same woman, whose name was Estha. For Mathan, the descendant of Solomon, had taken her first as his wife, and he died, leaving behind a single son named Jacob. After his death, because the law does not object to a widow marrying another man, Melchi, the descendant of Nathan, since he belonged to the same tribe but not to the same family, took her as his wife after Mathan's demise, and he also had a son by her named Eli. In this manner Jacob and Eli became uterine brothers by different fathers. One of them, namely Jacob, in keeping with the law's command,[451] took the wife of his brother Eli, who died childless, and he begot Joseph. But according to the teachings of the law, the latter becomes the son of Eli, whose wife his brother Jacob had taken in order to revive his brother's seed. For thus, by means of proof, he (*sc.* either the evangelist or Eusebius) expresses legal descent, which is established by a form of adoption, rather than by the reality of begetting. Thus far the Ecclesiastical History. From this we learn that Joseph was the son of two brothers, and we ascertain that a single woman was joined to men of different families. For if Estha was of Nathan's family, the family of Solomon is strange to her, though it is of the same tribe. But if she was of Solomon's family, the family of Nathan is strange with respect to her.[452]

That all the property of a father with no sons, is due to his daughter's husband after her death, in a single tribe[453]

And Tobias said: Where do you want us to stay? And the angel answered: Here is one whose name is Raguel, a near kinsman of your tribe. He has a daughter named Sara, but he has no son nor any other daughter beside her. All his substance is due to you, and you must accept her as wife. Ask her therefore of her father, and he shall give her to you.

Likewise, the same: Raguel gave Tobias half of all that he owned, and he made him a deed, that the half that remained should come to their ownership after their passing.

Likewise, at the end of the book one reads: And it came to pass that after the death of his mother, Tobias departed out of Nineveh with his wife and children and children's children, and returned to his father- and mother-in-law. And he found them both in health in old age, and he closed their eyes, and all the inheritance of Raguel came to him.

Likewise, in the book of Numbers one reads: And the princes of the families of Gilead, the sons of Machir, the sons of Manasseh, of the stock of the children of Joseph, came and spoke to Moses before the princes of Israel, and said: The Lord has commanded you, my lord, that you should divide the land by lot to the children of Israel, and that you should give to the daughters of Salphaad our father the due possession of their father. Now if men of another tribe take them to wives, their possession shall follow them, and being transferred to another tribe, will be removed from our inheritance. And thus it shall come to pass, that when the jubilee, that is, the fiftieth year of remission, is come, the distribution made by the lots shall be confounded, and the possession of one shall pass to another. Moses answered the children of Israel, and said by the command of the Lord: The tribe of the children of Joseph has spoken rightly. And this is the law promulgated by the Lord touching the daughters of Salphaad: Let them marry whom they will, only so that it be to men of their own tribe, etc., lest the possession of the children of Israel be mingled from tribe to tribe. For all men shall marry wives of their own tribe and kindred. And all women shall take husbands of the same tribe, that the inheritance may remain among the sons and in the families, and that the tribes be not mingled one with another, but remain so as they were separated by the Lord. And the daughters of Salphaad did as was commanded. And Maala, and Thersa, and Hegla, and Melcha, and Noa were married to the sons of their uncle by their father, of the family of Manasseh, who was the son of Joseph, and the possession that had been allotted to them remained in the tribe and family of their father.

42 Concerning places (*loca*)[454]

42.1 That a church must not be founded by infidels

A synod: If someone has entered a *locus*, let a church be founded by the church, not by infidels or laymen.[455]

Concerning building a monastery

The synod of Agde: Let no one dare commence building or found a new monastery except with the bishop's approval or command.

42.2 Concerning someone building a church in the territory of another bishop

The synod of Orange: If a bishop or anyone else has built a church in the territory of another bishop, the consecration of this church should be reserved for the one in whose territory it has been built, and its governance shall be entrusted to the same; or let him be excommunicated otherwise.

Likewise: But if a secular person built a church and invited another bishop in lieu of the one in whose territory he has built it, that bishop, as well as all the other bishops who are received at a dedication of this sort, should be excommunicated.

42.3 Concerning land received from infidels [for founding] a church

A synod said: Should anyone who builds a church have received the land from infidels, let him summon the bishop and elders, and let it be confirmed to the bishop, and let the bishop confirm it as an offering to God and newcomers.

Concerning *loca* without [relics of] martyrs

The synod of Nicaea: It has been decided that altars established all about for the memory of martyrs, in fields and besides roads, in which no body or relic of martyr are shown to be kept, should be destroyed by the bishops in charge of these *loca*. But if many ordinary people object to this, let the members of the community nevertheless be warned not to visit these *loca*, to prevent the sensible ones from perchance being drawn in by superstition. And under no circumstances should any memory of martyrs be admitted as credible, unless there be a body, or other relics, or unless the tradition concerning the habitation or the passion of someone be related by a highly credible source.

42.4 Concerning the way of life of a newcomer[456] who receives a *locus*

The synod of Patrick says: If a newcomer enters the community, let him not baptise, nor offer, nor consecrate, nor build a church, until he has received permission from the bishop of that province, for this is the way of humility. And one who turns to infidels or laymen without having received the bishop's permission is a stranger.

The synod of Orléans: No *monachus*, being driven by ambition or vanity, shall presume to found a cell without the will of his abbot.

That a newcomer cannot build a *locus* of his own will

A synod: It has been decided that a newcomer should not build a *locus* without the permission of the monastery to which he is subject.

42.5 Concerning a newcomer who is not able to occupy his *locus*

A Hibernian synod said: It is agreed that a newcomer may receive a *locus* among the monasteries. But when he is not able to occupy the *locus* given to him, he shall return to the monastery from which he came. If he received it from infidels and has not been able to occupy it, let him receive its price from the heirs, but it cannot be sold to others. If he has buried the relics of saints in it, he can give it to other clerics, but only if they are *perfecti*.

42.6 Concerning someone giving a *locus* to another, if they separate, they shall separate in the following manner

A Hibernian synod: It is necessary that a *princeps* who does not commit himself or his property but who, however, will put himself at the service of the church, if he is dismissed or wishes to withdraw, shall leave behind half the offspring of the livestock[457] of the church and what was given him (i.e. in connection with his office) he shall leave behind intact, apart from what the expenses of the *locus* demanded of him. And what he brought with him, he shall take away with him. If he brought in a *dominatrix*[458] or servants, they shall belong to his part. But if he brought them in to serve the *locus*, they shall go out with the *locus*'s part. And all the offerings of others (i.e. not the *princeps* or church) shall be divided [equally] between the *princeps* and the church on separation. But if the *princeps* is a catholic *sacerdos* (i.e. ordained) all the works he performed and all the ornaments of the *locus* will belong to the *locus*. And he shall not return what he expended of the property of the *locus* in the course of his work, except for the greatest things and the things belonging exclusively [to the church], namely the special vessels of the church. But according to the judgement of others, he shall not return on separation what he spent in the first year [of office] when he was needy.[459]

Concerning those who hold a *locus* temporarily, how ought they be separated upon their departure

A synod: They who hold a *locus* temporarily, if they wish to depart, they ought to leave behind a fourth of the movables for the *locus* and they ought to retain the same proportion of the movables as their own share.

Likewise: It has been established in ancient times that he should have half the offspring of the livestock with him, and leave the other half to the *locus*. And what was given him (i.e. in connection with his office), he shall leave in the ownership of the *locus* in good condition and intact, apart from what the expenses of the *locus* demanded of him. And what he brought with him, he shall take away with him. If, however, he brought in a *dominatrix*[460] or servants, they shall belong to his part. But if he brought them in to serve the *locus*, they shall go out with the *locus*'s part. All the offerings of others (i.e. not the *princeps* or church) shall be divided [equally] between the kinsmen and the church on separation. All the fruits of his labour shall belong to the *locus*. And he shall not return what he expended of the property of the *locus* in the course of his work. Other judges nevertheless maintain that he shall not return on separation what he spent in the first year [of office] when he was needy.

42.7 Concerning those who decry the lives of their neighbours, and therefore change the *locus*

Gregory says: Often, when we complain about the lives of [our] neighbours, we seek to change to another *locus*, to choose the retreat of a more isolated life, ignoring the fact that if there is no spirit, the *locus* itself is not helpful. For Lot was a holy man in Sodom. But he sinned on the mountain, for the *loca* do not protect the mind. The parent of the human race himself testifies to this, for he fell in paradise: but all the earthly things we talk about are less perfect. For were the *locus* helpful, Satan would not have fallen from heaven. The psalmist, seeing temptations everywhere in this world, sought a *locus* to which to escape. But he was unable to find protection without God. For which reason he asked that he (i.e. God) become his fortified *locus*, wherefore he sought a *locus*, saying: Be unto me Lord God a protector and a defended place, that you may make me safe. Therefore the wicked have to be endured wherever they are, for Abel would not have been able to be just, were Cain not to exercise his malice. But there is one reason why the company of the wicked ought to be avoided: lest, if they are perhaps unable to be reformed, they shall draw others to imitate them.

42.8 That God must not be sought from *locus* to *locus*

Augustine: God must not be sought from *locus* to *locus*, for if you love what you loved, you are where you were; and if you do not love what you loved, you are not where you were.

Likewise: The kingdom of heaven is among you, and kingdoms of heaven have been founded throughout the world. How do you expect to come across the earth to him, who fills the earth? Have faith in the Lord God and stay in your *locus*. If you have been in the habit of leaving, you will never lack a reason to leave when necessary.

Isidore: God must not be sought by the step of the feet, but the step of good conduct.

43 Concerning consecrated places (*loca*)

43.1 Concerning the consecration of a *locus*

In the Apocalypse: Alleluia shall be sung throughout the city and its quarters and its squares, and afterwards it is said: No unclean person shall pass through it. The same is said of the tabernacle: Every stranger who might have entered, shall be put to death.

43.2 Concerning the appropriate boundary[461] around every holy *locus*

Every city of refuge has been set up with its precincts.[462]

The law: The following was spoken to Moses in the plains of Moab by the Jordan, facing Jericho: Command the children of Israel that they give to the Levites out of their possessions cities to dwell in, and their precincts round about; that they may abide in the towns, and the precincts may be for their livestock and beasts of burden. Which precincts shall reach from the walls of the cities outward, a thousand paces on every side. The number of these cities is forty-seven.

Likewise: Every city was given to the priests with its precincts for feeding the livestock of the priests.

Likewise: Ezekiel, when measuring a city, sometimes measured a thousand paces, sometimes two thousand paces to the east, etc.

Likewise: Solomon's temple had an enclosure around it in which whoever committed an evil act, perished.

Likewise: Moses's tabernacle had a court around it.

Likewise: Ezekiel saw an angel with a reed in his hand, to measure the city round about and its precincts on the outside.

Likewise, in the Apocalypse: An angel came to measure the city and its precincts.

Likewise, in Zechariah: When they returned from Babylon, they built the temple and its environs, etc.

43.3 That the boundary of a holy *locus* is designated and bounded by three *personae*

A synod: All the consecrated boundaries of holy *loca* ought to have signs around them, that they may be separated from the fields of the members of the community (*plebiles*).

A Hibernian synod: The boundary of a holy *locus* should have signs around it.

Whence a synod says: Wherever you have found the sign of Christ's cross, you shall not offend.

Likewise: Three *personae* consecrate the boundary of a holy *locus*: the king, the bishop, the people.

Concerning the boundary of holy *loca*

The Lord through Ezekiel: In them the firstfruits of the firstfruits of the land shall be a holy of holies, by the boundary of the *sacerdotes*[463] twenty-five miles in length and ten in width. And they shall not sell thereof, nor exchange, neither shall the firstfruits of the land be alienated.

Concerning the three inhabitants of the *loca*

That no one shall be released on the day of judgement, except Noah for the sake of married people, Job for the sake of penitents, Daniel for the sake of virgins. Only they are the inhabitants of the kingdom of heaven. Let a holy *locus* not exceed the length and width of the exterior court of the tabernacle and of Solomon's temple, which measures 100 cubits after the measure of a man's hand in length, fifty cubits [in width].

43.4 Concerning the number of boundaries of a holy *locus*[464]

The same synod: He placed four boundaries around the holy *locus*: the first, to which laymen and women enter, another, to which only clerics come. The first is called holy, the second more holy, the third most holy. Note that a name for the fourth is missing.[465]

A synod: There ought to be two or three boundaries around a holy *locus*. The first, to which we strictly forbid entry to anyone except holy men; for no laymen and women approach it, only clerics. The second, to the precincts of which we allow entry to crowds of rustic *plebes* that are not much given to wickedness. The third, to which we do not refuse entry to laymen, killers, adulterers, and harlots, by permission and custom. On account of which the first is called most holy, the second more holy, the third holy, proclaiming their dignity by being distinct. Note that a name for the fourth is missing.[466]

43.5 That a holy *locus* must not be touched by the wicked

The law: Therefore Moses told the words of the people to the Lord, who said: Go to the people, and sanctify them today and tomorrow, and let them be ready on the third day. For on the third day the Lord may come down in the sight of all the people upon Mount Sinai, and you shall appoint certain boundaries to the people round about, and you shall say: Take heed you go not up into the mount and that you touch not its borders. Everyone who touches the mount shall be put to death; he shall be stoned to death, or shall be pierced with javelins, whether it be beast or man, he shall not live.

And a little later the Lord said to him: Go down and charge the people, lest they should have a mind to pass the boundaries to see the Lord, and a very great multitude of them should perish. The priests also that come to the Lord, let them be sanctified, lest he strike them, etc.

In Numbers: When it was time to set out, the Levites shall take down the tabernacle. When a camp is laid out, they shall set it up. Any stranger who shall approach it shall die.

The mount in which the law was given, it is commanded that no soul or beast should touch it. And he established a boundary between him and Moses, and between Moses and Joshua, and between Joshua and the elders, and between the elders and the multitude of the people.

Likewise: There was a space between the tabernacle and the people of the tribe of Levi, and the family of the priests in the courts, and between the tabernacle and the holy of holies.

In Ezekiel: There will be a wall and a rampart.

Likewise: Remove the shoes from your feet, etc. This signifies that worldly people may not enter holy *loca*. A similar thing is also said to Joshua.

That a holy *locus* must not be touched by profane people

The law: And the children of Israel said to Moses: Behold we are consumed, we all shall perish. Must we all come to an end by annihilation?

The Lord said to Aaron: You and your sons shall minister in the tabernacle of[467] the testimony, and the Levites shall observe your commands, and all the works of the tabernacle, insofar as they do not come near the vessels of the sanctuary nor the altar, lest they die. A stranger shall not join himself with you. Keep watch in the charge of the sanctuary and in the ministry of the altar, lest indignation shall arise.

If a stranger shall come to it, he shall be cut down.

43.6 That a violation of the temple of God must incur a sevenfold punishment

Paul: If any man violate the temple of God, God shall destroy him.

Jerome: Whoever has sinned in holy *loca* is deserving of death, and whoever has violated pure things is deserving of penance.

Likewise, Jerome: Whoever has polluted holy *loca* shall pay double in compensation.

Jeremiah: You have polluted the Lord's temple; therefore I shall repay your evils upon you.

Augustine: Do not touch sacred things; not only their insides, but also their outsides.

43.7 Concerning the decree of the *Hibernenses* in relation to those who violate relics

A Hibernian synod: Whoever has violated the relics of bishops or martyrs by homicide, let him do penance for seven years in exile. But if by theft, three years.

But if he has defiled the *loca* of presbyters or martyrs by homicide, let him do penance for three and a half years in special servitude. But if a killer has slain someone within the bounds of a holy place where there is a tomb of a bishop, let him do penance for three and a half years. But if the same enclosure was not previously frequented by a wicked crowd,[468] and if someone has violated the boundaries of a *locus* of presbyters by homicide, let the killer do penance for a full year and a half, but with the boundary nevertheless remaining inviolate. For if it should be violated, they should be permitted to do penance for a year and fifty days.[469] For a *locus* is not to be called holy in which killers with their spoils, and thieves with their loot, and adulterers, and perjurers, and fortune-tellers, and druids, and harlots, are accustomed to enter. For every holy *locus* ought to be purified not only from within, but its boundaries [also ought to be purified]. Those which have been consecrated by saints, ought to be pure.

But if he has killed within the bounds of a holy *locus* in which laymen receive hospitality [let him do penance] for one year. But we remit the posterior period, fifty days, for a *locus* is not to be called holy, which killers with their spoils, thieves with their loot, adulterers, and perjurers, and fortune-tellers, and druids enter. And every holy *locus* ought to be purified not only from within, but its boundaries [also ought to be purified]. Those which have been consecrated by saints ought to be pure.

43.8 That the pollution of a holy *locus* is worse the more saints there are in it[470]

Patrick said: Whoever offends the deities, namely the martyrs, offends God. For the more martyrs are buried in that *locus*, the more he offends God.

43.9 Concerning worshipping holy *loca*, and their dignity

The synod of Vercelli: By how much devotion must holy *loca* be honoured? Indeed for the living they offer protection,[471] for the dead refuge, for the wicked defence, etc.

Jerome: Jerusalem, the holy city, was a nurse for the young, a helper of the old, a refuge for all.

43.10 Concerning the diversity of punishment in holy and wicked *loca*

Jerusalem was deserted for seventy years. But Babylon will be uninhabited forever.

43.11 That it is not a *locus* that edifies, but Christ

Jerome says in his letters concerning Leo and his *locus*: The nobility of *loca* is the spirits of saints. For Jerusalem was cursed so long as the Jebusites dwelt in it.

43.12 Concerning the consecrations of Jerusalem, through which, albeit different, every holy place should be consecrated

Jerusalem is consecrated, first, by the spirit of the prophets; second, by holy sacrifices cleansing the sins of men; third, by the promulgation of the divine law, as [it is said]: The law and the word of the Lord shall emanate from Jerusalem; fourth, by the erection of the temple in it; fifth, by the blood of Zechariah the priest.

Concerning the oblivion of the consecrations of holy *loca* because of the sins of their inhabitants

Jerome: Five consecrations were forgotten by the Jews, since there were no good people in it. For which reason Christ, seeing the city, wept for it, saying: Woe to thee, harlot city.

43.13 That they are consecrated once more, but only after punishment

Jerome: Jerusalem is consecrated by the Lord's passion and the blood of Stephen, the first martyr, and Jacob, the first bishop of Jerusalem.

That, also on a feastday, a holy *locus* does not defend offenders[472]

In the chronicles: But for such a multitude to repair to Jerusalem, it is said that it was on account of the feast of the unleavened bread. For this reason Jews from all nations poured into the city, as if they were freed from prison.[473] And it was fitting that they be killed in the same days of the Pasch, in which they crucified Christ the saviour.

43.14 That a holy *locus* does not edify the wicked

Jerome: If the *locus* itself were to edify, Satan would not have fallen from heaven, and Adam would not have been cast out of paradise.

Concerning a *locus* for congregating for legal cases, namely the forum

In the nineteenth book of the etymologies: A *forus* is a place for conducting litigations, so called from 'speaking' (*fando*).[474] This place is also called *prorostra*, because after ships of the Carthaginians were captured in the Punic war, their curved bows (*rostra*) were carried off and fixed at the end of the Roman forum as a sign of this victory. A *forus*, however, consists of a legal case, the law, and a judge. 'Legal case' (*causa*) is so called from the event (*casus*) which occurred. For it is the basis and origin of a legal charge,[475] when it has not yet been laid open by the examination of a debate; while it is dealt with it is a *causa*, when it is finished it is justice.

Concerning the division of *loca* among catholics

The synod of Sardica: And if the old catholics shall claim it as their own, and the others, who have recently been converted, as theirs, let the will of the majority of catholics be preferred to the minority. But if the parts [of the community] are divided equally, let it be entrusted to the bishops of greater age, etc.[476]

Concerning not transgressing the boundaries of the forefathers

In Deuteronomy: Do not take up and move your neighbour's boundaries, which those who came before have set upon your possession.

43.15 That, also on a feastday, a holy *locus* must not defend the wicked[477]

Jerome: After the Lord's passion the Jews, growing in wickedness, crowded together in that city at Easter; since the dignity of neither the *locus* nor the feastday protected them, they were destroyed by the Romans.

43.16 That spilled sacrosanct blood is dearer to God than a *locus*

Jerome said: Children were killed in Jerusalem, in Bethlehem, [and] in Rome, but punishment was given to Herod for the slaying of the children, and not on account of these *loca*.

Likewise: Jacob was slain in Jerusalem, but Jerome said: Punishment is about to descend on the Jews for his slaying, not on account of the *locus*.

Jerome: The punishment that was inflicted on Herod was pronounced perhaps, on account of the slain children, not on account of the holy *loca* in which they were slain.

Likewise: The punishment pronounced against the Jews, which was executed immediately, is reported to have come on account of the slaying of Jacob, not on account of the holy *locus* in which he was slain.

43.17 Concerning the proof that holy blood is dearer than a holy *locus*

A synod: The blood of martyrs consecrates the place, not the place the blood. If someone has said 'the church is mine', you say to him that in the Canticle one reads: My dove is one and my beloved is one. And you shall say to him: It is fitting for a son to be slain in the bosom of the one who mothered and reared him, but know that only the one who reared is polluted, and on account of this pollution she is consecrated; but the son is dead.

A synod: Bishop Obius says: No one can pollute the relics of those whose souls, filled with the vision of God, forget worldly things. And the souls of the saints cry beneath God's altar, saying: Avenge our blood, etc.

43.18 Concerning the word '*basilica*' and its division

A Hibernian synod: *Basilion* is Greek for Latin *rex*, and hence *basilica regalis*, the name deriving from the fact that in the earliest times only kings were buried in it. For other men were committed either to fire or to a heap of stones.

Likewise: No one shall have the liberty to divide the *basilica* without the permission of the *princeps*. And if he has dared to do this, let him make restitution according to the dignity of the same *locus*.

That one must not sacrifice to the holy founders of *loca*, but to God

Isidore: Our forefathers founded festivities for martyrs, either to incite imitation, or that we may be joined to their merits so that we help [each other] by prayers, in such a fashion that 'to none of the martyrs, but to God himself'; and so forth, as far as: 'Whoever shall lapse into this error, let him be punished'.[478]

In the Apocalypse, the Angel: Do not adore me, for I am your fellow servant; adore God.

In Daniel: Why do you adore me? Adore God, etc.

44 Of matters concerning women

44.1 Concerning the praise of virginity in both sexes

Jerome: Virginity is the beauty of the church, the jewel of piety, the head of sanctity, the flower of chastity, the commencement of life, the guardian of moderation, the patroness of innocence, the friend of justice, the eradicator of vices, the conqueror of desires. It is steadfast in abstinence, unwavering in its humility, sincere in charity, the fortifier of prayer, assiduous in vigils, resolute in fasts, the victory of life, the consort of angels; virginity follows the lamb wherever he has gone, it always stays in the sight of the creator. It is a thing loftier than all others, and the Lord does not dare command it, saying: Not all men understand this word, except for those to whom it has been granted by my father.

In this matter it is necessary to be careful, lest pride should snatch [us].

Concerning those who curse marriage

The synod of Agde: If someone despises marriage and detests a faithful or religious woman sleeping with her husband or deems her blameworthy, as though she cannot enter the kingdom of God, let him/her be anathema.

44.2 That it is necessary to beware of pride in continence

A synod: If any of those who preserve their virginity on account of the Lord is puffed up against those who are married, let him/her be anathema.

Likewise: Let each and every person who preserves their virginity do so on account of the Lord, not on account of detesting marriage. Whoever despises a faithful husband and a religious wife, or deems them blameworthy, let him/her be anathema.

44.3 Concerning false virgins and their behaviour

Jerome: One blushes to say it, for the wickedness of it [and] sadly, it is true. Some walk around with upright necks and playful feet, but others drink sterilising potions, and slay an unborn person. And some, when they sense they are pregnant, contemplate the potions of the offence of abortion, and they frequently also perish, and they are led to the underworld, guilty of three offences: of slaying themselves and Christ, and adultery, and murder of an unborn child.

44.4 Concerning women killing their unborn children

Jerome in his letters: Any woman soever who has performed this act of abomination is considered doubly guilty, both for her soul and for murdering her child. We therefore decree that she should do fourteen years penance.

Augustine said in the homilies: A woman who either destroys her foetus or her child has committed homicide.[479] A woman or man who consented to her in this sin, should do seven years of severe penance.

Likewise: Let no woman receive a potion, nor kill her children, either conceived or born. For any woman who does this should know that she will render her account with homicides before Christ's tribunal.

Likewise: Women ought not accept any diabolical potions, by means of which they are then unable to conceive. But any woman who has done this, however many times she ought to have conceived or given birth, she shall acknowledge that she is guilty of as many homicides.

44.5 Concerning penance for women killing their unborn children

The synod of Ancyra: Concerning women who fornicate and kill their offspring, or do things to drive out their unborn children in their womb, there is indeed an ancient decision to remove them from the church until their death. However, we rule more charitably, that a period of fourteen years be given to them, according to the established grades of penance.

44.6 Concerning the origin of widows

The first widow was Dina, Jacob's daughter; the second Noami; the third, to whom Elijah was sent in Sarepta of Sidon; the fourth, the Samaritan woman,[480] who used to receive Elisha and give him food; the fifth Esther;[481] the sixth Judith, who triumphed over Holofernes, king of the

Assyrians. And in the New Testament the first widow was Anna, who recognised the infant Lord.

44.7 Concerning true widows

Paul says: Let a widow be chosen of no less than sixty years of age, the wife of one husband. Note that if she had more husbands, she would not be a widow. Let a widow be chosen of sixty years of age.

Jerome: In this matter, every precept concerns those widows who are fed by the alms of the church. And an age qualification is prescribed for the following reason: that only they who are no longer able to work may receive the foods of the poor. At the same time consider that one who had a number of men, though she be old and decrepit and needy, is not eligible to receive the church's support. But if almsbread be withheld from her, how much more so that bread that descends from heaven; any unworthy person who has eaten it shall be guilty of violating the body and blood of Christ.

Concerning a widow's status

Likewise: According to the same, a widow is chosen if she is proven in her good works, if she brought up children, if she gave hospitality, if she washed the feet of saints, etc.

Likewise: In holy dress, in temperament, in her walk; no criminal offenders, no garrulous women, not women given to much wine.

A synod: Widows of the sort that are sustained by a stipend from the church ought to be so persistent in God's work, that they help the church by their prayers and merits.

44.8 That the church ought to sustain its infirm widows

A synod says: Young widows, who are infirm in the body, should be sustained at the expense of the church whose widows they are.[482]

44.9 Concerning young widows

Paul: Young widows should either choose to marry whom they want, though only in the Lord, or dedicate themselves [to the church] and withdraw from men.

Concerning the separation of widows and clerics

Jerome said: Clerics should be careful not to be near the houses of widows; and widows should be careful to keep out of the clerics' sight. For a gaze is polluted by a gaze.

That an accomplice has only a little less blame than the defiler himself

The synod of Ancyra: A certain man having a fiancée defiled her sister and left her pregnant. Afterwards he married his fiancée. But the one who was defiled hanged herself. Those who were aware of the affair have been ordered to be received after making satisfaction for ten years, according to the established grades of penance.

44.10 Concerning the word 'veiled' (*palliatae*)[483]

A Hibernian synod: A veil (*pallium*) is so called from 'paleness' (*palliditas*), whence also 'veiled' is derived; and the goddess Pallas, who is also called Minerva, whose temple is pale, whose priestesses were veiled (*palliatae*) virgins, that is to say, veiled (*uelatae*). Whence it is transferred in the New Testament to *palliatae*, which is to say 'veiled women'.

44.11 Concerning the age in which young girls ought to wear a veil

A synod: Nuns, though their way of life and behaviour be worthy, should not be veiled before their twelfth year.

44.12 Concerning the two kinds of veiled women

Augustine in the book concerning the synclitic virgin: There are two kinds of veiled women: the first are the virgins who imitate Mary by their physical appearance and dress; the second are the penitents imitating Anna.[484]

They ought to live under the rule of a pastor until their death. Wherever they are, there is a church. The first kind represents the bishops, and the second grade corresponds to the presbyters, namely, the elders.

Jerome: Just as there are two kinds of men, holy men and penitents, so also of women, virgins and penitents.

44.13 Concerning the honour of veiled religious women

A Roman synod: The *palliatae*, namely the veiled, should be held in great honour. They overcome their sex, namely their fragility, and they renounce the affairs of the world.

44.14 Concerning the manner in which the two kinds of veiled women should live

The *Romani* say: Just as they have accepted the fragility of their sex, it is proper that women always live under a strict pastoral hand. Virgins wearing the dress of virginity should be separated from the sight of all men, and thus they should live until death. But penitents should be subject to obedience. And the more they know their own fragility, the more cautious they ought to become.

44.15 Concerning wicked women penitents

Jerome: There are certain[485] female penitents who want to live as depraved, garrulous, vagabond, gossiping, worthless women, who have nothing of value to offer to others.

44.16 Concerning the manner of life of young women

The synod of Arles: Young women, live thus: be mindful of nothing except your house and your parents. And when you parted from your parents, live a cloistered life under the rule of a presbyter until death.

44.17 That it does not harm the nuns to be oppressed by force

Jerome: The body of holy women is not blemished by force, but by will.

Likewise: Thus, when the purity and sanctity of the mind endure, the sanctity of the body, though defiled, is not lost even if the body is oppressed. By the same token, the sanctity of the body is lost when the purity of the soul is violated, even though the body is untouched.

44.18 That women do not teach men

Paul to Timothy: I do not allow women to teach.

Jerome: Some—how shameful!—learn from women that they should teach men.

44.19 Concerning women being silent in church

Paul to the Corinthians: May your women keep silence in the churches. For they are not allowed to speak, but to be subject, as the law says. But if they want to learn anything, let them ask their husbands at home. For it is a shame for a woman to be allowed to speak in church.

44.20 That wives and women do not receive any male or sacerdotal office

Isidore: Women are not permitted to speak or teach in church, nor[486] anoint or offer, nor claim for themselves a portion of any male function or sacerdotal office.

45 Concerning the law of matrimony[487]

45.1 Concerning the praise of matrimony

Jerome said: Unless matrimony had existed, virginity would not have existed; the earth is populated by matrimony, but heaven by virginity.

45.2 Concerning the sort of wife that must be had in matrimony

Augustine: Such ought the wife to be, that must be had according to the law, to wit: if she is a chaste virgin, if she has been betrothed while still a virgin, if she is provided with a dowry, namely by thirty shekels of silver, and lawfully given away by her kin, she must be accepted both by her bridegroom and his bridesmen. And thus according to the law and the Gospel she must be taken honourably in matrimony at a public wedding, and she must never be separated from her husband, unless she devote herself to God with his consent, and except because of fornication. For if she has fornicated, she must be left, but so long as she is alive, another wife must not be taken, for adulterers shall not obtain the kingdom of God.[488] And her penance must be accepted, but they must both be chaste for as long as she lives.[489]

45.3 Concerning the three lawful marriages

Jerome: One reads that there are three lawful marriages in scripture. The first marriage is of a virgin, chaste and betrothed while still a virgin, lawfully given with a dowry to a husband. The second is of a young girl apprehended by a man in a city and joined to him by force; if her father should wish it, that man shall provide her with a bride-price of fifty shekels given to her father, or as much as the father has decided, and the man shall give the price of her chastity. But if she had a fiancé before she was apprehended, she shall be given to him if the father and the daughter wish it. The third marriage: if the father of the aforesaid apprehended daughter should not wish it, she shall not be joined to the man who defiled her, but to him, whom the father, who shall give her a dowry, has chosen, and she shall be lawfully his. But the first marriage is preferable to these latter two.

45.4 Concerning the fourth known type of marriage

Jerome: Yet another, fourth lawful marriage is added: when a man's wife has died, he may take another, provided that she is not a widow, nor divorced, nor betrothed, but a young girl. The same applies to a woman.

On account of which Paul says: A woman who is under the power of a man, is lawfully bound by her husband's law while her husband lives.

Therefore she shall be regarded as an adulteress if she has been joined to another man while her husband lives. But if her husband died, she is free from the husband's law, so that she is not an adulteress even though she has been with another man.

45.5 Concerning the fifth [type of] marriage

Jerome: A fifth is added: if a man or woman has taken up the religious life by mutual consent, the other may take a new spouse, but only a young woman or a young man.

Concerning those who take wives after penance, if they join themselves to concubines

Augustine said: It is decreed that if in adolescence—because of pressure of fear, or the danger of captivity—he has done penance and afterwards, fearing the consequences of slipping back into youthful incontinence, he has chosen to unite with a wife, lest he be guilty of fornication, he should be deemed to have committed a venial sin, so long as he shall not know another apart from his spouse. We do not fix this as a rule, but only lay down what is more tolerable. For according to true knowledge, nothing befits a penitent more than persisting in both mental and bodily chastity.

Concerning *monachi* who undertake military service or take wives

Augustine: One cannot abandon the vocation of a *monachus* once it has been taken up by one's free will or desire without incurring sin. For he ought to render what he vowed to God. Therefore whoever resumed his military service or his marriage, forsaking his avowal of a solitary life, must be purged by the satisfaction of public penance, for even if his military service be innocent and the marriage respectable, it is an offence to turn one's back to the choice of better things.

Concerning the marriage of young women who were once in the religious vocation but were not consecrated[490]

Young women who enter the life and the vocation of virginity of their own free will without being forced by their kinsmen, if afterwards they have chosen to wed, they commit a sin, even if consecration has not yet taken place, the granting of which they would surely not have been deprived if they persisted in their vocation.

Concerning consecrated women who marry

It cannot be doubted that a great offence is committed, both where one's vocation is forsaken and the consecration violated. For if even things made by humans cannot be trampled on with impunity, what will be of them who shatter the terms of such a sacrament?[491]

Likewise, the *Romani*: If anyone gives his daughter to a husband, he shall receive a lawful dowry, i.e. thirty shekels. But if she loses him through death and she wishes to marry another, the sons should receive the dowry. If she has none, it is prescribed that it be given to her father.

Likewise: If a father has willingly joined his daughter in marriage of rightful law, and [the groom] dares have a slave girl as concubine beside her, let him be ousted from the church of God and the table of every Christian, unless he be called back to penance.

If anyone who is of independent legal standing wants to marry his slave woman, if he wishes to sell her afterwards, it shall not be permitted. But if he wishes to sell her nevertheless, we command that he be damned, and we place the slave woman under the power of a *sacerdos*.

Concerning a harlot wife

Adomnán explained that she will be a harlot who has broken[492] the yoke of her own husband, and is joined to a second husband or a third. Her husband shall not take another wife while she lives. For we do not know whether that verdict which we read in Questions to the Romans was attested by acceptable or false witnesses.[493]

45.6 That adultery must also be guarded against in lawful marriages

Jerome: In a lawful marriage adultery is to be guarded against: [marriage] is not so much about what desire covets but only about what a modest nature and posterity require.

Likewise: He may not have another wife besides his own. For if he should have one, the one who was lawful will no longer be lawful.

Paul said: Every sin that a man committed is outside the body. But he who committed fornication, sins against his own body. This is to say: he casts a blemish on his wife, so that she is not lawful to him, but an adulteress.

For a married man who has committed any sin soever does not blemish his wife if she does not consent to it. But if he fornicates with other women, he blemishes his own wife if he does not curb his lust in marriage. For one must not be a servant unto lust, but posterity. Otherwise: Every sin, etc.

Pelagius said: Every sin can be committed by a single partner, who can be called a limb but not the entire body. But in fornication two perish.

45·7 Concerning dissolving a marriage without blame

It is asked whether there are circumstances in which a wife may unite with another man, while the former [husband] is alive. Concerning this matter, there are three such circumstances. The first, coercive force, does not break the marriage.[494] The second, if there happens to be a need to depart to another, as Sarah did, lest Abraham be slain by the wicked king. Or as it has been done in the New Testament. Augustine says this: When a certain rich man exacted a payment in gold from another man, and the latter did not have the means to repay him, the rich young man told the other man's wife that if she gave herself to him, the debt will be repaid. And she, knowing she had no power over her own body, consulted her husband, who, giving thanks, gave her permission, saying that there is not adultery where there is no lust. The third, if she is sterile, as one reads in Genesis of Abraham and Jacob marrying their slave-women.

That an adulteress[495] should not return to her former husband

In Deuteronomy: If a man take a wife, and have her, and she find not favour in his eyes because of some uncleanness, let him write a bill of divorce, and shall put it in her hand, and send her out of his house. And when she is departed, and marries another husband, and he also hates her, and has given her a bill of divorce, and has sent her out of his house or if he is dead, the former husband cannot take her again to wife because she is defiled and has become abominable before the Lord.

Concerning virgins taken by force or seduced

In Exodus: If a man seduce a virgin not yet espoused, and lie with her, he shall endow her and marry her. If the virgin's father will not give her to him, he shall repay according to the bride-price, which virgins are wont to receive.

In Deuteronomy: If a man espoused a young woman who is a virgin, and someone find her in the city and lie with her, you shall bring them both out to the gate of that city, and they shall be stoned: the young woman because she did not cry out when she was in the city, the man because he humiliated his kinsman's wife.

Likewise: [But] if, in a field, a man find a young woman who is betrothed, and taking hold of her, lie with her, he alone shall die. The young woman shall suffer nothing.

Likewise, in Deuteronomy: If a man find a young woman who is a virgin, who is not espoused, and taking her, lie with her, and the matter come to judgement, he who lay with her shall give fifty shekels of silver, and shall marry her, because he has humiliated her, and he may not put her away all the days of his life.

45.8 Concerning a divorced woman

Moses says: 'If your wife shall not find favour in your eyes, write her a bill of divorce'. He did not instruct that she be put away outright, but that a bill of divorce be given her, for the Lord said in the Gospel that a woman may never be separated from her husband, except on account of fornication.

45.9 Concerning the causes that the bill of divorce specifies

Augustine: These are the causes for divorce that the bill of divorce specifies concerning the wife, to wit: if she is a drunk, if she is irascible, or immoderate, or quarrelsome, or a glutton, or slanderous, or if she is found not to be a virgin. But if these shall be false, the husband shall give his wife a hundred pounds of silver.

45.10 That she must not be divorced for these reasons

Isidore says: Well then, if she is barren, or deformed, or of advanced age, or smelly, or a drunk, or irascible, or [given to] wicked deeds, or immoderate, or a glutton, or quarrelsome, or slanderous, should she be kept or sent away? Whether you like it or not, she must be kept just as she was received.

45.11 Concerning the periods in which a married couple ought to be continent

In the law: The Lord spoke to Moses, saying: Speak to the children of Israel, and say to them: If a woman having received seed shall give birth to a boy, she shall be unclean seven days, as in the days of her menstruation. And on the eighth day the infant shall be circumcised. But she shall remain in the blood of her purification thirty-three days. She shall touch no holy thing, neither shall she enter into the sanctuary until the days of her purification be fulfilled. But if she shall give birth to a girl, she shall be unclean two weeks, as in her menstruation, and she shall remain in the blood of her purification forty-seven days. Afterwards she shall bring an immaculate lamb for her sin.

Likewise: In the three forty-day periods of the year they are separated in respect to the bed, and on Sundays, and on the fourth and sixth days of the week, and on all feastdays married couples ought to be continent. And in those days in which the wife is pregnant, namely from the time that the child moves in the womb and until birth, they ought not have intercourse.

A Hibernian synod: In the three forty-day periods of the year, and on Sunday, and on the fourth and sixth day of the week, married couples ought to be continent.

Likewise: On all feastdays, and in those days in which the wife is pregnant, namely from the time that the child moves in her womb and until its birth [they ought to be continent].

Likewise: For thirty-six days from birth if it is a boy, but if it is a girl, forty-six days.[496]

Likewise: Those living the religious life are not permitted to have intercourse.

45.12 Concerning men and women who must not be admitted into marriage

Augustine: Wives, do not have husbands whose previous wives are alive. For these marriages are adulterous. Nor are you permitted to take that woman, who has departed from her husband by divorce, while her husband is alive.

45.13 That second marriages must not be banned for fear of adultery

Augustine: The apostle prescribed second marriages because of incontinence, saying: It is better for a man to marry than to fornicate with many women to satisfy his lust. More often, to be sure, licence to marry is not [sought for the sake] of devotion but lewdness.

Jeremiah: At last I asked him and said: Lord, if a wife or husband should pass away, and one of them should remarry after the death of the other, will the one marrying be sinning or not by doing this? And he said: They[497] do not sin against me, but if they have been continent and remained in that state, they shall obtain great glory with God, but if they remarry, they do not sin.

45.14 That a wife must not be taken while the former is alive, even though she be an adulteress

The synod of Arles: It is decided that faithful young men who apprehend their wives in adultery should not take others as long as their wives are alive, even though they are adulteresses. This rule is observed lest, at any time, he deny the opportunity of penance to a penitent woman, and lest he pollute himself by many unions.[498]

45.15 Concerning not concealing a woman's adultery, and receiving her penance, and avoiding taking another wife

Hermas says to the pastor angel: Allow me, Lord, to ask you a few things. 'Speak', he said. If someone, Lord, should have a wife who was faithful at home, and later he caught her committing adultery, I ask whether he sin if he should live with her? And he said to me: So long as he is not aware of her wrongdoing, he shall not sin, but if he be aware of her sin and the wife should not do penance for her wrongdoing, but persist publicly in her wickedness, the man shall commit an offence if he continues to live with her, and be the accomplice of her conscience. What, I ask, shall a husband do if his wife remains in the same vice? He said to me: He should put her away and himself remain continent. But if after she has been put away he has taken another wife, he too shall be guilty of adultery. But my Lord, I say, if after the wife has been put away, she should do penance and want to return to her husband, should she be received by him or not? And he said to me: If she has not been received, her husband sins, and commits a great offence against himself. For each person who does penance for his sins receives pardon. Because one pardon for penance is granted to the Lord's servants. Thus far Hermas.

Therefore, after divorcing his wife, a husband ought not take another, lest he deprive his wife of her chance of penance. The same is true for both a man and a woman.

Patrick: If a man's wife has fornicated with another man, let him not take another wife for as long as the former lives. If perchance she has repented and should do penance, let him take her back and let her serve him as a slave for as long as she lives. And let her do penance for an entire year on bread and water, and let them not share the same bed.

Likewise, Innocent says: One is allowed to put away his wife only on account of fornication; but while she lives, he may not take another.

45.16 Concerning the chastity of the betrothed before the wedding

Augustine: Anyone who wishes to take a wife, just as he desires to find her a virgin, so should he guard his virginity up until the wedding. For to be polluted before the wedding is such a grave sin that when the wedding has arrived, he is not deemed worthy to receive a blessing together with his betrothed, and the following example is fulfilled in him: 'He refused a blessing, and it shall be withdrawn from him'.

Since a man (*uir*) takes his name from valour (*uirtus*) and a woman (*mulier*) from weakness (*mollitia*), namely fragility, how can anyone expect his wife to be victorious over lust, the cruellest of beasts, when he himself succumbs to the first blow of lust? For whatever women are not permitted to do against the catholic faith, men are entirely forbidden to do.

Concerning the ways in which husbands and wives are chosen

In the books of etymologies: In choosing a husband, four things are generally sought: valour, lineage, good looks, intelligence. Of these, intelligence is the more potent in arousing love.

Likewise: In choosing a wife four things impel a man to love: beauty, lineage, wealth, [good] character. It is better, however, to seek good character in her than beauty. But nowadays they seek women who are commended either by their wealth or beauty, not uprightness of character.

45.17 Concerning not having concubines before marriage

Augustine: How does it come about that many men are not ashamed to have concubines before marriage, whom they send away after a number of years, and thereafter take lawful wives; whence I testify and declare before the Lord and his angels that God has always prohibited that sort of union, and he never approved of it, and especially in Christian times it has never been permitted to have concubines, nor is it permitted, nor shall it ever be permitted.

45.18 Concerning not having concubines together with a lawful wife[499]

Jerome: No one seeks a number of women, except in order to satisfy a superfluous desire.

Likewise: Whoever desires a number of women, mixes what is permissible with what is illicit. For the apostle says: He who is joined to a harlot is made one body.

45.19 That a freeborn woman ought to be joined to a freeborn man after his concubine has been forsaken

The synod of Narbonne:[500] Cast the slave woman out of bed, and take a woman of undisputed free-status; this is not a second marriage, but an increase of respectability.

The same synod: If young women have married men with concubines, having been joined to the men by the wish of their fathers, they are blameless provided that the women, whom the men have, are not in a state of wedlock; for a wife is one thing, and a concubine another.

The same synod on the matter of a presbyter or deacon who has given his virgin daughter away to a man who already has a woman joined to him, by whom he also had children: Not every woman who is joined to a man is a wife, for not every son is an heir to the father. However, marriage agreements between the freeborn are lawful, and likewise between equals. This very same principle was instituted by the Lord before Roman law existed. Therefore a wife is one thing, and a concubine another, just as a free woman is one thing, and a slave woman another. For which reason, the apostle also gave testimony in order to demonstrate the distinction between these persons. In Genesis, Abraham: Cast out this slave woman and her son, for the son of the slave woman shall not be heir with my son Isaac. Whence also the marriage partnership was founded from the outset in such a way that, over and above a sexual union, it would also have in it the sacrament of Christ and his church. There is no doubt that a woman with respect to whom it is shown that the ministry of marriage was not performed is not married. And a little later on: Therefore, if a cleric of any place soever has given his daughter in matrimony to a man who has a concubine, she must not be accepted as though he has given her in marriage, lest perhaps that woman turns out to be freeborn and lawfully endowed and respectfully taken at a public marriage ceremony. The Roman rule, which forbids a marriage if it was corrupted in advance, did not permit this practice, which has been established from the beginning of time.[501]

45.20 That a wife ought to do penance if her husband does penance

Origen: Let women learn to follow their husbands from the examples of the patriarchs, for it is not without reason that it is written that Sarah outlived Abraham,[502] but in order to show that if a man precedes his wife to the Lord, his wife ought to follow him; for, if she sees that her husband stands by God, I say the wife ought to follow him in that.

45.21 That coercive force does not harm virginity in the New Testament

Jerome in the commentary on Matthew: In the Gospel, he said, the intention is sought, which, even if it has no effect, it nevertheless does not go unrewarded. Although the law[503] does not punish the intention, it punishes the outcome, lest you commit adultery. Suppose that a maiden becomes a prostitute during persecution. According to the Gospel, because the maiden did not sin intentionally, she is admitted [as a wife]; in the law, because she has been corrupted, she is rejected.

45.22 Concerning returning a debt between a husband and wife

Paul: It is good for a man not to touch a woman; for the sake of continence let every man have his own wife, and let every woman have her own husband.

Paul: Let the husband render the debt to his wife, and the wife also in like manner should render the debt to the husband.

The same, likewise: Do not be mutually defrauded, except, perhaps, by consent, at a particular point in time, that you may give yourselves to prayer; and get together again, lest Satan tempt you with your incontinency.

Likewise, Paul: A woman does not have power over her own body, but her husband does.

45.23 Concerning a woman and, moreover, a man not having power over their own body

Paul: A woman does not have power over her own body, but her husband does. In like manner, a man does not have power over his own body, but his wife does.

45.24 That a wife ought to be subjected to her husband

Augustine: A man (*uir*) takes his name from valour (*uirtus*), namely from war, struggle, defence, primacy, being the first to speak; a woman (*mulier*) from weakness (*mollitia*), namely fragility, infirmity, humility, subjection.

45.25 Concerning a wife being subjected to her husband

Paul: Let women be subject to their husbands, as to the Lord.

45.26 Concerning the names of spouses

Augustine: A man (*uir*) takes his name from valour (*uirtus*), namely from war, struggle, defence, primacy, being the first to speak; but a woman (*mulier*) from weakness (*mollitia*), namely fragility, infirmity, humility, subjection.

45.27 Concerning a wife being cast out for adultery

Isaiah: Our bed has narrowed, so that one must fall out, and a short covering cannot cover both.

Likewise: Shall I not be angry over these things? For you have uncovered yourself near me, and have received adultery.

45.28 Concerning no one leaving his wife, except for fornication, and on a fool retaining an adulteress

The Lord says in the Gospel: I say to you: whosoever shall put away his wife, except for fornication, commits adultery.

Jerome: Because she has divided one flesh into two and has been separated from her husband for fornication, she ought not be retained, nor shall the man be under that malediction, because the scripture says: The one who retains an adulteress is foolish and impious.

Therefore, where there is fornication or suspicion of fornication, the wife is put away without hindrance.

45.29 That a harlot does not have a husband of her own

Christ in John: Call your husband. The woman answered: I have no husband. Jesus says: You are right; for you had five husbands, and he whom you now have is not your husband.

Jerome: Where there was a number of husbands, there the one man who is her own ceases to be.

45.30 That a wife must not be cast out upon baptism

A Roman synod says: A man who married a virgin as his first wife before he was baptised may not have another after baptism, while the first lives. Offences are dissolved in baptism, not lawful marriage.

Concerning the guilt of an adulterer

The law: If any man has been an adulterer to [his own] wife and committed adultery with his neighbour's wife, let them be put to death, both the adulterer and the adulteress.

45.31 Concerning children begotten of adulterous wives with living husbands

Ezekiel: Cast out your fornicating mother and the children of fornication.

Augustine: An adulteress wife must be cast out together with the fruit of adultery, lest the blessed offspring be contaminated. Note that Abraham separated himself from Lot with his seed, because he had foreknowledge that Lot's seed would be cursed, and note that Hagar was cast out with her son, lest he be together with the blessed seed.

I heard the Lord say to Abraham: Cast out Hagar together with her son, for the son of a slave woman shall not be heir together with the son of a free woman.

Concerning children who are begotten despite men[504]

A Hibernian synod: If someone corrupts the lawful wife of another, and plants his seed, and the woman should fall pregnant, that child shall belong to the body from which it was born, but he shall nevertheless pay for the upkeep of the child and of his education, to the sum that judges have adjudicated. But if he has planted his seed by adultery, the corrupter shall render nothing, nor shall the adulterer give anything to the adulteress, except, perhaps, for the price of education, after the child has been acknowledged.[505]

45.32 Concerning excommunicating every adulterer

A Hibernian synod: Every adulterer must be excluded from celebrating together, from sharing a table, from cohabitation, from blessing, from absolution,[506] from socialising, until he does penance.

45.33 Concerning receiving an adulteress after penance and on the measure of penance

A synod: We rule that a woman joined to another man through adultery should be excommunicated until she complete her penance, and after penance let her be reconciled with her husband.

Patrick: If a man's wife has fornicated with another man, he shall not take another wife for as long as the former lives. If perchance she might repent and do penance, he shall take her back and let her serve him as a slave for as long as she lives. And let her do penance for an entire year on an allowance of bread and water, and let them not share the same bed.

But in another synod: She shall do penance for seven years, three of them strict, and four relaxed. These rulings must also be understood to apply to the man if he has committed adultery.

45.34 Concerning the chastity of a penitent spouse

Augustine: Her penance must be accepted, but through chastity of life to both of them, for as long as she should live.

Patrick: Let her do penance for an entire year on bread and water.

But in another synod: Seven years, of which three are strict, four relaxed. Similarly if a woman has been sent away by her husband.

45.35 That a bridegroom whose fiancée is chaste does not go to war

The law: What man is he, who espoused a wife, and has not yet taken her? Let him go and return to his house, lest he die in war and another man take her.

45.36 That a brother does not climb into the bed of his dead brother

The synod of Arles said: Let the surviving brother not climb into the bed of his dead brother; for if he has done this, let him be excommunicated.

The *Romani*: Let the surviving brother not climb into the bed of his dead brother, for the Lord said: They shall be two in one flesh. Therefore your brother's wife is your sister.

That a woman may not marry two brothers

A Neocaesarean synod: If a woman marries two brothers, let her be excluded until death, but on her deathbed, for mercy's sake, if she promises that made healthy she would dissolve the bonds of this union, let her do penance. But if a woman or man shall have died in such marriages, the penance shall be strict for the remaining one.[507]

Likewise: A woman who is joined to two brothers must be excommunicated, unless she does penance.

Jerome said: A woman should not climb into the bed of two brothers; for if she has done this, she has committed adultery.

45.37 Concerning betrothed young women who are also corrupted by others

A synod: It is proper that betrothed young women who have been corrupted by others be removed from them and given to those to whom they have previously been betrothed.

Concerning a husband who casts out his wife

Ursianus says: Get away from me woman, so long as the little flame is burning, take the chaff away.

That a man ought not cast out his wife

The Lord in Genesis: They shall be two in one flesh. Therefore what God has joined, man does not separate.

The apostle: You have been bound to a wife; seek not to be loosed.

Moses: Let him give her a bill of divorce. Note that Moses does not command but advises, because of the hardness of the people.

That in the law one reads of having two wives

In Exodus: If a man have two wives, one beloved, and the other hated, and they have had children by him, etc.

45.38 Concerning wives coming under suspicion [for adultery]

The law says: When a wife shall have gone astray, and slept with another man in contempt of her husband, and her husband fails to discover it, but the woman keep the adultery secret, and the woman cannot be accused by witnesses, because she was not caught in the act, if the spirit of jealousy stir up the husband against his wife, who either is defiled or is charged on false suspicion, he shall bring her to the priest, and shall offer an oblation for her, the tenth part of a measure of barley meal, he shall not pour oil thereon, nor put frankincense upon it, because it is a sacrifice of jealousy, and an oblation searching out adultery. The priest therefore shall offer it, and set it before the Lord. And he shall take holy water in an earthen vessel, and he shall cast a little earth of the pavement of the tabernacle, the tenth part, into it. And when the woman shall stand before the Lord, she shall uncover her head, and shall put on his hands the sacrifice of remembrance and the oblation of jealousy. And he himself shall hold the most bitter waters, whereon he has heaped curses with execration. And the priest shall adjure her, saying: If another man has not slept with you, and if you be not defiled in forsaking your husband's bed, these most bitter waters, in which I have heaped curses, shall not hurt you. But if you have gone aside from your husband, and are defiled, and have slept with another man, you shall be subject to these curses. May the Lord put a curse upon you as an example for all among your people; may he make your thigh rot, and may your belly swell and burst asunder. Let the cursed waters enter into your belly, and may your thigh rot as your womb swells. And the woman shall answer: Amen. And the priest shall write these curses in a notebook, and shall wash them out with the most bitter waters, upon which he has heaped the curses, and the priest shall give her the waters to drink. And when she has drunk them up, the priest shall take from her hand the sacrifice of jealousy, and shall elevate it before God, and shall put it upon the altar, yet so as first to take a handful of the sacrifice of that which is offered, and burn it upon the altar, and so give the most bitter waters to the woman. And when she has drunk them, if she be defiled, and having despised her husband be guilty of adultery, the waters of malediction shall go through her, and her belly swelling, her thigh shall rot, and the woman shall be cursed, and she shall be an example to all the people. But if she be not defiled, she shall not be hurt, and shall bear children. This is the law of jealousy.[508]

45.39 That a wife cannot accuse her husband of uncertain adultery

A Roman synod: A wife cannot accuse her husband of adultery, and hidden sins go unpunished; but a man can constantly charge her with adultery before the *sacerdos*.

The same synod said: An offence having been secretly committed, a man[509] is not easily separated [from the community] on suspicion [alone]; should his shameful deed be uncovered, he shall certainly be banished.

Matthew: Judge not, that you may not be judged.

We should [not] pass judgement quickly where there is doubt, but reserve the final decision to God, so that when the time of judgement will arrive, he will not cast out anyone by suspicion of an offence from the company of saints, but the obvious criminal.

46 Concerning penance

Concerning the word 'penance'

In the books of etymologies: Penance is like punishment (*punitentia*), because a man does penance within himself to punish (*punire*) the evil that he has let in.

46.1 Concerning the praise of penance

Augustine said: Just as water extinguishes fire, so penance washes away offences by fountains of tears, and just as in the shadows there is no light without a torch, so a sin cannot be absolved without penance. For that which the sin shuts, penance shall open. Whoever fears the Lord, is illuminated by penance. O penance, you remit sins with the help of God's mercy, you unlock paradise, you enliven a weary man and cheer a depressed man, you salvage from ruin, you restore integrity, you recover honour, you rebuild trust, you pour overflowing grace. O penance, I will say what I know of you. You release all things that are bound, you alleviate all misfortunes, you elucidate all things that are confused, you restore all abandoned things. O penance, more glittering than gold, more gleaming than the sun, sin never defeats it, penance repels the sin of avarice, it dreads excess, flees rage, strengthens love, crushes pride, checks the tongue, it cultivates good character, it hates malice, it keeps out envy.

46.2 Concerning the confession of sins

Augustine: Confess to the Lord, for he is good, for his mercy is eternal. We learn with the Holy Spirit teaching, said Augustine, that we are not entitled to the cures prepared for purging offences, unless we have confessed our offences, as God commands. What does a sinner keep secret that he has done in the sight of God? What is he ashamed to confess, who did not shy away from being contaminated by sins? And so, by confessing, he dissolves what he had done by sinning; by making amends he cleanses what he had tarnished by the filth of wrongdoing. Let the one who was too indifferent before the offence be more cautious after; let the one who used to follow the Devil with wicked deeds, follow Christ with good deeds. God does not want to punish the wickedness of a man who resolves to confess his offences.

Jacob: Confess your sins one to another, for the confession of a sin and the magnificence of penance are His work.

Gregory: The quantity of punishment shall correspond to the measure of sin, for just as the physician cannot work a cure unless he has examined the patient with his hands and eyes, so a wise man cannot heal the offences of sinners without confession. Confession from the heart is accepted for justification, confession by the mouth makes for salvation. One who conceals his offences shall not be set right. One who has confessed and forsaken them obtains mercy.

That the penance of a wicked man holds back punishment in his lifetime

In the books of Kings one finds [the following]: Therefore, when Ahab had heard these words, he tore his garments, and covered his flesh with haircloth, and fasted and slept in sackcloth, and walked with his head cast down. And the word of the Lord came to Elijah the Thesbite, saying: Have you not seen Ahab humbled before me? Therefore, because he has humbled himself for my sake, I will not bring the evil in his days, but in his son's days I will bring the evil upon his house.

46.3 Concerning accepting the penance of sinners

Jerome to Damasus, bishop of Rome: The untimely old lady in the Gospel, who confessed that she was no better than a dog, at last deserved to be heard, with the door shut to her fellow slaves. At midnight a friend received bread from a friend. God, whom no one can overcome by force, is won over by the prayers of the publican. The city of Nineveh, which was ravaged by sin, was left standing through tears. Christ brought the thief from the cross to paradise. Christ, I say, gladly embraces the returning prodigal son. After ninety-nine animals were left, the shepherd rejoices more when a single little sheep that had remained [lost] has been found. Paul was made from a persecutor into a vessel of election; he suffers blindness to his carnal eyes, that he may see better with his mind, that he who used to lead the shackled servants of Christ to the council of the Jews, should later take pride in bearing chains of his own.

That remission is granted only for correction

In the Gospel: And after the pieces of silver were scattered in the temple, he went out and, departing, he hanged himself.

Jerome: It was of no use to do penance for an offence that he cannot correct. If a brother sinned against his brother in such a way that it is still possible for him to make amends for his sin, it may be remitted to him. But should the effects remain, penitence is treated as a vain utterance.

Concerning penance for drunken clerics

The synod of Agde: Before all things, clerics must avoid drunkenness, for it is the tinder and fermenter of all vices. Therefore he whom it has been agreed was drunk suffers according to his [clerical] rank: we decree that he must either be banished from communion for a period of thirty days, or subjected to corporeal punishment.

Concerning the penance of those who resume their wicked ways

The synod of Arles: They who resume their wicked ways after confession and repent once more, should do penance for four years.

46.4 That a short penance is efficacious

Peter says in Clement: Each and every person can complete either a short or long period for his penance. And it is therefore up to you to decide when to come to our table, and it is not up to us to decide, we who are not permitted to take food with someone unless he be first baptised.

Likewise, another: It is possible to overcome long-term negligence by brief and assiduous diligence.

Likewise, Clement: Let no one think that proof of repentance is shown in the length of time, rather than in the strength of devotion and purpose. For the minds are laid open before God, because he does not take account of time, but of souls.

John Cassian says: Let us remember king David: two offences, of such gravity and such magnitude, were deleted by a single speech of penance.

46.5 That efficacious penance must be confessed solely to God

Paphnutius said in his 'conference': Finally, who is he who cannot say: I have acknowledged my sin to you; and so forth, as far as: I did not conceal [it]. So that by this confession we may deserve to add boldly: And you have forgiven; as far as: Mine. But if, being held back by shame, you are embarrassed to reveal these things in the presence of all, you should not cease to confess them with continuous supplication to him, from whom they cannot hide, and say: I acknowledge my iniquity; as far as: I have done. For he is wont to heal without public acknowledgment of one's shame, and to forgive sins without reproach.

Concerning correct penance

Jerome: I read of Peter's tears, not of his satisfaction. Therefore the tears wash away an offence [of] which one is ashamed to speak.

Likewise: We do not deny, however, that mortal offences are absolved also by secret penance, but only after the secular way of life has been reformed.

46.6 Concerning reflecting upon the cases and their subsequent undoing

Gregory the Roman said: The cases must be reflected upon, and then the power of binding and loosing must be exercised.

Likewise: Indeed, guilt must be contemplated, and the penance that should be followed after sin must also be contemplated, that the verdict of the shepherd may release those whom the omnipotent God visits through compunction.

Likewise, it is said elsewhere: Let no one strike with the sword a sore that the rod is able to heal; nor should anyone contemplate curing with a rod something that must be pierced by the sword.

46.7 That past evils do not harm true penitents

Augustine: Past evils do not harm if they are no longer welcome in the present, especially if they have been expiated by many almsgivings.

46.8 Concerning penance being performed with tears

David said: I have laboured in my groanings; and so forth, as far as: I will water.

Likewise: My eyes have sent forth springs of water.

Likewise: Upon the rivers of Babylon, there we sat, etc.

Jeremiah: Who will give water to my head, and a fountain of tears to my eyes?

The *Romani* say of penitents: It has been settled that after falling into ruin, the abbot shall oversee penance; and if it be with weeping, and lamentation, and a garment of grief, and under supervision, then performing a brief penance is better than one that is long and lax with fear in mind, in which nothing harsh is being undertaken.

Origen: Because we look upon the world with greedy eyes, we do penance with tears.

46.9 That penance is impossible in times of anguish

Jerome: Perform penance as long as you can; for when you are unwell, you do not perform penance, but observe anguish and groans.

Augustine: Penance bears fruit when you execrate vices; but when you are unwell, it is not you who denounces vices, but your vices that denounce you.

Likewise: When you are unwell, you do not heal the wounds of your body yourself, but you are healed by a healthy doctor; so too the wounds of souls are healed by someone who is healthy.

Likewise: But in hell, who will confess to you?

46.10 That forgiveness for penance at the end is uncertain

Augustine: They who perform penance with their last breath, I do not say to them that their sins shall be remitted, for I do not know this, nor do I take it for granted; but perform penance while you are healthy, and in doing this you shall be safe, because you have corrected your sins in time, for with your last breath you have not forsaken your sins, but your sins have forsaken you. But you say: Perhaps God will remit them. Perhaps what you say is true, but I do not know this, for were I to know, I would despair that nothing would help you. Therefore let go of what is uncertain, cling to what is certain.

Jerome says: When penance is efficacious, perform it. But if you lament between life and death, you shall have nothing certain; you prolong grief more than you observe penance.

46.11 That penance is also to be performed in one's last breath

In the dogmas of the church: We believe without doubt that penance abolishes sins, even if a sinner should do penance in his dying breath by publicly revealing his sins with lamentation. Since the intent of God, which had decreed to save what had perished, stands immutable, and for that reason, because his will does not change whether [penance occurs] by emendation of one's life—if time is conceded for this—or whether by simple confession, if life is quickly extinguished. The forgiveness of sinners is postulated because God does not wish for the death of a sinner. Should anyone argue against God's most just mercy, he is not a Christian but a Novitian.

Patrick: If someone is weak, let him do penance, also out of necessity, for God is merciful.

46.12 That the host must not be denied, not even to those doing penance in their last breath

The synod of Nicaea: As a rule, when someone who is dying asks to receive the grace of communion, the bishop probably ought to give him from the eucharist.

In the Ecclesiastical History: Dionysius, replying to the aforesaid Fabianus, recounted a certain story, saying that there was one Serapion among those who lapsed in Alexandria, and he often asked to be admitted [into communion], but his wish was never granted. He finally became afflicted with an illness, and he lay for three days without being able to speak at all. But on the fourth day, as he recovered a little, he called his little daughter and said: 'Why do you detain me? I ask you to quickly get someone to call in the presbyter, that I may finally be absolved'. And when he said that, he lost the power of speech once more. A slave boy hurried to the presbyter, but the presbyter fell ill during the night and could not come; nevertheless, because I (i.e. Dionysius of Alexandria) have ordered that no one should deny the solace of reconciliation to dying people who lapsed, and especially to those who previously demanded it, he gave the boy who came to him a bit of the eucharist, which he ordered him to administer, dissolved, to the old man. After the boy returned, before he entered the house, Serapion recovered once again, and asked: 'Are you back, boy? Even though the presbyter was not able to come, do as he told you, that I may depart'. And after the eucharist was administered, he cheerfully gave up the ghost, as if chains and fetters were broken. By which it is established beyond doubt that no one ought to be cheated of the efficacy of this good substance.

A Roman synod: Therefore the final communion is dispensed with penance, that men of this kind may be freed in their final moments from eternal ruin.

Likewise, a Roman synod: Communion is not to be denied to penitents in the last breath of their life.

Concerning those who engage in commerce during or after penance

The synod of Narbonne:[510] The quality of the profit either excuses the businessman or accuses him, for there is both honest and shameful business. Nevertheless, it is more fitting for a penitent to suffer losses than to be implicated in the dangers of commerce, for it is difficult not to contract sin among the buyers and sellers.

Concerning those who fornicate outside the boundaries of reason, namely have intercourse with beasts, or commit incest with their blood relatives, or pollute themselves with men

The synod of Ancyra: At whatever age before their twentieth year they have committed such an offence, let them be allowed back to the communion of prayer after fifteen years of penance. Thereafter they endure five more years in this form of communion, then finally they attain the eucharist. Let their lives be examined as to how they passed their time in penance, and let them be forgiven accordingly. But if they are insatiable in these offences, let them spend longer in penance. At whatever age after their twentieth year [and already] having wives, they lapsed into this form of sin, let them be received to the communion of prayer after doing penance for twenty-five years. In the fifth year of enduring, let them finally receive the eucharist. But if they have wives and they are over fifty years old, and they have reverted to this offence, let them be entitled to communion at the end of their lives.

Concerning those who have adulterous wives or are known adulterers themselves

The synod of Ancyra: If someone's wife committed adultery, or he has been implicated in adultery himself, let him do seven years penance. It is proper that he attain perfection according to [his] former grades.[511]

That it is not permitted to serve both God and the world

Paul: No man, being a soldier to God, entangles himself in secular businesses.

Likewise: He who wants to implicate himself in human occupations is not free from the snares of the devil.

Likewise: For they who want to become rich fall into temptation and into the snare of the devil.

Likewise: Whoever renounced human affairs ought not be bound (*sc.* to them) once more.

In the Gospel: No man putting his hand to the plough and looking back is worthy, lest we imitate Lot's wife.

The synod of Arles decreed: The charioteers among the faithful must be excommunicated for as long as they participate in races.

Concerning the good that is lost in a short time

Ezekiel: In what day soever a just man shall have sinned, all of his justices shall be cast into oblivion.

Solomon, the wisest of men, and the one found worthy of building a temple to the Lord and singing spiritual verses, quickly became worthy of a thousand deaths.

Constantine was a good emperor for thirty years and gave Christians licence to congregate freely and build basilicas in Christ's honour. But at the end of his life he was baptised by bishop Eusebius Nicomedes, and converted to the Arian dogma.

Whence it is said: Alas! Sadly he was good to begin with, and bad at the end.

Judas was good with the eleven apostles, and in one day he lost his goodness.

Jerome: It is not a virtue to begin, but it is a virtue to complete.

Concerning a protracted evil healed in an instant

Ezekiel: In what day soever the sinner shall be converted from sin, all of his evils shall be cast into oblivion.

Likewise, Daniel said to the wicked king: Let my counsel be acceptable to you, and redeem your sins with your alms.

Christ said to the thief who confessed to him: Today you will be with me, etc.

In the Gospel: A denarius is given to those late in coming.

Likewise: I shall judge each and every one according to his ways.

Likewise: Old improprieties are not imputed to the magi who adored Christ.

Likewise: The Ninevites are healed in three days from the recent retribution.

In the Gospel: You have been made whole, sin no more!

Concerning the ones who are unable to do penance

A synod: Penitents who carefully adhere to the law of penance, if perchance they died on the road or in the sea, where they could not have been succoured, let their memory be commemorated by prayers and offerings.

Likewise: If someone has been snatched by sudden death and was unable to do penance, the one who was with him, to whom he confessed his penance, shall be consoled, and his memory, or prayer, or offering, or alms should be sanctioned.

That adulterers are not permitted to cohabit after penance

A synod: Those who lived in an illicit marriage ought not live in the same house after penance, nor have intercourse with each other on account of love.

Patrick: Whoever gives up adultery should do penance; thereafter he shall not dwell in the same house, nor in the same estate.

A Hibernian synod: When a husband or wife have returned to the Lord after their sin, they shall not meet in the same church, nor should there be an exchange of greetings between them, nor kindness, nor glances, nor communication, nor should they drink from the same spring, nor should they foster together, though the punishment of both has been completed.[512]

Concerning their cohabitation in the same house

A synod: When both their desire to sin and the forbidden love fade, it does not harm them to dwell in a single church.

A Roman synod: Each one considers in his heart whether love of the sin and desire have ceased, for a dead body does not harm the body of a dead man. Otherwise let them be separated.

46.13 Concerning the place of penance

Ezechias prayed at the temple. The three youths prayed at the temple. Daniel prayed at the temple. As Origen said in the annals of the Hebrews: David did penance in the tabernacle. On account of which he says: I shall come into your house, etc. Aaron prayed in the tabernacle for his sins.

Augustine: Four things must be observed in penance: Confession, place, time, manner.

A synod says: A place of correcting and penitence is to be decided upon.

Concerning epithets for those who resume worldly affairs after penance

Solomon: A dog returning to his vomit, and a sow to her wallowing pit.

46.14 What is the last breath

Augustine said: It is a last breath when someone breathes unhealthily for as long as he can endure. Because when our flesh, which has become weak and fat by the nourishments of sin, is torn and enfeebled by the bitings of disease, it awaits its release.

The synod of Chalcedon: Penance must be prescribed even unto death, as a thief deserved. According to the prophet: If, having repented, you lament, then you will be saved.

46.15 Concerning the ones passing away imminently

The synod of Carthage says: If it be the case that the one who requires penance when he is ill has lost the power of speech because of his illness, when the *sacerdos* who has been called in comes to him, let them who have heard him testify whether he is [on the verge of] passing away imminently, and if he is believed to die immediately, let him be reconciled by the laying on of hands, and let the eucharist be poured on his lips. But if he has recovered, he is reminded by the aforesaid witnesses of the fulfilment of his petition, and he should be placed under the statutes of penance for as long as the *sacerdos*, who prescribed the penance, shall decide.

46.16 That a penance cannot be relaxed without confession preceding

Jacob said: Confess your sins one to another, for the confession of a sin and the magnificence of penance are the work of God.

Gregory: The form of punishment shall correspond to the measure of sin because, just as the medic cannot work a cure unless he has felt and examined the patient with his hands and eyes, so a wise man cannot heal the offences of sinners without confession. For one believes with his heart unto justice, but let confession with the mouth be unto salvation.

46.17 That doing penance for a single year is sufficient

The Lord said to Job concerning the whirlwind: Take courage in my angels and the throne of my kingdom; but had you reformed yourself in this world for a year, would I have remembered your former offences?

46.18 Concerning a single day's penance healing the person

Gregory: Behold everything you do is transient, and, whether you like it or not, without a moment's pause, you come closer [to death]. Why, then, is the time that remains loved?[513] If you acknowledge your sin, God forgives; the time changes from morning to evening.

46.19 Concerning the laying on of hands over the penitent during Lent, and that the same penitents should bury the dead, and that they should genuflect from Easter to Pentecost

A Roman synod: Let a hand be laid over the penitents by bishops in every time of fasting. Let the penitents carry the dead of the church and bury them. Penitents shall also genuflect during the days of forgiveness.

47 Concerning territories[514] subject to tribute[515]

That it must not be divided between the kingdom and the church, but they should share[516]

That it must be divided between the kingdom and the church[517]

47.1 Concerning dividing territories subject to tribute in three[518]

Joseph, being in possession of all of Egypt, dispensed of it very justly as he left behind a share [for his heirs], and gathered the tribute for Pharaoh, and rendered unto God the things that are God's. The people of Israel gave a share to God, and tribute to caesar, and reserved another part for themselves and their heirs after them.

A synod: Let every inheritance that is subject to the tribute of a king and is bound to a church be divided into three parts. The first part is given to the heirs without the casting of lots. The second to the kings, for Christ says: For me and for you, Peter. The third to God, for the earth is the Lord's, etc.

Jerome: It is fitting that they who live under three persons give a third to God, and a third to the king, who reigns and supports the church together with God and men. And one reads that there were three orders of columns in the temple: the first, of wood without any coating; these are the subjects; the second coated with silver, signifying the kings; the third with gold, signifying catholic *principes*.

Origen said: It must be noted that in the same manner that the silver and golden ones govern their part, so do the wooden ones. It must be noted that the silver- and golden-coated ones are built on wood, for the church and the kingdom are founded and supported by lay people.

47.2 That all free property is given to God

The Lord in the Gospel: If you want to be perfect, go and sell all that you have, etc., for the earth and its plenitude are the Lord's.

On account of which Peter said: We have abandoned all things because of you, etc. To these a hundredfold and eternal life are promised.

47.3 That, if all is given to God, the world's share must be left in the hands of the world

Jerome said: Each and every person who flees the world leaves his share in the hands of the world. For Joseph, fleeing, left his tunic in the hands of a woman. Thus also Christ resurrected, leaving the linen cloths that were laid on the ground. Thus also Peter, escaping prison, being roused by an angel, left behind the chains. Thus it is also said to Moses: Remove your shoes, for the place whereon, etc. Thus also Joshua, that he may go freely into the holy place.

47.4 That the king's entitlement is not withdrawn from the church

Jerome: Just as lawfully married people must not separate, for it is said, 'they two shall be in one flesh', and, 'what God has joined together, let no man separate', thus also what is given to the church as tribute to the king, or an act of sale, or a testament [must not be separated from it].

47.5 That the *census*[519] of a king and bishop are equal

A Hibernian synod said: Everyone who has dared to steal or seize things that belong to a king or bishop, or offend in any other way against them, caring not about despising them, shall pay the price of seven *ancillae*[520] or do penance with a bishop for seven years.

48 Concerning martyrs

Concerning the word 'martyrs'

In the books of etymologies: They are called 'martyrs' in Greek, 'witnesses' (*testes*) in Latin. Whence 'testaments' (*testimonia*) are called *martyria* in Greek. Witnesses (*testes*) are so called because they endured tribulations as testimony to Christ. There are two kinds of martyrdoms: one is found in overt suffering and the other in the hidden virtue of the soul.[521]

Augustine said: What is 'martyr' in Greek is 'confessor' in Latin. It is given this name because it suits one who confesses by blood and burning fire. For 'confessor' denotes many things.

48.1 Concerning the origin of martyrs

The first martyr was Abel, for whose blood the earth opened, [as it is said]: The voice of your brother's blood cries to me from the earth. Jerome: This was the second curse on the land after the first, which is proclaimed to Adam: Cursed is the earth in your work. The second was Zechariah, the son of Barachias, who was slain between the temple and the altar, whose blood brought captivity in an evil land to the sons of Israel. The third is Stephen, whose blood opened the heavens.

48.2 That there is no difference between a martyr and a baptised person

The synod of Nicaea: We do not distinguish between a confession of baptism and a confession of blood. Martyrdom is where all the sacred things of baptism are contained.

A baptised person confesses his faith before a *sacerdos* [and] replies when asked, and a martyr does the same before a persecutor. The former is sprinkled with oil or sprinkled with water after his confession, the latter is sprinkled with blood or washed with fire. The former receives the Holy Spirit by the laying on of the bishop's hand, the latter is made a mouthpiece of the Holy Spirit, while he himself does not speak, but the spirit of the Father speaks through him. The former receives the eucharist in the communication of the body of Christ, the latter himself dies together in Christ. The former renounces the acts of the world, the latter renounces life itself. The sins are remitted to the former, in the latter, they are utterly extinguished.

48.3 That the happiness of martyrs is attained through the unhappiness of martyrdom

Jerome: Martyrs are happy if they are temporarily unhappy. But they are happy for eternity because they have obtained in a short time what they desired for a long time. Whence brief sorrow must be endured, that eternal life might be obtained.

48.4 Concerning the different torments of martyrs

Jerome: There are many kinds of torments: some the sword lays low, buried in the throat by a surprise blow. Others, the pillory of the cross fastened, on which death is both repelled when asked for and asked for when repelled. Others, the saw cut through with rough teeth. Others, the iron hoof, furrowing, crushed. Others, the ferocious beast decapitated with its bites. Others, the force of the blows tore their inmost organs through the skin. Others, the earth buried alive. Others, who were thrown from high ground, the fall crushed to death. Others, who were tossed into it, the water swallowed. Others, the devouring flame, hungry, consumed until they turned into ash. Others, a suffocation delivered by the hands strangled. Others, a cruel dismembering of limbs with switches dismembered. Others, a cruel seclusion in prisons finished off.

48.5 Concerning the transmigration of martyrs, that is, of relics

The people of God returning from Egypt carried with it Joseph's bones to the land of Canaan.

The book of Matthew, written by his own hand, was translated together with his relics.[522]

The bones of Luke and Andrew were translated. The bones of John the Baptist were translated to Jerusalem and his head was found at the fourth milestone from the city.

Paul's head was translated from a lake and buried in Rome.

Concerning transporting martyrs

In the books of Hilarion: His disciple Hesychius stole his body, carrying it from the grave to his own monastery in Syria, and buried it immediately in the ground in the same garden.[523] But afterwards, in Palestine, the holy man Hesychius heard [of Hilarion's passing away], he journeyed to Cyprus, and, in order to take the suspicion of those watching carefully away from them, he pretended to want to live in the same garden; over the course of ten months he stole his body despite grave danger to his life. Carrying it away, he placed it in the ancient monastery, with all the monks and crowds of city dwellers following; the tunic, and hood, and cloak that were over the dead man's body were unharmed, and the entire body was intact as if he were still alive, and fragranced by such scents that it was believed to be anointed with ointments.

That it is twice the sin to do evil near martyrs

Augustine: It is twice the sin to do evil near [the relics of] martyrs, and a double punishment of preventing [the presence] of angels follows.

Likewise: Where there be evil men, there also malignant spirits reside.

48.6 Concerning martyrs interceding on our behalf

Gregory: When they recognise any of their virtues in us, then, without doubt, the holy martyrs intercede on our behalf.

48.7 That the feast days of martyrs are not celebrated during Lent

The synod of Laodicea: It is not permitted to celebrate the feast days of martyrs during Lent, but it is fitting for their holy commemoration to be held on Sabbaths and Sundays.

48.8 Concerning the three occasions[524] on which martyrs are translated

Augustine said: There are three occasions on which martyrs should be translated. The first, when the force of persecutors weighs down on their *loca*; the second, when the *loca* are experiencing hardship; the third, when they are weighed down by the company of evil men.

48.9 That the dignity of martyrs sometimes migrates with their relics, sometimes stays behind

Jerome: Note that when some of the martyrs are translated, their dignity migrates with them; but when others are translated, dignity does not depart from their *loca*.

48.10 Concerning the resurrection of translated martyrs

Origen said: Some believe they will resurrect in the *locus* of their ashes, others in the *locus* of their bones. Where the head shall be, that is where all the limbs shall be joined together.

Ezekiel saw bones drawing towards bones, each one to its joint, and he prophesied that they will grow nerves and flesh, and thereafter stretch skin, thence that a spirit would blow into it from the four winds.

48.11 That the dignity of God is not bestowed upon martyrs

Isidore: Our forefathers founded [festivities for martyrs], either to incite imitation or that we may be joined to their merits and be helped by prayers, that, nevertheless, honour be not given to any of the martyrs, but to God himself, who crowns the martyrs.[525] Although we erect altars in the memory of martyrs, what *sacerdos* says, 'we offer to you, Peter, and you, Paul'? But he says: 'We offer to God, who has crowned the martyrs'. For we revere martyrs by the same form of reverence by which holy men are worshiped in the present life, namely by uniting with them. For there is one God that a single form of worship applies to and is owed to, not to an angel, nor a martyr, nor a holy soul. Whoever shall lapse into this error, let him be corrected.

48.12 That the spirit of martyrs does not worry about the affairs of the world

Augustine: Every now and again men fall into great errors by false visions. For it is agreed that the dead do not know what takes place here, while it takes place here; later they shall hear from the ones who come to them in death.

Jerome: All who migrate from the body forget the affairs of the world. For when they see the preparation of their beatitude, being filled by the sight of heavenly things, they do not recall their worldly suffering; and when sinners remember their sufferings as they are tormented by punishments, they cannot recall the pleasures of the world and of loved ones.

48.13 That, when it is necessary, they see things that take place here

Jerome: Some think that the spirits of the dead can see some things that take place here; when there is need either for them or for us, not only the things of the present, but also past and future things are revealed by the spirit.

48.14 That not all dead persons are capable of this

Jerome: Not all dead persons are capable of seeing the things that take place here, just as not all people here have foresight, except prophets.

48.15 That martyrs who are prepared to be martyred are called martyrs

Gregory: When Christ asked Jacob and John and said: Can you drink the cup which I am about to drink? They replied: We can. And when Christ answers, 'you shall indeed drink my cup', he declares that they will suffer martyrdom. In which thing we are led to understand that John, whose blood was not shed, is to be regarded as a martyr.[526]

49 Concerning relics buried in a remote place[527]

49.1 That many men of God were buried in a remote place, that they might be visited by angels and avoided by the wicked

Origen said: Moses, the man of God, was buried on Mount Phasga, that he might always be visited by angels and avoided by the wicked.

Likewise: Aaron was buried on Mount Horeb.

Likewise: Paul the hermit and others are buried in the desert, for the Lord himself, being also beleaguered by the wicked, often fled either to the desert, or to a mountain, or to the sea.

49.2 That relics placed in a remote place are visited no less frequently by God and his angels

Christ says: I shall be with you all days, even to the consummation [of the world].

Origen: Not only do we know that the living are helped by God, but also that the dead are visited and helped.

In the Life of the Monks we read that certain martyrs buried in the desert were visited by angels every morning and evening, and they sung hymns by their graves.

49.3 That martyrs buried in a remote place are visited more than those buried among the wicked

In the Life of the Fathers[528] we read that martyrs buried among the wicked are visited by angels, but that the angels return sadly.

Whence the Lord said: Then the land enjoyed her Sabbaths.

Jerome: One must know which is more blameworthy: to defraud angels or men.

Likewise: After the resurrection many testified that they heard voices of angels saying: Let us go away from these places.

50 Concerning seeing the dead in a dream

50.1 Concerning the dead appearing to the living

Augustine: The dead appear to the living and they recall what they say through this dream.

50.2 Concerning the reason that the dead appear to the living in sleep

Augustine said: Some think that [the dead appear] by means of angelic graces either in order to comfort the living of their kin or in order to advise the human race that care should be shown towards the grave. And even if [such care] may not benefit the dead, one nevertheless complains if it is lacking in the religious order.[529]

50.3 That it sometimes happens that the dead are mistakenly seen in a dream

Augustine: Every now and again men fall into great errors by false visions, etc.

50.4 Concerning the reason that they appear to the living

Gregory said: Some are sent to us that we may believe there are heavenly rewards and infernal punishments. For just as a pregnant woman might be sent to prison and give birth to a child there and he would be nurtured and reared there: should his mother mention the sun and the moon and the stars and the mountains and the hills and flying birds and running horses, he would nevertheless know nothing but the darkness of the prison, so also in this, the blindness of their exile, mortals mistrust that what they hear is true.

50.5 Concerning the bodily form that the dead assume

Gregory: What kind of bodies do the dead assume? They are spiritual bodies, like [the bodies] after the resurrection and of Moses and Elijah on the mountain; or, as some say, ethereal bodies formed for this reason alone, that they may speak to men by means of a vision.

50.6 Concerning dreams

Gregory: Take note, Peter, that there are six ways in which dream visions touch the mind. Sometimes dreams are induced by a full stomach, sometimes by an empty one, sometimes by illusion, sometimes by thought and illusion at one and the same time, sometimes by revelation, sometimes by thought and revelation. The first two that we have mentioned, we all know through experience. And the latter four we find in the pages of holy scripture. For if it were not for the fact that most dreams emanated from our hidden enemy through illusion, the wise man would never have exclaimed, saying: For dreams cause many to err and they ruin those who believe in them. Or, indeed: You shall not divine nor observe dreams. By whose words it is clearly shown how detested are those things which are connected with augurs. Again, if it were not for the fact that they proceed at once from thought and illusion, the wise man would hardly have said that many worries follow dreams, and unless, sometimes, they arose out of the mystery of revelation, Joseph would not have seen dreams that he was to be preferred to his brothers, nor would an angel have warned Mary's husband in dreams that he should flee to Egypt, taking his boy with him. Again, unless sometimes dreams proceeded from thought and revelation at one and the same time, never would the prophet—while examining Nebuchadnezzar's vision—have commenced from the root of his thought, saying: You, O king, didst begin to think in your bed what should come to pass hereafter. And a little further: You, O king, saw, and behold there was a great statue, etc. But, undoubtedly, since dreams vary in accordance with so many different circumstances, just as it is not clear where they originate from, so it ought to be difficult to believe them. Holy men, by a certain subtle sensitivity, detect among illusions and revelations the echoes or images of visions, so that they know whether they learn something from a good spirit or whether they suffer some illusion. For if these things are not met with a cautious mind, the mind is overwhelmed by the many falsehoods of the deceiving spirit, which makes a habit of foretelling many true things from time to time, that, in the end, it may ensnare our soul by a single fallacy.

51 Concerning tonsure[530]

51.1 Concerning the origin of the ecclesiastical tonsure

Isidore said: The practice of ecclesiastical tonsure begins with the Nazarenes, who, having kept their hair intact, used to shave their heads after the continence of a noble life and throw the hair into the fire, that they might consecrate their devotion to the Lord. Whence the apostles, following this example, were consecrated to the Lord by cutting their hair, as if they were delivered for divine worship.

It is said to Ezekiel: Son of man, take a sharp sword and run it over your head. On account of which Priscilla and Aquila are said in the Acts of Apostles to have made a vow.

51.2 Concerning Peter, the first tonsured cleric

The *Romani* say: Peter was the first cleric to be tonsured, bearing in his head the image of Christ's crown of thorns.

51.3 Concerning the five reasons that Peter was tonsured

The *Romani* say that Peter was tonsured for five reasons. The first, that he imitate Christ's crown; the second, that clerics be discerned from laymen by their tonsure, appearance, and works, and that they be discerned by their appearance just as they are by their works; the third, that he might reprove the priests of the Old Testament by being tonsured in the same spot where the dove descended on Christ's head; the fourth, that he might endure mocking yelps in the Roman kingdom on account of God; the fifth, that he might distinguish the Christians from Simon Magus, whose head was shorn in front from ear to ear, when previously the magi had a curl on their forehead.

51.4 That the sacrament of the tonsure[531] must be held in the soul

Isidore said: The sign of the tonsure in clerics is now upon their body, but [the sacrament] is undertaken in the soul within, which is to say that we cast off the sins of the flesh as though they were hairs. And thus, having been renewed with respect to our mental faculties, that were like wild locks of hair, we begin to shine, shedding the old man with his deeds and putting on the new, who is renewed into the knowledge of God, a renewal that ought to take place in the mind, but finds expression on the head.

51.5 That the *corona*[532] signifies both the priesthood and the kingdom

Isidore says: The priesthood and the reign of the church are symbolised in a shorn head.[533] For among the elders, there was a tiara on the head of *sacerdotes*, namely of clerics.

Whence Peter said: You are a kingly and priestly race.

We do not groom our hair like the Nazarenes, i.e. because there is a great difference between the prophetic covering and the revelation of the Gospel.

Whence the apostle said: When you shall be converted to Christ, remove the veil.

51.6 Concerning the tonsure of the Britons and solemnity and mass

Gildas said: The Britons are in opposition to the whole world, enemies of Roman customs, not only in respect to mass, but also to tonsure, together with the Jews they worship the shadows of future things more than truth. They celebrate Easter with the Jews on the fourteenth moon.[534]

The *Romani* say: They say that their tonsure originated with Simon Magus, whose tonsure extended from ear to ear, standing for the excellence of the tonsure of the magi, by which only the foremost part of the forehead used to be covered. And the sermon of Patrick[535] attests that the first one to wear this tonsure in Ireland was the swineherd of king Lóegaire mac Néill[536] from whom nearly all the *Hibernenses* assumed their tonsure.

51.7 That clerics who are not tonsured in the Roman manner must be excommunicated

Patrick: If a cleric [be found], whose hair is not shorn in the Roman manner, he ought to be excommunicated.

That clerics who are not tonsured in the Roman manner must be excommunicated

Patrick said: Any cleric, from ostiary to *sacerdos*, who is seen without a tunic that covers his thighs, who does not cover the shame of his belly and his nakedness, and who has not been tonsured in the Roman manner, and if his wife parades with her hair unveiled, they shall both be condemned and separated from the church.[537]

That a woman ought not be tonsured

The synod of Gangra: A woman being tonsured in the name of Christianity should be anathema.

Jerome: It is not the locks of hair that ought to be shorn, but the vices that ought to be shaved. Hair was granted [her] for the sake of beauty and for veiling her head as a sign of obedience to her husband.

Origen on abuses: I have seen a man grooming his hair and a *sacerdos* not wearing white offering the bread to the Lord. And the third thing that is detestable to me and God are women who tonsure their hair, which is given to them as a veil.

Whence the apostle: A man ought to pray with his head uncovered, but let a woman pray with her head veiled.

That a woman ought to be tonsured

The law: Whoever swore an oath to the Lord tonsured his head and cast the hair into the fire as a sign of the cutting out of vices. Paul has also done this in Cenchrae. In the Old Testament they walked around in mourning garb, with shaven heads, in sign of commemoration and sadness.

A synod decreed in the matter of veiled women living under a rule who bear children, that they should tonsure their hair to symbolise the vices that depart from them.

Concerning spineless effeminates in scripture

Augustine: Those who changed over to having a feminine manner, are rightly [said] not to have manly strength. And it is to be believed that by a just judgement of God it comes about that they who deform themselves by taking on a feminine appearance should lose their manly strength.

52 Concerning tame beasts

52.1 Concerning the name and kinds of harmful beasts[538]

In the twelfth book of the etymologies: The word 'beast', properly speaking, includes lions, panthers, tigers, wolves, foxes, and dogs, and other animals that attack with their mouth or their claws, except for serpents. They are called beasts from the force with which they attack. And they are called 'wild' (*ferus*) because they enjoy a natural freedom and are driven (*ferre*) by their instinct.[539]

Jerome: Beasts are so called from *bessus*, namely from their habit (Old Irish *bés*) of being ferocious.[540]

Likewise: Whatever attacks with its claws or its wing is called beast.

52.2 That a beast must be confined, lest its owner pay for what it damages

The law says: Everyone who rears and has a beast, let him confine it.

Jerome: insomuch as it is a beast, it is reared in order to cause harm.

Augustine: Whoever does not wish to kill his neighbour should not rear a beast. For if it has caused harm, he shall render a life for a life, a loss for a loss.

Faustus: O prudent man, cultivate your land, yoke your oxen, take care, and so forth until he says: Do not rear a beast; insomuch as it may profit you, it is harmful to your neighbours.

In the Life of the Monks of Egypt: Someone fasted before the Lord asking that He restrain his beasts, and He prevented them from grazing upon the harvests of a hermit.

Likewise: Someone was feeding a number of hens, [and] a fox devoured [them]. And lifting his hand to the sky he said: Why do you feed these superfluous and harmful beings?

Likewise, someone said: Lord, return to me what your foxes have devoured—namely his mother's hens—and without doubt God restored them to him.

52.3 Concerning goring oxen

The law says: If a goring ox strike down a man or woman, the ox shall be stoned and not be eaten, and the owner of the ox shall be quit. But if the ox has gored yesterday and the day before, and its master did not confine it, and it shall kill a man, the ox shall be stoned and they shall kill its owner, unless he shall give for his life whatsoever judges have adjudged.

52.4 Concerning the three things that man requires

Jerome: Everyone needs three things: a slave, a dog, an ox. A slave for work, a dog for protection, an ox for ploughing. A slave lives off his master's property, a dog eats from everyone's crumbs, an ox grazes grasses and grain and chaffs.

52.5 Concerning dogs[541]

The *Hibernenses* say: A chained dog, whatever damage it has caused at night, shall not be paid for by its master. But if it hurt someone in daytime, its master shall pay. And a dog that watches over livestock, whatever damage it has caused in the cowshed or in the pastures of its livestock, it shall not be paid for by its master. But if it went outside the bounds, whatever damage it has caused shall be paid for.

In the books of etymologies: The Latin noun 'dog' (*canis*) seems to have a Greek etymology. For it is called *cinos*[542] in Greek, though some think it is named after the sound (*canor*) of barking, because it is loud, whence also 'to sing' (*canare*) is named. No animals are smarter than dogs, for they have more sense than others. And for they alone recognise their names, love their masters, defend the homes and properties of their masters, and they lay down their life for their masters, they willingly run after game with their master, they do not leave the body of their master even when he has died. Owing to their inferior nature they are not able to live apart from humans.[543]

For although on a family residence many animals are useful to the household, caring for the dogs is of no little importance, etc., until it is said: They have their own desire to understand, to love, to serve.

Likewise: They do not hate those whom they attack, but show zeal for whom they love.

Likewise: Note that we know that the angel did not disdain to have a dog as his travelling companion.

52.6 That a dog's first offence is not paid for

If a dog should devour something, on the first offence nothing is given in compensation, except, perhaps, the dog itself. But if it has offended again, let its master pay for what it devoured.

52.7 Concerning livestock killing other livestock

The law: If an ox wounded another man's ox and it die, they shall sell the live ox, and let them divide its price, and divide the carcass between them. But if his ox was wont to gore yesterday and the day before, and its master does not keep it in, he shall render ox for ox and shall take the whole carcass.

That an animal must not be reared if it may kill

Augustine: Anyone not wanting to torment his neighbour should not rear a beast. For if it has caused harm, let him render a life for a life, a loss for a loss.

52.8 Concerning watchdogs

The *Hibernenses* say: If a watchdog caused any harm at night, its master shall not pay. But if it harms during the day, he shall make good.

52.9 Concerning hens

The *Hibernenses* say: If hens have devastated the harvest, or the vineyard, or the garden in a *ciuitas* surrounded by a fence as high as a man's chin and with a thorned strip, their master shall pay; otherwise he shall not pay. But if they go out beyond the drying kiln,[544] the master shall pay if they caused harm.[545]

53 Concerning eating meats[546]

53.1 Concerning the time that they were permitted for human consumption

Isidore: Meats were permitted for human consumption after the deluge, because initially they were forbidden, that human eagerness might be curtailed. Whence: I have given you the fruit tree, and the herbs to eat. Afterwards, through Noah all animals were given for consumption, that nature might be sated by things that are lawful, and restrained from things not lawful. As it is said: Flesh with blood you shall not eat. But after the law of Moses has come, this licence is restricted, and clean and unclean were revealed.

Concerning the lawful consumption of flesh

Jerome: Everything that God created is good: grass for the consumption of livestock, flesh for human consumption.

The synod of Ancyra: Flesh is good, thus so that it be received with thanksgiving.

Concerning the unlawful consumption of flesh

Isidore: But after the appearance of Christ, who is the beginning and the end, that which he ordered[547] at the beginning, he also retracted at the end of time, saying through his apostle: It is a good thing not to eat flesh, nor drink wine or anything else, wherein is excess. And again: He that is weak, let him eat herbs. Therefore meats are not forbidden because they are said to be bad, but because feasting on flesh brings about excess, [which is] both the tinder and fosterer of all vices.

53.2 That meats are not prohibited, but their consumption brings about excess

Paul said: Meats are not bad, but their consumption brings about excess, [which is] the fosterer of all vices.

53.3 That food in which there is excess must not be eaten

Augustine: Do not eat food in which excess is brought about.

Whence Paul said: All things are lawful, but not all things are helpful.

53.4 Concerning abstaining from consuming meats

Jerome: The consumption of meats is lawful, but in this lawful deed we should preach abstinence.

53.5 Concerning taking care not to cause controversy in eating meats

Paul said: Let not him who eats, despise him who does not eat, and he who does not eat, let him not judge him who eats. For he who eats should eat in honour of God, giving thanks; and he who does not eat does not eat in honour of God.

53.6 That every animal that dies without its blood being shed, is carrion

Jerome said: If it has been suffocated either by the hand of man in the manner of pagans, or died of natural causes,[548] or was killed by beasts, or fire, or water, or met its death by any other cause, it is unlawful; for carrion is that which gives up its life without its blood being shed, and in which the soul perishes.

53.7 Concerning the decree of a synod concerning lawful and unlawful meats

The synod of Gangra said: If anyone shall condemn a man who, with devotion and catholic faith, eats flesh that has no blood and was neither offered[549] to idols nor suffocated, as though that man is without hope on account of this consumption, let him be anathema.

That meats were forbidden in the law

In the New Testament they have been cleansed.

Eucherius was asked: Why was the common food called 'unclean'? He replied: Because then, contrary to the prohibition, [the common food] was open to other men in common, who did not observe the law with respect to the differentiation of foodstuffs, by which observation the Jews boasted that they are God's party. It was cleansed when the Lord said to Peter: That which the Lord has cleansed, do not call common.

53.8 That eating fish is undoubtedly lawful

Isidore said: We may eat fish, which the Lord ate after the resurrection. Nor did the apostles forbid it.

Jerome: We accept and praise the eating of fish with great thanks, for the Lord received it in resurrection.

Augustine: There is a single flesh that does not bring about excess, namely fish; but the law teaches that some fish are unlawful, like the *inscamosus* and the hairy, etc.

Concerning rivers with fish

Likewise, *XLV titulos*: And they lay down that fish-weirs, which are called *correte*, shall be destroyed in rivers suitable for nets, so that there may be no seed of discord in the brotherhood for the sake of food, and so that their rancour-possessed hearts may not be saddened, in accordance with the example of the Gospels: If you offer your gift at the altar, etc. But in another part of the river unsuitable for nets, fish-weirs should be constructed in such a way that they are of the same measurement upon the water. And a channel for swimming should be built for the fish of the sea for the benefit of all men, right along the river from its lowest to its highest part, so that they (i.e. the sea-fish) may provide food for all, to whom it was said in common by the Creator: Rule over the fishes of the sea. How far the swimming channel next to the weir shall extend across [the river] shall, however, be as true judges adjudicate. For it is said: Woe to you who despoil, for you also will be despoiled.[550]

53.9 That the eating of birds is lawful

Jerome: The flesh of birds is lawful to clerics. For it does not nourish as much as it generates sorrow. And the law teaches that nearly all birds are lawful.

53.10 That the eating of wild animals, and especially deer, is lawful

The *Hibernenses* say: The flesh of wild animals is, according to many, permitted for consumption, because it causes belching from the intestines rather than saturation. Some say that it is similar to other kinds of flesh, because it satiates like any other flesh; the church has nevertheless consecrated these three kinds of meats for consumption.

That eating animals, namely swine, is lawful

In the Old Testament it is said of the priest: The hare also, for that too chews the cud but does not divide the hoof, and the swine, which divides the hoof and does not chew the cud: the flesh of these you shall not eat.

53.11 That eating swine is lawful

Origen said: Swine was previously unclean, but now, consecrated by the destruction of the pigs in the Gospel,[551] it is as though it has been sanctioned by a command in punishment.

In the books of etymologies: We call every animal that lacks human language and appearance 'livestock'.

Augustine: The word 'livestock' is appropriate to those animals that are of use for men, either by helping in labour, like oxen and horses and the like, or by being used for wool or consumption, like sheep and swine.

That swine meat is not permitted to all

Jerome, in the struggle against Jovinian: I heard therefore that soldiers, and athletes, sailors, and rhetors, and pourers of metal, and others who are given to hard work, eat swine, and wild boars, and deer, and other living creatures.

53.12 Concerning swine that devour men

Theodore said: Pigs that have had blood—but just a taste—are to be eaten; but if they should mutilate and eat the corpses of the dead, their flesh may not be eaten until it is macerated.

Likewise: If a pig drank blood, it is permitted if it only tasted, it is not.

53.13 That it is forbidden to eat horses[552]

In Deuteronomy: Every beast that has a hoof, but does not divide it, nor chews the cud, shall be unclean. The law forbids it.

But Jerome says in the conflict against Arnobius: Horse and dog are always unclean animals.

Theodore the bishop: They do not forbid horse, but it is the custom for it not to be eaten.

The synod of Carthage said: The church does not forbid horse but it is nevertheless unlawful to eat it.

53.14 Concerning carrion swine, and concerning animals that have consumed human blood, and meats chewed by wolves, concerning fish and suffocated animals, concerning meats chewed on by a hawk, and concerning the horse

The law: If any beast die, of which it is lawful for us to eat, he who touches the carcass thereof shall be unclean until the evening; and he who eats or carries away any of it shall wash his clothes.

Theodore the bishop says: The Greeks do not give carrion to their swine. However, they allow the skin of carrion to be used for shoes, but not for any sacred use. If pigs should consume carrion flesh or human blood, we believe they should not be cast out, nor, likewise, should hens. Animals that are chewed by wolves or dogs must not be eaten, except that they be thrown to swine and dogs, nor a deer or a goat, which have been found dead [be eaten]. Fish are permitted, for they have a different nature. Birds and other animals, if they are strangled in nets, must not be eaten. For Paul said: Abstain from suffocated blood and idolatry; and likewise from hawk carrion. He does not forbid horse, but it is not customary to eat it.

Concerning lawful use

Gregory in the homilies: Know that whoever does nothing unlawful is regarded by the law as though he does lawful things. Piety operates in such a manner that they do not relinquish the things of the world even if they do not want them.

53.15 Concerning eating flesh and all other foodstuffs, unless they scandalise one's neighbours

Paul says: One believes that he may not eat all things, for he who is weak should eat herbs. Let not him who eats despise him who does not eat, and he who does not eat, let him not judge him who eats. For the Lord has taken him; let he who eats in honour of the Lord eat. For he gives thanks to God. I believe and trust in the Lord Jesus Christ that nothing is unclean of itself; except to him who believes it is unclean. But you who have faith in your possession, have it before God! Should food scandalise my brother, I shall not eat flesh for all eternity.

53.16 That the foods of infidels do not harm according to the doctrine, if they are received with thanksgiving and if they do not scandalise one's brother, and, similarly, are not sacrificed to idols

Paul said: Whatsoever is sold in the market, eat, asking no question for conscience's sake. The earth is the Lord's, and the fullness thereof. If an infidel invites you for a meal and you wish to go with him, eat anything that is set before you, asking no question for conscience's sake. If any man say, 'this has been sacrificed to idols', do not eat of it for the sake of him that said this. I mean: for the conscience of the other; so you do not repute it to the idol, but to God.

54 Concerning true innocence

54.1 Concerning the praise of innocence

Augustine said: True innocence is that which harms no one, desires nothing, believes that all are better.

Likewise: Being content in all respects, it does not covet the things of others.

Likewise: Innocence surpasses fasting. Whoever fasts, chastises his own body. Innocence knows no corruption. It surpasses prayer. For whoever prays, fears being punished. But innocence knows no punishment, hence it does not fear. It surpasses almsgiving. For whoever gave alms either for his own sake or for his friends' sake, truly has no innocence, because he extinguishes (*sc.* an evil?) within himself through almsgiving. It surpasses reading. For whoever reads, reads that he may speak to the Lord. But innocence does not need to seek the Lord, for it never departs from him; for purity of mind discovers all the attainments of reading. On account of which it is said: He whose heart is pure, does not need to be taught letters. For purity of mind is a companion of the angels, conscious of the divine gift, nothing is invisible to it. They follow the lamb wherever he goes. Of them it is said: Their angels always see the face of the father.

54.2 Concerning the innocence of children

In the Gospel: Allow your young to come to me and do not hinder them. For the kingdom of heaven belongs to such as these.

When the Lord says 'the kingdom of heaven belongs to such as these', note that he does not say 'of such an age', for it was their merit that was expedient to him, not the age of such as these.

Jerome in his commentary on Matthew: 'To such as these'[553] is significant. He said 'such as these' not 'them' in order to show that it is not age that governs, but proper conduct. In a similar manner, one is not called a brother unless he is religious.

Jerome in the same commentary: But he also significantly added: Whoever calls his brother 'raca'. For no one is a brother to us, except he who holds the same share with us.

Likewise: Unless you do as these children, you shall not enter the kingdom of God.

54.3 Concerning wicked, but nevertheless innocent children

In the Life of the Fathers:[554] A child aged five who was brought up badly was accustomed to saying wicked things and doing wicked things. He was snatched by a demon in his nurse's bosom. Having spoken wickedly, he died, and he got nothing of merit after death.

In the Life of the Monks: A certain child who behaved badly was snatched from life by a fever and his father asked bishop Obius to offer a host for him. The latter said: He who behaved badly in life, is not entitled to or does not need an offering after death, for age does not earn merit, but merit helps age.

Paul said: When I was a child, I spoke as a child; when I became a man, I abandoned those thing that are childish, for the Lord says: The kingdom of heaven belongs to such as these. Note that he does not say 'of such an age'.

Jerome says: One must be mindful of character, not age; for age deceives.

54.4 Concerning vices pertaining to the innocence of children

Augustine: What qualities are childish? Deception, fickleness, greed for everything; a boy is insulting, perjurious, gluttonous, etc.

54.5 Concerning the two kinds of innocence

Augustine says: There are two kinds of innocence: false innocence, which age does not quash, and necessity, as in young children. True innocence is that which knows no malice, even in a man's body, as occurs rarely.

54.6 That the young are not counted among the perfect

Six thousand armed men of the people of God are counted, except children and women. Similarly, the five thousand in the Gospel, except women and children.

54.7 Concerning the age of a child in which no compensation is made

A Gallican synod: A child under fifteen shall not receive anything for an offence except discipline. But after this age he shall make compensation for any offence or theft.

A Gallican synod: A child under twelve shall not receive anything for an offence except discipline.

54.8 Concerning the age before which nuns should not be veiled, however much their way of life and manners be worthy

A synod: Nuns, though their way of life and manners be proven, should not be veiled before their twelfth or fifteenth year.

Concerning young children

That the ones abandoning young children in the church of God deserve punishments

A Hibernian synod: Let those who abandon young children in a church of God without the abbot's knowledge do penance for three and a half years if there are bishops buried or present in it. But if they committed homicide in it, let them do penance for seven years. This [rule] is occasioned by the fact that [the bishop] has seven grades, and the church is septiform. If, however, it has no bishop, but instead it is a small church, let them do penance for a year and a half.

Concerning those to whom belong children that have been abandoned in a church[555]

A child who has been brought to the church is its slave, unless he is redeemed through payment. Should he behave impudently, if he shall correct himself as best he can, his offensive behaviour shall not stain the church. But [if] a child that has been brought to the church has left it, blameless, within a period of one hundred days, the church shall have no power over him, but he will belong to the right of kindred. If the church received money from his parents in whatever amount, after the fashion of fosterers, it shall take the place of the parents. [If the child has died][556] through negligence, let those who were neglectful do penance for seven years for being negligent, for they have killed Christ. Hence others judge that they who abandon young children do penance for seven years, and they should endure as much trouble as they have inflicted on the church.

Concerning the defence of those who abandon young children in the church of God

Christ: Allow your young to come to me. He established Christ the infant by his example.

Abraham led the strangers to Sodom without blame. He led Christ the stranger in the same way.

Origen in the annals: A young child was placed in the temple. He was raised in the temple by a certain *sacerdos* with no blame to his parents.

In the Life of the Monks: Wherever there is a church of God, there you shall lead strangers. On account of this he led Christ to you, namely the vessel to his chosen people.

Gregory: Who shall show me mercy? For mercy is without a stumbling block. On account of which he created the merciful one.

That young children should not be separated from their mothers in their early years

Lactantius: And this has been proved most skilfully, that glistening and rich bodily fluid irrigates the tenderness of the new body, until it is both equipped with teeth to consume hard foodstuffs, and strengthened with powers.

That the young ought to make their wishes known when they reach puberty

A synod: It is proper that children, when they have reached puberty, are to be compelled to take wives or proffer continence. And girls of the same age should choose between chastity and marriage by paternal will.

55 Concerning hospitality

55.1 That hospitality must be observed

Paul to the Hebrews: Do not forget hospitality; for by this some have pleased angels received in their home.

In the Gospel: Bring the needy and the wanderers into your house.

Likewise: You who indulge in your riches, seek out the hungry! Note that he does not only say that they should receive them, but even seek them out.

55.2 Concerning the profit of hospitality

Abraham, through hospitality, deserved to hear the mysteries from God. Lot, through hospitality, deserved to be released from the Sodomites. Rahab, the harlot of Jericho, freed her household through hospitality. The faithful widow, also by showing hospitality to the prophets, deserved to have her son revived and her vessel of flour replenished. Abdias,[557] the servant of God, deserved to receive the grace of prophecy by ministering to the prophets.

Gregory in the homilies: A certain *princeps* gave water to strangers and washed their feet. And he saw five men, but when he returned he only found four. And in the following night he saw and heard the Lord saying: Up until now you have attended to my limbs, but you have done this to me instead. For the Lord said: Whoever received you, received me.

In the Life of the Monks:[558] Some thieves [disguised as strangers seeking hospitality] came to a *locus* with the intention of robbing it. And all the *monachi*, with candles in their hands, came to their service together with their *princeps*. Each and every one of them (i.e. the *monachi*), serving them (i.e. the thieves) the water of indulgence, saw clearly and pointed out to them [their wicked ways] and they confessed their guilt and did penance.

55.3 Concerning being careful of strangers

In the Life of the Fathers: A stranger came to the bishop, but he did not receive him. So he went to a certain married man and told him that he was not received by the bishop. And this married man took him in. The latter woke up in the middle of the night and he killed the former's son; for the stranger was possessed by demons, because the married man took him in insult to the bishop.

55.4 Concerning receiving wicked strangers

A Roman synod: They who present themselves as monastic disciples but are unknown should bring with them, from brethren to whom they are known, somebody who will commend them. But if they have not brought anyone who might testify in their favour, let them not be received, on account of fraudsters who pretend to be perfect disciples, but are rapacious wolves.

Concerning the reward [for hospitality]

The Lord in the Gospel: He who receives a prophet in the name of a prophet shall receive the reward of a prophet.

Likewise: Whoever feeds the just, it is as if he feeds God. Whoever feeds the sinner, it is as if he feeds the just, because he is a hungry man. Note that Christ did not turn away from Judas the traitor.

56 Concerning heretics

56.1 Concerning the word 'heretics' and the reason why they are called heretics

Jerome says: 'Heretic' is in Greek what '*elector*' is in Latin, because each and every one of them chooses his own doctrine. For 'heresy' is translated 'choice'. Cicero said that '*eresim*' ought to be written without phonetic aspiration.

56.2 Concerning the reason why they are heretics

Augustine said: They are heretics for no other reason, save that not understanding scripture correctly, they stubbornly defend their false opinions contrary to the sense [of scripture].

56.3 Concerning heresiarchs

Jerome: 'Heresiarch' is '*elector excelsus*' in Latin; they are the authorities of heretics, wherefrom their dogmas and schools emanate; they are called heresiarchs, like Arius, after whom the Arians and the dogma of the Arians are named.

56.4 That a heretic must be avoided after reproach

Paul said: Avoid a heretic after his second or third reproach; knowing that he is a subverter of such a kind, and having been condemned he offends by his own judgement.

A synod said: We decree that a heretic must be avoided, for just as cancer snakes through the body, so does his doctrine snake through our souls.

Likewise: Every heretic is persuasive and very sweet, and thus he must be avoided like fire.

56.5 That it is not necessary to avoid a heretic

Augustine said: Insofar as he is a heretic, he must not be avoided, but overcome with arguments, lest he believe that he has won rather than been defeated.

Jerome: Perversity must be refuted and overcome with arguments from scripture; just as it arises easily, so it convinces easily.

56.6 Concerning reading the books of heretics

A bishop should not read the books of pagans. But let him read the books of heretics if necessity and circumstance require it.

57 Concerning men's property

Whether men's property is to be punished or not for their offences

57.1 That man's property is punished for his offence

The Lord pronounces against nature: Cursed is the earth in your work. In the deluge all the property of the world was destroyed because of the offences of men. On account of the offence of Pharaoh and the Egyptians their firstborn were also slain. The swine of the Gerasenes, possessed by the devil because of their (i.e. the Gerasenes') sin are drowned. For previously they offended against Abraham's livestock.

Jerome: On account of a man's offence, all his possessions are held under the sign of offence; an ox and an ass are damned.

Jerome: What is more fitting for punishment in lieu of a man, than that by which he lives and which always sustains him?

Origen: When that man has offended, he shall forfeit[559] his property, and you shall drag him to judgement.

Augustine: When a man becomes corrupt he also damns everything so that he is dragged to judgement by his own devices.

57.2 That a man's property should not be punished for his offence

In Exodus: Although Pharaoh and his people were destroyed in the Red Sea, his livestock were spared.

Likewise: Although Amalek was destroyed, his livestock are not destroyed.

Likewise: Similarly, although the Amorrhites are destroyed, their livestock are not destroyed.

Origen: It is said in the homilies concerning the red cow: Livestock do not bear the blame for human offence, but bear it away.

Likewise, Origen: The more useful they are to all ends, the more they are free.

57.3 Concerning the three things that are free from the offence of another

A Hibernian synod: There are three who do not bear the offences of others: the generous man, if he holds his household with all in common; the livestock of the innocent whose fruit and labour are common to all, seeking nothing apart from food, and the food by which they live is not man's but God's; the slave faithfully serving his master.

Hence Jerome says: The offence of the master does not fall upon his slave. But the offence of the slave passes on to his master.

Hence Balaam was ready to kill, had he not been put right by the ass, and the ass was free.

In Deuteronomy: When the Lord your God shall deliver that city into your hands, you shall slay all that are therein of the male sex with the edge of the sword, but not women and children, cattle, and other things that are in the city.

57.4 That livestock must not be confiscated for anyone's offence save its own

A Hibernian synod says: Let no beast be punished except for its own offence, e.g. either for killing a man, or causing injury, or killing another beast, or for destroying preserved grass or the harvest.

Concerning livestock fasting with men

Although retribution was imminent, they were also freed in this manner, fasting as the Ninivites with their livestock.

Concerning livestock

The son of Sirach: You have cattle, tend to them; and if they be useful to you, keep them with you.

58 Concerning guiding barbarians[560]

58.1 That the one who guides barbarians is guilty of blood

Augustine: In my opinion shedding blood and guiding shall be punished in a similar way.

A synod: Whoever brought evil on his neighbour, is guilty of blood.

58.2 Concerning the punishment of those guiding barbarians

A Hibernian synod said: Whoever guides barbarians should do penance for fourteen years.[561] A barbarian, i.e. a foreigner. Who is a foreigner if not one who strikes down everybody cruelly and savagely?

58.3 Concerning the law by which the nobles[562] prescribed fourteen years of penance for the leaders

A Hibernian synod said: The nobles[563] decided on fourteen years for this reason: if they entered the burial places[564] of bishops, or if they killed or struck down a religious man or a nun, or dragged out innocents from the church, let the guide do penance for seven years for his own guilt, and seven years for the guilt of those whom he guided.

58.4 Concerning the leader who does not repent[565]

Origen said: Everyone who guides strangers assumes the guilt of all, if he cannot repent.[566]

Jerome: Anyone who engages in deceit contracts the guilt of blood-shedding.

58.5 Concerning the three guilts of Judas

A synod: Judas contracted three guilts, for he chose deceit, and guided strangers, and accepted the reward of deceit.

A psalm says: Bloody and deceitful men, etc.

Concerning cursing those who guide strangers

In the law: The Moabites are cursed because they led Balaam son of Beer to curse the people of God.

Likewise: Israel hated those who brought Rasin the king of Syria upon Jerusalem.

Do not lead the *allophyli*[567] into the land of God, lest a malediction cling to you.

Jerome: The Jews led a cohort of gentiles to Christ's passion, and a malediction remained upon them.

Concerning the punishment to those guiding barbarians

Augustine: The leader of a foreign race does not incur another penalty, except for his own leadership of foreigners. He who guides foreigners to his own neighbour deserves a double punishment: he is deserving of death.

Faustus: Brother, do not bring evil upon your neighbours, lest you too should perish.

Concerning those who guide foreigners going unpunished

In the law: Balaam, whom the Moabites brought in, was a magician, and the Moabites were outside the church of God; such people do not exist nowadays, rather all non-believers are in God.[568]

Likewise: Rasin was a gentile king of Syria and Israel worshiped idols. But nowadays they are not called 'gentiles', but 'the faithful', and they do not overturn the church of God [nor] inflict devastation on the saints.[569]

Likewise: These days they are not called barbarians, but the faithful of a single language. For punishments are reckoned for your people, when you do not know the language of your enemies. As Isaiah said: I shall bring upon you a faithless people whose language you do not know. And here there was not only one leader, but one's own cause and indignation have led each and every one, therefore all are leaders. Hence, according to the prophet: Everyone shall die for his own sin. For the father shall not die for the sin of his son, nor the son for the sin of the father, and certainly not for the sin of a stranger.

59 Concerning feasts

59.1 Concerning the three reasons[570] for which the church, according to the *Romani*, celebrates dedications

That the blessing of many may protect a new home, that the Lord may protect its dwellers through the prayers of the multitude, that property may increase through blessings.

59.2 Concerning preaching in feasts

Augustine: Whenever we invite others, we have arranged to provide food, whence the flesh is restored; it is fitting that we see to it either that a divine reading be re-read, or that something holy be recited for the nourishment of the soul, lest the slave woman be given precedent over the mistress, [with the consequence that] while the slave woman is made drunk, the mistress is not fed by the sweetness of the word of God. For man does not live on bread alone, but in every word of God. Just as the flesh does not live without food, neither does the soul without the word of God.

59.3 Concerning excluding buffoonery and dirty talk from the feast

Augustine: But some do not only ignore the divine reading, by which the soul is refreshed, but busy themselves with idle speech, for which they shall be accountable in the day of judgement; sometimes they either engage in slanderous and silly talk themselves, or gladly listen to others who speak in such a manner. If the soul does not receive that by which to live, why is that by which it dies forced upon it?

A synod: A cleric singing between courses at a meal, not edifying faith, should be excommunicated.

Concerning comparing those who work miracles and those who are less able to work miracles

Gregory says: There are many who do not work miracles; nevertheless, they are no different from those who work miracles.[571]

59.4 That one must not dine in the feasts of gentiles, but fast

Augustine: We fast, dearest brothers, on the feastdays of gentiles, and we lament the stupidity of these wretched men with true and perfect charity.

Concerning giving feasts to the poor

The synod of Gangra: If anyone despises those who, in a faithful manner, give *agapae*, i.e. feasts, to the poor, and invite the brethren in honour of God, and he does not want to acquiesce in these invitations, spurning that which is laid out [by the hosts], let him be anathema.

Concerning the three things that the dignity of a feast comprises

Every feast is deserving of three things: propriety, timeliness, kindness.

That it is inappropriate to hold feasts in a church

The synod of Laodicea: It is not appropriate that feasts, which are called *agapae*, be held in *dominici*, i.e. in the Lord's churches, nor is it appropriate to eat or spread out couches within the house of God.

60 Concerning maledictions

Concerning cursing enemies

60.1 How enemies ought to be cursed

Solomon: Let it not be well with the impious, neither let his days be prolonged, but as a shadow let him pass away, who fears not the face of God.

Paul: Would that they who trouble you were cut down.

Alexander the coppersmith has done me much evil; may the Lord reward him according to his work.

In a psalm: Render retribution to the proud. And these things are said not as a wish, but as a prophecy.

That one must fear cursing a just man

In the books of Kings: And Elisha went up to Bethel. And as he was going up the way, little boys came out of the city and mocked him, saying: Up you go, you bald head. And looking back, he saw them, and cursed them in the name of the Lord. And there came forth two bears out of the forest, and tore of them forty-two boys.

60.2 Concerning the two reasons[572] for praying for one's enemies

Augustine: We pray for our enemies for two reasons:[573] either that they may be reformed from their evils, or that they do not add evils to evils. On account of which the Lord said: I shall add evils to evils. And elsewhere: Their iniquities are not yet complete.

60.3 That one must not curse one's own enemy, but the enemy of God and the church

Origen: I do not curse my enemy, but the enemy of God and his church. For when one limb suffers, all limbs suffer together.

David: Arise, let not man be strengthened.

Augustine: When a man is strengthened, the church is weakened.

60.4 That one must not ask for the death of an enemy

Gregory says: Another demands the death of an enemy, and being unable to pursue him by the sword, he pursues him by prayer. The one cursed continues to live, and the one who cursed is held guilty of killing him. For the Lord says to love one's enemy, but that man nevertheless asked the Lord to kill his enemy. And they who pray thus wage war against their creator. On account of which it is said: May his prayer be turned to sin. It is clearly a sinful prayer to ask for things that God, who is the one being beseeched, forbids. For the truth says: When you shall stand to pray, forgive your debts.[574]

That one must not ask anything against the Lord

Jerome said: We must be careful not to ask for things that go against the Lord. David wept for his enemy Saul. Stephen prayed for his enemies.

Augustine: When we pray against an enemy, we pray against the Lord; and unless the Holy Spirit intervenes for us, the prayer is transformed against us into evil.

In the Life of the Fathers:[575] Florentius the hermit said about the four monks who killed his bear: I have faith in the Lord, that they shall receive punishment for their wickedness in this life, in the sight of all. And divine vengeance followed. They were struck down by leprosy and died. After this happened, the man of God panicked, and lamented all his life, declaring that he was a murderer.

60.5 Concerning the dialogue of Peter and Gregory

Peter says concerning malediction: Should we consider it a grave sin if, perchance, we curse someone when we are overcome with anger? Gregory: Why do you ask me whether it is a grave sin, when Paul would say: Nor shall cursers possess the kingdom of God. Think, therefore, how great the sin is, which keeps one out of the kingdom of God. Peter says: What if, perchance, not of malice, but of a careless or perturbed tongue, one verbally assaults the enemies of God or his neighbour? Gregory: If idle speech is reprehensible in the eyes of the harsh judge, then all the more so that speech which is harmful.

60.6 Concerning the curses of the law

These curses shall come upon you and overtake you. Cursed shall you be in the city, cursed in the field. Cursed shall be your barn, and cursed your kneading bowls.[576] Cursed shall be the fruit of your womb, and the fruit of your earth, and the herds of your oxen, and the flocks of your sheep. Cursed shall you be coming in, and cursed going out. The Lord shall send upon you famine and hunger, and a rebuke upon all your works. May the Lord set pestilence upon you. May the Lord afflict you with poverty, with fever and with cold, with burning and with heat, and with corrupted air and with rust, and pursue you until you perish. May the heaven that is above you be of bronze, and the ground you tread upon of iron. Let the Lord give dusty rain upon your land, and let ashes come down from heaven upon you, until you be consumed. Let the Lord betray you as you fall before your enemies. And let your carcass be food for all the fowls of the air and the beast of the earth, and let there be none to drive them away. Let the Lord strike you with the sores of Egypt, and with the scab and the itch that you are unable to heal. Let the Lord strike you with feeble mindedness and blindness and madness, and may you grope at midday, and not make straight your ways. And may you at all times suffer false accusations, and be oppressed with violence, and may you have no one to deliver you, etc.

Concerning those who are cursed by such things

Cursed be he who does not honour his father and mother, and may all the people say: Amen. Cursed be he who moves his neighbour's landmarks, and all the people shall say: Amen. Cursed be he who causes the blind man to wander in his journey, and all the people shall say: Amen. Cursed be he who perverts the judgement of the stranger, of the orphan, and the widow, and all the people shall say: Amen. Cursed be he who lies with the wife of his close kin and uncovers his bed, and all the people shall say: Amen. Cursed be he who lies with any beast, and all the people shall say: Amen. Cursed be he who lies with his sister, the daughter of his father, or his mother, and all the people shall say: Amen. Cursed be he who lies with his mother-in-law, and all the people shall say: Amen. Cursed be he who strikes down his neighbour, and may all say: Amen. Cursed be he who takes gifts to slay an innocent person, and all the people shall say: Amen. Cursed be he who abides not in the words of this law, and fulfills them not in actions, and all the people shall say: Amen.

61 Concerning benedictions

The law says: And all these blessings shall come upon you and take hold of you if you hear his precepts. Blessed shall you be in the city, blessed in the field, blessed shall be the fruit of your womb, and the fruit of your earth, and the fruit of your cattle, and the folds of your sheep, and the herds of your ploughing cattle, and blessed shall be your barns, and blessed your kneading bowls.[577] Blessed shall you be coming in and going out. The Lord shall cause your enemies that rise up against you to fall down before you. The Lord will send forth a blessing upon your storehouses and upon all the works of your hands, and will bless you in the land that you shall receive, etc.

Concerning showing kindness to neighbours

That everyone should show kindness to his neighbour, whether he be a layman, an ecclesiastic, not doing penance[578]

The law: Do not do evil to your neighbour. But if you have done, ask his forgiveness.

Job: I have harmed no one, and if I have harmed anyone, I made amends.

Christ: If you offer your gift at the altar, and there you remember that your brother had something against you, leave it there, etc.

Augustine: Should any cleric or *monachus* or layman, offend his neighbours, he ought not offer a host, nor plead [before God] without reconciling them, lest his prayer be transformed into sin.

Jerome: Whoever offends his neighbour ought to reconcile him, for unless he reconciles his neighbour, he cannot reconcile God. If he says to you, 'I am dead to the world', tell him what the synod decreed: Each and every *monachus* is dead to the world when he does not require any worldly thing and has taken care of all evils. And if he says, 'I am a penitent', tell him what the synod decreed: True penance with God and your neighbours is when there is no discord.

Thus, in the Life of the Monks: Someone was living as a penitent in a monastery, and another commoner, whom he defrauded, rebuked him, and thus saddened him. And the abbot seeing him sad, returned [to the penitent] the silver that he (*sc.* the penitent) cheated him (*sc.* the commoner) out of.

That everyone ought to forgive his neighbour

Christ: I have forgiven you, and you shall be forgiven.

If you have not forgiven, he will not forgive you, etc.

Likewise: Forgive your debts, etc.

Likewise: I know you are my disciples if you love each other.

Jerome: How can we ask for our sins to be forgiven when we do not forgive our neighbours?

Concerning this, that he who does evil to his neighbour should do penance and that he to whom it is done should forgive

Christ in the Gospel of Luke: Take heed to yourselves, if your brother sin against you. Reprove him, and if he do penance, forgive him. And if he sin against you seven times in a day, and seven times in a day he turns to you, saying, ‘I repent’, forgive him.

That one must not forgive once, nor seven times, but seventy times seven

Peter asked Christ how often he should forgive, whether till seven times. Christ replied: I say not to you up to seven times, but up to seventy times seven.

Concerning the difference between Christ’s household and the devil’s

Augustine: The household of Christ is distinguished by the following: when they remit others their debts, when they entreat for their enemies, when they have no property, when they take in guests, when they do not defraud, when they do not ask for their own things to be returned, when they do not seize the things of others.

Concerning a man having nothing to give his neighbour except peace

Origen: A man to whom the Lord forgives all his sins, what should he repay his neighbour, except the sign of peace?

Concerning defrauding one's neighbours

Gregory in his homilies: Three things defraud a neighbour: exile, *monachium*[579] with stripping away of property,[580] a death succeeded by life.[581]

Concerning being silent and raising one's voice

Concerning the manner in which one must keep silent

David: I said I will take heed to my ways, etc.

Likewise: A man full of tongue shall not be set straight upon the earth.

Augustine: Silence must be observed in all things, especially at the dining table and during mass

Likewise: It is better to pray with a silent heart without making a sound, than to use words alone without the attention of the mind.

Isidore: A river that fills beyond its capacity often carries mud.

Likewise: Silence is reverence of justice.

Concerning the things that are contained in silence

Many things are contained in silence. Wisdom, which says: In babble there shall not want sin. Fear of God, which says: Speak not much, lest you offend against God. Sobriety of the mind, which says: The art of silence must be observed at all times.

Concerning restraining and guarding one's mouth

Wisdom says: He who restrains his lips is most wise.

Likewise: Death and life are in the power of the tongue.

Likewise: He who guards his mouth preserves his soul. Let every man be quick to hear, slow to speak.

Concerning the manner in which the voice should be raised

Isaiah: Lift up your voice, etc.

In the Acts of the Apostles: Peter, standing with the eleven apostles, raised his voice.

In the Apocalypse: I heard a great voice saying to them: Come up hither. And they went up.

Concerning the four [reasons] for which the voice is raised

Augustine: There are four [reasons] for raising one's voice. The first, with those who are far off, as [it is said]: Salvation is far from sinners. The second, when you are deaf, as [it is said]: Like the deaf viper, etc. The third, when we are angry, as [it is said]: I am angry with you for you have not kept my commandments. The fourth: not by raising the voice, but by the compassion of the heart, as he exclaims: With my whole heart, etc.

62 Concerning the labour of craftsmen

Concerning the labour of craftsmen

In the books of Kings: Now when Hiram had heard the words of Solomon, he rejoiced, and Hiram sent to Solomon, saying: I have heard all you have desired of me, and I will do all your desire concerning cedar trees, and fir trees. My servants shall bring them down from Lebanon to the sea, and I will put them together in floats on the sea, and convey them to the place which you have indicated to me, and will land them there, and you shall provide the necessities to me, to furnish food for my household. So Hiram gave Solomon cedar trees, and fir trees, according to all his desire. And Solomon allowed Hiram twenty thousand measures of wheat, for provision for his house, and twenty measures of the purest oil; thus gave Solomon to Hiram every year. And the Lord gave wisdom to Solomon, as he promised him, and there was peace between Hiram and Solomon, and they two made a league together. And king Solomon chose workmen from all Israel, and the levy was of thirty thousand men. And he sent them to Lebanon, ten every month by turns, so that in two months they were at home, and they were to Hiram over these levies.[582] And Solomon had eighty thousand to carry burdens, and eighty thousand to hew stones in the mountain, besides the overseers who were over every work, three thousand in number, and three hundred that ruled over the people, and the ones who did the work. The king commanded that they should bring great stones, precious stones, for the foundation of the temple, and should square them, and the masons of Solomon, and the masons of Hiram hewed them.

And a little later it is laid down therein: And the house, when it was being built, was built of stones hewed and made ready, so that there was neither hammer nor axe nor any tool of iron heard in the house.

And thereafter one reads therein: And king Solomon sent, and brought Hiram from Tyre, the son of a widow of the tribe of Naphtali, whose father was a Tyrian, a craftsman in bronze and full of wisdom and understanding and skill to work all work in bronze, etc.

And thereafter it is laid down therein: And when twenty years were ended after Solomon had built the two houses, that is, the house of the Lord and the house of the king—Hiram the king of Tyre furnishing Solomon with cedar trees and fir trees, and gold according to all he had need of—then Solomon gave Hiram twenty cities in the land of Galilee. And Hiram came out of Tyre to see the towns which Solomon had given him, and it pleased him not. And he said: Are these the cities which you have given me, brother? And he called them the land of Chabul, unto this day. And Hiram sent to king Solomon a hundred and twenty talents of gold. This is the sum of the expenses which king Solomon offered to build the house of the Lord and his own house.

The law in Exodus: And Moses said to the children of Israel: Behold the Lord has called by name Beseleel the son of Uri the son of Hur of the tribe of Judah, and has filled him with the spirit of God, with wisdom and understanding to devise and to work in gold and silver and bronze, and in engraving stones, and in carpentry. Whatsoever can be devised artificially, he has given in his heart. Ooliab also, the son of Achisamech of the tribe of Dan, he has instructed both of them with wisdom to do the work of a goldsmith, and of a coppersmith, and of a weaver.

And when Moses had called them and every skilful man, to whom the Lord had given wisdom, and such as of their own accord had offered themselves to the making of the work, he delivered all the offerings of the children of Israel unto them.

62.1

The *Hibernenses* say: Should any craftsman do a clumsy job and ask for half the tools, he shall have half the wage; otherwise, he shall receive the third part of the value [of the contract], so that another third be given to the workmen, and another third for food and tools. Whence shall they have judges? To wit, a judge from the craftsmen, and a judge from the leaders of the church or the *castellum*,[583] and they shall judge in the matter of his asking price on the basis of the work done, not in accordance with the utility [value of the structure]. Afterwards the craftsman shall have the price of a blessing. Thus they shall judge also with respect to other men of art.[584] But anyone who does not abide by this council shall be excommunicated, and let no one receive him, and he shall die without communion.

62.2 Concerning the dedication of a new church building

In the dedication of the tabernacle there was a great feast among the Jews. Likewise in the dedication of the temple in Jerusalem, likewise in its rebuilding.

In the annals of the *Romani*: In the dedication of the church of Peter a great feast took place.

In the chronicles: Under Philip, in the dedication of Rome, after the rebuilding of the surrounding walls, there was a great feast. Likewise in the dedication of Constantinople under Constantine.

In the Gospel: A great dedication ceremony took place in Jerusalem, namely for the new dedication. Whence the church observes this rite.

Concerning the three reasons[585] for which the church celebrates dedications[586]

A synod: The church performs dedication ceremonies for three reasons: that God may protect a new home through the prayers of all, and that the Lord may keep the inhabitants safe through the prayers of the multitude, and that wealth may increase through blessings.

63 Concerning augury

63.1 That Christians ought not seek divinations or auguries

Augustine: I warn you in like manner that none of you should seek advice from among the magicians, [587] divinators, and fortune-tellers, for anyone who does this evil at once loses the sacrament of baptism, and immediately becomes profane and a pagan, and without considerable alms or a long penance, he shall be lost in perpetuity.

Augustine said: Similarly, do not become a follower of auguries, nor small birds singing, nor the diabolical divinations of their song.

63.2 That good works are useless while such things are observed

Augustine: Whoever shall believe in the aforesaid evil men—to wit, magicians, and divinators, and soothsayers, and dispensers of phylacteries, and other kinds of auguries—will perish, though he may fast, or pray, give alms generously, or torment his body by all sorts of afflictions. Nothing will help him as long as he continues to observe such things.

63.3 Concerning the punishment for divination

The law says: A man or woman in whom there is a pythonical or divining spirit, dying let them die, they shall stone them, and their blood be upon them.

63.4 Concerning those given to auguries and magical consultation of scripture[588]

The synod of Agde said: One must not pass over in silence that which has greatly infested the faith of religion, namely that so many clerics or laymen practise augury and predict the future by means of magical consultation of scripture. For as long as one persists in this offence, he is a stranger to the church.

63.5 Concerning the penance of Christians who observe divinations

The synod of Ancyra: They who, in the manner of pagans, consult divinations, should do penance for five years.

63.6 That auguries must not be observed, even if they are true

Augustine: What would we do if these auguries should pronounce the truth? Concerning this matter scripture gives testimony and warns us, saying: Even if they have said true things, do not believe them.

63.7 Concerning the reason that demons know more than men

Isidore said in the books of etymologies: They say demons are so called by the Greeks as if the word were *demnas* (Isidore: *δαήμων*), that is, knowledgeable in many things. Whence they are also accustomed to give some answers. And there is in them more knowledge of things than in fragile humanity, partly through the sharper acumen of their senses, partly through the experience of an extremely long life, partly through angelic revelation at God's command.[589]

63.8 Concerning Christian unruly behaviour

Augustine: Let none of you take notice of the day in which he leaves his house and the day in which he returns; for God made all days equal, as it is written: The first day was made, and the second, etc. But whenever you feel the need to set out in whatever way, make yourself a little symbol of the cross in the name of Jesus Christ, faithfully singing the creed and the Lord's prayer, confident of God's help, go on the journey, saying with the apostle: Who shall separate us from the love of Christ, etc. For good Christians are not separated from Christ by trials, nor by tribulations, but the lukewarm are both distracted by idle stories from time to time, and, if they endure so much as a little measure of harm, they are immediately scandalised.

64 Concerning the soul

64.1 Concerning the nature of the soul

Jerome says: I do not pronounce on the nature of the soul, whether it has fallen from heaven, as Pythagoras and all the Platonists and Origen [believe], or whether it is of the same substance of God, as the Stoics and Manicheans [believe], or whether souls, having been made a long time ago, are kept in a treasure chest, as some ecclesiastics foolishly believe, or whether they are created by the Lord every day and sent into bodies, as [it is written], 'my Father is at work until now, and I work', or whether they are born at the same time as the body: as a body proceeds from a body, so does a soul from a soul. But I do not say that the soul is from God, for God alone is immortal and unchangeable, and incorruptible, and incapable of suffering.

Lactantius said: Some have said that the soul is fire, others a spirit, others blood. They say it is fire because it animates the body; a spirit, because it blows (*spirat*) through our limbs; blood, because it moves with the blood.

Concerning the three parts of the soul

Thomas: Clearly there is a single wisdom in man, and the intellect and memory and skill proceed from a single wisdom.

For Gregory [said]: Skill exists that you may absorb what you have not learned, memory exists that you do not forget what you have learned, and intellect that you understand the things that can be shown or taught. If you, mortal, can possess these three within a single wisdom, how much more so God ought to be believed to have three persons in a single divinity.

That every soul has an angel to watch over it

In the Gospel: See that you do not despise any of these little ones. For I say to you that their angels always see the face of my father who is in heaven.

Jerome in his commentary on Matthew: The dignity of the souls is great, such that each and every one, from his inception, has an angel delegated to watch over him. And the apostle instructed that women's heads be veiled in churches on account of the angels.

64.2 Concerning the seven substances of the soul

Augustine says concerning the soul: So long as the spirit is contemplated upon, so long as the senses sense, so long as the mind understands, so long as reason discerns, so long as the will wishes, so long as memory remembers, so long as our limbs are strong, there is a soul.

64.3 Concerning the three parts of the soul

Abraham says: The soul comprises three parts: the rational, the irascible, the desirous. When, therefore, one of these dispositions is seized by a force of harmful passion, the name is given to the vice according to the disposition corrupted. For if the pest of vice infected its rational part, it shall beget the vices of vainglory, arrogance, envy, pride, presumption, heresy. And if it has wounded the irascible sense, it shall yield rage, impatience, depression, peevishness, pusillanimity, and cruelty. And if it has damaged the desirous part, it shall generate gluttony, fornication, love of money, avarice, and harmful and worldly desires.

64.4 Concerning the soul's dwelling-place

Augustine: Some say that the soul's dwelling place is in the chest, others in the skull, but many say that it is diffused throughout the whole body.

64.5 Concerning the life of the body and the soul

Isidore: The life of the body is the soul, the life of the soul is God. And just as the body is dead without the soul, so is the soul dead without God. As much as the body is broken down, by so much the mind is drawn away from illicit desire.

Jerome in his commentary on Matthew: From the heart, he said, evil thoughts emanate; therefore the principal dwelling-place of the soul is not in the brain, as Plato [believed], but in the heart, according to Christ.

64.6 Concerning the dialogue of Gregory and Peter

How can an incorporeal soul be harmed by a corporeal fire? Peter: How can an incorporeal thing be held and harmed by a corporeal thing, I do not know. Gregory replied: Tell me, I say, whether you perceive the apostate spirits that have been cast out from the glory of heaven as corporeal or incorporeal? Peter: What sane and wise man would say that these spirits are corporeal? Gregory: Would you say that hell fire is corporeal or incorporeal? Peter says: I do not doubt that hell fire is corporeal, in which it is certain that bodies are tortured. Gregory: The truth shall certainly say to the reprobates at the end of time: Go into the eternal fire, which has been prepared for the devil and his angels. If, therefore, the devil and his angels, though incorporeal, shall be tormented by corporeal fire, it is a small wonder that also souls, even before they receive bodies, endure real bodily torments.

64.7 Concerning the dialogue of Gregory and Peter on the matter of the place in which the souls of the just are received before judgement

Peter said: Are the souls of the just received in heaven now, before the resurrection of the bodies? Gregory: We cannot confirm this with respect to all the just, nor deny it with respect to all. For there are souls of certain just men which are as yet carried away from the heavenly kingdom to certain mansions. In which thing what other [cause] for delay[590] is there, save that they were somewhat short of possessing perfect justice.

Likewise: It is clearer than daylight that the souls of the perfect immediately, once they leave the prison of this flesh, are admitted to the heavenly thrones. This is attested by the same truth that says: Wheresoever a body shall be by itself, there shall the eagles also be gathered together. For where our redeemer rests his body, there, without doubt, the souls of the just are collected.

64.8 That the soul is not a part of the divinity and that it does not exist before it is joined to the body

Isidore: The soul is not a part of the divine substance or nature, nor does it exist before it is joined to the body. But it is created at that moment when the body, to which it is joined, is also created. The philosophers say that it exists before it is joined to the body; the truth of this is not confirmed by any evidence.

65 Concerning various cases

Augustine's statement concerning penance

Saint Jerome concerning penance

Concerning the moderation of fasting[591]

Augustine's statement concerning penance, instructing how it is to be performed[592]

Jerome's statement concerning penance to Damasus, the bishop of the city [of Rome], instructing that penitents be admitted

65.1 Concerning the need to restrain the clothes of Christians

Jerome said: Their clothing is neither too clean, nor too dirty, and not outlandish, lest a crowd of passers-by encounter you, and you should be pointed at.

Jerome: Surely, no one seeks special clothes for any other reason than vainglory: that he may appear more distinguished than others. That he seeks an expensive outfit only out of vainglory is borne out by the following fact, namely that no one wants to wear expensive clothes where he cannot be seen by others.

65.2 Concerning the three causes on account of which written things are neglected

Jerome: When you see a cupboard that is stacked with books and not often open, and the books within it are almost worn down by time, this usually comes about as a result of the uncleanly nature of the keepers, or the negligence of the readers, or the paucity of readers.

Concerning the three syllables that cleanse the sins of men

Augustine said: There are three syllables that can wash away the sin of men, just as the sin is cleansed by them. Augustine said: But they are not pronounced from an inner sacrifice, to wit: I have sinned (*pecc a ui*).[593]

65.3 Concerning idle speech

Augustine: Idle speech is that through which no good is attained in this world or the next.

Jerome: Idle speech is that which is conveyed to the hearers and speakers without utility.

Gregory: Idle speech is that which lacks either reason or peace.

Likewise: Idle speech is either that which is not needed for any justifiable reason, or has no intention to be useful.

Basil: Every speech that does not assist in attaining the grace of the faith of Christ, is idle, etc.

65.4 Concerning the Christian

Augustine says: Unless one holds human things in contempt, he cannot possess heavenly things. Who deems himself Christian save he who follows Christ's doctrine, and imitates his example? But you think he is a Christian whose bread never sates hunger, whose drink never quenches thirst, whose table no one knows, by whose help no pauper is supported, whose goodness no one is familiar with, whose pity no one knows. Let not someone like this be called a son of God. A Christian is he who shows mercy to all, a Christian is he who feels the grief of another as if it were his own, who is moved to tears by the tears of others, whose home is shared by all, whose door is closed to no one, whose table no pauper is a stranger to, whose goodness all know, who serves God by day and night, who is made poor to the world that he may become rich to God, who desires heavenly rather than earthly things, who spurns human things that he may know heavenly things.

65.5 Concerning the three requests of Patrick[594]

The *Hibernenses* say: There are three requests of Patrick, the first of which is that half or a third part of a region be given by them to the church that is closer to it;[595] the second, that nothing should be bound by oath by anybody on a weak church; the third, that a cleric be likewise examined in court by a layman.[596]

But now, render thanks to your God, for the four requests that you have made have been granted to you. The first request is that your preeminence shall be in Armagh. The second request is that whoever on the day of his separation from the body recites the hymn that has been composed for you, you shall adjudge him penance. The third request is that the descendants of Díchu, who kindly received you, shall find mercy both in this world and the next, and shall not perish. The fourth request is that all the *Hibernenses* on the day of judgement shall be judged by you, as it is said to the apostle: And you, sitting, shall judge the twelve tribes of Israel. That you may judge those whose apostle you have been.[597]

Concerning the true sacrifice

Gregory: The true sacrifice to God on our behalf will be when we shall make a sacrifice of ourselves.

65.6 That it benefits not to do anything against God's counsel

Jerome in his commentary on Jonah: The flight of the prophet can be a reference to him, who disregarded God's precepts and surrendered to the world, but this does not help him. From which example we know that things that men consider beneficial to them are turned into their ruin if God does not approve. Therefore human planning is of no use if it goes against God's will.

Indeed, the Egyptians were wiped out [for] providing help to detain Israel against God's will.

The ship was also put at risk for receiving the one who put it at risk.

Gregory Nazianzen said: How can one who is without possessions be detained?

The same says: There are two in heaven that cannot be detained: God and the angel. But the third is on earth, namely, the Christian, living in the flesh as though he were incorporeal.

65.7 That one must seek the advice of many

Origen: Ask many, but do not follow the example of many, as [it is said]: Be ye not many masters among you. This is said also of the wise men who teach by words and do not fulfil their teachings, as [it is said]: They go down alive into hell; as far as: Their.

Concerning dressing the feet of clerics

In the Acts of the Apostles: And the angel said to him: Gird yourself and bind on your sandals. And he did so. If an example was given by this [it is] that one ought not walk without sandals.

65.8 Concerning those who think they are righteous, but are not

Gildas in his letters: While they eat bread in moderation, they boast about it beyond measure; while they use water, at the same time they drink the cup of hatred; while they take holy dishes, they are given to disdains; while they expend themselves on vigils, they rebuke others who are overcome by sleep. They prefer fasting to charity, vigils to justice, their own contrivances to concord, the cell to the church, severity to humility, and, finally, man to God. They fast, which unless it is pursued through other virtues, profits nothing. But they who undertake charity, the holy spirits proclaim with a *cithara*.[598] All our justices are like the rag of a menstruous woman.

65.9 Concerning honouring the Sabbath

Jeremiah says: Take heed to your souls and carry no burdens on the Sabbath, and bring them not in by the gates of Jerusalem, and you shall not bring burdens out of your houses on the Sabbath, and do not do any work on it.

65.10 That the law of the Lord must be recited by day and night with assiduous prayer

Ezra says: And they read in the book of their Lord, and they confessed and adored the Lord their God four times in the day and four times in the night.

Concerning pride

Gregory in his homilies: A wondrous deed performed with pride does not exalt, but weighs one down. Whoever accumulates virtues without humility bears dust to the wind. Where it appears that something is attained, there it is in fact made more obscure.

That one must not respond to insults

Gregory: In which matter what is asked of us, if not that when we endure mendacious insults from our fellow men, we should be silent even about the truth of them, lest we convert the office of righteous reproach into the weapon of fury.

Likewise, Gregory: It is more glorious to walk away by being silent about an insult, than to prevail in reply.

Concerning the equal share of those who do battle and those who abide at the baggage

After they have done battle, David told his companions about the Amalekites: And let no man hearken to you in this matter. But equal shall be the portion of he who went down to battle and of he who abode at the baggage; let them divide alike.

That he who orders an execution himself performs the execution

Thus said the Lord God of Israel: I anointed you king over Israel and I delivered you from the hand of Saul, and gave you your master's house into your bosom, and gave you the house of Israel and Judah. And if these things be little, I shall add far greater things unto you. Why therefore have you despised the word of the Lord, to do evil in my sight? You have struck down Uriah the Hittite with his sword, and have taken his wife, and have slain him with the sword of the children of Ammon.

Concerning Sabbath and the fifth day[599]

Eusebius and Sylvester decreed that one must fast on Sabbath and on the fifth day. It must be observed as the Lord's day. On the Sabbath the Lord was placed in the grave, and all his disciples fasted. They rejoiced on the Lord's day just as much as they mourned. And therefore we say that whoever is able must fast on the Sabbath, but not the one who is not able; he does not seek what he cannot do. The fifth day is adorned for the ascent of Christ, to be associated with the day of resurrection.

65.11 That the city must not be opened in the morning

Nehemiah: Let not the gates of Jerusalem be opened until the sun be hot.

That neither they who are good enough, nor they who are evil enough, shall receive compensation in the day of judgement

John the metropolitan: Then, without doubt, there shall be a compensation for good and evil deeds, and as though they are placed on scales, and both parts sink, and the part on which the deeds sink low, shall pronounce the verdict. If, therefore, the multitude of evil deeds shall prevail, he shall be dragged to hell. But if the good deeds will be greater, they shall resist with greater force. And they shall oppose the evil deeds and their perpetrator, and they shall be called back to the place of the living even from the frontier of hell.

Concerning the one who is wrongly accused, how does he defend himself

A Roman synod: In regard to a dispute between two people with no witnesses, they decided that he shall testify by the four Gospels before he takes communion, by which he is approved. Then let him be subject to the ordeal by fire.[600]

65.12 Concerning the cause of our destitution

Ambrose says: The cause of our destitution is avarice. Therefore the birds of the sky do not lack nourishment, because they do not know to envy others.

65.13 Concerning perpetual health being obtained by no means other than work

Gregory said: Perpetual health that was shamefully lost by free will, is acquired through harsh labour; if there is nothing harsh in the work, there will be nothing valuable in the virtue [acquired].

That advice must not be given to all

Gregory says: To give advice to a fool is charity, to a wiser man pride.

That it is not permitted to discriminate in judgement

Solomon: He who discriminates in judgement does not do well. Such a man forsakes the truth even for a morsel of bread.

Likewise: It is not good to discriminate in judgement.

Likewise: He who stores up treasures by a lying tongue is vain; he is fattened up for the snares of death.

Likewise, Augustine: It is a sin to use words for deception and not for what they were created.

That the lion kills a sinner, protects the just

A lion that once killed a sinner afterwards guarded the body of a just man.

65.14 Concerning a gathering taking place a second time on account of stormy and rainy weather

In Ezra: And all the multitude answered and said with a loud voice: According to your word unto us, it shall be done, but as the people are many and it is raining, we are not able to stand outside, and it is a work of one day or two, [for] we have exceedingly sinned.

65.15 Concerning young boys

A Roman synod: It is proper that children, when they have reached puberty, are to be compelled to take wives or profess continence to the church. And girls of the same age should choose between chastity and marriage by paternal will.

65.16 That clerics are not tied to their places, unlike their superiors

The synod of Nicaea: Clerics must not be restricted to their own churches in times of danger, or persecution, or if their search for a better rule compels them to leave. Senior grades, however, ought not abandon their own churches, but ought to be burdened by every need of it.

65.17 That it is better to advise

Patrick says: We believe it is better to forewarn the negligent, lest offences abound, than to condemn the deeds once they are done.

Solomon: It is better to reprove than to be angry.

65.18 That one must not fast on Sunday

A Roman synod: Whoever fasts devoutly on Sunday is deemed not to be a catholic.

The synod of Gangra: If anyone fasts on Sunday on account of perceived continence, or defiance, let him be anathema.

66 Concerning contrary sources[601]

Concerning the example of manual labour not being performed by higher orders and, on the contrary, being performed by the bishop

Luke in the Acts of the Apostles: It would be wrong for us to leave the word of God and serve tables.

On the contrary, Paul in the Acts of the Apostles: For such things as were needful for me and them that are with me, these hands have furnished.

Concerning the example of living abroad and, on the contrary, of remaining in one's own *locus* and doing God's will there

God says to Abraham: Go forth out of your country, etc.

David: I have become a stranger to my brethren and an alien to the sons of my mother.

Wherefrom it emerges that every pilgrim is an heir of Abraham and also of David.

On the contrary, Augustine: The kingdoms of heaven have been founded throughout the world. How do you expect to come across the earth to him who fills the earth? The Lord did not say: Go forth to the east and seek justice, or sail to the west and seek mercy, but he said: Give and it shall be given to you, forgive, and you shall be forgiven, have faith in the Lord and stay in your *locus*.

Concerning the concession made to Christians with respect to foodstuffs and, on the contrary, the need to restrict it

And Christians have been given permission to eat what they desire with moderation and thanksgiving.

On the contrary, Paul: All things are lawful to me, but not all things edify.

Aponius: Only he who practises self-restraint also with respect to lawful things, does not stumble into the unlawful.

Concerning wishing evil on enemies and, on the contrary, not wishing evil

The Lord in the Law: You shall curse this people.

David: Have no mercy on all of Israel.

Job: Cursed be their fury, because it was stubborn.

On the contrary, the Lord in the Law: Revenge is mine, and I shall repay.

In the New Testament, Paul: Those who wish evil shall not possess the kingdom of God.

That books ought not be withheld and, on the contrary, not be given to evildoers

There are many, even religious men, who want to have many bound books and yet they keep them shut up in cupboards, so that they neither read them themselves, nor lend them to others to read, not understanding that there is no benefit in having books and yet being too busy to read them. For a clean and well bound book does not make the soul clean if it is not read. However, a book that is continually read, though it cannot be fair on the outside through being handled and read all the time, nonetheless makes the soul fair within.

On the contrary: Give not that which is holy to dogs, neither cast your pearls before swine.

Origen said this with respect to scripture.

Jerome: If you will give the scripture to a fool, he will despise it, and he will not read what is worthy, but he will deride what is bad, and wickedly misinterpret the author.[602]

A synod decreed: Books belonging to a community ought not be removed from the monastic establishment,[603] but should be confined for the use of those who would wish to read them.

The following was shown in the Annals of the Hebrews: In the time of Uziah, the five books of Moses were demanded by the twelve tribes, but Uziah replied that by no means ought they be handed over from the cupboard.

Concerning the immutability of doctrine and, on the contrary, its mutability

I do not come to destroy the law, but to fulfil.

Paul: If an angel of God should preach to you anything beyond what is already preached, do not believe him.

In the Ecclesiastical History: Let no new doctrine enter the caverns of your ears.

On the contrary: You have heard what was said by the authors of old: You shall love your neighbour and hate your enemy. But I say to you: Love your enemies.

Another says: There are two things in the error of men that are tolerated with great difficulty: that presumption of falsehood should prevail over the truth, and—even when the truth has revealed itself—that falsehood should be presumptuously defended.

That God ought not be forgotten in times of prosperity and, on the contrary, not forsaken in times of hardship

The Law: When the Lord your God shall have brought you into the land that he shall give you after its inhabitants have been expelled before you, into the cities that you did not construct, to the fruit that you did not water, to the cisterns that you did not dig, to the houses full of riches that you did not build, take heed diligently lest you forget the Lord, who brought you out of the house of servitude to these favours.

On the contrary, Paul: I speak the truth in Christ, I lie not, for neither death, nor life, nor the sword, nor hunger, nor nakedness, shall be able to separate me from the love of God, etc.

66.1 That every judge ought not be changeable in his judgement and, on the contrary, ought to overturn an injustice[604]

Pilate says: What I have written I have written.

Jerome: Let a judge give his verdict and let him not change it. For if he should change it, let him be demoted.

Paul, on the contrary: Every unjust bond shall be undone.

Jerome: It is better to change than to confirm what does not seem to be true.

66.2 Concerning the slowness of judging and its swiftness

Solomon: Judge, do not be hasty.

Likewise: Do not give a premature verdict.

Job: The case which I knew not, I examined most diligently.

Patrick: It is inappropriate for judges to be too swift in judgement before they know what is right. For it has been said: Judge, do not be hasty.

Isaiah, on the contrary: Woe to me, because I have been silent.

Jerome: It is surely a sin to withhold the truth for very long.

Solomon decided about the question of the women without delay.

Christ gave his verdict concerning caesar's tribute without delay.

Nathan judged David without delay.

Peter judged Ananias and Sapphira without delay.

66.3 That a judge ought to observe three things

Gregory Nazianzen: To inquire without discrimination, to judge without delay, not to withhold the truth.

Origen: A judge must overturn an injustice, condemn deceit, decide the truth without delay, and not seek praise for it.

66.4 Concerning the severity of punishment and, on the contrary, clemency

The Law: Whoever will shed innocent blood, his own blood shall also be shed.

David: God, the Lord God of revenge; as far as: You who judge the earth.

Likewise: The just man shall rejoice when he shall see the punishment; as far as: Of the sinner.

Jeremiah: Cursed be he who withholds his sword from blood.

In the New Testament: Ananias and Sapphira fall lifeless at Peter's words.

Jerome: So long as *sacerdotes* spare sinners, churches bring about death.

Likewise: He who does not kill a thief, himself destroys the helpless. He puts to death the souls that do not die, and revives the souls that do not live.

Likewise: He who strives to revive the unjust and tries to release a criminal from punishment puts the one who is not dying to death.

Likewise: He who kills by the sword ought to be killed by the sword.

Augustine: What is this vanity, to spare one and lead all others into danger? For the people are polluted by a single sinner.

The Law, on the contrary: Be not mindful of the injury of your citizens.

David: The Lord is gracious and merciful, patient and plenteous in mercy.

Likewise: And if his children forsake my law; as far as: I shall not move away from them.

Christ: Love your enemies.

Likewise: If you do not forgive men their sins, your heavenly father, who is in heaven, shall not forgive you.

Likewise: Mercy exalts itself above judgement.

Peter asked: If my brother offend against me, how many times shall I forgive him? Up to seven times? The truth responded: I say not to you, up to seven times, but up to seventy times seven.

The Lord pleaded on behalf of the Jews: Father, forgive them.

So Stephen also said: Lord Jesus, do not reckon this as their sin, for they know not what they do.

66.5 Concerning the guilt of offenders coming upon those who defend them and, on the contrary, not coming upon those who defend them in good faith[605]

The tribe of Benjamin is wholly annihilated and exterminated for defending the offenders of a single city.

Likewise: Josias, endeavouring to defend Charcamis, is slain by Pharaoh Necanor,[606] who communicated by means of messengers: I come not against you, but I fight against another house, against which the Lord has commanded me to go.

Jeremiah proclaimed: Do not defend the fugitives of God.

Likewise: The fugitives of God who fled to Egypt were annihilated, but the Egyptians who received them, likewise.

On the contrary: Not only did Abraham defend Lot the just and released him from the kings' captivity, but also the Sodomites, the enemies of God.

Likewise: Rahab the prostitute, defending Joshua's spies, the enemies of Jericho, is saved with all the members of her household.

Likewise: Joshua defends the Gabaonites, the enemies of God, and he is praised.

For we know that the city of refuge does not only defend the just, but also the unjust, that his case may be heard.

66.6 Concerning punishing theft severely and, on the contrary, leniently

Exodus: If any man steal an ox or a sheep, and kill or sell it; as far as: Being convicted of guilt, shall be put to death.

Solomon, on the contrary: The fault is not so great when a man has stolen; for he has stolen to fill his hungry soul.

Paul: He who stole, let him now steal no more, but labour with his hands, that he may have something to repay those in want.

66.7 Concerning dissolving an oath and, on the contrary, not dissolving it

If a woman, a girl in age, being in her father's house, bind herself by an oath, if her father knew the vows and immediately gainsaid them, both her vows and her oaths shall be void, and she shall not be culpable.

Saul vowed that Jonathan would be killed, and he was not killed, nor was he blamed for this, for he vowed according to his own will, not God's.

Avoid all iniquity, oppression, and injustice, for it is blood judgement; although it may not slay by the sword, it kills by means of the will; nor does it take heed of evil. For happy is the conscience that neither listens to nor looks at evil, and which displays its perfection more fully. For he says that he attains sublimity only on fortifications of unmovable rocks,[607] namely in Christ; and that he has received the bread of the apostles and the waters of faith, namely God's law.[608]

Thus far Cú Chuimne of Iona and Ruben of Dairinis.[609]

Commentary

[1]The omission of *plura... adserens* in HV is consistent with the injunction found in these copies (p. 120 ln. 12, p. 285 ln. 11, p. 286 ln. 1 of the present edition) against interpreting the Bible freely. See also nn 95, 183, 184.

[2]For other translations of the preface see N. Wright *apud* Dumville, 'Ireland, Brittany, and England', 92, and D. R. Howlett, 'The Prologue to the *Collectio*', 146.

[3]The foregoing Isidorian passsages have strained the interpretative faculties of many a medieval reader. Emendations by later readers were common, as with *Hib*'s replacing of the original *com-cilium* with *concilium* and Gratian's rendering of the same as *consilium* (*Decretum*, D. 15 c. 1: 7).

[4]This addition to the Isidorian text seems superfluous.

[5]For Isidore's interpretation of the word *princeps*, see *Etymol.* 9.3.21, cited here on p. 255 ln. 1. He does not use it exclusively to denote 'emperor'. For *principes* in the Irish church, see n 44.

[6]The dedication to bishop Stephen of Salona is from the so-called second recension of the *Dionysiana*.

[7]Here and throughout, *Sardinensis* was translated 'Sardican', because the reference is to the Council of Sardica of 343. *Hib* sometimes gives the correct form, but only in MS V.

[8]A *sacerdos* may well have been, as Charles-Edwards, *Chronicle*, 2:9, defined him, 'the chief resident priest in charge of a church, and especially perhaps its liturgical life', in both Ireland and Wales.

[9]The difference between presbyters and bishops, both of which are also designated *sacerdotes*, and between other members of the clergy, is developed in a citation from *Statuta ecclesiae antiqua* in chap. 3.3, where some are said to have had a *sacerdotium* and others, like deacons, a *ministerium*. According to Isidore, cited here and in chap. 2.4, the main difference is that a *presbyter* does not ordain clerics. For Isidore's understanding of the sacramental grades more generally, see *Etymol.* 7.12.

[10]Here and elsewhere, 'law' is synonymous with the Old Testament.

[11]See n 20.

[12]Lit. 'fruits of firstfruits'. The readings *poma addom* in V and *pomma addomus* in D only make sense if one takes *adom* in its literal Hebrew sense, meaning 'red'. The original text in the Apostolic Canons reads *ad domum*.

[13]To judge by the next sentence, which suggests that a bishop can be absent once but not twice, we may want to interpret the phrase *per unum dominicum* as a Latinisation of an Irish phrase with the Old Irish preposition *íar* ('across', 'along', but also 'after', 'beyond') meaning literally 'beyond one Sunday'. This interpretation is consistent with *Hib* 2.25, which states: *Sinodus Hibernensis decreuit ut sacerdos una tantum die ab æclesia defuerit.*

[14]The exegesis in this case is odd because according to Luke 3:23 Christ began preaching in his thirtieth year and did not live to be forty. However, the compilers may have been alluding to Numbers 4:3, *a tricesimo anno et supra usque ad quinquagesimum annum omnium qui ingrediuntur ut stent et ministrent in tabernaculo foederis.* It is further unclear in what sense *sacerdos* (on which see n 8) is meant to be understood. Following H (*sacerdos id episcopus*) and the Isidorian text on p. 4 ln. 17, a *sacerdos* can mean bishop, which is what the compilers might have had in mind. Indeed, the phrase about the *sacerdos* is out of sync with the chronology and appears to have been added at the end as an afterthought.

[15]See n 113.

[16]For Gildas, *sacerdotes* might simply have been another word for priests. *Hib*'s compilers, however, have employed the term with another sense in mind (nn 8, 9), hence here and elsewhere I preferred to retain the Latin untranslated.

[17]I.e. as one who confessed the faith during and despite persecution.

[18]Lit. 'how much more he ought to...' Perhaps what is meant is that the bishop's responsibility towards his community obliges him to ensure continuity in the episcopal office.

[19]This is a statement supporting the idea of a collective stake in running the ecclesiastical settlement.

[20]In an Irish context, a *parochia* or *paruchia* was an area or people served by a monastery or church settlement. See Sharpe, 'Some problems', 243–247.

[21]In Cormac's Glossary Old Irish *póc* is glossed: *quasi páx i.e. a páce, ar is airidhe sída in phóc* 'as though it were peace, namely from "peace" for the kiss is the sign of peace'.

[22]On priests, see n 8.

[23]I.e. pre-Christian law. See n 71.

[24]Preferring the reading *nunc* in DHOV, even though P's *sicut* and B's *sic* both serve the analogy but translate awkwardly into English.

[25]See n 9.

[26]This being the English verb that the Catholic Church uses for this action nowadays. However, the Latin verb employed by the latest edition of the Code of Canon Law is *conficio*. For both, see *Code of Canon Law: Latin-English Edition. New English Translation* (Washington, DC, 1998) §900.

[27]Lit. 'killer'. However, since it comes at the end of the list, it is unlikely to have been the sense intended here.

[28]An alternative translation, following the reading *in curam* found in most manuscripts (but appears inconsistent with the grammar) would be: 'he does not offer care to the poor without the bishop's consent'.

[29]I.e. pre-Christian law. See n 71.

[30]The Hiberno-Latin use of *immolare* in the sense of 'to offer', can be paralleled in writings of church Fathers and doctors, like Ambrose and Isidore. See Davies, 'Celtic charter tradition', 277; Stevenson, 'Literacy in Ireland', 30.

[31]See n 30.

[32]See n 102.

[33]Namely the presbyter.

[34]The variant in V, *apperuit*, seems like an attempt to form a subjunctive, giving the sense 'should not' as in my translation.

[35]Namely the presbyter.

[36]On Hiberno-Latin *ius* as the equivalent of Old Irish *dliged*, see Charles-Edwards, '*Dliged*', 71.

[37]Old Irish *airchinnech* 'head of the church'. See n 44.

[38]All copies of *Hib* depart from the Gregorian text to such an extent that the logic of the original argument is difficult to recover. I chose to follow P with minimal emendations.

[39]This appears to be the meaning intended in P, even though an *ab* is missing before *altaribus*. The Gregorian letter reads *admouendus*.

[40]The noun appears sometimes as *sedatium* (neut) and sometimes as *sedatio* (fem). Ó Corráin, Breatnach, and Breen, *Laws of the Irish*, 396, translate this 'mortuary tax'. However, Etchingham, *Church Organisation*, 240, 273, holds that 'a priest is entitled to a proportion of the property of every deceased person by way of what is called a *sedatium*, apparently a payment for administering the last sacrament'. He prefers not to render it 'mortuary tax' because 'it seems to be distinguished from the *pretium sepulchri*', which occurs here on p. 107 ln. 19 (*app. crit.*), p. 108 ln. 17. For *sedatium communis* or *communionis* as payment for administering the last sacrament, see chap. 2.16. The only other occurrence of *sedatium* in a Hiberno-Latin text known to me is in the canons of an Irish synod (Bieler, *Penitentials*, 170 §6), where it appears to denote compensation for physically harming a bishop.

[41]But according to DHV it was a Hibernian synod. The two attributions, however, are not necessarily mutually exclusive. The Irish Augustine, in the preface to *De mirabilibus sacrae scripturae*, dedicates his work to *uenerandissimis urbium et monasteriorum episcopis et presbyteris maxime Carthaginensium* 'the most venerated bishops and presbyters of the cities and monasteries, especially of the Carthaginians' (PL 35:2149). Grosjean, 'Sur quelques exégètes', 69–76, argued that the Carthaginians were the followers of St. Carthach (Mo Chutu) of Rathan in Co. Offaly. The Chronicle of Ireland gives the obit of a Saint Carthach in 637. In the Chronicle of Ireland, Carthach is said to have been expelled from Rathan in 636 and the Annals of Inisfallen add that he founded Lismore (Les Mór) in Co. Waterford in the same year. How much credence can be given to the annalistic record when it cannot be corroborated by independent sources is open to debate. However, it is clear that the tradition associating Carthach with Lismore dates from at least 833 (but no later than 911, the year in which the Chronicle of Ireland ends) for in that year the Chronicle of Ireland reports 'the burning of Lismore of Mo Chutu'.

[42]The implication seems to be that the charge is levied off the deceased's property alone, even if he was a *frater* himself. If this was the case, then a *frater* should probably be understood here as a property-owning *manach* (see n 115). The verb *aufugio* 'to shun, flee from' in its transitive form is difficult to translate in the present context. I have chosen to interpret it metaphorically.

[43]The eucharist given to the dying.

[44]In an Irish ecclesiastical context *princeps* corresponds to Old Irish *airchinnech* and denotes the head of an ecclesiastical institution, who can be either a layman or in orders. See Davies, 'Clerics as rulers'; Etchingham, *Church Organisation*, 50–59, 63–67.

[45]This is the only place-name in *Hib* which may be Irish, except for Armagh, which occurs only in BO (p. 460 ln. 4). For the possibility that it could, perhaps, be identified with Ferns, Co. Wexford, I owe thanks to Dr Fiona Edmonds. The orthography is not a problem, because the letter *n* in a parent text could easily have been mistaken for the letter *u*: a very common scribal blunder. For mention of a synod at Ferns in early medieval Ireland we have only hagiography to go by. The Latin Life of St. Maedoc tells of a synod that was purportedly convened by king Brandub (d. 605) of Leinster for the purpose of ordaining Maedoc archbishop and elevating Ferns to the status of a metropolitan see. However, Richard Sharpe's study of the relationship between the various recensions of the Life of Maedoc, conclude that the account of the synod and its decision to consecrate Maedoc archbishop, were interpolated in the thirteenth century. See his *Medieval Irish Saints' Lives*, 365.

[46]The following translation is adapted from Bieler, *Penitentials*, 185.

[47]I preferred 'service' to 'ministry' because of the technical meaning that the latter is given in *Hib* 3.3.

[48]For the distinction between *sacerdotium* and *ministerium*, see *Hib* 3.3.

[49]The second clause, from *ut* to *honorent*, does not appear in the *Statuta ecclesiae antiqua*.

[50]The word *Nazareni* (or variants thereof) does not occur in Ezra.

[51]The following chap. is loosely based on an Isidorian text, which *Hib* modified extensively.

[52]The reference here is to *κλῆρος* and *sors*, both of which were used in late antiquity to denote 'land-share'. For the Greek see Liddell, Scott, and Jones *Greek-English Lexicon*, and for the Latin see Niermeyer, *Mediae Latinitatis Lexicon*. These terms were ubiquitous in documents dealing with land in the fifth century. See Wickham, *Framing the Early Middle Ages*, 90.

[53]The pseudo-historical prologue to the *Senchas Már* §§4–6 (ed. and tr. Carey, 11–12/18) speaks of the church's right to defer judgement in cases of homicide to secular judges, who would judge according to traditional

Irish law. The pseudo-historical prologue does not say explicitly that the church itself should order capital punishment, but it suggests that the church is expected to condone it. Hagiography, however, makes an explicit reference to an ecclesiastical council condemning a thief to death. In the Life of Colmán Élo §30 (ed. Heist, 218) it is said that a *synodus monasteriorum* apprehended a thief and led him to the gallows, but he was eventually spared through the saint's intervention.

54Translation is adapted from Winterbottom, *Gildas*, 80–81.

55The word *peregrinatio* had diverse connotations in Ireland. The word *peregrinus* did not necessarily denote one who left the island or fulfilled the ascetic ideal. See Charles-Edwards, 'Social background to Irish peregrinatio', esp. 46, 57. Penitential *peregrinatio* is also well attested, e.g. in Adomnán's Life of Columba, 1.21, 1.30, 2.39. Some of these penitents would have been criminal offenders carrying out their sentence. See Geltner, '*Detrusio*'.

56There are 91 references in *Hib* to *Hibernenses*, *Synodus Hibernensis* and variants thereof. For a complete list, see table on p. 151*. Scholarship has tended to associate *Hibernenses* with a reactionary party within the Irish church, which resisted liturgical and institutional innovations that the churches in the south of Ireland began to introduce in the second third of the seventh century. *Hibernenses* are thus defined in opposition to their supposed adversaries, the *Romani* (on which see n 162), who acknowledged Rome as the highest authority within Christendom, and adopted the Victorian computistical reckoning in lieu of the 84-year calendar which the *Hibernenses* clung to until 716 when (according to Bede, *HE* 5.22) Iona was reformed. Mention of *Hibernenses* in early medieval Insular sources other than *Hib* is scant. The term occurs only in the titles of two penitentials: *De disputatione Hibernensis* and *Sinodus Hibernensis* (Bieler, *Penitentials*, 160, 170). For more on *Hibernenses* and Irish synods, see introduction, p. 70*.

57Sixth-century bishop of Hadrumentum in north Africa, who wrote a commentary on Reveleations, ed. A. W. Adams, CCSL 92 (1985).

58Translation adapted from *Etymologies*, tr. Barney *et al.*

59See previous note.

60See previous note.

61On the concept of 'natural law' in Irish legal culture, see n 71.

62Translation adapted from *Etymologies*, tr. Barney *et al.*

[63]See previous note.

[64]See previous note.

[65]See previous note.

[66]See previous note. In the final clause, see the *apparatus criticus* for disagreements between the reading from Isidore, which I printed in the main text, and the variants from *Hib* manuscripts which omit 'citizens', a concept unknown in Ireland.

[67]This appears to be *Hib*'s response to Romans 7, where Paul warns against the corrupting power of Old Testament law (7:8), a law which, according to him, became obsolete with the advent of the new, spiritual law (7:1–6). Much of Paul's criticism stems from his understanding of Old Testament law as a law that demanded genuine inner commitment from its followers, but due to human weakness, it could be followed only superficially through the rituals it prescribed. However, the new law that Paul preaches is said to be wholly spiritual. Eucherius makes a similar distinction between ritualised law (which already fulfilled its prefigurative role) and another, perhaps more worthy and more relevant law. This distinction is important, for it justifies the choice made by *Hib*'s compilers to admit material from the Old Testament as law, even though *Hib* addresses itself exclusively to Christians, who, according to Paul, are 'dead to the law' (Romans 7:4). Not only are a great many of *Hib*'s precepts drawn from the Old Testament, but book 19 explicitly places the Old and New Testaments side by side at the top of a hierarchy of authoritative Christian sources.

[68]The expression *nodum in scirpo quaerere* is well attested in Classical Latin. Jerome's original text reads: *in praeceptis quae ad uitam pertinent et sunt perspicua non debemus quaerere allegoriam, ne iuxta comicum modum quaeramus in scirpo.* I am indebted to Dr Sven Meeder for this reference and for the suggestion that the comic is likely to be Plautus, who uses the phrase in his *Menaechmi* 2.1.22. The manner in which *Hib* applies the citation from Jerome is significant for the fact that it authorises adjudicators to draw upon the Old Testament as a source for law, without having to depart from the literal sense of the text by, for example, treating it allegorically and thus complicating it. Like the previous citation, this citation can also be seen as an adaptation of Romans 7:1–6, where the laws of the Old Testament are portrayed as obsolete. *Hib*'s compilers were clearly looking for ways to justify their choice to rely heavily on the Old Testament.

[69]The error is not Isidore's, whose text rightly credits Lycurgus with the authorship of the Lacedaemonian rule and Solon with the laws of Athens.

[70]Translation adapted from *Etymologies*, tr. Barney *et al.*

[71]To judge by the occurrences of these expressions in chapters 2.5–2.7, 31.18, the 'law of nature' is the law that prevailed before Moses received the 'law of the letter' from God. Vernacular Irish law also draws a contrast between a 'law of nature' and a 'law of the letter'. It is most fully articulated in the pseudo-historical prologue to the *Senchas Már* §7 (ed. and tr. Carey, 12/18), and *Córus Bésgnai* §§35–37 (ed. and tr. Breatnach, 34/35). However, in both texts the 'law of nature' is identified with the vernacular law that held sway in pre-Christian Ireland. It is described therein as being not wholly incompatible with a Christian 'law of the letter', which is said to have been introduced into Ireland by St. Patrick. As Charles-Edwards ('Celtic kings', 67) put it, according to the pseudo-historical prologue, 'the law of nature written on men's hearts since Adam dug and Eve span had taken an Irish form in their vernacular law and had been purified of any taint of paganism by the collaboration between St. Patrick and the *filid*'. A similar attempt at syncretism can be found in *Synodus sapientium*, ed. Bieler, *Penitentials*, 168/9: *si inuenerimus iudicia gentium bona, que natura bona illis docet et Deo non displicet, seruabimus* 'if we find the *iudicia gentium* good, which their good nature teaches them, and it is not displeasing to God, we shall keep it'. For further discussion of these texts see Ó Corráin, Breatnach, and Breen, 'Laws of the Irish', 385–394; Ó Corráin, 'Irish vernacular law', 291–294. Here *iudicia gentium* echoes the basic division in Roman law between *ius ciuile* and *ius gentium*, distinguishing, respectively, the law of the Roman citizens and the laws of other nations, some of which also had force under Roman law. This division was known in Ireland thanks to Isidore's Etymologies, cited in *Hib* on p. 54 ln. 15 and p. 55 ln. 5.

[72]Translation adapted from *Etymologies*, tr. Barney *et al.*

[73]The original reads: *Ceteris ad integrum soluens ab omni conuentionis eorum molestia liberatus sum, uni satisfacere cotidie soluendo non possum.*

[74]On the fall from paradise as a recurrent motif in Irish law and exegesis, see Bracken, 'The Fall and the law'. Both Irish and patristic interpretations of the fall contributed to the shaping and articulation of fundamental moral concepts such as free will, malevolent intent, and awareness of the consequences of one's actions.

[75]The translation is by Winterbottom, *Gildas*, 80.

[76]This appears to be a misplaced comment on Matthew 17:20: *hoc autem genus non eicitur nisi per orationem et ieiunium.*

[77]The verb *iudicare* appears to be used in one sense in the Pauline citation and in another in the commentary on the citation. The exegesis in this case interprets the passage very creatively.

[78]Translation is adapted from Bieler, *Penitentials*, 189, 191. For discussion of the formula *locus, tempus, persona*, see n 188.

[79]*El* is in fact the Hebrew for 'God', but *mosyna* means nothing in Hebrew. Perhaps he intended *moshīa*, which means 'helping'/'saving'.

[80]*Recte* Osee.

[81]Perhaps the sarcasm is more poignant if the passage is rephrased as a chiding rhetorical question: 'Well then, did God make the tabernacle of the testimony for no reason?'

[82]Old Irish triads, wisdom texts in which certain ideas are arranged in thematic groups of three, often have a legal dimension. There are a number of passages in *Hib* that come in triadic form. The Old Irish triads have been edited and translated by Kuno Meyer, *The Triads of Ireland* (Dublin, 1906). For triads as a peculiar Irish and Welsh literary convention, see P. Sims-Williams, 'Thought, word and deed'.

[83]See n 102.

[84]See n 102.

[85]The two were elected to the papacy simultaneously in 498 but Laurence was made to cede office.

[86]Actually, according to the Bible, the Philistines were the ones who found the bodies on Mount Gelboe and placed them on the walls of Bethsan, whence the inhabitants of Jabesh Gilead removed them.

[87]In a legal gloss (*CIH* 961.38–39; 2094.4) it is equated with the Irish *screpul* 'scruple'. In *De disputatione Hibernensis synodi* §9 (Bieler, *Penitentials*, 160), thirteen shekels are said to be worth a *cumal* 'female slave'. For these references and analysis, see Kelly, *Farming*, 594.

[88]The eucharist given to the dying.

[89]Both H and V read *adiuuare*, but I wonder if they both erred, and the text should read *adiuuari*, meaning that the dying who do not receive communion cannot be helped.

[90]*Hib*'s version is unfaithful to the Isidorian original.

[91]Cf. Virgil, *Aeneid*, 4.569: *uarium et mutabile semper femina*.

[92]Translation adapted from *Etymologies*, tr. Barney *et al.*

[93]I.e. before they are thirteen years old, corresponding to the male age of legal maturity in the *Mishnah* (*Pirkei Avot* 5:25). In Irish law, a *fer midboth* had to be at least fourteen in order to swear in trivial cases: *Críth Gablach*, ed. Binchy §6, lines 32–37 (tr. MacNeill, 'Ancient Irish law' §68).

[94]Nowhere in *Hib* is there a description of what the rite of baptism consisted of. This is unusual given that late antique and early medieval texts of ecclesiastical law had much to say on the topic. See, e.g., Cresconius, *Concordia canonum* Bks 49–53 (Zechiel-Eckes, 555–558), *Vetus Gallica* Bk 21 (Mordek, 431–435). *Hib*'s silence on this topic invites speculations about the possible heterodox nature of the Irish baptismal rite, which the compilers might have deliberately glossed over.

[95]According to Luke 24:1–11, the apostles were wrong to disbelieve their testimony. There is no reason to assume that *Hib*'s compilers did not know the biblical story. However, here as elsewhere they were applying acontextual literal exegesis in order to give biblical censure to existing Irish laws. Irish law renders the oath of a woman (*bannoíll*) inadmissible, but there are a number of exceptions to this. See *GEIL*, 202, 207–208.

[96]Perhaps there is a deliberate ambiguity here, for *ueritas* can be another name for Christ, as on p. 456 ln. 23.

[97]*Fortach* 'overswearing' was the means by which a person of higher rank, e.g. a king or bishop, overrode the oath of a person of a lower rank in a legal dispute. The principle is expounded in *Di Astud Chirt 7 Dligid* (*CIH* 234.20–22=*AL*, vol. 5, 460.16–17). For this legal principle and further references, see *GEIL*, 199–200. On the Hiberno-Latin term normally used to translate overswearing, *superiurare*, see Binchy, *Studia Hibernica* 2 (1962): 62. The expression *malum testimonium* may refer to the testimony of an *anteist* 'bad witness', mentioned in *Gúbretha Caratniad* (*CIH* 2195.2–3 = *ZCP* 15 [1925]: 327 §19), on which see *GEIL*, 203.

[98]On the whole, Irish law forbids the testimony of a single witness and requires at least two or three (*Berrad Airechta*, *CIH* 596.4–5 = *Bürgschaft* 19 §58, tr. Stacey, *Lawyers and Laymen*, 210–233). Some exceptions are the testimony of a bishop between two acts of communion, the evidence of a dying man, and the evidence of an honest man who will gain nothing from lying (*CIH* 1570.1–8). For these and other examples see *GEIL*, 203.

[99]I take this to mean that they were not promised money in return for their testimony, but salvation.

[100]This was Origen's rendering of the name 'Joshua son of Nun'.

[101]The sense in which the verb *firmo* is intended here is not altogether clear. I take the passage to mean that if two people had a verbal contract, and one of them died, the heir of the dead party ought to honour his parent's obligation towards the living party. Perhaps the living party had to (re)confirm (*firmo*) the old agreement with the heir.

[102]A number of citations attributed in *Hib* to this source can in fact be traced to Gregory the Great. Perhaps the Gregorian material and texts such as the one cited in the present chapter, circulated together within a *florilegium* that was known by the title 'Life of the Fathers' (and is in fact cited as such on p. 201 ln. 17). The title is reminiscent of the *Apophthegmata patrum*, a collection of sayings attributed to various desert fathers and mothers, better known in its Latin transmission as *Vitas Patrum* (*sic*). Texts from this collection have been edited by Rosweyde in his *Vitae patrum*. According to B. Ward, *The Desert Fathers*, xxxi, the surviving Latin version of *Vitas Patrum* predates the surviving Greek version, but both ultimately derive from a lost Greek original. Analysis of the contents of the *Vitas Patrum* is provided by Rosenthal, *The 'Vitae Patrum'*, 10–21, and for the *Vitas Patrum* in early Irish literature, see C. Wright, *The Irish Tradition*, 175–180. I have been able to trace only one text to this source, on p. 23 ln. 16, where it is attributed to *Vita sanctorum*. However, *Hib* may contain more texts from it, but the wording might have changed so much that I was unable to identify them.

Like so many citations from hagiographical texts in *Hib*, much background information has been omitted when the text quoted in the present chapter was abridged from its source, making it difficult to recover the original context. The grammar, too, is flawed. In reconstructing the text I have departed from the literal sense in order to make the story more intelligible. The text appears to deal with a dispute between two *fratres* (perhaps monks or ascetics) over the right to be buried in the same grave. The cause for the conflict might have been that the two purchased a burial plot together, but one wanted to deprive the other from being buried there. The story seems to conclude with a happy end, although it is difficult to establish who promised what to whom and who cleared a space in the grave for whom.

[103]The exact legal sense of the verb *firmo* in this context is unclear to me.

[104]See previous note.

[105]This may be the sense which the verb *firmo* is intended to convey here.

However, here as elsewhere, the exact technical sense is unclear.

[106]Translation adapted from *Etymologies*, tr. Barney *et al.*

[107]See previous note.

[108]A special variety of ordeal (*fír*) in early Ireland was the *airderg* 'ordeal by heat'.

[109]I do not know of any place-name that *Consulentis* might refer to. *Consulinum*, now Stilo in Calabria, is an unlikely option.

[110]Ananias and Sapphira held back rather than took back, but *Hib* (and Isidore in the next section) appears to render the biblical story differently here.

[111]This is a possible meaning of this idiomatic phrase which literally translates as 'let an alien communion be imposed on him'.

[112]For the use of the term 'relic' to denote a tomb or cemetery, see Tírechán (Bieler, *Patrician Texts*, 130 line 18, 144 lines 25, 27). Compare the modern Irish word for graveyard, *reilig*. This usage may suggest a link between the emergence of Christian cemeteries, or the appropriation of existing cemeteries by Christians, and between the development of saints' cults. The translation of relics into cemeteries (see also *Hib* 18.2) would have created or reinforced a cemetery's Christian identity. See O'Brien, 'Pagan and Christian'; Ó Carragáin, 'Architectural Setting'.

[113]The term *ciuitas* (Old Irish *cathair*) denotes both a church and a church settlement with lay residents. For the use of the term in Irish saints' Lives, see Etchingham, *Church Organisation*, 93–97. It also occurs in the Chronicle of Ireland, 845.3. Charles-Edwards (*Ibid.* 2:2) believes that *ciuitas/cathair* designates a major church. In the present context *ciuitas* appears to be interchangeable with *ecclesia*.

[114]The *familia* (Old Irish *muintir*) had a dual meaning: it could denote the residents of a particular church or a wider community comprising the residents of different churches, who were subject to the authority of (and often economically linked to) a chief mother church, whose patron saint they venerated. Hence the *familia Choluim Chille* and the *familia Patricii*, the communities of Colum Cille and of Patrick, had their chief churches in Iona and Armagh, respectively. The word *familia* does not, however, denote a single, specific type of church organisation. See Etchingham, *Church Organisation*, 172–177.

[115]The *monachi* (Old Irish *manach* sgl., *manaig* pl.) were laypeople, often married, who sometimes lived on their own land and were subject to certain rules imposed on them by the monastery with which they were associated. Their relationship to the monastery was contractual: they received a loan of livestock or land, and in return provided labour or dues. For all intents and purposes they were the clients of an abbot, who acted as their lord (Charles-Edwards, *Early Christian Ireland*, 118–119; Etchingham, *Church Organisation*, 363–393). Although framed in the idiom of biblical exegesis, the present text constitutes a unique and important statement about the spatial division on what scholarship has come to refer to as an 'ecclesiastical estate' and the manner in which this division corresponded to different zones of habitation. See Flechner, 'Identifying monks'.

[116]This chapter opens with a genuine biblical citation, continues with an invented text, and concludes with exegesis of the two. Perhaps this is a form of speculative exegesis that had been practised in monastic schools as part of students' training in exegesis.

[117]This is how the Vulgate renders the Hebrew *omer*, which occurs in Exodus 16:16, 18, 22, 32, 33, 36. It was a unit of dry capacity, the equivalent of approximately four litres, according to Avraham Even Shoshan's Hebrew Dictionary (Jerusalem, 1984) [in Hebrew].

[118]Bread could be one of the provisions that a client owed his lord as food-rent. See, e.g., the food-rent to which an *ócaire* was entitled according to *Críth Gablach*, ed. Binchy §10 line 117 (tr. MacNeill, 'Ancient Irish law' §82).

[119]On the face of it, the combination 'slayers of the dead' (omitted in BHV) seems more of an oxymoron than derogatory.

[120]Lit. 'If someone removed God's gifts without penance to man, it is a small wonder that removing the gifts of men will go without penance'.

[121]See n 44.

[122]Which is to say that certain people might have been entitled to a life-share in church property, but upon their death the property was expected to revert back to the church. This echoes the principle expressed in the previous clause, which forbids property from being alienated from the church.

[123]See n 115.

[124]For the term *census*, see n 515. However, the reference here seems to be to an unfree or semi-free person, such as the *fuidir*.

[125]*accitamenta* is glossed in A with the Old Breton *clou*. For the interpretation 'key', see A. Fick and W. Stokes, *Vergleichendes Wörterbuch der indogermanischen Sprachen*, 3 vols. (Göttingen, 1890–1909).

[126]But the glossator in O appears to have thought the children are the ones who will be bound, because after *reus tenebitur* he added *aut rea erit*.

[127]The text may be playing with the ambiguous sense of *reatus*, whose classical sense is 'accused' or 'guilty'.

[128]Here it is likely to be a misrendering of *sinodus*. But see n 562 for another possible meaning.

[129]According to Irish law, contracts made with children or people of unsound mind are invalid. See *GEIL*, 80–82, 93.

[130]Jerome's original text, which reads 'scribes and priests', is an interpretation of Matt. 28:12–15, where the Jewish priests are said to have bribed the soldiers to say that Christ's body was stolen from the tomb by his disciples. Jerome believed that the bribe was made with money that had been offered to the temple.

[131]See previous note.

[132]Much of the following book is concerned with charges that the church demanded in return for burials. As noted by Etchingham, *Church Organisation*, 271–275, vernacular law also stipulates on the burial-charge (Old Irish *imnae*), and *Córus Bésgnai* §§46–47 (ed. and tr. Breatnach, 36–38/37–39) gives different rates corresponding to the deceased's honour-price (on which see n 263). In this respect vernacular law differs from *Hib*, which does not link legal status of laymen with the rate of the burial-charge. It does, however (*Hib* 18.6), prescribe different rates to property-owning *monachi*, according to their wealth. In total, 188 early medieval ecclesiastical cemeteries were excavated between 1970 and 2001. Most of these are 'unprotected burials', but many contain high status recumbent slabs with incised and carved crosses (O'Sullivan *et al.*, *Early Medieval Ireland*, 184), presumably marking the resting places of ecclesiastical and secular dignitaries. For a recent discussion see O'Brien, 'Literary insights into the basis of some burial practices'.

[133]An ancestral cemetery would be a cemetery of the *fert* variety mentioned by Tírechán (Bieler, *Patrician Texts*, 130 line 18, 144 lines 25, 27). Tírechán translates *fert* as *relic*, a word that occurs also in *Hib*, on which see n 112. Morphologically, a *fert* would be characterised by a round ditch, the earth from which was piled up to form a burial mound. As O'Brien

('Pagan and Christian', 'Literary insights') notes, archaeological evidence suggests that burial in ancestral graves and in ecclesiastical grounds coincided at least up to the eighth century, when ecclesiastical cemeteries began to proliferate. If ecclesiastical burial was indeed subject to payment, as *Hib* and *Córus Bésgnai* prescribe (see n 132), then we may have at least a partial (albeit reductionist) explanation as to why poorer individuals might be buried in non-consecrated ground. However, *fertae* also fulfilled important political and social functions, such as serving as boundary markers, and reinforcing community identity by providing a link with the ancestors. According to the present chapter in *Hib*, *fertae* were not to be regarded as necessarily non-Christian. Indeed, the chapter justifies burial in *fertae* with reference to the Bible.

[134]The purpose of this chapter seems to be to free a woman from the obligation or custom to be buried in the ancestral grave plot of her husband. She might instead be buried in a church, which could collect the burial charge. For various charges associated with burial, see chapters 2.14–16.

[135]According to Etchingham, *Church Organisation*, 386–388, the chapter is concerned with property-owning *manaig* of the highest social order, the value of whose property varied. The case discussed here concerns a *manach* who switched allegiance between two abbots.

[136]In translating *tacere* in this way I follow Etchingham, *Church Organisation*, 386.

[137]That is, if the first abbot did not tacitly approve the *manach*'s vow to the second abbot. A vow is likely to have entailed a pledge of the *manach*'s property to the second abbot, but such a pledge, as we have seen in chapter 17.9, could not have been made without the first abbot's consent. Hence the first abbot's prerogative to either overturn a vow or tacitly approve it.

[138]Note the similarity to the Anglo-Saxon 'heriot' (*heregeat*), namely the prerogative that a lord had to seize his dead client's horse and clothing. See Brooks, 'Arms, Status', 91–92.

[139]The Latin *habet in iure suo* is likely to be the equivalent of Old Irish *dliged*, which denotes both entitlement to something or an obligation to render something (i.e. to owe). See Charles-Edwards, '*Dliged*', 75–77.

[140]See n 138.

[141]According to *Hib* 43.18 *basilica* was another word for tomb.

[142]There are two distinct accounts of Iosias's death, in II Samuel 23:29 and in II Chronicles 35:20–27. According to the former, he was killed at

Megiddo, but according to the latter, he was fatally wounded there and then taken to Jerusalem to die.

[143]On *basilica* see n 141. Tírechán, *Collectanea* § 16 (Bieler, *Patrician Texts*, p. 136 lines 25–33), tells of a *presbyter*, Bruscus, whose remains were exhumed and translated by a member of the proprietary church of *genus Cotirbi* 'family of Cothirbe'.

[144]See n 40.

[145]Etchingham, *Church Organisation*, 387, suggests that the contrast is between an 'outsider or pilgrim entering a truly monastic state without worldly possessions... and a *monachus* possessed of assets'.

[146]See n 102.

[147]Lit. 'burial mounds'. The Old Irish for 'mound', *fert*, was used idiomatically to denote burial ground irrespective of whether it contained actual barrows or mounds. The original Gregorian text does not include this word. Instead, it reads: *Nam quos peccata grauia deprimunt, non ad absolutionem potius quam ad maiorem damnationis cumulum eorum corpora in ecclesiis ponuntur*. See also n 133.

[148]In the original story, it is made clear that it was the bishop who died: *Die autem trigesimo eiusdem ciuitatis episcopus, cum uespertina hora sanus atque incolumis ad lectum redisset, subita morte defunctus est*.

[149]A church administrator with mainly legal responsibilities. See Markus, *Gregory*, 114.

[150]Translating *causae* as 'cases' does not seem appropriate in this context, since cases cannot bind and loose, as *causae* are said to do in the opening sentence. For *causae* as 'sources', see *caussa* in *Thesaurus linguae Latinae*.

This book gives a hierarchy of authorities that should be consulted before invoking a council of the 'elders of the province' *seniores prouinciae* as a last resort. The list of authorities mentioned here, apparently arranged in a descending order of importance, gives pride of place to the Old Testament, exemplifying yet again the prominence that the Old Testament held among the sources drawn upon by *Hib*. On the manner in which the procedure prescribed in this book was (or was claimed to have been) implemented in practice, we have the testimony of Cumméne's Paschal letter, which, although dating from *c*. 630, contains remarkable parallels with book 19, suggesting that the protocol prescribed by the book predates the composition of *Hib*. As noted by Maura Walsh and Dáibhí Ó Cróinín, there are obvious similarities between the order of authorities Cumméne consulted before convening a synod and between the hierarchy of authorities mentioned here. For a whole year, Cumméne says, he studied what various authorities had to say about the date of Easter: first he consulted the Old and the New Testaments, then he inquired into the practices of the Hebrews, Greeks, 'Latins' and Egyptians, afterwards he sought advice from the writings of Greek and Latin Fathers (Origen, Jerome, Cyprian, Gregory) and only then he resorted to convening a synod. (See, respectively, Cumméne's Letter, ed. Walsh and Ó Cróinín, 58, 62, 64, 79, 83, 91.) A further likeness can be found in Cumméne's choice to summon a synod, which he justified by citing a scriptural passage, Deut. 32:7: *interrogaui patres meos ut annuntiarent mihi* 'I asked my elders to show me'. The same passage occurs in *Hib.B*'s version of book 19 (see *apparatus*). See also n 162.

[151]Although there is an overlap with the aforementioned twenty-two books of the Old Testament, this nevertheless appears to be a reference to the books belonging to the third division of the Old Testament, which commonly includes Psalms, Proverbs, Job, Ruth, Lamentations, Song of Songs, Ecclesiastes, Esther, Daniel, I and II Chronicles (also called Paralipomenon in the Vulgate), Ezra and Nehemiah (or II Ezra in the Vulgate). For Jerome's interpretation of this division, which omits Ruth and Lamentations, see his prologue to I Samuel (*Biblia Sacra iuxta Vulgatam uersionem*, ed. Weber and Gryson, 365). The Old Irish Treatise on the Psalter §61 (ed. Meyer, 22) gives a reduced list: Job, Proverbs, Song of Songs, and Ecclesiastes. Note that a glossator of the text of *Hib* in O interpreted *hagiographa* more broadly as 'sacred writings'.

[152]I take *historiae* to mean not only works of historiography like Eusebius's Ecclesiastical History or Orosius's Histories against the Pagans. Rather, this category may have the same semantic range as *senchas*, which encompasses, according to the *DIL*, history, tradition, and traditional law. Under 'traditions of the doctors' we may wish to include traditions of (patristic and other) biblical interpretation, namely exegesis (both historical and allegorical), which *Hib* frequently appends to biblical citations. In other words, book 19 may be saying that if a dispute cannot be settled with direct recourse to the OT or NT, perhaps an appeal to exegesis might help to clarify the biblical text and make it applicable in adjudication.

[153]To judge by the text spuriously attributed to Cicero on p. 2 ln. 5, this meeting is a synod. This interpretation is further supported by the opening of the present chapter in *Hib.B*, which reads *ipse uero Innocentius scripsit de senodis omnibus*.

[154]To judge by the description of a province which follows, the word can also be translated 'kingdom'. However, I preferred 'province' in order to retain the distinction with the jurisdiction discussed in book 24 *De regno.*

[155]I could not find any other occurrences of the expression *porro uicina,* except in Paschasius Radbertus's mid ninth-century *Expositio in Matheo,* Bk 1 lines 211–222. There he explains that verses in the Gospels which concur in sense but not in wording, are said to be *porro uicina.* The expression might therefore have been conventional within certain exegetical circles.

[156]This emulation of an Isidorian etymology appears to state that a province brings different or distant communities together in a relationship of 'vicinity', through the application of the same law, the use of a single language, and subjection to the same rule. On the concept of *uicinitas* in late antique canon law, see Flechner, 'Pope Gregory and the British: mission as a canonical problem'.

[157]This chapter offers what appears to be an idealised perspective on administrative divisions within a province. However, Charles-Edwards, *Early Christian Ireland,* 423, notes that the idea of a province comprising three kings, corresponds to *Críth Gablach*'s description of a 'mesne kingdom' ruled by an overking (ed. Binchy §32; tr. MacNeill §117). He draws attention to the fact that the territory of the Cruithni of modern Co. Antrim and the western parts of Co. Down had more than one kingdom and bishopric. The Life of Lugaid §19 (ed. Heist, 135) mentions that St. Comgall sent men of his *familia* to three provinces *tam in Hybernia quam in Britannia* 'in both Ireland and Britain', to search for a worthy candidate who would minister to him, whereupon they found Lugaid. The three provinces may be no more than an etiology, but the story should also serve as a reminder that, for the Irish, a *prouincia* settled by Irishpeople need not have designated a territory only within Ireland itself.

[158]Namely, *De ciuitate Dei.* See *apparatus.*

[159]See n 113.

[160]This ostensibly unrelated text appears to have been copied into *Hib.B* for no other reason than its mention of *prouincia* within a list of units of measurement.

[161]The expression *causae maiores* is best known for its incorporation into the Pseudo-Isidorian decretals (ed. Hinschius, 459, 712): *quod maiores causae cuiuscunque ecclesiae ad eam [sc. sanctam sedem Romae] referri debeant.*

[162]When read in conjunction with chapter 20.5, this chapter (a doublet of p. 114 ln. 7), with its attribution to *Romani*, confirms Sharpe's hypothesis that the main thing that distinguished *Romani* from *Hibernenses*, was 'the assertion of a belief in the oneness of Latin Christendom, with its hierarchy culminating in the papal primacy of the bishop of Rome' (Sharpe, 'Armagh and Rome', 68).

The protocol set out in this chapter appears to have been followed in Ireland before *Hib* was compiled. This may be inferred from the fact that Cumméne ends his account of a synod at Mag Léna with recounting how the *seniores* 'elders'—presumably the participants at the synod—decided that, in accordance with Innocent's injunction invoked in the present chapter (*ut maiores causae ad sedem apostolicam post episcopale iudicium referantur*), the question of the dating of Easter ought to be referred to 'the chief of cities', Rome, where a delegation was dispatched forthwith. Cumméne's letter can also be seen to describe a process of dispute settlement articulated in book 19, on which see n 150.

The instruction to refer difficult cases to the chief see echoes *Liber Angeli* §28: *Item quaecumque causa ualde difficilis exorta fuerit atque ignota cunctis Scotorum gentium iudicibus, ad cathedram archiepiscopi Hibernensium, id est, Patricii, atque huius antestitis examinationem recte refferenda.* The see designated by the *Liber Angeli* as the 'see of the archbishops of the Irish', is Armagh. However, before the twelfth century Ireland had no archbishop, in the sense of a metropolitan bishop of an ecclesiastical province on whom the pope conferred a pallium. The absence of metropolitans or archbishops did not prevent seventh-century Irish propagandists from making extravagant claims on behalf of their ecclesiastical patrons and endowing their predecessors retrospectively with archiepiscopal status. Not only Armagh, but also Kildare issued its own (rival) propaganda, claiming that it was the seat of *archiepiscopus Hibernensium episcoporum* 'the archbishop of the bishops of the Irish', for which see Cogitosus, *Vita S. Brigitae, praefatio* §32. For more on Armagh, the *Liber Angeli*, and the rivalry with Kildare, see Charles-Edwards, *Christian Ireland*, 420–429.

[163]For *ciuitas*, see n 113.

[164]See n 161.

[165]As in 20.3, here too we have an echo from *Liber Angeli*: *Si uero in illa cum suis sapientibus facile sanari non poterit talis caussa praedictae negotionis, ad sedem apostolicam decreuimus esse mittendam, id est, ad Petri apostoli cathedram auctoritatem Romae urbis habentem.* Charles-Edwards, *Christian Ireland*, 424, rightly notes that chapters 20.3 and 20.5 espouse different processes of

appeal. The latter envisages appeals to a lesser province, then to a greater see, then to a synod, and, finally to an authority outside Ireland, namely Rome. This process follows *Liber Angeli* closely. See also n 162.

[166]Cf. p. 117 ln. 10, p. 134 ln. 12.

[167]The Britons are condemned for not keeping Easter at the same date as the Roman and Gallic churches. If we are to believe Bede, *HE* 5.22, then the Irish themselves abandoned their controversial calendar only in 716, when Iona underwent a reform that included adopting a new computus (i.e. ecclesiastical calendar). However, the churches in the south of Ireland began to reform their paschal observance and apply the Victorian calendar already *c.* 630, when Cumméne wrote his Paschal letter (see n 150). The derogatory remark about the Britons suggests that this text originated either in a *Romani* milieu in southern Ireland before 716, or that it was written after 716, when all the Irish churches had already reformed. Interestingly, the present chapter distinguishes between Britons and heretics, suggesting that their error was not regarded as heresy.

[168]This is how Barney *et al.*, tr., *Etymologies*, interpret *modo actionem causę quod iurgium est litis.*

[169]The original Virgilian line (*Aeneid*, 12.898), reads: *limes agro positus litem ut discerneret aruis.*

[170]The original reads: *argutum inuentum*, translated by Barney *et al.*, *Etymologies*, 'clear discovery'.

[171]Some of the texts attributed to Gregory of Nazianzus, like this triad, appear to be of Irish origin. It is very likely that the name Gregory Nazianzen was appropriated by an Irish scholar, in the same manner that we find the names Augustine and Eusebius referring to Irish scholars in *De mirabilibus sacrae scripturae* (see also n 41). The Irish identity of the person referred to as Gregory Nazianzen is reinforced by a title of the constitution of an Irish synod, which reads: *De disputatione Hibernensis sinodi et Grigori Nasaseni* (Bieler, *Penitentials*, 160–162).

[172]To judge by this and other references to *scribae* in *Hib*, these were not mere copyists of manuscripts but, like '*sapientes*', held a prominent position in the Irish church. See Ireland, 'Aldfrith of Northumbria'; Charles-Edwards, *Christian Ireland*, 264–271.

[173]The expression '*contemtibilis omnibus negotis secularibus*' in the context of adjudication may be an allusion to Jethro's advice to Moses in Exodus 18:21, to appoint as judges those *qui oderint avaritiam* 'who hate avarice'.

The combination of *contemptibilis* and *saecularia* appears to be taken from I Corinthians 6:4: *saecularia igitur iudicia si habueritis contemptibiles qui sunt in ecclesia illos constituite ad iudicandum* 'if, therefore, you have judgements of things pertaining to this world, set them to judge, who are the most despised in the church' (cited here in chapter 21.26). The verse is intended to be ironic, but according to *Hib* 21.28 (see n 203), a *contemptibilis* in an Irish context was a holy man of some description.

[174]See n 173.

[175]The noun *periti* (pl.) / *peritus* (sgl.) is short for the expression *iuris peritus*, on which see note 177.

[176]On the identity of this Gregory, see n 171. The distinction between secular and ecclesiastical jurisdictions attributed to Gregory of Nazianzus in this and the previous text is also known from the *Codex Theodosianus* 16.11.1. The latter, however, is unlikely to have been a direct source for *Hib*.

[177]The expression *iuris peritus* was a technical Roman term for the legal expert who sat on a judicial panel as an adviser to the judges, usually Roman magistrates, who were not obliged to have legal training. Compare with the following Old Irish commentary on court procedure from the so-called *Airecht*-text §2, ed. Kelly, 'An Old-Irish text on court procedure', 85: 'The back court then, it is there that there are the king and the bishop and the expert in every legal language with the rank of master (*sai gacha berlai ollamand*)'. A possible example of a *iuris peritus* from Irish wisdom literature is the judge Caratnia of *Gúbretha Caratniad*, who advises the king, who sits in judgement.

[178]The glossator of the Old Irish commentary on court procedure (ed. Kelly, 'An Old-Irish text on court procedure') believed that one of the judges on the judicial panel, the *sai gacha berlai ollamand*, was a 'chief poet', but this expression could equally mean 'scribe' in the wider sense of the term, on which see n 172. See *GEIL*, 55, 193.

[179]An allusion to the dispute between Minerva and Neptune over the naming of Athens, mentioned in Ovid's Metamorphoses 6.1 and echoed by Isidore, Etymologies, 8.11.9

[180]The reading differs from the Vulgate text. It is difficult to gauge whether *Hib*'s compilers were being consistent about the sense in which they employed *contemptibilis*. After all, 'contemptuous of secular transactions', as on p. 116 ln. 14 (on which see n 173), and 'contemptuous of the

church', as in the present chapter, have entirely different meanings.

[181]This chapter contains a couple of triads (see n 82) on judges and adjudication. There are a number of Old Irish triads on these themes, e.g. §§77, 78, ed. and tr. Meyer, *Triads*.

[182]For an Old Irish equivalent of Latin *consensus*, see *comchétfaid* in *DIL*.

[183]Despite this injunction on leaving the sense of scripture unchanged, the Bible is interpreted quite liberally throughout *Hib*. It is not clear what form of interpretation the chapter is opposed to, because it does not explicitly advocate a literal interpretation, nor is it dismissive of allegorical interpretation. Chapter 37.15 also urges caution when interpreting scripture.

[184]Here ends the citation from Jerome, which has been abridged and decontextualised. My translation is interpretative. A fuller version of Jerome's original text is found on p. 286 ln. 1.

[185]On equality and inequality before the law see n 197.

[186]The orthography of the MSS is ambiguous, but reading *defferentiam* appears to make more sense in this context than *differentiam*.

[187]The verb *adoleo* is often used in the Bible in the combination *incensum adolere* 'to burn incense'. The expression is used both for burning incense in honour of the God of the Israelites and of other gods. The text may be drawing a contrast between *adolatio* and *ueritas* by punning on the dual sense of *ueritas*, a noun which is occasionally used to denote Christ by Augustine and other early Christian writers.

[188]The formula *'locus, tempus, persona'* and variants thereof was frequently used in Old and Middle Irish literature and law, on which see Breatnach, *Companion*, 355–361. Flower, *'Quidam Scotigena'*, 151–152, suggested that it might have become known to Irish authors through Boethius's commentary on Cicero's Topics. However, it is equally possible that *Hib*'s compilers knew it as an exegetical convention, in which case their use of it can be taken as another example of the manner in which they applied exegetical methods in their work. The combination *tempus et loca* echoes a classical formula that can be found in manuals on practical rhetoric, like Quintillian's *Institutio oratoria*, 6.3.101 (*persona, locus, tempus, casus*). We find the formula again in Isidore's *Etym.*, 2.16.1, where we are told that good forensic rhetoric should adapt arguments to suit *res, locus, tempus, persona*. By Gregory the Great's time it was already being applied to exegesis, as in his *Moralia in Iob*, 6.39: *In omni ergo quod dicitur, necesse est ut causa, tempus et*

persona pensetur; si uerba sententiae ueritas roborat, si hanc tempus congruum postulat, si et ueritatem sententiae et congruentiam temporis personae qualitas non impugnat. In *Hib* we also find it as an exegetical formula, on p. 306 ln. 11 (but it also occurs on p. 66 ln. 9, p. 66 ln. 11, where it seems to have no special significance beyond its literal meaning). In the present chapter, however, it is used as a formula to be observed by judges in adjudication.

[189]See book 66, *De contrariis causis.*

[190]*CPL* §872. The text excerpted from the work of this mid sixth-century author from Constantinople was miscopied in the surviving complete copies of *Hib.B*. Fortunately, Sedulius Scottus's *Collectaneum* 8.5.17, a secondary witness to a lost copy of *Hib.B*, preserves a better version.

[191]The embedded gloss in HV (*id est ut non intentio deprauatur a rectitudine*) does not seem to fit the context, so I left it untranslated in the *apparatus*.

[192]On equality and inequality before the law see n 197.

[193]The fifth reason is not in the Isidorian text. For the meaning 'idolatry', see n 187.

[194]See n 187.

[195]This is a truncated sentence from which I omitted *cum his* in order for it to make sense. The original passage from the *Recognitiones* reads: *et ideo cum in his omnia habeantur incerta, ad verum prophetam veniendum est, quem deus pater volens ab omnibus diligi, haec quae homines induxerunt, in quibus nihil potest adprehendi, noluit penitus extinguere, ut eo magis iste quaereretur et quam illi obcluserant, hic hominibus viam veritatis aperiret.*

[196]Lit. 'is removed'. The Vulgate reads *morietur*.

[197]This statement, which is on par with the rule set out on p. 465 ln. 3, is interesting for the fact that it advocates equality before the law, or at least before adjudicators. It is thus in sharp conflict with legal practice found in vernacular law which gave legal privileges to those of higher honour-price (on which see n 263), as well as to those of high religious or political status, like kings, bishops, or hermits. For a position that is more compatible with vernacular law, see chapter 31.23. A near-contemporary statement of equality before the law can be found in clause 2.1.2 of the Visigothic law.

[198]The text from *sed* to *est* does not occur in the original Ambrosian passage.

[199]Nebuchadnezzar's successor. Mentioned in II Kings 25:27 and Jeremiah 52:31.

[200]The *ut* at the beginning of this text is out of context, but serves as a connecting element in the original Gregorian text, which reads: *saecularia igitur iudicia si habueritis contemptibiles qui sunt in ecclesia, illos constituite ad iudicandum, ut ipsi uidelicet dispensationibus terrenis inseruiant, quos dona spiritalia non exornant.*

[201]I.e. Paul. This is an interpretation of I Corinthians 6:4, which precedes the present text in Gregory's Pastoral Rule 2.7.

[202]The translation is tentative. The original passage (below) was considerably altered by *Hib*'s compilers or the source they drew upon: *Si quis ab episcopo uel de ecclesiae uel de proprio iure credederit aliquid repetendum, si nihil conuicii aut criminationes obiecerit, eum pro sola conuentione a communione ecclesiae non liceat submoueri.*

[203]The symmetry between those mentioned in the title (*episcopi, scriba, contemptibilis*) and in the text below (*episcopi, scriba, contemptibilis*) suggests that a *contemptibilis* (on which see n 173) is a holy man of some description. Indeed, a variant in HV reads *sanctis* for *contemtibili.*

[204]See n 171.

[205]On *mendacium* as the equivalent of Old Irish *gáu*, see Charles-Edwards, 'The construction', 231.

[206]See n 604.

[207]Translating *inire iudicium*, which appears to be a variant of *subire iudicium* in Job 31:13, below.

[208]The expression *inire iudicium* in this chapter appears to differ in sense from the previous chapter.

[209]To judge by the previous two passages, this is a sarcastic phrase, rather than a phrase deliberately set in chiastic order.

[210]The context is the biblical verse above in which Christ professes to know God, his father. Augustine interprets this as positive arrogance.

[211]I preferred to leave *seruus* untranslated in order to retain the ambiguity 'slave'/'free client'.

[212]Canons of this synod directly precede the canons of the synod of Gangra in the *Dionysiana*, which explains why the text's provenance was confused.

[213]In this case *seruus* clearly means slave. See n 211.

[214]This chapter has often been connected with the story of St. Columba's ordination of Áedán Mac Gabráin, king of Dalriada, in Adomnán's Life of Columba 3.5. Since Adomnán, ninth abbot of Iona, was a contemporary of Cú Chuimne, one of *Hib*'s presumed compilers who was also from Iona, the two may have held a similar conception of kingship, which found expression in their works. Adomnán and Cú Chuimne might have belonged to a wider like-minded circle that espoused the subjection of temporal political powers to the church, or at least sought to secure a role for the church in legitimating and confirming kings. As Sharpe notes, the ordination episode in the Life, 'hints at a remarkable innovation in the idea of kingship. Instead of being inaugurated by pagan ritual, as Díarmait mac Cerbaill had been at the feast of Tara, Áedán is presented as being made king of Dalriada through "ordination" by the local holy man, Columba'. See Sharpe, *Life of St. Columba*, 355–456 n 358. It was Michael Enright, *Iona, Tara, and Soissons*, 5–78, who first suggested that Adomnán's view on kingship was informed by Samuel's anointment of Saul, described in the biblical scene cited in the present chapter.

[215]But the Amiatinus copy of the Vulgate reads *exigue*, hence 'sparingly will pity be granted to them'. I am grateful to Dr Richard Pollard for the reference and translation.

[216]There seems to have been no single procedure for regnal succession that was consistently observed in early medieval Ireland. The theory of succession, as propagated by early medieval Irish lawyers, took it for granted that a *tánaise ríg* 'heir apparent' would succeed to the kingship of a *túath*. An example is *Críth Gablach*, ed. Binchy §29. Other law tracts stipulate that in order to succeed to the kingship one had to be the son and grandson of a king, to be the son of a principal wife (preferably the eldest), to fulfil certain property qualifications, to be blameless, and physically unblemished. According to legend, the youngest could also succeed. See Ó Cróinín, *Early Medieval Ireland*, 63–71, esp. 70–71. For a more recent view on legal perspectives on the requisites for succession, see Warntjes, 'Regnal succession'.

[217]The cyclical movement expressed here is evocative of Polybius's idea of the rise and subsequent demise of constitutions in his Histories 6.8–9.

[218]According to the wisdom text on adjudication, *Gúbretha Caratniad*, if claimants to the kingship happen to be brothers of the same age, lots are cast between them. See Ó Cróinín, *Early Medieval Ireland*, 70.

[219]On what follows, see Meens, 'Politics, mirrors of princes', 349–352.

[220]Despite the doubling of the letter 'r', the verb intended here is *procuro-are* rather than *procurro-ere.*

[221]On the following text, see Meens, 'Politics, mirrors of princes', 349–352.

[222]See n 171.

[223]For the term *census,* see n 515.

[224]My emendation is based on Jerome's text, which reads: *post hunc surrexit in diebus census Iudas Galilaeus: qui inter caetera hoc quasi probabile proferebat ex lege, nullum debere Dominum nisi solum Deum vocari: et eos qui ad templum decimas deferrent, caesari tributa non reddere.*

[225]This allusion to Genesis 47:26, which also exempts the priests' land from tribute, anticipates the next chapter in *Hib.*

[226]In this case either the head of a church (on which see n 44), who placed his church under tribute, or a lay nobleman who exacted tribute. The context makes the first more likely. See discussion of this passage in Etchingham, *Church Organisation*, 218–219.

[227]The Vulgate and HV phrase this as a question, reading *usurasne*, rather than *ne ussuras.*

[228]Literally 'tax', because the original context is the Roman empire. However, *Hib*'s compilers are more likely to have been thinking in terms of tribute.

[229]A single manuscript, P, names the correct prophet, Jeremiah, in a gloss.

[230]Late Latin *sors* translates either as 'share' or 'inheritance'. See Niermeyer, *Mediae Latinitatis Lexicon.*

[231]The combination *manum mittere* is the equivalent of an idiomatic expression from the Hebrew Bible, meaning 'to strike', 'to slay'. The Vulgate uses this expression in its idiomatic Hebrew sense, e.g. in I Samuel 24:7, Nehemiah 13:21.

[232]The original Isidorian text reads *uincire.*

[233]The repetition of this clause does not occur in the Bible.

[234]This qualification is not in the biblical text.

[235]The reference appears to be to physical punishment. See n 53.

[236]The final sentence is not in Jerome's commentary.

[237]Augustine's text reads *flagrare* 'to inflame'.

[238]The allusion is to Proverbs 13:24: 'He who spares the rod hates his son'.

[239]For the passage to make sense I omitted *sed* from the translation.

[240]Augustine's text reads *non ipsa mors noceret sed peccatum* 'it was not death that harmed them, but sin'.

[241]See n 74.

[242]Sedulius Scottus's *Collectaneum* 25.8.10, a secondary witness to *Hib*, preserves a different version of this text (perhaps an emendation by Sedulius himself), which I used as an aid in editing and translating. His text reads: *Cain primus homicida septies punitur quia VII uindictas passus est, siue quod ex anima tripertita: racionabili, irascibili, concupiscibili, et corpore quadripertito, id est, terra, aqua, aere, igne; per VII peccans: I male audit, II inuidit, III iratus, IV occidit, V mentitus est, VI male credidit, VII disperauit, septies flagellatur; siue quia sub una poena per VII generationes usus est.*

[243]The ablative absolute *boue cadente* gives the impression that the ox, rather than the ark, fell over. I emended according to the biblical story.

[244]The reading 'forty-three' in P is strange, given that there were only forty-two to begin with. Only O gives an alternative figure, while all other manuscripts omit any mention of the number of boys who were devoured.

[245]This may be an allusion to the practice of commuting long penances for shorter and harsher ones. See, e.g. the Old-Irish Table of Commutations, tr. D. A. Binchy *apud* Bieler, *Penitentials*, 278–282.

[246]The ninth-century Jewish exegetical text *Midrash Tanhuma* (*Tanhuma* §11, tr. Berman, *Midrash Tanhuma-Yelammedenu*, 32) is witness to a tradition according to which Lamech killed his exceptionally long-lived ancestor Cain in a hunting accident.

[247]Lit. 'ways'.

[248]See previous note.

[249]See previous note.

[250]See previous note.

[251]Lit. 'deceiving'/'cheating'.

[252]Lit. 'alien punishment'.

[253]The expression *uagus Dei* 'God's wanderer', may be the Latin equivalent of *déorad Dé* (lit. 'exile of God'), which was an Old Irish term that denoted 'hermit' or 'anchorite'. As noted by *GEIL*, 41, these hermits enjoyed an exceptional status in the laws, which gave them the power to act as enforcing sureties for contracts that were bound by the Gospels or the eucharist. Refusal of hospitality to an anchorite is discussed in the text known as *De iectione eclesie graduum ab hospitio* 'Concerning the refusal of hospitality to persons of ecclesiastical rank' §11 (Bieler, *Penitentials*, 174). An anchorite is there equated with a *princeps* and *scriba* for the purpose of calculating the compensation due for refusal of hospitality which resulted in death.

[254]The present chapter and chapter 27.9, are the only texts from *Hib* that are known to have been used for settling a dispute in Carolingian Europe. They are both cited in a letter by Alcuin to Candidus and Nathanel, dated *c.* 801 (MGH Epist. IV, 396 lines 8–12), in which Alcuin defends his decision to give shelter at Tours to a delinquent monk who fled from imprisonment at Orléans. See Wallach, *Alcuin and Charlemagne*, 129–130; Meens, 'Sanctuary, Penance, and Dispute Settlement'. The church of St. Martin at Tours is mentioned a number of times in Gregory of Tours's Histories as a place of refuge. The concept of the church as sanctuary was well known and is attested in both canon law, e.g. the first canon of the Council of Orléans of 511, and secular law, e.g. the *Lex Alamannorum* §§2, 3 (Schott, 84–86).

[255]I take this to mean that the killer shall lose his freedom, which could be restored to him only with the consent of the victim's kin, and after making proper restitution. For as long as his freedom was suspended, his status would have been that of a *cimbid* 'captive', held by the kin of the person whom he has wronged, until such time that he could be ransomed. See *GEIL*, 97–98.

[256]*Recte*: Athalia, as in HV.

[257]See n 254.

[258]Such a penitent is described in Adomnán's Life of Columba, 2.39. Librán was convicted of manslaughter in Connacht, and was ordered by Columba to perform seven years of penance on the island of Tiree, in the Hebrides. See also n 55.

[259]See n 254.

[260]*contractio*, from *contraho*.

[261]The expression *pecunia mortalis* translates Old Irish *marbdil* 'dead chattels'. An identical stipulation is found in the Irish law tract on theft, *Bretha im Gatta, CIH* 478–89. See Hull, 'Bretha im gatta'; Ó Corráin, Breatnach, and Breen, 'Laws of the Irish', 409–413. However, because *Hib* favours a lenient punishment for theft and *Bretha im Gatta* a harsher one, Charles-Edwards, 'The construction', 225, believes the two texts are independent of each other.

[262]See n 261.

[263]*lóg n-enech* 'honour-price' (lit. 'price of a face'), was the Irish equivalent of the Frankish *wergeld*, the Anglo-Saxon *leodgeld*, and the Welsh *wynebwerth*. Other Old Irish words used for honour-price were *díre* and *eneclann*. All persons of independent legal status were assigned a *lóg n-enech* based on their wealth, political status or ecclesiastical rank. The honour-price was a measure of legal status, and as a consequence determined one's capacity to make and guarantee contracts, to testify, and to judge. It also determined the level and type of compensation to which one was entitled for offences committed against one's own person, property, kin, or clientele.

[264]See *logad*(d) in *DIL*.

[265]This alludes to the practice of storing goods in a church for safekeeping, discussed by Lucas, 'The plundering and burning of churches'.

[266]According to Charles-Edwards, 'The construction', 228, *damnum* corresponds to Old Irish *aithgein* 'restitution'.

[267]Literally, 'usury', but Charles-Edwards, 'The construction', 228, suggests it might be the equivalent of Old Irish *lóg n-enech* 'honour-price' or *díre* 'penalty'/'fine' corresponding to honour-price.

[268]See n 261.

[269]On harmonising 'law' and 'nature', see n 71.

[270]See n 263.

[271]The deposits and form of deposit vary throughout the book, but in general, these are chattels deposited for safekeeping with an individual or the church. See Ó Corráin, Breatnach, and Breen, 'Laws of the Irish', 415–416. On this book's influence on the twelfth-century Welsh law text *Cyfraith Hywel*, see Pryce, 'Early Irish canons'.

[272]This is a literal rendition of the biblical Hebrew *elohim*, literally meaning 'gods'. Despite its plural suffix, the Hebrew Bible treats it as a noun

in the singular: it is qualified by adjectives in the singular and governs verbs in the singular. A case in point is Gen. 1:1: *bara elohim*, lit. 'gods (pl.) created (sgl.)'.

[273]See previous note.

[274]See n 261.

[275]Or, alternatively, 'pay a fine'. Both interpretations seem to work in this case.

[276]What follows is exegesis of Exodus 22:7–9, cited at the beginning of the book.

[277]The combination *ablata sit* is meant to echo Exodus 22:7, cited at the beginning of the chapter, where the wording is slightly different: *sublatum fuerit*. The different versions may suggest that *Hib*'s compilers cited the exegesis and the biblical text from different sources.

[278]What follows is exegesis of Exodus 22:7–9, cited at the beginning of the book.

[279]This presumably implies swearing on the relics of martyrs.

[280]I was unable to trace this word in Greek or any other language.

[281]Translating *uerbi gratia*, lit. 'on account of the word'.

[282]See n 102.

[283]The premise of this chapter contradicts chapter 28.6.

[284]According to a variant in B, which reads *quae* for *qui*, the church is intended here.

[285]I take these rather opaque passages to mean that churches that were unable to protect property that was deposited in them risked losing their status as 'cities of refuge'. On Irish churches performing this function, see Lucas, 'The plundering and burning of churches'.

[286]The use of *quamuis* 'even if' implies that the depositors would be likely to claim compensation for a lost deposit although they deposited their property (e.g. movables, livestock, or perhaps even land) with the church, knowing very well that the property will never be returned to them. This suggests that deposited property would have continued to be of value to the depositor, perhaps yielding some form of income that the depositor could claim. The rule prescribed by the Hibernian synod cited in this text was taken up by the Old Irish tract *Bretha im Gatta* (*CIH* 2109.27–30). For discussion see Ó Corráin, Breatnach, and Breen, 'Laws of the Irish', 415.

[287]I.e. if it is not immediately obvious that the house was broken into. This is how this passage was interpreted in medieval Welsh law. See Pryce, 'Early Irish canons', 112.

[288]According to Sheehy, 'Influences of ancient Irish law', 39, *suffoderit* corresponds to Old Irish *fo-claid*.

[289]I.e. if the theft affected both the depositor and the owner of the house, it is deemed less likely that the owner was the one who stole the deposit.

[290]My translation is tentative. The original text from the synod of Vaison was: *secundum statuta fidelissimorum, piissimorum, augustissimorum principum, quisquis expositum colligit ecclesiam contestetur, contestationem colligat; nihilominus de altario domino die minister adnuntiet, ut sciat ecclesia expositum esse collectum, ut intra dies decem ab expositionis die expositum recipiat, si quis se comprobauerit agnouisse, collectori pro ipsorum decem dierum misericordia, prout maluerit, aut ad praesens ab homine aut in perpetuum cum deo gratia persoluenda. Sane si quis post hanc diligentissimam sanctionem expositorum hoc ordine collectorum repetitor uel calumniator extiterit, ut homicida ecclesiastica districtione feriatur.*

[291]Translation adapted from *Etymologies*, tr. Barney *et al.*

[292]Esau had one Israelite wife and two Canaanite wives.

[293]Emending *quibus* to *quae*.

[294]The only letter in which Jerome mentions Thecla of Iconium, St. Paul's companion in the apocryphal Acts of Paul and Thecla, is No. 22 to Eustochium. Her name is mentioned in passing but nothing at all is said of her. In his *De uiris illustribus* §5 (*CPL* §616) he dismisses the Acts as apocryphal. Another reference to Thecla, as a nickname for Melania the Elder, is in the continuation to the Chronicle of Eusebius, in the entry for AD 374. No letter to Melania survives.

[295]This seems a plausible translation, albeit not a literal one.

[296]This chapter makes some of the most explicit statements on distinctions between kin and church, two categories that could sometimes overlap in early Irish society.

[297]Hiberno-Latin *ratio* is here the equivalent of Old Irish *dliged*. See n 487.

[298]Here, *hereditas* is equivalent to Old Irish *fintiu*. I owe thanks to the late Professor Donnchadh Ó Corráin for this suggestion.

[299]Hiberno-Latin *ratio* is here the equivalent of Old Irish *dliged*. See n 487.

[300]This is not the ordinary meaning of the Latin adverb *secus*, which the compilers appear to be using here as a preposition corresponding to Old Irish *sech*.

[301]Irish law allowed women to have a life-share in their fathers' inheritance. A *banchomarbae* 'female heir', or dowager, was not permitted to alienate land, and after her death the property was to revert to her kin-group. In exceptional cases the laws permitted women to bequeath land to their sons and daughters. See Kelly, *Farming*, 415–417; Ó Corráin, 'Women and law'. It is unclear from the title of this chapter whether *post eam heredes* refers to the heiress's children or to other members of her kin-group who were entitled to her share of the inheritance. Vernacular prescriptions on female inheritance are most fully articulated in the poem *In-longat bantaid banchuru*, ed. and tr. Charles-Edwards, *Early Irish and Welsh Kinship*, 516–519.

[302]See *DIL* for the range of senses of Old Irish *ord*, derived from Latin *ordo*.

[303]This is one of a number of instances in *Hib* where the practice of concubinage is taken for granted.

[304]See n 74.

[305]I.e. pre-Christian law. See n 71.

[306]This implies marriage within the kin. See n 309.

[307]The terms *rata* and *stipulator* are discussed by Thurneysen, 'Aus dem irischen Recht V', 364–372, who concludes that they were the Hiberno-Latin terms corresponding to Old Irish *ráth* and *naidm*, two different types of sureties. A *ráth* surety guaranteed a contract with his own property, and was obliged to discharge the principal's obligations if the latter defaulted on the contract. The principal would then have been indebted to the *ráth* and also owed him an additional fine for his trouble. A *naidm*'s role was to force the principal to discharge his obligation by means of distress, i.e. threatening to seize his property. For both, see, respectively, Binchy, *Críth Gablach*, 102–104, 100–101. Contracts of any kind, including marriages and reciprocal arrangements between lords and clients, had to be guaranteed by sureties. Binchy (101): 'In a society where there is no public enforcement of legal claims, the *naidms*, pledged to levy execution against a defaulting debtor, offer a primitive substitute for the modern State-administered justice'.

The plural noun *stipulationes* should normally be thought of as distinct from *stipulatores* and translated 'assurances', as in the Vulgate's version of Jeremiah 32:11, cited in *Hib* 33.6. However, the phrase *si stipulationes inter se dissentiant sortientur* in *Hib* 33.7, suggests that in *Hib* both nouns apply to people, and should be translated 'enforcing sureties'.

[308]Understood by Ó Corráin, 'Women and the law', 54, to be a hereditary church.

[309]The translation of the last sentence follows Ó Corráin, 'Women and the law', 54. The implication is that property should not be alienated from the paternal kin (an idea echoed also on p. 334 ln. 15). The variant text in H is identical in sense: *si genuerint filium uiris de cognatione sua paterna, hereditas eorum erit filiis* 'and if they will have a son by men of their own kindred, their inheritance shall belong to the sons' (note that Wasserschleben emended the text from V, which he gave in a footnote). After *c.* 700, the kin-group that counted for the purpose of inheritance was the *gelḟine* 'white kindred', consisting of three generations (Charles-Edwards, *Early Christian Ireland*, 86). The system of inheritance, which clearly favoured spouses belonging to the same kin, would thus have encouraged marriage between members of the *gelḟine*, usually first cousins. Strictly speaking, such marriages counted as incest in the eyes of the church, which held that husband and wife ought to be separated by at least six degrees (see Council of Auxerre of 585 §31, ed. de Clerq, p. 269; Roman council of 721 §§8, 9, PL 67:343C–D). Although *Hib* mentions the six-degree rule on p. 331 ln. 2, it nevertheless endorses first-cousin marriage and, as Ó Corráin points out, *Hib* uses a biblical rationale in doing so, for which see chapter 31.19.

[310]On lots see chapter 25.

[311]Privileging the testimony of nobles is entirely consistent with Irish vernacular law. For a view that holds that all litigants should be treated as equals in adjudication, see n 197.

[312]Lit. 'are judged'.

[313]The combination *quos mouet* is not in the original Augustinian text.

[314]Translating *doctrina*. See *Etymologies*, tr. Barney *et al.*

[315]Pledges were chattels deposited by one party with another as security, e.g. to guarantee the fulfilment of contracts. Early Irish law, according to *GEIL*, 164, 'relies greatly on the use of pledges *gell* to ensure that legal obligations are carried out'.

[316]The literal translation 'to whom it is owed' does not fit the context because the examples given are actually concerned with cases in which the debtor rather than the creditor died.

[317]See n 102.

[318]*Recte* Elisha.

[319]Cf. *Hib* 33.6.

[320]See n 307.

[321]According to Ó Corráin (personal comment), *miserere* renders Old Irish *logaid* 'forgive', 'remit'. On a pledge in Irish law, see n 315. The present chapter appears to treat a pledge as a security deposited with a creditor in order to allow the temporary or indefinite deferral of a debt.

[322]Translating *usura*.

[323]On these terms, see n 307.

[324]Sheehy, 'Influences of ancient Irish law', 36, translates the expression *manum defigere* 'to undertake suretyship'.

[325]Perhaps used here by the compilers as an allusion to the Old Irish expression *gaib fort láim* 'take into your hand' (*Berrad Airechta* §51) which describes the joining of hands that sealed a contract. See Stacey, *Road to Judgment*, 34–36.

[326]Translation slightly adapted from Bieler, *Penitentials*, 55.

[327]My translation of the end of the clause is interpretative. In translating *domina* 'abbess', I follow Charles-Edwards, *Chronicle of Ireland*, 2:3, who derives this meaning from the description of the abbess of Kildare in 732 as *dominatrix*. For obits of other abbesses to which the term is applied, see: 758, 771, 773, 780. Jaski, 'Marriage laws in Ireland', 19, suggests that *domina* should be equated with a woman of high status (*bé cuitchernsa* or *cétmuinter*), and translates: 'nor a woman, unless she is the head of a household, or a holy virgin'. Kathleen Hughes, *Church*, 158, believed a *dominatrix* could be a female equivalent of *princeps*, on which see n 44.

[328]I assume the debt would, in this case, have been demanded from the debtor's heirs.

[329]Sheehy, 'Influences of ancient Irish law', 37, suggests that the expression *quantum fatigatus fuerit* corresponds to Old Irish *imluad*, and 'refers to the inconvenience suffered by the *ráth* by his having to discharge the debt for his principal'.

[330]In other words, usury is exacted, even though a number of texts in *Hib* explicitly forbid both laymen and clerics from practising usury. See book 10 and the following chapters: 24.14, 28.8, 32.12, 34.4.

[331]The sense of *ratis* and *stipulationibus* is ambiguous in this chapter. On the one hand, the text attributed to Augustine below, where they are contrasted with *scriptiones* 'written attestations', suggests that these are not different types of record but people. But in the following text, attributed to Jerome, they may be interpreted as forms of written record.

[332]I retained the Vulgate sense of *stipulationes* and *ratas* (here a feminine noun, but neuter in the Vulgate) because I was not sure whether the compilers of *Hib* intended readers to understand these terms in their biblical or contemporary sense as 'enforcing sureties' and 'paying sureties'.

[333]Cf. chapter 32.4. Although no complete Irish charters survive from our period, Wendy Davies, 'Celtic charter tradition', 268–269, 276–278, has argued that some seventh- and eighth-century Latin texts, including *Hib*, contain material that draws on charter formulae. However, the earliest vernacular charters, such as the land grants written into the Book of Kells and the Book of Durrow, might have been 'a response to the discovery of European Latin charters in the eleventh and twelfth centuries'. The early eighth-century inscription on the standing-stone at Kilnasaggart, Co. Armagh, which records a grant of land, evidences the use of rudimentary charter terminology, of the kind that contemporary Patrician hagiography gives an idealised account. See Herbert, 'Before charters', 108.

[334]The terms *ratae* and *stipulationes* do not seem to refer to people here. See n 331.

[335]For *ratio* as 'law' see n 487.

[336]Charles-Edwards (personal comment) suggests that this may afford evidence for a reversed system of penitential commutation, whereby payment could be substituted by penance, and not only penance by payment, as in, for example, *De arreis* (*BCLL* §603).

[337]Cited in Gratian's *Decretum*, C. 22 q. 4 c. 17.

[338]Cited in Gratian's *Decretum*, C. 22 q. 5 c. 15. Cf. p. 100 ln. 17, p. 245 ln. 9, p. 473 ln. 14.

[339]Emending *sit* to *intersit*.

[340]For the practice of swearing by the altar see Fith Fio's grant to Druim Lías: *Additamenta* to Tírechán's *Collectanea* §9 (Bieler, *Patrician Texts*, 172).

[341]See n 109.

[342]See n 108.

[343]On the function of the jubilee in early Irish society, see n 349.

[344]All manuscripts but P diverge from the Vulgate text by reading 'brothers' for 'fathers'.

[345]Here P diverges from the Vulgate text by reading 'six' for 'seven' against all other manuscripts.

[346]The sense would have been wider than that which is intended in the citation from Leviticus below.

[347]See previous note.

[348]Alternatively, an Irish readership might have preferred to interpret *stipulationes* as 'enforcing sureties' and *ratas* as 'paying sureties'.

[349]In other words, the former owner loses it. Admittedly, a literal translation of the title would be: 'Concerning the time at which neglected property falls into '*ius antiquum*''. However, such a literal translation would be inconsistent with the sense of *ius antiquum* on p. 102 ln. 8 and p. 317 ln. 3, where the expression clearly means 'former ownership'. As for my rendering of the verb *cadere* as 'forfeit', it can be justified thus: the Irish verb glossed as *cadere* in the St. Gall glosses on Priscian (Sg. 71a9) is *do-tuit*, which, according to *DIL* also includes 'forfeit' in its semantic range.

Stevenson, 'Literacy in Ireland', 31–32, points out that texts such as the one quoted in this chapter and the one on p. 253 ln. 6 constitute a reversal of the biblical jubilee principle which guaranteed that property would be restored to its former ownership on the fiftieth year. According to Stevenson, the unique Irish jubilee was devised by the church as a compromise between the church's need for land and traditional precepts that forbade the alienation of kin land to anyone outside the kin, including the church. The Irish jubilee was thus established as an interim period during which each party could withdraw from the agreement, in a way that was meant to ensure that 'land was not alienated without the full consent of the whole kin-group'. An altogether different jubilee principle was espoused by Irish vernacular law, which determined that after seven years of clientship a free client would be entitled to a *iubaile soíre* 'jubilee of freedom'. Thus, according to *Cáin sóerraith* 'the regulation of a free fief', every free clientship came to an end after seven years, when the client returned the cattle that his lord had given him on loan. See Charles-Edwards, 'Early Irish law', 358–360.

[350]The reference appears to be to the sayings attributed to the fourth-century ascetic St. Amma Syncletica, some of which are found in the *Vitas Patrum*, on which see n 102. I am unaware that Augustine had written anything about her.

[351]For this interpretation I follow the embedded gloss in B. I take the phrase to mean that one would find it difficult to prove ownership of a property alienated for a long period of time, without living witnesses.

[352]Lit. 'passing'.

[353]This principle is a reversal of the biblical jubilee principle. See n 349.

[354]Cf. Bieler, *Penitentials*, 197.

[355]See n 349. I am not sure whether the *ius proprium* of this title should be understood in opposition to *ius antiquum* of the heading of chapter 35.7. If so, then *ius proprium* must have had a technical legal sense, though I am unable to offer a good translation.

[356]Perhaps a reference to joint land ownership by the kin.

[357]See n 44.

[358]This was Origen's rendering of the name 'Joshua son of Nun'.

[359]Gregory is here referring to nuns of noble birth.

[360]The contrast is with the passage before last, beginning 'In the books of Kings', as the text immediately above occurs only in *Hib.B*.

[361]See n 36.

[362]The distinction between *parochia* and *monachi* suggests that the former consisted of lay tenants, and the latter of the religious brethren. The requirement that the clerics must give their consent to the bishop's choice implies that they had a stake in governing the ecclesiastical settlement.

[363]A *comarbae* (or *coarb*) 'heir', inherited the chief office in an ecclesiastical settlement, be it that of abbot or *princeps* (or an office combining both). Whereas *Hib* does not condition one's eligibility to inherit upon one's affiliation with a particular kindred, vernacular law, and in particular *Córus Bésgnai* §§91–92 (ed. and tr. Breatnach, 44/45), stipulates that the head of a proprietary church ought to be chosen from the family of the founding saint. See Ó Cróinín, *Early Medieval Ireland*, 162–163.

[364]Alternatively, this could be a misrendering of *sinodus*. See also n 562.

[365]My translation is tentative.

[366]See n 113.

[367]This is yet another statement supporting the idea of a collective stake in running the ecclesiastical settlement.

[368]This chapter returns to the theme of a collective stake in governing the ecclesiastical settlement.

[369]Lit. 'observe'.

[370]Lit. 'observe'.

[371]On the term 'relic' in early medieval Ireland, see n 112. Since this text cannot be traced to Cassian, it is likely that the attribution is spurious and that the text is, in fact, of Irish origin.

[372]*Recte* 'Rehoboam'. Only MS V gives the correct name whereas all others name his brother, Jeroboam.

[373]My translation is not literal, for it requires a possessive pronoun instead of the reflexive '*sibi*'. However, a literal translation—'reserved for himself'—seems awkward.

[374]This verse sets the principle that a mission should not be sent to a place already possessing of a bishop. See Flechner, 'Pope Gregory and the British'.

[375]The conjunctions *uel* and *aut* may be translated 'and' in this context, as in Pseudo-Hilary's Commentary on the Catholic Epistles, which mentions a similar form of excommunication, perhaps drawing on the same source as *Hib*. See commentary on II John 1:10, ed. McNally, CCSL 108B, p. 119 line 18: *Haec est excommunicatio in nouo testamento, ut a mensa et missa et communione donus aecclaesiae separetur infidelis, ut paulus ait, cum huiusmodi nec cibum quidem sumatis.* The text is commonly regarded as Irish and dated *c.* 700 (*BCLL* §346).

[376]See n 21.

[377]Reading *coinquinatus* for *quoinquinatus*.

[378]Emending *digna* to *dignitas*.

[379]For this sense of *pyra*, see Acts 28:2 in the Vulgate.

[380]Lit. 'her'.

[381]It is unclear whether the scholars described in this book are entirely distinct from *filid* or whether their identities may, to some extent, overlap. The *filid*, frequently translated 'poets', were members of a profes-

sional learned class patronised by aristocrats whom they served as teachers, praise poets, genealogists, and legal experts. Irish law ranked a career as a *fili* on par with an ecclesiastical or a political career for the purpose of attaining and retaining noble status. For example, the eighth-century *Uraicecht Becc* 'Small Primer', states that the honour-price of the highest grade of scholar, *ollam,* is equal to that of a king. The relatively high legal status (or 'honour-price') associated with scholarship and the social prestige that it brought, suggest that becoming a *fili* would have been a very desirable pursuit. Although access to the ranks of the *filid* was restricted by hereditary right, scholarly merit would have allowed some learned men to join as low-ranking members. According to Charles-Edwards, 'The context and uses of literacy', Irish laws seem to have recognised a single hereditary aristocracy, whose members were either royals, high-ranking ecclesiastics, or prolific scholars. The starting point for any discussion of the social and legal status of the *filid* is a legal text regulating their profession, *Uraiccecht na Ríar*, edited by Liam Breatnach.

[382]Lit. 'examples'.

[383]See Souter, *Glossary of Later Latin.*

[384]*Sc.* the church.

[385]For other admonitions against interpreting scripture carelessly, see p. 120 ln. 12, p. 285 ln. 11.

[386]This text has been altered from both Gregory's and Caesarius's, on which the Gregorian sermon draws, where it read: *Fortasse panem ut indigenti elimosinam porrigat non habet...*

[387]Jerome's text has *paucis additis uel mutatis.*

[388]See n 190.

[389]The relative pronoun *qui,* which seems out of place, occurs only in manuscripts AHS.

[390]In this book as elsewhere in *Hib,* the word *monachus* varies in sense, sometimes meaning 'monk' and sometimes *manach* (on which see n 115). In order to retain the ambiguity I leave the word untranslated throughout.

[391]This sentence is an addition to the Isidorian text. It is clearly meant to curb the enthusiasm of young *monachi* eager to leave their monasteries and become anchorites.

[392]Isidore's text reads *uiuere,* not *uenire.* Since *Hib* (or its immediate source) did not emend *illa regione* to *illam regionem* (which it should have

done for grammatical correctness) then it would appear that the change from *uiuere* to *uenire* was not deliberate, but an error.

393Reading *lucrosae* for *lucro* as in Isidore.

394This interpretation is supported by the gloss *uestibus* above *duplicibus* in H.

395Even though Jerome never wrote to Benedict, *Hib*'s mention of Benedict as an addressee invites attention to the possibility that the rule of Benedict, which opens with a citation from Jerome's letter to Eustochius, might have been known in Ireland in one form or another. This possibility gains support from the phrase *peius quam loqui*, on which see the next note.

396My translation of *peius quam loqui* is premised on the assumption that it is an abridged paraphrase of a text in the Benedictine rule, which reads *melius est silere quam loqui*. The fact that the letter by Jerome cited here and in the first book of the rule does not contain this phrase increases the likelihood that *Hib*'s compilers had a different copy of the rule itself.

397This is an excerpt from a letter written by Gildas in response to questions sent to him by the cleric Vinnian, founder bishop of Clonard, who sought advice on the matter of *monachi* who quit their monastery to seek a harsher form of asceticism. The correspondence between them is mentioned in Columbanus's letter to Pope Gregory (ed. Walker, 8 §7). Excerpts from Gildas's letter came to circulate independently and are also found in a direct source of *Hib*, a *florilegium* now in Cambridge, Corpus Christi College, MS 279. See Sharpe, 'Gildas as a father of the Church'.

398For the source of this text, see n 397. Translation is adapted from Winterbottom, *Gildas*, 81.

399Translation is adapted from Winterbottom, *Gildas*, 81.

400See previous note.

401See previous note.

402The dual excommunication is absent from the canon of the Council of Nicaea, on which the present text is loosely based, but is found in the fifth canon of the Council of Hertford, the acta of which are incorporated in Bede's *HE* 4.5.

403Cf. n 375.

404Since some of these expressions are *hapax legomena* in Hiberno-Latin, the translation is tentative. I am grateful to Dr Anthony Harvey for discussing this text with me.

[405]The meaning of *excommunicare* was extended from persons to foodstuffs in Hiberno-Latin Penitentials and saints' Lives. See Harvey, 'Non-Classical vocabulary', 93–94.

[406]*CIH* 1396.11–16, 2125.3–7. The Irish text clearly draws on *Hib*, but is not a verbatim translation. See Ó Corráin, Breatnach, and Breen, 'Laws of the Irish', 417–418.

[407]*CIH* 2122.5, 11–12, 15, 18, 20; 1558.28–31; 1097.2–3. See Ó Corráin, Breatnach, and Breen, 'Laws of the Irish', 418–420.

[408]Translation is adapted from Winterbottom, *Gildas*, 80.

[409]Cf. book 53, *De carnibus edendis.*

[410]I emended to *in diuinis libris*, which is the reading found in another witness to this text, the eighth-century Hiberno-Latin *Prebiarum de multorum exemplaribus* §81 (ed. McNally, 168). It is possible that *'diuinos libros'* was a title of a *florilegium* used by the compilers of Θ, who might also have been *Hib*'s compilers.

[411]The text appears to be incomplete.

[412]The first half of this book is concerned with bequests made by *monachi* and heads of ecclesiastical settlements, either abbots or *principes*, who could be laymen. The practice of making bequests of this kind is attested in the quasi-cartulary *Additamenta* to Tírechán's *Collectanea* §§9, 16 (ed. Bieler, *Patrician Texts*, 172, 178). These clauses record, respectively, grants made by the aging Fith Fio to the *familia* of Druim Lías and by bishop Áed of Sletty to Armagh. The conditional allowances for making bequests are largely consistent with prescriptions found in Chrodegang (d. 766) of Metz's *Regula canonicorum* §31 (ed. Pelt, *Études*, 11), but not directly dependent on them. These prescriptions permitted canons to hold their own property as *precaria* (revocable grants of land) before it passed to the church on their death, but forbade them from making bequests. Such concessions, which flatly contradicted the Benedictine Rule, were necessary for attracting aristocratic inmates. The reforms undertaken at Christ Church Canterbury by Archbishop Wulfred (805–832) make similar concessions, but also allow the head of the church to make bequests, as indeed does the *Hibernensis*. For an edition of documents relating to the proprietary aspects of the reform and a comparison with Frankish reforms, see Brooks, 'Cathedral reform'.

[413]This was Attalus III (d. 133 BC), who bequeathed Pergamon to Rome.

[414]The word *agipa* is glossed with Old Breton *gulcet* in P and *latic* in O. According to Stokes, 'Old-Breton glosses', 340, 343: 'Here *latic* is the equivalent of *gulcet*... It must be a loan from *lōdix* "a counterpane". Hence also the Ir. *loit* in *dia loit find* "two white blankets"...'

[415]Old Irish *cumal* 'female slave', was a unit of exchange, like *sét*, cattle, or ounces of silver. The sources are inconsistent with respect to fixing its value in relation to other units of value. A number of law texts equate it with three cows, but others say a *cumal* was worth up to ten cows. On units of value see Kelly, *Farming*, 587–599.

[416]*iniuriae* may have a technical sense here.

[417]For the term *census*, see n 515.

[418]I.e. a payment for a grave. On the law of burial see book 18.

[419]See n 138.

[420]The eucharist given to the dying.

[421]This and the following chapter are discussed in *Bretha Nemed Toísech* §22. See Breatnach, 'Canon law and secular law', 445–447. For an edition and translation of the Old Irish texts that drew upon *Hib*, see *ibid.* and Breatnach, 'The first third of *Bretha Nemed*', 8/9.

[422]See previous note.

[423]See n 149.

[424]The original text reads *iustum*, not *uissum*.

[425]Translating *delegentur* of the original text.

[426]This and the following chapter are discussed in *Bretha Nemed Toísech* §22. See Breatnach, 'Canon law and secular law', 447–449. For an edition and translation of the Old Irish texts that drew upon *Hib*, see *ibid.* 449–450, Breatnach, 'The first third of *Bretha Nemed*', 16/17, 18/19.

[427]Translating *peregrina communio*. See n 111.

[428]See n 426.

[429]Perhaps Nehemiah is intended here.

[430]Simpson, 'The '*Prouerbia Grecorum*'', 6, draws attention to a parallel between this passage and *Córus Bésgnai* §56 (ed. and tr. Breatnach, 40/41), which allows a dutiful son (*mac gor*), who supports the elderly members of his family, to benefit from the disinheritance of an undutiful son (*mac ingor*).

[431]See book 35.

[432]Presumably the value of half the estate.

[433]Emending *admittenda* to *amittenda*, on Charles-Edwards's advice.

[434]The division was meant to settle competing claims to episcopal sees in Africa after the reconciliation between Donatist and Catholic bishops.

[435]This exegesis also refers to the final section of the previous chapter.

[436]See n 74.

[437]This biblical precept is the opposite of what Irish law prescribed for a division of an inheritance, namely that the youngest brother should divide the land and that his brothers should choose by order of seniority: the elder got first choice and the youngest last. The method was meant to ensure a fair division of the land. See *GEIL*, 102.

[438]The following chapter is concerned with the distinction between children who were brought to a church to be fostered, and others who were abandoned on a church's doorstep and became its slaves. The former case conforms to the usual pattern of fosterage in early medieval Ireland, where mutual exchange of foster-children was a means of forging ties between families and wider kin-groups. In the case described in the present chapter, the ties that were formed were either between a particular kin and a particular church/monastery, or between a particular kin and another kin that owned or controlled a church/monastery. Because of the preponderance of proprietary churches in Ireland, fosterage by the church should not necessarily be seen as rivalling the native social institution of fosterage, but as working with it.

[439]Since the previous chapter is peculiar to S, then *eadem* can be assumed to refer to *synodus Hibernensis* of chapter 41.21.

[440]The emendation is based on a second occurrence of this text on p. 427 ln. 9.

[441]Charles-Edwards, 'The construction', 231, suggests regarding *uincula* as the equivalent of Old Irish *nadmann* 'binding sureties'.

[442]For the term *census*, see n 515.

[443]On whom see 41.24.

[444]Ó Corráin, 'Early Irish churches', 332, points to a parallel between this chapter and *CIH* 2011.12 ff., a text beginning *Do breitheamhnus forna huile chin do-ní gach cintach síosanadh*, translated by Breatnach, *Companion*, 82,

'On judgement on every wrongdoing which every wrongdoer does here below'.

[445]This seems a likely translation for *regiones* since it creates a contrast with the movable property. Possessing land was a requisite for being free, which may explain why the following compensations in the list are being claimed not from the offender himself, but from various persons to whom he might have been subordinate.

[446]I owe thanks for the interpretation of this chapter to Charles-Edwards.

[447]I.e. fourteen generations from Abraham to David.

[448]I.e. fourteen generations from the Babylonian exile (that begins with Jechonias) until Christ.

[449]Four names are omitted from Luke's genealogy: Mahath, Zorobabel, Phaleg, and Heber.

[450]There seems to be no way to reconcile this statement with the above genealogy.

[451]This would be the biblical law of *yebum* (Deuteronomy 25:5), which obliged a brother to marry his dead brother's widow. *Hib* forbids this practice. See n 507.

[452]This text, attributed by Eusebius to the chronographer Africanus, reached *Hib*'s compilers in Rufinus's translation. Rufinus altered the original text, and his translation was altered before or when it was cited in *Hib*. Conflicting genealogies would have been of interest to an early medieval Irish audience because Irish genealogists were in the habit of merging genealogies in order to forge political alliances, to assert various contemporary political claims by drawing on a synthetic history, or simply to embellish the pedigrees of kings. This practice is well attested in the Irish origin legends, whose roots can be traced to the seventh and eighth centuries. But we also find it in royal propaganda conducted through texts that sought to rehabilitate the image of groups of former vassal peoples that gained political power. Two well-known—albeit later—examples of this, are the spurious pedigree that links the Airgialla to king Áed mac Ainmirech of the Cenél Conaill, and the one that links the Dál Cais of Munster to the Éoganachta. Under both Irish and Roman law, adopted sons had the same right to an inheritance either in property or status as biological sons. One is tempted to speculate that some contemporaries would have been happy to see the same rule apply to 'adopted' dynasties. Genealogists could have relied on the Bible as a source for legitimising the practice of 'retroactive

adoption' of one dynasty by another. On genealogies and origin myths see Ó Corráin, 'Irish origin legends and genealogy'; *Idem*, 'Creating the past'; *Idem*, 'Church and secular society', 277–284; Carey, *The Irish origin-legend*.

[453]Cf. *Hib* 31.16–20 and n 309.

[454]The word *locus* (Old Irish *loc*) often means 'church', as in the Kilnasaggart stone (see n 333) and in an inscription at Whithorn which reads 'the *loc* of St. Peter the apostle'.

[455]I owe thanks to Charles-Edwards for the suggestion that this might be a reference to the practice of *tellach*, by which a claimant or heir, wishing to assert their claim over land, entered it in a ceremonial manner.

[456]As Bieler, *Penitentials*, 59, renders it.

[457]According to Ó Corráin, 'Irish law and canon law', 162–163, this is a Latin rendering of Old Irish *indoth*, which defined the terms of 'division of property on the dissolution of a contract in which property was held in common'.

[458]See n 327.

[459]The rule described here is analogous to the custom that gave a free member of the kin complete control over land that he had acquired independently, but not over his share of the kin land (*GEIL*, 100). I am indebted to the late Professor Ó Corráin for his help with editing and interpreting this difficult text and its equivalent in *Hib.B*, below. For another translation see Hughes, *Church*, 159.

[460]See n 327.

[461]*terminus*, Old Irish *termonn*, can also be translated 'enclosure'. The vast *termonn* of Armagh is famously described in the *Liber Angeli* (Bieler, *Patrician Texts*, 184/5).

[462]Like *terminus*, the term *suburbana* also occurs in the *Liber Angeli* (Bieler, *Patrician Texts*, 184/5) in relation to Armagh. Doherty, 'Monastic town', 57, argues that the biblical idea of *suburbana* was interpreted in contemporary Irish texts to mean 'the area immediately surrounding a church within which a person could take refuge or sanctuary. However, since Armagh's *paruchia* included "all the tribes of the Irish", her area of sanctuary would likewise have to be the most extensive in the country'.

[463]The Vulgate reads 'Levites' (*Leuitarum*).

[464]The pattern of enclosures described in this chapter has been the subject of several studies concerned with finding biblical precursors (e.g. Exodus

26:33; Ezekiel 45, 48), with identifying *comparanda* in contemporary Irish texts, especially the Life of Brigit by Cogitosus and the *Liber Angeli*, and with adducing physical evidence in the Irish landscape. The most recent study, which can also be used as a guide for pertinent historiography, is Jenkins, *'Holy, Holier, Holiest'*.

[465]This may refer to the fourth division mentioned on p. 95 ln. 15.

[466]See previous note.

[467]Lit. 'to'.

[468]Emending *turbae* to *turba*.

[469]The end of this sentence may be an embedded gloss. On subtracting fifty days from penance, see next section.

[470]Lit. 'is as severe as the number of saints in it'.

[471]But *custodia* can also mean 'custody' in the sense of imprisonment. On monasteries as places of penal incarceration see Geltner, *'Detrusio'*.

[472]Cf. p. 347 ln. 5.

[473]But Eusebius/Jerome's Chronicle reads *carcere sunt inclusi* 'locked-up in prison', which is to say that Jerusalem became a prison from which the Jews could not escape their fate of being slaughtered and exiled by Titus's forces after the destruction of the Second Temple in AD 70.

[474]This is the defective verb [*for*], *fatus*, *fari*.

[475]For this interpretation of *negotium*, see chapter 21.

[476]See n 434.

[477]Cf. p. 189 ln. 16.

[478]*Hib.A* has another, quite different version of this text in chapter 48.11.

[479]But compare with the Canons of Theodore of Canterbury, where a woman is considered a murderess only if she aborts a pregnancy forty days after conception or later. See recension G §105 (Finsterwalder, 263). This canon is also important for its implications for the legal definition of 'person': if a pregnancy that is terminated within forty days of conception is not considered murder, it follows that the foetus is not regarded as a person.

[480]*Recte* 'the Shunammite'.

[481]The Bible says nothing about Esther either being or becoming a widow.

[482]This chapter and chapter 44.7 are good illustrations of the manner in which the church took over social roles that were traditionally in the hands of the kin, in this case caring for widows. In a society undergoing conversion, this would have led to increased dependence on the church and its institutions. It is impossible to say if this dependence was the result of a deliberate missionary tactic designed to increase the church's influence.

[483]The text on p. 782 concerning 'veiled women living under a rule' removes any doubt that 'veiled women' is another name for nuns.

[484]A misspelling of Amma, as in Amma Syncletica, on which see n 350.

[485]Translating *aliæ* in the sense of Old Irish *aile*.

[486]The conjunction *sed* does not occur in Isidore and I omitted it from my translation.

[487]The noun *ratio* is often glossed by Old Irish *dliged*, which, according to *DIL*, has 'law', 'right' among its range of meanings. Charles-Edwards prefers to translate Hiberno-Latin *ratio* in the present heading as 'rightful order'. See his '*Dliged*', 71.

[488]Other Irish canons that forbid remarriage are, e.g. *Hib* 45.33, and *Canones Adomnani* §16 (Bieler, *Penitentials*, 178), cited in *Hib* on p. 361 ln. 2. By and large, Insular authorities are inconsistent on the question of remarriage. Four recensions of the Canons of Theodore permit it, two forbid it, and the council of Hertford, presided over by Theodore himself, also forbids it. The Irish *Synodus Patricii* §26 (Bieler, *Penitentials*, 194) drew upon Theodore when it permitted remarriage after divorcing a fornicating wife. See Charles-Edwards, 'Penitential of Theodore'; Flechner, 'Canons of Theodore'.

[489]For my interpretation of the final phrase, which occurs only in APV, see chapter 45.15.

[490]I avoided a literal translation, which would have been awkward.

[491]My translation follows a version of this text found in Gratian's *Decretum*, C. 20 q. 1 c. 8.

[492]Bieler's text has *decusso* for *discuso*.

[493]The translation is by Bieler, *Penitentials*, 179.

[494]In my translation I omitted *qua* on the authority of Sedulius Scotus's Commentary on Matthew 5:32, which witnesses the same unidentified

source. It reads: *Tres autem sunt causae quae matrimonium non separant: Prima coacticia uis.*

[495]The Old Irish term *adaltrach*, derived from Latin *adultera*, was used to denote both 'concubine' and 'second wife' (*GEIL*, 71, 79). In *Hib*, *adultera* is not used in the latter sense.

[496]The figures in all manuscripts depart from the biblical verse, which gives thirty-three days for a boy and sixty-six for a girl. Only S has the correct figure for a girl but not for a boy. The entire passage is omitted from *Hib.B*. The figures thirty-six and forty-six are not unique to *Hib*, but also occur in the Irish *Liber ex lege Moysi*, which has modified the text of Leviticus 12:4–5. See Meeder, '*Liber ex lege Moysi*', 202–203 and *apparatus* therein.

[497]The verbs in the original are in the singular, but I preferred the plural forms in order to retain the gender ambiguity.

[498]For women who do penance for adultery, see *Hib* 45.15, 45.33.

[499]Cf. chapter 45.13. Christianity's insistence on monogamous marriages often led to an increase in concubinage as a substitute for polygamy. In certain societies this had adverse consequences for women who would otherwise have enjoyed legitimate status as wives in polygamous relationships. See Goody, 'Polygyny', 178, 180. Irish laws on marriage, such as the ones found in the eighth-century *Cáin Lánamna*, continued to regulate polygamy well into the Christian era, suggesting that the church either failed or did not go out of its way to try to eradicate the practice for fear of challenging deeply rooted social practices.

[500]This attribution was given because the following text is from Leo's letter to Rusticus, bishop of Narbonne.

[501]My translation of the final clause (from *que prohibet*) is conjecture.

[502]But Genesis 23:19 clearly states that Abraham outlived Sarah.

[503]I.e. the Old Testament.

[504]The expression *de capitibus* renders the Old Irish idiom *di chiunn* (lit. 'from the head'). See *cenn*[37] in *DIL* and discussion in Thurneysen, *Studies in Early Irish Law*, 50.

[505]To judge by the alternative reading in H, the final sentence addresses a contingency whereby the adulterer unknowingly made a woman pregnant. But even with this caveat, the full sense of the sentence eludes me.

[506]Compare *conloquium pacificum* on p. 299 ln. 2. See n 404.

[507]This appears to be a prohibition of the Hebrew practice of *yebum* (Deuteronomy 25:5), whereby a brother was commanded to marry his dead brother's widow. A marriage of this kind would have ensured that property remained in the hands of the deceased's kin and was not alienated by the widow. This may explain the disaproval of the church, which would have stood to gain from alienated property.

[508]Cf. Stokes, 'Irish ordeals', 192–193.

[509]Lit. 'one of the men'.

[510]See n 500.

[511]Meaning, perhaps, that if the offender is a cleric, he should be restored to his grade.

[512]Emending *sentio* to *censio* on Dr Richard Pollard's advice.

[513]From this point the text departs from Gregory.

[514]The noun *regio* is variably glossed by Old Irish *com(ḟ)oisce* ('proximity', 'nearness'), *ferann* ('land', 'domain', 'territory', 'monastery'), and *flaithius* ('kingdom'). See *DIL*.

[515]Here the Latin *census* renders Old Irish *cís* (Thurneysen, *Grammar*, 172). In late antiquity *census* denoted land tax, but in the early medieval west, where taxation was virtually unknown, it sometimes came to mean rent-paying. See Wickham, *Framing the Early Middle Ages*, 107, 112. On the distinction between tribute and tax, see *ibid.* 70: '[tribute consisted of] lump sums due from communities or individuals, determined essentially by relations of armed force, and often arbitrary or irregular in their incidence; tax, by contrast, was based on assessments of relative wealth, in land or movables'. The use of the term *census* in *Hib* complies more or less with Wickham's definition of tribute, though coercion is not an essential component according to *Hib* 47.

[516]See *CIH* 38.21 for tribute given to either lord or church: *cís flatha nó ecalsa*.

[517]See previous note.

[518]See n 516.

[519]The exact meaning of *census* is not clear to me here. It could, as elsewhere, mean 'tribute', but also 'estimation'.

[520]See n 415.

[521]Irish attitudes towards actual and spiritual martyrdom are expressed in the Cambrai Homily, a text whose only surviving copy is interpolated into a manuscript of *Hib* from Cambrai. See Ó Néill, 'Background to the Cambrai Homily'; Stancliffe, 'Red, white and blue martyrdom'.

[522]The mention of the veneration of books is interesting because nearly all early medieval manuscripts that survive from Ireland, about fifteen altogether, owe their survival to their having been venerated as relics. For instance, the *Cathach* 'battler' (Royal Irish Academy MS 12 R 33), a psalter dating *c.* 600 which was believed to have been written by St. Columba, was treated as a contact relic and kept in a reliquary between the eleventh century and 1813. See Sims-Williams, 'The uses of writing in early medieval Wales', 20–22.

[523]This passage is a distorted version of a passage in the Life of Hilarion, where it is the saint himself, while still alive, who commands Hesychius to bury him immediately. The remainder of the story as told here is more or less faithful to the Life.

[524]Lit. 'ways'.

[525]The addition *honor defertur* in S is not in the Isidorian text, which reads: *ita tamen ut nulli martyrum sed ipsi Deo martyrum, quamuis in memoriis martyrum constituamus altaria.*

[526]See n 521.

[527]For *dísert* as 'monastery' or 'hermitage', see, e.g. *dísert Diarmata* in the Chronicle of Ireland 842.13, 843.5 and *dísert Ciarán* in 857.2. Although the annals only begin to use Old Irish *dísert* as another word for a religious settlement in the ninth century, it is nevertheless possible that this sense dates from earlier times. However, the sense 'monastery'/'hermitage' does not seem to fit all the instances of *desertus* below. In the absence of any deserts in Ireland I preferred to render *desertus* by the expression 'remote place', but I retained the literal sense when an actual desert appears to have been intended. On the possibility that the usage of Old Irish *dísert* as 'hermitage' derives from Latin, see *desertulum* in the Supplement to the *Non-Classical Lexicon of Celtic Latinity*.

[528]See n 102.

[529]The text departs significantly from the original and my interpretation is tentative. In translating *relegiositate* 'religious order' I follow Bieler, *Penitentials*, 329.

[530]The problem of the clerical tonsure, a corollary of the Easter controversy, was one of the main bones of contention between the pro-Roman reformers in Britain and Ireland and their opponents. The tonsure was also the most overt feature that distinguished the members of the two rival groups.

[531]See *DIL* for Old Irish *corann* 'tonsure', a noun derived from *corona.*

[532]See previous note. I left the Latin untranslated in order to preserve the deliberate ambiguity of *corona* in this phrase.

[533]I left out of the translation the final garbled sentence, which can roughly be rendered thus: 'the crown of the circle leaves below and above'. The original text reads: *quod uero, detonso superius capite, inferius circuli corona relinquitur.*

[534]This is the only reference in *Hib* to Easter. Given the derogatory tone of this and the following text, it can be argued that they were penned by the *Romani* at a time when the Easter controversy in Ireland and Britain was still raging. The accusation that the Britons (and, by association, the *Hibernenses*) were Quartodecimans—i.e. heretics who kept Easter with the Jews on the fourteenth of the Jewish month of Nisan—was false but tenacious. The Quartodeciman rhetoric in Anglo-Saxon England is discussed by Stancliffe, *Bede, Wilfrid, and the Irish.* The absence of more detailed and prescriptive references to the observance of Easter is noteworthy and may suggest that the compilers deliberately avoided the topic because of its explosive potential or because the Easter controversy had not been fully settled when *Hib* was completed. Late antique and early medieval texts of ecclesiastical law usually give Easter a prominent place. See, e.g., Cresconius, *Concordia canonum* Bk 10 (Zechiel-Eckes, 491–492), *Vetus Gallica* Bk 23 (Mordek, 438–442).

[535]But, according to H (see *apparatus*), the source is *Libri Patricii.* There are three other occurrences of *Libri Patricii* that I am aware of. In the Book of Armagh, fol. 22^r, St. Patrick's *Confessio* is introduced by the heading *Incipiunt libri sancti Patricii episcopi.* On fol. 15^r of Rawlinson B 512, the designation *Libri Patricii* was interpolated into the Tripartite Life within a passage concerning twelve brothers who appeal to Lóegaire to settle a dispute between them. This interpolation is identical to an episode concerning Patrick and Lóegaire passing judgement on the seven sons of Amolngid reported in Tírechán's *Collectanea,* section 15 of Bieler's edited text. On fol. 132^v of O_2 the combination *Libri Patricii* introduces a story on Patrick and two bishops who are named in the manuscript as *Cethianus* and *Conallus.*

The same story occurs in one of the notes preceding Tírechán's *Collectanea* in the Book of Armagh, where the bishops are given different names: *Caetiacus* and *Sachellus*. Thus *'Libri Patricii'* appears to have been the title by which a collection of Patrician material was known, a collection that was in existence before Tírechán's work.

536The legendary king of Tara and St. Patrick's nemesis according to the saint's seventh-century Lives by Muirchú and Tírechán.

537According to Ó Corráin, Breatnach, and Breen, 'Laws of the Irish', 408 n 1, the text describes a *clericus iuculator*, a cleric who made a spectacle of himself, of the kind that was condemned by fifth-century Gallic councils.

538Reading *bestiarum* as in HV.

539Translation adapted from *Etymologies*, tr. Barney *et al.*

540According to Herren, 'Some new light', 53, *bessus* derives from Old Irish *bés* 'custom' and is an etymological play on *more*.

541On guard dogs in early Ireland see Kelly, *Farming*, 114–117.

542*Recte*: *κύων*.

543Translation adapted from *Etymologies*, tr. Barney *et al.*

544Translating *siccatorium*, but there may be other meanings.

545On damage to crops by hens in Irish law, see Kelly, *Farming*, 140–141.

546This chapter deals largely with issues of ritual purity, on which see R. Meens, 'Pollution in the early middle ages'.

547But compare Isidore's text, which reads *suspenderat*.

548Translating *per se ipsum lege mortis*.

549See n 30.

550I owe thanks to Professor Michael Winterbottom and the late Professor Ó Corráin for their help with the translation of this text. The text, which occurs only in H, is obviously an interpolation. The words it uses to render 'fish-weirs' are *gurgitia piscium*, *correte*, and *correptam* (read *corretam*). Whereas *gurgitia* is derived from the Latin masculine noun *gurges* (gen. *gurgitis*) which the text treats as a neuter, the forms *correte* and *correptam* are not of Latin origin. A similar form, *coretis*, in the combination *cum coretis*, is found in the Cornish *Carta Maenchi comitis* (also known as the Lanlawren Charter. A transcript and translation is Padel, 'Lanlawren charter', 43–44. A commentary is Padel, 'Pre-conquest charters'). Charters from the Welsh Book of Llandaff contain references to cases where land was granted *cum coretibus suis* to the bishopric of Llandaff (*Book of Land Dâv*, 150, 156, 158, 183, 210, 221, 225, 226, 234, 236). According to John Gwenogvryn Evans and John Rhŷs, *Book of Land Dâv*, 394, the charters used *coretibus* to render Old Welsh *coret* 'weir'. The Book of Llandaff is unique in its treatment of this word as a noun of the third declension. A similar form, *cora*, is attested in Old Irish (See *cora*(b), *corr*[3] in *DIL*). Given the fact that three Celtic languages, Old Irish, Old Cornish, and Old Welsh, constructed the word for 'fish-weir' using the same root, it may well be the case that a cognate existed in Old Breton as well. The attestations of the root in three Celtic languages and the possibility that it also existed in a fourth, make it all the more difficult to establish the origin of our text. However, an Irish origin for the text on weirs can be postulated based on the fact that weirs were frequently mentioned in the laws as a common method of fishing in medieval Ireland. Some law tracts discuss in detail the manner in which weirs should be positioned, as well as other technical aspects. See Kelly, *Farming*, 287–290, for references.

551 An allusion to the drowning of the pigs that were possessed by the devil in Mark 5:11–14.

552 *De disputatione Hibernensis sinodi* §13 (Bieler, *Penitentials*, 160) prescribes four years of penance for eating horseflesh.

553 Not a literal translation, but the paraphrase was necessary in order to echo the verse from Mark, quoted above, which Jerome interprets here.

554 See n 102.

555 See n 438.

556 The emendation is based on another occurrence of this text on p. 326 ln. 18.

557 More commonly known in the transliteration from the Hebrew as Obadiah or Ovadiah.

558 Sedulius's *Collectaneum* 25.31 is another secondary witness to this story, but preserves a fuller and different version. I have interpreted the text with the help of that version, which I reproduce here: *In Vita Monacorum legitur: Quoniam quidam latrones ad alium locum uenerunt causa predandi qui in modum hospitum apparuerunt. At monachi cum suo abbate ad obsequium eorum uenerunt. Et abbas, qui multis annis cecus fuit, aquam obsequii circa oculos suos dedit et statim aperti sunt oculi eius et clare uidit. Vnde et latrones suam culpam confessi sunt et monachi facti.*

[559]Lit. 'he shall take away'.

[560]Cf. Old Irish *barbarach* 'barbarian'/'foreigner'. A note in *Críth Gablach*, ed. Binchy §38 (tr. MacNeill, 'Ancient Irish law' §123) mentions among the *rechtgai ríg* 'special laws of a king' the *rechtgae do indarbbu echtarchiníuil* 'special law for the expulsion of a foreign race'. This is followed by the embedded gloss *.i. fri Saxanu* 'namely, in respect to the Saxons'. The reference here may be to King Ecgfrith's invasion of Brega in 684, whence he took Irish captives (Bede, *HE* 4.26).

[561]This passage corresponds to *Synodus Luci Victorie* §4 and Cumméne's Penitential 9.13. However, neither source is cited anywhere else in *Hib*, which suggests the passage was not cited directly from either.

[562]This is the meaning of the noun *senatores* according to Ó Corráin, 'Congressio senadorum'. The expression *congressio senadorum* in AU 780, 804 designates a meeting of nobles held 'under the presidency of a leading ecclesiastic'.

[563]See previous note.

[564]According to 43.18 *basilica* was another name for tomb or cemetery.

[565]The expression *animi affectus* is used four times by Augustine with the sense of 'feeling' or 'emotion', e.g. in *De serm. dom. in mont.* 1.23 line 520: *has interiectiones grammatici uocant particulas orationis significantes commoti animi affectum, uelut cum dicitur a dolente 'heu' uel ab irascente 'hem'*. However, this sense does not seem to suit the present context. My translation is based on a similar expression, *caritatis affectus*, in the prologue to the Penitential of Cumméne §3 (Bieler, *Penitentials*, 108). The prologue classifies *caritatis affectus* as the second path towards attaining remission of sins. A similar sense may be appropriate here, because the present chapter follows two chapters concerned with punishment and penance for guiding foreign enemies.

[566]See previous note.

[567]Some versions of the Vulgate read *allophyli* for *Palesitini* in Psalm 55:1.

[568]This ostensible paradox would be consistent with Pelagian doctrine, which did not regard faith in the Christian God as a requisite for salvation.

[569]Perhaps an allusion to the sack of Rome by Alaric's Christian Goths in 410, who were said by Augustine (*De ciuitate Dei* 1.1–2, 7) to have spared churches and relics.

[570]Lit. 'ways'.

[571]My translation is aided by the Gregorian original, which reads: *Nam sunt plerique qui etsi signa non faciunt signa tamen facientibus dispares non sunt.*

[572]Lit. 'ways'.

[573]See previous note.

[574]I omitted the superfluous *inquit* from the translation.

[575]See n 102.

[576]The Hebrew Bible reads *mish'eret* 'kneading bowl', which Jerome mistook for a noun derived from the Hebrew verb *nish'eret* 'she remains'; hence his translation *reliquiae*.

[577]For this sense of *reliquiae* see previous note.

[578]My translation of this heading is tentative.

[579]Perhaps the noun *monachium* is a Latinisation of Old Irish *manchaine*, which denotes service owed by a layman or monk to a lay lord or an abbot. In this case the reference could be to a penitential *manchaine*. On the range of meanings of *manchaine*, see *DIL*.

[580]According to Ó Corráin (personal comment), this is Old Irish *co lommrad*.

[581]Emending *succido* to *succedo*.

[582]But the Vulgate reads: *Adoniram erat super huiuscemodi indictione*.

[583]Perhaps *castellum* (the reading in P, *castulum*, is a *hapax legomenon* according to Du Cange's *Glossarium*) may be the equivalent of Old Irish *dún*.

[584]According to Ó Corráin (personal comment), *dona* renders Old Irish *áes dána*, or simply *dána* 'crafts'.

[585]Lit. 'ways'.

[586]In MS P *encaenia* has a plural sense (and not just form), to judge by the use of the form *encaenium* in the final clause of the previous chapter.

[587]For this sense of *καρδάγιοι* see McNeill and Gamer, *Handbooks of Penance*, 69.

[588]Namely, fortune-telling by means of interpreting words or phrases picked at random from the Bible, a technique known as '*sortes biblicae*'. On the casting of lots and divination in the early middle ages, see Wood, 'Pagan religion and superstitions', 161ff.

[589]Translation adapted from *Etymologies*, tr. Barney *et al.*

[590]The Gregorian original reads: *in quo dilationis damno quid aliud innuitur.*

[591]See p. 522.

[592]See p. 759.

[593]The original Augustinian passage reads: *tres syllabae sunt: peccaui. Sed in his tribus syllabis flamma sacrificii cordis ascendit in coelum.*

[594]The texts that follow, which emerge straight out of seventh-century Armagh propaganda, bolster the primacy of the see of Armagh and edify a kin group that claimed its descent from a certain Díchu, who is said by Muirchú (Bieler, *Patrician texts*, 78) to have been the first nobleman in Ireland to have been converted by Patrick. The prerogative of saints to leave *petitiones* 'requests' to be fulfilled after their death appears to be a hagiographical convention. It is also found in the three *petitiones* of Colmán Élo, on which see the Life of Colmán Élo §50 (ed. Heist, 223).

[595]Perhaps an allusion to Armagh.

[596]My translation is tentative. In HV we find a different version of the final 'request' (see *app. crit.*): 'that in judgement, when a dispute arises between a cleric and a layman, the layman should seek a cleric who may dispute with the cleric'. In other words, the laymen may not debate directly with the cleric, but only via a representative who is himself a cleric.

[597]Translation adapted from Bieler, *Patrician texts*, 116.

[598]Translation adapted from Winterbottom, *Gildas*, 80–81.

[599]A fast was normally observed on the fourth rather than the fifth day, but perhaps a different reckoning of days is used here.

[600]See n 108.

[601]For *causae* as 'sources', see *caussa* in *Thesaurus linguae Latinae*.

[602]The passage is not entirely clear to me.

[603]For Hiberno-Latin *urbs* see Bieler, *Penitentials*, 243 n 9.

[604]The translation of this chapter follows in part Charles-Edwards, 'The construction', 209–210. For *mendacium* as the equivalent of Old Irish *gáu*, see *ibid.* 231.

[605]Cf. Charles-Edwards, 'Construction', 220.

[606]*Recte* Nechao.

[607]Cf. *Gúbretha Caratniad* (*CIH* 2199.5–6 = *ZCP* 15 [1925]: 361 §46), where a plaintiff's oath is upheld if an *ail anscuichthe* 'immovable rock' overswears with him. One of the glosses on the text takes the expression to mean written evidence, with reference to ogham inscriptions on rocks. See *GEIL*, 204; Herbert, 'Before charters', 108.

[608]This is the best I could do with what appears to be a garbled paraphrase of Isaiah and Jerome's commentary thereon.

[609]On the authorship of *Hib*, see section 1.1 in the introductory chapters.

Glossary

airchinnech: See *princeps*.

ancilla: Literal translation of Old Irish *cumal* 'female slave', but used in the sense of a unit of value sometimes equated with three cows. See n 415.

basilica: A tomb, according to chap. 43.18.

causa: In a juridical sense, a 'case', but more narrowly a 'source'.

census: Tribute. See n 515.

ciuitas: Ecclesiastical settlement.

contemptibilis: 'One who contemns the world', e.g. a holy man or hermit. See n 173.

dominatrix: Female equivalent of *princeps*.

enforcing surety: Latin *stipulator*, rendering Old Irish *naidm*. Vouched for the fulfilment of a contract by force of arms. See n 307.

familia: Old Irish *muintir*. Collective name for those living in an ecclesiastical settlement, either lay or in orders. See n 114.

frater: Member of a *familia* (see above), either lay or in orders.

Hibernenses: The Irish who adhered to the 84-year Easter cycle and to the 'Celtic' tonsure. See n 56.

honour-price: Old Irish *lóg n-enech* 'honour-price' (lit. 'price of a face'). Roughly the Irish equivalent of *wergeld*. See n 263.

lex: Usually a reference to the Pentateuch.

locus: Church, monastery, church settlement, its buildings (e.g. monastic cell), or a holy place of some description (e.g. chapel).

manach: pl. *manaig*, from Latin *monachus*. Could denote both lay tenant of an ecclesiastical settlement or a monk who took vows. See n 115.

manaig: See *manach*.

manchaine: Service owed by a layman to a lay lord or by a monk to an abbot.

monachus: See *manach*.

monk: See *manach*.

naidm: See 'enforcing surety'.

paying surety: Latin *rata*, rendering Old Irish *ráth*. Vouched for the fulfilment of a contract with his own property. See n 307.

plebs: Usually a reference to the lay community.

presbyter: Often interchangeable with *sacerdos* but sometimes indicates a higher grade, immediately below the bishop. See n 8.

princeps: Old Irish *airchinnech*. Head of a church (broadly defined); may be a layman. See n 44.

rata: See 'paying surety'.

Romani: Commonly regarded as reformers who opposed the *Hibernenses* (see above) and venerated Rome as the highest authority in Christendom. See n 162.

sacerdos: Often interchangeable with *presbyter* and translated 'priest'. Glossed *episcopus* in H: p. 13 ln. 5 (*apparatus*). See also n 8.

sapiens: Old Irish *ecna*. Scholar, either secular or ecclesiastical, with judicial responsibilities. See p. 56*.

Sardinensis sinodus: A frequent misrendering of *Sardicensis*, referring to the Council of Sardica of 343. Only MS V has the correct form.

scriba: Church scholar with judicial responsibilities. See p. 56* and n 172.

sedatium/sedatio: According to 2.16, this appears to be a payment for administering the last sacrament. There are, however, other interpretations. For debate, see n 40.

stipulator: See 'enforcing surety'.

surety: See 'enforcing surety', 'paying surety'.

urbs: See *ciuitas*.

Bibliography

Primary sources

Passion of Saint Peter (Pseudo-Abdias), ed. J. A. Fabricius, *Acta Apostolorum Apocrypha siue Historia Certaminis Apostolici adscripta Abdiae*. Repr. with tr. D. L. Eastman, *Ancient Martyrdom Accounts of Peter and Paul* (Atlanta, 2015), 171–188.

Acta Andreae, ed. M. Bonnet, *Passio Andreae*, in *Acta Apostolorum Apocrypha*, ed. R. A. Lipsius and M. Bonnet, 3 vols. (Leipzig, 1891–1903), 2:2–37.

Adomnán, Law of Innocents, ed. and tr. K. Meyer, *Cáin Adomnáin*, Anecdota Oxoniensia, Mediaeval and Modern Series 12 (Oxford, 1905).

Adomnán, *Vita S. Columbae*, ed. A. O. and M. O. Anderson, *Adomnán's Life of Columba* (Edinburgh, 1961; 2nd ed. Oxford, 1991).

Adomnán, *Vita S. Columbae*, tr. R. Sharpe, *Adomnán of Iona. Life of St. Columba* (London, 1995).

Airecht-text, ed. and tr. F. Kelly, 'An Old-Irish text on court procedure', *Peritia* 5 (1986): 74–106, at 84–87; ed. Binchy, *CIH* 601.20–601.33, 601.34–602.4.

Alcuin, Letter 245, to Candidus and Nathanel, ed. E. Dümmler, MGH Epist. 4 (1895), 393–398.

Aldhelm, Letter 4, to Geruntius, ed. R. Ehwald, MGH Auct. ant. 15 (1919), 480–486.

Ambrose, *Expositio de psalmo cxviii*, ed. M. Petschenig, CSEL 62 (1913).

Ambrose, *Expositio euangelii secundum Lucam*, ed. M. Adriaen, CCSL 14 (1957).

Annals of Clonmacnoise, ed. D. Murphy (Dublin, 1896).

Annals of the Four Masters, ed. J. O'Donovan, *Annals of the Kingdom of Ireland by the Four Masters*, 7 vols. (Dublin, 1848–1851).

Annals of Tigernach, ed. W. Stokes, *Revue Celtique* 16 (1895): 374–419; 17 (1896): 6–33, 119–263, 337–420; 18 (1897): 9–59, 150–197, 267–303. Repr. 2 vols. (Felinfach, 1993).

Annals of Ulster, ed. S. Mac Airt and G. Mac Niocaill (Dublin, 1983).

Ansegisus, *Collectio capitularium*, ed. G. Schmitz, MGH Capitularia regum Francorum, Nova series 1 (1996), 431–664.

Audacht Morainn, ed. and tr. F. Kelly (Dublin, 1976).

Augustine, *De ciuitate Dei*, ed. B. Dombart and A. Kalb, CCSL 47–48 (1955).

Augustine, *De consensu euangelistarum*, ed. F. Weihrich, CSEL 43 (1904).

Augustine, *De cura pro mortuis gerenda*, ed. J. Zycha, CSEL 41 (1900), 619–660.

Augustine, *De Genesi ad litteram*, ed. J. Zycha, CSEL 28(1) (1894).

Augustine, *De sermone Domini in monte*, ed. A. Mutzenbecher, CCSL 35 (1967).

Augustine, *De trinitate*, ed. W. J. Mountain, CCSL 50–50A (1968).

Augustine, *Enchiridion ad Laurentium de fide et spe et caritate*, ed. E. Evans, CCSL 46 (1969), 49–114.

Augustine, *Ennarationes in psalmos*, ed. E. Dekkers and J. Fraipont, CCSL 38–40 (1956).

Augustine, *In Iohannis euangelium tractatus cxxiv*, ed. A. Mayer, CCSL 124 (1954).

Augustine, *Quaestiones euangeliorum*, ed. A. Mutzenbecher, CCSL 44B (1980).

Augustine, *Sermo 74*, ed. Maurists, *Sancti Aurelii Augustini Hipponensis episcopi operum*, 11 vols. (Paris, 1679–1700). Repr. PL 38:472–474.

Augustine, *Sermones 1–50*, ed. C. Lambot, CCSL 41 (1961).

Augustine (and Pseudo-Augustine), *Sermones*, ed. A. Mai, *Spicilegium Romanum*, 10 vols. (Rome, 1839–1844), vol. 8. Repr. PL 47:1147–8.

Augustinus Hibernicus, *De mirabilibus sacrae scripturae libri tres*, PL 35:2149–2200.

Basil, Rule (tr. Rufinus), ed. K. Zelzer, CSEL 86 (1986).

Basil, *Asceticon* (tr. Rufinus), ed. L. Holste, *Codex Regularum* (Rome, 1661). Repr. PL 103:483–554.

Pseudo-Basil, *Admonitio ad filium spiritualem*, ed. L. Holsten, *Codex Regularum* (Paris, 1663), Appendix 20–34. Repr. PL 103:683–700; ed. P. Lehmann, 'Die *Admonitio S. Basilii ad Filium Spiritualem*', in *Erforschung des Mittelalters. Ausgewählte Abhandlungen und Aufsätze*, 5 vols. (Stuttgart, 1959–1962), 5:201–245.

Bede, *Historia ecclesiastica gentis Anglorum*, ed. C. Plummer, *Venerabilis Baedae opera historica* (Oxford, 1896), 3–387.

Bede, *Historia ecclesiastica gentis Anglorum*, ed. and tr. R. A. B. Mynors and B. Colgrave, *Bede's Ecclesiastical History of the English People* (Oxford, 1969).

Berrad Airechta, ed. R. Thurneysen, *Die Bürgschaft im irischen Recht*, Aus den Abhandlungen der preussischen Akademie der Wissenschaften, Jahrgang 1928. Phil-hist. Klasse Nr. 2 (Berlin, 1928), 6–32.

Berrad Airechta, tr. R. Stacey, '*Berrad airechta*: An Old Irish tract on suretyship', in T. M. Charles-Edwards *et al.* ed., *Lawyers and Laymen* (Cardiff, 1986).

Benedict, Rule, ed. R. Hanslik, CSEL 75 (1960; 2nd ed. 1977).

Benedict, Rule, ed. J. Neufville and A. de Vogüé, SC 181–182 (1972), 412–675.

Bible, Douay-Rheims translation (Rheims, Duoai 1582–1610), revised by R. Challoner (Douai, 1749–1752).

Bibelwerk → Das Bibelwerk.

Boniface, Letters, ed. R. Rau, *Briefe des Bonifatius und Wilibalds Leben* (Darmstadt, 1968).

Book of Llandaff, ed. J. Gwenogvryn Evans and J. Rhys, *The Text of the Book of Land Dâv reproduced from the Gwysaney Manuscript* (Oxford, 1893).

Bretha Crólige, ed. D. A. Binchy, '*Bretha Crólige*', *Ériu* 12 (1938): 1–77.

Bretha im Gata, ed. V. E. Hull, *ZCP* 25 (1956): 215–223.

Bretha Nemed Toísech, ed. and tr. L. Breatnach, 'The first third of *Bretha Nemed Toísech*', *Ériu* 40 (1989): 7–21.

Breuiarium Hipponense, ed. C. Munier, CCSL 149 (1974), 30–53.

Caesarius, *Sermones*, ed. G. Morin, CCSL 103, 104 (1953).

Caesarius, *Epist. de Concilio Massiliense*, ed. C. de Clerq, CCSL 148A (1963), 90–96.

Cáin Adomnáin → Adomnán.

Cáin Lánamna, ed. and tr. R. Thurneysen, *Studies in Early Irish Law*, ed. Thurneysen (Dublin 1936), 1–75.

Cáin Lánamna, ed. and tr. C. M. Eska, *Cáin Lánamna: an Old Irish Tract on Marriage and Divorce* (Leiden, 2010), 78–299.

Cambrai Homily, ed. W. Stokes and J. Strachan, *Thesaurus Palaeohibernicus* (Cambridge, 1901–1903), 2:244–247.

Canones Adomnani, ed. L. Bieler, *The Irish Penitentials*, SLH 5 (Dublin, 1963), 176–180.

Canones Apostolorum, ed. A. Strewe, *Die Canonessammlung des Dionysius Exiguus in der ersten Redaktion* (Berlin, 1931), 1–10. *EOMIA* 1:32a–32ii.

Canones in causa Apiarii, ed. C. Munier, CCSL 149 (1974), 101–149.

Canones Theodori → *Discipulus Vmbrensium*.

Capitula iudiciorum → *Poenitentiale XXXV Capitulorum*.

Carta Maenchi comitis, ed. O. J. Padel, 'The text of the Lanlawren charter', *Cornish Studies* 7 (1979): 43–44.

Cartularies → Landévennec, Redon.

Cassian, John, *Collationes*, ed. M. Petschenig, CSEL 13 (1886).

Cassian, *De institutis coenobiorum*, ed. M. Petschenig CSEL 17 (1888), 3–231.

Cassiodorus, *Expositio sancti Pauli Epistulae ad Romanos*, PL 68:415–506.

Cathwulf, Letter to Charlemagne, ed. E. Dümmler, MGH Epist. 4 (1895), 501–505.

Celestine I, Letter 4, *Ad episcopos per Viennensem et Narbonensem prouincias*, ed. P. Coustant, *Epistolae Romanorum Pontificum... ab anno Christi 67 ad annum 440* (Paris, 1721), 1065–1072.

Chrodegang, *Regula canonicorum*, ed. J.-B. Pelt, *Études sur la cathédrale de Metz: la liturgie, 1: la liturgie, Ve–XIIIe siècles* (Metz, 1937).

Pseudo-Clement, Letters, ed. P. Hinschius, *Decretales Pseudo-Isidorianae et Capitula Angilramni* (Leipzig, 1863), 30–66.

Pseudo-Clement, *Recognitiones* (tr. Rufinus), ed. B. Rehm and F. Paschke, GCS 51 (1965).

Codex Theodosianus, ed. T. Mommsen and E. Meyer, *Theodosiani Libri XVI cum Constitutionibus Sirmondianis*, 2 vols. in 3 (Berlin, 1905); tr. C. Pharr *et* al., *The Theodosian Code and Novels and the Sirmondian Constitutions* (Princeton, 1952).

Cogitosus, Life of Brigit, ed. J. Colgan, *Vita II S. Brigitae, Triadis Thaumaturgae seu Diuorum Patricii Columbae et Brigidae... Acta* (Louvain, 1647), 518–524.

Collectio Hibernensis, ed. F. W. H. Wasserschleben, *Die irische Kanonensammlung* (Giessen, 1874; 2nd ed. Leipzig, 1885).

Columbanus, Letters, ed. G. S. M. Walker, *Sancti Columbani Opera*, SLH 2 (Dublin, 1957), 2–59.

Columbanus, *Regula coenobialis*, ed. G. S. M. Walker, *Sancti Columbani opera*, SLH 2 (Dublin, 1957), 142–168.

Commentary on the Psalms in MS Palatinus Latinus 68, ed. and tr. M. McNamara, *Glossa in Psalmos. The Hiberno-Latin Gloss on the Psalms of Codex Palatinus Latinus 68 (Psalms 39:11–151)*, Studi e Testi 310 (Vatican, 1986).

Constitutio Syluestri, ed. P. Hinschius, *Decretales Pseudo-Isidorianae et Capitula Angilramni* (Leipzig, 1863), 449–451.

Cormac's Glossary → *Sanas Cormaic.*

Corpus genealogiarum Hiberniae, ed. M. A. O'Brien (Dublin, 1962).

Córus Bésgnai, ed. and tr. L. Breatnach, *Córus Bésgnai. An Old Irish Law Tract on the Church and Society*, Early Irish Law Series 7 (Dublin, 2017), 26–47; ed. Binchy, *CIH* 520.1–536.27, 903.37–905.9; 1812.33–1821.27.

Councils → See also *sinodus, synodus.*

Council of Agde, ed. C. Munier, CCSL 148 (1963), 192–228.

Councils of Ancyra, Antioch, Carthage, Chalcedon, Constantinople, Gangra, Laodicea, Neocaesarea, Nicaea → Dionysius Exiguus, *Collectio canonum Dionysiana.*

Councils of Ancyra, Gangra, Laodicea, Neocaesarea, Nicaea, Sardica → See also Turner, *Ecclesiae occidentalis monumenta iuris antiquissima.*

Council of Arles, ed. C. Munier, CCSL 148 (1963), 9–24.

Council of Auxerre, ed. C. de Clerq, CCSL 148A (1963), 265–272.

Council of Carthage (419), ed. C Munier, CCSL 149 (1974), 182–228, 230–232.

Council of Carthage → Dionysius Exiguus and *Registri ecclesiae Carthaginensis excerpta.*

Council of Orange, ed. C. Munier, CCSL 148 (1963), 78–93.

Council of Orléans, ed. C. de Clerq, CCSL 148A (1963), 4–19.

Council of Sardica, ed. G. Voell and H. Justel, *Bibliotheca Juris Canonici Veteris*, 2 vols. (Paris, 1661), vol. 1. Repr. PL 56:773–84. *EOMIA* 1:452–544.

Council of Vaison, ed. C. Munier, CCSL 148 (1963), 96–104.

Cresconius, *Concordia canonum*, ed. K. Zechiel-Eckes, *Die concordia canonum des Cresconius: Studien und Edition*, 2 vols. (Frankfurt, 1992).

Críth Gablach, ed. D. A. Binchy (Dublin, 1979); tr. E. MacNeill, 'Ancient Irish law: the law of status or franchise', *Proceedings of the Royal Irish Academy* 36C (1923): 265–316, at 265–316.

Cú Chuimne, *Cantemus in omni die*, ed. and tr. D. Howlett, 'Five experiments in textual reconstruction and analysis', *Peritia* 9 (1995): 1–50, at 19–30.

Cumméne, Letter to Ségéne, ed. M. Walsh and D. Ó Cróinín, *Cummian's Letter de controversia paschali and the De ratione computandi* (Toronto, 1988), 56–96.

Cumméne, Penitential, ed. L. Bieler, *The Irish Penitentials*, SLH 5 (Dublin, 1963), 108–134.

Pseudo-Cumméne → *Excarpsus Cummeani*.

Das Bibelwerk, ed. G. MacGinty, *The Reference Bible. Das Biblework. Inter pauca problesmata de enigmatibus ex tomis canonicis nunc prompta sunt praefatio et libri de Pentateucho Moysi*, CCCM 173 (2000).

De canibus sinodus sapientium, ed. L. Bieler, *The Irish Penitentials*, SLH 5 (Dublin, 1963), 174.

De duodecim abusivis saeculi, ed. S. Hellmann, *Pseudo-Cyprianus. De XII abusiuis saeculi*, Texte und Untersuchungen zur Gedichte der altchristlichen Literatur 34.1 (Leipzig, 1909), 32–60.

De episcoporum transmigratione et quod non temere iudicentur regule quadraginta quattuor, ed. G. P. Pozzi, 'Le manuscrit tomus XVIIIus de la Vallicelliana et le libelle *De episcoporum transmigratione et quod non temere iudicentur regule quadraginta quattuor*', *Apollinaris* 30 (1958): 313–350, at 329–348.

De iectione eclesie graduum ab hospitio, ed. L. Bieler, *The Irish Penitentials* (Dublin, 1963), 172–174.

De ordine creaturarum, tr. M. Smyth, 'The seventh-century Hiberno-Latin treatise *Liber de ordine creaturarum*. A translation', *Journal of Medieval Latin* 21 (2011): 137–222, at 164–209.

Dionysius Exiguus, *Collectio canonum Dionysiana* (recension I), ed. A. Strewe, *Die Canonessammlung des Dionysius Exiguus in der ersten Redaktion* (Berlin, 1931).

Dionysius Exiguus, *Collectio canonum Dionysiana* (recension II), ed. G. Voell and H. Justel, *Bibliotheca Juris Canonici Veteris*, 2 vols. (Paris, 1661), 1:107–174 (councils), 183–248 (decretals).

Dionysius Exiguus, *Collectio decretalium Dionysiana*, ed. Justel, *Codex Canonum Ecclesiasticorum* (1628), *Bibliotheca Juris Canonici* I (1661), repr. PL 67:230–546.

Dionysius Exiguus, *Praefatio ad Stephanum Episcopum*, ed. F. Glorie, CCSL 85 (1972), 38–42.

Discipulus Vmbrensium, *Iudicia Theodori*, ed. P. W. Finsterwalder, *Die Canones Theodori Cantuariensis und ihre Überlieferungsformen* (Weimar, 1929), 285–334.

Egbert, Penitential, ed. F. W. H. Wasserschleben, *Die Bussordnungen der abendländischen Kirche* (Halle, 1851), 231–247.

Eucherius, *Instructionum ad Salonium libri duo*, ed. C. Mandolfo, CCSL 66 (2004), 77–216.

Eusebius, *Chronicon* (tr. Jerome), ed. R. Helm, GCS 47 (1956).

Eusebius, *Ecclesiastica Historia* (tr. Rufinus), ed. E. Schwartz and T. Mommsen, GCS 9 (Berlin, 1903).

Eutropius, *Breuiarium ab urbe condita*, ed. C. Santini, MGH Auct. ant. 2 (Berlin, 1978), 4–182.

Excarpsus Cummeani, ed. F. W. H. Wasserschleben, *Die Bussordnungen der abendländischen Kirche* (Halle, 1851), 460–493.

Excerpta de libris Romanorum et Francorum, ed. L. Bieler, *The Irish Penitentials*, SLH 5 (Dublin, 1963), 136–148.

Fragmenta Gildae → Gildas.

Fulgentius Ferrandus, *Breuiatio canonum*, ed. C. Munier, CCSL 149 (1974), 287–306.

Gennadius, *Liber ecclesiasticorum dogmatum*, ed. C. H. Turner, 'The *Liber ecclesiasticorum dogmatum* attributed to Gennadius', *Journal of Theological Studies* 7 (1905/6): 78–99, at 89–99.

Gesta sanctorum Rotonensium, ed. and tr. C. Brett, *The Monks of Redon. Gesta sanctorum Rotonensium and Vita Conuuoionis* (Woodbridge, 1989), 106–219.

Gildas, Fragments, ed. M. Winterbottom, *Gildas. The Ruin of Britain and Other Documents* (London, 1978), 143–145.

Gratian, *Decretum*, ed. E. Friedberg, *Corpus iuris canonici*, vol. 1 (Leipzig, 1879).

Gregory I, *Dialogi*, ed. A. de Vogüé, *Grégoire le Grand. Dialogues*, SC 251, 260, 265 (1978–1980).

Gregory I, *Homiliae in Euangelia*, ed. R. Étaix, CCSL 141 (1999).

Gregory I, *Homiliae in Hiezechihelem Prophetam*, ed. M. Adriaen, CCSL 142 (1971).

Gregory I, Letters, ed. D. Norberg, *S. Gregorii magni registrum epistularum*, CCSL 140–140A (1982).

Gregory I, Letters, tr. J. R. C. Martyn, *The Letters of Gregory the Great*, 3 vols. (Toronto 2004).

Gregory I, *Moralia in Iob*, ed. M. Adriaen, CCSL 143 (1979).

Gregory I, *Regula pastoralis*, ed. F. Rommel, CS 381–382 (Paris, 1992).

Hermas, Shepherd (*Hermas Pastor*: 'Palatine' version), ed. A. Vezzoni, *Il Pastore di Erma* (Florence, 1994), 48–230.

Pseudo-Hilary, Commentary on the Catholic Epistles, ed. E. McNally, CCSL 108B (1973), 53–124.

Hispana collectio, ed. G. Martínez Díez, *La colección canónica Hispana*, 5 vols. (Madrid, 1966–1992).

In-longat bantaid banchuru, ed. and tr. T. M. Charles-Edwards, *Early Irish and Welsh Kinship* (Oxford, 1993), 516–519.

Innocent, *Decreta*, *Dionysiana* version, ed. C. Justel, *Codex Canonum Ecclesiasticorum Dionysii Exigui* (Paris, 1628). Repr. PL 67:238–62.

Innocent, Letter 2, to Victricius, ed. P. Coustant, *Epistolae Romanorum Pontificum... ab anno Christi 67 ad annum 440* (Paris, 1721), 746–758.

Innocent, Letter 6, to Exsuperius, ed. P. Coustant, *Epistolae Romanorum Pontificum... ab anno Christi 67 ad annum 440* (Paris, 1721), 789–796. ed. H. Wurm, *'Decretales selectae' Apollinaris* 12 (1939): 74–77.

Isidore, *Chronica*, ed. T. Mommsen, MGH Auct. ant. 11 (1894), 424–488.

Isidore, *De ecclesiasticis officiis*, ed. C. M. Lawson, CCSL 113 (1989).

Isidore, *De natura rerum*, ed. J. Fontaine, *Isidore de Séville, Traité de la nature, suivi de l'épître en vers du roi Sisebut à Isidore* (Bordeaux, 1960).

Isidore, *Etymologiae*, ed. W. M. Lindsay, *Isidori Hispalensis episcopi etymologiarum siue originum libri XX*, 2 vols. (Oxford, 1911).

Isidore, *The* Etymologies *of Isidore of Seville*, tr. S. A. Barney, W. J. Lewis, J. A. Beach, and O. Berghof (Cambridge, 2006).

Isidore, *Historia Gothorum, Wandalorum, Sueborum*, ed. T. Mommsen, MGH Auct. ant. 11 (1894), 267–302.

Isidore, Letter to Massona, PL 83:899–902.

Isidore, *Quaestiones de ueteri et nouo testamento*, PL 83:201–207.

Isidore, *Sententiae*, ed. P. Lazier, CCSL 111 (1998).

Pseudo-Isidore, ed. P. Hinschius, *Decretales Pseudo-Isidorianae et Capitula Angilramni* (Leipzig, 1863).

Iudicium culparum, ed. L. Bieler, *The Irish Penitentials*, SLH 5 (Dublin, 1963), 150–158.

Iunilius, *Instituta regularia diuinae*, ed. H. Kihn, *Theodor von Mopsuestia und Junilius Africanus als Exegeten* (Freiburg, 1880), 465–528.

Jerome, *Aduersus Iouinianum*, PL 23:211–338.

Jerome, *Commentarii in Danielem*, ed. F. Glorie, CCSL 75A (1964).

Jerome, *Commentarius in Ecclesiasten*, ed. M. Adriaen, CCSL 72 (1959), 250–361.

Jerome, *Commentarii in iv epistulas Paulinas*, PL 26:307–618.

Jerome, *Commentarii in Esaiam*, ed. M. Adriaen, CCSL 73–73A (1963).

Jerome, *Commentarii in euangelium Matthaei*, ed. D. Hurst and M. Adriaen, CCSL 77 (1969).

Jerome, *Commentarii in Ezechielem*, ed. F. Glorie, CCSL 75 (1964).

Jerome, *Commentarii in Prophetas minores*, ed. M. Adriaen, CCSL 76–76A (1969–1970).

Jerome, *Dialogus aduersus Pelagianos*, ed. C. Moreschini, CCSL 80 (1990).

Jerome, *In Hieremiam prophetam libri iv*, ed. S. Reiter, CCSL 74 (1960).

Jerome, Letters, ed. I. Hilberg, CSEL 54–56 (1910–1918).

Jerome, *Vita S. Hilarionis*, ed. A. Bastiansen, *Vite dei Santi* (Rome, 1975), 4:72–142.

John VIII, Letter 44, to Mahen of Dol, ed. E. Casper, MGH Epist. 7 (1912), 299–300.

Justinian, *Digestum*, ed. T. Mommsen and P. Krüger, *Corpus Iuris Civilis* I (Berlin, 1870).

Lactantius, *De opificio Dei*, ed. S. Brandt, CSEL 27 (1893), 3–64.

Landévennec Cartulary, ed. A. de La Borderie, *Cartulaire de l'abbaye de Landévennec* (Rennes, 1888).

Leges Alamannorum, ed. C. Schott, *Das Gesetz der Alemannen* (Augsburg, 1993), 70–164.

Leges Visigothorum, ed. K. Zuemer, MGH Legum sectio I.1 (Hannover, 1902).

Leo I, *Decreta*, *Dionysiana* version, ed. C. Justel, *Codex Canonum Ecclesiasticorum Dionysii Exigui* (Paris, 1628). Repr. PL 67:277–362.

Leo IV, Letter 16, *Ad episcopos Britanniae*, ed. A. von Hirsch-Gereuth MGH Epist. 5 (1898), 593–596. Repr. MGH Concilia 3:187–189.

Liber Angeli, ed. L. Bieler, *The Patrician Texts in the Book of Armagh*, SLH 10 (Dublin, 1979), 184–190.

Liber ex lege Moysi, ed. S. Meeder, 'The *Liber ex lege Moysi*: notes and text', *Journal of Medieval Latin* 19 (2009): 173–218.

Liber questionum in euangeliis, ed. J. Rittmueller, CCSL 108F (Turnhout, 2003).

Life of Áedán (Máedóc), *Vita S. Aedani seu Maedoc*, ed. W. W. Heist, *Vitae sanctorum Hiberniae e codice Salmanticensi* (Brussels, 1965), 234–247.

Life of Brigit, *Vita I S. Brigitae*, ed. J. Colgan, *Triadis Thaumaturgae seu Diuorum Patricii Columbae et Brigidae... Acta* (Louvain, 1647), 527–542.

Life of Colmán Élo, *Vita S. Colmani*, ed. W. W. Heist, *Vitae sanctorum Hiberniae e codice Salmanticensi* (Brussels, 1965), 209–224.

Life of Fintan, *Vita S. Munnu*, ed. W. W. Heist, *Vitae sanctorum Hiberniae e codice Salmanticensi* (Brussels, 1965), 198–209.

Life of Gregory, ed. and tr. B. Colgrave, *The Earliest Life of Gregory the Great by an Anonymous Monk of Whitby* (Lawrence, KS, 1968).

Louis the Pious, Diploma for Saint-Méen, 26 March 816, in H. Morice, *Mémoires pour servir de preuves à l'histoire ecclésiastique et civile de Bretagne*, 3 vols. (Paris, 1742–1746), 1:225–227.

Midrash Tanhuma, tr. S. A. Berman, *Midrash Tanhuma-Yelammedenu* (Hoboken, NJ 1996).

Pseudo-Macarius, Rule, ed. A. de Vogüé, SC 297 (1982), 372–388.

Muirchú, *Vita Patricii*, ed. Bieler, *The Patrician Texts in the Book of Armagh*, SLH 10 (Dublin, 1979), 61–122.

O'Davoren, D., Glossary (1563–1569), ed. W. Stokes, 'O'Davoren's Glossary', *Archiv für celtische Lexikographie*, 2 (1904): 197–504. Also printed in *CIH* 1466.11–1531.24.

Old-Irish Penitential, tr. D. A. Binchy *apud* L. Bieler, *The Irish Penitentials*, SLH 5 (Dublin, 1963), 259–274.

Old-Irish Table of Commutations, tr. D. A. Binchy *apud* L. Bieler, *The Irish Penitentials*, SLH 5 (Dublin, 1963), 278–282.

Old-Irish Text on Court Procedure → *Airecht*-text.

Old-Irish Treatise on the Psalter, ed. K. Meyer, *Hibernica Minora, Being a Fragment of an Old-Irish Treatise on the Psalter* (Oxford, 1894), 20–37.

Origen, *In Genesim homiliae*, ed. W. A. Baehrens, GCS 29 (1920), 1–144.

Orosius, *Historiarum adversus paganos libri VII*, ed. Marie-Pierre Arnaud-Lindet, *Histoires contre les païens*, 3 vols. (Paris, 1990–1991).

Paschasius Radbertus, *Expositio in Matheo*, ed., B. Paulus, CCCM 56, 56A, 56B (Turnhout, 1984).

Patrick, *Epistola ad milites Corotici*, *Epistola ad milites Corotici*, ed. L. Bieler, *Libri Epistolarum Sancti Patricii Episcopi*, 2 vols. (Dublin, 1952), 1:91–102.

Pelagius, *Expositiones XIII epistularum Pauli*, ed. A. Souter, *Pelagius's Expositions of Thirteen Epistles of St. Paul*, Texts and Studies IX, 3 vols. (Cambridge, 1922–1931).

Pelagius, *Liber de induratione cordis Pharaonis*, ed. G. de Plinval, *Essai sur le style et la langue de Pélage suivi du traité inédit De induratione cordis Pharaonis*, Collectanea Friburgensia nouv. sér. fasc. 31 (Freibourg, 1947).

'Poem on the Airgialla', ed. and tr. M. O. Daly, *Ériu* 16 (1952): 179–188.

Poenitentiale Remense, ed. F. W. H. Wasserschleben, *Die Bussordnungen der abendländischen Kirche* (Halle, 1851), 494–504; ed. F. B. Asbach, *Das Poenitentiale Remense und der sogen. Excarpsus Cummeani* (Regensburg, 1975), Anhang 4–77.

Poenitentiale Sangalense Tripartitum, ed. H. J. Schmitz, *Die Bussbücher und das kanonische Bussverfahren nach handschriftlichen Quellen* (Düsseldorf, 1898), 177–189; ed. R. Meens, *Het tripartite boeteboek. Overlevering en betekenis van vroegmiddeleeuwse biechtvoorschriften (met editie en vertaling van vier 'tripartita')* (Hilversum, 1994), 326–352.

Poenitentiale XXXV Capitulorum, ed. F. W. H. Wasserschleben, *Die Bussordnungen der abendländischen Kirche* (Halle, 1851), 505–26; [as *Capitula Iudiciorum*] ed. R. Meens, *Het tripartite boeteboek. Overlevering en betekenis van vroegmiddeleeuwse biechtvoorschriften (met editie en vertaling van vier 'tripartita')* (Hilversum, 1994), 434–484.

Prebiarum de multorum exemplaribus, ed. R. E. McNally, Scriptores Hiberniae Minores Pars I. CCSL 108B (Turnhout, 1973), 161–171.

Prouerbia Grecorum, ed. S. Hellmann, *Sedulius Scottus* (Munich, 1906), 122–135; ed. D. Simpson, 'The '*Prouerbia Grecorum*'', *Traditio* 43 (1987): 1–22.

Psalterium Suthantoniense, ed. P. Ó Néill, CCCM 240 (2012).

Pseudo- → Basil, Clement, etc.

Redon Cartulary, *Cartulaire de l'abbaye de Redon en Bretagne*, ed. A. de Courson (Paris, 1863).

Redon Cartulary [facsimile], ed. H. Guillotel *et al.*, *Cartulaire de l'abbaye Saint-Sauveur de Redon* (Rennes, 1998).

Reference Bible → Das Bibelwerk.

Registri ecclesiae Carthaginensis excerpta, ed. C. Munier, CCSL 149 (1974), 182–228.

Richerus of Rheims, Histories, ed. H. Hoffmann, *Righeri historiarum libri IIII*, MGH Scriptores 38 (Hannover 2006).

Rufus Festus, *Breuiarium rerum gestarum populi Romani*, ed. J. W. Eadie, *The Breviarium of Festus: a Critical Edition with Historical Commentary* (London, 1967).

Sanas Cormaic, ed. W. Stokes, *Three Irish Glossaries* (London, 1862).

Sedulius Scotus, *Collectaneum miscellaneum*, ed. D. Simpson, CCCM 67 (1988).

Sedulius Scotus, *In euangelium Matthaei*, ed. B. Löfstedt, *Kommentar zum Evangelium nach Matthäus*, 2 vols. (Freiburg, 1989–1991).

Senchas Már, pseudo-historical prologue, ed. and tr. J. Carey, 'An edition of the pseudo-historical prologue to the *Senchas Már*', *Ériu* 45 (1994): 1–32, at 11–12, 17–19.

Sinodus Autisioderensis, ed. C. de Clerq, CCSL 148 (1963), 265–272.

Sinodus Hibernensis, ed. L. Bieler, *The Irish Penitentials*, SLH 5 (Dublin, 1963), 170.

Siricius, *Decreta*, *Dionysiana* version, ed. C. Justel, *Codex Canonum Ecclesiasticorum Dionysii Exigui* (Paris, 1628). Repr. PL 67:231–238.

Statuta ecclesiae antiqua, ed. C. Munier, CCSL 148 (1963), 164–188.

Symmachus, Letter 15, to Caesarius, ed. A. Thiel, *Epistolae Romanorum Pontificum... Tomus I. a S. Hilaro usque ad Pelagium II, ann. 461–523* (Braunsberg, 1868), 723–728.

Synodus episcoporum, ed. L. Bieler, *The Irish Penitentials*, SLH 5 (Dublin, 1963), 54–58; ed. M. J. Faris, *The Bishops' Synod ("The First Synod of St. Patrick"). A symposium with text, translation and commentary* (Liverpool, 1976); ed. D. N. Dumville, *Councils and Synods of the Gaelic Early and Central Middle Ages*, E. C. Quiggin Memorial Lectures 3 (Cambridge, 1997), 6–16; ed. D. R. Howlett, '*Synodus prima Sancti Patricii*: an exercise in textual reconstruction', *Peritia* 12 (1998): 238–253.

Synodus Luci Victorie, ed. L. Bieler, *The Irish Penitentials*, SLH 5 (Dublin, 1963), 68.

Synodus Patricii, ed. L. Bieler, *The Irish Penitentials*, SLH 5 (Dublin, 1963), 184–196.

Synodus Patricii, ed. A. Breen, 'The date, provenance and authorship of the Pseudo-Patrician canonical materials', *ZRG* 81 (1995): 83–129, at 112–116.

Synodus sapientium de decimis, ed. L. Bieler, *The Irish Penitentials*, SLH 5 (Dublin, 1963), 166–168.

Theodore → *Discipulus Vmbrensium.*

Theodulf of Orléans, Episcopal Statutes, ed. P. Brommer, MGH Capitula episcoporum, 3 vols. (1984), 1:76–184.

Tírechán, *Vita Patricii*, ed. Bieler, *The Patrician Texts in the Book of Armagh*, SLH 10 (Dublin, 1979), 122–166.

Triads, ed. and tr. K. Meyer, *The Triads of Ireland* (Dublin, 1906).

Uraicecht Becc, tr. E. MacNeill, 'Ancient Irish law: the law of status or franchise', *Proceedings of the Royal Irish Academy* 36C (1923): 265–316, at 272–281.

Uraiccecht na Ríar: *The Poetic Grades in the Irish Church*, ed. L. Breatnach (Dublin, 1987), 102–115.

Vetus Gallica, ed. H. Mordek, *Kirchenrecht und Reform im Frankenreich: Die Collectio vetus Gallica, die älteste systematische Kanonessammlung des fränkischen Gallien: Studien und Edition*, Beiträge zur Geschichte und Quellenkunde des Mittelalters 1 (Berlin & New York, 1975), 343–617.

Vinnian, Penitential, ed. L. Bieler, *The Irish Penitentials*, SLH 5 (Dublin, 1963), 74–94.

Virgilius Maro Grammaticus, *Epitomae*, ed. B. Löfstedt, *Virgilius Maro Grammaticus: Opera Omnia* (Munich, 2003), 103–245.

Virtutes Iohannis (Pseudo-Abdias), ed. E. Junod, Corpus Christianorum Series Apocrypharum 2 (1983): 799–834.

Virtutes quas Dominus dominica die fecit, ed. R. E. McNally, '*Dies dominica*: two Hiberno-Latin texts', *Medieval Studies* 22 (1960): 355–361, at 359–360.

Vitae sine auctorum nominibus → 'Life of'.

Vitas Patrum, ed. H. Rosweyde, *Vitae Patrum* (Antwerp, 1615), vols. 5, 6. Repr. PL 73:855–1022. Translations of selected portions of the *Vitas Patrum* are by H. Waddell, *The Desert Fathers* (Ann Arbor, MI, 1957) and by B. Baker, *Vitae Patrum* at http://vitae-patrum.org.uk

Vulgate, ed. R. Weber and R. Gryson, *Biblia Sacra iuxta Vulgatam uersionem* (Stuttgart, 1994).

Wulfstan, Canon-Law Collection, ed. J. E. Cross and A. Hamer, *Wulfstan's Canon Law Collection* (Cambridge, 1999).

Zosimus, *Decreta, Dionysiana* version, ed. C. Justel, *Codex Canonum Ecclesiasticorum Dionysii Exigui* (Paris, 1628). Repr. PL 67:261–278.

Secondary sources

Ambrose, S., 'The *Collectio canonum Hibernensis* and the Literature of the Anglo-Saxon Benedictine reform', *Viator* 36 (2005): 107–118.

Ambrose, S., 'The codicology and palaeography of London, BL, Royal 5 E. xiii and its abridgement of the *Collectio canonum Hibernensis*', *Codices Manuscripti* 54/55 (2006): 1–26.

Ballerini, P., and G. Ballerini, *S. Leonis Magni opera*, 3 vols. (Venice, 1753–1757). Repr. PL 54:13–56.1182.

Barker-Benfield, B. C., 'Not St. Dunstan's book?', *Notes and Queries* 40.4 (December, 1993): 431–433.

Bieler, L., *The Irish Penitentials*, SLH 5 (Dublin, 1963).

Bieler, L., 'The Christianization of the insular Celts during the sub-Roman period and its repercussions on the continent', *Celtica* 8 (1968): 112–125.

Bieler, L., *The Patrician Texts in the Book of Armagh*, SLH 10 (Dublin, 1979).

Binchy, D. A., 'The fair of Tailtiu and the feast of Tara', *Ériu* 18 (1958): 3–38.

Binchy, D. A., 'The Old-Irish table of penitential commutations', *Ériu* 19 (1962): 47–72.

Binchy, D. A., 'Patrick and his biographers: ancient and modern', *Studia Hibernica* 2 (1962): 7–173.

Binchy, D. A., 'St. Patrick's "First Synod"', *Studia Hibernica* 8 (1968): 49–59.

Binchy, D. A., ed., *Corpus iuris Hibernici*, 6 vols. (Dublin, 1978).

Binchy, D. A., 'The pseudo-historical prologue to the *Senchas Már*', *Studia Celtica* 10/11 (1975/1976): 15–28.

Bischoff, B., 'Wendepunkte in der Geschichte der lateinischen Exegese im Frühmittelalter', *Sacris Erudiri* 6 (1954): 189–281. Revised in Bischoff, *Mittelalterliche Studien*, 3 vols. (Stuttgart, 1966–1981), 1:205–273. [An English translation of the revised version is by Colm O'Grady, *Biblical Studies, The Medieval Irish Contribution*, ed. Martin McNamara (Dublin, 1976), 74–160.]

Bischoff, B., *Die südostdeutschen Schreibschulen und Bibliotheken in der Karolingerzeit, Vol. 1: Die Bayrischen Diözesen* (Wiesbaden, 1960).

Bischoff, B., 'Die europäische Verbreitung der Werke Isidors von Sevilla', in his *Mittelalterliche Studien: Ausgewählte Aufsätze zur Schriftkunde und Literaturgeschichte*, 2 vols. (Stuttgart, 1966–1967), 1:171–194, at 186–187.

Bischoff, B., 'Panorama der Handschriftenüberlieferung aus der Zeit Karl der Grosse', in *Karl der Grosse. Lebenswerk und Nachleben*, ed. Bischoff, 5 vols. (Düsseldorf, 1965–1968), vol. 2 [*Das Geistige Leben*].

Bischoff, B., 'Frühkarolingische Handschriften und ihre Heimat', *Scriptorium* 12 (1968): 306–314.

Bischoff, B., *Latin Palaeography: Antiquity and the Middle Ages*, tr. D. Ó Cróinín and D. Ganz (Cambridge, 1990). Originally published as *Paläographie des römischen Altertums und des abendländischen Mittelalters* (Berlin, 1979; 2nd ed. 1986).

Bischoff, B., *Katalog der festländischen Handschriften des neunten Jahrhunderts*, 2 vols. (Wiesbaden, 2004).

Bishop, T. A. M., 'Notes on Cambridge manuscripts, part 7: the early minuscule of Christ Church, Canterbury', *Transactions of the Cambridge Bibliographical Society* 3 (1959–1963): 413–423.

Bracken, D., 'Latin passages in Irish vernacular law: notes on the sources', *Peritia* 9 (1995): 187–196.

Bracken, D., 'The Fall and the law in early Ireland', in *Ireland and Europe in the Early Middle Ages: Texts and Transmission*, ed. P. Ní Chatháin and M. Richter (Dublin, 2002), 147–169.

Bradshaw, H., Letter to Wasserschleben (28 May, 1885), printed in F. W. H. Wasserschleben, *Die irische Kanonensammlung*, 2nd ed. (Leipzig, 1885), lxiii–lxxv.

Bradshaw, H., *Collected Papers* (Cambridge, 1889).

Bradshaw, H., *The Early Collection of Canons Known as the Hibernensis. Two Unfinished Papers* (Cambridge, 1893).

Breatnach, L., 'Canon law and secular law in early Ireland: the significance of *Bretha Nemed*', *Peritia* 3 (1984): 439–459.

Breatnach, L., 'The first third of *Bretha Nemed Toísech*', *Ériu* 40 (1989): 1–40.

Breatnach, L., 'Lawyers in early Ireland', in *Brehons, Serjeants and Attorneys*, ed. D. Hogan and W. N. Osborough (Blackrock, 1990), 1–13.

Breatnach, L., 'On the original extent of the *Senchas Már*', *Ériu* 47 (1996): 1–43.

Breatnach, L., *A Companion to the Corpus Iuris Hibernici*, Early Irish Law Series 5 (Dublin 2005).

Breatnach, L., *The Early Irish Law Text Senchas Már and the Question of Its Date*, E. C. Quiggin Memorial Lectures 13 (Cambridge, 2011).

Breatnach, P. A., 'The pronunciation of Latin in medieval Ireland', *Scire litteras: Forschungen zum mittelalterlichen Geistesleben*, ed. S. Krämer and M. Bernhard (Munich, 1988), 59–72.

Breen, A., 'Some seventh-century Hiberno-Latin texts and their relationships', *Peritia* 3 (1984): 204–214.

Breen, A., 'The date, provenance and authorship of the Pseudo-Patrician canonical materials', *Zeitschrift der Savigny-Stiftung für Rechtsgeschichte: Kanonistische Abteilung* 81 (1995): 83–129.

Breen, A., '*De XII Abusiuis: text and transmission*', in *Ireland and Europe in the Early Middle Ages: Texts and Transmission*, ed. P. Ní Chatháin and M. Richter (Dublin, 2002), 78–94.

Brett, M., 'Theodore and the Latin canon law', in *Archbishop Theodore: Commemorative Studies on his Life and Influence*, ed. M. Lapidge (Cambridge, 1995), 120–140.

Brooks, N., 'Arms, status and warfare in late-Saxon England', in *Ethelred the Unready*, ed. D. Hill (Oxford, 1978), 81–103.

Brooks, N., 'Was cathedral reform at Christ Church Canterbury in the early ninth century of Continental inspiration?', in *Anglo-Saxon England and the Continent*, ed. H. Sauer, J. Story and G. Waxenberger (Tempe, 2011), 303–322.

Bruckner, A., *Scriptoria medii aeui Heluetica*, 14 vols. (Geneva, 1935–1978).

Bury, J. B., *The Life of St. Patrick and His Place in History* (London, 1905).

Carey, J., *The Irish Origin-Legend: A Synthetic Pseudohistory*, E. C. Quiggin Memorial Lectures 1 (Cambridge, 1994).

Carey, J., 'An edition of the pseudo-historical prologue to the *Senchas Már*', *Ériu* 45 (1994): 1–32.

Charles-Edwards, T. M., 'The social background to Irish *peregrinatio*', *Celtica* 11 (1976): 43–59.

Charles-Edwards, T. M., 'The pastoral role of the church in early Irish laws', in *Pastoral Care before the Parish*, ed. J. Blair and R. Sharpe (Leicester, 1992), 63–77.

Charles-Edwards, T. M., *Early Irish and Welsh Kinship* (Oxford, 1993).

Charles-Edwards, T. M., 'A contract between king and people in early medieval Ireland? *Críth Gablach* on kingship', *Peritia* 8 (1994): 107–119.

Charles-Edwards, T. M., 'The Penitential of Theodore and the *Iudicia Theodori*', in *Archbishop Theodore: Commemorative Studies on His Life and Influence*, ed. M. Lapidge (Cambridge, 1995), 141–174.

Charles-Edwards, T. M., 'The context and uses of literacy in early Christian Ireland', in *Literacy in Medieval Celtic Societies*, ed. H. Pryce (Cambridge, 1998), 62–82.

Charles-Edwards, T. M., 'The construction of the *Hibernensis*', *Peritia* 12 (1998): 209–237.

Charles-Edwards, T. M., *The Early Mediaeval Gaelic Lawyer*, E. C. Quiggin Memorial Lectures 4 (Cambridge, 1999).

Charles-Edwards, T. M., *Early Christian Ireland* (Cambridge, 2000).

Charles-Edwards, T. M., '*Dliged*: its native and Latinate usages', *Celtica* 24 (2003): 65–78.

Charles-Edwards, T. M., 'Early Irish Law', in *A New History of Ireland I*, ed. D. Ó Cróinín (Oxford, 2005), 331–370.

Charles-Edwards, T. M., tr., *The Chronicle of Ireland*, 2 vols. (Liverpool, 2006).

Charles-Edwards, T. M., 'Celtic kings: 'priestly vegetables'?', in *Early Medieval Studies in Memory of Patrick Wormald*, ed. S. Baxter, C. E. Karkov, J. L. Nelson, and D. Pelteret (Farnham, 2009), 65–80.

Chédeville, A., and H. Guillotel, *La Bretagne des saints et des rois Ve–Xe siècle* (Rennes, 1984).

Clarkson, C., 'Further studies in Anglo-Saxon and Norman bookbinding: board attachment methods re-examined', in R. Powell, *The Compleat Binder*, ed. J. L. Sharpe, Bibliologia 14 (Turnhout 1996), 154–214.

Coustant, P., ed., *Epistolae Romanorum Pontificum... ab anno Christi 67 ad annum 440* (Paris, 1721).

Crehan, J., 'The Seven Orders of Christ', *Theological Studies* 19 (1958): 81–93.

Cubitt, C. R. E., *Anglo-Saxon Church Councils c. 650–c. 850* (London, 1995).

D'Achéry, L., *Spicilegium, siue Collectio ueterum aliquot scriptorum qui in Galliae bibliothecis delituerant* (Paris, 1655–1677). Revised by S. Baluze, E.

Martène and L. F. J. De la Barre, *Spicilegium, etc.*, 3 vols. (Paris, 1723), vol. 1.

Davies, L. M., 'The *Collectio canonum Hibernensis* and its sources', D.Phil. dissertation, University of Oxford (1995).

Davies, L. M., 'The biblical text of the *Collectio canonum Hibernensis*', in *Ireland and Europe in the Early Middle Ages: Learning and Literature*, ed. P. Ní Chatháin and M. Richter (Stuttgart, 1996), 17–41.

Davies, L. M., 'Isidorian texts and the *Hibernensis*', *Peritia* 11 (1997): 207–249.

Davies, L. M., '*Statuta ecclesiae antiqua* and the Gallic councils in the *Hibernensis*', *Peritia* 14 (2000): 85–100.

Davies, L. M., 'The "mouth of gold": Gregorian texts in the *Collectio canonum Hibernensis*', in *Ireland and Europe in the Early Middle Ages: Texts and Transmission*, ed. P. Ní Chatháin and M. Richter (Dublin, 2002), 249–268.

Davies, W., *The Llandaff Charters* (Aberystwyth, 1979).

Davies, W., 'The Latin charter-tradition in western Britain, Brittany and Ireland in the early mediaeval period', *Ireland in Early Mediaeval Europe: Studies in Memory of Kathleen Hughes*, ed. D. Whitelock, R. McKitterick and D. N. Dumville (Cambridge, 1982), 258–280.

Davies, W., 'Clerics as rulers: some implications of the terminology of ecclesiastical authority in early medieval Ireland', in *Latin and the Vernacular Languages in Early Medieval Britain*, ed. N. Brooks (Leicester, 1982), 82–97.

Davies, W., 'The composition of the Redon cartulary', *Francia* 17/1 (1990): 69–90.

Deanesly M., and P. Grosjean, 'The Canterbury edition of the answers of pope Gregory I to St. Augustine', *Journal of Ecclesiastical History* 10 (1959): 1–49.

Dekkers, E., and E. Gaar, *Clavis patrum latinorum*, 3rd ed. (Steenbrugge, 1995).

Deuffic, J.-L., 'La production manuscrite des scriptoria bretons (VIIIe–XIe siècle)', in *Landévennec et le monachisme breton dans le haut moyen âge* (Landévennec 1986), 289–321.

Doherty, C., 'The monastic town in early medieval Ireland', in *The Comparative History of Urban Origins in Non-Roman Europe: Ireland, Wales, Denmark,*

Germany, Poland and Russia from the Ninth Century to the Thirteenth Century, ed. H. B. Clarke and A. Simms (Oxford, 1985), 45–75.

Du Cange, C., *Glossarium mediae et infimae Latinitatis*, 3 vols. (Paris, 1678); 3rd ed., 10 vols. (Nirot, 1882–1887).

Dumville, D. N., 'On the dating of the early Breton lawcodes', *Études Celtiques* 21 (1984): 207–221.

Dumville, D. N., 'St. Patrick at his 'First Synod'?', in Dumville *et al.*, *Saint Patrick. A.D. 493–1993* (Woodbridge, 1993), 175–178.

Dumville, D. N., *et al.*, *Saint Patrick. A.D. 493–1993* (Woodbridge, 1993).

Dumville, D. N., 'Ireland, Brittany, and England: transmission and use of *Collectio canonum Hibernensis*', in *Irlande et Bretagne: Vingt siècles d'histoire* (Rennes, 1994), 84–95.

Dumville, D. N., *Councils and Synods of the Gaelic Early and Central Middle Ages*, E. C. Quiggin Memorial Lectures 3 (Cambridge, 1997).

Elliot, M. D., 'New evidence for the influence of Gallic canon law in Anglo-Saxon England', *Journal of Ecclesiastical History* 64 (2013): 700–730.

Enright, M., *Iona, Tara, and Soissons: The Origin of the Royal Anointing Ritual* (Berlin, 1985).

Epistolae Romanorum Pontificum → Coustant, Thiel.

Etchingham, C., *Church Organisation in Ireland 650–1000* (Maynooth, 1999).

Etchingham, C., *The Irish 'Monastic Town': Is This A Valid Concept?*, Kathleen Hughes Memorial Lectures 8 (Cambridge, 2010).

Faris, M. J., ed., *The Bishops' Synod ("The First Synod of St. Patrick"). A Symposium with Text, Translation and Commentary* (Liverpool, 1976).

Firey, A., 'Ghostly recensions in early medieval canon law: the problem of the *Collectio Dacheriana* and its shades', *Tijdschrift voor rechtsgeschiedenis* 125 (2008): 63–82.

Firey, A., 'Mutating Monsters: Approaches to "Living Texts" of the Carolingian Era', *Digital Proceedings of the Lawrence J. Schoenberg Symposium on Manuscript Studies in the Digital Age*, vol. 2 (Kentucky, 2010), 1–14.

Flechner, R., 'The Making of the Canons of Theodore', *Peritia* 17–18 (2003–2004): 121–143.

Flechner, R., 'Paschasius Radbertus and Bodleian Library, MS. Hatton 42', *Bodleian Library Record* 18.4 (2004): 411–421.

Flechner, R., '*Libelli et commentarii aliorum*: The *Hibernensis* and the Breton bishops', in *Approaches to Religion and Mythology in Celtic Studies*, ed. K. Ritari and A. Bergholm (Newcastle, 2008), 100–119.

Flechner, R., 'Aspects of the Breton transmission of the Hibernensis', *Pecia* 12 (2008): 27–44.
On Open Access at http://researchrepository.ucd.ie/handle/10197/7020

Flechner, R., 'An Insular tradition of ecclesiastical law: fifth to eighth century', in *Anglo-Saxon/Irish Relations before the Vikings*, ed. J. Graham-Campbell and M. Ryan, *Proceedings of the British Academy* 157 (Oxford, 2009), 23–46.

Flechner, R., 'The problem of originality in early medieval canon law: legislating by means of contradictions in the *Collectio Hibernensis*', *Viator* 43 (2012), 29–47.

Flechner, R., 'Pope Gregory and the British: mission as a canonical problem', in *En marge*, ed. H. Bouget and M. Coumert (Brest, 2015).

Flechner, R., 'Identifying monks in early medieval Britain and Ireland: a reflection of legal and economic aspects', in *Monachesimi d'Oriente e d'Occidente nell'alto medioevo*, Atti delle Settimane di studio CISAM 64 (Spoleto, 2017), 805–844.

Fleuriot, L., *Dictionnaire des gloses en vieux Breton* (Paris, 1964).

Fleuriot, L., 'Un fragment en latin de très anciennes lois bretonnes armoricaines du VIe siècle', *Annales de Bretagne* 78 (1971): 601–660.

Flower, R., '*Quidam Scotigena .i. Discipulus Boëthii* or Boëthius and the four conditions of a tale', *Ériu* 8 (1916): 150–154.

Follet, W., Céli Dé *in Ireland. Monastic Writing and Identity in the Early Middle Ages* (Woodbridge, 2006).

Fornasari, M., 'Un manoscritto e una collezione canonica del secolo XI provenienti da Farfa', *Benedictina* 10 (1956): 199–210.

Fournier, P., 'De l'influence de la collection irlandaise sur la formation des collections canoniques', *Nouvelle revue historique de droit français et étranger* 23 (1899): 27–78.

Fournier, P., 'Le *Liber ex lege Moysi* et les tendances bibliques du droit canonique irlandais', *Revue Celtique* 30 (1909): 221–234.

Fournier, P., Auxilius[(3)], *Dictionnaire d'histoire et de géographie ecclésiastiques*, 5 vols. (Paris, 1930), 5:971–972.

Fournier, P., and G. Le Bras, *Histoire des collections canoniques en Occident, depuis les Fausses Décrétales jusqu'au Décret de Gratien*, 2 vols. (Paris, 1931–1932).

Fowler-Magerl, L., 'Fine distinctions and the transmission of texts', *Zeitschrift der Savigny-Stiftung für Rechtsgeschichte. Kanonistische Abteilung* 114 (1997): 146–186.

Fowler-Magerl, L., *Clavis canonum. Selected Canon Law Collections before 1140* (Hannover, 2005).

Frantzen, A. J., *The Literature of Penance in Anglo-Saxon England* (New Brunswick, NJ, 1983).

Friesen, B., 'Answers and echoes: the *Libellus responsionum* and the hagiography of the north-western European mission', *Early Medieval Europe* 14 (2006): 153–172.

Ganz, D., *Corbie in the Carolingian Renaissance* (Sigmaringen, 1990).

Gaudemet, J., *Les sources de droit de l'Église en occident du IIe au VIIe siècle* (Paris, 1985).

Gaudemet, J., *Église et cité. Histoire du droit canonique* (Paris, 1994).

Gaudenzi, A., 'Lo svolgimento parallelo del diritto longobardo e del diritto romano a Ravenna', in *Memorie della R. Accademia delle Scienze dell'Instituto di Bologna*, sez. giuridica, serie I, t. I (Bologna, 1906–1907), 37–164.

Geltner, G., '*Detrusio*: Penal cloistering in the middle ages', *Revue Bénédictine* 118 (2008): 89–108.

Gerriets, M., 'Theft, penitentials, and the compilation of the early Irish laws', *Celtica* 22 (1991): 18–32.

Giorgetti Vichi, A. M., and S. Mottironi, ed., *Catalogo dei manoscritti della Biblioteca Vallicelliana* (Rome, 1961).

Glathaar, M., *Bonifatius und das Sakrileg: Zur politischen Dimension eines Rechtsbegriffs* (Frankfurt, 2004).

Goody, J., 'Polygyny, economy and the role of women', in *The Character of Kinship*, ed. *Idem* (Cambridge, 1973), 175–190.

Gorman, M., 'Patristic and pseudo-patristic citations in the *Collectio Hibernensis*', *Revue Bénédictine* 120 (2011): 18–93.

Grosjean, P., 'Sur quelques exégètes irlandais du VIIe siècle', *Sacris Erudiri* 7 (1955): 67–98.

Haddan, A. W., and W. Stubbs, *Councils and Ecclesiastical Documents Relating to Great Britain and Ireland*, 3 vols. (Oxford 1869–1878).

Harvey, A., 'The non-Classical vocabulary of Celtic-Latin literature: an overview', in *Spoken and Written Language: Relations between Latin and the Vernacular Languages in the Earlier Middle Ages*, ed. M. Garrison, A. P. Orbán, and M. Mostert (Turnhout, 2013), 87–100.

Harvey, A., 'Some orthographic features of the Schaffhausen manuscript', in *The Schaffhausen Adamnán, Vol. II: Commentary*, ed. D. Bracken and E. Graff, Irish Manuscripts in Facsimile 1 (Cork, 2014), 99–101.

Harvey, A., ed., *The Non-Classical Lexicon of Celtic Latinity (A–H)* (Turnhout, 2006); *Supplement*, ed. A. Harvey and A. Malthouse (Dublin, 2015).

Hellmann, S., *Sedulius Scottus* (Munich, 1906).

Helmholz, R. H., *The Canon Law and Ecclesiastical Jurisdiction from 597 to the 1640s*, The Oxford History of the Laws of England I (Oxford, 2004).

Herbert, M., *Iona, Kells and Derry: the History and Hagiography of the Monastic Familia of Columba* (Oxford, 1988).

Herbert, M., 'Before charters? Property records in pre-Anglo-Norman Ireland', in *Charters and Charter Scholarship in Britain and Ireland*, ed. M. T. Flanagan and J. A. Green (Basingstoke, 2005), 107–119.

Herren, M. W., 'Some new light on the life of Virgilius Maro Grammaticus', *Proceedings of the Royal Irish Academy* 79C (1979): 27–71.

Herren, M. W., 'Insular Latin *c(h)arazare* (craxare) and its derivatives', *Peritia* 1 (1982): 273–280.

Herren, M. W., 'Sprachliche Eigentümlichkeiten in den hibernolateinischen Texten des 7. und 8. Jahrhunderts', in *Die Iren und europa im früheren Mittelalter*, ed. H. Löwe (Stuttgart, 1982), 1:425–433.

Herren, M. W., 'Old Irish lexical and semantic influence on Hiberno-Latin', in *Ireland and Europe: The Early Church*, ed. P. Ní Chatháin and M. Richter (Stuttgart, 1984), 197–209.

Herren, M. W., 'Latin and the vernacular languages', in *Medieval Latin: An Introduction and Bibliographical Guide*, ed. F. A. C. Mantello and A. G. Rigg (Washington, DC, 1996), 122–129.

Howlett, D. R., '*Synodus prima Sancti Patricii*: an exercise in textual reconstruction', *Peritia* 12 (1998): 238–253.

Howlett, D. R., 'The prologue to the *Collectio canonum Hibernensis*', *Peritia* 17–18 (2003–2004): 144–149.

Hughes, K., *The Church in Early Irish Society* (London, 1966).

Hughes, K., *Early Christian Ireland: Introduction to the Sources* (London, 1972).

Hughes, K., 'Synodus II S. Patricii', *Latin Script and Letters A.D. 400–900. Festschrift Presented to Ludwig Bieler on the Occasion of His 70th Birthday*, ed. J. J. O'Meara and B. Naumann (Leiden, 1976), 141–147.

Hull, V. E., 'Bretha im gatta', *ZCP* 25 (1956): 211–225.

Ireland, C., 'Aldfrith of Northumbria and the learning of a *sapiens*', in *A Celtic Florilegium: Studies in Memory of Brendan O Hehir*, ed. K. A. Klar, E. E. Sweester and C. Thomas, Celtic Studies Publications 11 (Lawrence, MA, 1996), 63–77.

Jackson, K. H., *Language and History in Early Britain* (Edinburgh, 1953).

Jaffé, P., *Regesta pontificum Romanorum ab condita ecclesia ad annum post Christum natum MCXCVIII. Editio tertia*, revised by M. Schütz *et al.*, 3rd ed. (Göttingen, 2016–2017).

Jaski, B., 'Marriage laws in Ireland and on the continent in the early middle ages', in *The Fragility of her Sex*, ed. C. E. Meek and M. Simms (Dublin, 1996), 16–42.

Jaski, B., 'Early medieval Irish kingship and the Old Testament', *Early Medieval Europe* 7 (1998): 329–344.

Jaski, B., 'Cú Chuimne, Ruben and the compilation of the *Collectio canonum Hibernensis*', *Peritia* 14 (2000): 51–69.

Jasper, D., and H. Fuhrmann, *Papal Letters in the Early Middle Ages* (Washington, DC, 2001).

Jenkins, D., *'Holy, Holier, Holiest'. The Sacred Topography of the Early Medieval Irish Church* (Turnhout, 2010).

Johnston, E., *Literacy and Identity in Early Medieval Ireland* (Woodbridge, 2013).

John Paul II (promulgator), *Code of Canon Law: Latin-English Edition. New English Translation* (Washington, DC, 1998).

Kelleher, J. V., *Too Small for Stove Wood, Too Big for Kindling. Collected Verse and Translations* (Dublin, 1979).

Kelly, F., 'An Old Irish text on court procedure', *Peritia* 5 (1986): 74–106.

Kelly, F., *A Guide to Early Irish Law*, Early Irish Law Series 3 (Dublin, 1988).

Kelly, F., *Early Irish Farming*, Early Irish Law Series 4 (Dublin, 1997).

Kenney, J. F., *The Sources for the Early History of Ireland: Ecclesiastical* (Columbia, NY, 1929).

Ker, N. R., 'The handwriting of Archbishop Wulfstan', in *England before the Conquest*, ed. P. Clemoes and K. Hughes (Cambridge, 1971), 315–332.

Ker, N. R., in E. G. W. Bill, *A Catalogue of Manuscripts in Lambeth Palace Library, MSS. 1222–1860* (Oxford, 1972).

Kéry, L., *Canonical Collections of the Early Middle Ages* (ca. 400–1140) (Washington, DC, 1999).

Keynes, S. D., 'Anglo-Saxon church councils', *Handbook of British Chronology*, 3rd ed., ed. E. B. Fryde, *et al.* (London, 1986), 583–589.

Keynes, S. D., 'The councils of Clofesho', Brixworth Lecture (1994).

Körntgen, L., 'Der *Excarpsus Cummeani*, ein Bussbuch aus Corbie?', in *Scientia Veritatis. Festschrift für Hubert Mordek*, ed. O. Münsch and T. Zotz (Sigmaringen, 2004), 59–75.

Kottje, R., *Studien zum Einfluss des Alten Testaments auf Recht und Liturgie des frühen Mittelalters: (6.–8. Jahrhundert)* (Bonn, 1964).

Kottje, R., 'Die frühmittelalterlichen kontinentalen Bussbücher: Bericht über ein Forschungsvorhaben an der Universität Augsburg (nunc Bonn)', *Bulletin of Medieval Canon Law*, n.s. 7 (1977): 108–111.

Kuttner, S. G., *A Catalogue of Canonical and Roman Law Manuscripts in the Vatican Library*, Studi e Testi 322, 328, 2 vols. (Vatican, 1986–1987).

Lapidge, M., and M. Herren, *Aldhelm: The Prose Works* (New Jersey, 1979).

Lapidge, M., and R. Sharpe, *A Bibliography of Celtic Latin Literature 400–1200* (Dublin, 1985).

Lapidge, M., ed., *Archbishop Theodore: Commemorative Studies on His Life and Influence* (Cambridge, 1995).

Lapidge, M., 'The career of Archbishop Theodore', in *Archbishop Theodore: Commemorative Studies on His Life and Influence*, ed. M. Lapidge (Cambridge, 1995), 1–29.

Le Bras, G., 'Sur la part d'Isidore de Séville et des Espagnols dans l'histoire des collections canoniques, à propos d'un livre récent (P. Séjourne)', *Revue des sciences religieuses* 10 (1930): 218–257.

Leumann, M., J. B. Hofmann, and A. Szantyr, *Lateinische Grammatik*, 2 vols. (Munich, 1965–1977).

Levison, W., Review of P. W. Finsterwalder, ed., *Die Canones Theodori Cantuariensis und ihre Überlieferungsformen* (Weimar, 1929), in *Zeitschrift der Savigny-Stiftung für Rechtsgeschichte: Kanonistische Abteilung* 19 (1930): 699–707.

Liddell, H. G., R. Scott, and H. S. Jones, *A Greek-English Lexicon* (rev. ed. Oxford, 1968).

Lindsay, W. M., 'Breton scriptoria: their Latin abbreviation-symbols', *Zentralblatt für Bibliothekswesen* 29 (1912): 264–272.

Lindsay, W. M., *Notae Latinae. An Account of Abbreviation in Latin MSS. of the Early Minuscule Period (c. 700–850)* (Cambridge, 1915).

Loew, E. A., *The Beneventan Script* (Oxford, 1914).

Loew, E. A., *The Beneventan Script: A History of the South Italian Minuscule*, 2nd enlarged edition prepared by V. Brown, Sussidi eruditi 33–34, 2 vols. (Rome, 1980).

Loofs, F., *Antiquae Britonum Scotorumque ecclesiae* (Leipzig, 1882).

Löfstedt, B., *Der hibernolatenische Grammatiker Malsachanus* (Uppsala, 1965).

Löfstedt, B., 'Some linguistic remarks on Hiberno-Latin', *Studia Hibernica* 19 (1979): 161–169.

Loth, J., 'Les gloses bretonnes d'Orléans', *Revue Celtique* 5 (1882): 104–115.

Lowe, E. A., ed., *Codices Latini antiquiores*, 12 vols. (Oxford, 1934–1972).

Lucas, A. T., 'The plundering and burning of churches in Ireland, 7th to 16th century', in *North Munster Studies: Essays in Commemoration of Monsignor Michael Moloney*, ed. E. Rynne (Limerick, 1967), 172–229.

Maassen, F., *Geschichte der Quellen und der Literatur des canonischen Rechts im Abendlande bis zum Ausgange des Mittelalters* (Graz, 1870).

Mabillon, J., *De re diplomatica* (Paris, 1681; supplement, 1704).

Mac Coisdealbha, P., *The Syntax of the Sentence in Old Irish: Selected Studies from a Descriptive, Historical and Comparative Point of View* (Tübingen, 1998).

Madan, F., E. H. Craster, and N. Denholm-Young, *A Summary Catalogue of Western Manuscripts in the Bodleian Library at Oxford* (Oxford, 1937).

Markus, R. A., *Gregory the Great and His World* (Cambridge, 1997).

Marstrander, C., E. G. Quin *et al.* ed., *Contributions to a Dictionary of the Irish Language* (Dublin, 1913–1976).

Maurus Inguanez, D., ed., *Codicum Casiensium manuscriptorum catalogus*, 3 vols. (Monte Cassino, 1915–1941).

McCone, K., *Pagan Past and Christian Present in Early Irish Literature* (Maynooth, 1990).

McKee, H., ed., *Juvencus Codex Cantabrigiensis Ff.4.42* (Aberystwyth, 2000).

McKitterick, R., *History and Memory in the Carolingian World* (Cambridge, 2004).

McLeod, N., *Early Irish Contract Law* (Sydney, 1992).

McNally, R. E., '*Dies dominica*: two Hiberno-Latin texts', *Medieval Studies* 22 (1960): 355–361.

McNeill J. T., and H. M. Gamer, tr., *Medieval Handbooks of Penance: a Translation of the Principal "libri poenitentiales" and Selection from Related Documents* (New York, 1938; repr. 1990).

Meeder, S., 'The early Irish Stowe Missal's destination and function', *Early Medieval Europe* 13 (2005): 179–196.

Meeder, S., 'The spread and reception of Hiberno-Latin scholarship on the Continent in the eighth and ninth centuries', Ph.D dissertation, University of Cambridge (2010).

Meeder, S., 'The *Liber ex lege Moysi*: notes and text', *Journal of Medieval Latin* 19 (2009): 173–218.

Meeder, S., 'Boniface and the Irish Heresy of Clemens', *Church History* 80 (2011): 251–280.

Meens, R., *Het tripartite boeteboek. Overlevering en betekenis van vroegmiddeleeuwse biechtvoorschriften (met editie en vertaling van vier 'tripartita')* (Hilversum, 1994).

Meens, R., 'Pollution in the early middle ages: the case of the food regulations in penitentials', *Early Medieval Europe* 4 (1995): 3–19.

Meens, R., 'Politics, mirrors of princes and the Bible: sins, kings and the well-being of the realm', *Early Medieval Europe* 7 (1998): 345–357.

Meens, R., 'The uses of the Old Testament in early medieval canon law. The *Collectio vetus Gallica* and the *Collectio Hibernensis*', in *The Uses of the Past in the Early Middle Ages*, ed., Y. Hen and M. Innes (Cambridge, 2000), 67–77.

Meens, R., 'The oldest manuscript witness of the *Collectio canonum Hibernensis*', *Peritia* 14 (2000): 1–19.

Meens, R., 'Sanctuary, penance, and dispute settlement under Charlemagne: the conflict between Alcuin and Theodulf of Orléans over a sinful cleric', *Speculum* 82 (2007): 277–300.

Meyvaert, P., 'Diversity within unity: a Gregorian theme', *Heythrop Journal* 4 (1963): 141–162.

Meyvaert, P., 'Bede's text of the *Libellus responsionum* of Gregory the Great to Augustine of Canterbury', in *England before the Conquest*, ed. P. Clemoes and K. Hughes (Cambridge, 1971), 15–33.

Meyvaert, P., 'Le Libellus responsionum à Augustine de Cantorbéry: une oeuvre authentique de saint Grégoire le Grand', in *Grégoire le Grand*, ed. J. Fontaine, R. Gillet and S. Pellistrandi (Paris, 1986), 543–550.

Migne, J.-P., ed., *Patrologia Latina*, 221 vols. (Paris, 1844–1864).

Moore, M., 'The Body of Pope Formosus', *Millennium. Jahrbuch zur Kultur und Geschichte des ersten Jahrtausends n. Chr.* 9 (2012): 277–297.

Mordek, H., *Kirchenrecht und Reform im Frankenreich: Die Collectio vetus Gallica, die älteste systematische Kanonessammlung des fränkischen Gallien: Studien und Edition*, Beiträge zur Geschichte und Quellenkunde des Mittelalters 1 (Berlin & New York, 1975).

Mordek, H., and Reynolds, R. E., 'Bischof Leodegar und das Konzil von Autun', in *Aus Archiven und Bibliotheken: Festschrift fur Raymund Kottje zum 65. Geburtstag*, ed. H. Mordek (Frankfurt, 1992), 71–92.

Mordek, H., *Bibliotheca capitularium regum Francorum manuscripta. Überlieferung und Traditionszusammenhang der fränkischen Herrschererlasse* (Munich, 1995).

Most, G., *The Syntax of the Vitae sanctorum Hiberniae* (Washington, DC, 1946).

Munier, C., *Les sources patristiques du droit de l'Église du VIIIe au XIIIe siècle* (Strasbourg, 1957).

Munier, C., *Les statuta ecclesiae antiqua. Édition, Études critiques* (Paris, 1960).

Naz, R., ed., *Dictionnaire de droit canonique*, 7 vols. (Paris, 1935–1965).

Nicholson, E. W. B., 'The origin of the "Hibernian" collection of canons', *ZCP* 3 (1899–1901): 99–103.

Ní Dhonnchadha, M., 'The guarantor list of *Cáin Adomnáin, 697*', *Peritia* 1 (1982): 178–215.

Niermeyer, F., and C. van de Kieft, *Mediae Latinitatis Lexicon Minus*, 2 vols. (Leiden, 1976).

Nürnberger, A. J., 'Über die Würzburger Handschrift der irischen Canonensammlung', *Archiv für katholisches Kirchenrecht* 60 (1888): 3–84.

Nürnberger, A. J., 'Über eine ungedruckte Kanonensammlung aus dem 8 Jahrhundert', in *Bericht der wissenschaftlichen Gesellschaft Philomathie in Neisse* 25 (1888–1890): 118–197.

O'Brien, E., 'Pagan and Christian burial in Ireland during the first millennium A.D.: continuity and change', in *The Early Church in Wales and the West: Recent Work in Early Christian Archaeology, History and Place-Names*, ed. N. Edwards and A. Lane (Oxford, 1992), 130–137.

O'Brien, E., 'Literary insights into the basis of some burial practices in Ireland and Anglo-Saxon England in the seventh and eighth centuries', *Aedificia Nova. Studies in Honor of Rosemary Cramp* (Michigan, 2008), 283–299.

Ó Carragáin, T., 'The architectural setting of the cult of relics in early medieval Ireland', *Journal of the Royal Society of Antiquaries of Ireland* 133 (2003): 130–176.

Ó Corráin, D., 'Nationality and kingship in pre-Norman Ireland', in *Nationality and the Pursuit of National Independence*, ed. T. W. Moody, Historical Studies 11 (Belfast, 1978), 1–35.

Ó Corráin, D., 'The early Irish churches: some aspects of organisation', in *Irish Antiquity: Essays and Studies Presented to Professor M. J. O'Kelly*, ed. D. Ó Corráin (Cork, 1981), 327–341.

Ó Corráin, D., 'Irish law and canon law', in *Ireland und Europe: The Early Church*, ed. P. Ní Chatháin and M. Richter (Stuttgart, 1984), 157–166.

Ó Corráin, D., L. Breatnach, and A. Breen, 'The laws of the Irish', *Peritia* 3 (1984): 382–438.

Ó Corráin, D., 'Irish origin legends and genealogy: recurrent aetiologies', in *History and Heroic Tale: a Symposium* (Odesne, 1985), 51–96.

Ó Corráin, D., 'Marriage in early Ireland', in *Marriage in Ireland*, ed. A. Cosgrove (Dublin, 1985), 5–24.

Ó Corráin, D., 'Irish vernacular law and the Old Testament', *Ireland and Christendom: The Bible and the Missions*, ed. P. Ní Chatháin and M. Richter (Stuttgart, 1987), 284–307.

Ó Corráin, D., 'Women and the law in early Ireland', in *Chattel, Servant or Citizen: Women's Status in Chruch, State, and Society*, ed. M. O'Dowd and S. Wichert (Belfast, 1995), 45–57.

Ó Corráin, D., 'Congressio senadorum', *Peritia* 10 (1996): 252.

Ó Corráin, D., 'Creating the past: the early Irish genealogical tradition', *Peritia* 12 (1998): 177–208.

Ó Corráin, D., 'Synodus II Patricii and vernacular law', *Peritia* 16 (2002): 335–343.

Ó Corráin, D., 'Ireland *c.* 800: aspects of society', in *A New History of Ireland I*, ed. D. Ó Cróinín (Oxford, 2005), 549–608.

Ó Corráin, D., 'The church and secular society', in *L'Irlanda e gli irlandesi nell'alto medioevo*, Atti delle Settimane di studio CISAM 57 (Spoleto, 2010), 261–323.

Ó Cróinín, D., 'Mo-Sinnu moccu Min and the computus of Bangor', *Peritia* 1 (1982): 281–295.

Ó Cróinín, D., *Early Medieval Ireland 400–1200* (London, 1995).

O'Donovan, J., *et al.*, ed., *Ancient Laws of Ireland*, 6 vols. (Dublin, 1865–1901).

O'Dwyer, P., *Céli dé: Spiritual Reform in Ireland 750–900* (2nd ed., Dublin, 1981).

Ó Néill, P., 'The Old-Irish treatise on the Psalter and its Hiberno-Latin background', *Ériu* 30 (1979): 148–164.

Ó Néill, P., 'The background to the Cambrai Homily', *Ériu* 32 (1981): 137–148.

Ó Néill, P., ed., *Psalterium Suthantoniense*, CCCM 240 (2012).

O'Sullivan, A., F. McCormick, T. Kerr and L. Harney, *Early Medieval Ireland, Archaeological Excavations 1930–2004*, Early Medieval Archaeology Project (EMAP) Report 2.1 (Dublin, 2008).
http://www.ucd.ie/t4cms/emap_report_2_1_complete.pdf

Pächt, O., and J. J. G. Alexander, *Illuminated Manuscripts in the Bodleian Library*, 3 vols. (Oxford, 1966–1973; concordance of shelfmarks, 1974).

Parkes, M. B., 'The handwriting of St. Boniface. A reassessment of the Problems', *Beiträge zur Geschichte der deutschen Sprache und Literatur* 98 (1976): 162–179.

Padel, O. J., 'The new pre-conquest charters from Cornwall', *Cornish Studies* 6 (1979): 20–27.

Pettiau, H., 'A prosopography of Breton rulership', *Journal of Celtic Studies* 4 (2004): 171–189.

Picard, J.,-M., 'The Schaffhaausen Adomnán: a unique witness to Hiberno-Latin', *Peritia* 1 (1982): 216–249.

Picard, J.,-M., Review of J. Chittenden, ed., *Donatus Orthographicus, Ars Grammatica*, CCCM 40D (1982) in *Peritia* 5 (1986): 427–430.

Picard, J.,-M., 'The Latin language in early medieval Ireland', in *The Languages of Ireland*, ed. M.. Cronin and C. Ó Cuilleanáin (Dublin, 2003): 44–56.

Picard, J.,-M., 'Christianisation et hiérarchie dans la société irlandaise des VIIe et VIIIe siècles', in *Hiérarchie et stratification sociale dans l'Occident médiéval (400–1100)*, ed. F. Bougard, D. Logna-Prat, R. LeJan (Turnhout, 2008), 23–38.

Pilone, R., 'Scrittura beneventana e scrittura carolina a proposito di un recente saggio', *Benedictina* 30 (1983): 203–208.

Pozzi, G. P., 'Le manuscrit tomus XVIIIus de la Vallicelliana et le libelle *De episcoporum transmigratione et quod non temere iudicentur regule quadraginta quattuor*', *Apollinaris* 30 (1958): 313–350.

Prothero, G. W., *A Memoir of Henry Bradshaw, Fellow of King's College, Cambridge, and University Librarian* (London, 1888).

Pryce, H., 'Early Irish canons and medieval Welsh law', *Peritia* 5 (1986): 107–127.

Quin, E. G., C. Marstrander, *et al.* ed., *Contributions to a Dictionary of the Irish Language* (Dublin, 1913–1976).

Reynolds, R. E., 'Excerpta from the *Collectio Hibernensis* in three Vatican manuscripts', *Bulletin of Medieval Canon Law* n.s. 5 (1975): 1–9.

Reynolds, R. E., *The Ordinals of Christ from their Origins to the Twelfth Century*, Beiträge zur Geschichte und Quellenkunde des Mittelalters 7 (Berlin & New York, 1978).

Reynolds, R. E., 'Unity and diversity in Carolingian canon law collections: the case of the *Collectio canonum Hibernensis* and its derivatives', in *Carolingian Essays*, ed. U.-R. Blumenthal (Washington, DC, 1983), 99–135.

Reynolds, R. E., 'Odilo and the *treuga Dei* in southern Italy: a Beneventan manuscript fragment', *Mediaeval Studies* 46 (1984): 450–462.

Reynolds, R. E., 'Law, Canon: to Gratian', in *Dictionary of the Middle Ages*, ed. J. R. Strayer *et al.*, 13 vols. (New York, 1982–1989), 7:395–413.

Reynolds, R. E., 'Clerics in the early middle ages: hierarchies and functions', in his *Clerics in the Early Middle Ages. Hierarchy and Image* (Aldershot, 1999), 1–31.

Reynolds, R. E., 'The "Isidorian" *Epistula ad Massonam* on lapsed clerics: notes on its early manuscript and textual transmission', *Grundlagen des Rechts: Festschrift für Peter Landau*, ed. R. Helmholz, P. Mikat, J. Müller, and M. Stolleis (Paderborn, 2000), 77–92.

Reynolds, R. E., 'The transmission of the *Hibernensis* in Italy: tenth to twelfth century', *Peritia* 14 (2000): 20–50.

Reynolds, R. E., 'Further evidence for the influence of the *Hibernensis* in Southern Italy: an early eleventh-century canonistic *florilegium* at Montecassino', *Peritia* 19 (2005): 119–135.

Reynolds, R. E., 'The influence of the Eastern patristic Fathers on the canonical collections of south Italy in the eleventh and early twelfth centuries', in *Canon Law, Religion, and Politics: Liber Amicorum Robert Sumerville*, ed. U.-R. Blumenthal, A. Winroth, and P. Landau (Washington, DC, 2012), 75–106.

Richter, M., 'Dating the Irish Synods in the *Collectio canonum Hibernensis*', *Peritia* 14 (2000): 70–84.

Rosenthal, C. L., *The 'Vitae Patrum' in Old and Middle English Literature* (Philadelphia, 1936).

Schüling, H., 'Die Handbibliothek des Bonifatius', *Archiv für Geschichte des Buchwesens* 4 (1963): 325–327.

Seckel, E., 'Studien zu Benedictus Levita VIII (Studie VIII, Teil I)', *Neues Archiv* 39 (1914): 327–431.

Sharpe, R., 'Vitae S. Brigitae: the oldest texts', *Peritia* 1 (1982): 81–106.

Sharpe, R., 'Some problems concerning the organization of the church in early medieval Ireland', *Peritia* 3 (1984): 230–270.

Sharpe, R., 'Armagh and Rome in the seventh century', in *Irland und Europa: die Kirche im Frühmittelalter*, ed. P. Ní Chatháin and M. Richter (Stuttgart, 1984), 58–72.

Sharpe, R., 'Gildas as a Father of the Church', in *Gildas: New Approaches*, ed. M. Lapidge and D. N. Dumville (Woodbridge, 1984), 191–206.

Sharpe, R., *Medieval Irish Saints' Lives: An Introduction to* Vitae Sanctorum Hiberniae (Oxford, 1991).

Sharpe, R., 'An Irish textual critic and the *Carmen paschale* of Sedulius: Colmán's letter to Feradach', *Journal of Medieval Latin* 2 (1992): 44–54.

Sharpe, R., 'Churches and communities in early medieval Ireland: towards a pastoral model', in *Pastoral Care before the Parish*, ed. J. Blair and R. Sharpe (Leicester, 1992), 81–109.

Sharpe, R., tr., *Adomnán of Iona. Life of St. Columba* (London, 1995).

Sheehy, M. P., 'Influences of ancient Irish law on the *Collectio canonum Hibernensis*', *Proceedings of the Third International Congress of Medieval Canon Law*, ed. S. Kuttner (Vatican, 1971), 31–41.

Sheehy, M. P., 'The *Collectio canonum Hibernensis*: a Celtic phenomenon', in *Die Iren und Europa im früheren Mittelalter*, ed. H. Löwe (Stuttgart, 1982), 525–535.

Sheehy, M. P., 'The Bible and the *Collectio canonum Hibernensis*', *Ireland and Christendom. The Bible and the Missions*, ed. P. Ní Chatháin and M. Richter (Stuttgart, 1987), 277–283.

Simpson, D., 'The "*Proverbia Grecorum*"', *Traditio* 43 (1987): 1–22.

Simpson, H., 'Ireland, Tours and Brittany: the case of Cambridge, Corpus Christi College, MS. 279', in *Irlande et Bretagne, vingt siècles d'histoire* (Rennes, 1993), 108–123.

Sims-Williams, P., 'Thought, word and deed: an Irish triad', *Ériu* 29 (1978): 78–111.

Sims-Williams, P., 'The uses of writing in early medieval Wales', in *Literacy in Medieval Celtic Societies*, ed. A. H. Pryce (Cambridge, 1998), 15–38.

Smith, J. M. H., *Province and Empire. Brittany and the Carolingians* (Cambridge, 1992).

Smyth, M., 'The seventh-century Hiberno-Latin treatise *Liber de ordine creaturarum*. A translation', *Journal of Medieval Latin* 21 (2011): 137–222.

Souter, A., *A Glossary of Later Latin to 600 A.D.* (Oxford, 1949).

Stacey, R. Chapman, *The Road to Judgment: From Custom to Court in Medieval Ireland and Wales* (Pennsylvania, 1994).

Stancliffe, C., 'Red, white and blue martyrdom', in *Ireland in Early Mediaeval Europe. Studies in memory of Kathleen Hughes*, ed. D. N. Dumville *et al.* (Cambridge, 1982), 21–46.

Stancliffe, C., *Bede, Wilfrid, and the Irish* (Jarrow, 2003).

Stevenson, J., 'Literacy in Ireland: the evidence from the Patrick dossier in the Book of Armagh', in R. McKitterick, ed., *The Uses of Literacy in Early Medieval Europe* (Cambridge, 1990), 11–35.

Stickler, A. M., *Historia Iuris Canonici Latini. Historia Fontium* (Rome, 1950).

Stokes, W., *Old-Breton Glosses* (Calcutta, 1879). Repr. *Revue Celtique* 4 (1879–1880): 324–348.

Stokes, W., ed., *The Breton Glosses at Orleans* (Calcutta, 1880).

Stokes, W., ed. and tr., 'The Irish ordeals', in *Irische Texte*, 3rd ser. 1 (Leipzig, 1891), 183–229.

Stokes, W., and J. Strachan, ed., *Thesaurus Palaeohibernicus*, 2 vols. (Cambridge, 1901–1903).

Stotz, P., *Handbuch zur lateinischen Sprache des Mittelalters*, 5 vols. (Munich, 1996–2004).

Stresser, I., 'Irisches im Althochdeutschen', in *Die Iren und europa im früheren Mittelalter*, ed. H. Löwe (Stuttgart, 1982), 399–424.

Supino Martini, P., 'Carolina romana e minuscola romanesca. Appunti per una storia della scrittura latina in Roma tra IX e XII secolo', *Studi medievali*, Serie terza 15.2 (1974): 769–794.

Thesaurus linguae Latinae → Von Wölfflin.

Thiel, A., *Epistolae Romanorum Pontificum... Tomus I. a S. Hilaro usque ad Pelagium II, ann. 461–523* (Braunsberg, 1868).

Thurneysen, R., 'Zur irischen Kanonensammlung', *ZCP* 6 (1908): 1–5.

Thurneysen, R., 'Aus dem irischen Recht IV: Zu den bisherigen Ausgaben der irischen Rechtstexte', *ZCP* 16 (1927): 167–230.

Thurneysen, R., ed., *Die Bürgschaft im irischen Recht*, Abhandlungen der preussischen Akademie der Wissenschaften, Phil.-Hist. Klasse. Nr. 2 (Berlin, 1928).

Thurneysen, R., 'Aus dem irischen Recht V: Zu der Etymologie von ir. *ráth* 'Bürgschaft' und zu der irischen Kanonensammlung und den Triaden', *ZCP* 18 (1930): 364–375.

Thurneysen, R., *Studies in Early Irish Law* (Dublin, 1936).

Thurneysen, R., *A Grammar of Old Irish*, tr. D. A. Binchy and O. Bergin (Dublin, 1961).

Tristano, C., 'Scrittura beneventana e scrittura carolina in manoscritti dell'-Italia meridionale', *Scrittura e civilità* 3 (1979): 89–150.

Turner, C. H., *Ecclesiae occidentalis monumenta iuris antiquissima*, 2 vols. (Oxford, 1899–1939).

Ullmann, W., 'On the use of the term *Romani* in the sources of the earlier middle ages', *Studia Patristica* 2 (1957): 155–163.

Ullmann, W., *The Growth of Papal Government in the Middle Ages. A Study in the Ideological Relation of Clerical to Lay Power*, 3rd ed. (London, 1970).

Ussher, J., *Britannicarum ecclesiarum antiquitates* (Dublin, 1639).

Van De Wiel, C., *History of Canon Law*, Louvain Theological and Pastoral Monographs 5 (Louvain, 1991).

Von Wölfflin, E., *et al.*, ed., *Thesaurus linguae Latinae: Editus auctoritate et consilio academiarum quinque Germanicarum Berolinensis, Gottingensis, Lipsiensis, Monacensis, Vindobonensis* (Leipzig, 1900–).

Wallach, L., *Alcuin and Charlemagne. Studies in Carolingian History and Literature* (Ithaca, 1959).

Ward, B., tr., *The Desert Fathers. Sayings of the Early Christian Monks* (London, 2003).

Ware [Waræus], J., *S. Patricio qui Hibernos ad fidem Christi conuertit adscripta Opuscula* (London, 1656).

Warntjes, I., 'Regnal succession in early medieval Ireland', *Journal of Medieval History* 30 (2004): 377–410.

Wasserschleben, F. W. H., *Die irische Kanonensammlung* (Giessen, 1874; 2nd ed. Leipzig, 1885; repr. 1966).

Webster L. and J. Backhouse, ed., *The Making of England: Anglo-Saxon Art and Culture, AD 600–900* (London, 1991).

Wickham, C., *Framing the Early Middle Ages. Europe and the Mediterranean 400–800* (Oxford, 2005).

Winterbottom, M., 'Notes on the text of Gildas,' *Journal of Theological Studies*, n.s. 27 (1976): 132–140.

Wood, I.N., 'Pagan religion and superstitions east of the Rhine from the fifth to the ninth century', in *After Empire*, ed. G. Ausenda (Woodbridge, 1995), 253–268.

Wood, S., *The Proprietary Church in the Medieval West* (Oxford, 2006).

Wormald, C. P., 'Archbishop Wulfstan and the Holiness of Society', in *Anglo-Saxon History: Basic Readings*, ed. D. A. E. Pelteret (New York, 2000), 191–224.

Wright, C. D., *The Irish Tradition in Old English Literature* (Cambridge, 1993).

Wurm, H., *Studien und Texte zur Dekretalensammlung des Dionysius Exiguus* (Bonn, 1939).

Young, P., *Catalogus Librorum Manuscriptorum Bibliothecae Wigorniensis* [prepared in 1622–1623], ed. I. Atkins and N. R. Ker (Cambridge, 1944).

Zechiel-Eckes, K., 'Die Hibernensis-Redaktion der Kölner Domhandschrift 210', *Zeitschrift der Savigny-Stiftung für Rechtsgeschichte. Kanonistische Abteilung* 131 (2014): 553–562.

Indexes

Wasserschleben to Flechner conversion table

• The coordinates below refer to Wasserschleben's 1885 edition

Praefatio

p. 3	p. 1

Liber I

Caput 1

a	p. 4 ln. 9
b	p. 4 ln. 12
c	p. 4 ln. 17

Caput 2

a	p. 5 ln. 11
b	p. 5 ln. 12
c	p. 5 ln. 14

Caput 3

p. 6 ln. 2

Caput 4

a	p. 6 ln. 12
b	p. 7 ln. 3

Caput 5

a	p. 7 ln. 8
b	p. 7 ln. 13

Caput 6

a	p. 7 ln. 17
b	p. 8 ln. 1

Caput 7

a	p. 8 ln. 6
b	p. 8 ln. 9
c	p. 8 ln. 11
d	p. 8 ln. 14
e	p. 9 ln. 5

Caput 8

a	p. 9 ln. 11
b	p. 9 ln. 21
c	p. 9 ln. 21

Caput 9

a	p. 11 ln. 2
b	p. 11 ln. 4
c	Only in K fol. 5^r

Caput 10

a	p. 11 ln. 9
b	p. 44 ln. 11
c	p. 11 ln. 12
d	p. 11 ln. 14
e	p. 11 ln. 16
f	p. 11 ln. 18
g	p. 12 ln. 1
h	p. 12 ln. 3
i	p. 12 ln. 4
k	p. 12 ln. 7
l	p. 12 ln. 9
m	p. 12 ln. 11
n	p. 12 ln. 14
o	p. 12 ln. 15
p	p. 12 ln. 17

Caput 11

a	p. 13 ln. 2
b	p. 13 ln. 8
c	p. 13 ln. 13

Caput 12

p. 14 ln. 10

Caput 13

p. 14 ln. 13

Caput 14

a	p. 14 ln. 18
b	p. 15 ln. 1

Caput 15

p. 15 ln. 7

Caput 16

a p. 15 ln. 10
b p. 15 ln. 13
c p. 15 ln. 15

Caput 17

a p. 16 ln. 3
b p. 16 ln. 6
c p. 16 ln. 10
d p. 16 ln. 14
e p. 16 ln. 16

Caput 18

a p. 17 ln. 3
b p. 17 ln. 5

Caput 19

p. 17 ln. 8

Caput 20

p. 18 ln. 2

Caput 21

p. 18 ln. 14

Caput 22

a p. 18 ln. 17
b p. 19 ln. 3
c p. 19 ln. 1

Liber II

Caput 1

a p. 19 ln. 13
b p. 19 ln. 13
c p. 19 ln. 18

Caput 2

p. 20 ln. 2

Caput 3

p. 20 ln. 9

Caput 4

p. 20 ln. 14

Caput 5

a p. 21 ln. 9
b p. 21 ln. 13

Caput 6

p. 22 ln. 3

Caput 7

p. 22 ln. 7

Caput 8

p. 23 ln. 3

Caput 9

p. 23 ln. 9

Caput 10

p. 23 ln. 13

Caput 11

a p. 24 ln. 9
b p. 24 ln. 11
c p. 24 ln. 14
d p. 24 ln. 16
e p. 24 ln. 17
f p. 25 ln. 1
g p. 25 ln. 3

Caput 12

p. 25 ln. 6

Caput 13

a p. 25 ln. 12
b p. 26 ln. 2
c p. 26 ln. 4

Caput 14

p. 26 ln. 9

Caput 15

a p. 26 ln. 13
b p. 26 ln. 16

Caput 16

p. 27 ln. 2

Caput 17

a p. 27 ln. 8
b p. 27 ln. 11

Caput 18

p. 27 ln. 17

Caput 19

p. 28 ln. 5

Caput 20

p. 28 ln. 2.20

Caput 21

p. 28 ln. 16

Caput 22

a p. 29 ln. 2
b p. 29 ln. 5
c p. 29 ln. 7

Caput 23

p. 29 ln. 11

Caput 24

p. 29 ln. 16

Caput 25

a p. 30 ln. 7
b p. 30 ln. 11

Caput 26

p. 30 ln. 15

Caput 27

p. 31 ln. 8

Liber III

Caput 1

p. 31 ln. 17

Caput 2

p. 32 ln. 2

Caput 3

p. 32 ln. 14

Caput 4

a p. 32 ln. 18
b p. 33 ln. 3

Caput 5

p. 33 ln. 8

Caput 6

a p. 34 ln. 2
b p. 34 ln. 5

Caput 7

p. 34 ln. 7

Caput 8

p. 34 ln. 10

Caput 9

p. 34 ln. 13

Caput 10

p. 34 ln. 15

Liber IV

Caput 1

p. 35 ln. 3

Caput 2

p. 35 ln. 6

Caput 3

p. 35 ln. 12

Caput 4

p. 36 ln. 2

Liber V

Caput 1

p. 36 ln. 8

Caput 2

p. 36 ln. 12

Caput 3

p. 37 ln. 2

Caput 4

p. 37 ln. 8

Liber VI

Caput 1

p. 37 ln. 14

Caput 2

p. 38 ln. 6

Liber VII

Caput 1

p. 38 ln. 12

Caput 2

p. 39 ln. 2

Caput 3

p. 39 ln. 6

Liber VIII

Caput 1

p. 39 ln. 13

Caput 2

p. 40 ln. 2

Liber IX

Caput 1

p. 40 ln. 14

Caput 2

a p. 41 ln. 2
b p. 41 ln. 12

Liber X

a p. 44 ln. 6
b p. 44 ln. 8
c p. 44 ln. 9
d p. 44 ln. 11
e p. 44 ln. 13
f p. 44 ln. 15
g p. 44 ln. 16
h p. 44 ln. 17
i p. 45 ln. 1
k p. 45 ln. 3
l p. 45 ln. 5
m p. 45 ln. 7
n p. 45 ln. 8
o p. 45 ln. 10
p p. 45 ln. 16
q p. 45 ln. 17
r p. 46 ln. 1
s p. 46 ln. 4
t p. 46 ln. 6
u p. 46 ln. 7
v p. 46 ln. 8
w p. 46 ln. 9
x p. 46 ln. 11
y p. 46 ln. 15

Liber XI

Caput 1

a p. 50 ln. 4
b p. 50 ln. 7

Caput 2

p. 50 ln. 15

Caput 3

p. 50 ln. 18

Caput 4

a p. 51 ln. 6
b p. 51 ln. 10

Caput 5

p. 52 ln. 3

Caput 6

p. 52 ln. 13

Liber XII

Caput 1

a p. 58 ln. 13
b p. 58 ln. 15

Caput 2

a p. 58 ln. 18
b p. 59 ln. 12
c p. 59 ln. 15
d p. 57 ln. 3
e p. 60 ln. 3
f p. 60 ln. 6

Caput 3

a p. 60 ln. 16
b p. 61 ln. 1
c p. 61 ln. 3

Caput 4

a p. 61 ln. 5
b p. 61 ln. 6
c p. 61 ln. 9
d p. 61 ln. 11

Caput 5

p. 61 ln. 18

Caput 6

a p. 62 ln. 6
b p. 62 ln. 8

Caput 7

p. 62 ln. 10

Caput 8

a p. 63 ln. 2
b p. 63 ln. 8
c p. 63 ln. 10

Caput 9

a p. 63 ln. 17
b p. 64 ln. 1
c p. 64 ln. 4

Caput 10

p. 64 ln. 7

Caput 11

p. 64 ln. 11

Caput 12

p. 64 ln. 15

Caput 13

p. 64 ln. 15

Caput 14

p. 65 ln. 6

Caput 15

a p. 65 ln. 11
b p. 65 ln. 15
c p. 66 ln. 6

Caput 16

p. 66 ln. 13

Liber XIII

Caput 1

p. 69 ln. 3

Caput 2

a p. 69 ln. 9
b p. 69 ln. 13
c p. 69 ln. 17

Caput 3

a p. 70 ln. 1
b p. 70 ln. 13
c p. 70 ln. 16

Caput 4

a p. 71 ln. 6
b p. 71 ln. 7

Caput 5

a p. 71 ln. 9
b p. 71 ln. 10

Caput 6

a p. 72 ln. 2
b p. 72 ln. 3
c p. 72 ln. 4
d p. 72 ln. 5
e p. 72 ln. 6
f p. 72 ln. 8

Caput 7

p. 72 ln. 12

Caput 8

p. 72 ln. 15

Liber XIV

Caput 1

p. 73 ln. 12

Caput 2

a p. 73 ln. 18
b p. 74 ln. 1

Caput 3

p. 75 ln. 2

Caput 4

p. 75 ln. 11

Caput 5

p. 75 ln. 15

Caput 6

a p. 76 ln. 5
b p. 76 ln. 7
c p. 76 ln. 8

Liber XV

Caput 1

p. 77 ln. 3

Caput 2

a p. 77 ln. 8
b p. 77 ln. 12
c p. 77 ln. 17

Caput 3

a p. 78 ln. 6
b p. 78 ln. 11
c p. 78 ln. 15

Caput 4

a p. 79 ln. 2
b p. 79 ln. 7

Caput 5

a p. 79 ln. 12
b p. 79 ln. 16

Caput 6

a p. 80 ln. 2
b p. 80 ln. 4
c p. 80 ln. 7

Caput 7

p. 80 ln. 12

Caput 8

a p. 81 ln. 3
b p. 81 ln. 6
c p. 81 ln. 8
d p. 81 ln. 12

Caput 9

p. 82 ln. 15

Liber XVI

Caput 1

a p. 84 ln. 6
b p. 84 ln. 7

Caput 2

p. 84 ln. 10

Caput 3

a p. 84 ln. 15
b p. 84 ln. 18
c p. 85 ln. 3
d p. 85 ln. 5

Caput 4

a p. 85 ln. 13
b p. 85 ln. 15
c p. 85 ln. 17

Caput 5

a p. 86 ln. 5
b p. 86 ln. 6

Caput 6

p. 87 ln. 5

Caput 7

a p. 87 ln. 10
b p. 87 ln. 11
c p. 87 ln. 13

Caput 8

a p. 87 ln. 15
b p. 87 ln. 17

Caput 9

a p. 87 ln. 15
b p. 88 ln. 7
c p. 88 ln. 8
d p. 88 ln. 9
e p. 88 ln. 10
f p. 88 ln. 12
g p. 88 ln. 14

Caput 10

a p. 89 ln. 2
b p. 89 ln. 8
c p. 89 ln. 21

Caput 11

a p. 90 ln. 3
b p. 90 ln. 6
c p. 90 ln. 10

Caput 12

p. 90 ln. 13

Caput 13

a p. 91 ln. 10
b p. 91 ln. 18
c p. 91 ln. 19
d p. 91 ln. 21
e p. 92 ln. 1

Caput 14

p. 92 ln. 6

Caput 15

p. 92 ln. 10

Liber XVII

Caput 1

p. 92 ln. 15

Caput 2

p. 93 ln. 3

Caput 3

a p. 93 ln. 8
b p. 93 ln. 13
c p. 93 ln. 15
d p. 93 ln. 16
e p. 94 ln. 6
f p. 94 ln. 8
g p. 94 ln. 10
h p. 94 ln. 12
i p. 94 ln. 14
k p. 94 ln. 16
l p. 94 ln. 18

Caput 4

p. 95 ln. 2

Caput 5

p. 97 ln. 17

Caput 6

p. 97 ln. 21

Caput 7

a p. 98 ln. 11
b p. 98 ln. 13

Caput 8

p. 98 ln. 15

Caput 9

a p. 99 ln. 9
b p. 99 ln. 11

Caput 10

p. 99 ln. 14

Caput 11

a p. 100 ln. 3
b p. 100 ln. 8

Caput 12

a p. 100 ln. 14
b p. 101 ln. 6

Caput 13

p. 101 ln. 13

Caput 14

a p. 101 ln. 20
b p. 102 ln. 2
c p. 102 ln. 6

Caput 15

a p. 102 ln. 10
b p. 102 ln. 16
c p. 103 ln. 4

Caput 16

p. 103 ln. 11

Liber XVIII

Caput 1

a p. 104 ln. 3
b p. 104 ln. 6
c p. 104 ln. 10
d p. 104 ln. 13
e p. 104 ln. 15

Caput 2

a p. 105 ln. 2
b p. 105 ln. 3
c p. 105 ln. 17

Caput 3

a p. 106 ln. 10
b p. 106 ln. 11

Caput 4

a p. 106 ln. 15
b p. 106 ln. 17

Caput 5

p. 107 ln. 3

Caput 6

a p. 107 ln. 9
b p. 107 ln. 20

Caput 7

a p. 108 ln. 15
b p. 109 ln. 4

Caput 8

a p. 109 ln. 11
b p. 109 ln. 16
c p. 110 ln. 1
d p. 110 ln. 7
e p. 110 ln. 11
f p. 110 ln. 15
g p. 110 ln. 17

Caput 9

p. 111 ln. 3

Liber XIX

p. 111 ln. 7

Liber XX

Caput 1

p. 112 ln. 3

Caput 2

a p. 112 ln. 6
b p. 112 ln. 11

Caput 3

a p. 113 ln. 6
b p. 113 ln. 8
c p. 113 ln. 10

Caput 4

a p. 114 ln. 3
b p. 114 ln. 9
c p. 114 ln. 10

Caput 5

a p. 114 ln. 13
b p. 114 ln. 16

Caput 6

p. 115 ln. 2

Liber XXI

Caput 1

a p. 116 ln. 13
b p. 116 ln. 18

Caput 2

p. 117 ln. 2

Caput 3

p. 118 ln. 16

Caput 4

p. 119 ln. 3

Caput 5

a p. 119 ln. 14
b p. 119 ln. 16

Caput 6

a p. 120 ln. 2
b p. 120 ln. 5

Caput 7

a p. 120 ln. 19
b p. 121 ln. 3
c p. 121 ln. 4
d p. 121 ln. 8
e p. 121 ln. 11

Caput 8

p. 121 ln. 14

Caput 9

a p. 122 ln. 11
b p. 122 ln. 14

Caput 10

a p. 124 ln. 2
b p. 124 ln. 5
c p. 124 ln. 8
d p. 124 ln. 13

Caput 11

a p. 124 ln. 16
b p. 125 ln. 6
c p. 125 ln. 11

Caput 12

p. 126 ln. 5

Caput 13

a p. 127 ln. 2
b p. 127 ln. 11

Caput 14

p. 128 ln. 2

Caput 15

a p. 129 ln. 2
b p. 129 ln. 9

Caput 16

p. 130 ln. 17

Caput 17

a p. 130 ln. 20
b p. 130 ln. 21
c p. 131 ln. 1
d p. 131 ln. 2
e p. 131 ln. 3
f p. 131 ln. 4
g p. 131 ln. 9

Caput 18

a p. 131 ln. 13
b p. 131 ln. 14

Caput 19

a p. 131 ln. 18
b p. 132 ln. 1

Caput 20

a p. 132 ln. 3
b p. 132 ln. 9
c p. 132 ln. 12
d p. 132 ln. 13
e p. 132 ln. 14
f p. 132 ln. 15

Caput 21

p. 133 ln. 17

Caput 22

p. 134 ln. 6

Caput 23

a p. 134 ln. 10
b p. 117 ln. 7
c p. 134 ln. 15
d p. 134 ln. 17
e p. 134 ln. 18

Caput 24

a p. 135 ln. 4
b p. 135 ln. 7

Caput 25

p. 135 ln. 11

Caput 26

a p. 135 ln. 15
b p. 136 ln. 6
c p. 136 ln. 8

Caput 27

a p. 136 ln. 14
b p. 136 ln. 18

Caput 28

p. 137 ln. 3

Caput 29

p. 137 ln. 11

Caput 30

p. 139 ln. 11

Caput 31

a p. 139 ln. 13
b p. 139 ln. 17
c p. 139 ln. 18

Liber XXII

Caput 1

p. 140 ln. 13

Caput 2

p. 140 ln. 15

Caput 3

a p. 141 ln. 14
b p. 141 ln. 15
c p. 141 ln. 17
d p. 141 ln. 18
e p. 142 ln. 1
f p. 142 ln. 2
g p. 142 ln. 3

Caput 4

p. 142 ln. 5

Caput 5

p. 142 ln. 12

Caput 6

p. 143 ln. 2

Liber XXIII

Caput 1

a p. 143 ln. 6
b p. 143 ln. 7

Caput 2

p. 143 ln. 9

Caput 3

a p. 143 ln. 11
b p. 143 ln. 12

Liber XXIV

Caput 1

p. 143 ln. 17

Caput 2

a p. 144 ln. 2
b p. 144 ln. 6

Caput 3

p. 144 ln. 9

Caput 4

a p. 144 ln. 12
b p. 144 ln. 15

Liber XXV

Caput 1

p. 145 ln. 12

Caput 2

p. 147 ln. 9

Caput 3

p. 147 ln. 14

Caput 4

a p. 148 ln. 8
b p. 149 ln. 5

Caput 5

p. 149 ln. 10
p. 149 ln. 11

Caput 6

a p. 149 ln. 13
b p. 149 ln. 15

Caput 7

p. 150 ln. 2

Caput 8

p. 150 ln. 6

Caput 9

a p. 150 ln. 12
b p. 150 ln. 13
c p. 151 ln. 1
d p. 151 ln. 4
e p. 151 ln. 5
f p. 151 ln. 9
g p. 151 ln. 12

Caput 10

a p. 151 ln. 14
b p. 151 ln. 15
c p. 152 ln. 14
d p. 152 ln. 19
e p. 152 ln. 21

Caput 11

p. 153 ln. 2

Caput 12

p. 153 ln. 6

Caput 13

a p. 154 ln. 2
b p. 154 ln. 9

Caput 14

a p. 155 ln. 8
b p. 155 ln. 19
c p. 156 ln. 1

Caput 15

a p. 156 ln. 13
b p. 156 ln. 17

Caput 16

a p. 157 ln. 2
b p. 157 ln. 3
c p. 157 ln. 5

Caput 17

a p. 157 ln. 13
b p. 158 ln. 1
c p. 158 ln. 3
d p. 158 ln. 5
e p. 158 ln. 6

Caput 18

a p. 74 ln. 1
b p. 158 ln. 12
c p. 158 ln. 16
d p. 158 ln. 17

Caput 19

a p. 159 ln. 5
b p. 159 ln. 7

Liber XXVI

Caput 1

a p. 159 ln. 11
b p. 159 ln. 13

Caput 2

a p. 160 ln. 4
b p. 160 ln. 5
c p. 160 ln. 6

Caput 3

a[b] p. 160 ln. 12
b p. 160 ln. 14

Caput 4

p. 161 ln. 6

Caput 5

p. 162 ln. 12

Liber XXVII

Caput 1

p. 162 ln. 16

Caput 2

p. 163 ln. 14

Caput 3

p. 163 ln. 18

Caput 4

p. 164 ln. 2

Caput 5

p. 164 ln. 6

Caput 6

p. 164 ln. 16

Caput 7

a p. 166 ln. 22
b p. 167 ln. 1
c p. 167 ln. 2
d p. 167 ln. 4

Caput 8

a p. 168 ln. 13
b p. 168 ln. 15
c p. 168 ln. 17
d p. 169 ln. 1
e p. 169 ln. 3
f p. 169 ln. 5

Caput 9

p. 169 ln. 8

Caput 10

p. 171 ln. 11

Caput 11

a p. 172 ln. 15
b p. 172 ln. 16
c p. 172 ln. 17
d p. 173 ln. 1
e p. 173 ln. 3
f p. 173 ln. 5
g p. 173 ln. 7

Caput 12

a p. 174 ln. 2
b p. 174 ln. 3
c p. 174 ln. 4
d p. 174 ln. 6
e p. 174 ln. 8
f p. 174 ln. 10
g p. 174 ln. 11
h p. 174 ln. 13
i p. 174 ln. 15
k p. 174 ln. 17

Caput 13

a p. 175 ln. 3
b p. 175 ln. 12
c p. 175 ln. 14
d p. 175 ln. 17

Caput 14

p. 176 ln. 2

Caput 15

a p. 176 ln. 13
b p. 176 ln. 17
c p. 177 ln. 1
d p. 177 ln. 2

Caput 16

p. 177 ln. 5

Caput 17

p. 177 ln. 14

Caput 18

p. 178 ln. 5

Caput 19

a p. 179 ln. 16
b p. 179 ln. 18
c p. 180 ln. 1
d p. 180 ln. 4
e p. 180 ln. 5
f p. 180 ln. 6
g p. 180 ln. 8

Caput 20

a p. 180 ln. 12
b p. 180 ln. 14
c p. 180 ln. 16
d p. 181 ln. 3
e p. 181 ln. 5
f p. 182 ln. 12, p. 182 ln. 13, p. 182 ln. 16

Caput 21

a p. 181 ln. 17
b p. 181 ln. 19
c p. 181 ln. 20

Caput 22

a p. 182 ln. 2
b p. 182 ln. 4

Caput 23

a p. 182 ln. 6
b p. 182 ln. 17

Caput 24

a p. 183 ln. 2
b p. 183 ln. 4

Caput 25

p. 183 ln. 8

Caput 26

p. 183 ln. 14

Liber XXVIII

Caput 1

p. 184 ln. 13

Caput 2

a p. 185 ln. 2
b p. 185 ln. 4

Caput 3

p. 185 ln. 13

Caput 4

p. 185 ln. 17

Caput 5

a p. 186 ln. 8
b p. 186 ln. 11

Caput 6

p. 186 ln. 4

Caput 7

a p. 186 ln. 16
b p. 187 ln. 1

Caput 8

p. 187 ln. 8

Caput 9

a p. 187 ln. 13
b p. 187 ln. 16

Caput 10

a p. 188 ln. 2
b p. 188 ln. 5
c p. 188 ln. 7

Caput 11

p. 188 ln. 12

Caput 12

a p. 189 ln. 4
b p. 189 ln. 7
c p. 189 ln. 9

Caput 13

a p. 189 ln. 13
b p. 189 ln. 14
c p. 189 ln. 15
d p. 189 ln. 18
e p. 190 ln. 1
f p. 190 ln. 2

Caput 14

a p. 190 ln. 9
b p. 190 ln. 11
c p. 190 ln. 11
d p. 190 ln. 15

Liber XXIX

Caput 1

p. 191 ln. 7

Caput 2

p. 192 ln. 3

Caput 3

a p. 192 ln. 19
b p. 193 ln. 8

Caput 4

a[b] p. 193 ln. 11
b p. 193 ln. 14

Caput 5

p. 194 ln. 4

Caput 6

p. 196 ln. 2

Caput 7

p. 196 ln. 10

Caput 8

a p. 196 ln. 18
b p. 197 ln. 1

Caput 9

a p. 197 ln. 4
b[c] p. 197 ln. 6
c p. 197 ln. 12

Liber XXX

Caput 1

a p. 198 ln. 10
b p. 199 ln. 3
c p. 199 ln. 4

Caput 2

a p. 200 ln. 2
b p. 200 ln. 4
c p. 200 ln. 6
d p. 200 ln. 8

Caput 3

a p. 201 ln. 6
b p. 201 ln. 17

Caput 4

a p. 202 ln. 2
b p. 202 ln. 5

Caput 5

a p. 203 ln. 2
b p. 203 ln. 4
c p. 203 ln. 5
d p. 203 ln. 7
e p. 203 ln. 11
f p. 203 ln. 15

Caput 6

p. 203 ln. 19

Liber XXXI

Caput 1

a p. 204 ln. 19
b p. 205 ln. 1

Caput 2

a p. 205 ln. 4
b p. 205 ln. 6

Caput 3

p. 205 ln. 8

Caput 4

a p. 205 ln. 16
b p. 206 ln. 3

Caput 5

a p. 206 ln. 6
b p. 206 ln. 8

Caput 6

p. 206 ln. 19

Caput 7

a p. 207 ln. 10
b p. 207 ln. 12
c p. 207 ln. 18
d p. 207 ln. 20
e p. 207 ln. 21

Caput 8

a p. 208 ln. 3
b p. 208 ln. 5
c p. 208 ln. 7
d p. 208 ln. 9
e p. 208 ln. 10
f p. 208 ln. 11
g p. 208 ln. 12
h p. 208 ln. 13
i p. 208 ln. 15

Caput 9

a p. 209 ln. 2
b p. 209 ln. 4

Caput 10

a p. 209 ln. 7
b p. 209 ln. 9
c p. 209 ln. 10

Caput 11

a p. 209 ln. 13
b p. 209 ln. 17
c p. 209 ln. 18

Caput 12

a p. 210 ln. 6
b p. 210 ln. 7
c p. 210 ln. 8

Caput 13

a p. 210 ln. 11
b p. 210 ln. 16
c p. 210 ln. 17
d p. 210 ln. 18
e p. 210 ln. 19
f p. 211 ln. 4

Caput 14

a p. 211 ln. 7
b p. 211 ln. 9
c p. 211 ln. 10

Caput 15

a p. 212 ln. 3
b p. 212 ln. 5
c p. 212 ln. 7

Caput 16

a p. 212 ln. 10
b p. 212 ln. 13
c p. 212 ln. 14
d p. 212 ln. 16
e p. 213 ln. 1
f p. 213 ln. 3

Caput 17

p. 213 ln. 7

Caput 18

p. 213 ln. 12

Caput 19

a p. 214 ln. 2
b p. 214 ln. 4
c p. 214 ln. 7

Caput 20

a p. 214 ln. 17
b p. 214 ln. 19
c p. 215 ln. 1
d p. 215 ln. 4

Liber XXXII

Caput 1

p. 215 ln. 9

Caput 2

a p. 216 ln. 10
b p. 216 ln. 11

Caput 3

p. 217 ln. 3

Caput 4

p. 217 ln. 8

Caput 5

p. 217 ln. 12

Caput 6

p. 217 ln. 12

Caput 7

p. 218 ln. 10

Caput 8

p. 218 ln. 13

Caput 9

p. 219 ln. 3

Caput 10

a p. 219 ln. 8
b p. 219 ln. 9,
p. 219 ln. 10,
c p. 219 ln. 11
d p. 219 ln. 12
e p. 219 ln. 13
f p. 219 ln. 14
g p. 219 ln. 15

Caput 11

p. 220 ln. 21

Caput 12

a p. 220 ln. 6
b p. 221 ln. 6
c p. 221 ln. 9

Caput 13

p. 221 ln. 11

Caput 14

p. 222 ln. 21

Caput 15

a p. 223 ln. 3
b p. 223 ln. 7
c p. 223 ln. 9
d p. 223 ln. 17
e p. 223 ln. 20

Caput 16

a p. 224 ln. 7
b p. 224 ln. 11
c p. 224 ln. 13

Caput 17

a p. 225 ln. 7
b p. 225 ln. 17

Caput 18

a p. 225 ln. 21
b p. 226 ln. 1
c p. 226 ln. 2
d p. 226 ln. 3
e p. 226 ln. 5

Caput 19

a p. 226 ln. 9
b p. 226 ln. 11
c p. 226 ln. 13

Caput 20

p. 227 ln. 16

Caput 21

a p. 228 ln. 9
b p. 228 ln. 13

Caput 22

p. 228 ln. 16

Caput 23

a p. 229 ln. 3
b p. 229 ln. 7
c p. 229 ln. 11

Caput 24

p. 318 ln. 2

Liber XXXIII

Caput 1

a p. 231 ln. 3
b p. 231 ln. 4
c p. 231 ln. 5
d p. 231 ln. 6
e p. 231 ln. 8
f p. 231 ln. 10

Caput 2

a p. 231 ln. 13
b p. 231 ln. 14
c p. 231 ln. 16
d p. 232 ln. 2

Caput 3

a p. 232 ln. 8
b p. 232 ln. 18
c p. 232 ln. 19
d p. 232 ln. 20
e p. 233 ln. 1

Caput 4

p. 233 ln. 6

Caput 5

a p. 234 ln. 2
b p. 234 ln. 6
c p. 234 ln. 7
d p. 234 ln. 14

Caput 6

a p. 234 ln. 16
b p. 234 ln. 18
c p. 234 ln. 19
d p. 235 ln. 1

Caput 7

p. 235 ln. 4

Caput 8

p. 235 ln. 13

Caput 9

p. 235 ln. 16

Caput 10

a p. 236 ln. 2
b p. 236 ln. 4
c p. 236 ln. 9

Caput 11

a p. 236 ln. 12
b p. 236 ln. 14
c p. 236 ln. 15

Caput 12

a p. 236 ln. 20
b p. 237 ln. 1
c p. 237 ln. 2
d p. 237 ln. 4
e p. 237 ln. 6
f p. 237 ln. 7
g p. 237 ln. 9

Liber XXXIV

Caput 1

a p. 237 ln. 17
b p. 237 ln. 18
c p. 237 ln. 19
d p. 237 ln. 19

Caput 2

a p. 238 ln. 2
b p. 238 ln. 3

Caput 3

p. 238 ln. 8

Caput 4

p. 238 ln. 12

Caput 5

p. 239 ln. 2

Caput 6

a p. 239 ln. 9
b p. 239 ln. 13
c p. 239 ln. 15
d p. 239 ln. 17

Caput 7

p. 240 ln. 2

Caput 8

a p. 240 ln. 8
b p. 240 ln. 10

Liber XXXV

a p. 240 ln. 13
b p. 241 ln. 11
c p. 241 ln. 13
d p. 241 ln. 16
e p. 241 ln. 18
f p. 241 ln. 19
g p. 241 ln. 20
h p. 241 ln. 22

Caput 2

a p. 242 ln. 2
b p. 242 ln. 7
c p. 242 ln. 8
d p. 242 ln. 9
e p. 242 ln. 11
f p. 242 ln. 15

Caput 3

p. 242 ln. 19

Caput 4

a p. 243 ln. 4
b p. 243 ln. 6
c p. 243 ln. 7
d p. 243 ln. 9

Caput 5

a p. 243 ln. 13
b p. 243 ln. 17
c p. 244 ln. 4
d p. 244 ln. 5
e p. 244 ln. 6
f p. 244 ln. 8
g p. 244 ln. 18
h p. 245 ln. 1
i p. 245 ln. 4

Caput 6

a p. 245 ln. 7
b p. 245 ln. 9
c p. 245 ln. 15

Caput 7

p. 245 ln. 18

Caput 8

p. 246 ln. 5

Caput 9

p. 246 ln. 10

Caput 10

p. 246 ln. 17

Caput 11

p. 247 ln. 2

Caput 12

p. 247 ln. 6

Caput 13

a p. 247 ln. 13
b p. 247 ln. 16

Caput 14

p. 248 ln. 2

Liber XXXVI

Caput 1

p. 248 ln. 12

Caput 2

p. 249 ln. 3

Caput 3

p. 249 ln. 9

Caput 4

p. 249 ln. 15

Caput 5

p. 250 ln. 9

Caput 6

p. 250 ln. 12

Caput 7

a p. 250 ln. 15
b p. 250 ln. 17
c p. 251 ln. 1

Caput 8

p. 252 ln. 13

Caput 9

p. 253 ln. 2

Caput 10

p. 254 ln. 2

Caput 11

p. 254 ln. 11

Liber XXXVII

Caput 1

p. 255 ln. 8

Caput 2

p. 255 ln. 15

Caput 3

p. 257 ln. 16

Caput 4

a p. 258 ln. 2
b p. 258 ln. 6
c p. 258 ln. 15
d p. 258 ln. 18
e p. 258 ln. 20

Caput 5

a p. 259 ln. 2
b p. 259 ln. 6

Caput 6

p. 259 ln. 14

Caput 7

p. 259 ln. 17

Caput 8

p. 260 ln. 2

Caput 9

p. 260 ln. 9

Caput 10

a p. 262 ln. 2
b p. 262 ln. 3
c p. 262 ln. 5
d p. 262 ln. 6
e p. 262 ln. 7
f p. 262 ln. 9

Caput 11

a p. 262 ln. 13
b p. 262 ln. 15

Caput 12

p. 263 ln. 3

Caput 13

p. 263 ln. 7

Caput 14

p. 264 ln. 4

Caput 15

p. 264 ln. 8

Caput 16

a p. 264 ln. 12
b p. 264 ln. 19

Caput 17

p. 265 ln. 2

Caput 18

p. 265 ln. 5

Caput 19

p. 265 ln. 10

Caput 20

a p. 265 ln. 14
b p. 266 ln. 3
c p. 266 ln. 5
d p. 266 ln. 6

Caput 21

p. 266 ln. 16

Caput 22

a p. 267 ln. 3
b p. 267 ln. 8
c p. 267 ln. 13
d p. 268 ln. 3

Caput 23

p. 269 ln. 3

Caput 24

a p. 269 ln. 7
b p. 269 ln. 9
c p. 269 ln. 10

Caput 25

a p. 269 ln. 18
b p. 270 ln. 1
c p. 270 ln. 2

Caput 26

p. 271 ln. 3

Caput 27

p. 271 ln. 7

Caput 28

p. 271 ln. 11

Caput 29

p. 271 ln. 15

Caput 30

p. 271 ln. 18

Caput 31

p. 272 ln. 5

Caput 32

a p. 272 ln. 10
b p. 272 ln. 11
c p. 272 ln. 13

Caput 33

a p. 272 ln. 16
b p. 272 ln. 18

Caput 34

p. 273 ln. 8

Caput 35

p. 273 ln. 11

Caput 36

p. 273 ln. 15

Caput 37

p. 274 ln. 12

Caput 38

p. 276 ln. 3

Caput 39

p. 277 ln. 12

Liber XXXVIII

Caput 1

a p. 277 ln. 17
b p. 277 ln. 18
c p. 278 ln. 1
d p. 278 ln. 6
e p. 278 ln. 8
f p. 278 ln. 13

Caput 2

a p. 278 ln. 15
b p. 278 ln. 17

Caput 3

p. 279 ln. 3

Caput 4

a p. 279 ln. 6
b p. 279 ln. 9
c p. 279 ln. 10
d p. 279 ln. 11
e p. 279 ln. 12
f p. 279 ln. 14
g p. 279 ln. 16
h p. 279 ln. 18

Caput 5

a p. 280 ln. 8
b p. 280 ln. 10
c p. 280 ln. 12
d p. 280 ln. 15
e p. 280 ln. 19
f p. 281 ln. 1

Caput 6

a p. 281 ln. 10
b p. 281 ln. 12
c p. 281 ln. 13
d p. 281 ln. 15

Caput 7

a p. 281 ln. 18
b p. 281 ln. 21

Caput 8

p. 282 ln. 5

Caput 9

a p. 282 ln. 10
b p. 282 ln. 12

Caput 10

p. 282 ln. 17

Caput 11

a p. 283 ln. 3
b p. 283 ln. 6

Caput 12

p. 283 ln. 10

Caput 13

a p. 283 ln. 15
b p. 283 ln. 18

Caput 14

a p. 284 ln. 6
b p. 284 ln. 7
c p. 284 ln. 9

Caput 15

a p. 284 ln. 12
b p. 284 ln. 16

Caput 16

p. 284 ln. 19

Caput 17

p. 285 ln. 2

Caput 18

p. 286 ln. 21

Caput 19

a p. 287 ln. 14
b p. 287 ln. 16

Liber XXXIX

Caput 1

p. 288 ln. 3

Caput 2

p. 288 ln. 7

Caput 3

a p. 289 ln. 2
b p. 291 ln. 5
c p. 292 ln. 1

Caput 4

a p. 292 ln. 10
b p. 292 ln. 12
c p. 292 ln. 15

Caput 5

p. 293 ln. 15

Caput 6

p. 294 ln. 2

Caput 7

p. 294 ln. 7

Caput 8

p. 295 ln. 13

Caput 9

p. 295 ln. 18

Caput 10

a p. 296 ln. 3
b p. 296 ln. 5

Caput 11

p. 296 ln. 8

Caput 12

a p. 296 ln. 12
b p. 296 ln. 14

Caput 13

p. 297 ln. 3

Caput 14

p. 297 ln. 9

Caput 15

p. 297 ln. 13

Caput 16

p. 298 ln. 3

Liber XL

Caput 1

a p. 298 ln. 7
b p. 298 ln. 14
c p. 298 ln. 16
d p. 299 ln. 1

Caput 2

a p. 299 ln. 5
b p. 300 ln. 4

Caput 3

a p. 300 ln. 7
b p. 300 ln. 8

Caput 4

p. 300 ln. 10

Caput 5

a p. 301 ln. 2
b p. 301 ln. 13

Caput 6

a p. 301 ln. 16
b p. 302 ln. 3

Caput 7

p. 302 ln. 6

Caput 8

p. 302 ln. 9

Caput 9

p. 302 ln. 13

Caput 10

a p. 302 ln. 17
b p. 303 ln. 2

Caput 11

a p. 303 ln. 8
b p. 303 ln. 10

Caput 12

p. 303 ln. 14

Caput 13

a p. 303 ln. 18
b p. 303 ln. 19
c p. 304 ln. 1
d p. 304 ln. 6

Caput 14

a p. 304 ln. 10
b p. 304 ln. 14
c p. 304 ln. 15
d p. 305 ln. 6

Caput 15

a p. 305 ln. 11
b p. 305 ln. 19
c p. 306 ln. 1
d p. 306 ln. 5

Caput 16

p. 307 ln. 2

Liber XLI

Caput 1

a p. 307 ln. 7
b p. 307 ln. 9
c p. 307 ln. 12
d p. 307 ln. 13

Caput 2

a p. 308 ln. 2
b p. 308 ln. 3

Caput 3

a p. 308 ln. 6
b p. 308 ln. 9
c p. 308 ln. 11

Caput 4

a p. 308 ln. 16
b p. 309 ln. 1
c p. 309 ln. 6

Caput 5

a p. 309 ln. 11
b p. 309 ln. 17
c p. 309 ln. 19

Caput 6

a p. 310 ln. 13
b p. 310 ln. 16

Caput 7

a p. 310 ln. 19
b p. 311 ln. 1

Caput 8

p. 311 ln. 8

Caput 9

p. 311 ln. 12

Caput 10

p. 312 ln. 2

Liber XLII

Caput 1

p. 313 ln. 12

Caput 2

p. 313 ln. 15

Caput 3

a p. 314 ln. 8
b p. 314 ln. 9
c p. 314 ln. 11
d p. 314 ln. 13

Caput 4

a p. 314 ln. 16
b p. 314 ln. 18
c p. 315 ln. 1
d p. 315 ln. 4
e p. 315 ln. 6
f p. 315 ln. 9
g p. 315 ln. 14
h p. 315 ln. 17

Caput 5

a p. 316 ln. 2
b p. 316 ln. 3
c p. 316 ln. 4

Caput 6

a p. 316 ln. 10
b p. 316 ln. 12
c p. 316 ln. 12
d p. 316 ln. 14
e p. 316 ln. 15

Caput 7

p. 317 ln. 2

Caput 8

p. 318 ln. 2

Caput 9

a p. 318 ln. 9
b p. 318 ln. 12
c p. 318 ln. 16

Caput 10

a p. 319 ln. 2
b p. 319 ln. 5
c p. 319 ln. 6
d p. 319 ln. 7
e p. 319 ln. 8

Caput 11

a p. 319 ln. 11
b p. 319 ln. 19

Caput 12

a p. 320 ln. 2
b p. 320 ln. 9
c p. 320 ln. 11
d p. 320 ln. 12
e p. 320 ln. 13
f p. 320 ln. 14

Caput 13

a p. 320 ln. 17
b p. 320 ln. 18
c p. 320 ln. 19
d p. 321 ln. 1
e p. 321 ln. 2
f p. 321 ln. 4
g p. 321 ln. 6

Caput 14

a p. 322 ln. 5
b p. 322 ln. 10
c p. 322 ln. 13

Caput 15

p. 322 ln. 18

Caput 16

a p. 323 ln. 2
b p. 323 ln. 11
c p. 323 ln. 14

Caput 17

p. 323 ln. 18

Caput 18

p. 324 ln. 3

Caput 19

p. 324 ln. 16

Caput 20

p. 325 ln. 11

Caput 21

a p. 325 ln. 16
b p. 325 ln. 20

Caput 22

p. 326 ln. 8

Caput 23

p. 326 ln. 15

Caput 24

p. 326 ln. 18

Caput 25

a p. 327 ln. 6
b p. 327 ln. 9
c p. 327 ln. 14

Caput 26

a p. 327 ln. 17
b p. 328 ln. 1

Caput 27

p. 328 ln. 11

Caput 28

p. 328 ln. 17

Caput 29

p. 328 ln. 22

Caput 30

p. 329 ln. 9

Caput 31

p. 329 ln. 19

Caput 32

p. 330 ln. 2

Liber XLIII

Caput 1

p. 335 ln. 19

Caput 2

a p. 336 ln. 5
b p. 336 ln. 9

Caput 3

p. 336 ln. 14

Caput 4

p. 337 ln. 4

Caput 5

p. 337 ln. 15

Caput 6

p. 338 ln. 3

Caput 7

p. 339 ln. 3

Caput 8

a p. 339 ln. 18
b p. 340 ln. 1
c p. 340 ln. 5

Liber XLIV

Caput 1

p. 340 ln. 8

Caput 2

a p. 340 ln. 12
b p. 340 ln. 18
c p. 341 ln. 1
d p. 341 ln. 3
e p. 341 ln. 5
f p. 341 ln. 6
g p. 341 ln. 8
h p. 341 ln. 9

Caput` 3

a p. 341 ln. 15
b p. 341 ln. 16
c p. 341 ln. 18

Caput 4

p. 342 ln. 7

Caput 5

p. 342 ln. 12

Caput 6

a p. 343 ln. 14
b p. 343 ln. 17
c p. 343 ln. 19
d p. 343 ln. 20

Caput 7

a p. 344 ln. 11
b p. 344 ln. 12
c p. 344 ln. 14
d p. 344 ln. 15
e p. 344 ln. 17

Caput 8

p. 344 ln. 19

Caput 9

p. 345 ln. 19

Caput 10

a p. 345 ln. 23
b p. 345 ln. 25

Caput 11

p. 346 ln. 2

Caput 12

p. 346 ln. 5

Caput 13

p. 346 ln. 10

Caput 14

p. 346 ln. 16

Caput 15

p. 347 ln. 2

Caput 16

p. 347 ln. 10

Caput 17

p. 348 ln. 9

Caput 18

a p. 348 ln. 18
b p. 349 ln. 1

Caput 19

a p. 349 ln. 6
b p. 349 ln. 11

Caput 20

a p. 349 ln. 16
b p. 349 ln. 19

Liber XLV

Caput 1

p. 350 ln. 10

Caput 2

a p. 351 ln. 6
b p. 351 ln. 8

Caput 3

p. 351 ln. 12

Caput 4

a p. 351 ln. 19
b p. 352 ln. 1
c p. 352 ln. 4
d p. 352 ln. 7

Caput 5

p. 352 ln. 12

Caput 6

p. 352 ln. 18

Caput 7

a p. 353 ln. 2
b p. 353 ln. 4
c p. 353 ln. 12
d p. 353 ln. 14
e p. 353 ln. 16

Caput 8

p. 353 ln. 19

Caput 9

a p. 354 ln. 2
b p. 354 ln. 5

Caput 10

p. 354 ln. 15

Caput 11

p. 355 ln. 2

Caput 12

a p. 355 ln. 5
b p. 355 ln. 10

Caput 13

p. 355 ln. 13

Caput 14

p. 355 ln. 16

Caput 15

p. 356 ln. 4

Caput 16

p. 356 ln. 7

Caput 17

a p. 356 ln. 11
b p. 356 ln. 12

Caput 18

a p. 356 ln. 16
b p. 356 ln. 17

Caput 19

p. 357 ln. 2

Caput 20

p. 357 ln. 8

Liber XLVI

Caput 1

p. 357 ln. 13

Caput 2

p. 357 ln. 16

Caput 3

p. 358 ln. 9

Caput 4

p. 359 ln. 2

Caput 5

p. 359 ln. 10

Caput 6

a p. 361 ln. 7
b p. 361 ln. 10
c p. 361 ln. 12

Caput 7

p. 362 ln. 2

Caput 8

p. 363 ln. 16

Caput 9

p. 364 ln. 2

Caput 10

p. 364 ln. 7

Caput 11

a p. 365 ln. 5
b p. 365 ln. 7
c p. 365 ln. 10

Caput 12

p. 365 ln. 13

Caput 13

a p. 365 ln. 18
b p. 366 ln. 1

Caput 14

p. 366 ln. 8

Caput 15

p. 366 ln. 14

Caput 16

p. 367 ln. 19

Caput 17

p. 368 ln. 16

Caput 18

a p. 369 ln. 2
b p. 369 ln. 4

Caput 19

a p. 369 ln. 9
b p. 369 ln. 11
c p. 369 ln. 14

Caput 20

p. 370 ln. 12

Caput 21

p. 370 ln. 17

Caput 22

a p. 371 ln. 7
b p. 371 ln. 9

Caput 23

p. 371 ln. 15

Caput 24

p. 372 ln. 6

Caput 25

p. 372 ln. 8

Caput 26

p. 372 ln. 12

Caput 27

a p. 373 ln. 3
b p. 373 ln. 5

Caput 28

a p. 373 ln. 10
b p. 373 ln. 13

Caput 29

p. 373 ln. 16

Caput 30

a p. 374 ln. 6
b p. 374 ln. 7
c p. 374 ln. 14

Caput 31

p. 375 ln. 2

Caput 32

a p. 375 ln. 7
b p. 375 ln. 10
c p. 375 ln. 15

Caput 33

p. 375 ln. 18

Caput 34

p. 376 ln. 5

Caput 35

a p. 376 ln. 9
b p. 376 ln. 11
c p. 376 ln. 14
d p. 377 ln. 3

Caput 36

p. 377 ln. 6

Caput 37

p. 378 ln. 2

Caput 38

a p. 379 ln. 13
b p. 379 ln. 16

Liber XLVII

Caput 1

p. 380 ln. 6

Caput 2

p. 380 ln. 20

Caput 3

p. 382 ln. 2

Caput 4

a p. 383 ln. 10
b p. 383 ln. 14
c p. 383 ln. 16
d p. 383 ln. 20

Caput 5

a p. 384 ln. 2
b p. 384 ln. 11
c p. 384 ln. 13

Caput 6

a p. 384 ln. 16
b p. 384 ln. 18
c p. 385 ln. 1

Caput 7

p. 385 ln. 4

Caput 8

a p. 385 ln. 7
b p. 385 ln. 9
c p. 385 ln. 10
d p. 385 ln. 12
e p. 385 ln. 16

Caput 9

a p. 386 ln. 2
b p. 386 ln. 4
c p. 386 ln. 6

Caput 10

a p. 386 ln. 10
b p. 386 ln. 17

Caput 11

a p. 387 ln. 2
b p. 387 ln. 10

Caput 12

a p. 387 ln. 16
b p. 388 ln. 13
c p. 388 ln. 15

Caput 13

a p. 392 ln. 4
b p. 392 ln. 8

Caput 14

p. 392 ln. 14

Caput 15

a p. 391 ln. 6
b p. 391 ln. 9

Caput 16

p. 393 ln. 6

Caput 17

a p. 393 ln. 15
b p. 393 ln. 17

Caput 18

p. 394 ln. 2

Caput 19

p. 394 ln. 6

Caput 20

p. 394 ln. 13

Liber XLVIII

Caput 1

p. 395 ln. 6

Caput 2

p. 396 ln. 2

Caput 3

p. 396 ln. 8

Caput 4

p. 396 ln. 15

Caput 5

p. 397 ln. 2

Liber XLIX

Caput 1

a p. 397 ln. 15
b p. 397 ln. 17

Caput 2

a p. 398 ln. 2
b p. 398 ln. 4

Caput 3

p. 398 ln. 13

Caput 4

p. 398 ln. 18

Caput 5

p. 399 ln. 7

Caput 6

p. 400 ln. 8

Caput 7

p. 400 ln. 11

Caput 8

p. 400 ln. 15

Caput 9

p. 401 ln. 3

Caput 10

p. 401 ln. 6

Caput 11

p. 401 ln. 12

Caput 12

a p. 402 ln. 3
b p. 402 ln. 6

Caput 13

p. 402 ln. 12

Caput 14

p. 402 ln. 16

Caput 15

p. 403 ln. 3

Liber L

Caput 1

a p. 403 ln. 11
b p. 403 ln. 13
c p. 403 ln. 14

Caput 2

a p. 403 ln. 19
b p. 404 ln. 1
c p. 404 ln. 3

Caput 3

a p. 404 ln. 7
b p. 404 ln. 10
c p. 404 ln. 11

Liber LI

Caput 1

p. 404 ln. 15

Caput 2

p. 405 ln. 2

Caput 3

p. 405 ln. 8

Caput 4

p. 405 ln. 11

Caput 5

p. 405 ln. 18

Caput 6

p. 406 ln. 4

Liber LII

Caput 1

p. 407 ln. 12

Caput 2

p. 408 ln. 2

Caput 3

p. 408 ln. 5

Caput 4

p. 409 ln. 2

Caput 5

p. 409 ln. 9

Caput 6

p. 409 ln. 17

Caput 7

p. 410 ln. 10

Liber LIII

Caput 1

p. 412 ln. 7

Caput 2

a p. 412 ln. 11
b p. 412 ln. 12
c p. 412 ln. 13
d p. 412 ln. 15
e p. 412 ln. 18
f p. 413 ln. 2

Caput 3

p. 413 ln. 5

Caput 4

p. 413 ln. 12

Caput 5

p. 413 ln. 17

Caput 6

p. 414 ln. 19

Caput 7

p. 414 ln. 22

Caput 8

p. 415 ln. 7

Caput 9

p. 415 ln. 10

Liber LIV

Caput 1

p. 415 ln. 17

Caput 2

p. 416 ln. 18

Caput 3

p. 416 ln. 21

Caput 4

p. 417 ln. 3

Caput 5

p. 417 ln. 6

Caput 6

p. 417 ln. 11

Caput 7

p. 418 ln. 2

Caput 8

a p. 418 ln. 14
b p. 418 ln. 16
c p. 418 ln. 18

Caput 9

p. 419 ln. 14

Caput 10

p. 419 ln. 17

Caput 11

a p. 420 ln. 6
b p. 420 ln. 10

Caput 12

a p. 421 ln. 2
b p. 421 ln. 5

Caput 13

a p. 421 ln. 9
b p. 421 ln. 11

Caput 14

p. 422 ln. 1

Caput 15

p. 422 ln. 17

Caput 16

p. 423 ln. 6

Liber LV

Caput 1

a p. 423 ln. 15
b p. 423 ln. 17
c p. 423 ln. 18

Caput 2

a p. 424 ln. 10
b p. 424 ln. 19

Caput 3

a p. 424 ln. 21
b p. 425 ln. 2
c p. 425 ln. 7
d p. 425 ln. 10

Caput 4

p. 425 ln. 12

Caput 5

p. 425 ln. 15

Caput 6

p. 425 ln. 15

Caput 7

p. 426 ln. 6

Liber LVI

Caput 1

a p. 428 ln. 16
b p. 428 ln. 18
c p. 428 ln. 19

Caput 2

a[c] p. 429 ln. 2
b p. 429 ln. 7
c p. 429 ln. 12

Caput 3

p. 430 ln. 2

Caput 4

a p. 430 ln. 8
b p. 430 ln. 14
c p. 430 ln. 16

Liber LVII

Caput 1

p. 431 ln. 3

Caput 2

p. 431 ln. 7

Caput 3

p. 431 ln. 11

Caput 4

a p. 431 ln. 15
b p. 431 ln. 18
c p. 432 ln. 1

Caput 5

a p. 432 ln. 4
b p. 432 ln. 6

Caput 6

p. 432 ln. 9

Liber LVIII

Caput 1

p. 432 ln. 14

Caput 2

p. 433 ln. 13

Caput 3

p. 434 ln. 2

Caput 4

p. 434 ln. 15

Caput 5

p. 434 ln. 19

Liber LIX

Caput 1

a p. 435 ln. 5
b p. 435 ln. 7

Caput 2

p. 435 ln. 9

Caput 3

p. 435 ln. 14

Caput 4

a p. 436 ln. 2
b p. 436 ln. 4

Caput 5

a p. 436 ln. 6
b p. 436 ln. 8

Liber LX

Caput 1

p. 437 ln. 16

Caput 2

p. 437 ln. 20

Caput 3

a p. 438 ln. 7
b p. 438 ln. 12

Caput 4

p. 439 ln. 3

Liber LXI

Caput 1

a p. 440 ln. 4
b p. 440 ln. 6
c p. 440 ln. 9

Caput 2

p. 440 ln. 17

Caput 3

a p. 441 ln. 3
b p. 441 ln. 5
c p. 441 ln. 6

Caput 4

a p. 441 ln. 8
b p. 442 ln. 4
c p. 442 ln. 6

Caput 5

p. 442 ln. 12

Caput 6

p. 443 ln. 18

Liber LXII

Caput 1

p. 444 ln. 8

Liber LXIII

Caput 1

p. 449 ln. 25

Caput 2

a p. 450 ln. 7
b p. 450 ln. 9
c p. 450 ln. 11
d p. 450 ln. 14

Liber LXIV

Caput 1

p. 451 ln. 4

Caput 2

p. 451 ln. 13

Caput 3

p. 451 ln. 18

Caput 4

p. 452 ln. 2

Caput 5

p. 452 ln. 7

Caput 6

p. 452 ln. 10

Caput 7

p. 452 ln. 14

Caput 8

p. 453 ln. 2

Liber LXV

Caput 1

a p. 453 ln. 13
b p. 454 ln. 1

Caput 2

p. 454 ln. 18

Caput 3

p. 455 ln. 2

Caput 4

p. 455 ln. 2

Caput 5

a p. 455 ln. 15
b p. 455 ln. 18

Caput 6

p. 456 ln. 2

Caput 7

a p. 456 ln. 15
b p. 456 ln. 21

Caput 8

p. 457 ln. 5

Liber LXVI

Caput 1

a p. 458 ln. 2
b p. 458 ln. 5

Caput 2

p. 458 ln. 10

Caput 3

a p. 458 ln. 18
b p. 458 ln. 20
c p. 458 ln. 22
d p. 459 ln. 1

Caput 4

p. 459 ln. 6

Caput 5

p. 459 ln. 20

Caput 6

p. 460 ln. 15

Caput 7

p. 461 ln. 8

Caput 8

p. 461 ln. 13

Caput 9

p. 461 ln. 16

Caput 10

p. 462 ln. 2

Caput 11

p. 462 ln. 7

Caput 12

p. 463 ln. 19

Caput 13

p. 464 ln. 14

Caput 14

p. 464 ln. 18

Caput 15

p. 465 ln. 13

Caput 16

p. 465 ln. 18

Caput 17

p. 466 ln. 2

Caput 18

a p. 466 ln. 7
b p. 466 ln. 9

Caput 19

a p. 466 ln. 11
b p. 466 ln. 13

Liber LXVII

Caput 1

a p. 469 ln. 19
b p. 469 ln. 20
c p. 470 ln. 1

Caput 2

a p. 470 ln. 4
b p. 470 ln. 5
c p. 470 ln. 6
d p. 470 ln. 7
e p. 470 ln. 10
f p. 470 ln. 11

Caput 3

p. 471 ln. 1

Caput 4

a p. 471 ln. 4
b p. 471 ln. 5
c p. 471 ln. 6
d p. 471 ln. 7
e p. 471 ln. 8
f p. 471 ln. 9
g p. 471 ln. 11
h p. 471 ln. 13
i p. 471 ln. 15
k p. 471 ln. 16
l p. 471 ln. 19
m p. 471 ln. 20
n p. 471 ln. 21
o p. 472 ln. 1
p p. 472 ln. 3
q p. 472 ln. 4

Caput 5

a p. 472 ln. 12
b p. 472 ln. 14
c p. 472 ln. 17
d p. 472 ln. 18
e p. 473 ln. 1
f p. 473 ln. 3

Caput 6

a p. 473 ln. 7
b p. 473 ln. 9
c p. 473 ln. 11

Caput 7

a p. 473 ln. 14
b p. 473 ln. 17

Bible and Apocrypha

Genesis

1:28 → p. 419 ln. 9
1:29 → cf. p. 416 ln. 1
2:19 → p. 225 ln. 22
2:24 → p. 376 ln. 12, p. 377 ln. 11
3:17 → p. 225 ln. 21, p. 397 ln. 17, p. 432 ln. 14
3:22 → cf. p. 175 ln. 12
3:23 → cf. p. 273 ln. 8
4:1–2 → cf. p. 304 ln. 16
4:7 → p. 225 ln. 22
4:10 → p. 397 ln. 15
4:23–4 → p. 172 ln. 1, cf. p. 175 ln. 5
5:5 → cf. p. 175 ln. 3
5:32 → cf. p. 304 ln. 18
6:21–23 → cf. p. 432 ln. 14
7:1 → cf. p. 305 ln. 11
7:13 → cf. p. 301 ln. 2
9:5 → p. 181 ln. 8
9:6 → cf. p. 168 ln. 4, cf. p. 471 ln. 4
9:7 → cf. p. 226 ln. 1
11:1–9 → cf. p. 172 ln. 2
11:10–26 → cf. p. 223 ln. 10
12:1 → p. 223 ln. 20, p. 467 ln. 5
13:9–11 → p. 326 ln. 15
14 → cf. p. 182 ln. 10, cf. p. 472 ln. 20
14:18–20 → cf. p. 21 ln. 9, cf. p. 23 ln. 13, cf. p. 319 ln. 18
14:24 → cf. p. 301 ln. 3
15:2 → cf. p. 264 ln. 12
17:19–21 → cf. p. 304 ln. 17
18:1–22 → cf. p. 429 ln. 2
18:12 → cf. p. 301 ln. 9
18:16 → cf. p. 427 ln. 21
18:22–27 → cf. p. 181 ln. 3
19 (*sic*) → cf. p. 301 ln. 4
19:1–3 → cf. p. 429 ln. 2
19:15–17 → cf. p. 305 ln. 12
19:24 → cf. p. 172 ln. 3
21:10 → p. 369 ln. 22, p. 374 ln. 11
23:9 → cf. p. 107 ln. 19
24:1–3 → p. 240 ln. 13
24:2 → cf. p. 263 ln. 14
24:9 → p. 240 ln. 13
25:5 → p. 219 ln. 8, cf. p. 260 ln. 13
25:5–6 → p. 220 ln. 21
25:19–34 → cf. p. 304 ln. 18
25:21 → cf. p. 67 ln. 18
25:23 → cf. p. 218 ln. 4
25:33 → cf. p. 100 ln. 10, cf. p. 219 ln. 9
26:18 → cf. p. 90 ln. 6
26:26 → cf. p. 301 ln. 5
26:26–28 → p. 241 ln. 3
26:30–31 → p. 241 ln. 3, cf. p. 301 ln. 6
27:9–36 → cf. p. 100 ln. 10, cf. p. 219 ln. 9
29 → cf. p. 182 ln. 16
29:31–35 → cf. p. 304 ln. 19
30:1–24 → cf. p. 304 ln. 19
31:38–39 → p. 202 ln. 2
31:42 → p. 208 ln. 1
31:43–45 → p. 240 ln. 19
31:53 → p. 240 ln. 19
34 → cf. p. 179 ln. 1
34:1–3 → cf. p. 352 ln. 18
34:6 → cf. p. 352 ln. 18
37:18–36 → cf. p. 304 ln. 19
37:21 → cf. p. 182 ln. 15
38:24 → p. 164 ln. 10
39:4 → cf. p. 263 ln. 17
41:40–44 → cf. p. 135 ln. 2, cf. p. 263 ln. 16, cf. p. 395 ln. 6
41 (*sic*) → cf. p. 301 ln. 8
42 (*sic*) → cf. p. 301 ln. 7

42:6 → cf. p. 395 ln. 6
42:25–26 → cf. p. 395 ln. 6
47:20–27 → cf. p. 221 ln. 20
47:26 → cf. p. 151 ln. 12
48:1–5 → p. 217 ln. 14
48:5–6 → cf. p. 219 ln. 10, cf. p. 307 ln. 7
48:13–20 → cf. p. 217 ln. 12
48:22 → p. 217 ln. 8
49:7 → cf. p. 218 ln. 10
50:24 → p. 105 ln. 7

Exodus

2:16–22 → cf. p. 182 ln. 14
2:21 → cf. p. 241 ln. 9
3:5 → p. 343 ln. 20, p. 396 ln. 12
3:17 → cf. p. 96 ln. 2
4:10–17 → cf. p. 218 ln. 6
7:7 → p. 218 ln. 7
7:14–12:36 cf. p. 172 ln. 4
11:1–6 → cf. p. 432 ln. 15
12:17–50 → cf. p. 58 ln. 19
13:19 → cf. p. 399 ln. 7
14 (*sic*) → cf. p. 180 ln. 5
14:28 → cf. p. 433 ln. 13
15:20 → cf. p. 53 ln. 1
16:18 → p. 97 ln. 10
17:11–12 → cf. p. 74 ln. 1
18:12 → p. 101 ln. 16
18:13 → cf. p. 119 ln. 3
18:18–23 → p. 117 ln. 10
19:9–13 → p. 343 ln. 2
19:12 → cf. p. 343 ln. 14
19:21–22 → p. 343 ln. 8
20:5 → p. 205 ln. 8
20:12 → p. 210 ln. 11, p. 211 ln. 2
20:15 → p. 191 ln. 7
20:17 → p. 191 ln. 10, p. 319 ln. 9
21:12 → p. 163 ln. 16
21:12–13 → cf. p. 185 ln. 2
21:14 → p. 186 ln. 16
21:15 → p. 211 ln. 7
21:16 → p. 193 ln. 8
21:17 → p. 172 ln. 16, p. 211 ln. 9
21:28–30 → p. 413 ln. 5
21:29–31 → cf. p. 412 ln. 11
21:33–34 → p. 122 ln. 4
21:35–36 → p. 414 ln. 22
22:1 → p. 192 ln. 19, p. 473 ln. 7
22:2–3 → p. 195 ln. 12
22:3 → cf. p. 195 ln. 1
22:3–4 → p. 193 ln. 3
22:4 → p. 194 ln. 9
22:5 → p. 122 ln. 1
22:6 → p. 122 ln. 7
22:7 → p. 193 ln. 6
22:7–9 → p. 198 ln. 10
22:10–13 → p. 202 ln. 5
22:14–15 → p. 199 ln. 22
22:16–17 → p. 363 ln. 2
22:26 → p. 236 ln. 9
22:28 → p. 132 ln. 15
22:29 → p. 96 ln. 14
23:1 → p. 86 ln. 17
23:2 → p. 88 ln. 9
23:2–3 → p. 124 ln. 8
23:6 → cf. p. 124 ln. 13
26:33 → cf. p. 342 ln. 12, cf. p. 342 ln. 16
27:9 → cf. p. 341 ln. 5
27:18 → cf. p. 342 ln. 10
28:38 → p. 27 ln. 17
29:4 → p. 6 ln. 4
32:11–13 → cf. p. 74 ln. 1, cf. p. 158 ln. 10
32:26–27 → p. 167 ln. 4
32:27 → p. 167 ln. 1
32:33 → cf. p. 305 ln. 15
33 (*sic*) → cf. p. 182 ln. 12
35:30–35 → p. 449 ln. 15
36:2–3 → p. 449 ln. 21
36:8–38 → cf. p. 24 ln. 19

Leviticus

1–7 (*sic*) → cf. p. 72 ln. 3

4:4 → cf. p. 25 ln. 1,
cf. p. 101 ln. 20

5:1 → p. 28 ln. 10,
p. 86 ln. 8,
p. 246 ln. 17

5:4–7 → cf. p. 23 ln. 13,
p. 247 ln. 2

6:2–6 → p. 200 ln. 11

8:12 → cf. p. 265 ln. 14

9:3 → cf. p. 23 ln. 13

9:10–20 → cf. p. 22 ln. 3

9:23–24 → cf. p. 392 ln. 7

10:1–2 → cf. p. 27 ln. 19,
cf. p. 51 ln. 19,
cf. p. 172 ln. 9,
cf. p. 176 ln. 3,
cf. p. 306 ln. 16

10:12–13 → cf. p. 95 ln. 2,
cf. p. 95 ln. 7

10:14 → p. 95 ln. 4,
cf. p. 95 ln. 8

11:6–8 → p. 420 ln. 2

11:26 → p. 421 ln. 7

11:39–40 → p. 421 ln. 19

12:2–6 → p. 364 ln. 12

12:4–5 → p. 365 ln. 10

19:3 → p. 211 ln. 3

19:15 → p. 124 ln. 5

19:18 → p. 167 ln. 8,
p. 471 ln. 18

19:26 → p. 406 ln. 12

19:32 → p. 132 ln. 7,
p. 143 ln. 6,
p. 143 ln. 7

20:10 → p. 374 ln. 2

20:10–21 → p. 166 ln. 5

20:27 → p. 451 ln. 18

22:11 → cf. p. 95 ln. 9

22:14→ p. 93 ln. 13

25:24 → cf. p. 250 ln. 12

25:29–30 → p. 253 ln. 2

26:34 → p. 404 ln. 9

27:2–8 → p. 80 ln. 12

27:14–15 → p. 93 ln. 3

27:16 → p. 249 ln. 15

27:28 → p. 97 ln. 13,
p. 102 ln. 6

27:28–29 → p. 92 ln. 15

Numbers

1:1–3 → p. 330 ln. 14

1:26–27 → p. 330 ln. 19

1:51 → p. 343 ln. 12,
p. 344 ln. 9

4:4 → cf. p. 25 ln. 3

5:7 → p. 235 ln. 17

5:9 → p. 24 ln. 9

5:12–29 → p. 378 ln. 2

8:24 → p. 32 ln. 6

11:14–17 → p. 118 ln. 7

11:28 → cf. p. 263 ln. 13

12 (*sic*) → cf. p. 259 ln. 6

12:3 → p. 262 ln. 5

12:10 → cf. p. 176 ln. 2

15:32 → cf. p. 172 ln. 15

16:23–33 →
cf. p. 28 ln. 2,
cf. p. 172 ln. 5,
cf. p. 173 ln. 14,
cf. p. 205 ln. 10

16:26 → cf. p. 305 ln. 13

16:36–40 →
cf. p. 319 ln. 16

17:12–13 → p. 344 ln. 2

18:1–5 → p. 344 ln. 4

18:18 → p. 24 ln. 14

18:20 → cf. p. 42 ln. 5

20:9–12 → cf. p. 173 ln. 3

22:5–20 → cf. p. 437 ln. 2

22:21–39 → cf. p. 434 ln. 9

25:7 → cf. p. 164 ln. 11

25:7–8 → cf. p. 189 ln. 13

26:3–22 → cf. p. 330 ln. 22

27:1–4 → p. 226 ln. 13

27:6 → p. 227 ln. 9

27:8–11 → p. 219 ln. 3

27:10 → p. 227 ln. 18

30:3 → p. 245 ln. 7

30:4–6 → cf. p. 100 ln. 17,
p. 244 ln. 18,
cf. p. 245 ln. 9,
cf. p. 473 ln. 14

30:11–15 →
cf. p. 100 ln. 17

35:1–4 → p. 340 ln. 13

35:3 → cf. p. 316 ln. 10

35:26–27 → p. 186 ln. 4

35:30 → p. 87 ln. 19

35:31 → p. 168 ln. 5,
cf. p. 314 ln. 1

36:1–12 → p. 334 ln. 28
36:5–12 → p. 226 ln. 17
36:7 → p. 227 ln. 13
36:8 → cf. p. 227 ln. 11

Deuteronomy

1:16–17 → p. 124 ln. 2
3:12 → cf. p. 224 ln. 7
6:6–9 → p. 73 ln. 13
6:10–12 → p. 469 ln. 9
9:9 → cf. p. 59 ln. 1
13:8–9 → p. 167 ln. 2
14:28 → p. 97 ln. 5
15:1–3 → p. 249 ln. 3
16:18 → cf. p. 163 ln. 14
16:19 → p. 88 ln. 14, p. 135 ln. 11, p. 140 ln. 10
17:6 → p. 87 ln. 13, p. 87 ln. 15
17:8–9 → p. 118 ln. 16
17:9–10 → p. 134 ln. 6
17:9–11 → p. 117 ln. 3
17:11 → cf. p. 124 ln. 13
17:12 → p. 25 ln. 6, p. 132 ln. 4
17:17 → p. 149 ln. 13
18:6–8 → p. 317 ln. 7
19:4–5 → p. 185 ln. 4
19:11–13 → p. 187 ln. 1
19:14 → p. 348 ln. 6
19:15 → p. 87 ln. 11, cf. p. 88 ln. 10, p. 163 ln. 18
19:16–21 → p. 91 ln. 10
19:17 → cf. p. 91 ln. 18
19:19 → cf. p. 91 ln. 19
20:7 → p. 376 ln. 5
20:13–14 → p. 434 ln. 11
21:7–8 → cf. p. 168 ln. 4, cf. p. 471 ln. 4
21:15 → p. 377 ln. 17
21:15–16 → p. 216 ln. 4
21:16–17 → p. 217 ln. 3
21:17 → p. 213 ln. 12, p. 215 ln. 13
21:18–21 → p. 166 ln. 22
22:23–24 → p. 363 ln. 5
22:25–26 → p. 363 ln. 9
22:28–29 → p. 363 ln. 11
23:3–6 → cf. p. 436 ln. 10, cf. p. 437 ln. 2
23:19 → p. 236 ln. 20
23:23 → p. 245 ln. 11
23:24–25 → p. 121 ln. 18
24:1 → p. 363 ln. 16
24:1–4 → p. 362 ln. 14
24:3 → p. 377 ln. 14
24:6 → p. 236 ln. 9
24:10 → cf. p. 235 ln. 13
24:10–13 → p. 236 ln. 4
24:14–15 → p. 234 ln. 2
24:16 → p. 204 ln. 19, p. 437 ln. 11
25:1 → p. 134 ln. 2
25:4 → p. 278 ln. 13
25:11–12 → p. 183 ln. 8
27:16 → p. 211 ln. 10
27:16–26 → p. 443 ln. 18
27:17 → p. 251 ln. 12
28:2–8 → p. 444 ln. 8
28:15–29 → p. 443 ln. 2
30:5–6 → cf. p. 100 ln. 14
32:7 → p. 111 ln. 14
32:35 → p. 92 ln. 4, cf. p. 468 ln. 1

Joshua

1:6 → p. 162 ln. 3
1:16–18 → p. 260 ln. 3
2:1–21 → cf. p. 180 ln. 12, cf. p. 305 ln. 16, cf. p. 429 ln. 3, cf. p. 473 ln. 1
6:17–18 → cf. p. 180 ln. 12
6:25 → cf. p. 180 ln. 12, cf. p. 226 ln. 9
7:14–18 → cf. p. 163 ln. 1
7:24–25 → cf. p. 161 ln. 15, cf. p. 164 ln. 6, cf. p. 195 ln. 16
9 → cf. p. 180 ln. 16, cf. p. 473 ln. 3
9:15 → cf. p. 241 ln. 10
10 → cf. p. 433 ln. 16
12:2 → cf. p. 224 ln. 7
13:9–10 → cf. p. 224 ln. 7
14:6 → p. 89 ln. 2
14:9 → p. 89 ln. 2
14:12–13 → p. 89 ln. 2

14:13 → cf. p. 219 ln. 11
15:16–19 → p. 225 ln. 8
15:46 → cf. p. 224 ln. 13
18:10 → p. 218 ln. 13
20:7–8 → p. 184 ln. 13
21:8 → cf. p. 316 ln. 10
21:12 → cf. p. 219 ln. 11

Judges

1:15 → cf. p. 225 ln. 7
2:1 → p. 241 ln. 12
2:9 → cf. p. 219 ln. 12
9:5 → cf. p. 256 ln. 5
14–16 (*sic*) → cf. p. 180 ln. 14
19:1–14 → p. 154 ln. 13
20:19–21 → cf. p. 180 ln. 6, cf. p. 472 ln. 12
21:5–13 → p. 154 ln. 16

Ruth

1:3 → cf. p. 352 ln. 18
4:2–6 → p. 224 ln. 16

I Samuel

1:11 → cf. p. 74 ln. 9
1:24–28 → cf. p. 427 ln. 23
2:12–36 → cf. p. 28 ln. 1, cf. p. 51 ln. 19, cf. p. 272 ln. 18
2:22–24 → p. 206 ln. 13
2:29 → p. 205 ln. 16, p. 269 ln. 20
3:13 → cf. p. 206 ln. 3, p. 206 ln. 6, p. 270 ln. 1
4:11 → cf. p. 176 ln. 4
6:3 → cf. p. 231 ln. 4
8:1–3 → p. 127 ln. 14
8:10–17 → p. 153 ln. 6
10:1 → p. 145 ln. 12, cf. p. 265 ln. 15
10:19–21 → p. 147 ln. 9
10:20–21 → p. 161 ln. 7
14:44 → cf. p. 244 ln. 10, cf. p. 473 ln. 17
14:44–45 → p. 244 ln. 13
16:10–13 → p. 146 ln. 7
16:13 → cf. p. 261 ln. 9, cf. p. 265 ln. 16
21:1–6 → cf. p. 197 ln. 9
22:22 → p. 184 ln. 3
24:22 → p. 241 ln. 14
26:9 → p. 150 ln. 9
26:16 → p. 150 ln. 6
27:5–7 → p. 253 ln. 8
30 (*sic*) → cf. p. 433 ln. 15
30:24 → p. 463 ln. 2
30:26–31 → cf. p. 319 ln. 15
31:6 → cf. p. 153 ln. 18
31:7–13 → cf. p. 79 ln. 12

II Samuel

1:14 → cf. p. 272 ln. 11
1:16 → cf. p. 272 ln. 11
3:2–5 → p. 333 ln. 10
5:14–16 → p. 333 ln. 13
6:1–7 → cf. p. 176 ln. 5
6:7 → p. 172 ln. 17
9:6–10 → p. 122 ln. 17
12:1–4 → p. 470 ln. 14
12:7–9 → p. 463 ln. 6
12:13–20 → cf. p. 392 ln. 5
12:15–18 → cf. p. 205 ln. 4
14:6–11 → p. 158 ln. 12
16:1–4 → p. 123 ln. 3
19:24–30 → p. 123 ln. 13
19:29 → p. 126 ln. 16, p. 138 ln. 17
21:8–10 → cf. p. 79 ln. 16
22:26 → p. 207 ln. 7
24:1–17 → cf. p. 172 ln. 7
24:12–10 → cf. p. 178 ln. 5

I Kings

1:2 → cf. p. 263 ln. 15
1:5–31 → cf. p. 218 ln. 5
2:5–6 → p. 157 ln. 13
2:12 → cf. p. 261 ln. 9
2:19–25 → p. 179 ln. 5
2:25 → p. 157 ln. 13
2:28 → p. 157 ln. 13
2:28–29 → p. 157 ln. 18
2:31 → p. 157 ln. 18
2:34 → p. 157 ln. 18
3:16–28 → cf. p. 119 ln. 4, cf. p. 119 ln. 12, cf. p. 138 ln. 2, cf. p. 470 ln. 11
5:3 → p. 269 ln. 9
5:7–18 → p. 448 ln. 6
6:7 → p. 449 ln. 1
6:20–35 → cf. p. 102 ln. 4
7:13–14 → p. 449 ln. 3
8 (*sic*) → cf. p. 102 ln. 4
9:10–15 → p. 449 ln. 6
11:9–13 → cf. p. 390 ln. 8
11:29–31 → cf. p. 205 ln. 6
11:43 → cf. p. 261 ln. 10
12:6–20 → cf. p. 153 ln. 19, cf. p. 175 ln. 8, cf. p. 205 ln. 6
12:18–19 → cf. p. 273 ln. 11
13:20–22 → p. 106 ln. 2
17:7–16 → cf. p. 352 ln. 18
20:42 → cf. p. 179 ln. 16, p. 180 ln. 1
21:27–29 → p. 381 ln. 15

II Kings

2:9 → cf. p. 74 ln. 7
2:23–24 → cf. p. 173 ln. 1, p. 440 ln. 12
4:7 → p. 232 ln. 6
4:18–37 → cf. p. 352 ln. 19, cf. p. 429 ln. 4
8:1–7 → p. 223 ln. 20
11:8 → cf. p. 341 ln. 3
13:23 → p. 207 ln. 10
14:5–6 → p. 205 ln. 1
16:5 → cf. p. 436 ln. 12, cf. p. 437 ln. 4
20:2–6 → cf. p. 74 ln. 5, cf. p. 74 ln. 8, cf. p. 392 ln. 4

I Chronicles

4:10 → p. 161 ln. 11
4:15 → cf. p. 219 ln. 11
4:43 → cf. p. 433 ln. 15
12:24 → cf. p. 426 ln. 2
16:22 → p. 132 ln. 8

II Chronicles

23:14 → p. 187 ln. 8
25:6–9 → p. 235 ln. 4
32:1–22 → cf. p. 67 ln. 19
35:20 → p. 180 ln. 9, p. 472 ln. 15

Ezra

1:1–5 → cf. p. 223 ln. 17
7:25–26 → p. 154 ln. 2
10:7–8 → p. 154 ln. 9
10:12–13 → p. 465 ln. 13

Nehemiah

2–6 → p. 341 ln. 9
5:1–12 → p. 155 ln. 8
7:3 → p. 463 ln. 19
9:3 → p. 462 ln. 7

Tobias

4:3 → p. 104 ln. 6
4:5 → p. 104 ln. 6
4:7 → cf. p. 72 ln. 4
4:11 → p. 70 ln. 1, p. 174 ln. 16
4:15 → p. 234 ln. 6, p. 234 ln. 11
6:10–13 → p. 334 ln. 17
8:24 → p. 334 ln. 21
13:22 → p. 340 ln. 8
14:14–15 → p. 334 ln. 24
14:15–17 → cf. p. 219 ln. 14

Judith

8:1 → cf. p. 352 ln. 20

Job

1:5 → p. 21 ln. 15, cf. p. 23 ln. 13

1:21 → p. 202 ln. 18, p. 315 ln. 14

2:10 → p. 21 ln. 17

29:16 → p. 138 ln. 13, p. 470 ln. 6

31:13 → p. 139 ln. 11

31:38–39 → p. 274 ln. 2, p. 274 ln. 4

42:15 → p. 225 ln. 15

Psalms (Gallican)

3:5 → p. 76 ln. 14

4:5 → p. 168 ln. 6

5:8 → p. 76 ln. 10, p. 392 ln. 6

6:7 → p. 385 ln. 7

7:12 → p. 118 ln. 5

9:2 → p. 448 ln. 3

9:20 → p. 441 ln. 5

14:5 → p. 237 ln. 2

15:6 → p. 162 ln. 4

21:19 → p. 162 ln. 9

23:1 → p. 94 ln. 13, p. 313 ln. 2

26:12 → p. 88 ln. 7

27:3 → cf. p. 305 ln. 18

31:5 → p. 384 ln. 3, p. 384 ln. 4

34:13 → p. 59 ln. 5

36:25 → p. 209 ln. 4

38:2 → p. 446 ln. 16

42:4 → p. 274 ln. 15

48:8 → cf. p. 82 ln. 13

50 → cf. p. 74 ln. 4

50:5–6 → p. 384 ln. 7

50:8 → p. 163 ln. 12

54:16 → p. 461 ln. 10

54:24 → p. 436 ln. 8

55:1 → cf. p. 436 ln. 14

57:5 → p. 448 ln. 1

57:11 → p. 168 ln. 7, p. 471 ln. 6

68:9 → p. 467 ln. 6

69:4 → p. 287 ln. 5

70:3 → p. 339 ln. 12

77:3–4 → p. 330 ln. 4

81:1 → p. 137 ln. 17

88:31–34 → p. 167 ln. 10, p. 471 ln. 20

88:32 → p. 208 ln. 18

93:1–2 → p. 168 ln. 2, p. 471 ln. 5

93:2 → p. 440 ln. 9

93:8 → p. 321 ln. 1

104:15 → p. 132 ln. 8

104:44 → p. 96 ln. 1

108:7 → p. 441 ln. 12

108:18 → p. 368 ln. 2

109:4 → p. 241 ln. 13

118:64 → p. 167 ln. 9

118:136 → p. 385 ln. 8

118:155 → p. 447 ln. 21

123:7 → p. 320 ln. 7

124:3 → p. 162 ln. 7

132:1 → p. 117 ln. 7

135:1 → p. 380 ln. 20

136:1 → p. 385 ln. 9

139:12 → p. 446 ln. 17

144:8 → p. 167 ln. 7, p. 177 ln. 6, p. 471 ln. 19

Proverbs

6:1 → cf. p. 237 ln. 17

6:30 → p. 197 ln. 6, p. 473 ln. 9

6:31 → p. 194 ln. 13

8:16 → p. 156 ln. 16

9:8 → p. 131 ln. 1

9:9 → p. 130 ln. 20

10:19 → p. 447 ln. 7, p. 447 ln. 11

11:15 → p. 237 ln. 18

12:19 → p. 84 ln. 6

13:3 → p. 447 ln. 13

13:4–6 → cf. p. 133 ln. 11

13:8 → p. 72 ln. 2

13:24 → cf. p. 169 ln. 14, p. 210 ln. 7

15:20 → p. 210 ln. 17

16:33 → p. 160 ln. 5

17:6 → p. 210 ln. 16

17:26 → cf. p. 133 ln. 11

18:18 → p. 161 ln. 9

18:21 → p. 447 ln. 12

20:16 → p. 237 ln. 19

20:21 → p. 270 ln. 16
20:28 → p. 149 ln. 7
20:29 → p. 19 ln. 15
21:6 → p. 465 ln. 7
22:26–27 → p. 237 ln. 14
22:28 → p. 251 ln. 9, p. 251 ln. 10
23:10 → p. 251 ln. 11
24:19 → p. 316 ln. 2
24:23 → p. 465 ln. 6
26:11 → cf. p. 392 ln. 12
27:17 → p. 131 ln. 2
27:19 → p. 143 ln. 2
28:21 → p. 465 ln. 4
30:9 → p. 191 ln. 12

Ecclesiastes

4:17 → p. 472 ln. 9
8:13 → p. 440 ln. 4
9:10 → p. 81 ln. 3
10:12 → p. 282 ln. 10
10:16 → p. 149 ln. 10
11:2 → p. 316 ln. 12

Canticles

2:2 → cf. p. 304 ln. 14
2:6 → p. 152 ln. 17
6:9 → cf. p. 349 ln. 7
8:3 → p. 152 ln. 17

Isaiah

1:15 → cf. p. 269 ln. 7
2:3 → p. 346 ln. 11
3:4 → p. 149 ln. 11
3:15 → p. 319 ln. 6
5:3 → p. 139 ln. 6
5:8 → p. 222 ln. 15
5:20 → p. 131 ln. 15
5:21 → p. 284 ln. 6
6:5 → p. 141 ln. 6, p. 279 ln. 9, p. 284 ln. 2, p. 470 ln. 9
6:8 → p. 270 ln. 6
10:14 → p. 284 ln. 9
11:14 → cf. p. 182 ln. 2
23:4 → p. 320 ln. 2
26:1 → cf. p. 343 ln. 19
26:10 → p. 189 ln. 14
28:20 → p. 372 ln. 12
29:10 → cf. p. 258 ln. 6
29:14 → p. 284 ln. 7
30:1 → cf. p. 176 ln. 14
30:10 → p. 141 ln. 14
33:16 → cf. p. 473 ln. 22
38:1 → p. 260 ln. 14
38:2–3 → cf. p. 74 ln. 5
41:1 → cf. p. 139 ln. 7
52:11 → p. 35 ln. 9
56:10 → p. 267 ln. 3, p. 284 ln. 3
57:6 → p. 372 ln. 14
57:8 → p. 372 ln. 14
58:1 → p. 36 ln. 8, p. 447 ln. 16
58:4 → p. 61 ln. 5, cf. p. 62 ln. 15, p. 316 ln. 3
58:6–7 → p. 64 ln. 7
58:7 → p. 214 ln. 5, p. 220 ln. 3, p. 428 ln. 18
61:6 → cf. p. 25 ln. 9
64:6 → p. 48 ln. 18, p. 461 ln. 23
65:2 → cf. p. 437 ln. 8

Sirach [Ecclesiasticus]

3:11 → cf. p. 216 ln. 10
3:22 → cf. p. 176 ln. 19
3:33 → p. 69 ln. 17, p. 174 ln. 3
7:24 → p. 435 ln. 2
7:29–30 → p. 210 ln. 13
12:1 → p. 300 ln. 13
19:18 → cf. p. 126 ln. 6
20:1 → p. 466 ln. 9
20:7 → p. 138 ln. 11
20:16 → p. 233 ln. 15
23:12–14 → p. 242 ln. 11
25:6 → p. 117 ln. 7, p. 134 ln. 13
29:4–9 → p. 233 ln. 10
30:1–6 → p. 229 ln. 15
34:23 → cf. p. 10 ln. 2, p. 29 ln. 5
34:30–31 → p. 61 ln. 14

Wisdom

1:1 → p. 121 ln. 1

4:8 → p. 134 ln. 15

6:2–7 → p. 145 ln. 16

6:7 → p. 146 ln. 5

Jeremiah

1:6 → p. 270 ln. 15

9:1 → p. 385 ln. 10

17:21–22 → p. 462 ln. 2

23:1 → p. 258 ln. 7

29:10 → cf. p. 223 ln. 17

32:6 → p. 239 ln. 9

32:7 → p. 239 ln. 9

32:11 → p. 239 ln. 9, p. 250 ln. 9

34:13–14 → p. 249 ln. 9

35:1–8 → p. 66 ln. 13

35:18–19 → p. 67 ln. 6, p. 215 ln. 9

37:16 → cf. p. 158 ln. 16

38:10 → cf. p. 158 ln. 16

38:16 → p. 241 ln. 20

38:20 → p. 241 ln. 20

38:24 → cf. p. 141 ln. 15

48:10 → p. 168 ln. 9, p. 471 ln. 7

50:8 → cf. p. 305 ln. 14

50:25 → cf. p. 177 ln. 10

Ezekiel

3:18 → p. 174 ln. 4

5:1 → p. 407 ln. 17

5:2 → cf. p. 411 ln. 11

5:6–8 → cf. p. 131 ln. 13

13:5 → p. 287 ln. 14

13:19 → p. 169 ln. 3, p. 471 ln. 11

16:3 → p. 205 ln. 13

18:4 → p. 204 ln. 18

18:7–8 → p. 237 ln. 4

18:9–13 → p. 208 ln. 5

18:14–22 → cf. p. 209 ln. 13

18:20–21 → p. 208 ln. 3

18:26 → cf. p. 209 ln. 17

28:28–30 → cf. p. 27 ln. 8

33:8 → p. 267 ln. 6

33:12–13 → p. 174 ln. 6, p. 390 ln. 6, cf. p. 390 ln. 17

34:2–5 → p. 258 ln. 9

44:28 → p. 28 ln. 5, p. 42 ln. 10

44:29–30 → p. 24 ln. 11

45:9 → cf. p. 258 ln. 6

45:16 → p. 260 ln. 9

48 (*sic*) → cf. p. 341 ln. 1

48:12–14 → p. 342 ln. 2

Daniel (Vulgate)

1:20 → cf. p. 135 ln. 1

2:29 → p. 406 ln. 21

2:31 → p. 407 ln. 1

2:48 → p. 101 ln. 13, cf. p. 319 ln. 14

3:29 → p. 207 ln. 21

3:29–45 → cf. p. 392 ln. 4

3:46–100 → cf. p. 60 ln. 13, cf. p. 172 ln. 11

3:32 → p. 207 ln. 21

4:24 → p. 70 ln. 13, p. 82 ln. 12, p. 174 ln. 2, p. 390 ln. 19

5:17 → p. 135 ln. 4, p. 140 ln. 5

6:16–23 → cf. p. 74 ln. 6, cf. p. 392 ln. 5

9:1–19 → cf. p. 207 ln. 20

9:23 → p. 60 ln. 1

10:11 → p. 60 ln. 1

10:19 → p. 60 ln. 1

12:3 → cf. p. 282 ln. 1

13 (*sic*) → cf. p. 163 ln. 5

13:5 → p. 143 ln. 12

14:3 → cf. p. 350 ln. 7

Osee

6:6 → cf. p. 69 ln. 15, p. 167 ln. 16

Joel

1:14 → p. 64 ln. 4, p. 64 ln. 13

2:15 → p. 64 ln. 4, p. 64 ln. 13

Amos

5:7 → p. 131 ln. 14

5:15 → cf. p. 119 ln. 11

Abdias [Obadiah]

1 → cf. p. 429 ln. 5

Jonah

1:4 → cf. p. 183 ln. 2

1:7 → p. 161 ln. 16, p. 163 ln. 4

2:1–9 → cf. p. 74 ln. 5

3:5 → cf. p. 391 ln. 3, cf. p. 434 ln. 19

3:7 → cf. p. 58 ln. 18, cf. p. 382 ln. 6

Habacuc

2:6 → p. 222 ln. 17, p. 319 ln. 5

Zechariah

8:19 → p. 120 ln. 19

Malachiah

2:7 → p. 51 ln. 11

II Maccabees

12:39–46 → cf. p. 80 ln. 4, cf. p. 307 ln. 4

Matthew

1:1–16 → p. 331 ln. 20

3:7 → p. 321 ln. 4

3:9 → p. 204 ln. 8

4:4 → p. 438 ln. 3

4:21–22 → cf. p. 266 ln. 1

5:7 → p. 460 ln. 7

5:9 → p. 121 ln. 8

5:13 → p. 131 ln. 18, p. 281 ln. 10

5:17 → p. 468 ln. 20

5:22 → p. 173 ln. 7, p. 424 ln. 17

5:23–24 → p. 444 ln. 22

5:31–32 → p. 363 ln. 18

5:33 → p. 241 ln. 22

5:34 → p. 243 ln. 4

5:34–35 → p. 242 ln. 19

5:40 → p. 315 ln. 17

5:44 → p. 167 ln. 12, p. 169 ln. 16, p. 191 ln. 9, p. 469 ln. 3, p. 471 ln. 21

5:45 → p. 329 ln. 23

5:48 → p. 329 ln. 23

6:2 → p. 71 ln. 10

6:3 → p. 71 ln. 9

6:4 → cf. p. 71 ln. 11

6:5 → p. 75 ln. 15

6:7 → p. 447 ln. 8

6:9 → p. 204 ln. 10

6:12 → p. 445 ln. 16

6:15 → cf. p. 167 ln. 14, cf. p. 445 ln. 15, cf. p. 472 ln. 1

6:16 → cf. p. 71 ln. 11

6:20 → p. 221 ln. 9

7:1 → p. 470 ln. 5

7:1–2 → p. 124 ln. 16

7:3 → p. 303 ln. 4

7:6 → p. 81 ln. 21, p. 468 ln. 10

7:21 → p. 75 ln. 11

8:20 → p. 49 ln. 11, p. 263 ln. 4

8:22 → p. 212 ln. 13

8:28 → cf. p. 433 ln. 1

9:10 → cf. p. 301 ln. 10

10:8 → p. 28 ln. 16, p. 135 ln. 9, p. 140 ln. 8

10:10 → p. 278 ln. 4

10:28 → p. 178 ln. 13

10:37 → p. 214 ln. 17

10:40 → p. 429 ln. 11

10:41 → p. 430 ln. 14

11:29 → p. 49 ln. 12

12:1–4 → cf. p. 197 ln. 11

12:49–50 → p. 70 ln. 10

13:30 → p. 304 ln. 13
14:10 → p. 158 ln. 1
14:13–21 → cf. p. 264 ln. 16, cf. p. 426 ln. 3
15:19 → p. 455 ln. 18
15:32 → p. 280 ln. 2
16:18 → p. 260 ln. 21
16:19 → p. 186 ln. 1
16:24 → cf. p. 152 ln. 21
17:1–4 → cf. p. 88 ln. 3
17:20 → cf. p. 62 ln. 13
17:25 → p. 151 ln. 14
17:26 → p. 150 ln. 15, p. 151 ln. 11, p. 221 ln. 18, p. 222 ln. 9, p. 395 ln. 11
18:3 → p. 424 ln. 19
18:5 → p. 49 ln. 15
18:10 → p. 424 ln. 7, p. 454 ln. 12
18:15–17 → p. 298 ln. 7
18:18 → p. 186 ln. 1
18:19 → p. 111 ln. 16
18:21 → cf. p. 167 ln. 17, cf. p. 446 ln. 3, cf. p. 472 ln. 4
18:21–22 → cf. p. 167 ln. 17
19:5–6 → p. 396 ln. 16
19:9 → cf. p. 358 ln. 3, p. 373 ln. 3
19:11 → p. 350 ln. 17
19:14 → p. 424 ln. 10, p. 427 ln. 19
19:21 → p. 49 ln. 14, p. 222 ln. 4, p. 293 ln. 12, p. 396 ln. 2
19:27 → p. 152 ln. 10, p. 222 ln. 5, p. 396 ln. 4
19:28 → cf. p. 460 ln. 9
19:29 → p. 214 ln. 17
20:2 → cf. p. 234 ln. 13, cf. p. 234 ln. 14
20:12 → cf. p. 234 ln. 13, cf. p. 234 ln. 14
20:22–23 → cf. p. 403 ln. 3
20:26 → p. 262 ln. 13
20:28 → p. 262 ln. 16, p. 263 ln. 9
21:12–17 → cf. p. 189 ln. 17
21:13 → p. 96 ln. 11, p. 275 ln. 5, p. 324 ln. 5, p. 324 ln. 7
21:17 → cf. p. 299 ln. 8
22:1–14 → p. 299 ln. 16, cf. p. 300 ln. 7
22:21 → cf. p. 133 ln. 14, p. 150 ln. 12, p. 222 ln. 2, cf. p. 395 ln. 8, cf. p. 470 ln. 13
22:39 → p. 170 ln. 9
23:2–3 → p. 280 ln. 8
23:4 → p. 279 ln. 12
23:5 → cf. p. 290 ln. 14
23:9 → cf. p. 71 ln. 14, p. 212 ln. 10
23:13 → p. 320 ln. 18
23:35 → cf. p. 346 ln. 13, cf. p. 397 ln. 16
24:28 → p. 456 ln. 23
24:35 → p. 251 ln. 17
25:21 → p. 264 ln. 19
25:34 → p. 306 ln. 19
25:36 → p. 228 ln. 11
25:40 → p. 70 ln. 3, p. 70 ln. 8
25:41 → p. 456 ln. 9
26:26 → cf. p. 23 ln. 14, cf. p. 39 ln. 16
26:28 → cf. p. 23 ln. 14
26:47–50 → cf. p. 305 ln. 2, cf. p. 390 ln. 14
26:52 → p. 190 ln. 11
26:60 → p. 88 ln. 8
26:60–61 → p. 285 ln. 13
26:67 → p. 133 ln. 4
27:5 → cf. p. 176 ln. 6, p. 382 ln. 14
27:38 → cf. p. 307 ln. 2
28:18 → p. 223 ln. 5
28:20 → p. 403 ln. 19

Mark

1:19–20 → cf. p. 266 ln. 1
5:11–13 → cf. p. 420 ln. 7, cf. p. 433 ln. 1
6:31–44 → cf. p. 264 ln. 16, cf. p. 426 ln. 3
7:21 → p. 455 ln. 18
9:1–4 → cf. p. 88 ln. 3
9:28 → p. 60 ln. 7
9:49 → p. 121 ln. 3
10:14 → p. 424 ln. 10, p. 427 ln. 19
10:35 → cf. p. 212 ln. 16
11:15 → cf. p. 189 ln. 17
11:17 → p. 96 ln. 11
11:20 → cf. p. 167 ln. 14, cf. p. 445 ln. 15, cf. p. 472 ln. 1
11:25 → cf. p. 441 ln. 14
12:17 → p. 150 ln. 12, p. 470 ln. 13
13:31 → p. 251 ln. 17
14:43–45 → cf. p. 305 ln. 2, cf. p. 390 ln. 14
15:27–28 → cf. p. 307 ln. 2
16:1 → cf. p. 264 ln. 1

Luke

1:20 → cf. p. 173 ln. 5
2:1 → p. 151 ln. 9
2:4 → cf. p. 151 ln. 3, p. 151 ln. 4
2:41–52 → cf. p. 119 ln. 9, cf. p. 134 ln. 18
3:23–38 → p. 332 ln. 12
4:4 → p. 438 ln. 3
4:17 → cf. p. 39 ln. 14
4:23 → p. 303 ln. 1
6:27 → p. 167 ln. 12, p. 169 ln. 16, p. 191 ln. 9, p. 469 ln. 3, p. 471 ln. 21
6:29–30 → p. 314 ln. 16
6:37 → cf. p. 167 ln. 13, cf. p. 445 ln. 14
7:47 → p. 174 ln. 8
8:2 → cf. p. 39 ln. 13
9:12–17 → cf. p. 264 ln. 16, cf. p. 426 ln. 3
9:28–30 → cf. p. 88 ln. 3
9:58 → p. 49 ln. 11
9:62 → p. 390 ln. 1
10:7 → p. 277 ln. 17
12:13 → cf. p. 220 ln. 1
14:26 → p. 215 ln. 2
15:4–6 → cf. p. 382 ln. 8
15:11–32 → cf. p. 382 ln. 7
17:3 → p. 445 ln. 21
17:37 → p. 456 ln. 23
18:11 → p. 48 ln. 19
18:16 → p. 424 ln. 10, p. 427 ln. 19
18:22 → p. 72 ln. 5
19:8 → p. 193 ln. 1
19:23 → cf. p. 236 ln. 14
19:45–48 → cf. p. 189 ln. 17
19:46 → p. 96 ln. 11
20:25 → p. 470 ln. 13
22:19 → p. 23 ln. 10
22:48 → cf. p. 305 ln. 2, cf. p. 390 ln. 14
23:33 → cf. p. 307 ln. 2
23:34 → cf. p. 167 ln. 19, cf. p. 472 ln. 7
23:43 → cf. p. 382 ln. 6, p. 390 ln. 21
23:56 → cf. p. 264 ln. 1
24:1–11 → cf. p. 85 ln. 10
24:50 → cf. p. 39 ln. 17

John

1:11 → p. 223 ln. 5
1:32 → cf. p. 408 ln. 9
1:47 → p. 36 ln. 5
2:8–9 → cf. p. 39 ln. 15
2:13–16 → cf. p. 189 ln. 17
2:19 → p. 285 ln. 19
2:25 → cf. p. 64 ln. 4
4:16–18 → p. 373 ln. 10
4:38 → p. 96 ln. 4
5:14 → p. 174 ln. 9, p. 391 ln. 4
5:17 → p. 453 ln. 17
5:31 → cf. p. 88 ln. 1
5:36 → cf. p. 88 ln. 1
6:1–14 → cf. p. 264 ln. 16, cf. p. 426 ln. 3
8:1–11 → cf. p. 181 ln. 1, cf. p. 182 ln. 13

8:39 → p. 209 ln. 9

8:55 → p. 142 ln. 8

10:22 → p. 450 ln. 14

12:6 → cf. p. 263 ln. 10

12:48 → p. 118 ln. 3

13:5 → cf. p. 39 ln. 15

13:14 → cf. p. 445 ln. 17

13:29 → cf. p. 273 ln. 3

14:15 → p. 96 ln. 5

14:27 → p. 121 ln. 2

18:13–40 → cf. p. 273 ln. 1

18:36 → p. 152 ln. 9

19:11 → p. 181 ln. 13

19:18 → cf. p. 307 ln. 2

19:22 → p. 126 ln. 16, p. 138 ln. 16, p. 251 ln. 16, p. 469 ln. 19

19:23–24 → cf. p. 308 ln. 9, cf. p. 325 ln. 20

20:23 → cf. p. 167 ln. 14, cf. p. 445 ln. 15, cf. p. 472 ln. 1

Acts

1:18 → cf. p. 176 ln. 6

1:23 → cf. p. 266 ln. 2

1:23–26 → p. 255 ln. 8

1:24–25 → p. 160 ln. 8

1:26 → p. 161 ln. 11, cf. p. 261 ln. 11

2:14 → cf. p. 447 ln. 17

4:32 → p. 274 ln. 21, cf. p. 289 ln. 7

4:32–35 → p. 292 ln. 18

5:1–5 → cf. p. 293 ln. 5, cf. p. 470 ln. 15

5:3 → cf. p. 163 ln. 7

5:5–10 → cf. p. 93 ln. 8, p. 104 ln. 15, cf. p. 138 ln. 3, cf. p. 170 ln. 11, cf. p. 173 ln. 9, cf. p. 176 ln. 7, cf. p. 471 ln. 8

6:2 → p. 466 ln. 18

6:2–4 → p. 32 ln. 8

6:3–5 → cf. p. 264 ln. 2, cf. p. 305 ln. 4

6:5 → cf. p. 264 ln. 17

7:58 → cf. p. 397 ln. 19

7:59 → p. 167 ln. 20, p. 472 ln. 8

8:20 → p. 26 ln. 2, p. 135 ln. 4, p. 270 ln. 18

8:21 → p. 162 ln. 5

9:3–9 → cf. p. 174 ln. 11, cf. p. 382 ln. 9

10:15 → p. 418 ln. 11

12:8 → p. 461 ln. 13

15:29 → p. 422 ln. 8

18:18 → p. 407 ln. 18, cf. p. 411 ln. 12

20:11 → cf. p. 301 ln. 13

20:34 → p. 467 ln. 1

21:25 → p. 422 ln. 8

27:33 → p. 58 ln. 13

27:35 → p. 58 ln. 15

Romans

1:32 → p. 181 ln. 10

2:1 → p. 177 ln. 7

2:11 → p. 126 ln. 11

2:24 → p. 320 ln. 11

7:2–3 → p. 359 ln. 5

8:35 → p. 453 ln. 7

8:38–39 → p. 469 ln. 14

9:1 → p. 241 ln. 16, p. 469 ln. 14

9:12 → cf. p. 218 ln. 4

9:22 → cf. p. 177 ln. 10

10:3 → p. 48 ln. 20

10:9 → cf. p. 174 ln. 10

11:33 → p. 177 ln. 1

12:17 → p. 320 ln. 12

12:19 → p. 199 ln. 20, p. 247 ln. 16, cf. p. 468 ln. 1

13:1–4 → p. 144 ln. 15

13:7 → p. 151 ln. 1, cf. p. 221 ln. 22, p. 231 ln. 5

14:2 → p. 416 ln. 13

14:2–3 → p. 422 ln. 17

14:3 → p. 417 ln. 6

14:5 → p. 64 ln. 11

14:6 → p. 417 ln. 6, p. 422 ln. 17

14:14 → p. 422 ln. 17

14:22 → p. 422 ln. 17

15:20 → p. 275 ln. 23

I Corinthians

1:10 → p. 122 ln. 11, p. 328 ln. 7
3:3 → p. 316 ln. 4
3:13 → p. 118 ln. 4
3:16 → p. 86 ln. 3
3:17 → p. 189 ln. 18, p. 344 ln. 11
3:19 → p. 126 ln. 7
5:5 → p. 170 ln. 14, cf. p. 177 ln. 16
5:11 → p. 276 ln. 8
5:13 → p. 135 ln. 15, p. 137 ln. 8
6:1–4 → p. 135 ln. 15
6:4 → p. 117 ln. 15
6:5–6 → p. 117 ln. 16
6:7–8 → p. 314 ln. 18
6:9–10 → cf. p. 245 ln. 14, cf. p. 442 ln. 14
6:10 → p. 468 ln. 2
6:12 → p. 417 ln. 1, p. 467 ln. 16
6:16 → cf. p. 369 ln. 5
6:18 → p. 361 ln. 12, p. 361 ln. 18
7:1–2 → p. 371 ln. 5
7:3 → p. 371 ln. 7
7:4 → p. 371 ln. 12, p. 371 ln. 15
7:5 → p. 371 ln. 9
7:9 → cf. p. 354 ln. 2, cf. p. 365 ln. 19
7:27 → p. 377 ln. 13
7:39 → p. 106 ln. 17
9:11 → p. 277 ln. 20
9:13 → p. 24 ln. 16, p. 278 ln. 5
9:14 → p. 278 ln. 6
9:27 → p. 279 ln. 14
10:25–26 → p. 303 ln. 8
10:25–29 → p. 423 ln. 6
10:26 → p. 395 ln. 11
10:27 → p. 303 ln. 10
11:4–5 → p. 411 ln. 9
11:10 → cf. p. 454 ln. 16
12:21–22 → p. 143 ln. 15, p. 273 ln. 15
13:5 → p. 197 ln. 14
13:11 → p. 134 ln. 17, p. 425 ln. 7
14:34–35 → p. 357 ln. 2
15:50 → p. 65 ln. 3

II Corinthians

3:16 → p. 409 ln. 15
5:17 → p. 253 ln. 18
6:3 → p. 320 ln. 9
6:14–15 → p. 298 ln. 14
6:15 → cf. p. 298 ln. 14
9:10 → p. 279 ln. 3
12:14 → p. 71 ln. 7

Galatians

1:9 → cf. p. 468 ln. 21
2:11–13 → p. 321 ln. 8
3:1 → p. 320 ln. 19
4:16 → p. 141 ln. 17
4:19 → p. 204 ln. 12
4:30 → cf. p. 369 ln. 20
5:12 → p. 440 ln. 6

Ephesians

4:28 → p. 174 ln. 13, p. 197 ln. 4, p. 473 ln. 11
5:18 → p. 416 ln. 12
5:22 → p. 372 ln. 6
6:1 → p. 210 ln. 18
6:4 → p. 210 ln. 8
6:5–8 → p. 144 ln. 2
6:9 → p. 143 ln. 17

Philippians

3:19 → p. 191 ln. 11

Colossians

3:9–10 → p. 409 ln. 4
4:6 → p. 287 ln. 2

I Thessalonians

5:17 → p. 73 ln. 12
5:21 → p. 131 ln. 3

I Timothy

2:1 → p. 74 ln. 13

2:4 → cf. p. 130 ln. 9

2:12 → p. 356 ln. 16

3:1 → p. 4 ln. 16

3:1–2 → p. 8 ln. 6

3:2–3 → cf. p. 21 ln. 4, p. 144 ln. 9

3:5 → p. 270 ln. 2

3:6 → p. 8 ln. 11, p. 8 ln. 14

3:8–10 → p. 32 ln. 18

4:8 → p. 210 ln. 19

5:1–4 → p. 321 ln. 14

5:9 → p. 353 ln. 2

5:10 → p. 353 ln. 12

5:20 → p. 320 ln. 17

5:22 → p. 8 ln. 9

5:23 → p. 64 ln. 1

6:9 → cf. p. 389 ln. 21, p. 389 ln. 22

II Timothy

2:4 → p. 389 ln. 20

2:20 → cf. p. 306 ln. 18

2:24 → p. 262 ln. 9

3:1–5 → p. 271 ln. 18

4:2 → p. 287 ln. 11

4:14 → p. 440 ln. 7

Titus

2:15 → p. 287 ln. 10

3:10–11 → p. 431 ln. 15

Philemon

1:10–17 → cf. p. 181 ln. 20

Hebrews

9:13–14 → p. 23 ln. 6

9:17 → p. 90 ln. 17, p. 261 ln. 12

11:31 → cf. p. 180 ln. 12

12:6 → p. 169 ln. 17

13:2 → p. 428 ln. 16

Jacob

2:13 → p. 472 ln. 3

3:1 → p. 461 ln. 8

5:14 → p. 74 ln. 11

5:16 → p. 73 ln. 18, p. 174 ln. 15, p. 381 ln. 7, p. 393 ln. 15

5:17–18 → cf. p. 74 ln. 3

I Peter

1:12 → p. 268 ln. 6

2:9 → p. 409 ln. 12

2:13–14 → p. 144 ln. 12

2:18 → p. 144 ln. 6, p. 272 ln. 16

2:23 → p. 49 ln. 16

I John

5:16 → p. 81 ln. 12

II John

10–11 (*sic*) → p. 300 ln. 10

Apocalypse

2:5 → p. 51 ln. 6

3:19 → p. 321 ln. 2

5:1 → cf. p. 78 ln. 17

6:10 → p. 178 ln. 1

11:12 → p. 447 ln. 18

13:10 → p. 168 ln. 10, p. 471 ln. 15

14:4 → p. 424 ln. 6

17:1 → cf. p. 346 ln. 18

18:16 → cf. p. 346 ln. 18

18:19 → cf. p. 346 ln. 18

19:10 → p. 350 ln. 6

21:15 → p. 341 ln. 6, p. 341 ln. 8

22:11 → p. 177 ln. 11

Hermas, the Shepherd

4:1 → p. 366 ln. 14

4:4 → p. 366 ln. 1

Acta Andreae

pp. 24–25 (ed. Bonnet) → p. 164 ln. 17

Passion of St. Peter (Pseudo-Abdias)

15 → p. 261 ln. 1

***Virtutes Iohannis* (Pseudo-Abdias)**

7 → p. 118 ln. 1

Index of sources

- If edition coordinates are too broad or ambiguous then page numbers are given in the apparatus and occasionally in the index
- A colon in the coordinates of some commentaries indicates division by biblical verse

Acta Andreae (Pseudo-Abdias)

See Bible and Apocrypha

Aldhelm

Epist. 4, *Ad Geruntium*, ed. R. Ehwald, MGH Auct. ant. 15 (Berlin, 1919), 480–6

pp. 483–4 → cf. p. 407 ln. 10

Ambrose

De spiritu sancto
ed. O. Faller, CSEL 79 (1963)

3.6.36 → p. 133 ln. 17

Expositio euangelii secundum Lucam
ed. M. Adriaen, CCSL 14 (1957)

20:24 → p. 152 ln. 8

6:25, 26 → p. 159 ln. 5

Expositio de psalmo cxviii
ed. M. Petschenig, CSEL 62 (1913)

Sermo 12.32 → p. 125 ln. 11,
p. 127 ln. 11

Augustine

De ciuitate Dei
ed. B. Dombart and A. Kalb, CCSL 47–8 (1955)

16.17 → cf. p. 112 ln. 13

22.30 (p. 862 ln. 22–3) → p. 276 ln. 20

De consensu euangelistarum
ed. F. Weihrich, CSEL 43 (1904)

2.3 (pp. 84–5) → p. 230 ln. 2

De cura pro mortuis gerenda
ed. J. Zycha, CSEL 41 (1900), 619–60

10.12 (p. 641) → p. 402 ln. 3,
p. 405 ln. 8

De Genesi ad litteram
ed. J. Zycha, CSEL 28(1) (1894)

3.11 (p. 75) → p. 420 ln. 10

De sermone Domini in monte
ed. A. Mutzenbecher, CCSL 35 (1967)

1.20.63 (p. 72) → p. 169 ln. 8

1.20.64–5 (pp. 73–5) → p. 170 ln. 1

2.8.28 (p. 117) → p. 233 ln. 1

2.8.28 (p. 117) → p. 232 ln. 18

De trinitate
ed. W. J. Mountain, CCSL 50–50A (1968)

2.1 (p. 80) → p. 469 ln. 4

4.6 (p. 175) → p. 131 ln. 9,
p. 141 ln. 2

Enchiridion ad Laurentium de fide et spe et caritate
ed. E. Evans, CCSL 46 (1969), 49–114

39 → p. 230 ln. 16

72 → p. 171 ln. 5

110 (p. 109 ln. 26) → cf. p. 77 ln. 8,
p. 77 ln. 12

Ennarationes in psalmos
ed. E. Dekkers and J. Fraipont, CCSL 38–40 (1956)

3.4 (p. 8 ln. 1–6) → p. 76 ln. 15

7.8 (p. 41 ln. 24–25) → p. 423 ln. 15

30.2.2.13 (p. 211 ln. 4–5) → cf. p. 159 ln. 11
p. 159 ln. 13

30.2.2.13 (p. 211 ln. 13–14) → p. 160 ln. 4

In Iohannis euangelium tractatus cxxiv
ed. A. Mayer, CCSL 36 (1954)

19:23 → cf. p. 159 ln. 15

43:12 (p. 378 ln. 26) → p. 178 ln. 15

Quaestiones euangeliorum
ed. A. Mutzenbecher, CCSL 44B (1980)

1.23 → p. 151 ln. 15

Sermones 1–50
ed. C. Lambot, CCSL 41 (1961)

9.20 → p. 216 ln. 14,
p. 220 ln. 6,
p. 221 ln. 2

Sermo 4 (*apud* Mai)
ed. A. Mai, *Spicilegium Romanum* (Rome, 1839–44), vol. 8
Repr. PL 47:1147–8 (*CPL* §372)

PL 47:1148 → p. 76 ln. 5,
p. 76 ln. 7

Sermo 74
ed. Maurists, *Sancti Aurelii Augustini Hipponensis episcopi operum*, 11 vols. (Paris, 1679–1700), vol. 5
Repr. PL 38:472–4

PL 38:473 → p. 158 ln. 5

Sermo 392 (*CPL* §285)
PL 39:1709–13

2.2 → p. 365 ln. 13,
p. 367 ln. 16

Sermo 393
PL 39:1713–15 (*CPL* §285)

PL 39:1714 → p. 458 ln. 14

Augustinus Hibernicus

De mirabilibus sacrae scripturae
PL 35:2149–2200

3.17 (PL 35:2200) → p. 93 ln. 10

Basil (tr. Rufinus)

Regula
ed. K. Zelzer, CSEL 86 (1986)

9 (pp. 46–7) → p. 65 ln. 6

77 → p. 125 ln. 6

120 → p. 181 ln. 11

Asceticon
ed. L. Holste (Rome, 1661)
Repr. PL 103:483–554

Interrog. 40 (PL 103:513) → p. 459 ln. 3

Interrog. 89 (PL 103:524) → p. 58 ln. 8

Interrog. 130 (PL 103:534) → p. 43 ln. 17

Pseudo-Basil

Admonitio ad filium spiritualem
ed. L. Holsten, *Codex Regularum* (Paris, 1663) Appendix 20–34
Repr. PL 103:683–700 (*CPL* §1155*a*)

3 (PL 103:687) → p. 213 ln. 3

Benedict

Regula
ed. A. de Vogüé and J. Neufville, *La régle de Saint Benoît, Sources chrétiennes* 181–6 (Paris, 1972)

1 (pp. 436–40) → cf. p. 292 ln. 1

Caesarius of Arles

Sermones
ed. G. Morin, CCSL 103, 104 (1953)

1.8 → p. 285 ln. 6

1.17 → p. 437 ln. 20

33.2 (p. 145) → p. 96 ln. 15

43.1 (p. 190) → p. 368 ln. 3

54.1 → p. 451 ln. 5,
p. 451 ln. 9,
p. 453 ln. 2

54.3 → p. 452 ln. 10

54.5 → p. 451 ln. 13

192.4 → p. 68 ln. 18

199.2 → p. 73 ln. 2

Epist. de Concilio Massiliense 533
ed. C. de Clerq, CCSL 148A (1963), 90–6

pp. 91–2 ln. 147–8 → p. 169 ln. 1,
p. 471 ln. 16

Canones Adomnani

ed. L. Bieler, *The Irish Penitentials*, SLH 5 (Dublin, 1963), 176–80

14, 17 → cf. p. 417 ln. 11

16 → p. 361 ln. 2

Canones apostolorum

Dionysiana I, ed. A. Strewe, *Die Canonessammlung des Dionysius Exiguus in der ersten Redaktion* (Berlin, 1931), 1–10
EOMIA 1:32a–32ii

3 → p. 10 ln. 13

4 → p. 10 ln. 16

5 → p. 10 ln. 19

7 → p. 31 ln. 8

14 → p. 19 ln. 5

17 → p. 5 ln. 4,
p. 14 ln. 2

18 → p. 14 ln. 5

20 → p. 238 ln. 2

21 → p. 18 ln. 7

22 → p. 18 ln. 7

39 → p. 310 ln. 1,
p. 310 ln. 9 (*app. crit.*)

Canones in causa Apiarii c. 420

ed. C. Munier, CCSL 149 (1974), 101–49

30 → p. 247 ln. 13

Cassian

De institutis coenobiorum
ed. M. Petschenig, CSEL 17 (1888), 3–231

5.35 → p. 65 ln. 13

12.11 → p. 383 ln. 20

Collationes
ed. M. Petschenig, CSEL 13 (1886)

2.26 → cf. p. 252 ln. 1

5.11 → p. 57 ln. 8
5.21 → p. 57 ln. 14
5.24 → p. 223 ln. 11
18.8 → p. 290 ln. 5
20.8 (p. 564) → p. 384 ln. 2
24.15 → p. 455 ln. 2

Cassiodorus

Expositio sancti Pauli Epistulae ad Romanos
PL 68:415–506 (*CPL* §902)

1:29 (PL 68:421) → p. 316 ln. 7

Celestine I

Epist. 4, *Ad episcopos per Viennensem et Narbonensem prouincias* (J³ 821)
ed. P. Coustant, *Epistolae Romanorum Pontificum* (Paris, 1721), 1065–72

4.7 → p. 14 ln. 10
4.8 → p. 14 ln. 13

Pseudo-Clemens Romanus

Epist. ad Iacobum (tr. Rufinus)
ed. B. Rehm and F. Paschke, GCS 51 (1965)

3.2 → p. 15 ln. 1, p. 261 ln. 5
10.1 → p. 136 ln. 10
10.2–4 → p. 201 ln. 2

Recognitiones (tr. Rufinus)
ed. B. Rehm and F. Paschke, GCS 51 (1965)

1.67 → p. 140 ln. 15
2.5 → p. 130 ln. 13, p. 142 ln. 15
2.25 → p. 129 ln. 2
2.36 → p. 121 ln. 11
2.72 → p. 383 ln. 10
3.19 → p. 130 ln. 11
4.16 → p. 64 ln. 15
4.21 → p. 141 ln. 8
5.4 → p. 130 ln. 4
6.2 → p. 383 ln. 14
6.6 → p. 213 ln. 7
7.37 → p. 67 ln. 12, p. 67 ln. 14, p. 67 ln. 15
8.61 → p. 129 ln. 16
9.7 → p. 232 ln. 8
9.19 → p. 55 ln. 20
10.44 → p. 383 ln. 16

Councils

See also *canones, Registri eccl. Carth., sinodus, Statuta, synodus*

Council of Agde 506

ed. C. Munier, CCSL 148 (1963), 192–228

4 → p. 94 ln. 2
5 → p. 94 ln. 6, p. 314 ln. 9
6 → p. 30 ln. 15, p. 31 ln. 3, p. 277 ln. 12
7 → p. 309 ln. 1
10 → p. 45 ln. 17
16 → cf. p. 388 ln. 15

18 → p. 321 ln. 20

19 → p. 355 ln. 2,
p. 426 ln. 12

27 → p. 293 ln. 19,
p. 336 ln. 2

32 → p. 136 ln. 18

38 → p. 297 ln. 13

41 → p. 383 ln. 2

42 → p. 452 ln. 2

Council of Ancyra 314

Dionysiana I, ed. A. Strewe, *Die Canonessammlung des Dionysius Exiguus in der ersten Redaktion* (Berlin, 1931), 31–8
EOMIA 2:54–115

10 → p. 377 ln. 6

20 → p. 352 ln. 12

21 → p. 188 ln. 2

22 → cf. p. 186 ln. 8

23 → cf. p. 452 ln. 7

24 → p. 354 ln. 10

Council of Antioch 341

Dionysiana I, ed. A. Strewe, *Die Canonessammlung des Dionysius Exiguus in der ersten Redaktion* (Berlin, 1931), 44–52

20 → p. 3 ln. 14

22 → cf. p. 9 ln. 21

24 → p. 275 ln. 12,
p. 309 ln. 11,
p. 309 ln. 19

Council of Arles 314

ed. C. Munier, CCSL 148 (1963), 9–24

4 → cf. p. 390 ln. 3

11 → p. 366 ln. 8

15 → p. 92 ln. 1

Council of Carthage 419

Dionysiana I, ed. A. Strewe, *Die Canonessammlung des Dionysius Exiguus in der ersten Redaktion* (Berlin, 1931), 70–85

29 → p. 113 ln. 8

ed. C. Munier, CCSL 149 (1974), 230–2

131 → p. 84 ln. 15,
p. 85 ln. 1

Council of Chalcedon 451

Dionysiana I, ed. A. Strewe, *Die Canonessammlung des Dionysius Exiguus in der ersten Redaktion* (Berlin, 1931), 98–105

3 → p. 31 ln. 10,
p. 46 ln. 18

9 → p. 42 ln. 17,
p. 43 ln. 2,
p. 43 ln. 13

10 → p. 297 ln. 3

18 → p. 317 ln. 17

Council of Gangra *c.* 343

Dionysiana I, ed. A. Strewe, *Die Canonessammlung des Dionysius Exiguus in der ersten Redaktion* (Berlin, 1931), 41–4
EOMIA 2:147–214

2 → p. 418 ln. 2

3 → p. 145 ln. 2

8 → p. 99 ln. 6

11 → p. 439 ln. 6

15 → p. 214 ln. 2

16 → p. 212 ln. 3

17 → p. 411 ln. 2

18 → p. 68 ln. 9,
p. 466 ln. 13

Council of Laodicea 4th cent.

Dionysiana I, ed. A. Strewe, *Die Canonessammlung des Dionysius Exiguus in der ersten Redaktion* (Berlin, 1931), 52–60

EOMIA 2:322–400

28 → p. 324 ln. 3

51 → p. 400 ln. 11

53 → p. 43 ln. 6

54 → p. 43 ln. 8

Council of Neocaesarea 315

Dionysiana I, ed. A. Strewe, *Die Canonessammlung des Dionysius Exiguus in der ersten Redaktion* (Berlin, 1931), 38–40

EOMIA 2:12–14, 116–141

2 → p. 376 ln. 14,
cf. p. 377 ln. 1

Council of Nicaea 325

Dionysiana I, ed. A. Strewe, *Die Canonessammlung des Dionysius Exiguus in der ersten Redaktion* (Berlin, 1931), 24–31

EOMIA 1:103–273

13 → p. 387 ln. 14

16 → cf. p. 296 ln. 3

17 → p. 46 ln. 9,
p. 197 ln. 12

Council of Orange 441

ed. C. Munier, CCSL 148 (1963), 78–93

5 → p. 322 ln. 2

9 → p. 336 ln. 5,
p. 336 ln. 9

30 → p. 18 ln. 2

Council of Orléans 511

ed. C. Munier, CCSL 148A (1963), 4–19

1 → p. 188 ln. 12

6 → p. 136 ln. 14

18 → p. 376 ln. 9

22 → p. 298 ln. 3,
p. 337 ln. 9

23 → p. 318 ln. 9

Council of Sardica 343

ed. G. Voellus & H. Justel, *Bibliotheca Juris Canonici* (Paris, 1661), I
Repr. PL 56:773–84

EOMIA 1:452–544

15 → p. 11 ln. 2

Council of Vaison 442

ed. C. Munier, CCSL 148 (1963), 96–104

4 → p. 97 ln. 21,
p. 314 ln. 13

9 → p. 203 ln. 19

10 → p. 203 ln. 19

Cumméne

Paenitentiale, ed. L. Bieler, *The Irish Penitentials*, SLH 5 (Dublin, 1963), 108–34

9.13 → cf. p. 435 ln. 9

De canibus sinodus sapientium

ed. L. Bieler, *The Irish Penitentials*, SLH 5 (Dublin, 1963), 174

1 → p. 413 ln. 17

2 → p. 414 ln. 19

De duodecim abusiuis saeculi

ed. S. Hellmann, *Ps. Cyprian. De XII abusivis saeculi*, Texte und Untersuchungen 34.1 (Leipzig, 1909), 32–60

9 (pp. 51–3) → p. 148 ln. 8

9 (pp. 52–3) → p. 147 ln. 14

Dionysius Exiguus

Praefatio ad Stephanum Episcopum
ed. F. Glorie, CCSL 85 (1972), 38–42

4–5 → cf. p. 3 ln. 8

Eucherius

Instructionum ad Salonium libri duo
ed. C. Mandolfo, CCSL 66 (2004), 77–216

1 (p. 92) → p. 125 ln. 17

1 (p. 97) → p. 56 ln. 2

1 (p. 173) → p. 74 ln. 15

1 (p. 179) → p. 418 ln. 8

Eusebius

Chronicon (tr. Jerome)
ed. R. Helm, GCS 47 (1956)

Olymp. 162 (pp. 145–6[h]) → p. 307 ln. 12

Olymp. 184 (p. 158[f]) → p. 156 ln. 5

Olymp. 195 (p. 169[k]) → p. 348 ln. 14

Olymp. 210 (pp. 182–3[k]) → p. 348 ln. 16

Olymp. 212 (p. 187[a]) → p. 183 ln. 14, p. 189 ln. 16, p. 347 ln. 5

Olymp. 219 (pp. 192–3[d]) → p. 230 ln. 6

Olymp. 239 (pp. 207–8[d–f]) → p. 156 ln. 8

Olymp. 256 (p. 217[d]) → p. 450 ln. 11

Ecclesiastica Historia (tr. Rufinus)
ed. E. Schwartz and T. Mommsen, GCS 9 (Berlin, 1903)

1.3.17 → p. 47 ln. 11

1.7.7–10 → p. 333 ln. 16

3.31.3 → p. 105 ln. 17

4.14.6 → p. 304 ln. 1

4.14.7 → p. 304 ln. 6

5.3.2–3 → p. 65 ln. 15

6.5.5 → p. 243 ln. 9

6.8.7 → p. 16 ln. 3

6.11.1–2 → p. 16 ln. 6

6.19.7 → p. 117 ln. 11

6.44.1–6 → p. 387 ln. 16

7.30.20–21 → p. 16 ln. 10

9.10.11 → p. 102 ln. 10, p. 252 ln. 4, p. 318 ln. 12

10.2 → p. 15 ln. 10, p. 137 ln. 11

10.5 → p. 201 ln. 6

Eutropius

Breuiarium ab urbe condita
ed. C. Santini, MGH Auct. ant. 2 (Berlin, 1978), 4–182

8.18.1 → p. 147 ln. 2

Excerpta de libris Romanorum et Francorum

ed. L. Bieler, *The Irish Penitentials*, SLH 5 (Dublin, 1963), 136–48

26 → cf. p. 426 ln. 6

27 → cf. p. 195 ln. 4

47 → cf. p. 360 ln. 17

59 → cf. p. 360 ln. 20

60 → cf. p. 360 ln. 23

Gennadius

Liber ecclesiasticorum dogmatum
ed. C. H. Turner, *J Theological Studies* 7 (1905/6): 89–99

22 → p. 384 ln. 13

40 → p. 398 ln. 4

46 → p. 387 ln. 2

Gildas

Fragmenta Gildae
ed. M. Winterbottom, *Gildas. The Ruin of Britain and Other Documents* (London, 1978), 143–5

1 → p. 301 ln. 2

2 → p. 61 ln. 18

3 → p. 48 ln. 11

4 → p. 293 ln. 15,
p. 294 ln. 7

5 → p. 15 ln. 13,
p. 294 ln. 2,
p. 295 ln. 18

6 → p. 272 ln. 5

7 → p. 15 ln. 15,
cf. p. 276 ln. 3,
p. 276 ln. 6

8 → p. 140 ln. 13

9 → p. 259 ln. 6

10 → p. 295 ln. 11

Gregory I

Dialogi
ed. de Vogüé, *Grégoire le Grand. Dialogues*, SC 251, 260, 265 (1978–80)

1.1.6 → p. 256 ln. 18

1.4.19 → p. 256 ln. 21

1.5.6 → p. 256 ln. 23

1.9.18 → p. 413 ln. 2

1.10.7 → p. 257 ln. 4

1.12.4 → p. 438 ln. 15

2.3.10 → p. 257 ln. 7

2.23.2 → p. 257 ln. 14

2.23.4–5 → p. 78 ln. 6

2.24.1–2 → p. 78 ln. 11

2.34.2 → p. 111 ln. 3

3.15.7 → p. 442 ln. 6

3.15.9–10 → p. 442 ln. 12

3.15.17 → p. 76 ln. 2

3.26.8 → p. 403 ln. 3

3.37.20 → p. 283 ln. 10

4.12.3 → p. 377 ln. 9

4.19.1 → cf. p. 424 ln. 21

4.25.2–4.26.1 → p. 456 ln. 15

4.26.1 → p. 456 ln. 21

4.27.14 → p. 177 ln. 2

4.30.4–5 → p. 456 ln. 2

4.42.3 → p. 79 ln. 2

4.44.10 → cf. p. 78 ln. 17

4.50.2–6 → p. 406 ln. 4

4.53.1–2 → p. 109 ln. 16

4.53.3 → p. 110 ln. 15

4.54.1–2 → p. 110 ln. 1

4.55.2–3 → p. 110 ln. 7

4.55.4 → p. 109 ln. 11,
p. 110 ln. 17

4.56.1–2 → p. 110 ln. 11

4.57.14 → p. 78 ln. 15

Homiliae in Euangelia
ed. R. Étaix, CCSL 141 (1999)

6.6 (pp. 43–4) → p. 285 ln. 6

7.4 → p. 462 ln. 10

14.2 → p. 287 ln. 16

15.2 → p. 394 ln. 6

17.5 → p. 267 ln. 20

17.7 → p. 277 ln. 18,
p. 278 ln. 1

17.8 → p. 274 ln. 2,
p. 274 ln. 4

18.2 → p. 462 ln. 14

18.4 → p. 462 ln. 17

22.9 → cf. p. 8 ln. 1

23.2 → cf. p. 429 ln. 7

26.5 → p. 14 ln. 18,
p. 169 ln. 5,
p. 471 ln. 13

27.7–8 → p. 441 ln. 13

39.2 → p. 26 ln. 4

40.3 → p. 49 ln. 4,
p. 458 ln. 5

Homiliae in Hiezechihelem Prophetam
ed. M. Adriaen, CCSL 142 (1971)

9.14 → p. 159 ln. 7,
p. 299 ln. 5

9.22–23 → p. 339 ln. 3

11.10 → p. 267 ln. 8

11.12–15 → p. 286 ln. 21

Moralia in Iob
ed. M. Adriaen, CCSL 143 (1979)

5.11 → p. 467 ln. 17

32.15 → p. 398 ln. 18

Registrum epistularum
ed. D. Norberg, *S. Gregorii Magni registrum epistularum*,
CCSL 140–140A (1982)

Epist. 1.24 (p. 23) ad Iohannem *et al.* (J³ 2099) → p. 279 ln. 18

Epist. 9.219 (pp. 783–4) ad Suagrium *et al.* (J³ 2863) → p. 25 ln. 12

Epist. 9.219 (p. 786) ad Suagrium *et al.* (J³ 2863) → p. 269 ln. 10

Epist. 9.219 (p. 787) ad Suagrium *et al.* (J³ 2863) or *Epist*. 11.46 (p. 943) ad Brunigildam (J³ 2964) → p. 27 ln. 11,
cf. p. 28 ln. 9

Regula pastoralis
ed. F. Rommel, CS 381–2 (1992)

1.2 → p. 27 ln. 12

1.10 → p. 256 ln. 14

1.11 → p. 256 ln. 14

2.2 → p. 128 ln. 16

2.7 (pp. 220–2) → p. 19 ln. 18, p. 136 ln. 3

2.10 (p. 250) → p. 257 ln. 12

3.2 → p. 302 ln. 3

3.4 → p. 259 ln. 2

3.14 (p. 348) → p. 459 ln. 1

3.23 (p. 414) → p. 121 ln. 8

Hermas

See Bible and Apocrypha

Pseudo-Hilary

Commentary on Catholic Epistles
ed. E. McNally, CCSL 108B (1973)

II John 1:10 → cf. p. 276 ln. 4, p. 298 ln. 16

Innocent I

For the decretals below see also *Dionysiana* version, ed. C. Justel, *Codex Canonum Ecclesiasticorum Dionysii Exigui* (Paris, 1628) §§ 10, 13, 22, 23, 24. Repr. PL 67:238–62

Epist. 2, *Ad Victricium* (J[3] 665)
ed. P. Coustant, *Epistolae Romanorum Pontificum* (Paris, 1721), 746–58

2.6 → p. 113 ln. 13, p. 114 ln. 7

Epist. 6, *Ad Exsuperium* (J[3] 675)
ed. P. Coustant, *Epistolae Romanorum Pontificum* (Paris, 1721), 789–96

6.6 → p. 388 ln. 13

6.8 → p. 45 ln. 10

6.10 → p. 379 ln. 13, p. 379 ln. 16

6.11 → p. 45 ln. 14

6.13 → cf. p. 111 ln. 7

Isidore

Chronica
ed. T. Mommsen, MGH Auct. ant. 11 (1894), 424–88

252, 255 → p. 156 ln. 1

272–3 → p. 155 ln. 19

325, 327, 329–30 → p. 102 ln. 16, p. 252 ln. 9, p. 318 ln. 16, p. 390 ln. 10

390, 395–6 → p. 103 ln. 4

De ecclesiasticis officiis
ed. C. M. Lawson, CCSL 113 (1989)

1.35.1–4 → p. 350 ln. 2, p. 401 ln. 12

1.37 [36].4–5 → p. 57 ln. 18

1.43 [42].3 → p. 60 ln. 16

1.45.1 → p. 415 ln. 17, p. 416 ln. 10

1.45.2 → p. 418 ln. 14

2.1.1 → p. 42 ln. 14

2.4.1–2 → p. 407 ln. 12

2.4.3 → p. 409 ln. 2

2.4.4 → p. 409 ln. 9

2.5.1 → p. 20 ln. 5

2.5.2 → p. 6 ln. 2

2.5.3 → p. 6 ln. 6

2.5.5 → p. 6 ln. 8

2.5.7 → p. 256 ln. 7

2.5.8 → p. 4 ln. 9, p. 4 ln. 12, p. 4 ln. 17

2.5.9 → p. 6 ln. 12

2.5.10 → p. 13 ln. 5

2.5.11 → p. 7 ln. 8

2.5.12 → p. 7 ln. 17, cf. p. 8 ln. 9, p. 8 ln. 11

2.5.13 → p. 8 ln. 14

2.5.15 → p. 5 ln. 7, p. 10 ln. 9

2.5.16 → p. 10 ln. 10, p. 10 ln. 12

2.5.17–19 → p. 9 ln. 11

2.5.19 → p. 124 ln. 11

2.6.1 → p. 8 ln. 3

2.7.1 → cf. p. 19 ln. 13, p. 20 ln. 2, p. 134 ln. 16

2.7.1–2 → p. 20 ln. 14

2.7.4 → p. 19 ln. 13

2.8.1 → p. 32 ln. 2

2.8.3–4 → p. 33 ln. 8

2.8.4 → p. 34 ln. 2

2.8.5 → p. 33 ln. 3

2.10.1 → p. 35 ln. 3, p. 36 ln. 2

2.10.2 → p. 35 ln. 6

2.11.1 → p. 36 ln. 8

2.11.2 → p. 37 ln. 2

2.11.5 → p. 37 ln. 8

2.12.1, 2 → p. 41 ln. 2

2.13.1, 3 → p. 37 ln. 14

2.15 [14].1 → p. 38 ln. 12, p. 39 ln. 2

2.16.1 → p. 288 ln. 7

2.16.2–9 → p. 289 ln. 2

2.18.11 → p. 357 ln. 8

2.20.4 → p. 365 ln. 18

2.20.9 → p. 368 ln. 9, p. 368 ln. 11

2.20.12 → p. 364 ln. 7

Epist. ad Massonam
PL 83:899–902

2–3 → p. 52 ln. 3

7–9 → p. 51 ln. 10

10–11 → p. 52 ln. 13

Etymologiae
ed. W. M. Lindsay, *Isidori Hispalensis episcopi etymologiarum siue originum libri XX*, 2 vols. (Oxford, 1911)

2.10.1–3 → p. 53 ln. 8

2.10.4 → p. 54 ln. 2

2.30.14–16 → p. 83 ln. 7

5.1.1–3 → p. 56 ln. 9

5.2.1 → p. 54 ln. 10

5.3.1–2 → p. 54 ln. 15

5.3.3 → p. 53 ln. 8

5.4.1–2 → p. 54 ln. 19

5.5 → p. 55 ln. 3

5.6 → p. 55 ln. 5

5.20.1 → p. 54 ln. 6

5.21 → p. 55 ln. 15

5.24.2 → p. 83 ln. 4, p. 90 ln. 13

5.24.3 → p. 91 ln. 6

5.25.2–3 → p. 55 ln. 8

5.26.1 → p. 192 ln. 16

5.26.18 → p. 191 ln. 3

5.27.4 → p. 164 ln. 14, p. 165 ln. 11

5.39.35–6 → cf. p. 102 ln. 16

6.16.5–9 → p. 2 ln. 8
6.16.11–13 → p. 1 ln. 16
6.19.65 → p. 57 ln. 3,
p. 59 ln. 19
6.19.67–68 → p. 59 ln. 19
6.19.70 → p. 59 ln. 19
7.12.1–2 → cf. p. 42 ln. 3,
cf. p. 42 ln. 9
7.12.11 → p. 4 ln. 10
7.12.22 → cf. p. 31 ln. 17
8.1.1 → p. 313 ln. 7
8.3.1–2 → cf. p. 431 ln. 2
8.11.15–16 → p. 452 ln. 14
9.3.1, 3 → p. 145 ln. 7
9.3.5 → p. 147 ln. 5
9.3.21 → p. 255 ln. 3
9.4.5 → p. 331 ln. 13
9.4.7 → p. 330 ln. 9
9.5.2 → p. 230 ln. 21
9.5.3, 15, 16 → p. 204 ln. 4,
p. 230 ln. 14
9.5.17 → p. 204 ln. 13
9.5.20 → p. 230 ln. 8
9.6.1 → p. 331 ln. 6
9.6.2 → p. 331 ln. 9
9.6.29 → p. 331 ln. 2
9.7.28 → p. 368 ln. 9
9.7.29 → p. 368 ln. 11
12.2.1 → p. 412 ln. 3
12.1.5 → p. 420 ln. 8
12.2.25–6 → p. 414 ln. 4
15.2.1–3 → p. 184 ln. 8
15.15.1–7 → p. 112 ln. 13
18.15.1–2 → p. 347 ln. 13
18.15.2 → p. 115 ln. 9
18.15.9 → p. 83 ln. 19

Historia Gothorum, Wandalorum, Sueborum
ed. T. Mommsen,
MGH Auct. ant. 11 (1894), 267–302

81–2 → cf. p. 103 ln. 4

Quaestiones de ueteri et nouo testamento
PL 83:201–7

In Leuit. 6.1 → p. 22 ln. 7
In Exod. 50.2 → p. 305 ln. 6

Sententiae
ed. P. Lazier, CCSL 111 (1998)

1.12.1 → p. 455 ln. 15
1.12.4 → p. 457 ln. 5
2.14.1 → p. 340 ln. 5
2.30.1 → p. 84 ln. 13,
p. 86 ln. 6
2.31.1, 2 → p. 242 ln. 2
2.31.2 → p. 242 ln. 7
2.31.4, 5 → p. 245 ln. 18
2.31.6, 7 → p. 246 ln. 10
2.31.8 → p. 246 ln. 5
2.31.9 → p. 243 ln. 17
2.31.10 → p. 247 ln. 6
2.42.7 → p. 60 ln. 13
2.44.3 → p. 60 ln. 10
2.44.8 → p. 61 ln. 11
2.44.13 → p. 63 ln. 2
2.44.15 → p. 63 ln. 2
2.44.16 → p. 63 ln. 2
3.8.1–2 → p. 75 ln. 2
3.8.3 → p. 75 ln. 8
3.37.4 → p. 280 ln. 19

3.37.5–6 → p. 281 ln. 1

3.52.10 → p. 128 ln. 4

3.52.13 → p. 128 ln. 9

3.52.14 → p. 128 ln. 12

3.52.16 → p. 128 ln. 12

3.54.7 → p. 127 ln. 2

3.55.2 → p. 84 ln. 10

3.55.6 → p. 86 ln. 11

3.56.1–2 → p. 129 ln. 9

Iunilius

Instituta regularia diuinae
ed. H. Kihn, *Theodor…und Junilius Africanus* (Freiburg, 1880), 465–528

2.28 → p. 125 ln. 20,
p. 286 ln. 12

Jerome

Aduersus Iouinianum
PL 23:211–338

1.14 → p. 353 ln. 4

2.6 → p. 420 ln. 14

2.15 → p. 59 ln. 12,
p. 60 ln. 3

2.37 → p. 142 ln. 2

Commentarii in Danielem
ed. F. Glorie, CCSL 75A (1964)

4:24 (pp. 816–7) → p. 70 ln. 16

5:17 (pp. 824–5) → p. 135 ln. 7

Commentarius in Ecclesiasten
ed. M. Adriaen, CCSL 72 (1959), 250–361

10:12 → p. 282 ln. 12

11:2 → cf. p. 316 ln. 12

Commentarii in iv epistulas Paulinas (Ad Galatas, Ad Ephesios, Ad Titum, Ad Philemonem)
PL 26:307–618

Ephes. 2.3 (PL 26:490) → cf. p. 61 ln. 9

Tit. 2:9–10 (PL 26:585) → p. 192 ln. 3

Tit. 3:1–2 (PL 26:590) → p. 151 ln. 5

Commentarii in Esaiam
ed. M. Adriaen, CCSL 73 (1963)

23:1–4 (p. 308) → p. 320 ln. 4

33:13–19 (pp. 414–16) → cf. p. 473 ln. 22

Commentarii in euangelium Matthaei
ed. D. Hurst and M. Adriaen, CCSL 77 (1969)

5:13 → p. 132 ln. 1,
p. 281 ln. 12,
p. 284 ln. 14

5:22 → p. 424 ln. 17

13:30 → p. 124 ln. 18,
p. 379 ln. 19

15:32 → p. 280 ln. 4

17:26 → p. 152 ln. 2

17:27 → p. 153 ln. 2

21:13 → p. 324 ln. 9

22:21 (p. 204) → p. 150 ln. 13

25:40 → p. 70 ln. 5

26:57 → p. 133 ln. 5

26:61 → p. 85 ln. 3,
p. 285 ln. 15

27:5 → p. 382 ln. 16

28:12–15 → p. 103 ln. 11,
p. 103 ln. 14

Commentarii in Ezechielem
ed. F. Glorie, CCSL 75 (1964)

9:1 (p. 103) → p. 168 ln. 13

44:22–31 (p. 669) → p. 267 ln. 13

Commentarii in Hieremiam prophetam
ed. S. Reiter, CCSL 74 (1960)

22:3 → cf. p. 168 ln. 17

32:11 → cf. p. 239 ln. 17

Commentarii in Prophetas minores
ed. M. Adriaen, CCSL 76–76A (1969–70)

Osee 7:11 → p. 315 ln. 6

Iona 1:4 → p. 183 ln. 4,
p. 460 ln. 15

Iona 1.7 → p. 160 ln. 14

Zachar. 2:8 → p. 56 ln. 6

Epistulae
ed. I. Hilberg, CSEL 54–6 (1910–18)

6.1 → p. 84 ln. 13,
p. 86 ln. 6

14.9 → p. 5 ln. 11,
p. 258 ln. 15,
p. 267 ln. 17

16.1 → p. 382 ln. 2

22.9 → p. 59 ln. 15

22.13–14 → p. 351 ln. 12

22.17 → p. 63 ln. 10

22.27 → p. 49 ln. 2,
p. 458 ln. 2

22.34 → cf. p. 292 ln. 1

36.5 → cf. p. 172 ln. 1

36.6 → cf. p. 171 ln. 19

52.12 → p. 63 ln. 17

53.3 → p. 281 ln. 18

53.7 → p. 120 ln. 13,
p. 286 ln. 2

54.4 → p. 392 ln. 12

64.4 → p. 212 ln. 14,
p. 213 ln. 1,
p. 301 ln. 16

107.10 → cf. p. 63 ln. 8

126.1 → p. 453 ln. 13

Vita S. Hilarionis
ed. A. Bastiansen, *Vite dei Santi* (Rome, 1975), 4:72–142

46 (PL 23:52) → p. 399 ln. 14

Lactantius

De opificio Dei
ed. S. Brandt, CSEL 27 (1893), 3–64

12 (pp. 46–7) → p. 428 ln. 6

Leo I

Decreta (J^3 1098)
Dionysiana version, ed. C. Justel, *Codex Canonum Ecclesiasticorum Dionysii Exigui* (Paris, 1628). Repr. PL 67:277–362

18 → p. 369 ln. 11,
p. 369 ln. 14

19 → p. 369 ln. 9

23 → p. 388 ln. 18

24 → p. 359 ln. 14

25 → p. 360 ln. 2

Muirchú

Vita Patricii
ed. L. Bieler, *Patrician Texts*, SLH 10 (Dublin, 1979), 61–122

II.5, 6 → p. 460 ln. 3

Old-Irish Penitential

tr. D. A. Binchy *apud* Bieler, *The Irish Penitentials*, SLH 5 (Dublin, 1963), 259–74

36 → p. 365 ln. 1,
p. 365 ln. 5

Origen

In Genesim homiliae
ed. W. A. Baehrens, GCS 29 (1920), 1–144

4.4 (p. 54) → p. 370 ln. 12

Orosius

Historia aduersus paganos
ed. M.-P. Arnaud-Lindet, *Histoires contre les païens*, 3 vols. (Paris, 1990–1991)

prolog. 3–4 → p. 414 ln. 12

prolog. 5 → p. 414 ln. 15

prolog. 7 → p. 414 ln. 16

4.13.17–18 → p. 192 ln. 11

5.15.3 → p. 230 ln. 11

7.4.4 → p. 157 ln. 5,
p. 157 ln. 8

Passion of St. Peter (Pseudo-Abdias)

See Bible and Apocrypha

Pelagius

Expositiones XIII epistularum Pauli
ed. A. Souter, *Pelagius's Expositions of Thirteen Epistles of St. Paul* (Cambridge, 1922–31)

Rom. 2:4 → p. 175 ln. 17

I Cor. 6:7 → p. 315 ln. 1

I Cor. 6:18 → p. 361 ln. 19

Liber de induratione cordis Pharaonis
ed. G. de Plinval, *Essai sur le style et la langue de Pélage suivi du traité inédit De induratione cordis Pharaonis* (Freibourg, 1947)

2 (p. 139) → p. 1 ln. 5

Liber de uita Christiana
PL 40:1031–46 (*CPL* §730)
(also attributed to Fastidius. See *BCLL* §1179)

6 → p. 49 ln. 19

14 → p. 47 ln. 20,
p. 459 ln. 6

Patrick

Epistola ad milites Corotici
ed. L. Bieler, *Libri Epistolarum* (Dublin, 1952), 1:91–102

8 → cf. p. 10 ln. 2,
cf. p. 29 ln. 5,
cf. p. 29 ln. 14,
cf. p. 291 ln. 7,
cf. p. 313 ln. 15

Prouerbia Grecorum

ed. D. Simpson, 'The '*Prouerbia Grecorum*'', *Traditio* 43 (1987): 1–22

References here are to other secondary witnesses to the *prouerbia*

I 1 → p. 286 ln. 16

I 2 → p. 286 ln. 17

I 65 → p. 300 ln. 1

I 69 → p. 317 ln. 13

IV 1 → p. 146 ln. 13

Registri ecclesiae Carthaginensis excerpta

ed. C. Munier, CCSL 149 (1974), 182–228

75 → p. 314 ln. 3

83 → p. 336 ln. 18

118 → p. 324 ln. 16,
p. 348 ln. 2

122 → p. 132 ln. 9

Sinodus Hibernensis

ed. L. Bieler, *The Irish Penitentials*, SLH 5 (Dublin, 1963), 170

9 → p. 397 ln. 2

Siricius

Decreta (J[3] 605)
Dionysiana version, ed. C. Justel, *Codex Canonum Ecclesiasticorum Dionysii Exigui* (Paris, 1628). Repr. PL 67:231–8

9 → p. 13 ln. 8

10 → cf. p. 13 ln. 2,
p. 13 ln. 13

Statuta ecclesiae antiqua

ed. C. Munier, CCSL 148 (1963), 164–88

1 → p. 7 ln. 13,
p. 9 ln. 5,
p. 11 ln. 9

2 → p. 11 ln. 12

3 → p. 11 ln. 10

4 → p. 11 ln. 14

5 → p. 11 ln. 16

6 → p. 11 ln. 18

7 → p. 12 ln. 1

8 → p. 12 ln. 3

9 → p. 12 ln. 4

10 → p. 12 ln. 9

11 → p. 12 ln. 7

12 → p. 12 ln. 14

14 → p. 12 ln. 11

15 → p. 12 ln. 15

16 → p. 12 ln. 17

20 → p. 393 ln. 6

22 → p. 82 ln. 15,
p. 391 ln. 6

25 → p. 46 ln. 7

26 → p. 44 ln. 6

27 → p. 44 ln. 8

28 → p. 44 ln. 9

29 → p. 44 ln. 11

30 → p. 136 ln. 8

32 → p. 90 ln. 10

34 → p. 44 ln. 13

36 → p. 353 ln. 19

40 → p. 302 ln. 6

42 → p. 44 ln. 15
44 → p. 46 ln. 1
46 → p. 84 ln. 7
50 → p. 18 ln. 14
52 → p. 85 ln. 13
57 → p. 34 ln. 7
58 → p. 34 ln. 10
60 → p. 34 ln. 5
61 → p. 34 ln. 13
65–7 → p. 394 ln. 13
71 → p. 44 ln. 17
72 → p. 46 ln. 4
74 → p. 46 ln. 6
75 → p. 45 ln. 1, p. 438 ln. 12
76 → p. 45 ln. 3
77 → p. 68 ln. 7, p. 466 ln. 11
79 → p. 45 ln. 7
80 → p. 45 ln. 5, p. 303 ln. 18
82 → p. 303 ln. 19
86 → p. 97 ln. 21
88 → p. 45 ln. 8
90 → p. 7 ln. 3
91 → p. 20 ln. 9
92 → p. 32 ln. 14
93 → p. 35 ln. 12
94 → p. 40 ln. 14
95 → p. 38 ln. 6
96 → p. 36 ln. 12
97 → p. 39 ln. 6
98 → p. 41 ln. 12
102 → p. 353 ln. 16

Sulpicius Severus

Dialogi
ed. C. Halm, CSEL 1 (1866), 152–216
3.11 → p. 181 ln. 5
3.14 (p. 212) → p. 29 ln. 16

Symmachus

Epist. 15, *Ad Caesarium* (J^3 1460)
ed. A. Thiel, *Epistolae Romanorum Pontificum* (Braunsberg, 1868), 723–8
15.2 → p. 98 ln. 15

Synodus episcoporum

ed. L. Bieler, *The Irish Penitentials*, SLH 5 (Dublin, 1963), 54–8
praef. → p. 466 ln. 7
1 → p. 327 ln. 14
3 → p. 296 ln. 8
4 → p. 327 ln. 17
5 → p. 327 ln. 17
6 → p. 410 ln. 10, p. 410 ln. 13
8 → p. 238 ln. 3, p. 240 ln. 10
11 → p. 296 ln. 5
12 → p. 302 ln. 9
13 → cf. p. 72 ln. 15
14 → p. 188 ln. 7
15 → p. 196 ln. 18
17 → p. 391 ln. 16
20 → p. 231 ln. 8
24 → p. 337 ln. 4

27 → cf. p. 302 ln. 13

28 → p. 302 ln. 13

31 → p. 46 ln. 11

34 → p. 296 ln. 8

Synodus Luci Victorie

ed. L. Bieler, *The Irish Penitentials*, SLH 5 (Dublin, 1963), 68

4 → cf. p. 435 ln. 9

Synodus Patricii

ed. L. Bieler, *The Irish Penitentials*, SLH 5 (Dublin, 1963), 184–96

2 → p. 29 ln. 11

3 → p. 385 ln. 12

4 → cf. p. 18 ln. 17,
p. 298 ln. 16

9 → p. 190 ln. 15

10 → p. 50 ln. 12

11 → p. 392 ln. 1

12 → p. 81 ln. 19

14 → p. 66 ln. 6

24 → p. 92 ln. 6,
p. 248 ln. 6,
p. 464 ln. 10

25 → p. 376 ln. 11

30 → cf. p. 252 ln. 7,
p. 252 ln. 13

Synodus Sapientium de decimis

ed. L. Bieler, *The Irish Penitentials*, SLH 5 (Dublin, 1963), 166–8

1 → p. 97 ln. 12

8 → cf. p. 117 ln. 10

Theodore, *Canones*

ed. P. W. Finsterwalder, *Die Canones Theodori Cantuariensis und ihre Überlieferungsformen* (Weimar, 1929), 239–334

D 19–22, 168 → p. 422 ln. 1

D 22 → p. 421 ln. 11

D 23 → p. 421 ln. 2

D 79 → p. 19 ln. 3

U i.11.2 → cf. p. 466 ln. 11

U i.11.3 → cf. p. 68 ln. 7

U i.14.24 → cf. p. 365 ln. 7

U ii.14.1 → cf. p. 400 ln. 11

Vinnian, Penitential

ed. L. Bieler, *The Irish Penitentials*, SLH 5 (Dublin, 1963), 74–94

25 → p. 197 ln. 1

43–5 → p. 367 ln. 12,
p. 375 ln. 10,
p. 375 ln. 20

Virgilius Maro Grammaticus, *Epitomae*

ed. B. Löfstedt, *Virgilius Maro Grammaticus* (Munich, 2003), 103–245

11 (p. 230) → p. 412 ln. 7

Vitas Patrum

ed. H. Rosweyde (Antwerp, 1615), vols. 5, 6. Repr. PL 73:855–1022

9.11 → p. 23 ln. 16

Virtutes Iohannis

See Bible and Apocrypha

Zosimus

Decreta (J³ 745)
Dionysiana version, ed. C. Justel, *Codex Canonum Ecclesiasticorum Dionysii Exigui* (Paris, 1628). Repr. PL 67:261–78

3 → p. 13 ln. 2

Translation index

- For biblical books as sources, see the index of Bible and Apocrypha
- For authors and church councils as sources, see the index of sources and tables 1–4

Aaron, biblical figure 514–15, 550, 634, 665, 699
 burial of 776
 as chief *sacerdos* 482, 491, 493–7, 500, 601, 670, 673, 708, 711, 730
 foods of 545, 696
 sins of 768
 sons of 491, 514, 545, 600, 602, 626, 700, 730
abandonment of children 794
Abel, biblical figure 727, 772
Abimelech, son of Gideon, biblical figure 663, 696
Abiron, biblical figure 600–1, 624, 699
Abisai, nephew of King David 584
Abner, uncle of King Saul 584
Abraham, biblical patriarch 491, 623, 625–7, 638, 669, 695–6, 699, 710, 745
 and altar 715
 as ancestor of Jesus Christ 720–1
 burial of 551, 554
 and Hagar his slave 754
 and inheritance 634–5, 666
 and oaths 651–2
 as pilgrim 825
 and property 798
 and Sarah his wife 751
 and Sodom 606–7, 794, 830
Absalom, son of King David 625–6
Achan 592–4
Achis, Philistine king 652, 661
acolytes, ordination of 506
Adam, biblical patriarch 520, 599, 601, 640, 699
 as ancestor of Jesus Christ 721
 burial of 551
 curse on 772
 paradise, expulsion from 638, 659, 676
Adomnán, abbot of Iona 744
Adonias, brother of Solomon 604–5
Adonibezec, biblical figure 594–5
adultery 794 → *See also* matrimony; penance
Ahab, biblical king 583, 605, 760
Alexander, bishop of Jerusalem 489, 560
almsgiving 601, 685
 and excommunicants 697
 practice of 527–9
 praise of 527–8
 word 526–7
Amalek 799
Amasias, king of Israel 624, 647, 720
Ananias, biblical figure 598, 600, 602, 689, 691, 828–9
Anatolius, bishop of Laodicea 489–90
anchorites 689–90

Andrew, apostle 595, 670, 773
animals → *See* beasts; livestock
Anna, biblical figure 738–9
Annam, biblical priest 676
Anthony, saint 688
Antoninus Pius, Roman emperor 588
Arianism 480, 602, 766, 797
Arius → *See* Arianism
Armagh 820
Artaxerxes, Persian king 587
Asaph, psalmist 506
augury 813–14
Axa, biblical figure 639

Balaam, biblical figure 799, 801
Balthasar, king of Babylon 576
baptism 481, 487, 504–5, 509, 513, 519, 538, 549, 697, 713, 715, 725, 754, 761, 766, 772, 813
barbarians, guiding of 800–2
Barsabas 592, 662
Bathsheba 604, 624
beasts → *See also* food; livestock
  confining of 783
  definition of 782
  dogs 784–5
  hens 785
  oxen 783–4
benedictions 807–8
bequests
  of bishops 701–3
  of children 704
  and *monachi* 701, 703–5
  of *principes* 701–3
  of women 704–5
Beseleel, craftsman of the Tabernacle 811
bishops 678–9
  age, episcopal 486–7
  bequests of 701–3
  census of 771
  Christ, as image of 488, 505
  and church building 724
  and church property 490, 709
  conduct of 484–5
  duties of 485–6, 488, 492, 505
  eunuchs as 490
  and excommunication 490–1
  infirmity of 490
  and judgements 574–6
  laying on of hands 482
  manual labour by 825
  marriage of 481, 487
  ordination of 483, 487–8
  and provinces 557
  relics of 731
  as sinners 513
  successors to 489, 667
  word 481
blessings → *See* benedictions
Boaz 639, 720–1
books 818, 826–7
Bosor 608
burial → *See also* dead, caring of
  ancestral cemeteries 552–3
  and *monachi* 553–5

law of 551–6
of martyrs 554
of spouses 551–3, 556
of the wicked 555–6
payment for 554
retaining the dead 554–5

Cain, biblical figure 599, 601, 727
Caiphas, biblical priest 572, 592, 676
Caleb, biblical figure 634, 639
Cerinthus, heresiarch 698
Childeric, barbarian king 551
children → *See* abandonment of children; fathers and children
Christ → *See* Jesus Christ
Christians, general
conduct of 511–12, 819
word 511
Christmas 712
church → *See also loca*
and blasphemy 711
children in 715–16
dedication of 812
defensores of 706
and fostering 712–13
foundation of 723–5, 812
gifts to 709–11
and inheritance 708–9
money collection in 716–17
parochia 714–15
and payments 713–14
plotting in 709
plundering of 706–7
and portion of 708
and prisoners 717
and secular persons 711–12, 718
and sinners 717–18
word 705–6
circumcilliones 689–90
Clement I, pope 488, 667, 671
clerics 678, 824
conduct of 508–10
judgement of 507, 574–5
and neighbours, offending of 807
and provinces 557
slaves of 712
as sureties 649
voice of 508
word 507
clothing
of deacons 501
footwear 821
restraint in 818
coenobia 688–90
Commodus, Lucius Aurelius, Roman emperor 588
communio 496
concubines → *See* matrimony
Constantine I the Great, Roman emperor 488, 550–1, 575, 660, 766
and Constantinople, dedication of 812
and Nicaean synod 480
Constantinople 812
Core, biblical figure 600–1, 624, 710
craftsmen, labour of 810–12

Cú Chuimne of Iona, presumed compiler of *Hib* 831 → *See also* Ruben (2)

cursing → *See* maledictions

Curtius, consul of Salassus 588

Damasus I, pope 760, 818

Daniel, biblical prophet 520, 593, 695, 768

as judge 573

and judgement day 729

in lions' den 530, 590

Dathan, biblical figure 600–1, 624, 699

David, son of Jesse, king of Israel 617, 661, 673, 710

as ancestor of Jesus Christ 585, 720–2

and fasting 519

as lawgiver 564–5, 567, 572, 576, 590, 627

ministers of 669

and oaths 652

ordination of 667,670

as pilgrim 825

and prayer 530, 532

as psalmist 506

and Saul 593, 608, 665, 675, 695, 805, 822

sin of 600, 604, 624, 626, 768, 828

and Solomon 589, 634

sons, names of 721

deacons → *See also* subdeacons

and bequests 703

Christ as 505

conduct of 500–2

dress of 501

duties of 501–2

ordination of 500

origin of 500

dead, caring of 532–6 → *See also* burial

debts

interest 648–9

pledges 647–8

remission of 645

repayment of 644–5

sureties 649–51

deposits

and churches 622–3

and the dead 621

livestock 621

loans 619

loss of 620, 622

restitution of 620

theft of 618–19

uncertain 623

Díchu mac Trichim, Patrick's first convert 820

Dina, daughter of Jacob, biblical figure 639, 737

Diocletian, Roman emperor 550, 660, 710

Dionysius, bishop of Alexandria 764

divination → *See* augury

doorkeepers 504–6

dreams

of the dead 777–8

prophetic 592

types of 778–9

Easter 480, 712, 769
  date of 558
  and Jews 519, 612, 733, 734, 781
elders 479, 515, 556, 560–2, 570–1, 576, 579, 583, 587, 589, 592, 596, 629, 639, 666, 668, 690, 709, 720, 724, 730, 740, 780
Eleazar, biblical priest 710
Eli, biblical priest 497, 624–5, 673, 676
Elijah, biblical prophet 540, 598, 645, 737, 760, 778
  fasting of 520
  as *monachus* 688–9
  prayer of 530
Elisha, biblical prophet 530, 600, 638, 688, 737
Ephraim, biblical figure 633
Esau, biblical figure 549, 625–6
Esther, biblical figure 737
Eusebius of Nicomedia 766
Eusebius, pope 822
Eutyches, presbyter at Constantinople 480
Eve, biblical matriarch 551, 640
excommunication, excommunicants
  associations with 696–7, 699–701
  and heretics 698
  manner of 695
  of *monachi* 693, 697
  persons subject to 695–8
  regulation of 694
  of untonsured clerics 781
exorcists 504–5
Ezekiel 695, 775
Fabianus, bishop of Antioch 764
fasting 818
  of Christ 519
  and feasts of gentiles 803
  and gluttony 518
  and livestock 800
  and penance 769
  practice of 518–26
  praise of 520–1
  on Sundays 825
  word 518
fathers and children → *See also* inheritance
  and concubines 635
  correction of children 625
  duty and honour 628–31
  first-born rights 630, 632
  and patience 628
  and sin 624–5
  truth, telling of 626–7
  word 623
Faustus of Alexandria, saint 555
feasts 802–3
Florentius, hermit 805
food 826 → *See also* fasting; feasts
  of Aaron, biblical priest 545, 696
  birds 788
  carrion 787, 790
  fish 787–8
  horses 789
  meat, flesh 785–6, 788–90
  swine 788–90
  time for 785

of the wicked 695

wild animals 788

Galerius, Roman emperor 550, 660, 710

Gideon, son of Joash, biblical figure 674

Gothoniel, biblical figure 663

gyrovagi 690

Ham, son of Noah, biblical figure 625–6, 638, 659, 696

Hannah, mother of Samuel, biblical figure 530, 532

Hebron 608

heresy 480, 685, 797–8 → *See also* Arianism; Manicheans

Hermas 748–9

hermits 688–90

Herod, biblical king 572, 590, 734

Hesychius, disciple of Hilarion 773

Hezekiah, king of Judah 530, 627, 652, 768

Hilary, saint 688, 773

Hiram, king of Tyre 810–11

Holofernes, Babylonian general of Assyrian origin 735

hospitality 795–6

inheritance 630, 632–44

and adopted sons 643–4

daughters as heirs 639–41, 722

and tribes 722–3

innocence

of children 792–5

and nuns 793

praise of 791

Isaac, biblical patriarch 491, 541, 549 625–6, 696

as ancestor of Jesus Christ 720–1

burial of 551

and fasting 525

inheritance of 634–5

Jacob, blessing of 482

and oaths 652

Isaiah 530, 590, 670

ius → *See* law

Jacob, biblical patriarch 491, 540–2, 586, 601, 604, 607, 621, 626, 696, 699, 712–13, 737, 759, 769

as ancestor of Jesus Christ 720–1

blessing by Isaac 482

burial of 551–2

and grandchildren 633, 643

inheritance of 549, 634, 639, 701

and oaths 652

sins of 602

and slave-women 745

Jacob, bishop of Jerusalem 482, 489, 670, 702

Januarius, saint, bishop of Benevento 556

Joakim, king of Judah 525

Jericho 608

Jeroboam, biblical king 583, 676

Jesus Christ

on alms 528

apostles, blessing of 482

bishops as image of 488

Cana, miracle at 505
crucifixion of 526, 594–5, 733
as exorcist 505
fasting of 519
as figure of Moses 482
on forgiveness 808
genealogy of 720–2
and grades of participation 505
on inheritance 635
as judge 572–3
on mercy 596, 601, 605, 607
as first *sacerdos* 493–4
in the temple 562, 612
on tribute 585–6
Jethro the Midianite, father-in-law of Moses 550, 560, 573, 607, 652, 696, 701
Jezebel, biblical figure 520
Joab, nephew of King David, biblical figure 589–90
Job, biblical patriarch 576, 589, 644, 646, 667, 676, 769
daughters of 639
and judgement day 729
offering to God 492–4
John the Baptist, saint 520, 590, 688, 711
John the Evangelist, saint 519, 586, 698, 701
Jonathan, son of King Saul, biblical figure 654, 831
Jonah, biblical prophet 530, 592–3
Joseph, biblical patriarch 552, 573, 590, 607, 633, 643, 699, 771
dreams of 779
inheritance of 634, 636, 701
as judge 573
as prefect of Egypt 585, 669, 696, 770
relics of 773
Joseph, saint 585, 713, 720, 779
Joshua 540–1, 605, 652, 663, 669, 771, 830
blessing by Moses 482, 484
and fasting 519
and lots 593, 634
and tabernacle 730
on theft 616
and tribe of Judah 719
Josias, king of Judah 525, 554, 605, 830
Jovinian 631, 789
jubilees
property, restitution of 657, 659–61
reasons for 662
remission of land 657–9
slaves, freeing of 657–8
Judas Iscariot 527, 586, 602, 663, 667–8, 672, 676, 696, 797
apostleship, loss of 513, 591, 662, 766
three guilts of 801
Judas Maccabee 534, 695, 701
judgements 829–30 → *See also* judges
and clerics 574–6
conflict in 564–5
justness of 565–7, 573, 824
and *monachi* 576–7
and peace 563
perversion of 567–9, 573
place of 561–2
and *principes* 576–7
and provinces 557–9

types 559–61
way of making 562–3
word 559
judges
conduct of 567
culpable 572
decisions of 571, 828
disposition of 570
good 571–2
ignorance of 569–70
swiftness of 575–6, 828
testing of 570
Judith, biblical figure 737

kings, kingship
and flattery 591
marriage 584
moderation of rule 586–90
obedience to 587–90
ordination of 581–2
quality of kings 582–5
regicide 584
succession, order of 582
tribute 585–6, 588–9
word 581

Laban, biblical figure 541–2, 607, 620, 626, 651
Lamech, biblical figure 599, 602
Laurence, Roman archpriest 533
law → *See also* judgements; judges
authors of 517
definition of 515–16
ius 516–17
lex 516
maledictions 806
mos 516
transgression of 517
lectors 503–6
Lent 518, 520, 690, 769, 774
Levi, biblical figure 624, 634
lex → *See* law
Lia, wife of Jacob, biblical figure 551
livestock 798–800
loca → *See also* church
basilica 735
boundaries of 728–30, 734
and churches 723–5
consecration of 727, 732–3
departure from 725–7
and feastdays 733–4
and holy blood 734–5
and Jerusalem 732–3
and legal cases 733
and living abroad 823
and monasteries 724-5
and newcomers 725
profanation of 729–34
and relics 724–5, 731–2
worshipping 732
Lóegaire mac Néill, legendary king of Tara 781
lordship and subjection 580–1 → *See* kings, kingship
lots, casting of 591–3
Luke, saint, relics of 773

Lycontius, presbyter 498

Macarius, saint 688
Macedonius I, bishop of Constantinople 480
maledictions
 of enemies 804–6, 826
 of just men 804
 and the law 806
 limitations on 805, 826
 and Peter and Gregory 805
Manasseh, king of Judah 627
Manasseh, son of Joseph, biblical figure 633, 640–1
Manicheans 815
Marcian, Eastern Roman emperor 480
Marcion of Sinope 698
Marcus Antonius, Roman consul 588
Mardochai, biblical figure 590
Mark, bishop of Jerusalem 489
Mark the Evangelist, saint 490
marriage → *See* matrimony
martyrs, martyrdom
 as baptism 772
 intercession of 774
 origin of 772
 spirits of 775–6
 torments of 773
 translation of 774–5
 transmigration of relics 773
 word 771
Mary Magdalene, saint 505
Mary, Virgin 713, 739, 779
Matthias, apostle 592, 662, 667, 670
matrimony 824
 adultery 595–6, 742, 744–5, 748, 752–5, 757–8, 765, 767
 of bishops 481, 487
 chastity before marriage 742, 749, 755
 and concubines 481, 487, 625, 635, 743–4, 750–1
 and consecrated women 743–4
 continence in marriage 747
 dissolution or divorce 745–7
 of kings 584
 lawful 742–3
 marital debt 752
 and penance 751, 755
 praise of 741–2
 remarriage to husband's brother 756
 seduction or rape 746, 751–2
 slave women 744–5, 749–51
 subjection of wife 752
Matthew, saint, relics of 773
Maximian, Roman emperor 550, 589
Melchisedech, biblical king-priest 491–2, 494, 710
Mephibosheth, biblical figure 564–5
Miriam, sister of Moses and Aaron, biblical figure 514–15, 665, 674
monachi/monks
 abbots 690–4, 705–5
 and bequests 701, 703–5
 and children 694
 and excommunication 693, 697

fugitive 691–3, 717
kinds of 688–90
and neighbours, offending of 807
origin of 688
as plotters 709
property, non-ownership of 691
word 688

mos → *See* law

Moses, biblical patriarch 514–15, 540, 550, 558, 589, 601–2, 668–9, 696, 699, 771, 778, 811
and bequests 701
burial of 776
chair of 682
and fasting 519
as figure of Jesus Christ 482
and Joshua 482, 484, 540, 669
as lawgiver 500, 517, 560–1, 572–3, 596, 640–1, 644, 663, 666, 674, 723, 728–30, 746–7, 757
and oaths 652
and Pharoah 634, 695
and prayer 530, 607
as *princeps* 670–1, 674
sin of 600
and the tabernacle 495
and tribe of Judah 719
wife of 665

Narcissus, bishop of Jerusalem 489

Nathan, biblical figure 828

Nebuchadnezzar, king of Babylon 527–8, 550, 592, 600–1, 779

Nechao, Pharoah 605, 830

neighbours 807–9

Nestorius, archbishop of Constantinople 480

Noah, biblical patriarch 640, 666, 699–700, 785
and altar 715
as ancestor of Jesus Christ 721
and Ham, his son 625–6, 696
and judgement day 729

Noami, biblical figure 737

Numa Pompilius, king of Rome 517

oaths
dissolution of 654–5, 831
false 655–6
perjury 656
swearing of 651–4, 656–7

offences
and apostates 605–6
and church as defender 607
and consent 606
and festive days 608
forgiveness of 605
and fugitives 607
and intention 604–5
punishment for 594–604
theft 613–19

offerings 543–6 → *See* tithes

Olympius, Arian bishop 602

Onesimus, slave 692

Ooliab, Israelite craftsman 811

Pasch → *See* Easter

Patrick, saint, three requests of 819–20
Paul, saint 636, 665, 670, 692, 696
 conversion of 601, 760
 fasting of 519
 and heresy 598
 as *monachus* 688
 and oaths 652
 relics of 733
 and tonsure 782
Paul the Hermit, saint 776
penance 818
 acceptance of 760
 and adultery 765, 767
 of clerics 761
 duration of 761, 769
 in illness and death 763–5, 768
 and intercourse, unlawful 765
 place of 768
 praise of 758–9
 for theft 616
 true 762
 word 758
Peter, saint 490, 540, 585–6, 665, 672, 692, 712
 and Ananias and Sapphira 598, 600, 691, 828–9
 and bequests 702
 fasting of 519
 on mercy 597
 ordination of 667, 670
 as pope 482, 671
 prison, escape from 771
 and Simon Magus 495, 593, 674
 tonsure of 780
Phineas, biblical priest 594, 612
Phoroneus, legendary Greek king 517
Polycarp, bishop of Smyrna 698
Pontius Pilate, governor of Judaea 575, 606
Potiphar, biblical figure 669
prayer
 for enemies 804
 practice of 530–2, 679, 821
presbyter 481–2, 484, 501, 557, 680, 740, 751
 age of 487
 and bequests 703
 and councils 480
 conduct 492, 494, 620, 731
 duties of 485–6, 490, 492, 499, 502, 506, 530, 574, 764
 offerings by 485, 532
 ordination of 492
 origin 491
princeps
 and bequests 701
 and church property 677, 679, 718
 conduct of 663–5, 667–9, 671–2, 674–5
 heirs to 666–7, 670–1
 and hospitality 796
 and *loca* 725–6
 opposition to 670, 674
 ordination of 662–3, 667, 670–1
 and personal property 678–9
 rights of 666

subjection to 665–6, 669, 676
wicked 675–6, 678
word 662
worthiness of 672–5
Priscilla and Aquila, biblical figures 779
property
of Abraham 798
and *monachi*, non-ownership by 691
and offences 798–9
of *princeps* 678–9
restitution of in jubilees 657, 659–61
of *sacerdos* 497–9
province 557–9
psalmists 506
punishment of offences → *See* offences
Pythagoras 815

Rahab, biblical figure 605, 640, 830
Rasin, king of Syria 801–2
Rebecca, wife of Isaac, biblical figure 525, 551
refuge, cities of 608–13
Rehoboam, king of Judah 624, 626, 667, 720
relics 724–5, 731–2
of bishops 731
remote burial of 776–7
translation of 774–5
transmigration of 773
Ruben, biblical figure 607, 624, 633, 665
Ruben of Dairinis, presumed compiler of *Hib* 831 → *See also* Cú Chuimne
Ruth, biblical figure 639

Sabbath 600, 821–2
and martyrs, feast days of 774
of years 658
sacerdos 481, 483, 545, 548, 555, 572, 597, 611, 619, 657, 663, 726, 729, 744, 772, 794
absence of 499
age of 487
and bequests 702, 704
Christ as 505
conduct of 496–7, 514–15, 682
duties 501, 505, 768, 829
entitlements of 494–7, 708
as judge 560, 575, 616, 642, 758
offerings by 492–4, 775, 782
origin of 482, 491
property and gifts 497–9
and provinces 558
purchase of office by 495–6, 674
resistance to 495
as sinners 514–15
as teachers 680
and tonsure 780–1
Samson, biblical figure 605–6
Samuel, biblical prophet 532, 582, 586, 670–1, 689
and Saul 581, 592, 670
sons of 568
Sapphira, biblical figure 598, 600, 602, 689, 691, 828–9
sarabites 689–90
Sarah, wife of Abraham 551, 745, 751
Saul, king of Israel 534, 564–5, 583–4, 592, 602, 665
and David 593, 608, 675, 695, 805, 822

- death of 587, 667
- and oaths 652, 654, 831
- ordination of 581–2, 670

Sem, son of Noah, biblical figure 638, 721

Severus, Roman emperor 582

silence 809–10

Simeon, biblical figure 604, 624, 633–4, 721

Simon Magus 495, 593, 674, 780–1

Sodom and Gomorrha 600, 696, 699, 726, 794–5, 830

Solomon, king of Israel 589–90, 602, 604–5, 625–6, 634
- as ancestor of Jesus Christ 720–2
- death of 667
- as judge 593, 615, 626, 828
- temple of 504, 638, 728–9, 766, 810–11

soul 815–17

speech, idle 802–3, 819

Spyridon, bishop of Cyprus 621

Stephen, bishop of Salona 480

Stephen, saint 597, 603, 669, 672, 772, 805

Stoics 815

subdeacons → *See also* deacons
- Christ as 505
- duties of 502, 505
- ordination of 502–3
- origin of 503
- word 505

Susanna, biblical figure 532

Sylvester, pope 822

Symmachus, pope 533

synods 479–80

Syrus, saint 555

teachers
- conduct of 681, 687
- entitlements and reward 680–1
- and heresy 685
- and scripture 684, 686
- wicked 682

testimony
- practice of 537–43
- types of 536–7
- word 536

Thamar, biblical figure 594

theft
- in a church 615–16
- compensation for 614, 618
- of deposits 618–19
- lenience towards 617
- penance for 616
- punishment for 613–15
- word 613

Theodosius the Elder, Roman emperor 480

Theotechnus, bishop of Caesarea Maritima 489

Thomas, saint 599–600

Tiberius, Roman emperor 589

tithes
- and *monachi* 548
- removal or reclamation of 547–8
- of sinners 550–1
- time of payment 546

Titus, Roman emperor 588, 687
Tobias 635, 695, 722–3
tonsure 779–82
Thrasamund, king of the Vandals 551
tribe
  and consanguinity 719–20
  and genealogies 720–2
  and inheritance 722–3
  Judah 719–21
  populus and plebs 720
  word 719
tribute 770–1
truth 577–9

Uriah the Hittite 822
Uziah, biblical king 600, 602, 720, 827

wages 646–7
women → *See also* matrimony
  in church 741
  inheritance of 639–41, 722
  penitents 740
  unborn children, killing of 737
  veiled and nuns 739–41, 743–4
  virginity 736–7, 741
  widows 737–9

Zachary, father of John the Baptist 600
Zacheus, biblical tax collector 614
Zechariah, priest, son of Barachios 732, 772
Zedechiah, king of Judah 578, 590
Ziba, biblical figure 565

Also in the Studies in Medieval and Early Modern Canon Law Series

Kenneth Pennington, General Editor

The Hibernensis
Book 2: *Translation, Commentary, and Indexes*
Book 1: *A Study and Edition*
Roy Flechner, editor

The Uses of the Dead
The Early Modern Development of Cy-Près Doctrine
Caroline R. Sherman

Bonds of Wool
The Pallium and Papal Power in the Middle Ages
Steven A. Schoenig, SJ

Gratian and the Development of Penitential Thought and Law in the Twelfth Century
Atria A. Larson

Gratian the Theologian
John C. Wei

Liberty and Law
The Idea of Permissive Natural Law, 1100–1800
Brian Tierney

Marriage on Trial
Late Medieval German Couples at the Papal Court
Ludwig Schmugge
Translated by Atria A. Larson

Medieval Public Justice
Massimo Vallerani
Translated by Sarah Rubin Blanshei

A Sacred Kingdom
Bishops and the Rise of Frankish Kingship, 300–850
Michael Edward Moore